Handbook Bibliometrics

Handbook Bibliometrics

Edited by
Rafael Ball

DE GRUYTER
SAUR

ISBN 978-3-11-108900-3
e-ISBN (PDF) 978-3-11-064661-0
e-ISBN (EPUB) 978-3-11-064259-9

Library of Congress Control Number: 2020945307

Bibliographic information published by the Deutsche Nationalbibliothek
The Deutsche Nationalbibliothek lists this publication in the Deutsche Nationalbibliografie; detailed bibliographic data are available on the Internet at http://dnb.dnb.de.

© 2022 Walter de Gruyter GmbH, Berlin/Boston
This volume is text- and page-identical with the hardback published in 2021.
Cover image: imaginima / E+ / Getty Images
Printing and binding: CPI books GmbH, Leck

www.degruyter.com

Preface

Handbooks may well seem old-fashioned. In the age of split second Internet communication and bite-size information, to some they might even look out of place. While we all use and enjoy swift access to tiny morsels of information, we also – and especially against this backdrop – need an overview and structuring of knowledge and the classification of perspectives and overall contexts. As Ernst Cassierer already put it at the beginning of the twentieth century in his extensive work *The Problems of Knowledge: Philosophy, Science and History since Hegel:* "The need for synthesis and synopsis, for an overview and a comprehensive perspective... still exists."[1]

No tweet can deliver this; no blog entry can render redundant how important and valuable this might be.

As a result, it makes sense to publish this handbook. It is important to keep forming the overview and bringing together the themes of the broad-based special research. Even if – and precisely because – there are other handbooks on the topic, every editor has his or her own perspective and contributes towards the diversity of the opinions and views in tandem with his or her authors.

As editor of this handbook, first of all I would like to thanks the precious and outstanding work of the experts who contributed to the text. My special thanks to all of you who provided your specialist knowledge and experience, your curiosity and research questions, but also your answers and explanations in this handbook. I am convinced that the topic of bibliometrics will continue to be heard and noticed, perceived in its entirety and keep on developing thanks to the collection and compilation of these valuable specialist articles.

My special thanks go to Dirk Tunger, who not only provided relevant contributions to the book, but who also helped me with his know-how and his network during the conception and discussion of the contents.

My thanks also go to the publishing house for supporting this edition. At a time when the importance of professional publishing cannot be stressed often enough, I thank Claudia Heyer and Jana Fritsche on behalf of the publishing house De Gruyter for making this bibliometrics handbook possible.

My gratitude also goes to the proofreader John Ryan, who provided the authors with expert, professional and laid-back advice, and gave me the support I needed, especially when it came to formal issues regarding the design and layout.

Rafael Ball
Zurich, summer 2020

---

[1] Hans-Jörg Rheinberger, Natur und Kultur im Spiegel des Wissens, Marsilius Kolleg Band 12, Universitätsverlag Winter, Heidelberg, 2015: Ernst Cassirer, *Problem of Knowledge*, 19 (here 42).

Contents

Introduction —— 1
Rafael Ball

1 History and Institutionalization of Bibliometrics

1.1 A Historical Overview of Bibliometrics —— 7
     Farshid Danesh and Ali Mardani-Nejad

1.2 Institutionalization and Professionalization of Bibliometrics —— 19
     Niels Taubert

1.3 Eugene Garfield and the Institute for Scientific Information —— 27
     David A. Pendlebury

1.4 Derek De Solla Price: The Father of Scientometrics —— 41
     Frashid Danesh and Ali Mardani-Nejad

1.5 Coevolution of Field and Institute: The Institutionalization of Bibliometric Research Illustrated by the Emergence and Flourishing of the CWTS —— 53
     Anthony van Raan

1.6 International Conferences of Bibliometrics —— 65
     Grischa Fraumann, Rogério Mugnaini, and Elías Sanz-Casado

2 Theory, Principles and Methods of Bibliometrics

2.1 Peer Review and Bibliometrics —— 77
     Bernhard Mittermaier

2.2 Jurisdiction of Bibliometrics —— 91
     Arlette Jappe and Thomas Heinze

2.3 National Research Evaluation Systems —— 99
     Michael Ochsner, Emanuel Kulczycki, Aldis Gedutis, and Ginevra Peruginelli

2.4   The Mathematical Embedding of Bibliometrics —— 107
      Leo Egghe

2.5   Bibliometrics in the Humanities, Arts and Social Sciences —— 117
      Michael Ochsner

2.6   Relationship between Peer Review and Bibliometrics —— 125
      Michael Ochsner

3 (Classical) Indicators

3.1   Measuring the Impact of Research – from Scholarly Communication to Broader Impact —— 135
      Wolfgang Glänzel, Pei-Shan Chi, and Koenraad Debackere

3.2   From Simple Publication Figures to Complex Indicators: Bibliometrics and the Dilemma of Methodological Correctness, Significance, and Economic Necessity —— 149
      Dirk Tunger, Heinz Ahn, Marcel Clermont, Johanna Krolak, and Andreas Meier

3.3   The Journal Impact Factor: A Bibliometric Indicator with a Long Past —— 159
      Dirk Tunger

3.4   The h-index —— 169
      Grischa Fraumann and Rüdiger Mutz

4 Alternative Metrics (Altmetrics)

4.1   The Future Has Already Begun: Origin, Classification, and Applications of Altmetrics in Scholarly Communication —— 181
      Dirk Tunger and Andreas Meier

4.2   History, Development and Conceptual Predecessors of Altmetrics —— 191
      Clemens Blümel and Stephan Gauch

4.3   Social Media and Altmetrics —— 201
      Kaltrina Nuredini, Steffen Lemke, and Isabella Peters

4.4   Altmetric.com: A Brief History —— 215
        Ben McLeish

4.5   PlumX Metrics (Plum Analytics) in Practice —— 221
        Juan Gorraiz and Christian Gumpenberger

4.6   PLOS Article-Level Metrics —— 235
        Steffen Lemke, Kaltrina Nuredini, and Isabella Peters

4.7   Eigenfactor —— 245
        Grischa Fraumann, Jennifer D'Souza, and Kim Holmberg

4.8   Academic Social Networks and Bibliometrics —— 255
        Clemens Blümel

4.9   ResearchGate and the Academic Social Network Sites: New Environments for New Bibliometrics? —— 265
        Enrique Orduña-Malea and Emilio Delgado López-Cózar

4.10   Mendeley —— 281
        Robin Haunschild

5 Applications, Practice and Special Issues in Bibliometrics

5.1   An Ecology of Measures and Indicators: Bibliometrics in Resource Allocation —— 291
        Björn Hammarfelt and Fredrik Åström

5.2   Benchmarkings and Rankings —— 299
        Ronald Rousseau

5.3   Technological Trend Analysis —— 311
        Miloš Jovanović

5.4   Research Collaboration and Bibliometric Performance —— 319
        Tindaro Cicero and Marco Malgarini

5.5   On the Need for Accessibility, Standardization, Regulation, and Verification in Bibliometrics: The Leiden Manifesto and Beyond —— 329
        Dirk Tunger

5.6 Gender and Bibliometrics: A Review —— 335
Tahereh Dehdarirad

5.7 Visualization of Research Metrics —— 365
Hélène Draux

5.8 Regional Distribution of Research: The Spatial Polarization in Question —— 377
Marion Maisonobe

5.9 Bibliometrics and Co-Authorship —— 397
Dorte Drongstrup

6 The Data Basis in Bibliometrics

6.1 Web of Science, Scopus and Further Citation Databases —— 409
Ingrid Bauer

6.2 Expanding Dimensions: A New Source in the Bibliometrician's Toolbox —— 421
Juergen Wastl

6.3 The Islamic World Science Citation Center (ISC): The Construction and Application —— 431
Jafar Mehrad and Mohammad Reza Ghane

6.4 Institutional Repositories and Bibliometrics —— 455
Valeria Aman

7 Teaching and Training

7.1 Institutions for Bibliometric Qualification —— 465
Simone Fühles-Ubach and Miriam Albers

7.2 Bibliometrics in the Curriculum —— 475
Simone Fühles-Ubach, Miriam Albers, and Mandy Neumann

7.3 The Competent Bibliometrician – A Guided Tour through the Scholarly and Practitioner Literature —— 485
Sabrina Petersohn

8 The Future of Bibliometrics

8.1 The Future of Bibliometrics: Where is Bibliometrics Heading? —— 499
Rafael Ball

8.2 Open Science and the Future of Metrics —— 507
Tamara Heck

List of Contributors —— 517

Index —— 527

Introduction
Rafael Ball

The development of academia, its structure and systems, its communication, and above all its questions to the world is a fascinating research field in itself. The fact that, over its 2,000-year history, academia has blossomed from an individual commitment and the interests of individuals into an institutionalised form is of particular importance. The foundation of academies and universities at the end of the Middles Ages, the enthusiasm for new things and the open-mindedness during the Renaissance, still fascinate to this day. Universities and all the other parallel structures of institutionalised academia and research evolved into a veritable "mass phenomenon" in the early twentieth century. A growing number of people are interested in the vast range of issues concerning humans, society and the world around them. However, ever more people also have the option of choosing academia for a living and research as a career, which is yielding ever more answers, insights and new products. Research and academic questions are going into increasing depth. However, the horizon in which the findings need to be embedded is also becoming broader and more complex; for many issues, only collaboration between the various disciplines produces the right solutions. A network of comprehensive answers to academic questions is taking shape, although the academic knowledge process will never be completed. Academia does not provide definitive answers; they are only ever valid until new findings are able to refute, modify or improve on the explanation. Karl Popper describes this as the falsification theory in his book *The Logic of Scientific Research* (first published as *Logik der Forschung* in 1934; English translation 1959).[1]

According to Popper, one fundamental principle of academia is that it shares its results, discusses with other scientists and thus keeps moving forward. However, this also means that academic results are never generated purely for one's own personal development, but always have to be published as well. Otherwise, in the best case scenario it involves research in private industry to develop products and, in the worst case, "secret science", exactly like the "maverick scholars" portrayed in poor television series.

Since the mid-twentieth century, the number of publications has boomed. Increasing numbers of scientists are producing more and more findings and publishing more and more results in books and journals, at conferences and, ever since the early 2000s, in or on blog entries, websites, databases or in other state of the art electronic forms of (social) media, such as the meanwhile highly successful social academic networks that are increasingly being used. The volume of academic output has

---

[1] Karl Popper, Logik der Forschung, Akademieverlag, 2013.

Dr. **Rafael Ball**, Director ETH Libraries and Collections, ETH Zurich, Rämistrasse 101, 8092 Zuerich, Switzerland. Email: rafael.ball@library.ethz.ch.

reached a scale which the individual often can no longer fathom. Already today, twenty per cent of all academic publications in Germany are not even cited once. The number of journals, books and conferences has ballooned. Digital publishing formats and social media are being discovered as additional or new publishing platforms and used massively.

On the one hand, this has created a wonderful situation for knowledge gains in academia; on the other hand, however, it has become impossible to obtain an overview (even a rough one) of the results published and their quality and importance for the respective subject.

In this respect, the bell tolls for bibliometrics. Anyone who is no longer able to read or perceive everything that is published in or even beyond his or her discipline has to choose. Due to the sheer volume, however, in most cases a quantitative selection is no longer possible. Bibliometrics offers a way out here. It gauges the perception of academic publications via the roundabout route that citations take and uses this to draw inferences about their quality. If academic publications are cited frequently, it is safe to assume that they are important papers (and worth reading in detail). By the same token, a paper that is cited seldomly, if at all, seems less relevant.

This fundamental principle of inferring the quality of a paper indirectly from the number of citations is the basis of bibliometrics, the requirements, methods and results of which are the subject of this handbook.

The first attempts to establish a link between citations of publications and the quality of the papers were made as early as 1927.[2] However, the actual development and eventual broad usage of bibliometrics only really took off with the advent of the digital age. Only in this way can a mass evaluation of analysis data on citations made be realised. The fact that this spawns a broad field of statistical "variant forms" meant it was inevitable that bibliometrics itself would blossom into a (virtually incomprehensible) science. Nowadays, bibliometrics refers to a vast number of forms of metrics, which measure the perception and importance of academic publications in statistical form. In the process, today citations are merely one gauge among many other attention indicators. As a result, however, the consideration of bibliometrics has long since become part of scholarly communication and must also be embedded in current developments such as open access or open science.

This handbook examines all these different topics related to bibliometrics.

In the chapter entitled 'History and Institutionalization of Bibliometrics', articles on the historical development of bibliometrics and its methods are described and explained. The institutionalization of bibliometrics in the course of this historical development also features extensively, based on selected people and institutions that can be regarded as milestones of bibliometrics. They have been instrumental in bib-

---

[2] Gross, PLK & Gross, EM 1927, College libraries and chemical education, *Science* 66, pp. 385–389.

liometrics becoming an accepted part of the variety of methods used to evaluate academia.

The chapter 'Theory, Principles and Methods of Bibliometrics' addresses the methodical foundations of bibliometrics, which are essentially mathematical and statistical in character. An attempt is also made at a heuristic assessment of what measuring attention can actually tell us about the quality of academic publications (and what it cannot).

Besides offering an overview of the basic indicators and their importance and calculation, the chapter '(Classical) Indicators' also singles out individual core indicators such as the h-Index and analyses them in depth.

The chapter 'Alternative Metrics (Altmetrics)' focuses on social media and their metrics, which have emerged since the birth of digitalisation. It is no longer anywhere near enough to measure citations in the quantitative analysis of publications and there has long been a wealth of serious publications, such as in social media, where the classical indicator canon has ceased to be applicable. This is where alternative metrics, which are explained in detail and their use described in this chapter, come in.

The chapter 'Applications, Practice and Special Issues in Bibliometrics' outlines a colourful bouquet of special examples and prospects of bibliometric research. These include concepts and initiatives, as well as issues concerning the visualisation of and connections between innovation, regional consolidation and trends in bibliometrics.

Bibliometrics would not have been feasible if the data basis of this academic research had not been constantly expanded and optimised. It constitutes a crucial foundation for automatic analysis systems and the processing of vast quantities of data to work in bibliometrics. The chapter 'The Data Basis in Bibliometrics' discusses various commercial and non-commercial databases like those used in bibliometrics, including their pros and cons.

Bibliometrics grew out of the suspicion of being a "sideline" of sociologists, philosophers, mathematicians or librarians. Whilst it has become a core research and application field at various institutions, it has not yet really established itself as a discipline in its own right. In the chapter 'Teaching and Training', we summarise the current state of affairs, where the next generation of scholars can learn from bibliometrics and how the topic is rooted in university curricula.

The handbook concludes with the chapter 'The Future of Bibliometrics', which attempts to provide an outlook from various perspectives as to where bibliometrics might develop alongside the latest developments of academic communication.

Finally, an index should enable core topics and keywords to be found more easily.

1 History and Institutionalization of Bibliometrics

1.1 A Historical Overview of Bibliometrics

Farshid Danesh and Ali Mardani-Nejad

Abstract: Bibliometrics is one of the few methods that analyze data on a large scale. The development and growth of bibliometrics as an area of research have been remarkable in recent decades. However, bibliometrics is not a new phenomenon as it originated from statistical bibliography. The primary purpose of this chapter is to present a historical view of bibliometrics as well as the significant events that took place in this field from the late nineteenth century to the late twentieth century (1870–1980). The chapter will explore 116 years to illustrate the advent of bibliometrics, its essential definitions, its pioneers, its theories, and the influential works of this field, from 1873 to the end of 1989.

Keywords: bibliometrics, bibliometrics trend, bibliometric rule, bibliometric theories.

Introduction

As a word, bibliometrics appears to have its roots in "Biblio" and "metric." The term "Biblio" derived from the combined Latin and Greek word "biblion," which is similar to the word Bybel (os), meaning book. Paper derived from the word Byblos, a city of Phoenicia, noted for its export trade in the paper. The word "metrics," on the other hand, indicates the science of measurement, and is derived either from the Latin or Greek word "metricus" or "metrikos," each respectively meaning measurement (Sengupta, 1992). The metric word also specifies the science of measurement, derived from the Greek or Latin word metric, meaning measurement. In this chapter, the historical background of bibliometrics from origin to the formation of theories studied, and the foundations, thoughts, rules, and publications during the eighteen and nineteenth centuries in bibliometrics, is introduced. This historical overview dates back to the early 1870s when the initial idea of bibliometrics was sparked into life in 1873 and progresses to the late 1980s when it matured. This chapter will focus on the first significant bibliometrics events from the 1870s, which lasted more than a century until the end of the 1980s.

Farshid Danesh, Regional Information Center for Science & Technology (RICeST), Shiraz, Iran, farshiddanesh@ricest.ac.ir
Ali Mardani-Nejad, Young Researchers and Elite Club, Najafabad Branch, Islamic Azad University, Najafabad, Iran

Alphonse Pyramus de Candolle 1806-1893 　　Vilfredo Pareto 1848-1923 　　Felix Auerbach 1856-1933 　　Jean Baptiste Estoup 1868-1950

Fig. 1

The 1870s

1873: The first bibliometrics documentary, entitled "Histoire des Sciences et des Savants Depuis Deux Siècles," was published by French-Swiss botanist Alphonse de Candolle in 1873. He described the changes made in the scientific ability of nations in terms of their membership in scientific communities. His goal in this study was to identify the factors influencing the scientific success of a nation (van Raan, 2004).

The 1890s

1896: Conceptual bibliometrics derived from statistical bibliography and its application dates back to the 1890s. The work of Campbell (1896), which uses statistical methods to study the subject scattering in publications, may be considered as the first attempt in bibliometrics studies (Osareh, 1996).

1896: Pareto, the Italian economist (University of Lausanne), recognized the 80/20 principle in 1896. In a paper entitled "Cours d'économie politique," he published on this principle. Pareto believed that approximately 80% of the land in Italy was owned by 20% of the population (Moore, 1897). He then carried out surveys on a variety of other countries and found to his surprise that a similar distribution applied (Backhaus, 1980).

The 1910s

1913: German physicist Felix Auerbach presented German cities' population ranking according to the distribution law. The law that we now refer to as "Zipf's Law" was founded in those years (Auerbach, 1913).

Alfred J. Lotka 1880-1949   Edward Condon 1902-1974   George Kingsley Zipf 1902-1950   Samuel C. Bradford 1878-1948

Fig. 2

1916: French stenographer J.B. Estoup noted that rank (r) and frequency (F) in a French text were related by a "hyperbolic" law, which states that r · F is approximately constant, cf. (Estoup as cited in Harremoës and Topsoe, 2005).
1917: Cole and Eales used a statistical bibliography in 1917 to study citations of comparative anatomical texts from 1550 to 1860 (Cole and Eales, 1917).

The 1920s

1923: Hulme performed a statistical analysis of science history in 1923. His analysis was based on journals that had reached the International Bookkeeping Directory in 17 disciplines. Hulme was the first to invent the term "statistical bibliography" (Hulme, 1923).
1926: Lotka provided a basis for the scientific productivity of the authors. Lotka believed that few authors produce a high percentage of scientific works in scientific subjects. Of course, this does not necessarily reflect the impact and content of these authors' publications (Lotka, 1926; Garfield, 1995).
1927: Gross and Gross also used the citation analysis method for the first time. They used previous periodicals as sources of chemistry citations. Their citation analysis method as a model and sample was used up to 50 years later (Gross and Gross, 1927).
1928: E. Condon, a physicist from the Bell Telephone Company, found regularity in the research on raising the capacity of telephone lines for communication. Condon found that the distribution relationship between lgr & lgnr is close to a straight line AB, with an angle α between line AB and the χ-coordinate. If tgα=γ, then log (rγ · nr) = log K (Qiu et al., 2017).
1929: Zipf defended his Ph.D. dissertation entitled "Relative Frequency as a determinant of phonetic change" (Zipf, 1929).

Paul Otlet 1868-1944 Claude Shannon 1916-2001 S. R. Ranganathan 1892-1972 Eugene Garfield 1925-2017

Fig. 3

The 1930s

1932: Zipf published a book entitled *Selected Studies of the Principle of Relative Frequency in Language* (Zipf, 1932).

1934: Bradford published his articles on scientific journals. He reported that a relatively small number of journals published a high percentage of all papers. Bradford divided journals into two groups: (1) a central core of the journals with their most relevant articles; and (2) several groups around the core (Bradford, 1948).

1934: Paul Otlet, the Belgian librarian, was one of a few people called the Father of Information Science. He added "DOCUMENTATION" to the field of information science, while the Universal Decimal Classification (UDC) was another of his achievements. He also used the term bibliometrics for the first time in the Traité de Documentation book (Rousseau, 2014).

1935: In a book entitled *The Psychobiology of Language: An Introduction to Dynamic Philology*, Zipf stated that the word length is inverse with its relative frequency. This exploration led to the discovery of a law known as Zipf's law, which, in his opinion, and in general, tends to be based on the size of the words, which has an inverse (not necessarily proportional) relation to the number of occurrences (Zipf, 1935).

The 1940s

1948: Herman Fussler characterized the literature of chemistry and physics, the use of "key journals" (Fussler, 1949).

1948: Samuel C. Bradford published "Documentation" in 1948 (Bradford, 1948).

1948: In 1948, Claude Elwood Shannon presented an article entitled "A Mathematical Theory of Communication," which had a striking effect on information science. In this paper, he considers the fundamental problem of communication in reproducing the message sent by the sender to the receiver (Shannon, 1948).

1948: The term "librametrics" was first introduced by Siyali Ramamrita Ranganathan (S.R.R.) in 1948 at the annual Slip Conference in Spain (Ranganathan, 1948).

Derek J. de Solla Price 1922-1983　　Vasily Nalimov 1910-1997　　Robert K. Merton 1910-2003　　Alan Pritchard 1941-2015

Fig. 4

1949: Zipf made the first attempt at vocabulary within the text. By studying the abundance of words used in English texts, Zipf found some examples of the principle of least effort (Zipf, 1949).

The 1950s

1955: Eugene Garfield devised a bibliographic system for scientific texts called the "Science Citation Index." The citation index scheme compiled information that was more convenient than the conventional index called "subject index" and could bridge the gap between authors and researchers (Garfield, 1955).
1956: Fano and Kessler introduced the first idea of the bibliographic coupling. The "Bibliographic couple" is one of the bibliometric methods that examine the critical works of authors, documents, and prestigious journals and identifies the relationship between the author's major works and references and essential documents and journals (Sen and Gan, 1983).
1958: Miller and Newman clarified the statistical explanation between the rank and frequency of words in English texts (Miller and Newman, 1958).

The 1960s

1963: Garfield published the Science Citation Index (SCI). The use of this resource has flourished as a tool for various studies and analyses, and today it is one of the most reputable sources for bibliometric studies.
1963: Price published his book entitled *Little Science, Big Science*. For the first time, he used statistical data, "the phenomenon of progressive text growth." He showed that between 1660 and 1960, the number of scientific articles had doubled every 15 years (Price, 1963).
1963: Eugene Garfield and Irving Sher introduced Journals Impact Factor (IF) in the Institute for Scientific Information (ISI) to select journals for the Science Citation Index (Garfield and Sher, 1963; Garfield, 1999). At that time, nobody thought that

the index would be so affected. Now, Impact Factor is an extensive guide to selecting the best journals for the Science Citation Index.

1964: Goffman and Newill presented the "GENERALIZATION OF EPIDEMIC THEORY." They believed that the movement of an idea over time was the same as an infectious virus. The virus grew at a particular time, with some infected, transmitting this idea (TRANSMISSION OF IDEAS), with a feverish peak of awareness in it (Goffman and Newill, 1964). This process may gradually be reduced and improved, leading to the death of thought or ending with its incubation. This model can be used with ISI analyses to predict the prevalence of a research subject, the duration of an outbreak, the number of people affected, and whether an information retrieval system should facilitate the communication of relevant scientific information (Garfield, 1980).

1965: Derek de Solla Price called for the link between articles as the network of scientific articles (Price, 1965).

1967: Leimkuhler presented a mathematical model for explaining the efficiency of publications (Leimkuhler, 1967).

1968: Co-citation of authors was introduced as co-mention by Rosengren in 1968 (Rosengren, 1968). Co-citation studies are the correct representation of the logical mind-body structures of science, and a tool for observing the current state of science and for predicting its future direction.

1968: Merton unveiled a phenomenon called the "Matthew Effect." He believed that the amount of citation received by researchers with an organizational affiliation was as large as the organization, meaning that researchers from large organizations received more citation than those from small organizations (Merton, 1968).

1969: The term Nakometria, later renamed Scientometrics, was first used in the Soviet Union by Vasily Nalimov (Nalimov and Mul'chenko, 1969).

1969: The term "bibliometric" was used in 1969 by Pritchard. He believed that the term bibliography was statistically ambiguous because it may be interpreted as a statistical analysis of bibliographies in statistics. Therefore, the term "bibliometrics" is more effective and comprehensive than the "statistical bibliographic" term and suggests the use of mathematics and statistical methods in the quantitative analysis and aspects of librarianship and information science (Pritchard, 1969).

1969: The term "bibliometrics," as far as is verifiable, was first used in the 1969 issue of *Documentation Journal*. In that issue, the paper by Robert Fairthorne was published, entitled "Bibliometric Description." In its first paragraph, Fairthorne noted that Alan Pritchard was the inventor of the term bibliometrics (Fairthorne, 1969).

The 1970s

1970: By 1970, bibliometrics had become a heading in both Library Literature and Library and Information Science Abstracts (Peritz, 1984, quoted in Hood and Wilson, 2001).

1972: Ortega hypothesis: in an original Spanish language book published in English in 1932, Jose Ortega and Gasset presented a hypothesis that was used, 40 years later, by two American sociologists named Jonathan R. Cole and Stephen Cole, in 1972, in an article entitled "The Ortega Hypothesis," published in Science Journal. They examined his hypothesis about physics scientists and concluded that Ortega's hypothesis did not approve in their research populations. However, they did not reject the hypothesis and suggested that it could be considered in other sciences (Cole and Cole, 1972).

1973: The Social Science Citation Index (SSCI) was published at the Institute for Scientific Information (ISI) in Philadelphia, the USA, for social science research areas, under the supervision of Eugene Garfield.

1973: Using methods of group analysis, Small studied co-citation couples. The identification and mapping of the structure of a scientific discipline also became possible through the study of co-citation coupling (Small, 1973).

1975: Moravcsik and Murugesan proposed the first approach to categorizing citations in 1975. Their most important work at that time was weighting citations based on function and context, which had not been carried out until then. They began their studies from 1975 and their first article entitled "Some Results on the Function and Quality of Citations" was published in 1975. They classified scientific papers' citations based on being (a) conceptual or operational, (b) organic or perfunctory, (c) evolutionary or juxtapositional, or (d) confirmatory or negational (Moravcsik and Murugesan, 1975; Jörg, 2008)

1975: Brookes organized the first International Research Forum in Information Science (IRFIS) at University College London to discuss the theoretical aspects of information science (Brookes, 1976).

1976: Price, in his article about a "Cumulative Advantage Distribution," proposed a model in which, statistically, success breeds success in a specific situation. It is common in bibliometric matters and many diverse social phenomena that success seems to breed success. A paper that has been cited many times is more likely to be cited again. In this theory, it would appear that the course of future citation successes is determined statistically by the history of the cited paper, suggesting that citations are generated by a pull mechanism from the previous citation rather than from a push mechanism of the papers that do the citing (Price, 1976).

1976: After publishing the Science Citation Index at the Institute for Scientific Information (ISI), Garfield published citations in order to rank journals and present a regular and analytical report on their status and ranking in a variety of thematic areas and disciplines.

1978: Scientometrics Journal was founded, and the concept of Scientometrics was introduced at the same time in Budapest. According to Bensman, Scientometrics Journal acted as a bridge between the East and the West (Garfield, 2007).

1978: After the publication of two citation indexes of science and social sciences, the Institute for Scientific Information (ISI) found it necessary to view studies in the art

and human sciences using the indexing and organizing method. This led to the arts and humanities citation index being published for the first time (Komatsu, 1999).
1979: Prof. Otto Nacke introduced the term infometric. He defined this concept as the use of mathematical methods to understand phenomena related to information through the description and analysis of these phenomena and the discovery of the rules governing them (Sengupta, 1992).

The 1980s

1981: Based on the analysis of co-citation coupling, White and Griffith presented a new tool for exploring the intellectual structure of science (White and Griffith, 1982).
1983: The co-word analysis, introduced by Callon in 1983, was based on the assumption that the presence of words or concepts together represents the content of that document. By measuring the amount of this co-occurrence, the network can draw the concepts of a scientific field (Callon, 1983).
1983: The Price Award was the first and most prestigious international infometric award, given to individuals with proven and extraordinary achievements in quantitative science studies and applications. Tibor Braun, the founder and editor-in-chief of the Scientometrics journal, created the Price Award in 1983, to keep the memory of Price alive (Derek John De Solla Price Award of the Journal Scientometrics, 2016). One of the goals of this award was to acknowledge the individuals who played a vital role in the development of science.
1984: The first Price medal was awarded to Eugene Garfield in 1984.
1984: In 1984, FID (International Federation for Information and Documentation) set up the Committee on Infometrics to provide valid data for research and development, policymaking, planning, management of institutions, and projects, programs, and scientific activities.
1987: The first international conference on Bibliometrics, Scientometrics, and Infometrics was held in Belgium in 1987 and the second conference in London in 1989.

Conclusion

In this chapter, a historical approach to bibliometrics and a century of essential events were reviewed. From the first efforts of researchers in this field, such as Candolle's attempt to publish the first bibliometrics documentary in 1873, to the studies of White and Griffith and Callon at the beginning of the 1980s for both co-citation and co-word studies, all such scholars published works in this area whose influence would be long-lasting.

The first attempts to record the concept of bibliometrics to the internationalization of this area of human knowledge and the establishment of the world's first scientific organization, named *Institute for Scientific Information (ISI)*, was undertaken by Eugene Garfield (September 16, 1925–February 26, 2017), in particular for citation indexing, abstracting, and citation analysis of reputable papers and publications discussed globally. He also published the first science, social sciences, and arts and humanities citation indexes, while for the ranking of scholarly journals based on valid indicators such as the Impact Factor (IF) he published the first *Journal Citation Report (JCR)*.

Also of note is the publishing of the first specialized journal, *Scientometrics*, the organizing of national and international conferences on the topic of metrics, and quantitative researches and the attention of international communities and associations such as FID and the Committees of Infometrics establishment in FID. All of this resulted in a heightened understanding of the world of science, such as the global importance and necessity of this field as well as its capabilities as an interdisciplinary research area in solving the problems and challenges of research-related areas and macro policymaking, and observing the scientific status of countries, organizations, and scientists at the national and international levels.

References

Auerbach, F 1913, 'Das Gesetz der Bevölkerungskonzentration', *Petermann's Geographische. Mitteilungen*, vol. 59, pp. 7–74.
Backhaus, J 1980, 'The Pareto Principle', *Analyse & Kritik*, vol. 2, no. 2, pp. 146–171.
Bradford, SC 1948, *Documentation*, Crosby Lockwood, London.
Brookes, BC 1976, 'A personal note', in *International Research Forum in Information Science: the Theoretical Basis of Information Science*, pp. 6–7, BLR & D Report 5262, British Library, London.
Callon, M, Courtial, JP, Turner, WA & Bauin, S 1983, 'From translations to problematic networks: an introduction to co-word analysis', *Social Science Information*, vol. 22, no. 2, pp. 191–235.
Campbell, F 1896, *Theory of the National and International Bibliography*, Library Bureau, London.
Cole, FJ & Eales, NB 1917, 'The history of comparative anatomy. Part I: A statistical analysis of the literature', *Sei. Prog*, vol. 11, pp. 578–596.
Cole, JR, & Cole, S 1972, 'The Ortega Hypothesis', *Science*, vol. 178, no. 4059, pp. 368–375.
Derek John de Solla Price Award of the Journal Scientometrics [Website], http://issi-society.org/awards/derek-de-solla-price-memorial-medal/ (July 15, 2020).
Fairthorne, RA 1969, 'Empirical hyperbolic distribution (Bradford-Zipf-Mandelbrot) for bibliometric description', *Journal of Documentation*, vol. 25, no. 4, pp. 319–343.
Fussler, HH 1949, 'The Library Quarterly: Information', *Community. Policy*, vol. 19, no. 1, pp. 19–35.
Garfield, E 1955, 'Citation indexes for science: a new dimension in documentation through association of ideas', *Science*, vol. 122, pp. 108–111.
Garfield, E 1980, 'The epidemiology of knowledge and the spread of scientific information', *Essays of an Information Scientist*, vol. 4, pp. 586–591.
Garfield, E & Sher, IH 1963, 'New factors in the evaluation of scientific literature through citation indexing', *American Documentation*, vol. 14, no. 3, pp. 195–201.
Garfield, E 1995, 'New International Professional Society Signals The Maturing Of Scientometrics And Informetrics', *The Scientist*, vol. 9, no. 16, p. 11.

Garfield, E 1999, 'Journal impact factor: a brief review', *Canadian medical association journal*, vol. 161, no. 8, pp. 979–980.

Garfield, E 2007, 'From the science of science to scientometrics: Visualizing the history of science with histcite software', *Proceedings of ISSI. 1, P. 21–26, 11th International conference of the international society for scientometrics & informetrics, CSIC,* June 25–27, Madrid, Spain.

Goffman, W & Newill, VA 1964, 'Generalization of Epidemic Theory', *Nature*, vol. 204, no. 4955, pp. 255–228.

Gross, PLK & Gross, EM 1927, 'College libraries and chemical education', *Science*, vol. 66, pp. 1229–1234.

Harremoës, P & Topsoe, F 2005, 'Zipf's law, hyperbolic distributions, and entropy loss', *Electronic Notes in Discrete Mathematics*, vol. 21, pp. 315–318.

Hood, WW & Wilson, CS 2001, 'The literature of bibliometrics, scientometrics, and informetrics', *Scientometrics*, vol. 52, no. 2, pp. 291–314.

Hulme, FW 1923, *Statistical Bibliography in relation to the growth of modern civilization*, Grafton, London.

Jörg, B 2008, 'Towards the Nature of Citations', in *Poster Proceedings of the 5th International Conference on Formal Ontology in Information Systems (FOIS 2008)*, http://www.dfki.de/~brigitte/publications/FOIS08_Poster_BrigitteJoerg.pdf (July 15, 2020).

Komatsu, S 1999, 'Arts & Humanities Citation Index', *Journal of Information Processing and Management*, vol. 41, no. 12, pp. 989–997.

Leimkuhler, FF 1967, 'The Bradford distribution', *Journal of documentation*, vol. 23, no. 3, pp.197–207.

Lotka, AJ 1926, 'The frequency distribution of scientific productivity', *Journal of the Washington Academy of Science*, vol. 16, no. 12, pp. 317–323.

Merton, RK 1968, 'The Matthew effect in science', *Science*, vol. 159, no. 3810, pp. 56–63.

Miller, GA & Newman, EB 1958, 'Tests of a statistical explanation of the rank-frequency relation for words in written English', *American Journal of Psychology*, vol. 71, pp. 209–218.

Moore, HL 1897, 'Cours d'Économie Politique', by V. Pareto, Professeur à l' Université de Lausanne, vol. I, p. 430, 1896; vol. II. p. 426, 1897; Lausanne: F. Rouge, *The Annals of the American Academy of Political and Social Science*, vol. 9, no. 3, pp. 128–131.

Moravcsik, MJ & Murugesan, P 1975, 'Some Results on the Function and Quality of Citations', *Social Studies of Science*, vol. 5, no. 1, pp. 86–92.

Nalimov, VV & Mul'chenko, ZM 1969, *Naukometriya. Izuchenie nauki kak informatsionnogo protsessa (scientometrics: Study of science as an information process.)*, p. 192, Nauka, Moscow.

Ortega, JY y Gasset 1932, *The Revolt of the Masses*, pp. 84–85, Norton, New York.

Osareh, F 1996, 'Bibliometrics, Citation Analysis, and Co-Citation Analysis: A Review of Literature I', *Libri*, vol. 46, pp. 149–158.

Price, DJdS 1965, 'Networks of Scientific Papers', *Science*, vol. 149, no. 3683, p. 515.

Price, DJdS 1963, *Little Science, Big Science*, Columbia University Press, New York.

Pritchard, A 1969, 'Statistical Bibliography or Bibliometrics', *Journal of Documentation*, vol. 25, pp. 348–349.

Price, DJdS 1976, 'A General Theory of Bibliometric and other Cumulative Advantage Processes', *Journal of the American Society for Information Science*, vol. 27, no. 5, pp. 292–306.

Qiu, J, Zhao, R, Yang, S & Dong, K 2017, *Informetrics: Theory, methods, and applications*, pp. 121–143, Springer, Singapore.

Ranganathan, SR 1948, Proc. of the Aslib's Ann. Conf., Leamington Spa, Great Britain.

Rosengren, KE 1968, *Sociological aspects of the literary system*, Nature och Kultur, Stockholm.

Rousseau, R 2014, 'Forgotten founder of bibliometrics', *Nature*, vol. 510, p. 218.

Sen, SS & Gan, SS 1983, 'A Mathematical Extension Of The idea of bibliographic coupling and its application', *Annals of library science and documentation*, vol. 30, no. 2, pp. 78–82.

Sengupta, IN 1992, 'Bibliometrics, Informetrics, Scientometrics, and bibliometrics. An Overview', *Libri*, vol. 42, no. 2, pp. 75–79.

Shannon, CE 1948, 'A Mathematical Theory of Communication', *Bell System Technical Journal*, vol. 27, no. 3, pp. 379–423.

Small, H 1973, 'Co-citation in the scientific literature: A new measure of the relationship between two documents', *Journal of the American Society for information science banner*, vol. 24, no. 4, pp. 256–269.

van Raan, AF 2004, 'Measuring science: Capita Selecta of current main issues', in H. Moed, W. Glänzel & U. Schmoch, *Handbook of quantitative science and technology research: the use of publication and patent statistics in studies of S&T systems*, Kluwer, Dordrecht.

White, HD & Griffith, BC 1982, 'Authors as markers of intellectual space: Co-citation in studies of science, technology, and society', *Journal of documentation*, vol. 38, no. 4, pp. 227–255.

Zipf, G. 1949, *Human behavior and the principle of least effort*, Addison Wesley, Boston.

Zipf, GK 1929, 'Relative frequency as a determinant of phonetic change', *Harvard Studies in Classical Philology*, vol. 40, pp. 1–95.

Zipf, GK 1932, *Selected studies of the principle of relative frequency in language*, Harvard University Press, Cambridge, Mass.

Zipf, GK 1935, *The psycho-biology of language*, Houghton Mifflin, Oxford, England.

1.2 Institutionalization and Professionalization of Bibliometrics

Niels Taubert

Abstract: This article offers an overview as to what extent bibliometrics is an institutionalized field of research and to what extent it is a professional practice. After different dimensions of institutionalization (stabilization of a cognitive core, evolvement of a social structure, development of a communication network) have been reviewed an overview of the dimension of professionalization is given. These include the formation of a specific type of expertise and the establishment of a claim for jurisdiction for a social problem. The article concludes with the following diagnosis: although bibliometics has been established as a field of research, the process of professionalization has to be characterized as incomplete. The reason for this has both to do with missing tracks of formal qualifications together with the proliferation of automated bibliometric tools to non-experts.

Keywords: bibliometrics, communication system, professionalization, institutionalization, infrastructures, professional code.

Introduction

This article offers both an overview as to what extent bibliometrics is an institutionalized field of research and to what extent it is a professional practice. It therefore builds upon two sociological concepts: from a viewpoint of the sociology of the professions (Abboth, 1988; Petersohn, 2016; Petersohn and Heinze, 2018), professions share some common features. First, they comprise a cognitive core of a specific expertise that is usually based on academic knowledge. Second, they address a societally relevant problem for which they put forward cognitive and social claims for jurisdiction and control. Third, such claims are often contested by competing groups. Fourth, expertise is institutionalized in the form of professionals, organizations as well as commodities such as databases, classification, and other artifacts.

The institutionalization of the cognitive core of the profession in which academic knowledge is developed can be described with reference to the sociology of science. Within this tradition it is commonplace that the epistemic process of the establishment of a field of knowledge goes hand in hand with the formation of a social structure. An institutionalized field of knowledge therefore finds its expression in research institutes and groups dedicated to the field that forms a community of scholars and are connected by a network of communication. The community is reproduced by a specific (academic) training which introduces future members to the field. Institu-

---

Dr. **Niels Taubert,** head of the working group Bibliometrics and a sociologist of science, technology, and digital media by training, niels.taubert@uni-bielefeld.de

tionalized communities are organized by scholarly societies (Weingart and Schwechheimer, 2007) and share common criteria of excellence for the evaluation of contributions to the knowledge. If a professional field of application exists, it is likely that professional norms or ethics are codified.

In what follows, the complementary dimensions of the two concepts mentioned above are used as a heuristics to describe the degree of institutionalization and professionalization of bibliometrics. In drawing a multifaceted picture, it will be shown that bibliometrics today is an institutionalized field of research in which the reproduction of the social structure of the bibliometrics community in terms of training is lacking. Because of the absence of a formal qualification together with the availability of bibliometric tools for non-experts, the claim for jurisdiction and control is contested, especially in the field of research evaluation. With respect to control, the degree of professionalization tends to be low.

Cognitive Core, Communication System, and Social Structure in Academic Bibliometrics

Bibliometrics, i.e., methods that deal with the analysis of large numbers of scientific publications and the relations between them – the citations –, has a long tradition. Although the term bibliometrics was invented by Alan Prichard in 1969, bibliometric studies are much older. Besides the seminal and well known works of Alfred Lotka (1926) on the distribution of productivity and of Derek de Solla Price (1963) on the growth of science, one should note that systematic studies on the development of publications and citations have been conducted in psychology (Godin, 2006) as well as in chemistry (Gross and Gross, 1927). Since these first bibliometric studies were based on manual collections of data, the availability of a database that is continuously updated and can be reused for different purposes is of critical relevance. Therefore, the Science Citation Index (published first in 1963 for the year 1961) played a major role for the institutionalization of bibliometric research. The consolidation of the cognitive core of the field began during the 1970s with a large expansion since the 2000s (Yang et al., 2016; Petersohn and Heinze, 2018). The field has developed and a diverse range of topics have been studied, including, for example, scientific productivity, citation networks, co-operations, disciplinary profiles of institutions, mobility and career of researchers, performance indicators, and so on. Regarding its location in the scientific landscape, it is often stated that it has been differentiated as a subfield in the library and information sciences (LIS) but it also holds strong links to the social studies of science.

The institutionalization of a cognitive core of bibliometrics went hand in hand with the foundation of communication channels for the dissemination of research in the field. For years there was no alternative to *Scientometrics* (founded in 1978) and the *Journal of the American Society for Information Science and Technology*. This changed in 1991, when *Research Evaluation* was first published. During this period, the publication output of *Scientometrics* grew enormously: the journal started with five issues in one volume, changed to six issues in two volumes in 1986, then published nine issues in three volumes, and ended up with 12 issues in four volumes on an annual basis from 2005 onwards. The increase of the publication output of the bibliometrics community is also reflected by the foundation of new journals such as the *Journal of Informetrics* and *Collnet Journal of Scientometrics and Information Management*, which both appeared from 2007 onwards, and the *Journal of Scientometric Research and Publications*, which started in 2012. With respect to institutionalization, it is interesting to note that there is still no journal that is exclusively dedicated to bibliometrics. The main journals have a wider scope and address a broader community as they refer to more comprehensive terms like "scientometrics" or "quantitative analysis of science" in their self-descriptions (aims and scope). Besides these core-journals of the field, there are a large number of channels with a more general scope that are also open to contributions from bibliometrics. These journals usually cover library and information studies, documentation, management and use of information technologies or librarianship in general.

Like other fields of research, the bibliometrics community has also developed institutionalized forms of face to face exchanges in conference series. The oldest series is the yearly conference of the *International Society for Scientometrics and Informetrics* (ISSI), first conducted in 1987. A second conference series is the Science and Technology Indicators (STI) Conference that was initiated in 1988 by the Lisbon Institute. The community is represented by two major scholarly societies, the *International Society for Scientometrics and Informetrics* and the *American Society for Information Science*.

Bibliometric research is conducted at many places. Among important locations are the Leiden Centre for Science and Technology Studies (CWTS), the Centre for R&D Monitoring at KU Leuven, the Scimago Lab in Spain, the Karolinska Institute in Sweden, and the contract research company Science Metrics in Canada. In Germany, institutions that work in the field of bibliometrics form a network connected by the Competence Centre for Bibliometrics. In some contrast to the cognitive core, the established institutions, and the communication channels, the institutionalization of the reproduction function of the community is rather low. Bibliometric competencies are often developed in workshops run by the database providers at CWTS (Cox et al., 2019) or at the *European Summer School on Scientometrics* (ESSS) in combination with training on the job. There is some evidence that the inclusion of bibliometrics in the curricula of LIS programs is weak (Corrall, Kennan, and Afzal, 2013; Petersohn, 2016; Cox et al., 2019).

The institutionalization of academic bibliometrics can be summarized as follows: there is an epistemic core that has been established on the scientific landscape with paradigmatic "example" works and a clear-cut methodology together with institutes that – among others – conduct research in bibliometrics. Institutionalized channels for the communication of research also exist, as do scholarly societies that organize the community. The only shortfall in the institutionalization is that there is a considerable lack of formal ways of qualifications and a lack of certificates signaling qualification in bibliometrics to clients interested in expertise.

Infrastructures for Bibliometrics

Citation databases act as important infrastructures, both for bibliometric research as well as for professional practice. Therefore, their development is sketched in the next step. For more than 40 years the databases of the Institute for Science Information – at the beginning the Science Citation Index only, later also including the Social Science Citation Index, the Arts and Humanities Citation Index, the Conference Proceedings Citation Index, and the Book Citation Index – virtually held a monopoly for the provision of data for citation analysis. From 2000 onwards, a noticeable diversification of sources for citation information has taken place: Elsevier launched Scopus in 2004, Google published Google scholar in 2004 and the Digital Science (part of the Holtzbrinck Publishing Group) came up with Dimensions in 2018. Aside from the large interdisciplinary databases, subject-specific databases such as, for example, the Astrophysics Data System (ADS) (Eichhorn, 2004), zbMATH (Teschke, 2015), and MathSciNet (Davis and Fromerth, 2007) also include citation information as well as academic social network sites like ResearchGate and Academics (both launched in 2008). The increase in the number of sources of citation information is based on digital publishing and the possibility to automatically collect, process, and extract publication and citation information (de Rijcke and Rushforth, 2015), allowing a new regime to measure science that can be called "Quantification 2.0" (Krüger, 2020).

In addition, proprietary products like SciVal and InCite as well as free bibliometric tools like Publish or Perish (Harzing, 2010) and Google Scholar Metrics (Jascó, 2012) were released. What is momentous about this development is that they provide easy-to-use instant bibliometric analysis and off-the-shelf indicators that can be used by anyone, including non-bibliometric experts like research administrators or scientists themselves.

Bibliometrics and its References to Societally Relevant Problems

From its very beginning the problems to which bibliometrics should respond to were manifold. First, there was an interest in understanding the dynamics of science as described above. Second, there was (and still is) a perceived flood of scientific publications resulting in an information crisis (Wouters, 2000, p.66). As far as bibliometrics is concerned, the problem has at least two dimensions. On the one hand, there is the problem of decision-making for librarians, about which journals should be included in library collections, especially if funds and physical space are limited. On the other hand, there is the problem for scientists to find and select interesting and relevant publications, especially if time for reading is limited. Following the initial conception of the Science Citation Index, this was the problem Eugene Garfield wanted to create a solution for. The Science Citation Index was understood as an association-of-ideas-index (Garfield, 1955) and should help scientists to track the take-up of scientific ideas and research in other publications. The Journal Citation Report (JCR) introduced in 1975 refers to the second dimension – the decision-making problem of libraries – and provides information for selecting journals.

From the 1980s onwards, a third problem originated that is today most strongly associated with bibliometrics: to inform external stakeholders about the performance of different entities of the research system and to inform decision-makers about research funding. In this context of application, bibliometrics is used to measure scientific "productivity" and "impact". Evaluative bibliometrics is applied on different levels and at different occasions. Besides formal research evaluation in the context of performance-based funding systems (Butler, 2010) on the national level, evaluative bibliometrics is also used within research organizations for monitoring or informed decision-making and also on the level of individual researchers (e.g., appointment committees, tenure decisions, application for third party funding). Today, the allocation problem can be regarded as the most important societal problem that bibliometrics refers to (Taubert, 2013). Nevertheless, the jurisdictional claim for professional control in that field is by no means uncontested (Petersohn, 2016; Petersohn and Heinze, 2018). First, it competes with the mechanisms of self-regulation of science that the relevance and impact can only be assessed by peer scientists of the field. Second, it competes with non-trained groups using tools that offer instant bibliometric analysis. In many cases this kind of use does not thereby meet the professional standards, and has been criticized as not being well informed and being ill applied (Gingras, 2014). With respect to the extent of control over the field of research evaluation, the degree of professionalization of evaluative bibliometrics tends to be low.

Professional Code as a Reaction to Incomplete Professionalization

The contestation of bibliometrics evaluation can also be observed in different resolutions that refer to this type of use. While the statement of the board of directors of the IEEE (2014) refers to the malpractice in the use of bibliometric indicators (and supports calls for professionalization), The San Francisco Declaration on Research Assessment (DORA, 2012) addresses both (possible) extensive claims for jurisdiction of evaluative bibliometrics as well as malpractice. It likewise calls for not using the Journal Impact Factor as a surrogate for the measurement of individual articles (malpractice) and for assessing the quality of a contribution on the ground of the scientific content and not on metrics (restriction of extensive claims of evaluative bibliometrics).

The bibliometrics community also reacted to the contested nature of their claim with a resolution that can be regarded as the codification of professional norms. In its ten principles, it self-restricts the role of bibliometric analysis in the context of research evaluation, on the one hand, by stating that bibliometric analysis should support but not substitute expert assessment. The control over the field of evaluation should be exercised by both the self-regulating mechanisms of science (qualitative assessment by peers) and evaluate bibliometrics. On the other hand, the claim for jurisdiction is defended against groups without competencies in bibliometrics by the formulation of standards (e.g. careful selection of indicators that measure the performance against the mission of the entity that is evaluated, selection of field adequate indicators taking different publication and citations practices into account, regular updating of indicators (Hicks et al. 2015)). Such demands exclude research evaluation based on automated tools for bibliometric analysis.

Missing tracks of formal qualifications in bibliometrics and missing certificates that could signal competencies together with the proliferation of automated bibliometric tools to non-experts make it likely that claims of jurisdiction on research evaluation will also be contested in the future.

References

Abboth, A 1988, *The System of Professions. An Essay on the Division of Expert Labor*, The University of Chicago Press, Chicago and London.

Butler, L 2010, 'Overview of models of performance based research funding systems', in OECD (ed.), Performance-based Funding for Public Research in Tertiary Education Institutions, Workshop Proceedings, pp. 23–52, OECD Publishing.

Corrall, S, Kennan, MA & Afzal, W 2013, 'Bibliometrics and Research Data Management Services: Emerging Trends in Library Support for Research', *Library Trends*, vol. 61, no. 3, pp. 636–674.

Cox, A, Gadd, E, Petersohn, S & Sbaffi, L 2019, 'Competencies for bibliometrics', *Journal of Libarianship and Information Science*, vol. 51, no. 3, pp. 746–762.

Davis, PM & Fromerth, MJ 2007, 'Does the arXiv lead to higher citations and reduced publisher downloads for mathematics articles?', *Scientometrics*, vol. 71, no. 2, pp. 203–215.

De Solla Price, D 1963, *Little Science, Big Science*, Columbia University Press, New York et al.

De Rijcke, S & Rushforth, A 2015, 'To intervene or not to intervene; is that the question? On the role of scientometrics in research evaluation', *Journal of the Association for Information Science and Technology*, vol. 66, no. 9, pp. 1954–1958.

DORA 2012, *San Francisco Declaration on Research Assessment*, https://sfdora.org/read/ (July 15, 2020) Fehler! Hyperlink-Referenz ungültig..

Eichhorn, G 2004, 'Ten Years of the Astrophysics Data System', *Astronomy and Geophysics*, vol. 45, pp. 3.7–3.9.

Garfield, E 1955, 'Citation Indexes for Science. A new dimension in documentation through association of Ideas', *Science*, vol. 122, no. 3159, pp. 108–111.

Gingras, Y 2014, *Bibliometrics and Research Evaluation. Uses and Abuses*, The MIT Press, Cambridge (Mass.) et al.

Godin, B 2006, 'On the origins of bibliometrics', *Scientometrics*, vol. 68, no. 1, pp. 119–133.

Gross, PLK & Gross, EM 1927, 'College Libraries and Chemical Education', *Science*, vol. 66, no. 1713, pp. 385–389.

Harzing, AW 2010, *Publish or Perish. Your guide to effective and responsible citation analysis*, Tarma Software Research, Melbourne.

Hicks, D, Wouters, P, Waltman, L, de Rijcke, S & Rafols, I 2015, 'Bibliometrics: The Leiden Manifesto for research metrics', *Nature*, vol. 520, no. 7548, pp. 429–431.

IEEE 2014, 'Appropriate Use of Bibliometric Indicators for the Assessment of Journals, Research Proposals, and Individuals', *IEEE Computer Graphics and Application*, vol. 34, no. 2, pp. 86–87.

Jascó, P 2012, 'Google Scholar Metrics for Publications. The software and content features of a new open access bibliometric service', *Online Information Review*, vol. 36, no. 4, pp. 604–619.

Krüger, AK 2020, 'Quantification 2.0? Biblilometric Infrastructures in Academic Evaluation', *Politics and Governance*, vol. 8, no. 2, forthcoming.

Lotka, AJ 1926, 'The frequency distribution of scientific productivity', *Journal of the Washington Academy of Sciences*, vol. 16, no. 12, pp. 317–323.

Petersohn, S 2016, 'Professional competencies and jurisdictional claims in evaluative bibliometrics: The educations mandate of academic librarians', *Education for Information*, vol. 32, no. 2, pp. 165–193.

Petersohn, S & Heinze, T 2018, 'Professionalization of bibliometric research assessment. Insights from the history of the Leiden Centre for Science and Technology Studies (CWTS)', *Science and Public Policy*, vol. 45, no. 4, pp. 565–578.

Prichard, A 1969, 'Statistical Bibliography or Bibliometrics?' *Journal of Documentation*, vol. 25, no. 4, pp 348–349.

Taubert, N 2013, 'Bibliometrie in der Forschungsevaluation. Zur Konstitution und Funktionslogik wechselseitiger Beobachtung zwischen Wissenschaft und Politik', in JH Passoth & J Wehner (eds.), Quoten, Kurven und Profile. Zur Vermessung der sozialen Welt, pp. 197–204, Springer VS, Wiesbaden.

Weingart, P & Schwechheimer, H 2007, 'Institutionelle Verschiebungen der Wissensproduktion – Zum Wandel der Struktur wissenschaftlicher Disziplinen', in Weingart, P (ed.), Nachrichten aus der Wissensgesellschaft. Analysen zur Veränderung der Wissenschaft, pp. 41–54, Velbrück Wissenschaft.

Wouters, P 2000, 'Garfield as alchemist', in B Cronin & HB Atkins (eds.), The Web of Knowledge, pp. 65–71, Information today, Medford.

Yang, S, Han, R, Wolfram, D & Zhao, Y 2016, 'Visualizing the intellectual structure of information science (2006–2015): Introducing author keyword coupling analysis', *Journal of Informetrics*, vol. 10, no. 1, pp. 132–150.

1.3 Eugene Garfield and the Institute for Scientific Information

David A. Pendlebury

Abstract: Eugene Garfield and his Institution for Scientific Information (ISI) helped revolutionize information retrieval in the second half of the twentieth century by introducing the concept of citation indexing for scientific literature. *Science Citation Index* data also served as a foundation for quantitative studies in the history and sociology of science and eventually gave birth to the field of scientometrics. From its founding in 1960 until its sale to Thomson Corporation in 1992, ISI introduced a range of current awareness and information retrieval products and services covering the literature of the sciences, social sciences, and humanities. Other products, such as the *Journal Citation Reports*, permitted analysis of citations as measures of communication and research performance. ISI colleague Henry Small, with the support of Garfield, introduced science mapping in the 1970s to reveal the socio-cognitive structure of research. Clarivate Analytics acquired the ISI product range from Thomson Reuters Corporation in 2016 and today continues the original business and intellectual legacy of Garfield.

Keywords: citation analysis, citation indexing, Clarivate Analytics, *Current Contents*, Eugene Garfield, history and sociology of science, impact factor, Institute for Scientific Information (ISI), *Science Citation Index (SCI)*, *Web of Science (WoS)*.

Eugene Garfield (1925–2017) established the Institute for Scientific Information (ISI) in Philadelphia, Pennsylvania, USA, in 1960 as a commercial entity to produce a wide range of current awareness and information retrieval products, including *Current Contents* and the *Science Citation Index*. ISI (1960–1992) proved to be an innovative and risk-taking organization that pioneered many new concepts while rapidly adopting the latest technology in information processing, storage, and methods of information dissemination (Lazerow, 1974; Cawkell and Garfield, 2001; Lawlor, 2014). Its products were progressively transitioned from print to magnetic tape, to diskette, to CD-ROM, and to the World Wide Web. For more than three decades, the man and the business were inseparable in the eyes of customers and the research community at large.

David A. Pendlebury, Institute for Scientific Information, Clarivate Analytics, 160 Blackfriars Road, London SE1 8EZ, United Kingdom, david.pendlebury@clarivate.com

The Path to an Idea

The notion of a citation index for the sciences upended traditional ideas of indexing and information retrieval, which were previously focused on subject indexing by professionally trained personnel using controlled vocabularies. In the 1950s the increase in the production of scientific information put great strain on traditional indexing methods, resulting in delays of several years from publication to availability of the information in an index.

At the beginning of the decade, in 1951, after obtaining a B.S. in Chemistry at Columbia University in 1949 and working in the lab of physical chemist Louis P. Hammett, Garfield joined the Welch Medical Indexing Project at Johns Hopkins University, funded by the Army Medical Library, the predecessor of the National Library of Medicine. He explored machine methods to speed indexing of the scientific literature. In 1953 he organized the first symposium on this subject. It was after this that Garfield learned about citation indexing employed in the legal profession in *Shepard's Citations*. This index, in existence since 1873, served lawyers and judges by showing which legal decisions had been subsequently affirmed, overturned, or modified. Although Garfield made significant contributions to advancing traditional indexing using the then new IBM 101 Electronic Statistical Machine, his discovery of citation indexing was transformative in his thinking about automating indexing and improving information retrieval.

He immediately grasped the benefits of applying this method to the scientific literature: by recording references given by authors in their papers, one could reliably and precisely find related publications and, moreover, search "forward" to identify later papers that cited an earlier one of interest. After receiving his M.S. degree in library science from Columbia University in 1954, Garfield published a paper in *Science* in 1955 proposing a citation index for the sciences, which he called an "association-of-ideas" index and the researchers supplying the citations his "army of indexers." Citation indexing did not require professional indexing using subject headings and controlled vocabulary and was also independent of changing terminology. Moreover, citation indexing, he stated, broke the "subject index barrier" of conventional monodisciplinary indexes since citations could and did point to literature outside the boundaries of any defined coverage (Garfield, 1955; Weinstock, 1971; Garfield, 1979; McVeigh, 2017; de Araújo, 2019).

The *Science Citation Index*

So unconventional was Garfield's proposal that he met with indifference or opposition. In 1959, Joshua Lederberg, the 1958 Nobel laureate in Physiology or Medicine, wondered what happened to Garfield's proposal of 1955 and contacted him to ask about the development of a citation index, for which he expressed support. Lederberg's advocacy proved essential and a prototype focusing on genetics (*Genetics Ci-*

tation Index), with support from the US National Institutes of Health (NIH), was developed in 1962 and 1963 (Lederberg 1963). Garfield's suggestion to NIH and the National Science Foundation (NSF) to publish the full *Science Citation Index* (the name was Lederberg's suggestion) was not adopted, so Garfield took the risk to produce this himself in 1963 (Wouters, 1999; De Bellis, 2009).

The next year saw the first commercial version of the *Science Citation Index (SCI)*, issued in quarterly fascicles (Garfield, 1964). Garfield traveled the world to spread the gospel of citation indexing. Institutional subscriptions steadily increased. In 1973, he introduced the *Social Sciences Citation Index (SSCI)* and, in 1978, added the *Arts & Humanities Citation Index (A&HCI)* . The publication of the citation indexes in book form made for challenging manual searching as one consulted a Source Index of items listed by first author, a Permuterm Subject Index (from 1966 onwards) which listed pairs of title words, and a Citation Index – each section an entry point to, respectively, indexed papers, subjects and subtopics, and cited works and their citing papers. Online access via dial-up vendor services such as Dialog in the 1970s ameliorated manual searching through multiple and heavy printed volumes. A CD-ROM version of the *SCI* was introduced in 1988. Following the sale of ISI to the Thomson Corporation in 1992, a web version, bringing together the *SCI*, *SSCI*, and *A&HCI* and named the *Web of Science (WoS)*, appeared in 1997 (Schnell, 2018).

As of the beginning of 2020, and under the ownership of Clarivate Analytics (since 2016), the *WoS* Core Collection indexed more than 21,000 journals and, in total, included about 77 million source items and some 1.5 billion cited references. Coverage for the *SCI* and *SSCI* extends back to 1900, whereas the *A&HCI* spans from 1975 to present. In addition to the flagship databases, *WoS* also includes the *Conference Proceedings Citation Index* (1990-present), introduced in 2008; the *Book Citation Index*, (2005-present), introduced in 2011; and, the *Data Citation Index*, introduced in 2012. The *Emerging Sources Citation Index* (2005-present), which focuses on journals of regional importance and in emerging fields, was added to *WoS* in 2015.

The Journal Impact Factor

In the early 1960s, Garfield and his ISI colleague Irving H. Sher (1924–1996) examined patterns of journal-to-journal citations to identify the most-cited journals in each field (Garfield, 2000a). These data fed back into decisions about the journals to be indexed in the *SCI* if they were not already. Garfield and Sher formulated an indicator of journal importance and influence: the impact factor (Garfield and Sher, 1963; Garfield, 1972; Garfield, 1976; Bensman, 2007; Archambault, 2009; Pendlebury and Adams, 2012; Larivière and Sugimoto, 2019). The impact factor was first published in the *Journal Citation Reports (JCR)*, a volume appended to the 1975 *SCI*. The *JCR* has always included a wealth of information apart from the impact factor, including total papers, total citations, self-citations, citing and cited journal data, cited and citing half-life data, an immediacy index, and other statistics. In 1990 the *JCR* became a separate product. It offered two editions, for the sciences and for the social sciences, and over the years has been delivered in print, microfiche, CD-ROM, and on the web.

The journal impact factor became one of the most popular but most controversial of the company's offerings. What was designed to aid ISI itself in journal selection, librarians in collection development, and information scientists and other scholars in understanding scientific and scholarly communication patterns among journals turned into a proxy for the quality of individual papers published in a journal and a surrogate measure of performance in the evaluation of individuals. Publication in a high-impact journal, however, does not mean a paper or person will be highly cited, owing to the characteristic skewed distribution of citation statistics. Garfield pointed out the misuse, in public and print, but was nevertheless frequently blamed for applications of the impact factor that were never intended (Garfield, 2006).

Current Contents

While at Johns Hopkins in the early 1950s, Garfield created *Contents in Advance*, a publication that reproduced tables of contents of journals in library and information science. He produced it for his own interests and needs but offered it to others as a product. This was the origin of *Current Contents*. His solution to the problem of current awareness was "ridiculously simple" (Grimwade, 2018): provide in compact form a listing of just-published journal literature to alert researchers to articles of interest even before journals arrived on library shelves. In 1955 he started a contents-page service for management science which he titled *Management's DocuMation Preview*. It was later renamed *Current Contents in Management* but failed to earn a market. In 1956, and related to consulting work for pharmaceutical companies, Garfield started *Current Contents of Pharmaco-Medical, Chemical & Life Sciences*. *Current Contents of Space, Electronic & Physical Sciences Including Pure & Applied Chemistry* appeared in 1960, and thereafter the *Current Contents* business took off. In fact, it was the success of *Current Contents* that allowed Garfield to underwrite the development of the *SCI* and other products, such as *Index Chemicus*, in the 1960s. Editions, under various names, appeared and merged over the years (Lawlor, 2014; Grimwade, 2018). Eventually, there were seven editions of *Current Contents: Life Sciences*; *Clinical Medicine*; *Physical, Chemical & Earth Sciences*; *Agriculture, Biology & Environmental Sciences*; *Engineering, Computing & Technology*; *Social and Behavioral Sciences*; and *Arts & Humanities*.

One appeal of *Current Contents* was Garfield's own writing in the form of essays appearing sporadically in the 1960s but weekly from 1972. His essays, and other materials, are collected in 15 volumes (Garfield, 1977–1993) and available on his personal website (http://www.garfield.library.upenn.edu/).

Selective Dissemination of Information and Document Delivery

Another area of activity for Garfield and Sher in the 1960s dealt with what was then known as Selective Dissemination of Information (SDI) services. Drawing on the data recorded for *SCI* and *Current Contents*, a new service was introduced in 1965: *Automatic Subject Citation Alert* (*ASCA*). With *ASCA*, a researcher would create a search profile including any combination of author names, title words, organization names, journals, and, importantly, cited references that represented the researcher's interests. The search profile was run against the ISI data weekly and a printed report was then mailed to the researcher (Garfield and Sher, 1967).

In the days before transmission of digital forms of journals, ISI received multiple copies of the journals it indexed. These copies were cannibalized to provide copies of specific articles requested by ISI customers, and a royalty would be paid to the publisher. This document delivery service, launched in the 1960s, was originally called *OATS*, for *Original Article Tears Sheet Service*, but was later called *The Genuine Article*.

Chemical Information Products

Educated in chemistry, Garfield took interest at the Welch Medical Indexing Project in "chemical nomenclature used in Medical Subject Headings (MESH) and understanding the need for new approaches to retrieving chemical information" (Garfield, 2000b). Later, in 1958, working as a consultant to the Pharmaceutical Manufacturers' Association, Garfield indexed steroid compounds in the literature and recognized the possibility of algorithmically locating and identifying newly reported compounds. At this time, he invented a method for converting chemical names to molecular formulas, earning a Ph.D. in structural linguistics from the University of Pennsylvania for this work in 1961. He introduced *Index Chemicus* in 1960 as the first product of ISI. It reported new compounds and included graphical abstracts along with chemical formulas. It eventually became *Current Abstracts of Chemistry and Index Chemicus* in 1970. A range of chemical information products followed *Index Chemicus*: *Index Chemicus Registry System*, in 1968, which permitted computer searching of chemical structures using Wiswesser Line Notation; *Chemical Substructure Index*, in 1971; *Automatic New Structure Alert*, an SDI service, in 1973; *Current Chemical Reactions*, in 1979; and *Reaction Citation Index*, in 1995 (Garfield, 2001). These products were offered in a variety of media as technology changed through the years. The *WoS* Core Collection today includes *Current Chemical Reactions* (since 1985) and *Index Chemicus* (since 1993).

The History, Sociology, and Structure of Science: Derek Price, Robert Merton, and Henry Small

In his 1955 paper Garfield emphasized the importance of citation indexing for information retrieval but noted the value of citation data for the historian, both to reveal the transmission of ideas and the extent that a paper had been cited (Garfield, 1955). He returned to the theme in 1963 and expressed his interest in computer-generated "topological network diagrams which show the chronological and derivational relationships between scientific papers and therefore scientific discoveries" (Garfield, 1963). This paper references personal communication the previous year with two individuals who would figure largely in the use of ISI's citation data for historical and sociological research: Derek J. de Solla Price (1922–1983) of Yale University and Robert K. Merton (1910–2003) of Columbia University.

Price, a physicist by training and historian of science, had published *Science Since Babylon* and would publish *Little Science, Big Science* the year after his contact with Garfield (Price, 1961; Price, 1963). In both he demonstrated his interest in using the "tools of science on science itself." Once made aware of the new *Science Citation Index*, he asked for and received data from Garfield related to his interests, including the nature of the research front which he described as a growing "epidermal layer" of papers (Price, 1965) and cumulative advantage processes in citation that contribute to characteristic skewed distributions (Price, 1976). Price laid a foundation in quantitative studies of science using ISI citation data and in doing so helped establish the field of scientometrics. He also advocated strongly for the use of publication and citation analysis in planning, policymaking, and funding. When the NSF produced its first *Science Indicators* report issued in 1973, it included *SCI* data on national publication output and citation impact.

Merton, the leading sociologist of science, also lent support to Garfield and ISI by describing citation as part of the normative behavior of scientists with respect to acknowledging intellectual property rights. He called the citation a "pellet of peer recognition" and noted the moral imperative to cite one's colleagues in the repayment of intellectual debts (Merton, 1988). Harriet Zuckerman, a student of Merton, has summarized the influence of Garfield and citation analysis in the sociology in science (Zuckerman, 2018).

Henry Small (1941-), an historian of science, arrived at ISI in 1972. He soon introduced the technique of co-citation clustering to define specialty research areas (Small, 1973). The next year, with Belver Griffith (1931–1999), he demonstrated science mapping of the literature representing its socio-cognitive structure as determined by researchers themselves through their patterns of citation. In the following years, Small extended and improved techniques of science mapping, studied the validity of the maps in relation to expert opinion, and explored the connections from one realm to another, noting how these links are "threads that hold the fabric of science together" (Small and Garfield, 1985). Price welcomed Small's work in mapping science, calling it "revolutionary in its implications" and a step toward defining a natural order of research that could be used to create a "giant atlas of the corpus of scientific papers that can be maintained in real time for classifying and monitoring developments as they occur" (Price, 1980). In the 1980s, ISI introduced the *Atlas of Science*, first in book form and thereafter as a series of review journals (Grimwade, 2018). In retrospect, these products may be called experimental since they were not commercially successful. The *Atlas of Science* is emblematic of ISI in several ways. It was a cutting-edge venture rooted in a desire to understand the nature and potential of citation data, and it was a product offered without knowing whether there was any market for it. But Garfield valued the results of Small's research and took a risk.

Small synthesized the interests and perspectives of Price (mapping the research front), Merton (revealing socio-cognitive relationships and structures), and Garfield (exploiting the full richness of citation data), and he then extended these by describing the symbolic function of highly cited papers, exploring changing structures over time including identification of emerging topics, probing the context of citations, and more (Small, 2003; Pendlebury, 2013).

Citation Data in Research Evaluation

The use of citation data in the assessment of research performance relies heavily on Merton's description of the normative behavior of scientists as represented in the literature: the papers and people accruing many "credits" do so because the research community has depended on them more than others, signifying influence, impact, significance, utility, and other such notions (Garfield and Welljams-Dorof, 1992; Moed, 2005; Moed, 2017; Aksnes et al., 2019)

With the appearance of NSF's *Science Indicators* (1973), Francis Narin's *Evaluative Bibliometrics* (Narin, 1976), and *Toward a Metric of Science* (Elkana et al., 1978), interest in and use of publication and citation data as research performance indicators gathered pace. The launch of the journal *Scientometrics* (1978), initiated by Tibor Braun (1932-) of the Hungarian Academy of Sciences, also signaled that there was now a critical mass of scholars focusing on quantitative studies of science (and drawing on *SCI* data for their research). In the 1980s Braun's Information Science and Scientometrics Unit (ISSRU) focused on studies comparing the performance of nations. The ISSRU team demonstrated the use of relative citation impact and other measures. Meanwhile, the Centre for Science and Technology Studies (CWTS) at Leiden University, under the direction of Anthony F.J. van Raan (1945-), explored applications of publication and citation data to gauge performance at the meso level, that is, of universities and research groups within them. Both groups used ISI's data, but they modified and edited the data for the purposes of scientometric studies, since the data were indexed and organized for the different purpose of information retrieval.

Sociologist Jonathan Cole (1942-) of Columbia University, another student of Merton, noted that "the creation of the *SCI* represents a good case study of how technological innovations very frequently create the necessary conditions for advance in scientific fields" (Cole, 2000). In this case, it gave birth to the field of scientometrics.

Meanwhile at ISI, its research department, under the direction of Small, launched the newsletter *Science Watch: Tracking Performance and Trends in Basic Research* in 1990. The monthly publication included a feature story based on publication and citation data, an interview with a top-cited scientist, and top-ten lists of hot papers in biology, clinical medicine, chemistry, and physics, which resembled music pop-charts or bestseller book lists. During the 1990s at ISI, the research group began to produce products, first issued on diskette and then CD-ROM, for PC use: *National Science Indicators, University Science Indicators, Journal Performance Indicators, Highly Cited Papers, Local Journal Utilization Report* (used for journal collection development), and others including custom versions. In 2001, under the ownership of Thomson Corporation, Small and colleagues developed *Essential Science Indicators (ESI)*, a web product that provides data on most-cited authors, institutions, nations, and journals in 22 broad fields, as well as highly cited and hot papers. Small's research front data were also included, with the fronts derived from co-citation analysis of ESI's highly cited papers. In 2009, under ownership of Thomson Reuters, *InCites*, a web platform for research performance analysis, was introduced.

Fueling the activity of the ISSRU, CWTS, ISI, and other groups in the 1990s was demand from government agencies and universities responding to a new regime of accountability and increasing competition for research funding. New Public Management, in Australia, the UK, and US, dramatically changed the administration of universities, moving control from the faculty senate to professional administrators who employed business models in running their institutions. Publication output and citation impact data supplied the need for so-called hard evidence about research performance and demonstrations of "value for money."

Garfield watched the sea change in use of citation data and in 1998 asked, "Is the tail now wagging the dog?" (Garfield, 1998). The dog was citation data for information retrieval and the tail scientometric data on research performance. Garfield's intellectual interests in use of his own data were, in order: information retrieval, the history and sociology of science including science mapping, and, last, research evaluation.

Garfield frequently wrote about most-cited scientists and pointed out that citation data could balance instances of biased peer review, adding fairness to an assessment. But mostly he considered the use of citation data in the appointment, promotion, and funding of researchers complex and, with Merton, "ancillary to detailed judgments by informed peers" (Merton, 1979). While he did not proscribe the use of citation data for evaluating individuals, Garfield realized that when used at scale by non-experts misuse was inevitable and would have profound career and personal consequences. As early as 1963, Garfield condemned "promiscuous and careless use of quantitative citation data for sociological evaluations, including personnel and fellowship selection" (Garfield, 1963; also Garfield, 1983).

At a presentation in Dalian, China in 2009, Garfield said the tail of scientometrics had grown into a "monster." Developments contributing to this expansion in the last two decades, among others, have been the proliferation of university rankings following the appearance of the *Academic Ranking of World Universities* in 2003, the introduction of *Google Scholar* in 2004, and the arrival of the h-index in 2005.

Researchers themselves, who in past decades opposed evaluation by citations measures, increasingly display and even tout their total citation count or h-index, a sign of the institutionalization of "metrics." In some evaluative contexts, rewards are so outsized that researchers, albeit a minority, engage in strategic behavior in publishing and citing, effectively destroying the meaning and value of the performance indicators (de Rijcke et al. 2016). On the other hand, the robust development of science mapping during the last two decades is a salutary counterweight to runaway research assessment schemes and citation gaming, as well as a return to original notions of Garfield and of Small on the meaning, richness, and value of the data.

After ISI

After the sale of ISI in 1992, Garfield served as Chairman Emeritus to the company he founded. He continued a program of personal research and publishing and frequently traveled to lecture and receive honors.

A lifelong interest in communicating scientific information within the profession inspired Garfield in 1986 to create *The Scientist*, a newspaper for researchers. When ISI was sold to Thomson Corporation, he retained *The Scientist* and developed it further in partnership with publisher Vitek Tracz (1940-) after 2002 (Grimwade, 2018). It continues today under different ownership.

In addition to his work with *The Scientist*, Garfield returned to research begun in 1964, when he mapped direct citation links between key papers on the structure of DNA research, ordered chronologically to show descendants and antecedents (Garfield et al., 1964). In the first decade of the twenty-first century Garfield and colleagues developed the software tool *HistCite*. This PC program analyzed a collection of papers imported from *WoS* and drew a map of direct citations between papers arranged by year. He called this type of analysis algorithmic historiography (Garfield et al., 2003; Garfield, 2009; Grimwade, 2018). *HistCite* has now been superseded by *CitNetExplorer*, whose developers acknowledged inspiration from *HistCite* (van Eck and Waltman, 2014).

Accolades

In recognition of his research contributions, Garfield received several honorary doctoral degrees and numerous awards, including the first Derek J. de Solla Price Memorial Medal of the journal *Scientometrics* (1984). He was a Fellow of the American Association for the Advancement of Science (1966), the American Academy of Arts and Sciences (2005), and a Member of the American Philosophical Society (2007). During 1998–2000, he served as President of the American Society for Information Science & Technology.

In 2000, Garfield received a festschrift volume from colleagues entitled *The Web of Knowledge* (Cronin and Atkins, 2000). He died in February 2017, at the age of 91 (Clarivate Analytics, 2017; Small. 2017; Wouters, 2017).

Transcriptions of two in-depth interviews and an extensive video interview conducted by Small provide further information on his life and career (Garfield, 1987; Garfield, 1997; Garfield, n.d.). The Science History Institute, Philadelphia, maintains an archive of Garfield's professional papers.

As mentioned, the Thomson Corporation acquired ISI in 1992. Thomson merged with Reuters in 2008 to become Thomson Reuters. In 2016, Thomson Reuters sold its intellectual property and science business, including the substance of the original ISI, to two private equity firms in partnership, Onex Corporation and Baring Private Equity Asia. The company was then rebranded as Clarivate Analytics. The ISI identity was revived at the beginning of 2018 to designate a new research division within Clarivate.

References

Aksnes, DW, Langfeldt, L & Wouters, P 2019, 'Citations, Citation Indicators, and Research Quality: An Overview of Basic Concepts and Theories', *Sage Open*, vol. 9, no. 1, article number 2158244019829575, https://journals.sagepub.com/doi/full/10.1177/2158244019829575 (July 15, 2020), doi: https://doi.org/10.1177/2158244019829575.

Archambault, E & Larivière, V 2009, 'History of the Journal Impact Factor: Contingencies and Consequences', *Scientometrics*, vol. 79, no. 3, pp. 639–653, doi: https://doi.org/10.1007/s11192-007-2036-x.

Bensman, SJ 2007, 'Garfield and the Impact Factor', *Annual Review of Information Science and Technology*, vol. 41, pp. 93–155, http://garfield.library.upenn.edu/bensman/bensmanegif2007.pdf (July 15, 2020), doi: https://doi.org/10.1002/aris.2007.1440410110.

Cawkell, T & Garfield, E 2001, 'Institute for Scientific Information', in EH Fredricksson (ed.), *A Century of Scientific Publishing*, pp. 149–160, IOS Press, Amsterdam, http://www.garfield.library.upenn.edu/papers/isichapter15centuryofscipub149-160y2001.pdf (July 15, 2020), ISBN 13: 9781586031480.

Clarivate Analytics, *Commemoration and Celebration of the Life of Eugene Garfield, 1925–2017*, program for event, September 15–16, 2017, Clarivate Analytics, Philadelphia, PA.

Cole, JR 2000, 'A Short History of the Use of Citations as a Measure of the Impact of Scientific and Scholarly Research', in B Cronin & HB Atkins (eds.), *The Web of Knowledge: A Festschrift in Honor of Eugene Garfield*, pp. 281–300, Information Today, Inc., Medford, NJ, http://www.garfield.library.upenn.edu/webofknowledge.html (July 15, 2020), ISBN-13: 978–1573870993.

Cronin, B & Atkins, HB (eds.) 2000, *The Web of Knowledge: A Festschrift in Honor of Eugene Garfield*, Information Today, Medford, NJ, http://www.garfield.library.upenn.edu/webofknowledge.html (July 15, 2020), ISBN-13: 978–1573870993.

de Araújo, PC, Castanha, RCG & Hjørland, B 2019, 'Citation Indexing and Indexes', in B Hjørland & C Gnoli (eds.), *ISKO Encyclopedia of Knowledge Organization*, ISKO, https://www.isko.org/cyclo/citation (July 15, 2020).

De Bellis, N 2009, *Bibliometrics and Citation Analysis: From the Science Citation Index to Cybermetrics*, The Scarecrow Press, Inc., Lanham, MD, ISBN-13: 978–0810867130.

de Rijcke, S, Wouters, PF, Rushforth, AD, Franssen, TP & Hammarfelt, B 2016, 'Evaluation Practices and Effects of Indicator Use – A Literature Review', *Research Evaluation*, vol. 25, no. 2, pp. 161–169, doi: https://doi.org/10.1093/reseval/rvv038.

Elkana, Y, Lederberg, J, Merton, RJ, Thackray, A & Zuckerman, H 1978, *Toward a Metric of Science: The Advent of Science Indicators*, John Wiley & Sons, New York, ISBN: 471 98435–3.

Garfield, E 1955, 'Citation Indexes for Science: A New Dimension in Documentation through Association of Ideas', *Science*, vol. 122, no. 3159, pp. 108–11, http://garfield.library.upenn.edu/papers/science1955.pdf (July 15, 2020), doi: https://doi.org/10.1126/science.122.3159.108.

Garfield, E & Sher, IH 1963, 'New Factors in the Evaluation of Scientific Literature Through Citation Indexing', *American Documentation*, vol. 14, no. 3, pp. 195–201, http://www.garfield.library.upenn.edu/essays/v6p492y1983.pdf (July 15, 2020), doi: https://doi.org/10.1002/asi.5090140304.

Garfield, E 1963, 'Citation Indexes in Sociological and Historical Research', *American Documentation*, vol. 14, no. 4, pp. 289–91, http://www.garfield.library.upenn.edu/essays/V1p043y1962-73.pdf (July 15, 2020), doi: https://doi.org/10.1002/asi.5090140405.

Garfield, E 1964, '*Science Citation Index* – A New Dimension in Indexing', *Science*, vol. 144, no. 3619, pp. 649–654, http://www.garfield.library.upenn.edu/essays/v7p525y1984.pdf, doi: https://doi.org/10.1126/science.144.3619.649 (July 15, 2020).

Garfield, E, Sher, IH & Torpie, RJ 1964, 'The Use of Citation Data in Writing the History of Science', Institute for Scientific Information, Philadelphia, PA, http://www.garfield.library.upenn.edu/papers/useofcitdatawritinghistofsci.pdf (July 15, 2020).

Garfield, E & Sher, IH 1967, 'ASCA (Automatic Subject Citation Alert): A New Personalized Current Awareness Service for Scientists', *American Behavioral Scientist*, vol. 10, no. 5, pp. 29–32, http://www.garfield.library.upenn.edu/essays/v6p514y1983.pdf (July 15, 2020), doi: https://doi.org/10.1177/000276426701000507.

Garfield, E 1972, 'Citation Analysis as a Tool in Journal Evaluation', *Science*, vol. 178, no. 4060, pp. 471–479, http://www.garfield.library.upenn.edu/essays/V1p527y1962-73.pdf (July 15, 2020), doi: https://doi.org/10.1126/science.178.4060.471.

Garfield, E 1976, 'Significant Journals of Science,' *Nature*, vol. 264, no. 5587, pp. 609–617, http://www.garfield.library.upenn.edu/essays/v3p130y1977-78.pdf (July 15, 2020), doi: https://doi.org/10.1038/264609a0.

Garfield, E 1993, *Essays of an Information Scientist. Vols. 1–15*, ISI Press, Philadelphia, PA, http://www.garfield.library.upenn.edu/essays.html (July 15, 2020).

Garfield, E 1984, 'How to Use Citation Data for Faculty Evaluation, and When is it Relevant? Part 1', *Current Contents*, vol. 44 (October 31, 1983), reprinted in E Garfield, *Essays of an Information Scientist. Vol 6 (1983)*, pp. 354–362, ISI Press, Philadelphia, PA, http://www.garfield.library.upenn.edu/essays.html (July 15, 2020).

Garfield, E 1987, interview by Arnold Thackray and Jeffrey L. Sturchio, Beckman Center for the History of Chemistry, November 16, http://www.garfield.library.upenn.edu/oralhistory/interview.html (July 15, 2020).

Garfield, E 1979, *Citation Indexing – Its Theory and Application in Science, Technology, and Humanities*, http://www.garfield.library.upenn.edu/ci/title.pdf (July 15, 2020), John Wiley & Sons, New York, ISBN-13: 978–0471025597.

Garfield, E & Welljams-Dorof, A 1992, 'Citation Data: Their Use as Quantitative Indicators for Science and Technology Evaluation and Policymaking', *Science and Public Policy*, vol. 19, no. 5, pp. 321–327, http://www.garfield.library.upenn.edu/papers/sciandpubpolv19%285%29p321y1992.html (July 15, 2020), doi: https://doi.org/10.1093/spp/19.5.321.

Garfield, E 1997, interview by RV Williams, Chemical Heritage Foundation, July 29, http://garfield.library.upenn.edu/papers/oralhistorybywilliams.pdf (July 15, 2020).

Garfield, E 1998, 'From Citation Indexes to Informetrics: Is the Tail Now Wagging the Dog?', *Libri*, vol. 48, no. 2, pp. 67–80, http://www.garfield.library.upenn.edu/papers/libriv48%282%29p67-80y1998.pdf (July 15, 2020), doi: https://doi.org/10.1515/libr.1998.48.2.67.

Garfield, E 2000a, 'Recollections of Irving H. Sher 1924–1996: Polymath/Information Scientist Extraordinaire', *Journal of the American Society for Information Science and Technology*, vol. 52, no. 14, pp. 1197–1202, http://garfield.library.upenn.edu/papers/sherjasis&t52%2814%29p1197y2001.pdf (July 15, 2020), doi: https://doi.org/10.1002/asi.1187.

Garfield, E 2000b, 'From Laboratory to Information Explosions. The Evolution of Chemical Information Services at ISI', *Journal of Information Science*, vol. 27, no. 2, pp. 119–125, http://www.garfield.library.upenn.edu/papers/jis27%282%29p119y2001.pdf (July 15, 2020), doi: https://doi.org/10.1177/0165551014233626.

Garfield, E, Pudovkin AI &. Istomin, VS 2003, 'Why Do We Need Algorithmic Historiography?', *Journal of the American Society for Information Science and Technology*, vol. 54, no. 5, pp. 400–412, http://garfield.library.upenn.edu/papers/jasist54%285%29400y2003.pdf (July 15, 2020), doi: https://doi.org/10.1002/asi.10226.

Garfield, E 2006, 'The History and Meaning of the Journal Impact Factor,' *JAMA – Journal of the American Medical Association*, vol. 293, no. 1, pp. 90–93, http://garfield.library.upenn.edu/papers/jamajif2006.pdf (July 15, 2020), doi: https://doi.org/10.1001/jama.295.1.90.

Garfield, E 2009, 'From the Science of Science to Scientometrics: Visualizing the History of Science with *HistCite* Software', *Journal of Informetrics*, vol. 3, no. 3, pp. 173–179, http://garfield.library.upenn.edu/papers/issispain2007.pdf (July 15, 2020), doi: https://doi.org/10.1016/j.joi.2009.03.009.

Garfield, E, personal webpages, http://www.garfield.library.upenn.edu/ (July 15, 2020).

Garfield, E n.d., video interview, Web of Stories, https://www.webofstories.com/play/eugene.garfield/1 (July 15, 2020).

Grimwade, A 2018, 'Eugene Garfield – 60 Years of Invention and Innovation', *Frontiers in Research Metrics and Analytics*, vol. 3, no. 14, https://www.frontiersin.org/articles/10.3389/frma.2018.00014/full (July 15, 2020), doi: https://doi.org/10.3389/frma.2018.00014.

Lawlor, B 2014, 'The Institute for Scientific Information: A Brief History', in LR McEwen & RE Buntrock (eds.), *The Future of the History of Chemical Information*, ACS Symposium Series 1164, pp. 109–136, American Chemical Society, Washington, ISBN-13: 978–0841229457.

Larivière, V & Sugimoto, CR 2019, 'The Journal Impact Factor: A Brief History, Critique, and Discussion of Adverse Effects', in W. Glänzel, HF Moed, U Schmoch & M Thelwall (eds.), *Springer Handbook of Science and Technology Indicators*, pp. 3–24, Cham, Switzerland, Springer Nature, ISBN-13: 978–3030025106.

Lazerow, S 1974, 'Institute for Scientific Information', in A Kent, H Lancour & JE Daily (eds.), *Encyclopedia of Library and Information Science*, vol. 12, pp. 89–97, Marcel Dekker, New

York, http://www.garfield.library.upenn.edu/essays/v2p197y1974-76.pdf (July 15, 2020), ISBN-13: 9780824720124.

Lederberg, J 1963, 'Preface', in E Garfield & IH Sher, *Genetics Citation Index*, Institute for Scientific Information, Philadelphia, PA, http://garfield.library.upenn.edu/essays/v2p189y1974–76.pdf (July 15, 2020).

McVeigh, ME 2017, 'Citation Indexes and the Web of Science', in JD McDonald & M Levine Clark (eds.), *Encyclopedia of Library and Information Sciences*, fourth edition, vol. 2, 940–950, CRC Press, Boca Raton, FL, ISBN-13: 978–1466552593.

Merton, RK 1979, 'Foreword', in E Garfield, *Citation Indexing – Its Theory and Application in Science, Technology, and Humanities*, pp. xiii-xv, John Wiley & Sons, New York, http://garfield.library.upenn.edu/ci/foreword.pdf (July 15, 2020), ISBN-13: 978–0471025597.

Merton, RK 1988, 'The Matthew Effect in Science, II: Cumulative Advantage and the Symbolism of Intellectual Property', *ISIS*, vol. 79, no. 4, pp. 606–623, http://garfield.library.upenn.edu/merton/matthewii.pdf (July 15, 2020), doi: https://doi.org/10.1086/354848.

Moed, HF 2005, *Citation Analysis in Research Evaluation*, Springer Nature, Dordrecht, Netherlands, ISBN-13: 978–1402037139.

Moed, HF 2017, *Applied Evaluative Informetrics*, Springer Nature, Cham, Switzerland, ISBN-13: 978–3319605210.

Narin, F 1976, *Evaluative Bibliometrics: The Use of Publication and Citation Data in the Evaluation of Scientific Activity*, Computer Horizons Inc., Cherry Hill, NJ.

Pendlebury, DA & Adams, J 2012, 'Comments on a Critique of the Thomson Reuters Journal Impact Factor', *Scientometrics*, vol. 92, no. 2, pp. 395–401, doi: https://doi.org/10.1007/s11192-012-0689-6.

Pendlebury, DA 2013, 'Research Fronts: In Search of the Structure of Science', in C King & DA Pendlebury, *Research Fronts 2013: 100 Top-Ranked Specialties in the Sciences and Social Sciences*, pp. 29–31, Thomson Reuters Philadelphia, PA, http://garfield.library.upenn.edu/papers/pendleburykingresearchfronts2013.pdf (July 15, 2020).

Price, DJ de Solla 1961, *Science Since Babylon*, Yale University Press, New Haven, CT, ISBN 13: 9780300017984.

Price, DJ de Solla 1963, *Little Science, Big Science*, Columbia University Press, New York, NY, ISBN-13: 978–0231085625

Price, DJ de Solla 1965, 'Networks of Scientific Papers', *Science*, vol. 149, no. 3683, pp. 510–515, http://garfield.library.upenn.edu/papers/pricenetworks1965.pdf (July 15, 2020), doi: https://doi.org/10.1126/science.149.3683.510.

Price, DJ de Solla 1976, 'General Theory of Bibliometric and other Cumulative Advantage Processes', *Journal of the American Society for Information Science*, vol. 27, nos. 5–6, pp. 292–306, http://garfield.library.upenn.edu/price/pricetheory1976.pdf (July 15, 2020), doi: https://doi.org/10.1002/asi.4630270505.

Price, DJ de Solla 1980, 'Foreword', in E Garfield, *Essays of an Information Scientist. Volume 3. 1977–1978*, pp. v-ix, ISI Press, Philadelphia, PA.

Schnell, JD 2018, 'Web of Science: The First Citation Index for Data Analytics and Scientometrics', in FJ Cantú-Ortiz (ed.), *Research Analytics: Boosting University Productivity and Competitiveness through Scientometrics*, pp. 15–29, CRC Press, Boca Raton, FL, ISBN-13: 978–1498785426.

Small, H 1973, 'Co-citation in the Scientific Literature: A New Measure of the Relationship between Two Documents', *Journal of the American Society for Information Science*, vol. 24, no. 4, pp. 265–269, http://www.garfield.library.upenn.edu/essays/v2p028y1974-76.pdf (July 15, 2020), doi: https://doi.org/10.1002/asi.4630240406.

Small, H & Garfield, E 1985, 'The Geography of Science: Disciplinary and National Mappings,' *Journal of Information Science*, vol. 11, no. 4, pp. 147–159, http://www.garfield.library.upenn.

edu/essays/v9p325y1986.pdf (July 15, 2020), doi: https://doi.org/10.1177/016555158501100402.

Small, H 2003, 'Paradigms, Citations, and Maps of Science: A Personal History', *Journal of the American Society for Information Science and Technology*, vol. 54, no. 5, pp. 394–399, doi: https://doi.org/10.1002/asi.10225.

Small, H 2017, 'A Tribute to Eugene Garfield: Information Innovator and Idealist', *Journal of Informetrics*, vol. 11, no. 3, pp. 599–612, doi: https://doi.org/10.1016/j.joi.2017.04.006.

van Eck, NJ, & Waltman, L 2014, 'CitNetExplorer: A New Software Tool for Analyzing and Visualizing Citation Networks', *Journal of Informetrics*, vol. 8, no. 4, pp. 802–823, doi: https://doi.org/10.1016/j.joi.2014.07.006, see https://www.citnetexplorer.nl/ (July 15, 2020).

Weinstock, M 1971, 'Citation Indexes', in A Kent (ed.), *Encyclopedia of Library and Information Science*, vol. 5, 16–40, Marcel Dekker, New York, http://www.garfield.library.upenn.edu/essays/V1p188y1962-73.pdf (July 15, 2020), ISBN 13: 9780824721053.

Wouters, P 1999, *The Citation Culture*, PhD thesis, University of Amsterdam, Amsterdam, http://garfield.library.upenn.edu/wouters/wouters.pdf (July 15, 2020).

Wouters, P 2017, 'Eugene Garfield (1925–2017): Inventor of the *Science Citation Index*', *Nature*, vol. 543, no. 7646, p. 492, https://www.nature.com/articles/543492a (July 15, 2020), doi: https://doi.org/10.1038/543492a.

Zuckerman, H 2018, 'The Sociology of Science and the Garfield Effect: Happy Accidents, Unanticipated Developments and Unexploited Potentials', *Frontiers in Research Metrics and Analytics*, vol, 3, no. 20, https://www.frontiersin.org/articles/10.3389/frma.2018.00020/full (July 15, 2020), doi: https://doi.org/10.3389/frma.2018.00020.

1.4 Derek De Solla Price: The Father of Scientometrics

Frashid Danesh and Ali Mardani-Nejad

Abstract: The 1960s was a golden age in the quantitative sciences. The decade we witnessed was the age of different disciplines and studies expansion in science. One of the great pioneers and avant-gardes in the development of these fields can be called Derek De Solla Price. Price's descriptions of "science of science" have led to the definition of scientometrics and he is famous as the father of this field. Price was one of those first who introduced "x number of authors" as one of the indicators of scientific activities in different countries. The costly activities of scientometrics were so valuable that Tibor Brown, the founder and editor-in-chief of the journal *Scientometrics*, created a prize in 1983 to commemorate Price's work. This prize is the first and foremost international infometric prize awarded every two years. This chapter will cover his biography and his activities, and topics such as science of science, citation and referencing, the Price index, and his scientific growth pattern.

Keywords: understanding De Sola Price, scientometrics, Price index, scientific growth pattern, biology, science of science, citation and referencing.

Derek J. de Solla Price Biography

Derek John Price was born on January 22, 1922, in Leyton, a suburb of London, England, to Fanny Marie de Solla, a singer, and Philip Price, a tailor. Both of his parents were descended from Jewish immigrant families. He spent the 1946–1947 academic year at Princeton University as a Commonwealth Fund Fellow in mathematical physics and married Ellen Hjorth of Copenhagen, Denmark, in 1947. They had two sons and a daughter. Derek Price died in September 1983, after suffering a massive heart attack.

Introduction

After presenting a description of De Sola Price biography and a glimpse at a timeline of his activities during his lifetime, there will be some explanation of his fundamentals, thoughts, and important works in this chapter. Discussion of topics will include

---

Farshid Danesh, Assistant Professor, Information Management Research Department, Regional Information Center for Science & Technology (RICeST), Shiraz, Iran, farshiddanesh@ricest.ac.ir (Corresponding Author)
Ali Mardani-Nejad, Young Researchers and Elite Club, Najafabad Branch, Islamic Azad University, Najafabad, Iran

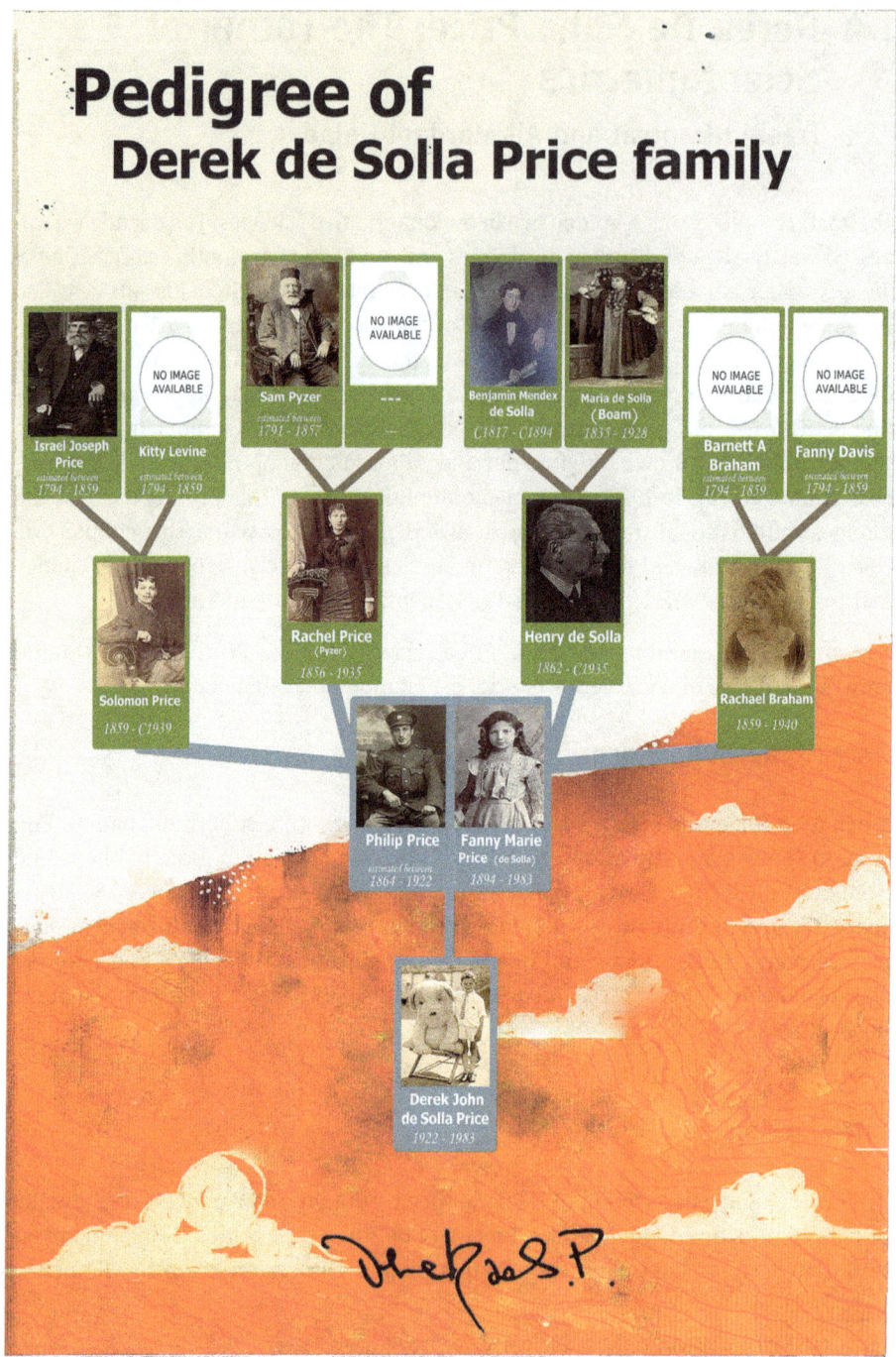

Figure 1: Pedigree of Derek de Solla Price family (MyHeritage Company, 2019).

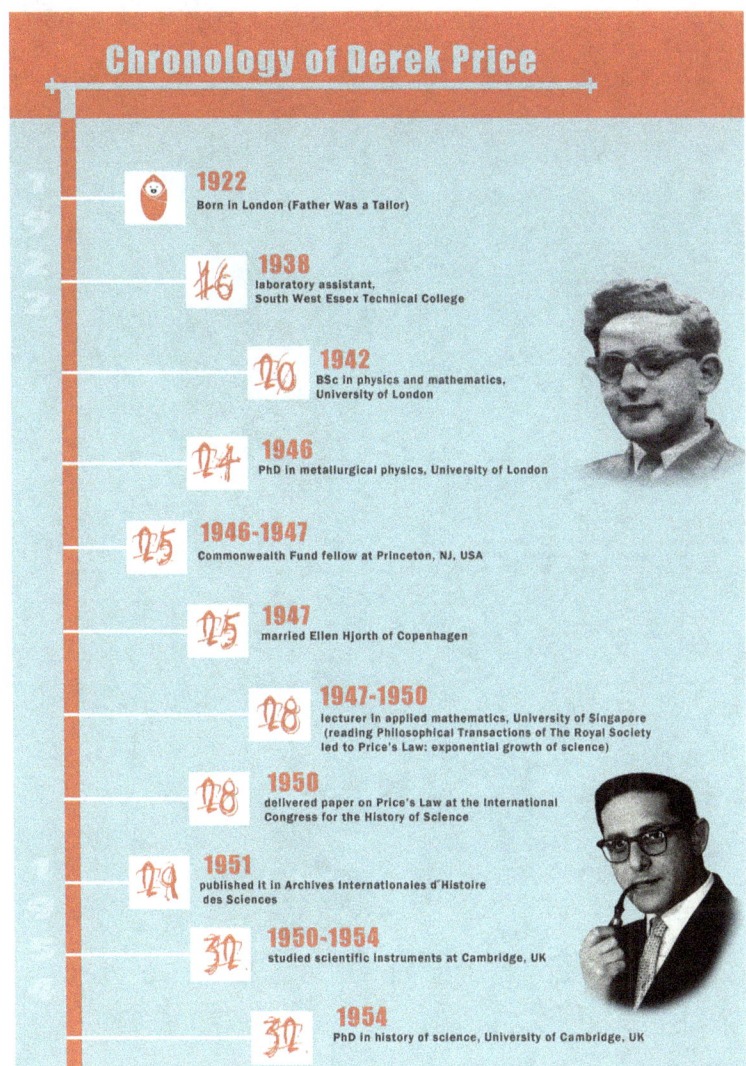

Figure 2: Chronology of Derek De Solla Price's life and profession (Alchetron Free Social Encyclopedia, 2018; McGill University, 1976).

science of science, citation and referencing, scientific growth pattern, and, at the end, the Price index, which he has a very colorful role in. During this chapter, these issues will indicate the secret of his immortality in scientometrics.

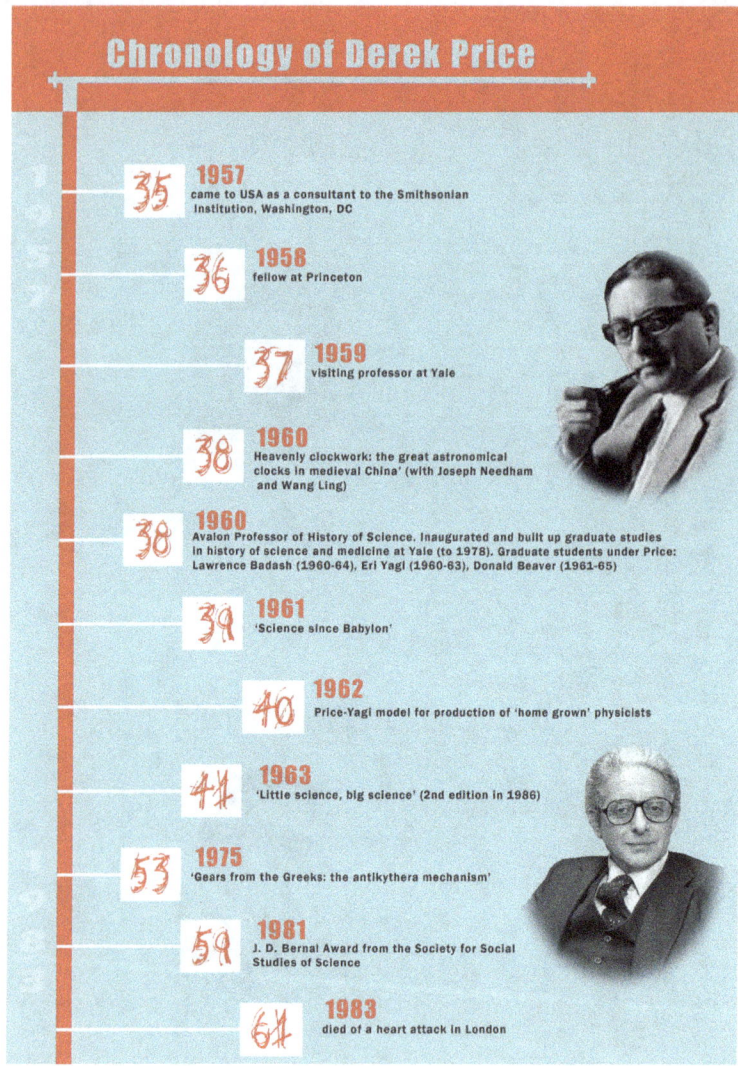

Figure 2 (continued): Chronology of Derek De Solla Price's life and profession (Alchetron Free Social Encyclopedia, 2018; McGill University, 1976).

Science of Science – Scientometrics

Price is one of the founders of science of science, and is one of the prominent representatives of the physical approach in quantitative studies of science and scientific activity as well as the creation of scientometrics indicators. A few years before the Russian scientist Vasiliy Vasilievich Nalimov (Nakometria, 1969) invented scientometrics, which led to the creation of a journal of the same name (1978), the description of the science of science led to the definition of scientometrics. Price's definition of the science of science is that the various scientific indicators must link with simple laws, in such a way that their phenomenological interpretation is possible.

The first chapter in Price's 1963 book, *Little Science, Big Science*, is called "A Science of Science." The fourth sample reference quotes from the Preface:

Price, on morphology of the term "scientometrics", in the third sample reference, comments on some of this etymology. He is quoted from the enlarged 1975 edition of a book originally published in 1961:

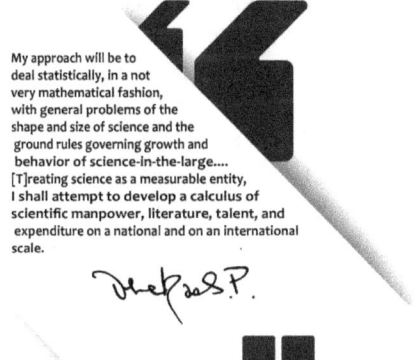

My approach will be to deal statistically, in a not very mathematical fashion, with general problems of the shape and size of science and the ground rules governing growth and behavior of science-in-the-large.... [T]reating science as a measurable entity, I shall attempt to develop a calculus of scientific manpower, literature, talent, and expenditure on a national and on an international scale.

Figure 3: Price, 1963, p. viii quoted in Diodato 1994, p. 147.

The material covered in this chapter has probably undergone more development and change than any other. It rapidly proved to have a life of its own, so that it grew first into a separate book (*Little Science, Big Science*) and then touched off a continuing series of research papers exploring many different quantitative investigations based on the counting of journals, papers, authors, and citations. In no time at all there were bibliographies and conventions devoted to bibliometrics and scientometrics, and even a meeting of the invisible college or people studying invisible colleges. ... [T]he term "science of science" achieved an almost explosive popularity. Unfortunately, though it came readily to the tongue and pleased those who desired objective investigations of the workings of science in society, the term rapidly became debased by being used in as many different ways, as there were users, and by being taken as a promise to deliver goods that were by their very nature undeliverable. (Price, 1963, p. viii, quoted in Diodato, 1994, p. 146)

Derek de Solla Price asserted that the primary aim of scientometrics is to do scientific analysis of science mathematically. He lucidly described that however successful we are in understanding the productivity of scientists and the mechanics and pattern of coherence of scientific creativity, we shall still need historians, sociologists, and psychologists of science for those types of analyses that cannot be expressed in metric terms (Sengupta, 1992, p. 86). Elsewhere, he asserted that: "Somewhat cautiously, it may be suggested that we need a social scientific equivalent of the

Newtonian masterstroke that took such vaguely used terms as force, work, and energy, redefined them with simple equations [...] and brought order into previous meanderings" (Price, 1980b, p. 1, quoted in Moed, 2005, p. 195).

Citation and Referencing

Derek De Solla Price stated that citation and referencing to earlier works in the West have been used since 1850 in scientific journals. The evidence suggested that the predecessors were aware of the necessity of using citation and referencing, and in their works they cited past works (Haghighi, 2003).

Derek De Solla Price studied how to conduct scientometrics and a network of citations among academic papers. He indicated that articles cited many times are likely to be cited in the future. The opposite is also true of this phenomenon; articles not cited regularly will not likely be cited in the future, which led to a model for this phenomenon. He also studied scientometrics to evaluate research. On this basis, Derek De Solla Price opened the door to a valuable contemporary bibliometric (Glanzel, 2008): "It seems to me a great pity to waste an excellent technical term by using the words citation and reference interchangeably. I therefore propose and adopt the convention that if Paper R contains a bibliographic footnote using and describing Paper C, then R contains a reference to C, and C has a citation from R. The number of references a paper has measured by the number of items in its bibliography as endnotes and footnotes, etc., while the number of citations a paper has is found by looking it up on some sort of citation index and seeing how many other papers mention it" (Price, 1970, p. 3, quoted in Moed, 2005, p. 114).

Price's Model

In 1963, Derek De Solla Price offered a model for explaining the productivity of authors in a thematic field. After analyzing the ideas of Francis Galton in the characterization of the elite and Alfred Lotka in productivity in chemistry and physics, he proposed a particular model (Sotudeh and Yaghtin, 2014).

Price's Law

This describes the number of prolific authors in a subject field. In a given field during a given period, the number of prolific authors is equal to approximately the square root of the total number of authors in the field. In particular, the prolific authors account for about half the publications in the field. This was named for Derek J. de Solla Price, and is also called Price's square root law (Diodato 1994, p. 131). Rousseau's law is one of the sources for Price's law of authorship, which in turn also draws ideas from Lotka's law of authorship. The sample references below suggest that the naming of the law may be more of attribution of an idea rather than a claim that Rousseau discussed square roots (Diodato 1994, p. 138).

Price's law, as said also known as the Price's Square Root Law, focuses on the relationship between the literature and the number of authors in the subject area. He stated that half of the publications come from the square root of all contributors. Thus, if 25 authors write 100 papers, five authors will have contributed 50 papers (Nicholls, 1988). Derek de Solla Price predicted that the number of elites in science is small compared to the total number of scientists. In his law, he claimed that any population of size N contains a capable elite of size $\sqrt{N}$. Alternatively, in other words, "One-half of all scientific papers contributed by several authors equal to the square root of the total number of scientific authors" (Sengupta, 1992, p. 80).

In the first sample reference, Price (1963) derived the law after discussing the ideas of Francis Galton (on elitism) and Alfred Lotka (on authorship in chemistry and physics). Price said: "If one computes the total production of those who write in papers, it emerges that a large number of low producers account for about as much of the total as the small number of large producers. In a simple schematic case, symmetry may be shown to a point corresponding to the square root of the total number of men, or the score of the highest producer" (Price, 1963, p. 46, quoted in Diodato 1994, 131).

Text Growth Rate

Price (1963), in the *Little Science, Big Science*, a fundamental work in the philosophy of science and scientometrics, for the first time, using statistical and objective data, depicted the phenomenon of Text Growth Rate. He showed that the number of scientific articles had doubled every 15 years between the 1660s, from scientific journal creation until the 1960s when Derek de Solla Price's book was written. That is, if in 1660, there was only one article in a specific subject, in 1977, this number would reach 3.2 million articles (Heidari, 2011).

Price suggested the total number of journals in 1980 to be about 40,000 (Price, 1980a). To paraphrase Eugene Garfield and Robert Merton, who laughed at him in a posthumous work, an expanded version of *Little Science, Big Science*, we can hardly doubt that Derek de Solla Price is, indeed, the Father of Scientometrics (Fernández Cano, Torralbo, and Vallejo, 2004).

When he taught applied mathematics at Raphael College, Derek de Solla Price developed a formula for calculating the growth of science, as well as calculating the half-life of scientific papers, which played a significant role in the formation and expansion of scientometrics (Furner, 2003). The following figure visualizes the growth of the number of scientific journals and review journals since 1665. The growth rate is such that the size of science has doubled every 10 or 15 years since the seventeenth century (Fernández Cano, Torralbo, and Vallejo, 2004)

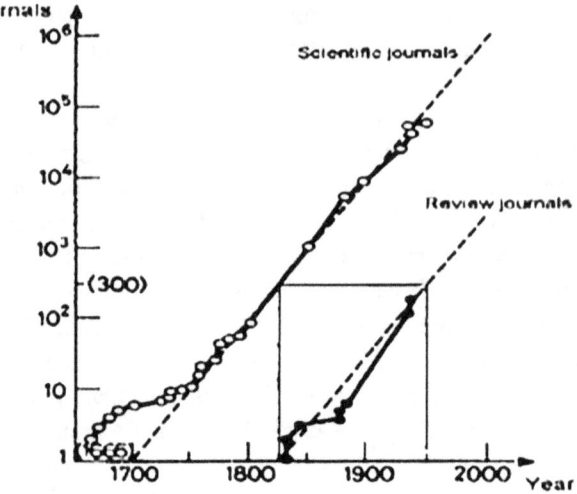

Figure 4: Total Number of Scientific Journals and Abstract Journals Founded, as a Function of Date (Price, 1963, p. 8).

Interacting with Countries with Common Scientific and Cultural Backgrounds

Using the results of scientific research, one can identify the scientific and cultural interactions of their country with other countries in recent years and the highest frequencies of such. Accordingly, recognizing the factors affecting the establishment of these communications and interactions can be necessary in order to strengthen the positive points and resolve weaknesses. In addition, this information can lead to the recognition of common areas of scientific and cultural cooperation among countries (quoted in Price, 1963; Noroozi Chakoli, 2012). It should be noted that Price was one of the first to count the number of authors as an indicator of scientific activities in different countries.

Scientific Growth Pattern

It was in 1986 when Derek de Solla Price for the first time, in his book *Little Science, Big Science*, made this discussion using scientific growth pattern. He believed that since the study of all scientific publications is not possible, it is necessary to know about science growth's rise, fall, and measurement, and he therefore suggested a study on measuring scientific growth using quantitative methods. He subsequently designed a two-variable intrinsic model that demonstrated scientific growth over time (Fernandez Cano, Torralbo and Vallejo, 2012), which gradually became more complicated with the entry of other explanatory variables, and evolved into a dynamic and vibrant promotional model.

Derek de Solla Price proposed three stages in his Scientific Growth Pattern: a) a primary stage with small increments; b) in second stage knowledge having a pure exponential growth; and c) a period of inalterable development. However, while it was argued that there is a period during which both the rates of increase and the absolute increase decline and eventually approach zero, nothing had been encountered in Derek de Solla Price's works to prove the claim (Fernández Cano, Torralbo, and Vallejo, 2004)

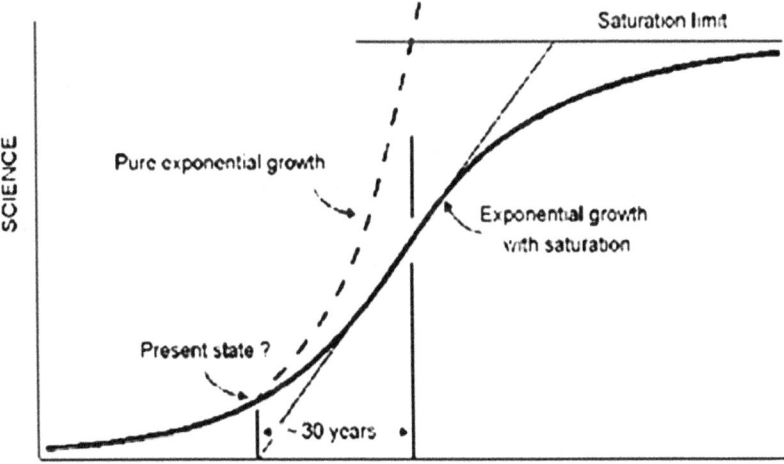

Figure 5: Price's model of scientific growth (Fernández et al., https://www.researchgate.net/profile/Antonio_Cano72004).

Finally, in an article published in 1971, Price empirically verified his complete model, using data on Ph.D. production and on scientific and manpower funds to show that there is a transition period of almost linear growth extending for two or three decades between the free exponential growth and the onset of adequate saturation (Fernández Cano, Torralbo, and Vallejo, 2004).

Price's index

According to Price (1970), this is a measure of the recency of references in a document, journal, or an entire subject field. It is the ratio of the number of references that are no more than five years old to the total number of references. It was frequently known as Price's immediacy index, but should not be confused with the measure known merely as the Immediacy Index (II); it can be compared with currency, half-life, median citation age, and recency score (Price, 1970).

The Last Word

This chapter opened using Derek de Solla Price's infographic based on his chronology, an in-depth and comprehensive look into his family life and professionalism. Derek de Solla Price was born in England in 1922 and died of a heart attack in the United States in 1983 at the age of 61. His life, in terms of length and number of years, was concise, but in terms of studying science and knowledge, he had a profound depth and various aspects.

His scientific life began with mathematics and physics and ended with scientometrics and science history. Immigration to the United States could be considered as one of the most critical events in his life; elsewhere, continuing to study at the University of Cambridge and working at Yale University, educating many students, many of whom were famous names of their era, gave Price's life, as a university professor, a great glory.

Awareness of the laws of physics allowed Derek de Solla Price to apply these rules to scientometrics. The first issue that calls his name around the world is "Science of Science." One of the things that makes him well known is his belief in scientometrics being interdisciplinary. He believed that it was possible to use the laws and principles of other sciences in scientometrics. Among Derek de Solla Price's most prominent works was *Little Science, Big Science*, as well as concepts such as "Science of Science," "progressive growth of texts," and "scientific growth pattern." Despite more than 30 years since Derek de Solla Price's death, reviewing Web of Science and Scopus suggests that his scientific production and publications are of interest to scientometrics scholars today and still feature valuable articles, books, and seminars. Peace Be Upon Him.

References

Alchetron Free Social Encyclopedia 2018, Derek J de Solla Price, https://alchetron.com/Derek-J-de-Solla-Price (Sept 22, 2020).

Diodato, V 1994, *Dictionary of bibliometrics*, The Haworth Press, New York.

Fernandez Cano, A, Torralbo, M & Vallejo, M 2012, 'Time series of scientific growth in Spanish doctoral theses (1848–2009)', *Scientometrics*, vol. 91, no. 1, pp. 16–36.

Fernandez Cano, A, Torralbo, M & Vallejo, M 2004, 'Reconsidering Price's model of scientific growth: An overview', *Scientometrics*, vol. 61, no. 3, pp. 301–321.

Furner, J 2003, 'Little book, big book: Before and after little science, big science: A review article, part II', *Journal of Librarianship and Information Science*, vol. 35, no. 3, pp. 189–201.

Glanzel, W 2008, 'De Solla Price, and the evaluation of scientometrics', *Research Trends*, September (7), pp. 4–5.

Haghighi, M 2003, 'Usage of citation in scholarly writing', *Iranian Journal of phycology and education*, vol. 32, no. 2, pp. 215–232.

Heidari, GR 2011, *Epistemology in Scientometrics*, Islamic World Science Citation Center (ISC), Shiraz.

McGill University. 1976. Articles by Beatty Lecture Archive: Derek de Solla Price, https://www.mcgill.ca/beatty/digital-archive/past-lectures/derek-de-solla-price-1976 (Sept 22, 2020).

Moed, HF 2005, *Citation analysis in research evaluation*, Springer, Netherlands.

MyHeritage company 2019, Professor, Ph.D. Derek John de Solla Price, https://www.geni.com/people/Professor-Ph-D-Derek-John-de-Solla-Price/6000000003340469413 (Sept 22, 2020).

Nalimov, VV & Mul'chenko, ZM 1969, *Naukometriya. Izuchenie nauki kak information nogo protsessa (scientometrics: Study of science as an information process)*, Nauka, Moscow.

Nicholls, PT 1988, 'Price's square root law: empirical validity and relation to Lotka's Law', *Information processing and management*, vol. 24, no. 4, pp. 469–477.

Noroozi Chakoli A 2012, 'The Role and Situation of the Scientometrics in Development', *Iranian Journal of Information Processing Management*, vol. 27, no. 3, pp. 723–736.

Price, DJD 1963, *Little Science, Big Science*, Columbia University, New York.

Price, DJD 1970, 'Citation measures of hard science, soft science, technology, and non-science', in CE Nelson & DK Pollock (eds.), *Communication among scientists and engineers*, Heath, Lexington, MA.

Price, DJD 1975, *Science since Babylon*, Yale University, New Haven.

Price, DJD 1980a, *The citation cycle*, in BC Griffith, *Key papers in information science*, pp. 195–210, Knowledge Industry Publications, White Plains, NY.

Price, DJD 1980b, 'Towards a Comprehensive System of Science Indicators', *Paper presented to the Conference on Evaluation in Science and Technology – Theory and Practice*, Dubrovnik, July 1980.

Sotudeh, H & Yaghtin, M 2014, 'Indicators and models for measuring researchers' scientific productivity', *Science and Technology Policy Letters*, vol. 4, no. 1, pp. 47–62.

1.5 Coevolution of Field and Institute: The Institutionalization of Bibliometric Research Illustrated by the Emergence and Flourishing of the CWTS

Anthony van Raan

Abstract: The quantitative study of science is mostly referred to as scientometrics. Within scientometrics, the research on scientific communication, particularly with data from publications, patents, citations, and journals, is called bibliometrics. The development of a new field of science as an "accepted" field within the academic community goes hand in hand with the rise and flourishing of institutes that shape the new field. In this chapter we illustrate this type of coevolution by a brief outline of the history and institutionalization of scientometric and particularly bibliometric research by one of the world's pioneering institutes, the Centre for Science and Technology Studies (CWTS) at Leiden University. We highlight the origin of the field, its institutionalization, the acceptance of the field within a critical academic community, the fate and fortunes of the new institute, the interplay of chance and seizing opportunities, the role of practical applications as the driving force of the development of the field, the crucial support of both public (university, ministries, research councils) and private companies, and especially of key figures who acted as champions for the promotion of the careful application of bibliometrics. The CWTS case tells of the successful synergy of pioneering work, the inspiring dynamics of bibliometrics as an internationally emerging interdisciplinary field, applications, theoretical underpinning, education, and commercialization.

Keywords: short history of scientometrics, institutionalization, CWTS, Leiden University, Elsevier, bibliometrics, research evaluation, science maps.

The quantitative study of science is mostly referred to as scientometrics. Within scientometrics, the research on scientific communication, particularly with data from publications, citations, and journals, is called bibliometrics. The development of a new field of science as an "accepted" field within the academic community goes hand in hand with the rise and flourishing of institutes that shape the new field. In this chapter we illustrate this type of coevolution by a brief outline of the history and institutionalization of scientometric and particularly bibliometric research by one of the world's pioneering institutes, the Centre for Science and Technology Studies (CWTS) at Leiden University. For comprehensive overviews of the early develop-

---

Dr. **Ton (A.) F.J. van Raan**, Centre for Science and Technology Studies, Leiden University, Leiden, The Netherlands, vanraan@cwts.leidenuniv.nl

ments in the quantitative studies of science we refer to Francis Narin in his seminal report *Evaluative Bibliometrics* (Narin, 1976), and to reviews of this author (van Raan, 2004; 2019).

Most of the research in bibliometric analysis was concentrated in the US until the early 1970s. This research was tremendously stimulated by the crucial breakthrough in the history of the quantitative studies of science, the creation of the *Science Citation Index* (SCI, now the Web of Science) by Eugene Garfield in his Institute for Scientific Information (ISI) (Garfield, 1955; Wouters, 1999). Cees le Pair, physicist and the then director of research at the physics research council (FOM) of the Netherlands Organization for Scientific Research (NWO), played a crucial role in the early development of bibliometric analysis outside the US. After a working visit in 1975 at the National Science Foundation and discussions with Derek de Solla Price and Eugene Garfield, le Pair immediately grasped the importance of the SCI as a support instrument for science policy by using publication and citation data in research evaluation. An important decision was made on an issue that is still current today: one of the first things we want to know is how bibliometric analysis will work in basic versus applied research. Two studies were carried out, the first in the basic research field of magnetic resonance (Chang, 1975), and the second in the applied research field of electron microscopy (Bakker, 1977).

The results of these studies clearly showed the potential as well as the limitations of bibliometric, and particularly citation, analysis. For magnetic resonance, high correlations were found for the identification of important breakthroughs based on citation analysis and based on peer assessments. For electron microscopy, however, citation analysis did not reveal all important developments and it became clear that patent analysis was indispensable in fields of applied research. In addition, towards the end of the 1970s one of the most important pioneers in bibliometrics, the Hungarian chemist Tibor Braun, established a bibliometric research group at the Academy of Sciences in Budapest. He made a crucial step for the academic emancipation of the field: the creation in 1978 of *Scientometrics*, the first journal for the quantitative research of science and technology.

How did the field of scientometrics reach Leiden University? Certainly, it was not a new university, looking for new departments. So why was this new field – often viewed with suspicion by the academic community – rapidly institutionalized in this centuries old, traditional and internationally renowned research university? What happened? In 1979 the Leiden University Executive Board decided that the allocation of the direct government funding to departments should be based, next to student numbers, on the proven quality of the research in the departments. For that time, this was a revolutionary step. I was involved in the development of this model, and as a physicist knowing Cees le Pair, I proposed using citation analysis in the assessment of research performance. Perhaps not that surprising, the research intensive Faculties of Natural Sciences and of Medicine were quite enthusiastic about the idea and in 1980 an extensive study was started: a citation analysis of all research groups in physics, astronomy, chemistry, biology, mathematics, and pharmacy, followed by all medical research groups. In total we analyzed 140 research groups, and with that it was the first large-scale bibliometric analysis at the "working floor" level. Moreover, this study also included interviews about the results with the researchers involved and, where possible, comparisons with peer review. All in all, the responses were encouraging and the Executive Board decided in 1983 to create a small group on bibliometric indicators development. The (predecessor of) CWTS was born. The report of this study (Moed et al., 1983), followed by a series of highly cited papers based on the report, catapulted the Leiden group to instant fame within the field of scientometrics. But we were not alone. I already mentioned the group of Braun in Budapest and at the University of Sussex Martin and Irvine carried out their groundbreaking bibliometric research of radio-astronomy groups in Europe (Martin and Irvine, 1983). Two more important bibliometric studies were conducted in the Netherlands around the same time: an analysis of biochemistry (Over Leven 1982) and of medical research in the Netherlands (Rigter 1983, 1986).

From 1983 onwards the brand-new Leiden group could count on continuous support of the Executive Board, the Ministry of Education, Culture and Science, and the publishing company Elsevier, mostly via contract-research projects. We also enjoyed a rapidly increasing international interest followed by increasing numbers of contract research assignments. The university provided us with a small basic financing, but otherwise we had to be self-supporting. In the beginning the SCI was only available in printed version, in very thick books, and thus, for each analysis, we had to visit the University Library. We started to use the new character-recognition facilities of the University in an attempt to transfer the printed version into a computer-readable version. This turned out to be a very cumbersome path. Fortunately, ISI soon provided us with the SCI on magnetic tapes. From that moment on we immediately started developing algorithms for data cleaning, data organization, and, the ultimate goal, to create our "enriched" SCI-based bibliometric database suitable for the accurate calculation of a broad set of bibliometric indicators.

Especially in these early days, Elsevier was particularly generous in the allocation of contract research. The Elsevier support came from the highest level: Pierre Vinken, the then CEO of Elsevier and professor of medical informatics at Leiden University was very much in favor of the development of the young bibliometric research group. In addition to typical publisher-related studies such as bibliometric analyses of journals, Elsevier gave us room to greatly broaden our bibliometric research and at the same time to go into depth, and to publish the results. This enabled us to work on increasingly advanced bibliometric methods. Particularly in the first half of the 1980s, important topics were co-citation analysis; statistics of bibliometric indicators; application of citation analysis in the social sciences and humanities; comparison of the results of bibliometric indicators with the outcomes of peer assessments; and bibliometric analysis of interdisciplinary research. Throughout this chapter we present in text boxes the topics of influential CWTS papers ranging from 1981 to 2019 in periods of five years.

Publications can be characterized by their list of references, and this forms the basis of co-citation analysis (Small, 1973). Another way to characterize publications is a list of characteristic terms, for instance specific concepts in the text of the publications, or author- and database-given keywords. This opened the way to a new development: co-word analysis, mathematically similar to co-citation analysis (Callon et al., 1983). It took quite a while, as computer power was not sufficient in the early 1980s, but finally co-word analysis became one of the basic methods to create science maps. The Leiden group played a crucial role in this development.

1981–1985
Research performance evaluation; field- and time dependence of indicators; development of the crown indicator, our flagship citation impact measure.

Initially the Leiden bibliometrics group was part of the staff of the Executive Board. However, the Board decided that given the increasing research activities the group should have a more academic basis. Sociology professor Mark van de Vall recognized the importance of quantitative research of science and technology in relation to the sociology of science and in 1986 the young group became a research unit in his Institute of Social Policy Research, Faculty of Social and Behavioral Sciences. This turned out to be a healthy basis. The new research unit was rapidly growing, albeit for about 90% "living" from contract research. It also made a further, strategically crucial next step possible: institutionalizing bibliometric research as an internationally recognized academic research field. In order to achieve this, it was crucial to set up a series of regular conferences with the highest possible standards. As discussed earlier, the field already had its own journal, *Scientometrics*, and this could be used to publish the best papers of a conference.

The Belgian mathematician Leo Egghe organized in 1987 the first international conference on bibliometrics and the theoretical aspects of information retrieval. This conference became the forerunner of today's ISSI[1] conferences. For the Leiden group this first international bibliometrics conference was the perfect place to extensively present the results of our research, and so we did. A year later we published the first *Handbook of Quantitative Studies of Science and Technology* (van Raan, 1988) and organized the first international conference specifically devoted to science and technology indicators in Leiden. From that time, this STI conference has been organized every two years, and since recently every year.

In 1989 the Leiden group acquired its formal name, *Centre for Science and Technology Studies* (CWTS), and after several organizational restructuring operations CWTS became an autonomous research department with this author as director. Important work at the end of the 1980s and early 1990s focused on bibliometric anal-

---

[1] ISSI: International Society for Scientometrics and Informetrics, https://www.issi2019.org/ (July 15, 2020).

yses in the humanities and social sciences, the further development of co-word and co-citation analysis, and analysis of science and technology interactions on the basis of citations to the scientific literature in patents. At the same time, we further improved our standard bibliometric analyses for research performance evaluation of university departments and institutes. This work formed the firm basis of our contract research. Our applied work was much more than the use of routines: it became a source of innovation and inspiration for the continuous development of new methods and the improvement of our data analytical tools. Through this fruitful combination of applications and basic research we were able to become one of the most active and influential bibliometrics research institutes worldwide.

1986–1990
Cross-field impact; impact delay; peer review and bibliometric analysis; validation studies; quasi-correspondence analysis and multidimensional scaling of bibliometric matrices; co-word mapping; patent analysis, science and technology interface, science base of technology; co-subfield analysis; citation balances of journal relations; fractal structure of the co-citation landscape; integrating multiple sources of information.

What was the secret behind this success? Next to the competence and ambitions of our staff, I think two elements were crucial. First, our heavy investments in computers and ICT personnel. Bibliometrics is a data-intensive field that cannot function without massive computing power and development of effective data-analytical algorithms. In addition, the fact that I am a physicist may also have been instrumental in being taken seriously in a sometimes quite averse academic environment. And what has proved indispensable is that the Leiden University Board has always been well-disposed towards CWTS in terms of organizational and policy support. After a successful take-off, our task was to consolidate and further reinforce the position of CWTS.

The 1990s was a decade of numerous CWTS achievements. From the perspective of institutional academic status, the appointment of this author in 1991 to Professor of Quantitative Studies of Science, probably the first chair in this field worldwide, was crucial. It put CWTS at the level of a well-established university department, and enabled us to organize PhD work largely autonomously. In particular, the Faculties of Medicine and of Natural Sciences strongly supported the establishment of the chair. After the appointment, an annual series of lectures for MSc students was set up which has evolved into what is now the CWTS international *Graduate Course on Measuring Science*.

1991–1995
international collaboration; bibliometric analysis and interdisciplinary research; quality judgement of journals in the humanities and social sciences; co-word analysis with combined clustering and multidimensional scaling; economics research, comparison with peer review; determinants of citation scores; patent co-classification mapping

of technology; the CWTS bibliometric database; combined co-citation and word mapping; cognitive resemblance in citation relations.

In the 1990s contract research commissioned by organizations and institutions worldwide, particularly within the European Union (universities, research councils, charities), further increased. We developed standardized procedures for the execution of performance analyses in which participation of the departments or institutes is a crucial element, particularly to verify the correct assignment of publications to research groups, as well as the completeness and correctness of publications sets. Meanwhile, ISI had become part of Thomson Reuters and the SCI was migrated from CD-ROMs to internet-based facilities which eventually led to the Web of Science (WoS).

A new development was the foundation of the *Netherlands Observatory for Science and Technology* (NOWT), established in 1992 as a joint venture of CWTS and MERIT,[2] Maastricht University. Its purpose was to compile the biannual Science and Technology Indicators (WTI) Report for the Ministry of Education, Culture and Sciences. CWTS produced the WTI reports until 2010. From 1994 CWTS was involved in the VSNU national research assessment procedures.[3] For a number of major disciplines, particularly medicine, biology, chemistry, physics, and psychology, we performed extensive bibliometric analyses of all research groups. These research evaluations of many hundreds of university institutes, departments and research groups provided us with an extensive experience and expertise in the application of bibliometric research performance analysis. The presentation of our results, part of the standardized procedure, often evoked emotional reactions, particular in the sense that bibliometric analysis, especially citations, cannot capture all aspects of scientific quality. Bibliometric analysis enables the assessment of one, but certainly an important aspect of quality, international impact. I often felt like a missionary, preaching with full devotion about our methodology and at the same time warning about the pitfalls and pointing out limitations. In this context a new commandment was formulated: never apply bibliometric analysis as a standalone tool, but always use it in combination with peer review.

1996–2000
Impact factor problems; dynamic mapping of research fields; peer review compared with a set of bibliometric indicators; influence of international collaboration on impact; growth, ageing and fractal differentiation of science; patent citation analysis; cross-disciplinary citation flows; better journal impact indicators; measuring scientific excellence; publication delays.

---

2 Maastricht Economic and Social Research Institute on Innovation and Technology, https://www.maastrichtuniversity.nl/research/united-nations-university-maastricht-economic-and-social-research-institute-innovation (July 15, 2020).
3 VSNU: Association of Universities in the Netherlands, https://www.vsnu.nl/en_GB (July 15, 2020).

Due to the steady increase of contract work, it was decided in 2002 to set up *CWTSbv* as a spin-off company of CWTS. This was a very important step in the institutionalization of CWTS. Setting up a spin-off company in a field such as bibliometrics with a well-arranged personnel and financial connection between company and university is no easy task. To find and get support from the right people proved, again, essential. My Leiden colleague astronomy professor, ESO[4] Director-General Harry van der Laan, and LURIS[5] director Ben Hiddinga all played a decisive role in the creation of CWTSbv.

But we still had one final step to go and that would take several years. Meanwhile, the internet had changed scientific communication. More and more data on all types of publications and other research outlets became available in institutional and personal websites. The use of these data, webometrics, and later the use of social media data, altmetrics, provided new opportunities in scientometric research and evaluation studies next to the WoS and, since 2004, Scopus data. As discussed earlier, books and in particular handbooks produced by an institute are, next to publications in international journals, an important sign of institutionalization. In a period of two years two CWTS-based (hand)books appeared (Moed et al., 2004; Moed, 2005).

An important and far-reaching event in the scientometric world was the emergence of *university rankings*, with the Shanghai Ranking[6] as the first in 2003. Shortly after that the Times Higher Education launched its ranking[7] and CWTS introduced the Leiden Ranking.[8]

2001–2005
Effect of language biases in international comparisons; benchmarking scientific excellence; research performance of China; inventor opinions on science dependence of technologies; scientific basis of applied research; Sleeping beauties in science; effects of commercialization of research on public knowledge production; conceptual and methodological problems in university rankings; relation between downloads and citations; inter-field knowledge transfer.

Then, in 2008, the Minister of Education, Culture and Sciences decided to grant CWTS a substantial amount of ear-marked financing in order to improve its innovative power. For the first time CWTS received a permanent direct university funding support of substantial size. This funding made it possible to set up a long-term research program with multiple themes and to initiate PhD work on a larger scale.

---

4 European Southern Observatory, https://www.eso.org/ (July 15, 2020).
5 LURIS is the Knowledge Exchange Office for Leiden University and Leiden University Medical Center, https://luris.nl/ (July 15, 2020).
6 http://www.shanghairanking.com/index.html (July 15, 2020).
7 http://www.timeshighereducation.co.uk/world-university-rankings (July 15, 2020).
8 http://www.leidenranking.com/ (July 15, 2020).

The then dean of the Faculty of Social and Behavioral Sciences, Theo Toonen, professor of public administration, played a crucial role in the Minister's decision. Also, in 2008, we moved to the renovated Willem Einthoven[9] building with a complete floor of our own. In my opinion, these events in 2008 can be seen as the actual completion of the institutionalization of our research and as the crowning glory of years of efforts to get scientometric research recognized as a scientific field with professional practitioners in an academic context.

2006–2010
Measuring research performance in the social science and the humanities; non-source citation analysis; comparison of h-index with crown indicator; effects of Open Access on citation impact; international mobility of Chinese researchers; normalization of co-occurrence data; spatial patterns of scientific collaboration; contextual citation impact; research performance at the individual level, influence of age; VOSviewer mapping tool.

Therefore, I conclude this history of the institutionalization of scientometrics illustrated by the issues that CWTS had to face. Of course, life goes on after 2008, new chairs were created (science policy; science and innovation studies), and this author retired in 2010 as Director of CWTS. Paul Wouters was appointed as Professor of Scientometrics and became the new director. He energetically took over the responsibility for CWTS. New research themes were developed such as responsible evaluation practices, scientific careers, social impact of science, innovation studies, and open science. In particular, the development of new mapping software (van Eck and Waltman, 2010; 2014) and a redefinition of our crown indicator (Waltman et al., 2011a; 2011b) has been of great importance.

2011–2015
New crown indicator; inconsistency h-index; publication-level classification; methodology of the Leiden Ranking; percentile-based indicators; clinical research underestimated in citation analysis; community detection in large networks; altmetrics, social media mentions and citation impact; CitNetExplorer; document properties and collaboration.

After the retirement of Paul Wouters in 2018 the triumvirate of Sarah de Rijcke, Ludo Waltman and Ed Noyons is now in charge of CWTS. For the newest developments we refer to the website of CWTS.[10] To conclude, Figure 1 shows a co-word landscape of the recent CWTS activities in scientometric research based on the 2016–2019 publi-

---

9 Our building is named after Willem Einthoven, Professor of Physiology at Leiden, inventor of the electrocardiograph, Nobel Prize 1924.
10 https://www.cwts.nl/ (July 15, 2020).

2.5 Coevolution of Field and Institute

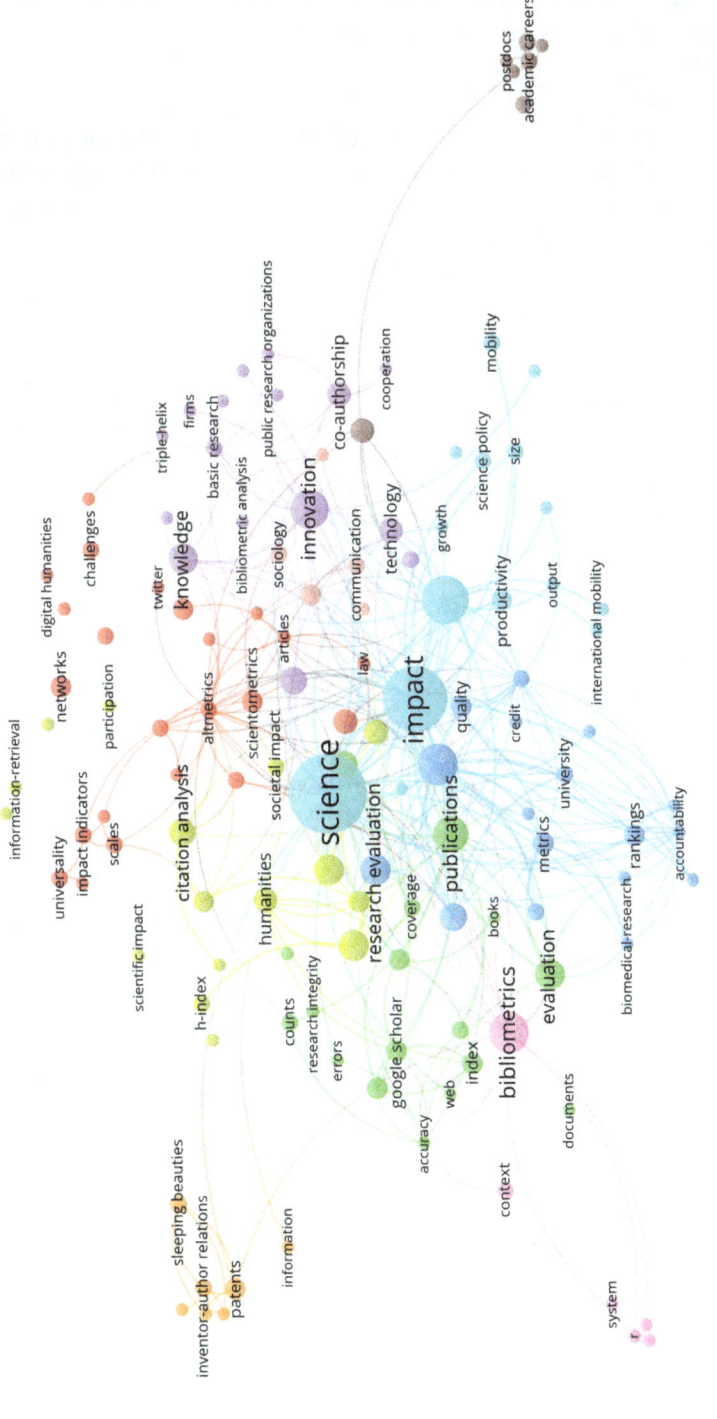

Figure 1: Map of CWTS research in recent years (co-word analysis, occurrence threshold=2, full counting modality).

cations. We clearly see thematic clusters (indicated by different colors) of both the long-standing core issues as well as the new developments.

2016–2019
Evaluation practices; citation-based clustering; social media metrics; Google Scholar and evaluation of social science and humanities research; funding acknowledgements; self-citations and impact factor; career attitudes; full versus fractional counting; in-text citations; university-industry R&D linkages.

References

Bakker, CJG 1977, *Elektronenmicroscopie in Nederland*, FOM, Utrecht, FOM-Report 43105.

Callon, M, Bauin, S, Courtial, JP & Turner W 1983, 'From translation to problematic networks: an introduction to co-word analysis', *Social Science Information*, vol. 22, pp. 191–235.

Chang, KH 1975, *Evaluation and survey of a subfield of physics: magnetic resonance and relaxation studies in the Netherlands*, FOM, Utrecht, FOM-Report 37175.

Garfield E 1955, 'Citation indexes for science: A new dimension in documentation through association of ideas', *Science*, vol. 122, no. 3159, pp. 108–111.

Martin, BR & Irvine J 1983, 'Assessing Basic Research: Some Partial Indicators of Scientific Progress in Radio Astronomy', *Research Policy*, vol. 12, pp. 61–90.

Moed, HF, Burger, WJM, Frankfort, JG & Van Raan, AFJ 1983, *On the Measurement of Research Performance: The Use of Bibliometric Indicators*, Science Studies Unit, Leiden.

Moed, HF, Glänzel, W & Schmoch, U (eds.) 2004, *Handbook of Quantitative Science and Technology Research*, Kluwer, Dordrecht.

Moed, HF 2005, *Citation Analysis in Research Evaluation*, Springer, Dordrecht.

Narin, F 1976, *Evaluative Bibliometrics: The Use of Publication and Citation Analysis in the Evaluation of Scientific Activity*, National Science Foundation, Washington D.C.

Over Leven (About Life) (1982). Report of the Verkenningscommissie Biochemie (National Survey Committee on Biochemistry). The Hague: Staatsuitgeverij (in Dutch).

Rigter H (1983). *De prestaties van het Nederlandse gezondheidsonderzoek* (Performance of health research in the Netherlands). RAWB (Council for Science Policy), Series Background Studies, Report 9. The Hague: Staatsuitgeverij (in Dutch).

Rigter H (1986). *Evaluation of the performance of health research in the Netherlands*. Research Policy 15, 33–48.

Small, H 1973, 'Co-citation in the scientific literature: a new measure of the relationship between two documents', *Journal of the American Society for Information Science and Technology*, vol. 24, pp. 265–269.

van Eck, NJ & Waltman, L 2010, 'Software survey: VOSviewer, a computer program for bibliometric mapping', *Scientometrics*, vol. 84, no. 2, pp. 523–538.

van Eck NJ & Waltman, L 2014, 'CitNetExplorer: A new software tool for analyzing and visualizing citation networks', *Journal of Informetrics*, vol. 8, no. 4, pp. 802–823.

van Raan, AFJ (ed.) 1988, *Handbook of quantitative studies of science and technology*, North Holland, Amsterdam.

van Raan, AFJ 2004, 'Measuring Science. Capita Selecta of Current Main Issues', in HF Moed, W Glänzel & U Schmoch (eds.), *Handbook of Quantitative Science and Technology Research*, pp. 19–50, Kluwer, Dordrecht.

van Raan, AFJ 2019, 'Measuring Science: Basic Principles and Application of Advanced Biliometrics', in W Glänzel, HF Moed, U Schmoch & M Thelwall (eds.), *Handbook of Science and Technology Indicators*, Series: Springer Handbooks, Springer, Heidelberg.

Waltman, L, van Eck, NJ, van Leeuwen, TN, Visser, MS & van Raan, AFJ 2011a, 'Towards a new crown indicator: An empirical analysis', *Scientometrics*, vol. 87, no. 3, pp. 467–481.

Waltman, L, van Eck, NJ, van Leeuwen, TN, Visser, MS & van Raan, AFJ 2011b, 'Towards a new crown indicator: Some theoretical considerations', *Journal of Informetrics*, vol. 5, no. 1, pp. 37–47.

Wouters, PF 1999, The Citation Culture, PhD thesis, University of Amsterdam.

1.6 International Conferences of Bibliometrics

Grischa Fraumann, Rogério Mugnaini, and Elías Sanz-Casado

Abstract: Conferences are deeply connected to research fields, in this case bibliometrics. As such, they are a venue to present and discuss current and innovative research, and play an important role for the scholarly community. In this article, we provide an overview on the history of conferences in bibliometrics. We conduct an analysis to list the most prominent conferences that were announced in the newsletter by ISSI, the International Society for Scientometrics and Informetrics. Furthermore, we describe how conferences are connected to learned societies and journals. Finally, we provide an outlook on how conferences might change in future.

Keywords: international conferences, bibliometrics, scientometrics, informetrics, altmetrics, history, learned societies, ISSI.

Introduction

Conferences are deeply connected to research fields, in this case bibliometrics. As such, they are a venue to present and discuss current and innovative research, and play an important role for the scholarly community. They also serve as a venue to play a variety of roles, strengthening the so-called invisible colleges (Zuccala, 2006), and are important for gaining scientific reputation (Söderqvist and Silverstein, 1994). Furthermore, conference awards and committee memberships are a marker of prestige among scholars (Jeong, Lee and Kim, 2009). This chapter provides an overview on international conferences in bibliometrics, and what role they play in the history and institutionalization of bibliometrics. Proceedings papers are published in conference proceedings, and such proceedings are also indexed, for example, since 1990 by the *Conference Proceedings Citation Index (CPCI)* (Sugimoto and Larivière, 2018) and in *Scopus* (Gingras, 2016). Apart from books and journal articles, proceedings papers have a long tradition in disseminating research (Sugimoto and

---

Grischa Fraumann, Research Assistant at the TIB Leibniz Information Centre for Science and Technology in the R&D Department, PhD Fellow at the University of Copenhagen in the Department of Communication, Research Affiliate at the "CiMetrias: Research Group on Science and Technology Metrics" at the University of São Paulo (USP), gfr@hum.ku.dk

Rogério Mugnaini, Professor of Library and Information Science at the University of São Paulo (USP), where he leads the research group "CiMetrias: Research Group on Science and Technology Metrics", mugnaini@usp.br

Elías Sanz-Casado, Full Professor in the Department of Library and Information Science at the Carlos III University of Madrid, Director of the research group "Laboratory for Metric Information Studies" (LEMI), leads the "Research Institute for Higher Education and Science" (INAECU) which is made up of members of Carlos III University of Madrid and Autonomous University of Madrid, elias@bib.uc3 m.es

Larivière, 2018), and are used as datasets for bibliometric (Glänzel et al., 2006; Lisée, Larivière, and Archambault, 2008) and altmetric studies (Thelwall, 2019). On the one hand, not all conference proceedings are indexed, which makes such citation indexes sometimes incomplete (Sugimoto and Larivière, 2018). On the other hand, some conferences publish their proceedings as journal special issues or books, which can lead to the indexing of proceedings papers. Proceedings papers play a particular role in natural sciences and medicine (Ball, 2017). They represent an important means of publication in computer science (Fathalla et al. 2018), while they might be rather irrelevant in other disciplines, such as sociology (Jeong, Lee and Kim, 2009). As such, they also contribute to faster knowledge sharing than journal articles.

A Historical Sketch on Conferences in Bibliometrics

There are several examples of early conferences in bibliometrics. In 1946, two international conferences on scientific information were the first events, organised by the Royal Society of London (Gingras, 2016). The goal was to develop new forms of indexing scientific literature. This was also related to the exponential amount of scientific literature that led to the foundation of a citation index as part of Garfield's Institute for Scientific Information (ISI) in 1963. The first international conference was held in 1974, titled "Toward a Metric of Science: The Advent of the Science Indicators" (Gingras, 2016). 1987 is considered as the start of a new era in international conferences, since a predecessor of the conferences organised by the International Society for Scientometrics and Informetrics (ISSI) was held for the first time.

This led in 1993 to the foundation of a learned society, namely ISSI (Gingras, 2016). Conferences, journals, and learned societies go in line with a consolidation of an academic discipline, as the foundation of the journal *Scientometrics* in 1978 demonstrates (Gingras, 2016). Most conferences nowadays also experience other forms of scholarly communication, such as the live tweeting about conference presentations and discussions (Holmberg, 2015). Such tweets may also lead to collaborations for researchers that do not physically attend a conference (Holmberg, 2015). Furthermore, conference reports are often also communicated via blogs. Other forms of communication are live streams or archived videos of conference presentations that are available on dedicated online platforms (Plank et al., 2019).

An Overview of International Conferences and its Relation to Learned Societies

ISSI is one of the largest learned societies in bibliometrics, among others. Established in 1993 by a group of researchers during a conference in Berlin, the Netherlands-based association coordinates the ISSI Conference, a members' directory, a blog, and a quarterly newsletter. Conference participants and society members get access to the ISSI conference proceedings, which contain all proceedings papers. ISSI also advocates for several international initiatives, such as the Initiative on Open Citations (I4OC), which has been supported by ISSI in an open letter (Sugimoto, Murray, and Larivière, 2018).

The influence by the society on the research fields can be observed by its significant number of members and conference participants. The conferences used to run independently (ISSI, 2019), and in 2019 were held for the first time together with the European Network of Indicators Designers (ENID). The biennial conference is held in different locations around the world, and the abovementioned first conference in 1987 was called "International Conference on Bibliometrics and Theoretical Aspects of Information Retrieval". As happens often within the scholarly community, anecdotal evidence suggests that the conference was started by a discussion between two researchers, and the question "Shouldn't we start a biennial international conference on informetrics?" (ISSI, 2015). Since 1993 it bears the same name as of today (Hood and Wilson, 2001; ISSI, 2019). The conference is reported to be one of the world's largest and most prestigious conferences (Gorraiz et al., 2014).

Considering the influence of ISSI, the quarterly newsletter is used as a dataset to query past and ongoing international conferences in this research field. A related data collection method has been carried out, for instance, by Söderqvist and Silverstein (1994) for conferences in immunology and Jeong et al. (2009) for conferences in bioinformatics. The *ISSI Quarterly Newsletter* started in 2005, and published 59 issues until September 2019, as of October 28, 2019. All newsletters are publicly available also for non-members. The newsletter in PDF has an ISSN and is curated by 10 members of an editorial board according to guidelines and potential authors need to submit proposals. This is to say the structure is rather similar to a magazine than to a newsletter. Apart from discussions on current research and the introduction of members as well as other news of the society, the newsletter includes conference announcements, call for papers and conference reports. Formats such as workshops, meetings, symposia, forums, summer schools, PhD courses, seminars, and other training courses were excluded from the selection in this article. All quarterly newsletters since the start were downloaded. This approach might have some limitations. For example, certain conferences might be excluded, because they were announced somewhere else. Still, the approach provides a glimpse into the world of conferences on bibliometrics. The conferences were ordered according to the frequency or status, and additional information on their listing in *Conference Proceedings Citation Index (CPCI)* as well as from conference websites was provided if available (see Table 1). The conferences that were discontinued over time are not included in Table 1, except for the UK Social Networks Conference that was merged with two other conferences.

Table 1: International conferences in bibliometrics (*N*=11) ordered by frequency/ status including information on their listing in *CPCI* (source: *ISSI Quarterly Newsletter* March 2005 until September 2019, number 1–59, retrieved from http://issi-society.org/publications/issi-newsletter/ [July 15, 2020]).

Conference name	Frequency/ Status	Listed in CPCI	Description
International Conference "Impact of Science" – Measuring and Demonstrating the Societal Impact of Science	Several times per year	-	"[A] conference [...] to discuss measuring and demonstrating the societal impact of science" (https://scienceworks.nl/impact-of-science-2015/ [July 15, 2020])
Triple Helix Conference	Annually	+	"The Triple Helix model presents an opportunity to achieve innovation outcomes for the socio-economic good through collaboration with multi-stakeholders within academia, industry and government spheres." (https://triple-helix.co.za/ [July 15, 2020])
S&T Indicators Conference	Annually	+	Conference on Science and Technology Indicators
InSciT Conference	Annually	-	Conference on Science of Team Science
WissKom conference	Annually	-	Conference of the Central Library at Forschungszentrum Jülich, Germany
CARMA: International Conference on Advanced Research Methods and Analytics	Annually	+	"Research methods in economics and social sciences are evolving with the increasing availability of Internet and Big Data sources of information. As these sources, methods, and applications become more interdisciplinary, the [...] International Conference on Advanced Research Methods and Analytics (CARMA) aims to become a forum for researchers and practitioners to exchange ideas and advances on how emerging research methods and sources are applied to different fields of social sciences as well as to discuss current and future challenges." (http://www.carmaconf.org/ [July 15, 2020])
iConference	Annually	+	"[...] insights on critical information issues in contemporary society." (https://ischools.org/iConference [July 15, 2020])

Table 1 *(Continued)*

Conference name	Frequency/ Status	Listed in CPCI	Description
International Conference on Webometrics, Informetrics and Scientometrics (WIS) & COLLNET Meeting	Annually	+	"[...] all aspects of webometrics, informetrics and scientometrics." (http://collnet2019.dlut.edu.cn/meeting/index_en.asp?id=2676 [July 15, 2020])
International Conference on Scientometrics and Informetrics (ISSI)	Biennial	+	"The goal of [the] ISSI [conference] is to bring together scholars and practitioners in the area of informetrics, bibliometrics, scientometrics, webometrics and altmetrics to discuss new research directions, methods and theories, and to highlight the best research in this area." (https://www.issi2019.org/ [July 15, 2020])
Atlanta Conference on Science and Innovation Policy	Biennial	+	"The Atlanta Conference on Science and Innovation Policy provides a showcase for the highest quality scholarship from around the world addressing the challenges and characteristics of science and innovation policy and processes." (http://www.atlconf.org/ [July 15, 2020])
UK Social Networks Conference	Discontinued	-	The UK Social Networks Conference merged with the Applications of Social Network Analysis to form the European Conference on Social Networks (EUSN) (https://www.eusn2019.ethz.ch/ [July 15, 2020])

To the best of the authors' knowledge, there is no comprehensive discipline-specific database available that includes all conferences in bibliometrics, while there are several databases worldwide, for example discipline-specific ones, such as *dblp computer science bibliography* (Ley, 2002). Generally speaking, these databases list proceedings papers that are linked to, for example, authors and conferences. Apart from the conferences mentioned in Table 1, one could add the Altmetrics Conference, an annual conference that provides a venue for research and other initiatives on altmetrics, that is metrics to track research articles online (Priem et al., 2010), but only the related Altmetrics Workshop was mentioned in the *ISSI Quarterly Newsletter*, and workshops were excluded from this selection. Other available databases on a national level might include the Brazilian *Lattes Platform* (Marques 2015) that shows CVs of researchers and their publications as well as the attended national and international conferences (Mugnaini et al., 2019). A similar database might also be provided by institutional, national or international CRIS (Current Research Information Systems) (Sivertsen, 2019), such as *DSpace-CRIS* (Palmer et al., 2014) or *VIVO* (Börner et al., 2012; Conlon et al., 2019). Nevertheless, there are certain ongoing initiatives that might provide in future a more nuanced view on international conferences. One example is the *ConfIDent platform* that is developed as part of a research project funded by the German Research Foundation (DFG). The project objective is to develop a Wiki-based platform that takes into account the needs of scholarly communities, and offers a curated list of conferences. By structuring the conference data according to requirements of interoperability on the technical side and to academic demands on the social side, the system aims to present the possibility for a sociotechnical quality assessment of the content (Hagemann-Wilholt, Plank, and Hauschke, 2019; Hagemann-Wilholt, 2019; Sens and Lange, 2019). Generally speaking, proceedings papers may also be linked to ORCID IDs of researchers, that is personal identifiers (Dreyer et al., 2019). There are also other existing online platforms, such as *Open Research* (Fathalla et al., 2019) and *ConfRef.* Additionally, there are further initiatives to develop persistent identifiers (PIDs) for conferences (Crossref, 2019). There are also initiatives underway to develop a semantic representation of scientific events (Fathalla and Lange, 2018) in knowledge graphs, and to make structured queries available to the wider public (Fathalla, Lange, and Auer, 2019a). Such datasets may also be used to rank conferences or explore the impact of these events (Fathalla, Lange and Auer, 2019b; Hansen and Budtz Pedersen, 2018; Hauschke, Cartellieri, and Heller, 2018; Altemeier, 2019).

Conclusions

Conferences are important vehicles to disseminate research and to network with peers. Conferences aligned with journals and learned societies serve an important role in the institutionalization of bibliometrics. Bibliometricians and altmetricians also develop metrics based on data from conferences. There are ongoing initiatives to develop persistent identifiers for conferences. How will the future of conferences look like? Live streaming and other online tools, among others, might have changed the importance of traveling to conferences, and social media makes it possible to join the discussion remotely, but conferences will most probably remain prominent in the academic world, because the social component of meeting other researchers is one of the most important aspects. However, the climate crisis and coronavirus pandemic will most probably require fundamental changes for most academic conferences, and will accelerate digital alternatives and make it less necessary to physically attend these events (Viglione, 2020).

References

Altemeier, F, 'Konferenzmetadaten als Basis für szientometrische Indikatoren', in *VIVO Workshop 2019*, Hannover.

Ball, R 2017, *An Introduction to Bibliometrics: New Development and Trends*, Elsevier Science.

Börner, K, Conlon, M, Corson-Rikert, J & Ding, Y 2012, 'VIVO: A Semantic Approach to Scholarly Networking and Discovery', *Synthesis Lectures on the Semantic Web: Theory and Technology*, vol. 2, no. 1, pp. 1–178, https://doi.org/10.2200/S00428ED1 V01Y201207WBE002.

Conlon, M, Woods, A, Triggs, G, O' Flinn, R, Javed, M, Blake, J & Gross B et al. 2019, 'VIVO: A System for Research Discovery', *Journal of Open Source Software*, vol. 4, no. 39, p. 1182, https://doi.org/10.21105/joss.01182.

Crossref, 'PIDs for Conferences & Projects', https://www.crossref.org/working-groups/conferences-projects/ (July 15, 2020).

Dreyer, B, Hagemann-Wilholt, S, Vierkant, P, Strecker, D, Glagla-Dietz, S, Summann, F, Pampel, H & Burger, M 2019, 'Die Rolle Der ORCID ID in der Wissenschaftskommunikation: Der Beitrag des ORCID-Deutschland-Konsortiums und das ORCID-DE-Projekt', *ABI Technik*, vol. 39, no. 2, pp. 112–21, https://doi.org/10.1515/abitech-2019–2004.

Fathalla, S & Lange, C 2018, 'EVENTSKG: A Knowledge Graph Representation for Top-Prestigious Computer Science Events Metadata', in NT Nguyen et al. (eds.), *Computational Collective Intelligence*, vol. 11055, pp. 53–63, Lecture Notes in Computer Science, Springer International Publishing, Cham.

Fathalla, S, Lange, C & Auer, S 2019a, 'A Human-Friendly Query Generation Frontend for a Scientific Events Knowledge Graph', in A Doucet (ed.), *Digital Libraries for Open Knowledge*, vol. 11799, pp. 200–214, Lecture Notes in Computer Science, Springer International Publishing, Cham.

Fathalla, S, Lange, C & Auer, S 2019b, 'EVENTSKG: A 5-Star Dataset of Top-Ranked Events in Eight Computer Science Communities', in P Hitzler et al. (eds.), *The Semantic Web*, vol. 11503, pp. 427–442, Lecture Notes in Computer Science, Springer International Publishing, Cham.

Fathalla, S, Vahdati, S, Auer, S & Lange, C 2018, 'Metadata Analysis of Scholarly Events of Computer Science, Physics, Engineering, and Mathematics', in E Méndez et al. (eds.), *Digital Libraries for Open Knowledge*, vol. 11057, pp. 116–128, Lecture Notes in Computer Science, Springer, Cham.

Fathalla, S, Vahdati, S, Auer, S & Lange, C 2019, 'The Scientific Events Ontology of the OpenResearch.Org Curation Platform', in C-C Hung & GA Papadopoulos (eds.), *Proceedings of the 34th ACM/SIGAPP Symposium on Applied Computing – SAC '19*, pp. 2311–13, ACM Press, New York.

Gingras, Y 2016, *Bibliometrics and Research Evaluation: Uses and Abuses*, History and foundations of information science, The MIT Press, Cambridge Massachusetts.

Glänzel, W, Schlemmer, B, Schubert, A & Thijs, B 2006, 'Proceedings Literature as Additional Data Source for Bibliometric Analysis', *Scientometrics*, 68, no. 3, pp. 457–73, https://doi.org/10.1007/s11192–006–0124-y.

Gorraiz, J, Gumpenberger, C, Hörlesberger, M, Moed, H & Schiebel E 2014, 'The 14th International Conference of the International Society for Scientometrics and Informetrics', *Scientometrics*, vol. 101, no. 2, pp. 937–38, https://doi.org/10.1007/s11192-014-1438–9.

Hagemann-Wilholt, S, Plank, M & Hauschke C 2019, 'ConfIDent – for FAIR Conference Metadata: Development of a Sustainable Platform for the Permanent and Reliable Storage and Provision of Conference Metadata', in *21st International Conference on Grey Literature*.

Hagemann-Wilholt, S 2019, *ConfIDent – Eine Verlässsliche Plattform Für Wissenschaftliche Veranstaltungen*, WissKom 2019, Jülich, Germany, 4 Jun 2019–6 Jun 2019, http://juser.fz-juelich.de/record/863207 (July 15, 2020).

Hansen, TT & Pedersen, DB 2018, 'The Impact of Academic Events – A Literature Review', *Research Evaluation*, vol. 27, no. 4, pp. 358–66, https://doi.org/10.1093/reseval/rvy025.

Hauschke, C, Cartellieri, S & Heller, L 2018, 'Reference Implementation for Open Scientometric Indicators (ROSI)', *Research Ideas and Outcomes*, vol. 4, p. 59, https://doi.org/10.3897/rio.4.e31656.

Holmberg, K 2015, *Altmetrics for Information Professionals: Past, Present and Future*, Chandos Publishing, Oxford.

Hood, WW & Wilson, CS 2001, *Scientometrics*, vol. 52, no. 2, pp. 291–314, https://doi.org/10.1023/A:1017919924342.

ISSI 2015, 'Quarterly E-Newsletter of the International Society for Scientometrics and Informetrics', 42, http://issi-society.org/media/1043/newsletter42.pdf (July 15, 2020).

ISSI, 'Conferences', http://issi-society.org/conferences/ (July 15, 2020).

Jeong, S, Lee, S & Kim, H-G 2009, 'Are You an Invited Speaker? A Bibliometric Analysis of Elite Groups for Scholarly Events in Bioinformatics', *Journal of the American Society for Information Science and Technology*, vol. 60, no. 6, pp. 1118–31, https://doi.org/10.1002/asi.21056.

Ley, M 2002, 'The DBLP computer science bibliography: Evolution, research issues, perspectives', in *International symposium on string processing and information retrieval*, pp. 1–10, Springer, Berlin, Heidelberg.

Lisée, C, Larivière, V & Archambault, E 2008, 'Conference Proceedings as a Source of Scientific Information: A Bibliometric Analysis', *Journal of the Association for Information Science and Technology*, vol. 59, no. 11, pp. 1776–84, https://doi.org/10.1002/asi.v59:11.

Marques, F 2015, 'Valuable Records: Data Compiled from the Lattes Platform Provide Fuel for Studies on Science in Brazil and Reveal Trends', Pesquisa FAPESP 233, FAPESP, https://revistapesquisa.fapesp.br/en/2015/07/15/valuable-records/ (July 15, 2020).

Mugnaini, R, Damaceno, RJP & Mena-Chalco, JP 2019, 'An empirical analysis on the relationship between publications and academic genealogy', in *17th International Conference on Scientometrics & Informetrics (ISSI 2019)*, pp. 2376–86 proceedings of ISSI 2019, Sapienza University, Rome.

Palmer, DT, Bollini, A, Mornati, S, & Mennielli, M 2014, 'DSpace-CRIS@HKU: Achieving Visibility with a CERIF Compliant Open Source System,' *Procedia Computer Science*, vol. 33, pp. 118–123, https://doi.org/10.1016/j.procs.2014.06.019.

Plank, M, Drees, B, Hauschke, C, Kraft, A & Leinweber, K 2019, 'Now or Never: Innovative Tools and Services for Scientists', in IFLA (ed.), *IFLA World Library and Information Congress (WLIC) 2019: Libraries: Dialogue for Change*, http://library.ifla.org/2504/ (July 15, 2020).

Priem, J, Taraborelli, D, Groth, P & Neylon, C 2010, 'Altmetrics: A Manifesto', http://altmetrics.org/manifesto/ (July 15, 2020).

Sens, I & Lange, C 2019, 'ConfIDent – a Reliable Platform for Scientific Events', https://gepris.dfg.de/gepris/projekt/426477583?language=en (July 15, 2020).

Sivertsen, G 2019, 'Developing Current Research Information Systems (CRIS) as data sources for studies of research', in W Glänzel, HF Moed, U Schmoch & M Thelwall (eds.), *Springer Handbook of Science and Technology Indicators*, Springer, Heidelberg.

Söderqvist, T & Silverstein, AM 1994, 'Studying leadership and subdisciplinary structure of scientific disciplines', *Scientometrics*, vol. 30, p. 243, https://doi.org/10.1007/BF02017226.

Sugimoto, CR, Murray, DS & Larivière, V 2018, 'Open Citations to Open Science', http://issi-society.org/blog/posts/2018/april/open-citations-to-open-science/ (July 15, 2020).

Sugimoto, CR & Larivière, V 2018, *Measuring Research: What Everyone Needs to Know®*, Oxford University Press, New York.

Thelwall, M 2019, 'Mendeley Reader Counts for US Computer Science Conference Papers and Journal articles', *Quantitative Science Studies*, pp. 1–16, https://doi.org/10.1162/qss_a_00010.

Viglione, G 2020, A year without conferences? How the coronavirus pandemic could change research, Nature 579, 327–328. https://doi.org/10.1038/d41586-020-00786-y.

Zuccala, A 2006, 'Modeling the invisible college', *Journal of the American Society for information Science and Technology*, vol. 57, no. 2, pp. 152–168.

2 Theory, Principles and Methods of Bibliometrics

2.1 Peer Review and Bibliometrics
Bernhard Mittermaier

Abstract: Peer review is an established process supporting decisions made on journal publications, grant applications, and tenure, but also helping to assess research groups. For several reasons, peer review is currently being debated, and bibliometrics could serve as its substitute. A large number of studies comparing both approaches has been published, with an overview of their results presented and discussed in this chapter. Although there are good reasons to be hesitant about utilizing bibliometric approaches to assess single persons (e.g. for tenure), the situation is different when assessing research groups. In the STM area, bibliometric indicators could be used as a replacement for peer review.

Keywords: peer review, peer judgement, research assessment, grants, tenure.

Introduction

Peer review is an evaluation of a manuscript or a research proposal, for example. It is carried out by one or more people with expertise similar to that of the producers of the work, i.e. peers (Weller, 2001). The term also includes the retrospective evaluation of the past performance of a scientist or a group of scientists (Gemma, 2017). In a slightly broader sense, the term "peer review" is also used to assess, for example, teaching (Chism and Chism, 2007; Samson and McCrea, 2008; Snavely and Dewald, 2011; van Valey, 2011) or medical staff and practices (Chop and Eberlein-Gonska, 2012; Ertel and Aldridge, 1977; Hadian et al., 2018; Lang, 1999). The latter forms are not discussed here. This chapter opens with an overview of peer review, before presenting a selection of studies comparing peer review and bibliometric indicators. It concludes with a discussion of the findings.

Peer Review

The Development of Peer Review

It is often claimed – probably for the first time by Zuckerman and Merton (1971) – that peer review was invented by the first secretary of the Royal Society, Henry Oldenburg (1610 – 1677). Further occurrences of this narrative can be found in Baldwin (2018), which has led to the impression that peer review is more or less inextricably linked with scholarly publishing. However, Melinda Baldwin showed that it was only

---

Dr. **Bernhard Mittermaier**, Forschungszentrum Jülich, Central Library, 52425 Jülich, Germany, b.mittermaier@fz-juelich.de

over the course of the nineteenth and early twentieth centuries that a number of learned societies adopted the practice of systematically consulting anonymous reviewers about submitted papers. For instance, the Royal Society of Chemistry adopted reviewing systems in the nineteenth century. The American Physical Society implemented this practice in the early twentieth century, though it was not until the 1960s that all submissions to their flagship journal *Physical Review* were peer-reviewed. At this time, the editors of *Nature* still abstained from consulting external reviewers if papers were submitted or recommended by scientists whom they trusted. It was not until 1973 that external peer review became mandatory for manuscripts submitted to *Nature* (Baldwin, 2015). As late as 1989, an editorial in *The Lancet* revealed a huge inner distance to peer review:

> In the United States far too much is being demanded of peer review. Careers and the viability of whole departments now depend on publication in peer-reviewed journals. In the public domain the process is sometimes seen as a guarantee of truth, which is silly; (...) Journals do things differently, and long live those differences, but there was consensus that turning away papers within the editorial board or 'in house' without an outside opinion by no means disqualified a journal from calling itself peer reviewed and that reviewers are advisers (always The Lancet's preferred term) not decision makers. (Anonymous, 1989)

The Peer-review Process

Probably the most important type of peer review occurs when a manuscript is submitted to a journal (Paltridge, 2017). Journals that have implemented a peer review process are referred to as "peer-reviewed journals" or "refereed journals"; sometimes only publications in such journals are considered "real" scientific output. The first step in the process after submission is assessment by the editor. At this stage, some submissions are rejected ("desk rejection") because they are of low quality or because they are beyond the journal's scope. Once they pass this initial screening, articles are sent to external reviewers. In some cases, authors are invited to suggest reviewers. The number of reviewers ranges from one to three or even more at the discretion of the editor or depending on the regulations of the journal. The standard procedure is "blind peer review", where the author receives the reviewers' comments, but the reviewers themselves remain anonymous. In "double-blind peer review", the author is also anonymized. However, this is not always an easy task, for instance if information about the author's affiliation is necessary to understand the article. The rationale here is to enable reviewers to express their opinions openly and, in the case of double-blind peer review, to avoid any bias with regard to the authors' gender, age, reputation, etc. "Open peer review" is the opposite approach, applied for example by journals published by Copernicus. Here, manuscripts are published in their initial form and then undergo a public review (everybody can comment) in addition to invited and more in-depth reviews. All comments can be read free of charge.

In most cases, reviewers are asked to express their opinion in a structured manner. The intention is to help the editor in judging the cmments and the authors in implementing them. Most often, reviewers have to opt for one final recommendation: for example, "accept as is"; "accept with minor revisions"; "accept with major revisions"; or "reject". If – in the case of two reviewers – there is a substantial disagreement between the recommendations, editors either make the final decision themselves or invite a third reviewer.

If a revision is deemed necessary, authors are advised to follow the reviewers' suggestions, though it is possible in principle for the authors to discuss changes they may consider unreasonable with the editor. It is common practice for authors to provide a detailed response to each reviewer, explaining how they have followed the reviewer's advice or, if they have not, their reasons for not implementing certain suggestions. After revision and resubmission, the editor again decides whether the article will be published or not. Overall, rejection rates differ hugely between journals, e.g. between 2% and 68% in the atmospheric sciences (Schultz, 2010).

The peer review process for books is rather heterogeneous (Goldfinch and Yamamoto, 2012). External peer review by one reviewer (or even more than one) is often substituted by an editorial review, particularly in the case of edited books, where a number of different authors write the chapters. In the case of monographs and particularly in the case of textbooks, the publisher provides the editing through his staff.[1]

Grant proposals can be reviewed in exactly the same way as journal articles, with the exception that here reviewers are not asked to improve the text of the proposal but rather to suggest a different experimental setting etc. Often, grant proposals are judged by a review panel in quite a different setting: the reviewers do not act independently of each other but discuss the proposal together after questioning the applicants. This process often comprises a single session in which a number of proposals for the same tender are reviewed. As a grant application not only includes the research proposal itself but also curriculum vitae of the participating scientists along with their publication records and letters of recommendations, the review also takes the past performance of the applicants into account.

An even greater shift towards past performance assessment occurs in the evaluation of research groups or institutions. For instance, in Germany, universities participating in the German federal and state governments' Excellence Initiative undergo a rigorous assessment carried out by scientists from abroad. The same applies to the extramural research institutions of the Leibniz Association and the Helmholtz Association. They are evaluated every seven years to decide whether they can continue as a member of the Leibniz Association or, in the case of Helmholtz, to what extent the

---

[1] In contrast to this, journal editors are usually not staff members of the publisher, but scientists who pursue this work in addition to their research and teaching duties. They get no or only minimal compensation for their editorial duties (de Knecht, 2019).

research programmes will be financed. I will elaborate using the example of the Helmholtz Association: Helmholtz pools its research activities in six strategic programmes, which typically extend across the Association's research centres. Programme evaluation happens in two stages: first, each centre's past performance is evaluated in relation to the programme; then, two years later, the proposals for future research are assessed. On average, each programme has a publication output of 20,000 journal articles in a seven-year period (Helmholtz, 2018). The key questions here are: what is the most suitable method for assessing such a volume of scientific output and is such an assessment even feasible?

Peer Review Under Criticism

Peer review is extremely important in scholarly communication, and there are a number of supporting arguments in its favour. First, there is the (mistaken) assumption that peer review has always been linked to scholarly publishing. Furthermore, article quality is considered to be improved by the process (Jefferson, Wager, and Davidoff, 2002; Pierie, Walvoort, and Overbeke, 1996). Finally, peer review is regarded as a form of self-regulation within a field: author and reviewer are on an equal footing and could theoretically swap roles. This distinguishes peer review from the examination of a thesis by a supervisor and from the application process in an office.

Nevertheless, criticism of peer review has been growing in recent years (Bornmann, 2011; Eysenck and Eysenck, 1992; Gould, 2013; Smith, 2006). Some of the criticized aspects include:

(1) Peer review is inefficient, time-consuming, and expensive. Publications are often delayed, and innovative and unconventional ideas can be prohibited.
(2) Reviewers might deliberately reject the paper or at least slow down the process and in the meantime steal and publish the results on their own (Retraction Watch, 2016).
(3) A plurality of reviewers rarely agree on their recommendations, so reproducibility and reliability are poor (Bornmann, Mutz, and Daniel, 2010).
(4) The fate of a particular proposal is only partially determined by its scientific value; random elements appear to play an important role as well (Cole and Simon, 1981).
(5) Reviewers' recommendations are often biased, which means that the fairness of the process is questionable.

Peer Review and Bibliometrics

In light of this critique, alternatives to peer review would be worth testing, even though the aforementioned approach of open peer review could overcome a number of problems associated with peer review (Godlee, 2002; Walsh et al., 2000). In the case of grant applications, a system known as the "peer-reviewed-productivity formula system" (Roy, 1985) has been proposed, but it apparently has never been adopted. Another option is to utilize bibliometric indicators instead of peer review. This approach has been the subject of many investigations (for overviews, compare e.g. (Aksnes, Langfeldt, and Wouters, 2019; Vieira and Gomes, 2018; Gallo and Glisson, 2018; Wouters et al., 2015; Bornmann, 2011). For historical reasons (Wouters et al., 2015), the majority of these studies aim to compare results derived from bibliometric indicators with peer review, thus taking peer review as the gold standard. However, the subsequent overview starts with studies which test peer review using bibliometric parameters.

Peer Review Versus Journal Impact Factor

It is commonly accepted that there is a hierarchy of journals. This is sometimes conveyed using the image of a pyramid: there are a few high-ranking journals (defined as such by their Journal Impact Factor (JIF), according to the Journal Citation Reports published by Clarivate Analytics), followed by a larger number of middle-tiered journals and an even larger number of low-impact journals (McKiernan et al., 2019): "To succeed in science, one must climb this pyramid: in academia at least, publication in the more prestigious journals is the key to professional advancement" (Jennings 2006). According to this assumption, authors will submit their manuscript to one of the highest ranked journals and in the case of a rejection move down the pyramid and submit to journals with a lower JIF. Bornmann (2011) cites a dozen studies that have compared the quality of the rejecting and the subsequent accepting of journals by means of the JIF. Up to 70% of the rejected manuscripts could be tracked as having been published later in a journal with a higher JIF. Hence, "authors do not necessarily move from 'leading' journals to less prestigious journals after a rejection" (Weller, 2001).

Peer Review Versus Citation Analysis

Sir Theodore F. Fox, former editor of *The Lancet*, was rather sceptical about the predictive value of editorial decisions: "When I divide the week's contributions into two piles – one that we are going to publish and the other that we are going to return – I wonder whether it would make any real difference to the journal or its readers if I exchanged one pile for another." (Fox, 1965). However, evidence-based investigations reveal a significant effect of these decisions for a number of journals: Bornmann and Daniel (2008) tracked 878 articles accepted by *Angewandte Chemie – International Edition* and 959 rejected articles that were then published elsewhere. Their results show that being accepted by *Angewandte Chemie – International Edition* increased the expected number of citations by up to 50%. Similar results were obtained in investigations on the *American Journal of Neuroradiology* (McDonald, Cloft, and Kallmes, 2007; 2009), *Cardiovascular Research* (Opthof et al., 2000), *F1000* (Bornmann and Leydesdorff, 2013), and *Journal of Clinical Investigation* (Wilson, 1978). Broader investigations were conducted by Cicchetti (1991) and Benda and Engels (2011), confirming these findings. Thus, citation analysis suggests that peer review tends to select "the better pile" of manuscripts, which is subsequently cited more often.

Grant Decisions

Some studies have analysed grant peer reviews with the aim of assessing whether applicants who have been awarded funding were cited more often than unfunded applicants: van Leeuwen and Moed (2012) analysed the correlation between funding from three funding councils in the Netherlands and citation impact in the physical sciences, chemistry, and the geosciences. Successful applicants tended to generate a higher citation impact on the international level than those whose applications were rejected. A number of other studies (Armstrong et al., 1997; Bornmann and Daniel, 2006; 2008; Cabezas-Clavijo et al., 2013) also revealed a positive correlation between grant peer review and citation impact. Other studies, however, showed no or only a low correlation between successful grant applications (DFG's Emmy Noether Programme (Germany), the Swedish Foundation for Strategic Research, and the Council for Social Scientific Research of the Netherlands) and subsequent citation impact (Hornbostel et al., 2009; Melin and Danell, 2006; van den Besselaar and Leydesdorff, 2007). Thus, the results of the comparison of grant peer review and bibliometric indicators are mixed. Further to this, whether the selection of applicants might be a self-fulfilling prophecy was also questioned:

> They reward prior excellence [...], but they also afford the successful applicants resources that might enable them to do excellent scientific work in their future careers. If a study establishes significant performance advantages for accepted applicants but not rejected ones, one can argue [...] that the funding organization gives the fellows such an advantage in training, prestige, self-confidence, and so on that they later become superior scientists because of the fellowship, not because they were particularly promising at the point of application. Rather than picking the 'best' scientists, the selection committee might, in this view, create them. (Bornmann, 2011)

Tenure Decision

Vieira, Cabral, and Gomes (2014) analysed 27 professor recruitment processes that took place between 2007 and 2011 at six Portuguese universities with 174 candidates who had published a total of 7,654 documents indexed in the Web of Science in the 10 years prior to their applications. The disciplines of chemistry, physics, biology, mathematics, mechanics, geology, and computer science were involved. When any two applicants in a given recruitment process were compared using a combination of two bibliometric indicators (an h-index variant and the percentage of highly cited documents), the outcome of the ranking of those two applicants by peers could be predicted in 75% of cases. Jensen, Rouquier, and Croissant (2009) explored the correlation between bibliometric indicators (h index, h index divided by "scientific age", number of citations, number of publications, and average number of citations per publication) and the results of a peer review process concerning the promotion of about 600 researchers at France's Centre Nationale de la Recherche Scientifique (CNRS). The authors found that

> no single indicator is the best predictor for all disciplines. Overall, however, the Hirsch index h provides the least bad correlations, followed by the number of papers published. It is important to realize however, that even h is able to recover only half of the actual promotions. The number of citations or the mean number of citations per paper are definitely not good predictors of promotion. (Jensen, Rouquier, and Croissant, 2009).

Evaluation of Research Groups

There are several studies comparing peer review of research groups with bibliometric indicators. In general, these studies found a (sometimes weak) positive correlation. Wouters et al. (2015) explain "the imperfect correlations between bibliometric indicators and peer review (partly) by variation in qualitative peer-based judgements". For example, Aksnes and Taxt (2004) compared the peer ratings of 34 research groups at the University of Bergen (Norway) with a set of five bibliometric indicators. The highest Pearson's correlation was observed between peer ratings and an indicator called "relative publication strategy". It compares the average citation rate of the journals in which the group's articles were published with the average citation rates of the subfields covered by each journal. Meho and Sonnenwald (2000) analyzed the relationship between citation ranking and peer evaluation in assessing senior Kurdologists' research performance. Normalized citation ranking and citation content analysis were highly correlated with peer ranking, both for high-ranked and low-ranked senior scholars. Anthony van Raan et al. performed a number of investigations in this area: Nederhof and van Raan (1993) analyzed the relationship between bibliometric indicators and peer review for six research groups in economics. Peer review and bibliometric findings were generally in agreement. Rinia et al. (1998) showed the correlation between different bibliometric indicators and the outcomes of peer review made by expert panels of physicists in the Netherlands. In the field of physics, they assessed a set of 56 research programmes with approximately 5,000 publications and 50,000 citations. They found the strongest correlation to be between bibliometric indicators and the judgement of the researchers and the research team. Later, van Raan investigated the correlation between standard bibliometric indicators and peer judgement for 147 chemistry research groups in the Netherlands (Van Raan, 2006). He found that both h index and CPP/FCSm discriminate very well between the sets of documents that received a rating of 3 ("satisfactory") and the sets of documents that received ratings of 4 ("good") and 5 ("excellent").

National Research Assessments

A comparative analysis of citation indicators and peer ratings in the Italian research evaluation assessment Valutazione Triennale della Ricerca (VTR) revealed a significant correlation between the two approaches (Ancaiani et al., 2015), though this conclusion was later questioned for methodological reasons (Baccini and De Nicolao, 2016). The latter study concluded that bibliometrics and peer review do not produce similar results. Both studies by Abramo, D'Angelo, and Caprasecca (2009) and Franceschet and Costantini (2011) describe positive correlation between peer decisions and the impact factor of the journals in which the documents were published at the Italian VTR, though they did identify differences between the scientific fields. A number of investigations have been performed with data from the British Research Assessment Exercise (RAE) and its successor, the Research Excellence Framework (REF). For the 1992 RAE, Oppenheim (1997) found for three subject areas (anatomy, archaeology, and genetics) statistically significant correlations between the total number of citations received, or the average number of citations per member of staff, and the RAE score. Similar results were obtained from the 2001 RAE data for the field of archaeology by Norris and Oppenheim (2003). While some experts criticized the conclusions (e.g. Warner, 2000), others replicated the results for the areas of political science and chemistry. However, "no single model will apply across science and non-science disciplines. Any metrics approach to performance evaluation has to use a discipline-specific suite of indicators" (Butler and Mcallister, 2011). Butler and Mcallister (2011) used the mean citation rate, the department size, the research culture, and the presence of staff from the department being evaluated on the RAE panel as predictors of the peer decisions. They concluded that citations alone are no surrogate for a peer review. Work reviewing the bibliometrics of the RAE 2001 data came to the same conclusion. There were huge differences between the scientific fields, and even within a field with a statistically significant correlation between citation and RAE score such as chemistry, the ranking of institutions that emerged from the two measures was far from identical (Mahdi, D'Este, and Neely, 2008). The subsequent RAE and REF assessment exercises have been subject of further investigations; for an overview, see Traag and Waltman (2019). For example, the outcome of REF 2014 was compared with 15 bibliometric and altmetric indicators (HEFCE, 2015). The authors found that the quantitative indicators with significant impact in predicting peer evaluation differed between scientific disciplines. Consistently high correlations were found for several metrics in clinical medicine, economics, and econometrics. The study concludes that metrics cannot provide a like-for-like replacement of REF peer review. However, the study does not analyze department-level average scores, which, according to Traag and Waltman (2019), are more relevant for the REF.

Conclusion

Overall, most of the comparative studies found a moderately positive correspondence between peer review and bibliometric indicators, but the correlations identified have been far from perfect and have varied among the studies. Inter alia, the correlations depend on the scientific field, the bibliometric indicators, and the subject of the review:

- The results of studies focusing on grant decisions are mixed. While a number of studies revealed a positive correlation between grant peer review and citation impact, other studies showed no or only a low correlation between the success in grant applications and subsequent citation impact.
- The results of investigations on tenure decisions are not convincing either. At best, bibliometric indicators can predict the correct ranking of any two applicants in 75% of cases, which is only halfway between the actual result (100%) and a random decision (50%). Reviews of research group assessments generally revealed better correspondence between peer review and bibliometrics, often depending on the scientific field and the indicator in question.
- Investigations on national research assessments revealed results similar to the studies on research group assessments. As a rule of thumb, correlations in the area of science, technology, and medicine (STM) are better than in the social sciences and humanities, and correlations are better for field-normalized indicators than for basic indicators like the citation count.

Therefore, there is generally little empirical support for the hypothesis that bibliometrics reflects the same aspects of impact or research quality as peer review. However, the extent to which the correlation between the two approaches is considered sufficient depends on the nature and the goals of the evaluation. The statement by Abramo and D'Angelo (2011) regarding national research assessments could hold true for the evaluation of research groups as well: "Accepting that there is no one infallible evaluation method, the position of the authors is that for the natural and formal sciences, the bibliometric methodology is by far preferable to informed peer review." This may first appear as a daring thesis, but it can be justified for the following reasons:

- Peer review is far from perfect, as was shown, for example, in the section "Peer Review Versus Journal Impact Factor". Therefore, a deviation in the results of a bibliometric approach from a peer decision does not necessarily indicate that the bibliometric approach led to a "wrong" result.

- Peer review is very labour intensive and hence expensive. This can be justified for tenure decisions, for example, but must be questioned for the production of rankings.
- While there are good reasons to be hesitant about utilizing bibliometric approaches as the only method for evaluating single persons (e.g. tenure, grant), the situation for assessing groups is different, and here bibliometric analyses could replace peer review.

References

Abramo, G & D'Angelo, CA 2011, 'Evaluating research: from informed peer review to bibliometrics', *Scientometrics*, vol. 87, no. 3, pp. 499–514, https://doi.org/10.1007/s11192-011-0352-7.

Abramo, G, Andrea D'Angelo, C & Caprasecca, A 2009, 'Allocative efficiency in public research funding: Can bibliometrics help?', *Research Policy*, vol. 38, no. 1, pp. 206–15, https://doi.org/10.1016/j.respol.2008.11.001.

Aksnes, DW, Langfeldt, L & Wouters, P 2019, 'Citations, Citation Indicators, and Research Quality: An Overview of Basic Concepts and Theories', *Sage Open*, vol. 9, no. 1, p. 17, https://doi.org/10.1177/2158244019829575.

Aksnes, DW & Taxt, RE 2004, 'Peer reviews and bibliometric indicators: a comparative study at a Norwegian university', *Research Evaluation*, vol. 13, no. 1, pp. 33–41, https://doi.org/10.3152/147154404781776563.

Ancaiani, A, Anfossi, AF, Barbara, A, Benedetto, S, Blasi, B, Carletti, V, Cicero, T, Ciolfi, A, Costa, F, Colizza, G, Costantini, M, di Cristina, F, Ferrara, A, Lacatena, RM, Malgarini, M, Mazzotta, I, Nappi, CA, Romagnosi, S & Sileoni, S 2015, 'Evaluating scientific research in Italy: The 2004–10 research evaluation exercise', *Research Evaluation*, vol. 24, no. 3, pp. 242–55, https://doi.org/10.1093/reseval/rvv008.

Anonymous 1989, 'PEERS REVIEWED', *The Lancet*, vol. 333, no. 8647, pp. 1115–16, https://doi.org/10.1016/S0140-6736(89)92390-8.

Armstrong, PW, Caverson, MM, Adams, L, Taylor, M & Olley, PM 1997, 'Evaluation of the Heart and Stroke Foundation of Canada Research Scholarship Program: research productivity and impact', *The Canadian journal of cardiology*, vol. 13, no. 5, pp. 507–516, http://europepmc.org/abstract/MED/9179090 (July 15, 2020).

Baccini, A & De Nicolao, G 2016, 'Do they agree? Bibliometric evaluation versus informed peer review in the Italian research assessment exercise', *Scientometrics*, vol. 108, no. 3, pp. 1651–71, https://doi.org/10.1007/s11192-016-1929-y.

Baldwin, M 2015, 'Credibility, peer review, and Nature, 1945–1990', *Notes and Records: the Royal Society Journal of the History of Science*, vol. 69, no. 3, pp. 337–52, https://doi.org/doi:10.1098/rsnr.2015.0029.

Baldwin, M 2018, 'Scientific Autonomy, Public Accountability, and the Rise of "Peer Review" in the Cold War United States', *Isis*, vol. 109, no. 3, pp. 538–58, https://doi.org/10.1086/700070.

Benda, Wim GG & and Engels, TCE 2011, 'The predictive validity of peer review: A selective review of the judgmental forecasting qualities of peers, and implications for innovation in science', *International Journal of Forecasting*, vol. 2, no. 1, pp. 166–82, https://doi.org/10.1016/j.ijforecast.2010.03.003.

Bornmann, L 2011, 'Scientific Peer Review', *Annual Review of Information Science and Technology*, vol. 45, pp. 199–245, https://doi.org/10.1002/aris.2011.1440450112.

Bornmann, L & Daniel, H-D 2006, 'Selecting scientific excellence through committee peer review – A citation analysis of publications previously published to approval or rejection of post-doctoral research fellowship applicants', *Scientometrics*, vol. 68, no. 3, pp. 427–40, https://doi.org/10.1007/s11192-006-0121-1.

Bornmann, L & Daniel, H-D 2008, 'Selecting manuscripts for a high-impact journal through peer review: A citation analysis of communications that were accepted by Angewandte Chemie International Edition, or rejected but published elsewhere', *Journal of the American Society for Information Science and Technology*, vol. 59, no. 11, pp. 1841–52, https://doi.org/10.1002/asi.20901.

Bornmann, L & Leydesdorff, L 2013, 'The validation of (advanced) bibliometric indicators through peer assessments: A comparative study using data from InCites and F1000', *Journal of Informetrics*, vol. 7, no. 2, pp. 286–91, https://doi.org/10.1016/j.joi.2012.12.003.

Bornmann, L, Mutz, R & Daniel, H-D 2010, 'A Reliability-Generalization Study of Journal Peer Reviews: A Multilevel Meta-Analysis of Inter-Rater Reliability and Its Determinants', *PLOS ONE*, vol. 5, no. 12, e1433, https://doi.org/10.1371/journal.pone.0014331.

Butler, L & Mcallister, I 2011, 'Evaluating University Research Performance Using Metrics', *European Political Science*, vol. 10, no. 1, pp. 44–58, https://doi.org/10.1057/eps.2010.13.

Cabezas-Clavijo, A, Robinson-Garcia, N, Escabias, M & Jimenez-Contreras, E 2013, 'Reviewers' Ratings and Bibliometric Indicators: Hand in Hand When Assessing Over Research Proposals?', *Plos One*, vol. 8, no. 6, p. 12, https://doi.org/10.1371/journal.pone.0068258.

Chism, NVN & Chism GW 2007, *Peer review of teaching: a sourcebook*. 2nd ed., Bolton, Anker Pub. Co. MA.

Chop, I & Eberlein-Gonska, M 2012, 'Übersichtsartikel zum Peer Review Verfahren und seine Einordnung in der Medizi', *Zeitschrift für Evidenz, Fortbildung und Qualität im Gesundheitswesen*, vol. 106, no. 8, pp. 547–52, https://doi.org/10.1016/j.zefq.2012.08.017.

Cicchetti, DV 1991, 'The reliability of peer review for manuscript and grant submissions: A cross-disciplinary investigation', *Behavioral and Brain Sciences*, vol. 14, no. 1, 119–35, https://doi.org/10.1017/S0140525X00065675.

Cole, S, JR & Simon, GA 1981, 'Chance and consensus in peer review', *Science*, vol. 214, no. 4523, pp. 881–86, https://doi.org/10.1126/science.7302566.

de Knecht, S 2019, 'So what about editor compensation?', https://medium.com/@SiccodeKnecht/so-what-about-editor-compensation-89fccaf10d71 (July 15, 2020).

Ertel, PP & Aldridge, MG 1977, *Medical peer review: theory and practice*, Mosby, St. Louis.

Eysenck, HJ & Eysenck, SBG 1992, 'Peer review: Advice to referees and contributors', *Personality and Individual Differences*, vol. 13, no. 4, pp. 393–99, https://doi.org/10.1016/0191-8869(92)90066-X.

Fox, TF 1965, *Crisis in communication: the functions and future of medical journals*, Athlone Press, London.

Franceschet, M & Costantini, A 2011, 'The first Italian research assessment exercise: A bibliometric perspective', *Journal of Informetrics*, vol. 5, no. 2, pp. 275–91, https://doi.org/10.1016/j.joi.2010.12.002.

Gallo, SA & Glisson, SR 2018, 'External Tests of Peer Review Validity Via Impact Measures', *Frontiers in Research Metrics and Analytics*, vol. 3, no. 22, https://doi.org/10.3389/frma.2018.00022.

Gemma, D 2017, *The evaluators' eye: impact assessment and academic peer review*, 1st edition. ed., Springer Berlin Heidelberg, New York.

Godlee, F 2002, 'Making Reviewers Visible: Openness, Accountability, and Credit', *JAMA*, vol. 287, no. 21, pp. 2762–65, https://doi.org/10.1001/jama.287.21.2762.

Goldfinch, S & Yamamoto, K 2012, *Prometheus assessed?: Research measurement, peer review, and citation analysis*, Chandos Publishing, Oxford.

Gould, THP 2013, *Do we still need peer review?: an argument for change*, The Scarecrow Press, Inc., Lanham.

Hadian, M, Iwrey, RS, Meyer, C & Souter, PD 2018, *What is … medical staff peer review?*, American Bar Association, Chicago.

HEFCE 2015, *The Metric Tide: Correlation analysis of REF2014 scores and metrics (Supplementary Report II to the Independent Review of the Role of Metrics in Research Assessment and Management)*.

Helmholtz 2018, *Annual Report*, https://www.helmholtz.de/fileadmin/user_upload/04_mediathek/18_Helmholtz_Geschaeftsbericht_ENGLISCH_epaper.pdf (July 15, 2020).

Hornbostel, S, Böhmer, S, Klingsporn, B, Neufeld, J & von Ins, M 2009, 'Funding of young scientist and scientific excellence', *Scientometrics*, vol. 79, no. 1, pp. 171–190, https://doi.org/10.1007/s11192-009-0411-5.

Jefferson, T, Wager, E & Davido F 2002, 'Measuring the Quality of Editorial Peer Review' *JAMA*, vol. 287, no. 21, pp. 2786–2790, https://doi.org/10.1001/jama.287.21.2786.

Jennings, CG 2006, 'Quality and value: The true purpose of peer review', Springer Nature, accessed April 14, 2019.

Jensen, P, Rouquier, J-B & Croissant, Y 2009, 'Testing bibliometric indicators by their prediction of scientists promotions', *Scientometrics*, vol. 78, no. 3, pp. 467–479, https://doi.org/10.1007/s11192-007-2014-3.

Lang, DA 1999, *Medical staff peer review : motivation and performance in the era of managed care*. rev. ed., Health Forum, Inc., Chicago.

Mahdi, S, D'Este, P & Neely A 2008, *Citation counts: are they good predictors of RAE scores? A bibliometric analysis of RAE 2001* (AIM Research), https://www.bl.uk/collection-items/citation-counts-are-they-good-predictors-of-rae-scores-a-bibliometric-analysis-of-rae-2001 (July 15, 2020).

McDonald, RJ, Cloft, HJ & Kallmes DF 2007, 'Fate of Submitted Manuscripts Rejected from the American Journal of Neuroradiology: Outcomes and Commentary', *American Journal of Neuroradiology*, vol. 28, no. 8, pp. 1430–1434, https://doi.org/10.3174/ajnr.A0766.

McDonald, RJ, Cloft, HJ & Kallmes DF 2009, 'Fate of Manuscripts Previously Rejected by the American Journal of Neuroradiology: A Follow-Up Analysis', *American Journal of Neuroradiology*, vol. 30, no. 2, pp. 253–256, https://doi.org/10.3174/ajnr.A1366.

McKiernan, EC, Schimanski, LA, Muñoz Nieves, C, Matthias, L, Niles, MT & Alperin, JP 2019, 'Use of the Journal Impact Factor in academic review, promotion, and tenure evaluations', *PeerJ Preprints*, vol. 7, e27638v2, https://doi.org/10.7287/peerj.preprints.27638v2.

Meho, LI & Sonnenwald, DH 2000, 'Citation ranking versus peer evaluation of senior faculty research performance: A case study of Kurdish scholarship', *Journal of the American Society for Information Science*, vol. 51, no. 2, pp. 123–138, https://doi.org/10.1002/(sici)1097-4571(2000)51:2<123::Aid-asi4>3.0.Co;2-n.

Melin, G & Danell, R 2006, 'The top eight percent: Development of approved and rejected applicants for a prestigious grant in Sweden', *Science and Public Policy*, vol. 33, no. 10, pp. 702–712, https://doi.org/10.3152/147154306781778579.

Nederhof, AJ & van Raan, AFJ 1993, 'A bibliometric analysis of six economics research groups: A comparison with peer review', *Research Policy*, vol. 22, no. 4, pp. 353–368, https://doi.org/10.1016/0048-7333(93)90005-3.

Norris, M & Oppenheim, C 2003, 'Citation counts and the Research Assessment Exercise V: Archaeology and the 2001 RAE', *Journal of Documentation*, vol. 59, no. 6, pp. 709–730, https://doi.org/10.1108/00220410310698734.

Oppenheim, C 1997, 'The correlation between citation counts and the 1992 research assessment exercise ratings for British research in genetics, anatomy and archaeology', *Journal of Documentation*, vol. 53, no. 5, pp. 477–487, https://doi.org/doi:10.1108/EUM0000000007207.

Opthof, T, Furstner, F, van Geer, M & Coronel, R 2000, 'Regrets or no regrets? No regrets! The fate of rejected manuscripts', *Cardiovascular Research*, vol. 45, no. 1, pp. 255–258, https://doi.org/10.1016/s0008-6363(99)00339-9.

Paltridge, B 2017, *The discourse of peer review : reviewing submissions to academic journals*, Palgrave Macmillan, London.

Pierie, J-PEN, Walvoort, HC & Overbeke, AJPM 1996, 'Readers' evaluation of effect of peer review and editing on quality of articles in the Nederlands Tijdschrift voor Geneeskunde', *The Lancet*, vol. 348, no. 9040, pp. 1480–1483, https://doi.org/10.1016/S0140-6736(96)05016-7.

Retraction Watch 2016, 'Dear peer reviewer, you stole my paper: An author's worst nightmare', https://retractionwatch.com/2016/12/12/dear-peer-reviewer-stole-paper-authors-worst-nightmare/ (July 15, 2020).

Rinia, EJ, van Leeuwen, ThN, van Vuren, HG & van Raan, AFJ 1998, 'Comparative analysis of a set of bibliometric indicators and central peer review criteria: Evaluation of condensed matter physics in the Netherlands', *Research Policy*, vol. 27, no. 1, pp. 95–107, https://doi.org/10.1016/S0048-7333(98)00026-2.

Roy, R 1985, 'Funding science: The real defects of peer-review and an alternative to it', *Science, Technology, & Human Values*, vol. 52, no. 3, pp. 73–81, https://doi.org/10.1177/016224398501000309.

Samson, S & McCrea, DE 2008, 'Using peer review to foster good teaching', *Reference Services Review*, vol. 36, no. 1, pp. 61–70, https://doi.org/10.1108/00907320810852032.

Schultz, DM 2010, 'Rejection Rates for Journals Publishing in the Atmospheric Sciences', *Bulletin of the American Meteorological Society*, vol. 91, no. 2, pp. 231–244, https://doi.org/10.1175/2009bams2908.1.

Smith, R 2006, 'Peer review: a flawed process at the heart of science and journals', *Journal of the Royal Society of Medicine*, vol. 99, no. 4, pp. 178–182, https://doi.org/10.1258/jrsm.99.4.178.

Snavely, L & Dewald, N 2011, 'Developing and Implementing Peer Review of Academic Librarians' Teaching: An Overview and Case Report', *Journal of Academic Librarianship*, vol. 37, no. 4, pp. 343–351, https://doi.org/10.1016/j.acalib.2011.04.009.

Traag, VA & Waltman, L 2019, 'Systematic analysis of agreement between metrics and peer review in the UK REF', *Palgrave Communications*, vol. 5, no. 1, p. 29, https://doi.org/10.1057/s41599-019-0233-x.

van den Besselaar, P & Leydesdorff L 2007, *Past performance as predictor of successful grant applications: A case study. Report to the board of the Netherlands Social Science Research council (MaGW/NWO)*.

van Leeuwen, TN & Moed HF 2012, 'Funding decisions, peer review, and scientific excellence in physical sciences, chemistry, and geosciences', *Research Evaluation*, vol. 21, no. 3, pp. 189–198, https://doi.org/10.1093/reseval/rvs009.

van Raan, AFJ 2006, 'Comparison of the Hirsch-index with standard bibliometric indicators and with peer judgment for 147 chemistry research groups', *Scientometrics*, vol. 67, no. 3, pp. 491–502, https://doi.org/10.1556/Scient.67.2006.3.10.

van Valey, TL 2011, *Peer review of teaching: lessons from and for departments of sociology*, American Sociological Association, Washington DC.

Vieira, ES, Cabral, JAS & Gomes JANF 2014, 'Definition of a model based on bibliometric indicators for assessing applicants to academic positions', *Journal of the Association for Information Science and Technology*, vol. 65, no. 3, pp. 560–577, https://doi.org/10.1002/asi.22981.

Vieira, ES & Gomes, JANF 2018, 'The peer-review process: The most valued dimensions according to the researcher's scientific career', *Research Evaluation* vol. 27, no. 3, pp. 246–261, https://doi.org/10.1093/reseval/rvy009.

Walsh, E, Rooney, M, Appleby, L & Wilkinson G 2000, 'Open peer review: A randomised controlled trial', *British Journal of Psychiatry*, vol. 176, no. 1, pp. 47–51, https://doi.org/10.1192/bjp.176.1.47.

Warner, J 2000, 'A Critical Review of the Application of Citation Studies to the Research Assessment Exercises', *Journal of Information Science*, vol. 26, pp. 453–460, https://doi.org/10.1177/016555150002600607.

Weller, AC 2001, *Editorial peer review: its strengths and weaknesses.ASIST monograph series*, Information Today, Medford, N.J.

Wilson, JD 1978, 'Peer review and publication. Presidential address before the 70th annual meeting of the American Society for Clinical Investigation, San Francisco, California, 30 April 1978', *The Journal of Clinical Investigation*, vol. 61, no. 6, pp. 1697–1701, https://doi.org/10.1172/JCI109091.

Wouters, P, Thelwall, M, Kousha, K, Waltman, L, de Rijcke, S, Rushforth, A & Franssen T 2015, *The Metric Tide: Literature Review (Supplementary Report I to the Independent Review of the Role of Metrics in Research Assessment and Management)* (HEFCE).

Zuckerman, H & Merton RK 1971, 'Patterns of evaluation in science: Institutionalization, structure and functions of the referee system', *Minerva*, vol. 9, no. 1, pp. 66–100, https://doi.org/10.1007/bf01553188.

2.2 Jurisdiction of Bibliometrics

Arlette Jappe and Thomas Heinze

Abstract: The "professional jurisdiction" is a sociological term referring to tasks and activities that societies entrust to experts. This article applies a sociology of professions framework to the field of evaluative bibliometrics and presents new empirical findings on the emerging profession of bibliometric research assessment.

Keywords: profession, competition, research assessment, reputational control, expert organizations.

According to the Oxford English Dictionary, "jurisdiction" refers to the "official power to make legal decisions and judgements", which is further differentiated as referring either to "the extent of the power to make legal decisions and judgements", to "a system of law courts, a judicature", or to "the territory or sphere of activity over which the legal authority of a court or other institution extends". This legal term has been adapted and modified by sociologists to "professional jurisdiction" as a technical term referring to spheres of activity that are under more or less exclusive authority of certain professional groups in society at a given time in history (Abbott, 1988). The sociological usage is broader in that it does not only refer to the legal sphere, but also to a large variety of tasks and activities that societies entrust to experts. The extent of the professional authority, the scope of the relevant activities, as well as the precise character of the institutions securing that authority are left open by the sociological definition as these characteristics are regarded as historically variable objects of empirical research. Consequently, the purpose of sociological research on the professions is to investigate how expertise is institutionalized in modern societies.

In contrast to earlier studies that often described the historical development leading to the formation of formal associations and the establishment of ethics codes, Abbott (1988) postulated that sociological research should focus on the actual work of professionals. Abbott proposed a theoretical framework at a high degree of abstraction to encompass such diverse activities as carried out by lawyers, doctors, clergymen, psychologists, architects, engineers, librarians, or accountants. A basic theoretical distinction is between layperson and expert. According to Abbott, the

---

Selected empirical findings and text passages were taken from earlier publications (Jappe, 2020; Jappe, Pithan, and Heinze, 2018; Petersohn and Heinze, 2018).

Dr. **Arlette Jappe**, University of Wuppertal, Interdisciplinary Centre for Science and Technology Studies IZWT, Gaußstraße 20, 42119 Wuppertal, Germany, jappe@uni-wuppertal.de
Univ.-Prof. Dr. **Thomas Heinze**, Fakultät für Human- und Sozialwissenschaften, Bergische Universität Wuppertal, Gaußstr. 20, 42119 Wuppertal, theinze@uni-wuppertal.de

https://doi.org/10.1515/9783110646610-010

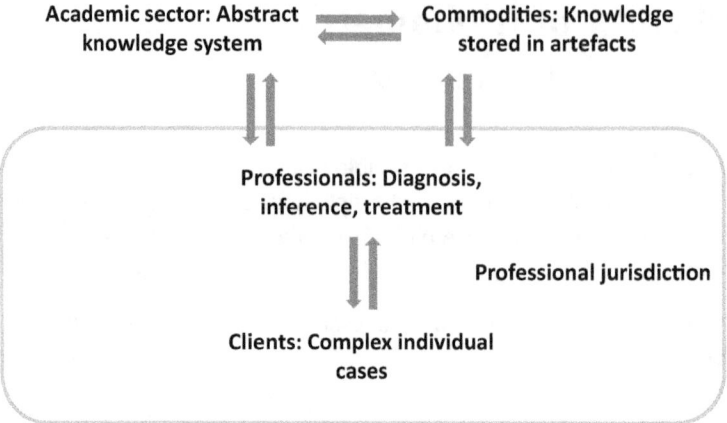

Figure 1: Theoretical framework of a mature profession according to Andrew Abbott. From Jappe, Pithan, and Heinze (2018), published under CC BY 4.0 license.

work of professionals in modern societies can be generally described as the application of abstract knowledge to complex individual cases. The theory thus posits a basic division of labour between an academic sector producing abstract knowledge and professional actors who apply this knowledge in their daily work with clients or patients (Figure 1). The application of abstract knowledge includes diagnosis, inference, and treatment. In fully established professions, this threefold professional practice is carried out in particular workplaces, such as hospitals or professional service firms. Abstract knowledge lends legitimacy to claims of jurisdiction, tying professional work to the general values of logical consistency, rationality, effectiveness, and progress. Such scientific legitimacy includes definition of the nature of problems, rational means of diagnosing these problems, and delivery of effective treatment. Moreover, abstract knowledge enables the instruction and training of students entering the profession, and facilitates the generation of new methods of diagnosis, inference, and treatment. Abstract knowledge is frequently and increasingly stored in specialized artefacts, such as manuals, libraries, instruments, databases or software (Abbott, 1991).

The concept of a professional jurisdiction extends beyond the mere economic notion of a market for expert services in that it asks for the process of establishing expert authority regarding problem definitions and treatments that are accepted as appropriate and legitimate by clients but also by society at large. Abbott identifies three social arenas in which professionals must establish and defend their jurisdictional claims: the legal system, the public, and the workplace. Yet, it would be misleading to think of professionalization as a uniform development process. Abbott criticized that earlier process models failed to account for the historical variety in the evolution of professions. In search of a more open framework that could support a comparative research perspective, he argued that the professions should be viewed as an interde-

Figure 2: Bibliometric research assessment as an emerging profession. From Jappe, Pithan, and Heinze (2018), published under CC BY 4.0 license.

pendent system. From a system perspective, competition among professional groups takes center stage. Hence, professional groups compete for recognition of their expertise and seek to establish exclusive domains of competence (professional jurisdictions). In view of the historical variety in jurisdictional settlements in modern societies, Abbott does not make specific assumptions of the role of the nation state, but argues for historical case studies of jurisdictions and jurisdictional disputes.

This theoretical framework has been applied to the development of evaluative bibliometrics in order to investigate how and to what extent professional groups have been successful in establishing jurisdictional claims in the area of bibliometric research assessment (Jappe, Pithan, and Heinze, 2018; Petersohn and Heinze, 2018; Petersohn, 2016; Jappe, 2020). The purpose of this research is to offer a new perspective on the ongoing debate on research metrics. Rather than giving advice for more professional, better, more effective or more legitimate means of research assessment, this sociological analysis aims, first, to describe to what extent evaluative bibliometrics has been institutionalized as a professional activity, and second, to explain what may be important obstacles or challenges to the ongoing professionalization process.

Applied to the field of evaluative bibliometrics, we assume that two main types of clients are potentially interested in bibliometric assessment services: organisations conducting research and research funders (Figure 2). These organizations require reliable information concerning the performance of their scientists, research groups, and funded projects for decision-making purposes (Miller, 2013; Moed, 2005), as well as for accountability and legitimacy (Power, 1997; Strathern, 1996). A universal reason why such organizations would be interested in quantitative assessment techniques is the rapid growth of science (Bornmann, and Mutz 2015). Since the knowledge base in most areas of science grows faster globally than the financial resources of any individual organisation, these organisations are routinely faced with resource allocation problems. Organisations have to make selection decisions on hiring and promotion of research staff, and when selecting research funding applications. There seems to exist an increasing demand for routine assessment techniques that are relatively cheap and universally applicable.

On the other hand, there are important reasons why research metrics are strongly contested within scientific communities (Aksnes, Langfeldt, and Wouters, 2019; Adler, Ewing, and Taylor, 2009; Cagan, 2013; Hicks et al., 2015). First, they pose a threat to the basic principle that only scientific colleagues from the same research area are competent judges of the merit of scientific contributions ("peer review"). The exclusive reliance on evaluation by scientific colleagues who are at the same time competitors within the same field is what sociologist Richard Whitley called "reputational control" (Whitley, 2000). While bibliometric indices are dependent on peer review because they build on peer-reviewed journal publications, the resulting performance metrics can be used by administrators, policymakers, or anybody else without any specific understanding of the work to be evaluated. Therefore, bibliometric assessment is perceived by many scientists as an intrusion on basic mechanisms of reputational control and thus on their professional autonomy.

Faced with this tension between an increasing demand for relatively objective performance assessment on one hand and considerable contestation on the other, the questions are, first, how and to what extent particular assessment techniques have been established, and second, where these techniques have been implemented as professional practice. What follows below are selected findings with regard to these two research questions, from studies conducted in the framework of Abbott's theory of professions, using a variety of quantitative and qualitative methods (Jappe, Pithan, and Heinze, 2018; Petersohn and Heinze, 2018; Jappe 2020).

The first study investigates whether the academic sector confers legitimacy to bibliometric assessment practice (Jappe, Pithan, and Heinze, 2018). We investigated reputational control in evaluative citation analysis (ECA), an academic sector closely related to research assessment practice, by delineating the field of ECA as all publications in the Web of Science citing any citation impact indices to have been proposed since the Journal Impact Factor (1972). Based on such citations, we constructed inter-organisational citation networks and showed that in these networks, peripheral actors contribute the same number of novel bibliometric indicators as central actors. In addition, the share of newcomers to the academic sector is high, the Hirsch-index being the most significant example of an outsider contribution which rapidly surpassed any previous metrics in terms of citation impact. The generally high share of outsiders indicates that ECA can be mastered with rather generalist scientific competencies, such as knowledge of statistical methods. Consistent with Whitley's definition, openness to outsider contributions can be considered a manifestation of weak reputational control.

These findings suggest that the growth in the volume of ECA publications has not been accompanied by the formation of an intellectual field with strong reputational control. Therefore, the academic sector has failed (so far) to provide scientific authority for research assessment as a professional practice. This finding is relevant for understanding the present state of professionalization in bibliometric evaluation techniques. If reputational control were high, we would expect recommendations for improved research assessment to be launched by the field as a result of the recent intensification of research on this topic. Yet, in the present situation of limited reputational control, even carefully drafted academic contributions appear unlikely to have a significant impact on research assessment practice since these inventions are not supported by an organized scientific community (ECA) that would select and amplify cognitive claims for jurisdiction.

Yet, Abbott's framework allows for other social mechanisms of how jurisdictional claims could be established among potential clients. In this regard, the second study investigates the field of professional actors through their work products (Jappe, 2020). In evaluative bibliometrics, the role of professionals is usually performed either by individual researchers from the academic sector or by specialized expert organizations, including bibliometric contract research institutes or consulting firms (Figure 2). Based on a large number of professional evaluation reports, this study investigates to what extent the field of research assessment practice displays certain methodological standards and which social actors defined such standards. A broad search yielded 138 professional evaluation studies targeting either research organizations or research funding instruments from 21 European countries plus EU framework programs. The sample only includes assessments conducted for purposes of decision-making in research policy or research management that were published as reports (grey literature) or journal articles in the period 2005–2019. Methodologically, the study resembles a "meta-evaluation" (Cooksy and Caracelli, 2005; Stufflebeam, 2001) in that a structured content analysis was used for a detailed comparison of individual evaluation studies.

The second study finds that bibliometric research assessment was most frequent in the Netherlands, the Nordic countries, Italy, and the United Kingdom. Although the studies originate from diverse national policy settings, we found significant methodological convergence. During the observation period, the Web of Science (WoS) was the dominant database for the assessment of public research in Europe (87% of study sample). We found that some expert organizations were able to set technical standards with respect to data quality through investments in in-house databases with improved WoS data. Citation impact was most frequently assessed with reference to international scientific fields. In addition, WoS classification of science fields functioned as a de-facto reference standard for research performance assessment.

Furthermore, the second study supports the notion that leading expert organizations function as role models and thus assume a legitimizing role for other professional actors who imitate them. Not only does the sample document a high market share of the Centre for Science and Technology Studies (CWTS) at the University of Leiden as the leading expert organization in Europe, but CWTS also seems influential in popularizing the field normalized citation means, a concept that has been adopted by other expert organizations in building expensive in-house databases. Perhaps more importantly, Jappe (2020) documents the influential role of database providers in defining and promulgating professional de-facto standards. The few examples of alternative or supplementary data sources, such as the citation database Medline/Pubmed and the Norwegian research documentation system CRISTIN, further underline that bibliometric evaluation depends on the accessible data sources. For example, even though the suitability of WoS subject categories as reference for performance evaluation has been repeatedly questioned in the field of ECA, methodological alternatives have had little influence in professional practice because they are not available alongside with citation data. This underlines the relevance of Abbott's warning regarding potential threats to professional autonomy through corporate control of expert commodities (Abbott, 1991).

The third study recasts the history of the expert organization CWTS in the context of Dutch research and higher education policy (Petersohn and Heinze, 2018). Drawing on a large data set, including both archival and interview data, the study shows how the Dutch science policy arena has stimulated the formation of quantitative research assessment as a new professional jurisdiction since the late 1960s. The professional responsibility for quantitative research assessment was institutionalized predominantly in the form of an expert organization that both built up expertise in the academic field of evaluative bibliometrics and provided professional services in assessing research quality: CWTS. Since the 2010s, CWTS has been challenged by ready-made bibliometric solutions by large database providers and publishing houses that increasingly attract non-experts to perform bibliometric assessments. The study also argues that the new professional field of quantitative research assessment experts in the Netherlands is subordinate to the older jurisdiction of peer review and may develop into an advisory jurisdiction in the future.

Taken together, empirical studies conducted in the framework of Abbott's theory of professions illustrate how professional jurisdictions can be examined, and they present insights into the formation of bibliometrics as a new professional jurisdiction. The analytical clarity and the richness of detail vindicate the attempt to thoroughly apply and utilize existing sociological theory. The main practical policy implication regarding professional control in evaluative bibliometrics is the apparent need for creating a public bibliometric infrastructure for all scientific disciplines that fulfils high demands of data quality, is fully transparent in terms of the methods used, and implements a strong form of expert advice and participation in developing open access tools.

References

Abbott, A 1988, *The system of professions: An essay on the division of expert labor*, University of Chicago Press, Chicago.

Abbott, A 1991, 'The Future of Professions: Occupation and Expertise in the Age of Organisation', *Research in the Sociology of Organisations*, vol. 8, pp. 17–42.

Adler, R, Ewing, J & Taylor, P 2009, 'Citation Statistics: A Report from the International Mathematical Union (IMU) in Cooperation with the International Council of Industrial and Applied Mathematics (ICIAM) and the Institute of Mathematical Statistics (IMS)', *Statistical Science*, vol. 24, no. 1, pp. 1–14.
Aksnes, DW, Langfeldt, L & Wouters P 2019, 'Citations, Citation Indicators, and Research Quality: An Overview of Basic Concepts and Theories', *Sage Open*, vol. 9, no. 1, pp. 1–17.
Bornmann, L & Mutz, R 2015, 'Growth Rates of Modern Science: A Bibliometric Analysis Based on the Number of Publications and Cited References', *Journal of the Association for Information Science and Technology*, vol. 66, no. 11, pp. 2215–22.
Cagan, R 2013, 'The San Francisco Declaration on Research Assessment', *Disease Models & Mechanisms*, vol. 6, editorial.
Cooksy, LJ & Caracelli VJ 2005, 'Quality, Context, and Use. Issues in Achieving the Goals of Metaevaluation', *American Journal of Evaluation*, vol. 26, no. 1, pp. 31–42.
Hicks, D, Wouters, P, Waltman, L, de Rijke, S & Rafols, I 2015, 'The Leiden manifesto for research metrics', *Nature*, vol. 520, pp. 429–431.
Jappe, A 2020, 'Professional standards in bibliometric research evaluation? A meta-evaluation of European assessment practice 2005–2019', *PloS One*, vol. 15 no. 4, e0231735.
Jappe, A, Pithan, D & Heinze, T 2018, 'Does bibliometric research confer legitimacy to research assessment practice? A sociological study of reputational control, 1972–2016', *PLoS One*, vol. 13, no. 6, e0199031.
Miller, P, & Power, M 2013, 'Accounting, organizing and economizing: connecting accounting research and organization theory', *The Academy of Management Annals*, vol. 7, no. 1, pp. 557–605.
Moed, HF 2005, *Citation Analysis in Research Evaluation*, Springer, Dordrecht.
Petersohn, S 2016, 'Professional competencies and jurisdictional claims in evaluative bibliometrics: The educational mandate of academic librarians', *Education for Information*, vol. 32, no. 2, pp. 165–93.
Petersohn, S & Heinze T 2018, 'Professionalization of bibliometric research assessment. Insights from the history of the Leiden Centre for Science and Technology Studies (CWTS) ', *Science and Public Policy*, vol. 45, pp. 565–78.
Power, M 1997, *The Audit Society: Rituals of Verification*, Oxford University Press, Oxford.
Strathern, M 1996, *Audit Cultures: Anthropological Studies in Accountability, Ethics and the Academy*, Routledge, London.
Stufflebeam, DL 2001, 'The Metaevaluation Imperative', *American Journal of Evaluation*, vol. 22, no. 2, pp. 183–209.
Whitley, R 2000, *The Intellectual and Social Organization of the Sciences. 2nd Edition*, Oxford University Press, Oxford.

2.3 National Research Evaluation Systems

Michael Ochsner, Emanuel Kulczycki, Aldis Gedutis, and Ginevra Peruginelli

Abstract: In current societies, research takes an important role as a driver of economic and social development. Therefore, research becomes more strategically relevant than ever. Consequently, research evaluation procedures have been implemented to monitor and steer research. This chapter offers an overview of national research assessment practices and reveals that they differ across countries and even research institutes as evaluations evolved over time. It comes to the conclusion that evaluation designers and research policymakers should establish an explicit link between policy goals and a specific research evaluation procedure taking the national evaluation system into account.

Keywords: research evaluation, evaluation systems, country comparison, peer review, social sciences and humanities, knowledge society, new public management, performance-based research funding.

Introduction

Recent decades have been marked by the transformation to a knowledge society. Knowledge generation has been seen as the major driver of economic development as well as an important means for reaching social goals. In such a knowledge society, universities and research institutions began to play an important role (see, e.g., Välimaa and Hoffman, 2008), which led to political demands for their accountability. Politicians, taxpayers, research agencies and managers became more interested in how the money provided to universities and research institutions is spent because the benefit of science was no longer just seen as the provision of highly qualified workers (e.g., Hoenack, 1993) but also as the provision of actual services and economic outputs (Gibbons et al., 1994; Etzkowitz and Leydesdorff, 1998). The development towards the knowledge society was linked with a shift in how public institutions were managed: rather than assuring high professional standards of public service procedures, public institutions now had to provide a service to the customer. Thus, the way in which such institutions were controlled changed considerably. Instead of procedures, outcomes were evaluated (Child, 2005): was there a "return on investment"? This came with institutionalised distrust (Deem, Hillyard and Reem

---

Michael Ochsner, D-GESS, ETH Zurich, Zurich (Switzerland) and FORS, Lausanne (Switzerland), ochsner@gess.ethz.ch
Emanuel Kulczycki, Adam Mickiewicz University Poznań, Poznań (Poland), emek@amu.edu.pl
Aldis Gedutis, Klaipėda University, Klaipėda (Lithuania), aldis.gedutis@ku.lt
Ginevra Peruginelli, Istituto di Informatica Giuridica e Sistemi Giudiziari – IGSG-CNR, Florence (Italy), peruginelli@igsg.cnr.it

https://doi.org/10.1515/9783110646610-011

2007): public servants had to be controlled regarding their efficiency and efficacity. This development also reached the universities (Deem et al., 2007; Hamann, 2016; Readings, 1996; Rolfe, 2013) and changed the way accountability was achieved here. In the past, quality assurance was guided by the principle of scientific freedom (peer review and rigid appointment procedures), but this no longer sufficed for being accountable to the public in the context of increased public and private spending on higher education and the rising importance of research for society and the economy. New Public Management thus asks for systematic evaluation procedures for publicly funded research on the institutional or national level (see, e.g., Geuna and Martin, 2003). At the same time, the share of competitively distributed funding for research increased considerably (Lepori, Reale and Spinello, 2018; Lepori et al., 2007). Thus, we argue in this chapter that research today is evaluated on different levels and in different time frames by various actors, leading to complex systems of evaluation procedures.

Given the logic of New Public Management, evaluation procedures were implemented in a top-down manner by governments and university administrations with the goal of the measurement of the direct achievements of research. Peer review was often criticised for being subjective (see, also critically, Daniel, Mittag and Bornmann, 2007; Peters and Ceci, 1982) and a more objective approach needed to be applied. Therefore, most of those procedures were – and still are – based on bibliometric and scientometric methods that pretend to facilitate a comparison of performances across departments, fields or countries.

These indicators, however, reflect only the research practices in a few disciplines of the natural and technical sciences and do not work well for many disciplines, being especially inadequate for the social sciences, humanities and arts (van Leeuwen, 2013; Nederhof, 2006). Moreover, the use of the indicators has been shown to have negative steering effects on researchers (see, e.g., de Rijcke et al., 2016). Therefore, not all countries implemented a bibliometric evaluation procedure. A well-known example is the UK where repeatedly a discussion was held on whether peer review could be replaced by indicators (see, e.g., Wilsdon et al., 2015), but the cornerstone of the evaluation stayed officially peer review.

Typologies of Evaluation Procedures

Several scholars set out to classify different types of research evaluation procedures or to present overviews of how research is evaluated across countries (Coryn et al., 2007; Galleron et al., 2017; Geuna, Hidayat and Martin, 1999; Geuna and Martin, 2001; 2003; Hicks, 2010; 2012; Jonkers and Zacharewicz, 2016; Lepori et al., 2007; Lepori, Reale and Spinello, 2018; Ochsner, Kulczycki and Gedutis, 2018; von Tunzelmann and Kraemer Mbula, 2003).

Three differentiations of evaluation procedures have been established (see also Whitley, 2007): the stage of evaluation (ex-ante vs. ex-post evaluation); link to funding (summative vs. formative evaluation); and method of evaluation (metric vs. peer review and different levels of evaluation). The first differentiates between procedures that evaluate research at the proposal stage, i.e. before the research has been carried out (ex-ante evaluation, e.g. for project funding) and procedures that evaluate research already conducted (ex-post evaluation, e.g. institutional evaluation). The second differentiates between procedures that allocate funding (summative) and procedures that aim at improving processes without any consequences regarding funding (formative). The third differentiates across different methods of evaluation, the most prominent being metric, indicator-based evaluation and peer review-based evaluation. Classifications differ as to which of the three differentiations they take into account. Most consider only one or two of those aspects.

The first group of classifications takes funding allocation to institutions into account and differentiates according to different methods of evaluation (Coryn et al., 2007; Geuna, Hidayat and Martin, 1999; Geuna and Martin, 2001; 2003; Hicks, 2012; von Tunzelmann and Kraemer, Mbula 2003). The studies of this first group of classification suggest that performance-based research funding systems (PRFSs) are implemented to enhance research excellence. Yet, both Hicks (2012) and Geuna and Martin (2003) raise the question of whether PRFSs are helping to achieve this goal as, for example, they are not encouraging interactions with industry (Hicks, 2012, p. 259) and they are costly and come with diminishing returns after the initial increase at the time of implementation (Geuna and Martin, 2003, p. 303).

The second group of classifications focuses on project funding, i.e. ex-ante evaluation (Lepori et al., 2007; Lepori et al., 2018; Zacharewicz et al., 2018). They show that competitively funded research projects gain rapidly in importance. They find that, first, there is considerable diversity across countries regarding funding instruments, agencies and beneficiaries. Second, there are many commonalities. In all countries, project funding is the second main channel of public funding of research and the share of competitive funding is growing. Furthermore, there is a common shift towards funding instruments oriented towards specific topics.

The typologies presented so far concern only a few specific evaluation procedures in the respective countries and do not take fully into account the three aspects of evaluation procedures identified above. If the goal of research evaluation is to influence research practice (if it wasn't, why would you evaluate in the first place; see, e.g., Hicks, 2012; Jonkers and Zacharewicz, 2016; Zacharewicz et al., 2018), it is not efficient to look at isolated research evaluation procedures or funding schemes. Researchers are influenced by many evaluation procedures and if policy aims at influencing research practice, it needs to take this diversity into account. Therefore, we focus in the next section especially on the third group of typologies, that focus on research evaluation systems (Galleron et al., 2017; van Gestel and Lienhard, 2019; Giménez-Toledo et al., 2019; Ochsner et al., 2018).

National Research Evaluation Systems

The combination of evaluation procedures in a country is complex. So complex that even experts can disagree about how research is evaluated in their countries (Galleron et al., 2017; Ochsner et al., 2018). Formal definitions of evaluation procedures can differ from actual practice, evaluation procedures evolve over time, and, most importantly, different evaluation procedures can be combined to balance out potential negative steering effects of the procedures (Ochsner et al., 2018). The studies showed that there is no dominant evaluation procedure in a country nor a coherent set of procedures. Rather, each country has a national evaluation system in place, i.e. a complex combination of different evaluation procedures with different aims, objects, scope and governing bodies (see also a similar conclusion regarding evaluation in law studies in van Gestel and Lienhard, 2019).

Ochsner et al. (2018) focus on eight characteristics regarding three types of evaluation procedures (institutional evaluation, project funding and national career promotion) and identify five ideal types. They are not real but rather abstract representations of evaluation systems. Actual national evaluation systems are rather combinations of the five ideal types. The first type is named "no national database, non SSH-specific" (not having a national publication database, using mainly non-metric evaluation procedures and not allowing for SSH adaptations). The second ideal type is named "non-metric, SSH-specific" (not having a publication database, not relying on metrics for their evaluations, not incentivising publications in English and having dedicated funding programs for SSH disciplines). The third ideal type is called "performance-based funding, non-metric" (having a PRFS in place that allows for SSH-specific adaptations and is based on metrics derived from a national publication database; funding link being either established through informed peer review or through a combination of a metric PRFS with an evaluation based on peer review to counterbalance the metric nature of the PRFS). The fourth type is named "performance-based funding, metric" (PRFSs being based on a national database and a metric evaluation that allows for SSH adaptations and not incentivising publications in English). Finally, the fifth type is named "metric, push for English" (metric evaluation based on a national publication database linked to funding and not allowing for SSH adaptations and incentivising publications in English). Table 1 shows how countries can be attributed to the five ideal types. It is remarkable that countries cluster regionally, which suggests that historical and political structure play a role in how research is evaluated. Similar results are reported regarding the role of books in evaluation procedures (Giménez-Toledo et al., 2019).

Table 1: Five ideal types of national evaluation systems and classification of countries.

Ideal Type	Countries closest to the ideal type	Countries difficult to classify, closest type chosen
No national database, non SSH-specific	Cyprus, France, Iceland, Macedonia, Malta, Montenegro, Portugal, Spain	Bulgaria, Italy
Non-metric, SSH-specific	Austria, Germany, Ireland, the Netherlands, Serbia, Switzerland	
Performance-based funding, non-metric	Lithuania, Norway, South Africa	Denmark, Israel
Performance-based funding, metric	Czech Republic, Croatia, Poland	Finland
Metric, push for English	Bosnia-Herzegovina, Estonia, Hungary, Slovakia, Slovenia, Romania	Latvia

Note: variables used for the classification (yes/no): institutional evaluation results affect funding; main method of institutional evaluation are metrics; system incentivises English language publications; institutional evaluation procedures reflect gender issues; existence of national publication database; SSH-specific institutional evaluation procedures; SSH-specific project funding programmes; existence of national career promotion procedure.

These results are based on how evaluation systems are perceived by experts. In the follow-up study, the experts from the countries collected national regulations on evaluation procedures to further systematise actual evaluation policies. The discussions showed that the three procedures used so far do not suffice to adequately describe the evaluation systems. The analysis of regulations identified seven different types of evaluation procedures: accreditation, formative national evaluation, performance-based national evaluation, excellence initiatives, national career promotion, government project funding and evaluation of academies of sciences or research institutes. Each country has its own mix of two to six evaluation procedures on the national level (see Ochsner, 2020), showing that national research evaluation procedures are complex and diverse and different types of evaluation procedures serve different goals.

Conclusion

Research is a complex endeavour and, therefore, research evaluation practices are diverse. There is no such thing as "the evaluation procedure" in a country but each country has a distinct set of evaluation procedures making up a national evaluation system. The situation of research is different in each country and so are research policies. Evaluation procedures need to reflect the needs of the research landscape in the country, its research policy and the academic structure in the country.

Consequently, it makes sense that each country has its own set of evaluation procedures in place rather than to try to standardise evaluation procedures across countries. Nevertheless, countries striving to achieve similar goals with their evaluation procedures can learn from each other's experiences.

Still, in practice, an explicit link of policy goals with a specific set of evaluation procedures in a country is missing. Many evaluation procedures seem to have evolved more or less arbitrarily, which can be seen by the geographical clustering among types of evaluation systems. We therefore encourage evaluation designers and research policymakers to establish an explicit link between policy goals and a specific research evaluation procedure, taking the national evaluation system into account.

Acknowledgements

This chapter is based upon work from COST Action CA 15137 'European Network for Research Evaluation in the Social Sciences and the Humanities (ENRESSH)', supported by COST (European Cooperation in Science and Technology).

References

Child, J 2005, *Organisation: contemporary principles and practices*, Blackwell, Malden, MA and Oxford.

Coryn, CLS, Hattie, JA, Scriven, M & Hartmann, DJ 2007, 'Models and Mechanisms for Evaluating Government-Funded Research: An International Comparison', *American Journal of Evaluation*, vol. 28, no. 4, pp. 437–457.

Daniel, HD, Mittag, S & Bornmann, L 2007, 'The potential and problems of peer evaluation in higher education and research', in A Cavalli (ed.), *Quality assessment for higher education in Europe*, pp. 71–82, Portland Press, London.

de Rijcke, S, Wouters, PF, Rushforth, AD, Franssen, TP & Hammarfelt, B 2016, 'Evaluation practices and effects of indicator use – a literature review', *Research Evaluation*, vol. 25, no. 2, pp. 161–69.

Deem, R, Hillyard, S & Reed, M 2007, *Knowledge, higher education, and the new managerialism. The changing management of UK universities*, Oxford University Press, Oxford.

Etzkowitz, H & Leydesdorff, L 1998, 'The endless transition: a "Triple Helix" of university-industry-government relations', *Minerva*, vol. 36, no. 3, pp. 203–08.

Galleron, I, Ochsner, M, Spaapen, J & Williams, G 2017, 'Valorizing SSH research: Towards a new approach to evaluate SSH research' value for society', *fteval Journal for Research and Technology Policy Evaluation*, vol. 44, pp. 35–41.

Geuna, A, Hidayat, D & Martin, BR 1999, *Resource Allocation and Research Performance: The Assessment of Research*, Report prepared for the Higher Education Funding Council of England, SPRU, Brighton.

Geuna, A & Martin, BR 2001, *University Research Evaluation and Funding: An International Comparison*, SPRU Electronic Working Paper Series (vol. 71), SPRU, Brighton, http://www.sussex.ac.uk/Units/spru/publications/imprint/sewps/sewp71/sewp71.pdf (July 15, 2020).

Geuna, A & Martin, BR 2003, 'University Research Evaluation and Funding: An International Comparison', *Minerva*, vol. 41, no. 4, pp. 277–304.

Gibbons, M, Lomoges, C, Nowotny, H, Schwartzmann, S, Scott, P & Trowm, M 1994, *The new production of knowledge. The dynamics of science and research in contemporary societies*, Sage.

Giménez-Toledo, E, Mañana-Rodríguez, J, Engels, TCE, Guns, R, Kulczycki, E, Ochsner, M, Pölönen, J, Sivertsen, G & Zuccala, AA 2019, 'Taking scholarly books into account, part II: a comparison of 19 European countries in evaluation and funding', *Scientometrics*, vol. 118, no. 1, pp. 233–251.

Hamann, J 2016, 'The visible hand of research performance assessment', *Higher Education*, vol. 72, no. 6, pp. 1–19.

Hicks, D 2012, 'Performance-based university research funding systems', *Research Policy*, vol. 41, no. 2, pp. 251–61.

Hicks, D 2010, 'Overview of models of performance-based research funding systems', in OECD (ed.), *Performance-based Funding for Public Research in Tertiary Education Institutions*, OECD Publishing, Paris, pp. 23–52.

Hoenack, SA 1993, 'Higher Education and Economic Growth', in WE Becker & DR Lewis (eds.), *Higher Education and Economic Growth*, pp. 21–50, Springer, Dordrecht.

Jonkers, K & Zacharewicz, T 2016, *Research Performance Based Funding Systems: a Comparative Assessment*, European Commission, Brussels.

Lepori, B, Reale, E & Spinello, AO 2018, 'Conceptualizing and measuring performance orientation of research funding systems', *Research Evaluation*, vol. 27, no. 3, pp. 171–83.

Lepori, B, van den Besselaar, P, Dinges, M, Poti, B, Reale, E, Slipersæter, S, Thèves, J & van der Meulen, B 2007, 'Comparing the evolution of national research policies: What patterns of change?', *Science and Public Policy*, vol. 34, no. 6, pp. 372–88.

Nederhof, AJ 2006, 'Bibliometric monitoring of research performance in the social sciences and the humanities: A review', *Scientometrics*, vol. 66, no. 1, pp. 81–100.

Ochsner, M 2020, *WG1. Aligning research evaluation with policy goals: Risks and opportunities. Presentation of the final results at the ENRESSH final meeting*, ENRESSH, Paris, https://enressh.eu/wp-content/uploads/2018/04/Stakeholders_PolicyGoals_v04.pdf (July 15, 2020).

Ochsner, M, Kulczycki, E & Gedutis, A 2018, 'The Diversity of European Research Evaluation Systems', in Proceedings of the 23rd International Conference on Science and Technology Indicators, CWTS, Leiden, pp. 1234–41.

Peters, DP & Ceci, SJ 1982, 'Peer-review practices of psychological journals: The fate of published articles, submitted again', *The Behavioural and Brain Sciences*, vol. 5, no. 2, pp. 187–95.

Readings, B 1996, *The university in ruins*, Harvard University Press, Cambridge, MA.

Rolfe, G 2013, *The university in dissent. Scholarship in the corporate university*, Routledge, Abingdon.

van Gestel, R & Lienhard, A, eds. 2019, *Evaluating academic legal research in Europe. The advantage of lagging behind*, Edward Elgar, Cheltenham.

van Leeuwen, TN 2013, 'Bibliometric research evaluations, Web of Science and the Social Sciences and Humanities: a problematic relationship?', *Bibliometrie – Praxis und Forschung*, vol. 2, no. 8, pp. 1–18.

von Tunzelmann, N & Kraemer Mbula, E 2003, *Changes in research assessment practices in other countries since 1999: final report*, http://www.ra-review.ac.uk/reports/Prac/Changing Practices.pdf (July 15, 2020).

Välimaa, J & Hoffman, D 2008, 'Knowledge society discourse and higher education', *Higher Education*, vol. 56, no. 3, pp. 265–285.

Whitley, R 2007, 'Changing governance of the public sciences', in R Whitley & J Gläser (eds.), *The changing governance of the sciences. The advent of research evaluation systems*, pp. 3–27, Springer, Dordrecht.

Wilsdon, J, Allen, L, Belfiore, E, Campbel, P, Curry, S, Hill, S, Jones, R, Kain, R, Kerridge, S, Thelwall, M, Tinkler, J, Viney, I, Wouters, P, Hill, J & Johnson, B 2015, *The metric tide. Report of the independent review of the role of metrics in research assessment and management*, HEFCE, London.

Zacharewicz, T, Lepori, B, Reale, E & Jonkers, K 2018, 'Performance-based research funding in EU Member States – a comparative assessment', *Science and Public Policy*, vol. 46, no. 1, pp. 105–115.

2.4 The Mathematical Embedding of Bibliometrics

Leo Egghe

Abstract: We treat the mathematical embedding of bibliometrics by means of the pseudo-convex bibliometric vector. We then show that the decreasing power function is the only function to describe and model bibliometric phenomena in a mathematical way. This is illustrated by treating two important examples: concentration and impact.

Keywords: convex, power function, Zipf, Lotka, concentration, inequality, Lorenz-curve, impact, Hirsch-index.

Introduction

Mathematical embedding of bibliometrics involves the quantitative (i.e. number-wise) treatment of bibliometric phenomena such as author-publication analysis and publication-citation analysis (leading to research evaluation), possibly embedded in network aspects (collaboration and citation networks).

The simplest description of bibliometric phenomena is achieved by using one-dimensional mathematics, i.e. describing bibliometric aspects by single numbers ("one-dimensional bibliometrics") (possibly in a time-dependent setting but that is not necessary). Examples include: number of (co-)authors, number of publications, number of citations or links (in a network, in- or out-links) or number of downloads. When putting these numbers in a time-dependent setting, one is able to perform growth or obsolescence (aging) studies.

We can study bibliometric phenomena on a higher level (literally a higher dimension) by using two-dimensional mathematics ("two-dimensional bibliometrics"). Here one not only considers two one-dimensional bibliometric phenomena (as described above) but also their mutual interaction. For example, one can combine author (or journal) counts with citation counts (to or from the publications of this author or journal). In this context, one talks about "source-item" studies, featuring in an "Information Production Process" (IPP) (Egghe, 2005) and references therein. In such systems one is interested in sources and the number of items they have (or produce) (e.g. authors or journals and how many publications (articles) they have, or articles and how many citations they give or receive).

In the next section we will show that two-dimensional bibliometrics is described by a convexity property of decreasing vectors (i.e. part of convex mathematics), leading to aspects of inequality in the source-item relationship (concentration, elitarism,

---

Leo Egghe, Universiteit Hasselt, Universitaire Campus, B-3590 Diepenbeek, Belgium, leo.egghe@uhasselt.be.

skewness). In this sense, bibliometric phenomena are in no way different from other source-item relations as, e.g., in sociometrics, econometrics (rich, poor), biometrics (species abundance), demography (e.g. sizes of cities), astronomy (e.g. sizes of galaxies) etc. Yet, the treatment of these phenomena in the different fields yields field-specific tools and techniques, as will become clear (for bibliometrics) in the sequel.

Real-life two-dimensional bibliometrics (described by decreasing vectors, see earlier and the next section) can be modelled in a continuous setting, as is generally done in probability theory. The most classical example is the distribution of the intelligence quotient of humans by means of the continuous Gauss-curve or clock- (or bell-) curve: the so-called normal density distribution. Here, however, we deal with skew (i.e. unequal) situations which hence have to be described by skew distributions. Based on the discrete aspects (see earlier and the next section) we model two-dimensional bibliometrics using convexly decreasing density functions. This will be done in the third section. There we will show that the decreasing power function (i.e. Zipf's or Lotka's law, see below) is best suited to study these elitary (unequal) phenomena as a mathematical model.

The last section is devoted to the description of "derived properties" of these skew distributions, such as concentration and impact measurement systems (the former originating from econometrics, the latter centered around Hirsch-type indices, defined for research evaluation (i.e. bibliometrics) purposes (Hirsch, 2005)).

Convexity of Bibliometric Vectors

The general source-item relationship can be described by a simple decreasing vector $X = (x_1, x_2, \ldots)$ with positive terms x_i and i a natural number (i.e. $i = 1, 2 \ldots$). Here x_i is a substitute for the number of items in the source on rank i. When we want to focus on the total number N of sources, we limit the index i to N. Such a finite vector can be considered as an infinite one by adding zeroes infinitely. Since X decreases, we assume that the sources are ranked in decreasing order of the number of items they have (or produce).

Such a vector $X = (x_1, x_2, \ldots)$ is called convex if the line segment connecting the points $X = (x_1, x_2, \ldots)(i, x_i)$ and $(i+1, x_{i+1})$ is more decreasing than the line segment connecting the points $(i+1, x_{i+1})$ and $(i+2, x_{i+2})$ for all i (more decreasing in the sense of a smaller ($\leq$) slope of the line segment). Convexity is an expression of (but not the same as) inequality (concentration, skewness) between sources in terms of their number of items. Indeed, convex functions decrease faster in the more productive sources, a fact that is the case in all unequal (bibliometric) phenomena: there is a larger difference (in the number of sources) between highly productive sources than between lowly productive sources (often there are many sources with an equal number of items such as 1, 2..., while, in the high productivity, there are large "gaps" between the production quantities of sources).

General bibliometric vectors X are not convex due to individual irregularities between the production numbers of sources. However, we have the following definition and basic convexity result.

Definition

A vector $X = (x_1, x_2, \ldots)$ is called pseudo-convex if there exists a subsequence $i_1 < i_2 < \ldots$ of natural numbers such that the vector $(x_{i_1}, x_{i_2}, \ldots)$ is convex.

Result

A decreasing vector $X = (x_1, x_2, \ldots)$ with $x_i \geq 0$ for all i is pseudo-convex.

Proof

If X is a constant vector then, obviously, X itself is convex. Now we assume that X is not constant. There are many ways to construct a convex subsequence out of X. Here we present the "most natural way" to enlight the type of convexity of X (to become clear in the sequel).

Take $i_1 = 1$ and let $i = i_2 > i_1$ be such that the slope of the line segment between $(1, x_1)$ and (i, x_i) is the smallest for all i, $i > 1$ (if there are ties, we take i_2 the smallest index). Note that this slope, if it exists (see below), equals

$$(x_{i_2} - x_{i_1})/(i_2 - i_1) = (x_{i_2} - x_1)/(i_2 - 1) < 0$$

(< 0 since X is not constant). Such a smallest slope exists. Indeed, let k be the smallest index such that $x_k < x_1$ (this exists since X is not constant). Alternatively, $(x_k - x_1)/(k - 1)$ is this smallest slope or there exists $i > k$ such that

$$(x_i - x_1)/(i - 1) < (x_k - x_1)/(k - 1)$$

There are only finitely many versions of i (and then we can pick the smallest one): indeed, if it supposed that there are infinitely many $i > k$ such that the above inequality is valid then

$$x_i < (i - 1)((x_k - x_1)/(k - 1)) + x_1 < 0$$

as soon as

$$i > x_1(k - 1)/(x_1 - x_k) + 1$$

contrary to the fact that all $x_i \geq 0$. We will then show, by induction, how we proceed further. If it is supposed that there are the points $(i_1, x_{i_1}) = (1, x_1), (i_2, x_{i_2}), \ldots, (i_k, x_{i_k})$ for which the slopes

$$(x_{i_j} - x_{i_{j-1}})/(i_j - i_{j-1})$$

are increasing ($\geq$), yielding a convex polygonal line up to index i_k. Now note that, for all $i > i_k$

$$(x_i - x_{i_k})/(i - i_k) \geq (x_{i_k} - x_{i_{k-1}})/(i_k - i_{k-1}) \quad (*)$$

Indeed, if it is supposed that there is a $i > i_k$ such that

$$(x_i - x_{i_k})/(i - i_k) < (x_{i_k} - x_{i_{k-1}})/(i_k - i_{k-1})$$

then

$$(x_i - x_{i_{k-1}})/(i - i_{k-1}) < (x_{i_k} - x_{i_{k-1}})/(i_k - i_{k-1}) \quad (**)$$

Indeed, the last two inequalities are equivalent with

$$i_k x_i - i_{k-1} x_i + i_{k-1} x_{i_k} < i x_{i_k} - i x_{i_{k-1}} + i_k x_{i_{k-1}}$$

as is readily seen. However (**) contradicts the choice of i_k (starting with i_2 as defined above). So (*) is valid for all $i > i_k$. Now we pick $i = i_{k+1}$ such that the slope

$$(x_i - x_{i_k})/(i - i_k)$$

is the smallest for all $i > i_k$ (if there are ties we take i_k the smallest index, which is not necessary but is a possible choice: keeping the maximum number of the original coordinates of X). Again, such a smallest slope exists, which will now be shown. Let $j > i_k$ be the smallest index such that $x_j < x_{i_k}$ (if this j does not exist then X is constant from $i = i_k$ onwards and the construction is then finished). Alternatively, $(x_j - x_{i_k})/(j - i_k)$ is this smallest slope or there exists $i > j$ such that

$$(x_i - x_{i_k})/(i - i_k) < (x_j - x_{i_k})/(j - i_k)$$

There are only finitely many versions of j (and then we pick the smallest one): indeed, if it is supposed that there are infinitely many $i > j$ such that the above inequality is valid then (since $i > j > i_k$)

$$x_i < (i - i_k)\,(x_j - x_{i_k})/(j - i_k) + x_{i_k} < 0$$

as soon as

$$i > x_{i_k}\,(j - i_k)/(x_{i_k} - x_j) + i_k$$

contrary to the fact that all $x_i \geq 0$.

This ends the induction process. This yields the convex sequence $(x_{i_1}, x_{i_2}, \ldots)$ which is a subsequence of the vector X proving that X is pseudo-convex.

Remarks

(i) The above construction is a kind of optimal way to exhibit the overall convex aspects of the bibliometric vector X since it focusses in a maximal way on the differences between the terms x_i while keeping a maximum of the original coordinates.

(ii) The curve constructed in the above proof is convexly decreasing but not smooth (i.e. not all derivatives exist) since it is a polygonal line. However, based on the constructed polygonal line we can derive a smooth curve, arbitrarily close to this polygonal line. This occurs as follows: for each corner point of the polygonal line a circle of arbitrary small radius is constructed that is tangent to the legs of the angle in the corner point, and these legs are replaced by the part of the circle between the tangent points of the circle and the legs. This yields a convexly decreasing smooth curve that is arbitrarily close to the original polygonal line by making the radius of the tangent circle as small as is preferred.

(iii) A similar construction for a subsequence $i_1 < i_2 < \ldots$ such that $(x_{i_1}, x_{i_2}, \ldots)$ is concave is not possible since all $x_i \geq 0$ and hence negative slopes that are arbitrarily close to zero exist for i (natural number) large enough. Hence the above result is not valid if "pseudo-convex" is replaced by "pseudo-concave".

The above result shows the real nature of bibliometric vectors X: bibliometric phenomena are described through pseudo-convexity of the vector X. This gives a sound basis for the convex continuous theory of bibliometrics as described in the next section.

Continuous Convex Bibliometric Theory

If a mathematical model to describe bibliometric inequality is searched for it is now clear from the previous section that a convexly decreasing (smooth) function of a continuous variable must also be looked for: $Z(r) \geq 0$ for $r \geq 0$ (a so-called rank-frequency function). In a discrete setting one could say that $Z = X = (x_1, x_2, \ldots)$ as above, with $Z(i) = x_i$ (with $i = r$) the number of items in the source on rank i. In a continuous setting, $Z(r)$ hence denotes the density of items in the source density $r \geq 0$ (or $0 \leq r \leq T$ if we want to focus on the finite total number of sources). Here "density" $Z(r)$ means that the cumulative value up to r ($\int_0^r Z(r')dr'$) equals the actual number of items up to r (comparable with $\sum_{j=1}^{i} x_j$ in the discrete setting with $i = r$).

The least number of parameters for such a function Z is two, since we are working with two-dimensional data. This is similar with the two parameters needed to perform a linear regression on data in the plane: one for the intercept (i.e. height) (a) and one for slope (b) in the equation $y = a + bx$ of a regression line. Here a convexly decreasing function Z should be dealt with, so a linear equation is not suited but also here two parameters should suffice: again one for height and now one to express curvature or, in other words, the degree of convexity. Of course, as stated above, two parameters are the minimum, so if a good convexly decreasing smooth function with two parameters can be obtained, there is an optimal solution in the sense of mathematical simplicity and efficiency.

There are several possible solutions to this challenge. The two simplest ones are mentioned: an exponential function

$$Z(r) = Ca^r$$

with $C > 0$ (for positive values and height) and $0 < a < 1$ (for decreasing convexity) and a power function

$$Z(r) = B/r^\beta$$

with $B > 0$ (for positive values and height) and $\beta > 0$ (for decreasing convexity).

Both functions are simple but there are several advantages of the power function model which will be highlighted below.

(i) The power function has the property that its inverse is also a power function:

$$r(Z) = (B/Z)^{1/\beta}$$

and even with the same convexity if $\beta = 1$: then we have $Z(r) = B/r$, the classical function of Zipf (Zipf, 1949; Egghe, 2005). In Egghe (2005), based on this, it is revealed that Z as a power law is equivalent with $f(j)$, a power function, where f(j) is the density of sources with item-density j: the so-called "law of Lotka" (Lotka, 1926; Egghe, 2005) where

$$f(j) = B/j^\alpha$$

($D > 0$, $\alpha > 1$) where ? and ? relate as

$$\beta = 1/(\alpha - 1)$$

Note that for an exponential function, its inverse is a logarithmic function, hence very different from an exponential one and also more difficult to use than a power function since the latter is algebraic while the former is transcendental.

While (i) is interesting from a mathematical point of view, the next advantage of the power law above **any other law** is more fundamental.

(ii) The power function is scale-free: for every $E > 0$

$$Z(Er) = B/(Er)^\beta = (B/E^\beta)/r^\beta = B'/r^\beta$$

i.e. again a power law with the same convexity expressed by the same exponent ?. In fact, one can prove (less trivially) that **any** scale-free function must be a power function (Luce, 1959; Roberts, 1979; Egghe, 2005) so that power functions are the only scale-free functions. The importance of this property cannot be overestimated. Indeed, scale-free means that no matter which part of the system we inspect as an individual unit we will encounter the same power law, i.e. the same convexity. This is important to notice since, due to human limits, one is often limited to inspect only a part of the complex system (or one even does not know what is the entire system) as is clear in e.g. the case of large bibliographies or in the case of the astronomical universe of galaxies and solar systems. In this interpretation, scale-free-ness is a necessity in order to be able to perform bias-free investigations.

Scale-free systems are abundant in all aspects of human life: too many examples exist for description in this short text. We contend ourselves with the general references (Egghe, 2005; Rousseau, Egghe, and Guns, 2018) and those (Rousseau, 1997; Faloutsos, Faloutsos, and Faloutsos, 1999; Barabàsi, Albert, and Jeong 2000) on the Internet.

This scale-free property of power functions is directly linked with so-called fractals, being geometric objects in which every infinite part is similar to the entire object (Mandelbrot, 1977; Feder, 1988). This is reflected in the above description of the scale-free property of complex systems.

It is hence clear that decreasing power laws are best suited to (simply) explain diverse aspects of inequality of general convex functions. Moreover, they yield clear formulae for these skew phenomena as will be shown in the last section.

Derived Properties Of Convex Bibliometric Functions

There are many aspects that can be derived from convexly decreasing functions. In this concluding section there will be focus on the two (in the view of this author) most important ones: concentration (inequality) and impact measures.

(i) Concentration Aspects
As mentioned above, inequality does not only occur in bibliometrics. It is initially described in econometrics and further developed in bibliometrics: concentration theory. Let $X = (x_1, x_2, \ldots, x_N)$ be a decreasing vector. A Lorenz-curve (Lorenz, 1905; Egghe, 2005, Rousseau, Egghe, and Guns, 2018) is built by linearly connecting the points $(i/N, \sum_{j=1}^{i} a_j)$, $i = 1, \ldots, N$ where $a_j = x_j / \left(\sum_{i=1}^{N} x_i \right)$. Lorenz-curves have the property that the larger this curve, the more unequal are the terms x_i in X. Originally, in econometrics, this was expressed by the transfer principle that taking away from the poor (small x_i) and giving it to the rich (large x_i) (i.e. an increase of the inequality) is equivalent to an increase of the Lorenz-curve (Egghe, 2005).

In the continuous framework with convexly decreasing function Z on the interval $[0,T]$, the Lorenz-curve of Z, denoted $L(Z)$, equals (by definition, to be compared with the discrete case) $L(Z)(r/T) = \left(\int_0^r Z\right)/A$, where $A = \int_0^T Z$, the total number of items.

$L(Z)$ is concavely increasing since Z is positive and decreasing. From this it is clear that $L(Z)''$ (the third derivative of the Lorenz-curve $L(Z)$) is proportional to Z''. Hence

Z is convex if and only if $L(Z)''' \geq 0$

which is a characterization of convex bibliometrics in terms of concentration theory (via the Lorenz-curve).

Based on the Lorenz-curve one can construct "good" concentration (inequality) measures that satisfy the transfer principle. Examples include the variation coefficient ($V = \sigma/\mu$, i.e. the standard deviation divided by the average of the bibliometric vector X or the rank-frequency function Z) and the Gini-index based on the area under the Lorenz-curve.

It is relatively easy to study concentration aspects using power functions, yielding inequality formulae in function of the power ? (which is bijectively related to the average number $\mu = 1/(1-\beta) = (\alpha-1)/(\alpha-2)$ of items per source (Egghe, 2005)). One example is when a fraction x of top-sources (i.e. most productive sources) produce a fraction $x^{1/\mu}$ of the items, a result which comes from the equation of the Lorenz-curve $y = x^{1/\mu}$ for power functions (again a power function!). This result shows that the higher ?, the more unequal are the bibliometrics data in X (or Z).

(ii) Impact Aspects

Using the bibliometric vector X or its continuous analogue Z, the simplest measure to derive is the average ?, called in bibliometrics (in the citation context) the impact factor (Garfield and Sher, 1963). Since X and Z are skew, it is, however, more useful, in order to describe "impact", to work with dispersion type measures (to be described below): indeed, only using ? does not describe skew data very well since very different skew situations can have the same averages. As in general statistics, one could use percentiles but they do not yield model-theoretic insights since they are only used to crunch raw data. The standard deviation (?) (mentioned in the previous subsection) is very important in a model-theoretic context and to measure inequality (cf. the variation coefficient V above) but cannot be used to measure impact (intuitive notion here (based on the idea of the impact factor) but further explained in the sequel).

A major breakthrough was realized in 2005 by the physicist (non-bibliometrician) Jorge Hirsch (Hirsch, 2005) who introduced his so-called Hirsch-index (or h-index): for a decreasing vector $X = (x_1, x_2, \ldots)$, $i = h$ is the highest index such that $x_i \geq i$ (i.e. $x_i < i$ for all $i > h$). This is a remarkable definition in which one looks at the "intersection point" of the decreasing (x_i)-sequence (of items) with the increasing (i)-sequence (of sources). In a continuous framework the Hirsch-index is simply defined as the unique $r = h$ such that $Z(r) = r$ (hence the fixed point of Z).

In this context we can illustrate in a clear way the "power" of power functions (Egghe and Rousseau, 2006). If we have a power function for $Z(r)$ then the Hirsch-index of Z, denoted $h = h(Z)$, is

$$h = T^{1/\alpha}$$

where T is the total number of sources and α is the exponent appearing in the law of Lotka. Equivalently we can use ?, the exponent appearing in the formula of Z, using that (see above)

$\beta = 1/(\alpha - 1)$ or $1/\alpha = \beta/(1 + \beta)$.

This is a typical example of the use of power functions in the general understanding of bibliometric phenomena. The formula above shows that the Hirsch-index is concavely (i.e. not too fast) increasing in the total number T of sources (since $\alpha > 1$) but that h not only depends on T (which is logical) but also on the power function exponent ? or ?, i.e. on the degree of convexity (?) of the rank-frequency function Z: h increases with ? (since it decreases in ?) (and convexly, i.e. faster than linearly, for T, not too small but fixed). Here we described "degree of convexity" by means of the exponent ?, which is intuitively logical.

Rousseau, Egghe, and Guns (2018) and Egghe (2010) are referred to for reviews of the vast literature on h-type indices and their applications. In Egghe and Rousseau (2019) a purely mathematical application of h-type indices (similar to the average) is given for the first time, inside and outside the power function setting.

Conclusions And Final Remarks

We showed that convexity plays a central role in bibliometrics in the discrete setting (with the biliometric vector X) as well as in the continuous setting (with the rank-frequency function Z).

Convexity is not the same as inequality (= concentration) or impact but is the basic ingredient to be used in the description of these two (and other) phenomena since it is the basic property of the vector X and the function Z.

The simplest way to describe convex bibliometric situations is by using decreasing power functions since they yield a simple tool to study basic bibliometric properties (such as inequality or impact) which are valid in any discrete or continuous bibliometric situation (properties that are difficult (and even impossible) to study in a general bibliometric context).

References

Barabàsi, A-L, Albert, R & Jeong, H 2000, 'Scale-free characteristics of random networks: The topology of the world-wide-web', *Physica A*, vol. 281, no. 1–4, pp. 69–77.

Egghe, L 2005, *Power laws in the information production process: Lotkaian informetrics*, Elsevier, Oxford.
Egghe, L 2010, 'The Hirsch-index and related impact measures', in B Cronin, *Annual Review of Information Science and Technology*, vol. 44, pp. 65–114.
Egghe, L & Rousseau, R 2019, Solving a minimum problem in $L^2[0,T]$ and a theory of generalized continuous h- and g-indices. Preprint.
Faloutsos, M, Faloutsos, P & Faloutsos, C 1999, 'On power-law relationships of the internet topology', *Proceedings of the Conference on Applications, Technologies, Architectures and Protocols for Computer Communication*, pp. 251–62, ACM, New York.
Feder, J 1988, *Fractals*, Plenum, New York.
Garfield, E & Sher, IH 1963, 'New factors in the evaluation of scientific literature through citation indexing', *American Documentation*, vol. 14, no. 3, pp. 195–201.
Hirsch, JE 2005, 'An index to quantify an individual's scientific research output', *Proceedings of the National Academy of Sciences of the United States of America*, vol. 102, no. 46, pp. 16569–72.
Lorenz, MO 1905, 'Methods of measuring concentration of wealth', *Journal of the American Statistical Association*, vol. 9, pp. 209–19.
Lotka, AJ 1926, 'The frequency distribution of scientific productivity', *Journal of the Washington Academy of Sciences*, vol. 16, no. 12, pp. 317–23.
Luce, RD 1959, 'On the possible psychophysical laws', *The Psychological Review*, vol. 66, no. 2, pp. 81–95.
Mandelbrot, B 1977, *The fractal geometry of nature*, Freeman, New York.
Roberts, FS 1979, *Measurement theory with applications to decisionmaking, utility and the social sciences*, Addison-Wesley, Reading (MA).
Rousseau, R 1997, 'Sitations: An exploratory study', *Cybermetrics*, vol. 1, no. 1.
Rousseau, R, Egghe, L & Guns, R 2018, *Becoming metric-wise. A bibliometric guide for researchers*, Chandos (Elsevier), Cambridge (MA).
Zipf, GK 1949, *Human behavior and the principle of least effort*, Addison-Wesley, Cambridge (MA) (reprinted 1965, Hafner, New York).

2.5 Bibliometrics in the Humanities, Arts and Social Sciences
Michael Ochsner

Abstract: Bibliometric methods are used in many evaluation procedures. They have been developed in the so-called Science, Technology, Engineering and Medicine (STEM) disciplines but are increasingly applied generally, thus also in the Humanities, Arts and Social Sciences (HASS). However, the bibliometric methods do not reflect research practices in the HASS disciplines and their use is therefore challenged. This chapter gives an overview on the issues of the use of evaluative bibliometrics in the HASS disciplines, outlines the value of bibliometric analysis for the HASS disciplines and discusses the potential of bibliometrics in informed peer review.

Keywords: humanities, arts and social sciences, altmetrics, informed peer review, coverage, citation practices, performance-based research funding, language, societal impact.

Introduction

Bibliometric indicators are an established tool for the evaluation of research in the so-called Science, Technology, Engineering and Medicine (STEM) disciplines. Bibliometric indicators have been deemed more objective, comparable, less burdensome and costly, and more responsive to current trends than the different forms of peer review that have been dominant in evaluation procedures. They help to monitor research performance over time and are an important steering tool for science administrators (KNAW, 2011). The application of bibliometrics concerned first the STEM fields but in the last decade the Humanities, Arts and Social Sciences (HASS) were also subject to bibliometric evaluation (Guillory, 2005; Ochsner, Hug and Daniel, 2016). However, in the HASS disciplines, the idea of parametrically steering research is challenged (KNAW, 2011) and bibliometric performance assessment for these disciplines is seen as problematic (Nederhof, 2006). Therefore, several bottom-up procedures have been initiated by HASS scholars (Ochsner, Hug and Galleron, 2017). In the following, an overview of the issues of the use of bibliometrics in the HASS disciplines will be given, the value of bibliomtetric analyses for the HASS disciplines will be presented and the potential of bibliometrics in informed peer review will be discussed.

Michael Ochsner, D-GESS, ETH Zurich, Zurich (Switzerland) and FORS, Lausanne (Switzerland), ochsner@gess.ethz.ch

https://doi.org/10.1515/9783110646610-013

Issues of Bibliometrics in the Arts and Humanities

The use of bibliometrics for the disciplines falling under the HASS umbrella has been challenged not only by the HASS scholars themselves but also by bibliometricians. Below, a short overview of the more technical issues with the use of bibliometrics in the HASS disciplines identified by bibliometricians is followed by a focus on more fundamental criticism by HASS scholars.

The Bibliometric Issues with the HASS Disciplines

In his seminal review on bibliometric monitoring in the social sciences and humanities, Nederhof (2006) points to five main differences in publication behaviour leading to problems using the same bibliometric methods as in the STEM fields: the first point, national or regional orientation, reflects that many HASS disciplines address issues that are relevant in a restricted geographical area. Language plays a crucial role as English does not serve as a lingua franca in all disciplines. Most HASS scholars therefore publish in more than one language (Kulczycki et al., 2020) and internationality is seen as being multilingual; moreover, international languages differ between disciplines and are not limited to English (Sivertsen, 2016a).

Second, the STEM disciplines mainly publish in English journals reflecting a hierarchical communication structure where a limited set of important journals cover the majority of highly cited articles (Bonaccorsi, 2018; Nederhof, 2006). The HASS disciplines publish in a diverse range of publication types; journal articles are not the most prestigious output but rather monographs or books (Hicks, 2004; Engels et al., 2018; Kulczycki et al., 2018). These are not covered by the dominant publication databases Web of Science and Scopus, even though both made considerable efforts to cover books. However, coverage remains low and technical deficiencies hinder the use for evaluative bibliometrics (Gorraiz, Purnell and Glänzel, 2013).

Third, bibliometricians identified a different pace of theoretical development, as Nederhof (2006) puts it. This diagnosis stems from the insight from bibliometric analyses that HASS publications contain an important fraction of citations older than five, ten or even fifteen years, and also that the obsolescence of articles, i.e. when an article is not cited anymore, is reached much later (Cole, 1983; Thomson, 2002).

Fourth, whereas in the STEM fields, research projects and teams are the dominant form of scientific inquiry (Thompson, 2002), research in HASS disciplines is often centred around the idea of a single scholar. While co-authorship increases also in the HASS disciplines, co-authored articles still have relatively few authors and often still follow the idea that each individual adds its own perspective; moreover, single-authorship remains important (Ossenblok, Verleysen and Engels, 2014).

Fifth, the HASS disciplines publish more outputs directed at a non-scholarly public because of a more direct interchange with society (Hicks, 2004; Nederhof, 2006). Contrary to patents or other interactions with industry, interactions with society do not lead to citations that can be harvested by bibliometricians. Often, boundaries between scholarly and non-scholarly work are not clear (van Gestel and Lienhard, 2019).

These five issues pose problems for the application of standard bibliometric measures. The main issue is the coverage of data. Not only is the coverage of all output massively lower in the relevant scientific citation databases, there is also a language bias to the coverage (Hug and Brändle, 2017; Sivertsen and Larsen, 2012); and worse, the internal coverage, i.e. the citations detected in the indexed articles referencing other articles indexed in the database, is very low in the HASS disciplines, rarely going beyond fifty per cent, pointing to the fact that many relevant articles are not indexed (van Leeuwen, 2013). Also, common indicators, like the Impact Factor, need to be adapted to the slower citation pace in the HASS disciplines as the two years citation window is too small (Nederhof, 2006).

If coverage is the main problem of bibliometric analysis in the HASS disciplines, the solution seems rather simple: databases have to increase coverage. Many countries have adopted such a strategy and have created a centralised national publication database containing all scholarly publications (Sivertsen and Larsen, 2012; Sīle et al., 2018). Different ways of knowledge production, however, do not only affect publication types but also citation practices, which are more diverse in the HASS fields, while citations are not always explicit (Bonaccorsi, 2018). Thus, bibliometric approaches to monitoring research performance are still contested among HASS scholars who put forward additional reservations about bibliometrics.

The Problems HASS Scholars have with Bibliometrics

Hug, Ochsner and Daniel (2014) summarise arts and humanities scholars' reservations about quantitative assessments of research performance into four main points. The first point states that bibliometric methods stem from the STEM fields, on which the social studies of sciences focused for a long time. Methods for identifying research performance are not easily transferable. For example, the language and coverage issues are not only of technical nature but also reflect the fact that scholarly discourses can differ not only between STEM and HASS fields but also between communities publishing in different languages, leading even to (or reflecting) epistemological differences within disciplines across regions (Bonaccorsi, 2018; Keller and Poferl, 2017). This concerns especially the arts (Lewandowska and Smolarska, 2019), which are understudied (Lewandowska and Stano, 2018). While the STEM fields largely follow the idea of a linear progress of knowledge, the HASS disciplines are based on interpretations, and knowledge is produced complementary, segmented or even alternative to each other (Bonaccorsi, 2018; Mallard, Lamont and Guetzkow, 2009). Citations thus take different functions and the number of citations is not meaningful as it depends on the subject matter (Bonaccorsi, 2018): a study on Mozart receives more citations than one on an unknown local composer. Second, humanities scholars are less open towards quantification as it is perceived as an unacceptable simplification (Hammarfelt and Haddow, 2018; KNAW, 2011) and that a focus on numbers neglects the important intangible and social benefits of HASS research (Hellström, 2010; McCarthy et al., 2004). Third, HASS scholars fear that the reductionist focus on numbers comes with negative steering effects, such as favouring spectacular research, citation cartels, goal displacement, neglect of societal interactions or academic freedom in the sense of serendipity (van Gestel and Lienhard, 2019; Hellström, 2010). Citations and numbers of publications do not measure the relevant object of interest, research performance or quality, which is much more complex (Ochsner, Hug and Daniel, 2012). Fourth, there are different standards of quality and a single measure of scientific merit is highly questionable against the background of epistemological diversity (Bonaccorsi, 2018; Ochsner, Hug and Daniel, 2014).

Altmetrics as a Better Option?

Given the critics on bibliometric indicators regarding their narrow focus on one of several possible ways of practicing and disseminating research, scholars suggested indicators taken from the social web as an alternative, the so-called altmetrics, such as Twitter mentions, libcitations (library holdings), good reads, or the altmetric doughnut (Konkiel, 2016; Zuccala et al., 2015). However, similar problems apply: first, it is not clear what those indicators measure (Bornmann, 2016), and second, there are severe technical problems such as reliability and reproducibility (Gumpenberger, Glänzel and Gorraiz, 2016).

Use of Bibliometrics in Evaluation Procedures

Despite the issues pointed out by the scientific communities, bibliometric measures are used in many evaluation situations, also for the HASS disciplines. Ochsner, Kulczycki and Gedutis (2018) identify five types of national evaluation systems, three of which rely on bibliometrics. One type represented by seven Eastern European countries is of particular concern for the HASS disciplines as it does not take HASS specificities into account but uses data from the international citation databases favouring English publications. In some other cases, the use of bibliometric indicators is adapted to SSH publication patterns by using national publication databases and/or involving the scientific community in the definition of which outputs or publishers are more prestigious than others (Sivertsen, 2016b). Independently of the evaluation systems in place, HASS scholars call for a shift of perspective on evaluations, from accountability to valorisation of research (Galleron et al., 2017), especially when it comes to arts (Hellström, 2010).

Effects on Scholarly Behaviour

Pointed out as a main reservation about the use of bibliometrics by HASS scholars, the risk of negative steering effects is widely discussed, especially when the methods do not correspond to research practices in the respective fields. Such negative steering effects have been discovered for the HASS in the sense that in contexts where journal publications are highly valued, certain research approaches are favoured over others (Lewandowski and Stano, 2018) and create tensions for young scholars who are pushed by their national system to publish English journal articles, while in their field monographs are important (Hammarfelt and de Rijcke, 2015; Xu, 2020). In their review, de Rijcke et al. (2015) found evidence for goal displacement, strategic behaviour, task reduction and focus on monodisciplinarity across STEM and HASS fields. Negative effects do not only concern behavioural changes of researchers; university administrators also might take decisions to improve rankings instead of enhancing the quality or the mission of the institution (Johnston and Reeves, 2017).

A "Bibliometrics for the Arts and Humanities"

Given all the issues mentioned above, should bibliometrics be banned for the HASS disciplines? Such a conclusion would be throwing the baby out with the bathwater. Bibliometric indicators are not only useful for evaluative purposes. Indeed, they have not been developed for such purposes; rather, they are a tool to study how research is conducted. Hammarfelt (2016) thus suggests developing a "bibliometrics for the arts and humanities". As knowledge production and dissemination is different in HASS fields and STEM fields and bibliometric research focused rather on the latter than the former, much has yet to be studied. Bibliometrics can help describe and understand differences in research and dissemination practices across (sub)disciplines. Thanks to bibliometric analyses, we have insights on the importance of multilingualism (Kulczycki et al., 2020) or the persistence of the importance of books (Engels et al., 2018), despite the claims that it will disappear (Thompson, 2002).

Research Quality and Bibliometrics or the Opportunity of Informed Peer Review

Even if research quality in HASS is a very complex construct that is not adequately represented by publication numbers and citations (Ochsner, Hug and Daniel, 2012), bibliometrics can still enhance evaluation procedures. Peer review also has its problems and is seen as subjective and having a low reliability. These deficits could be amended with the so-called informed peer review where the different aspects of quality are judged by the peers who can take indicators linked to these aspects as information to guide their judgement. The results from the studies by Ochsner, Hug and Daniel (2014) suggest that such a procedure will find more acceptance among HASS scholars.

References

Bonaccorsi, A 2018, 'Towards an Epistemic Approach to Evaluation in SSH', in A Bonaccorsi (ed.), *The evaluation of research in social sciences and humanities. Lessons from the Italian experience*, pp. 1–29, Springer, Cham.

Bornmann, L 2016, 'What do altmetrics counts mean? A plea for content analyses', *Journal of the Association for Information Science and Technology*, vol. 67, no. 4, pp. 1016–17.

Cole, S 1983, 'The hierarchy of the sciences?', *American Journal of Sociology*, vol. 89, no. 1, pp. 111–39.

Engels, TCE, Starcic, AI, Kulczycki, E, Pölönen, J & Sivertsen, G 2018, 'Are book publications disappearing from scholarly communication in the social sciences and humanities?', *Aslib Journal of Information Management*, vol. 70, no. 6, pp. 592–607.

Galleron, I, Ochsner, M, Spaapen, J & Williams, G 2017, 'Valorizing SSH research: Towards a new approach to evaluate SSH research' value for society', *fteval Journal for Research and Technology Policy Evaluation*, vol. 44, pp. 35–41.

Gorraiz, J, Purnell, PJ & Glänzel, W 2013, 'Opportunities for and limitations of the Book Citation Index', *Journal of the American Society for Information Science and Technology*, vol. 64, no. 7, pp. 1388–98.

Gumpenberger, C, Glänzel, W & Gorraiz, J 2016, 'The ecstasy and the agony of the altmetric score', *Scientometrics*, vol. 108, no. 2, pp. 977–82.

Hammarfelt, B & Haddow, G 2018, 'Conflicting measures and values: How humanities scholars in Australia and Sweden use and react to bibliometric indicators', *Journal of the Association for Information Science and Technology*, vol. 24, no. 2, pp. 924–35.

Hammarfelt, B 2016, 'Beyond Coverage: Toward a Bibliometrics for the Humanities', in M Ochsner, SE Hug & H-D Daniel (eds.), *Research Assessment in the Humanities. Towards Criteria and Procedures*, pp. 115–31, Springer International Publishing, Cham.

Hammarfelt, B & de Rijcke, S 2015, 'Accountability in context: effects of research evaluation systems on publication practices, disciplinary norms, and individual working routines in the faculty of Arts at Uppsala University', *Research Evaluation*, vol. 24, no. 1, pp. 63–77.

Hellström, T 2010, 'Evaluation of artistic research', *Research Evaluation*, vol. 19, no. 5, pp. 306–16.

Hug, SE & Brändle, MP 2017, 'The coverage of Microsoft Academic: analyzing the publication output of a university', *Scientometrics*, vol. 113, no. 3, pp. 1551–71.

Hug, SE, Ochsner, M & Daniel, H-D 2014, 'A framework to explore and develop criteria for assessing research quality in the humanities', *International Journal of Education Law and Policy*, vol. 10, no. 1, pp. 55–68.

Johnston, J & Reeves, A 2017, 'Assessing research performance in UK universities using the case of the economics and econometrics unit of assessment in the 1992–2014 research evaluation exercises', *Research Evaluation*, p. 28–40.

Keller, R & Poferl, A 2017, 'Soziologische Wissenskulturen zwischen individualisierter Inspiration und prozeduraler Legitimation. Zur Entwicklung qualitativer und interpretativer Sozialforschung in der deutschen und französischen Soziologie seit den 1960er Jahren', *Historical Social Research*, vol. 42, no. 4, pp. 301–57.

KNAW 2011, *Quality Indicators for Research in the Humanities*, Royal Netherlands Academy of Arts and Sciences, Amsterdam.

Konkiel, S 2016, 'Altmetrics: diversifying the understanding of influential scholarship', *Palgrave Communications*, vol. 2, no. 16057.

Kulczycki, E, Guns, R, Pölönen, J, Engels, TCE, Rozkosz, EA, Zuccala, AA, Bruun, K, Eskola, O, Starcic, AI, Petr, M & Sivertsen, G 2020, 'Multilingual Publishing in the Social Sciences and Humanities: A Seven-Country European Study', *Journal of the Association for Information Science and Technology*, vol. 26, no. 1, p. 41.

Kulczycki, E, Engels, TCE, Pölönen, J, Bruun, K, Duskova, M, Guns, R, Nowotniak, R, Petr, M, Sivertsen, G, Starcic, AI & Zuccala, A 2018, 'Publication patterns in the social sciences and humanities: evidence from eight European countries', *Scientometrics*, vol. 116, no. 1, pp. 463–86.

Lewandowska, K & Smolarska, Z 2019, 'Striving for Consensus: How Panels Evaluate Artistic Productions', *Qualitative Sociology*, vol. 70, no. 9, pp. 1–22.

Lewandowska, K & Stano, PM 2018, 'Evaluation of research in the arts: Evidence from Poland', *Research Evaluation*, vol. 27, no. 4, pp. 323–334.

Mallard, G, Lamont, M & Guetzkow, J 2009, 'Fairness as Appropriateness: Negotiating Epistemological Differences in Peer Review', *Science, Technology & Human Values*, vol. 34, no. 5, pp. 573–606.

McCarthy, KF, Ondaatje, EH, Zakaras, L & Brooks, A 2004, *Gifts of the Muse*, Rand Corporation, Santa Monica.

Nederhof, AJ 2006, 'Bibliometric monitoring of research performance in the social sciences and the humanities: A review', *Scientometrics*, vol. 66, no. 1, pp. 81–100.

Ochsner, M, Hug, SE & Daniel, H-D 2012, 'Indicators for Research Quality in the Humanities: Opportunities and Limitations', *Bibliometrie – Praxis und Forschung*, vol. 1, 4.

Ochsner, M, Hug, SE & Daniel, H-D 2014, 'Setting the stage for the assessment of research quality in the humanities. Consolidating the results of four empirical studies', *Zeitschrift für Erziehungswissenschaft*, vol. 17, no. 6, pp. 111–132.

Ochsner, M, Hug, SE & Daniel, H-D (eds.) 2016, *Research Assessment in the Humanities. Towards Criteria and Procedures*, Springer International Publishing, Cham.

Ochsner, M, Hug, SE & Galleron, I 2017, 'The future of research assessment in the humanities: bottom-up assessment procedures', *Palgrave Communications*, vol. 3, no. 17020.

Ossenblok, TLB, Verleysen, FT & Engels, TCE 2014, 'Coauthorship of Journal Articles and Book Chapters in the Social Sciences and Humanities (2000–2010)', *Journal of the Association for Information Science and Technology*, vol. 65, no. 5, pp. 882–97.

Sīle, L, Pölönen, J, Sivertsen, G, Guns, R, Engels, TCE, Arefiev, P, Duskova, M, Faurbæk, L, Holl, A, Kulczycki, E, Macan, B, Nelhans, G, Petr, M, Pisk, M, Soòs, S, Stojanovski, J, Stone, A, Šušol, J & Teitelbaum, R 2018, 'Comprehensiveness of national bibliographic databases for social sciences and humanities: Findings from a European survey', *Research Evaluation*, vol. 27, no. 4, pp. 310–22.

Sivertsen, G 2016a, 'Patterns of internationalization and criteria for research assessment in the social sciences and humanities', *Scientometrics*, vol. 107, no. 2, pp. 357–68.

Sivertsen, G 2016b, 'Publication-Based Funding: The Norwegian Model', in M Ochsner, SE Hug & H-D Daniel (eds.), *Research Assessment in the Humanities. Towards Criteria and Procedures*, pp. 79–90, Springer International Publishing, Cham.

Sivertsen, G & Larsen, B 2012, 'Comprehensive bibliographic coverage of the social sciences and humanities in a citation index: an empirical analysis of the potential', *Scientometrics*, vol. 91, no. 2, pp. 567–575.

Thompson, JW 2002, 'The Death of the Scholarly Monograph in the Humanities? Citation Patterns in Literary Scholarship', *Libri*, vol. 52, no. 3, pp. 121–36.

van Gestel, R & Lienhard, A 2019, 'Conclusion and discussion', in R van Gestel & A Lienhard (eds.), *Evaluating academic legal research in Europe. The advantage of lagging behind*, pp. 422–59, Edward Elgar, Cheltenham.

Xu, X 2020, 'Performing under "the baton of administrative power"? Chinese academics' responses to incentives for international publications', *Research Evaluation*, vol. 29, no. 1, p. 87–99.

Zuccala, AA, Verleysen, FT, Cornacchia, R & Engels, TCE 2015, 'Altmetrics for the humanities', *Aslib Journal of Information Management*, vol. 67, no. 3, pp. 320–36.

2.6 Relationship between Peer Review and Bibliometrics

Michael Ochsner

Abstract: Peer review as the cornerstone of academic quality control has been accused of several biases. As a less subjective and biased alternative, bibliometric methods have been developed and implemented in evaluation procedures. This chapter discusses the relationship between peer review and bibliometrics, showing that bibliometrics is dependent on peer review and not free of its biases. Using three examples of interrelating peer review and bibliometrics, it concludes that rather than playing the two methods of evaluation off against each other, efforts should focus on the interplay and combination of the two.

Keywords: Open Science, altmetrics, informed peer review, bias, citation practices, performance-based research funding, predictive validity, interrater reliability, research quality.

Introduction

Peer review is generally seen as the cornerstone of academic quality control and is often said to date back to the dawn of modern science in the eighteenth century (e.g. Bornmann, 2011). However, Kronick (1990) argues that peer review, depending on how one defines it, has occurred "ever since people began to identify and communicate what they thought was new knowledge. That is because peer review [...] is an essential and integral part of the process of consensus building" (Kronick, 1990, p. 1321). Whenever the exact start of peer review, peer review is the predominant method of evaluation for allocation of grants, the selection of manuscripts, academic recruitment, institutional evaluation, prizes, study programmes etc. (Bornmann, 2011; Daniel, Mittag and Bornmann, 2007; Ochsner et al., 2020). In their roles of "gatekeepers" (Lamont, 2009) or "guardians of science" (Daniel, 1993), peers thus assure the high standards of scientific endeavour and assign merit.

Being so important in academic life, peer review is criticised regularly and its use is challenged. Often, more objective evaluation methods using bibliometric indicators are suggested because peer review is deemed biased and socially contested and accused of slowing down the publication process (Bornmann and Leydesdorff, 2014). Still, peer review is inherent in all evaluation of scientific work, also in indicator-based approaches, simply because evaluation procedures that do not directly rely on peer review still use data on scientific works that include peer review as a central mechanism of evaluation (Ochsner et al., 2020).

Michael Ochsner, D-GESS, ETH Zurich, Zurich (Switzerland) and FORS, Lausanne (Switzerland), ochsner@gess.ethz.ch

In the following, the relationship between peer review and bibliometrics will be explored, giving a short overview on several issues and challenges peer review is facing and explicating bibliometrics' dependency on peer review. The chapter will show that bibliometrics and peer review should not be seen as mutually exclusive alternatives but as complementary methods of evaluation.

Biases associated with Peer Review

While peer review has been the most established method of evaluation of scientific works at least since the eighteenth century, it has nevertheless been criticised strongly and has come under pressure, especially during the last thirty years, given the availability of biblio- and scientometric data (Bornmann and Leydesdorff, 2014). At the same time, the criticism of peer review is not unchallenged. Rather, peer review is still seen as the most adequate form of evaluation of scientific merit (Hicks, 2012). In the following the literature on biases in peer review is summarised, with the arguments then presented for peer review.

Different Types of Biases

In the literature, several types of criticisms of the peer review process are discussed (Bornmann, 2011; Lee et al., 2013): The first, *low interrater reliability*, refers to when reviewers disagree on whether a manuscript is good enough for publishing or a project merits funding. The low agreement between reviewers is seen as a problem of the reliability of the process (Bornmann and Daniel, 2008). Second, *issues of fairness* of peer review are raised: criteria other than the merit of the manuscript, project or research might influence the decision, such as gender, the prestige of the author's or applicant's institution, their country or their (former) supervisor or the language of the article, meaning that native English speakers are rejected less often (Cronin, 2009; Wennerås and Wold, 1997). Third, *low predictive validity*, claims that reviewers' judgements might not be linked to the work's later appreciation, for example if reviews for highly cited papers were not more positive than those for less cited ones (Gottfredson, 1978) or if there are no differences between funded or rejected grant proposers regarding citation success (Melin and Danell, 2006). Fourth, the *efficiency* of peer review is questioned as it takes time to review and revise. This can delay research, is said to inhibit innovation and puts much burden on the scientific community (Cowen et al., 1987; Eysenck and Eysenck, 1992). Fifth, the *conservative bias* suggests that peer review leads to preference for established knowledge as peers tend to prefer research similar to their own and experts are often older than submitting authors (Lee et al., 2013). Sixth, experts might prefer research from their own discipline and are often not cognisant in related fields, which might punish research that crosses disciplinary boundaries, leading to *de-valuing of interdisciplinary research*

(Langfeldt, 2006). Seventh, the review process can be *stressful and frustrating*, especially for new authors, and thus can keep talents from doing research (Eysenck and Eysenck, 1992). Women are thereby more vulnerable to this process and seem to let their work be more influenced by evaluators, potentially damaging their own profile as a researcher (Lendák-Kabók and Ochsner, 2020). Eighth, review is said to lead to demonstration of *positive outcome bias*, meaning that only if an outcome is found is it published, while if an expected outcome is not found it is not published, leading to biased reporting, or so-called publication bias (Lee et al., 2013).

Issues with the Biases

While criticism is an integral part of scientific knowledge production and helps improve the peer review process, many scholars challenge the biases often attributed to peer review. Regarding the often-cited issue of fairness of peer review, especially regarding discrimination of women, many studies cannot replicate such biases (Friesen, 1998; Mutz, Bornmann and Daniel, 2012). Also, at least for prestigious journals, manuscripts rejected but published elsewhere receive less citations than those accepted (Bornmann et al., 2011), contesting the claim of low predictive validity. Langfeldt et al. (2015), however, criticise that studies on biases in peer review, especially regarding fairness and predictive validity, compare outcomes without having a clear concept of what the outcome should be: for example, does one really expect that a person who receives an open-mode research grant will be relatively more cited after the grant? Isn't it likely that the person is already chosen because of a higher impact potential? Ochsner (2020) goes further and challenges the methodology behind the studies. First, a high interrater reliability is not necessarily desirable as it might just be a sign of an unfortunate choice of experts following the same paradigm and thus rejecting research drawing from another paradigm. Without the reasons behind the different ratings, it cannot be interpreted as bias. Second, a high predictive validity, usually measured by citations, might just point to the fact that being published in this specific journal or having received a prestigious grant bolsters the citation rate of the article or scholar. Citations are not a good outcome indicator and not a valid measure for a functioning peer review process because citing a source can have many different meanings (Tahamtan and Bornmann, 2018). Third, if in a peer review process a bias can be identified, it might not be the problem inherent in the peer review but might lie in conditions external to it: e.g. if women are less self-confident and submit understated proposals or researchers at prestigious institutions have more time to write proposals and men work more often at prestigious institutions, peer review would be in favour of men in both conditions even though the peer reviewers would not favour men as such (see, e.g., Ceci and Williams, 2011; Enserink, 2015). Lipworth et al. (2011) even argue that the social and subjective dimensions of peer review are in fact the very essence of peer review, simply because the decisions to be taken are always choices against the background of many valuable, sometimes contradictory, information and as gatekeepers, reviewers and editors are expected to play this social role (see also Eysenck and Eysenck, 1992).

Most interestingly, even the authors cited above evoking the biases of the review process and also the researchers surveyed or interviewed in several studies on the perceptions of the peer review process confirm that peer review is still seen as the best, or least bad, way of improving research (be it manuscripts or research proposals) or gatekeeping (Cowen et al., 1987; Eysenck and Eysenck, 1992; Lendák-Kabók and Ochsner, 2020; Vanholsbeeck, 2020).

Links between Bibliometrics and Peer Review

Given that bibliometric assessments are advertised as a less biased and costly alternative to peer review, especially among policymakers (Taylor, 2011), it is worthwhile to reflect on the links between peer review and bibliometrics. First, some critics of peer review base their argument upon bibliometric measures: the amount of citations or correlations with citations are used to "validate" peer review procedures. However, citations have not been validated as good measures of scientific performance (Ochsner, Hug and Daniel, 2012) and it seems tautological to argue that bibliometrics are better suited because peer review outcomes do not correspond to bibliometric outcomes. Second, it is obvious that there is a strong link between peer review and bibliometrics because the main data sources for bibliometric analysis, Web of Science and Scopus, include only peer-reviewed publications. Additionally, performance-based research funding models relying on comprehensive national publication databases include only publications that were peer-reviewed (Verleysen and Engels, 2013). Third, indicator-driven performance-based research funding models can also involve a peer review component: peers decide which publication channels are considered first or second level (Sivertsen, 2016). Thus, bibliometric measures are not free of the biases ascribed to peer review.

Therefore, the question should not be whether bibliometrics should replace peer review but how to disburden and improve peer review processes, and evaluation procedures in general; and bibliometrics can play a role in this quest. Peer review can take many roles in evaluation procedures, appearing in different forms, and the decisions taken by the peers can be of varying significance (Ochsner 2020). Therefore, the interlinks between bibliometrics and peer review should come more into focus. I mention three examples worthy of further investigation.

Open Peer Review

With Open Science as a main policy goal, new versions of peer reviewing and publishing attract interest. Open Access (OA) journals that are not published in print anymore are not limited in space. Reviews can be made public and linked to different versions of the same article. Different models of Open Peer Review processes have been identified (Ross-Hellauer, 2017). This leads to new possibilities for bibliometric indicators, taking into account hitherto mostly hidden aspects of scientific work: the writing of reviews. Publons, recently integrated into Clarivate's Web of Science, already implemented a new indicator, the ratio of articles published and reviews submitted (publons.com). Other indicators are likely to emerge as well. However, it is most likely they will suffer from similar problems as other bibliometric measures, such as issues of coverage, disciplinary differences and the risk of gaming.

Ambiguity of Peer-reviewed Publications

Given that peer review is an important cornerstone of academic quality assurance, it also takes on an important role in evaluation practices. Whether a publication is peer-reviewed is often a criterion in evaluation procedures, for example performance-based funding systems, recruitment or grant funding; researchers are thus often asked to identify their peer-reviewed publications. However, even experts disagree whether a certain journal or book publisher applies peer review (Pölönen, Engels and Guns, 2020). This has consequences for the use of peer-reviewed publications in performance-based evaluation systems, which is why a label for peer-reviewed publications was created (Verleysen and Engles, 2013). It is somewhat amusing that an indicator for peer review helps assure the quality of a bibliometric indicator.

Informed Peer Review

However, not only peer review can be used to improve or innovate bibliometric indicators. Vice versa, bibliometric and scientometric indicators can also be used to improve peer review. As research quality is a complex construct, reviewers often disagree in their judgement, not because they disagree about single aspects of quality but because they apply different weightings of those aspects (Eysenck and Eysenck, 1992). Moreover, given the often high volume of works or profiles to evaluate, indicators assigned to aspects of research quality can help to take an informed decision. Ochsner, Hug and Daniel (2014) therefore suggest assigning indicators to different aspects of research quality and letting reviewers rate each aspect. Such a procedure will lead to more reliable and fair judgements (Thorngate, Dawes and Foddy, 2009).

Conclusions

The evaluation of research is a complex endeavour. Neither bibliometrics nor peer review are without problems or flaws. Instead of playing peer review and bibliometrics off against each other, more efforts should be spent on how the two interact and how they are best combined.

References

Bornmann, L & Leydesdorff, L 2014, 'Scientometrics in a changing research landscape', *EMBO reports*, vol. 15, no. 12, pp. 1228–32.

Bornmann, L, Mutz, R, Marx, W, Schier, H & Daniel, H-D 2011, 'A multilevel modelling approach to investigating the predictive validity of editorial decisions: do the editors of a high profile journal select manuscripts that are highly cited after publication?', *Journal Of The Royal Statistical Society Series A-Statistics In Society*, vol. 174, no. 4, pp. 857–79.

Bornmann, L 2011, 'Scientific Peer Review', *Annual Review of Information Science and Technology*, vol. 45, no. 1, pp. 199–245.

Bornmann, L & Daniel, H-D 2008, 'The Effectiveness of the Peer Review Process: Inter-Referee Agreement and Predictive Validity of Manuscript Refereeing at Angewandte Chemie', *Angewandte Chemie International Edition*, vol. 47, no. 38, pp. 7173–78.

Ceci, SJ & Williams, WM 2011, 'Understanding current causes of women's underrepresentation in science', *Proceedings of the National Academy of Sciences*, vol. 108, no. 8, pp. 3157–62.

Cowen, EL, Spinelli, A, Hightower, AD & Lotyczewski, BS 1987, 'Author reactions to the manuscript revision process', *American Psychologist*, vol. 42, no. 4, pp. 403–05.

Cronin, B 2009, 'Vernacular and vehicular language', *Journal of the American Society for Information Science and Technology*, vol. 60, no. 3, pp. 433.

Daniel, H-D 1993, *Guardians of science: Fairness and reliability of peer review*, VCH Verlagsgesellschaft.

Daniel, H-D, Mittag, S & Bornmann, L 2007, 'The potential and problems of peer evaluation in higher education and research', in A Cavalli (ed), *Quality assessment for higher education in Europe*, pp. 71–82, Portland Press, London.

Enserink, M 2015, 'Dutch sexism study comes under fire', *Science*, vol. 364, no. 6446.

Eysenck, HJ & Eysenck, SBG 1992, 'Peer review: Advice to referees and contributors', *Personality and Individual Differences*, vol. 13, no. 4, pp. 393–99.

Friesen, HG 1998, 'Equal opportunities in Canada', *Nature*, vol. 391, no. 6665, p. 326.

Gottfredson, SD 1978, 'Evaluating psychological research reports: Dimensions, reliability, and correlates of quality judgments.', *American Psychologist*, vol. 33, no. 10, pp. 920–34.

Kronick, DA 1990, 'Peer review in 18th-century scientific journalism', *Journal of the American Medical Association*, vol. 263, no. 10, pp. 1321–22.

Lamont, M 2009, *How professors think: Inside the curious world of academic judgment*, Harvard University Press.

Langfeldt, L, Bloch, CW & Sivertsen, G 2015, 'Options and limitations in measuring the impact of research grants – evidence from Denmark and Norway', *Research Evaluation*, vol. 24, no. 3, pp. 256–70.

Langfeldt, L 2006, 'The policy challenges of peer review: managing bias, conflict of interests and interdisciplinary assessments', *Research Evaluation*, vol. 15, no. 1, pp. 31–41.

Lee, CJ, Sugimoto, CR, Zhang, G & Cronin, B 2013, 'Bias in peer review', *Journal of the American Society for Information Science and Technology*, vol. 64, no. 1, pp. 2–17.

Lendák-Kabók, K & Ochsner, M 2020, 'A gender and geopolitical perspective on peer review', in M Ochsner, N Kancewicz-Hoffman, M Hołowiecki & J Holm (eds.), *Overview of peer review practices in the SSH. ENRESSH Report. European Network of Research Evaluation in the Social Sciences and Humanities*, pp. 78–86.

Lipworth, WL, Kerridge, IH, Carter, SM & Little, M 2011, 'Journal peer review in context: A qualitative study of the social and subjective dimensions of manuscript review in biomedical publishing', *Social Science & Medicine*, vol. 72, no. 7, pp. 1056–63.

Melin, G & Danell, R 2006, 'The top eight percent: development of approved and rejected applicants for a prestigious grant in Sweden', *Science and Public Policy*, vol. 33, no. 10, pp. 702–12.

Mutz, R, Bornmann, L & Daniel, H-D 2012, 'Does Gender Matter in Grant Peer Review?', *Zeitschrift für Psychologie*, vol. 220, no. 2, pp. 121–29.

Ochsner, M 2020, 'Place, role, form and significance of peer review in national research evaluation systems', in M Ochsner, N Kancewicz-Hoffman, M Hołowiecki & J Holm (eds.), *Overview of peer review practices in the SSH. ENRESSH Report. European Network of Research Evaluation in the Social Sciences and Humanities*, pp. 55–60.

Ochsner, M, Hug, SE & Daniel, H-D 2014, 'Setting the stage for the assessment of research quality in the humanities. Consolidating the results of four empirical studies', *Zeitschrift für Erziehungswissenschaft*, vol. 17, no. 6, pp. 111–32.

Ochsner, M, Hug, SE & Daniel, H-D 2012, 'Indicators for Research Quality in the Humanities: Opportunities and Limitations', *Bibliometrie – Praxis und Forschung*, vol. 1, p. 4.

Ochsner, M, Kancewicz-Hoffman, N, Holm, J & Hołowiecki, M 2020, 'Conclusions', in M Ochsner, N Kancewicz-Hoffman, M Hołowiecki & J Holm (eds.), *Overview of peer review practices in the SSH. ENRESSH Report. European Network of Research Evaluation in the Social Sciences and Humanities*, pp. 99–100.

Pölönen, J, Engels, TCE & Guns, R 2020, 'Ambiguity in identification of peer-reviewed publications in the Finish and Flemish performance-based research funding systems', *Science and Public Policy*, vol. 47 no. 1, pp. 1–15.

Ross-Hellauer, T 2017, 'What is open peer review? A systematic review', *F1000Research*, vol. 6, no. 588.

Sivertsen, G 2016, 'Publication-Based Funding: The Norwegian Model', in M Ochsner, SE Hug & H-D Daniel (eds.), *Research Assessment in the Humanities. Towards Criteria and Procedures*, pp. 79–90, Springer International Publishing, Cham.

Tahamtan, I & Bornmann, L 2018, 'Core elements in the process of citing publications: Conceptual overview of the literature', *Journal of Informetrics*, vol. 12, no. 1, pp. 203–16.

Taylor, J 2011, 'The Assessment of Research Quality in UK Universities: Peer Review or Metrics?', *British Journal of Management*, vol. 22, no. 2, pp. 202–17.

Thorngate, W, Dawes, RM & Foddy, M 2009, *Judging merit*, Psychology Press, New York, NY.

Vanholsbeeck, M 2020, 'Peer review in the context of the new modes of knowledge production, dissemination and evaluation', in M Ochsner, N Kancewicz-Hoffman, M Hołowiecki & J Holm (eds.), *Overview of peer review practices in the SSH. ENRESSH Report. European Network of Research Evaluation in the Social Sciences and Humanities*, pp. 87–93.

Verleysen, FT & Engels, TCE 2013, 'A label for peer-reviewed books', *Journal of the American Society for Information Science and Technology*, vol. 64, no. 2, pp. 428–30.

Wennerås, C & Wold, A 1997, 'Nepotism and sexism in peer-review', *Nature*, vol. 387, pp. 341–43.

3 (Classical) Indicators

3.1 Measuring the Impact of Research – from Scholarly Communication to Broader Impact

Wolfgang Glänzel, Pei-Shan Chi, and Koenraad Debackere

Abstract: The last two decades in the evolution of bibliometrics mark a significant turn towards the quantification and measurement of scientific communication beyond the scholarly one and towards a broader assessment of its various impacts on science and society. This chapter summarizes the background and the main characteristics of this evolution, and focusses on the latent and real challenges in the use of the new metrics designed for the measurement of the broader impact of research. In addition to the critical review several examples are given to illustrate the large potential and added value of the new metrics when used judiciously and correctly.

Keywords: Scientometrics 2.0, usage, downloads, captures, social media, citation impact, broader impact.

Introduction

Scientometrics – defined as "the application of mathematical and statistical methods to books and other media of communication" (Pritchard, 1969) – although not designed to directly evaluate research performance, has been successfully used to develop and provide tools to be applied to monitor and measure quantitative outputs of scholarly communication, above all in fundamental research on the nature and development of science. Statistical methods have been applied to measure and model processes and specific phenomena of present-day scientific communication since the 1970s and 1980s. Recently, open science, open access, as one important platform and instrument, and "altmetrics" (i.e., alternative metrics), as its possible assessment tool, have gained major attention since their emergence during the last decade. They also extended both the perspective and the domain of traditional scientometrics' studies. In particular, the social web provided an additional dimension of public opinion information to academic research and scholarly communication. These new sources led to the extension of traditional scientometrics captured by the early development of webometrics (Almind and Ingwersen, 1997) and altmetrics (Priem et al., 2010) to focus on assessing non-academic impacts originating from the web and

---

Wolfgang Glänzel, ECOOM and Faculty of Economics and Business, KU Leuven, Leuven, Belgium, and Dept. Science Policy and Scientometrics, Library of the Hungarian Academy of Sciences, Budapest, Hungary, wolfgang.glanzel@kuleuven.be
Pei-Shan Chi, ECOOM, KU Leuven, Leuven, Belgium, peishan.chi@kuleuven.be
Koenraad Debackere, ECOOM and Faculty of Economics and Business, KU Leuven, Leuven, Belgium, koenraad.debackere@kuleuven.be

the social web, respectively. Above all, altmetrics articulated the big promise of providing tools for assessing broader societal impacts of academic research beyond the scholarly one. Priem and Hemminger (2010) have outlined this new concept, compiled a comprehensive list of relevant services and provided a critical look at uses, limitations, and future challenges. In their article they also heralded the emergence of a new paradigmatic "Scientometrics 2.0" model. The expectations for the new metrics are enormous and so is the enthusiasm for their use. Unfortunately, their use is, at present, even less critical (and sometimes careless) than it was about three decades ago in the case of the emergence of their predecessor metrics. Bibliometricians have already raised their voice (e.g., Wouters and Costas, 2012; Gumpenberger at al., 2016) to admonish of latent and real challenges and dangers in the use of the new metrics. Before we give a short summary of the recent discussion, we briefly review the development from scientometrics to its recent overture towards a possible broader discipline called "Scientometrics 2.0" that sallied forth to measure scientific communication beyond the scholarly one and to assess broader impacts of scientific research.

Scientometrics 1.0 – From Information to Evaluation

From the historical viewpoint, scientometrics expresses the development of methods, indicators (metrics) for monitoring and measuring quantitative aspects of scholarly communication. It was originally developed for application to the basic sciences, first within the framework of scientific information. With time elapsing, the increasing demand for indicators in research evaluation resulted in a "perspective shift" (Glänzel, 2006). Due to the exponential growth of scientific literature, the increasing complexity of scholarly communication, and the crisis of the peer review system, scientometrics took a sharp rise in the 1970s and 1980s and found a new orientation. The main field of application of the metrics was now laid in evaluation and assessment of scientific research. As the first consequence of this shift, both scientometricians and users were faced with a change in application contexts and interpretation of indicators. Indicators became gradually used in contexts for which they never were designed (cf. Journal Impact Factors) and measures of scholars' communication patterns (cf. author self-citations) were, in the light of the new focus, re-interpreted. Inevitably, first limitations became apparent, uninformed use occurred and earned the attention of both researchers and users. This was the era of scientometrics 1.0.

The conceptual framework of scientometrics 1.0 was created for modelling and measuring the research impact on scientific communities and documented scholarly communication in basic sciences, mainly on the basis of journal literature, but was never designed to directly evaluate research performance and neither did it aim to correct/replace qualitative by quantitative methods. Being a truly interdisciplinary field, it evolved under the influence of sociology, economics, and other related fields from a sub-discipline of information science to an instrument for evaluation and benchmarking of scientific activity. Besides information science and sociology of science, science policy became the third driving force in the evolution of scientometrics. The science policy drive provided a major push to scientometrics, which resulted in the evolution from "little scientometrics" to "big scientometrics" (Glänzel and Schoepflin, 1994). This means the scientometrics' applications were oriented from little science, which is conducted by individual scientists or small teams linked to universities, to big science, which is characterized by teamwork, huge budgets, complex collaborations, and interdisciplinarity. Due to the dynamics of the evaluation processes, the focus of the applications shifted from macro-level studies downwards to meso-level and micro-level studies. This shift, and the conceptual shift from scientific information to research evaluation, all required a higher precision in data retrieval. However, the appropriate data sources and the new methods required were not yet fully available in the 1990s and therefore brought a sense of crisis to scientometrics.

Scientometrics 1.x – A Historical Sketch

Following the pioneering days of the field and its coming of age, a new challenge was issued to the meanwhile established discipline: the necessary extension towards applied sciences, and later on also to the social sciences and humanities (SSH) and technology. According to Glänzel and Chi (2018), bibliometricians observed in the last two decades of the twentieth century that scientific communication and research impact in fields like medical sciences (e.g., Lewison, 2000) or applied sciences (e.g., van Els et al., 1989), let alone in the social sciences and the humanities (SSH), are not sufficiently depicted by methods and metrics developed within the framework of traditional scientometrics. Researchers pointed to the fact that, e.g., in SSH and technology-related fields, a large share of both sources and targets are located outside documented scholarly communication published in periodicals, thus citations based on periodicals can only be considered an insufficient measure of impact and use of information. When scientometrics opened towards new data sources (including conference proceedings and books) and broadened towards the measurement of research performance in other fields than basic research, it became apparent that the above-mentioned framework proved too narrow for those fields. Scientometricians attempted to catch up with this challenge and to keep pace with the new developments in research evaluation by broadening the scope and improving their methods.

The extension of data sources and the partial broadening the scope of scientometrics resulted in what can be considered scientometrics 1.x versions of the traditional concept of scientometrics. It has two main characteristics: on the one hand the already mentioned "perspective shift" and on the other hand the trend of the applications focusing on lower levels of aggregation, away from the macro-level down to the meso-level and increasingly to the evaluation of individual scientists (challenges of individual-level bibliometrics – cf. Wouters et al., 2013). In short, the changes are not only seen in the shift to different types of targeted samples but also in the scale and scope of the scientometric analyses.

The advanced features of Scientometrics 1.x and the challenges they pose result in several issues. The opening and inclusion of new data sources has become an essential prerequisite to meet those challenges. New data sources including proceedings, books, national databases, and the web became integrated in the traditional foundation of bibliometrics. Hence also data-related issues arose, including big-data related issues, such as data cleaning, name disambiguation, and the need to cope with redundancies. Other issues arising from broadening the scope of scientometrics were of a more conceptual and methodological nature as they were closely related to specific cultures in scholarly communication of various fields, notably in the technology-related sciences, the social sciences, and the humanities, especially their subject-specific communication behavior with their specific publication types and channels, and the different function that citations may have across and within these domains; but also meso- and micro-level specific issues like individual co-authorship, gender, publication in Open Access (OA) requiring new qualities of data processing, and a higher granularity of information.

Beyond doubt, the traditional scientometric 1.x model had undeniable strengths. First, as to data sources it was based on a dynamic but closed universe: unique, mostly multidisciplinary bibliographic databases such as The ISI Science Citation Index, and later on, its successor, Thomson Reuters Web of Science, or Elsevier's Scopus. While these databases are growing, they form a closed dynamic universe. The system thus is dynamic but still remains closed in the sense that all the citation counts are from the same database. Any links with objects and items outside the databases such as so-called "non-source" items in references can be filtered out and excluded from the analysis. This has offered a significant potential for standardization and integration of quality consistent indicators, which, in turn, facilitate comparability of scientometric results by having a clear definition of exposure and scholarly impact. Since it was restricted to the measurement of scholarly communication, it furthermore provides clear definitions of actors, of impact and of the users of information within this framework (i.e., scholars themselves). This facilitates the interpretation of the scientometric results obtained. Because of the general availability of the mostly proprietary data products it shows a high level of reproducibility and documentability. The high-level replicability, of course, depends on transparent documentation and description to allow users to replicate the result using the same data. Furthermore, it proved to work at any level of aggregation and has been useful in combination with peer review system also at lower levels of aggregation. Thus, analysis at the (inter-)national and (inter-)institutional level, as well as analysis of individual researchers and research teams, can be conducted within this model. Finally, mathematical-statistical models for a variety of processes (publication activity, citation impact, co-authorship, citation-based networks, literature growth and evolution, etc.) could successfully be applied to the empirical results. The capability for extension to an open dynamic universe can therefore be obtained as soon as some new sources are added. This has been done already by matching databases with external sources even when their information may not suffice.

For instance, some external information like Mesh heading from the Medline can be used, by creating corresponding links, to assign individual papers to individual topics on the subject classification system of the Web of Science based on journals. The accuracy of author and affiliation assignment can also be improved by adding external information on detailed affiliation at the department level. For the case of name disambiguation at several levels additional information from the institution and individual curricula vitae would be needed to match the database for evaluative purposes. The match with external data sources conduces the regionalisation of data, linking funding and research output for verifying the efficiency of the funding process, and identifying and linking information sources and targets beyond scientific communities and the respective, relevant bibliographic databases. For instance, an important aspect of the real impact of medical research may be found in the medical guidelines used to improve treatment, which are not cited in the literature. The other side of the coin is the limitations of the Scientometrics 1.x model that should not be ignored. Various opportunities and limitations have been discussed among others by Glänzel and Debackere (2003). Most of those are of methodological or technical nature and concern the use and application of results and indicators. Apart from these, perhaps the most general and conceptual limitation is due to the excessive focus on scholarly communication since many of the results are used outside of this construct, even though web-based data sources go, at least in part, already beyond this framework (cf. Google Scholar, webometrics). However, as an example described in a small-scale study, Hoffman et al. (2014) observed no correlation of online communication activity with any of the more established impact measures.

Scientometrics 2.0 – Promises, Challenges and Limitations

Recently, the concept of Scientometrics 2.0 was proposed to embrace a big step towards the measurement of societal impact and "broader impacts" of research and to cover "open science" – "social media metrics" or "alternative metrics" as groundwork and components of a "Scientometrics 2.0" foundation (Priem and Hemminger, 2010). As possible sources Priem and Hemminger recommended to include bookmarking, reference managers, recommendation systems, comments on articles, microblogging, Wikipedia, blogging, and other sources such as social networks, video, and open data repositories.

Promises

One of the most important promises is, of course, to overcome a number of limitations of the scientometrics 1.x model, above all, the restriction to the measurement of scholarly communication and impact. Within this broader scope of Scientometrics 2.0, in general, and altmetrics, in particular, a number of important features and promises have been addressed. Thus Sugimoto (2016) pointed to the increasing demand for showing impact of research beyond academia and democratizing the impact construct by giving greater voice and vote, e.g., to underrepresented groups (gender, ethnicity, disability, geographic etc.) in determining impact. The recognition of the relevance of underrepresented groups leads to a more democratic way of articulating their presence and visibility inducing less discrimination. The other main promise of Scientometrics 2.0 stems from social networks. Network-based approaches based on social media data, e.g. communities of attention, hashtag coupling analysis, and reader pattern analysis (Wouters et al., 2019), may also contribute to a more diversified system of scientific impact assessment by adding a relational and social capital-based perspective (Hoffman et al., 2014).

Challenges and Limitations

The promises are contrasted by a number of challenges and limitations that have been summarized by Wouters and Costas (2012), Sugimoto (2016), and Gumpenberger et al. (2016), including:
- Analyses are usually conducted at the individual (micro) level and most benefits of Scientometrics 2.0 are at the micro-level. However, the aggregation at higher levels is questionable, so that the validity, reliability, and feasibility of large-scale studies are one of the main challenges.
- A number of assumptions are not yet validated and tested but the high dynamics and rapid development of online and electronic communications (Web 2.0 – and beyond?) will increase the difficulties for altmetrics to keep pace with their development in scientometrics once validated and implemented. In fact, a development might be outdated by the time of its implementation because the members and the social networks evolve so fast.
- More transparency and clarity in the data covered is needed. There is not yet any clear definition of actors on both sides. Thus, if we talk about impact – impact upon whom is meant? And what are the potential biases in terms of actor and user profiles? Without clarification the standardization and normalization of measures is hardly conceivable.
- Data quality: not only source-related reliability of input and assignments needs to be taken into account, but also that of the results as, for instance, automated processes may produce errors and influence social media metrics.
- In contrast to the previous scientometrics model, altmetrics still lacks mathematical background and proper models, which impede the clear interpretation of indicators. Issues caused by the use of composite indicators and the arbitrariness of their construction make their interpretation and comparability even more difficult. One of the goals of the altmetrics movement was to overcome the flaws of

the traditional citation-based indicators but instead new "all-in-one" indicators are created. We should resist any temptation to create new "all-in-one" indicators, notably for ranking ("old habits die hard", cf. Gumpenberger et al., 2016).

Scientometrics 2.0 – Approaches

In the following, we will give some examples from altmetrics to illustrate the specific requirements in dealing with data and effects of this – in many regards – open concept that lacks strict rules, reviewing, and partially even knowledge about particular usage and users in the communication processes. We will focus on our altmetrics research because that was always linked to and analyzed in the light of results of traditional bibliometrics.

Altmetrics

As an alternative method to extend the concept and application of traditional scientometrics, altmetric indicators calculate the scholarly impact based on diverse online research output, such as social media, online news media, online reference managers, and so on. Konkiel (2013) summarized five types of altmetrics: Shares, Saves, Reviews, Adaptations, and Social usage statistics. As already discussed by Glänzel and Chi (2019), Cave (2012) categorized Altmetrics using a similar approach in the following five ways: Usage, Captures, Mentions, Social media, and Citations. "Usage" comprises, for instance, clicks, downloads or views and could rather be considered measures of the intention to use something than their actual usage (Gorraiz et al., 2014). It reveals little about motivation. "Captures" expresses somewhat more as it indicates repeated usage, for instance, as bookmarks, favourites, readers or watchers. "Mentions" estimates measurement of activities such as news articles, Wikipedia links, or blog posts about research. "Social media" metrics are heterogeneous and partially just express acknowledgements and simple comments. This category includes the tweets, Facebook likes, etc. that reference the research. "Citation" represents the highest level and can be considered an extension of the concept of citations within the framework of traditional bibliometrics as this category reaches out beyond the framework of scholarly communication. It contains both traditional citation indexes such as Scopus or patent citations, as well as citations that help indicate societal impact such as clinical citations or policy citations. These five categories were adopted in PlumX Metrics (2020) as different impact measuring dimensions but still form just a minor part of what can be covered by broader or societal impact (cf., Lewison, 2004; 2008).

In terms of the relationship between the traditional scientometric indicators and altmetric ones, most of the previous studies have found some degree of correlation between altmetrics and citation indicators, suggesting that these two approaches are somehow related but not the same, and support the hypothesis that they should rather be considered as complementary sources providing different points of view (Zahedi, Costas, and Wouters, 2014; Costas, Zahedi, and Wouters, 2015; Gorraiz, Blahous, and Wieland, 2018). However, altmetrics is more prone to inflationary effects than traditional bibliometrics (cf. Persson et al., 2004) as we have seen that extreme usage value can easily reach a hundred thousand users in a couple of months. The context of altmetrics which tells us little about motivation is even more important for the interpretation of the measures than for traditional citations, since the numbers easily come to extreme out of regional nature. On the other hand, altmetrics data show a strong effect of the often discussed zero-inflated data phenomenon (cf., Bornmann and Haunschild, 2018) as well, that is, the extremely large share of zero frequency in several altmetrics distributions that contrasts the above-mentioned large numbers and that seem to go beyond the traditional communication models. The reasons for this effect are heterogeneous, but some are explicable: low coverage of papers on social media platforms (cf. Zahedi et al., 2014), low visibility, restricted access for public use or unmatched data.

Previous Results and Related Studies

Downloads were one of the first statistics to supplement citation indicators (Bollen et al., 2005) and are considered measures of usage – or rather measures of the intention to use something rather than their actual usage (Gorraiz et al., 2014). Despite their limited availability and interpretation, they provide interesting information about usage processes. In a previous study, (full text) download processes generally mirror the characteristics of citation processes but not always to the same extent and mostly with a certain field specific "translation coefficient" (cf. Glänzel and Heeffer, 2014). Downloads are of about two orders of magnitude more frequent than citations in an initial phase. Glänzel and Chi (2018) stressed in their recent study that this implies that one citation roughly corresponds to a certain number of downloads, which amounted to about 100 in our Elsevier sample of 80,000 journal documents put online in 2008 and followed up for downloads and citations with a five-year window (see Figure 1).

The citation process mirrors the increments of downloads, however with a certain "phase shift" in accordance to our expectations. The correlation between the impact and the usage measure proved very strong, which partially confirmed results of earlier studies by others (e.g., Moed, 2005; Brody et al., 2006; Thelwall, 2012). Further studies by Chi and Glänzel (2018; 2019) and most recently by Chi et al. (2019) could confirm and deepen these results. However, downloads are not closely related to documented scholarly communication as citations are by nature. Documents might be downloaded by anybody who has access without using or incorporating downloaded information in own publishable research.

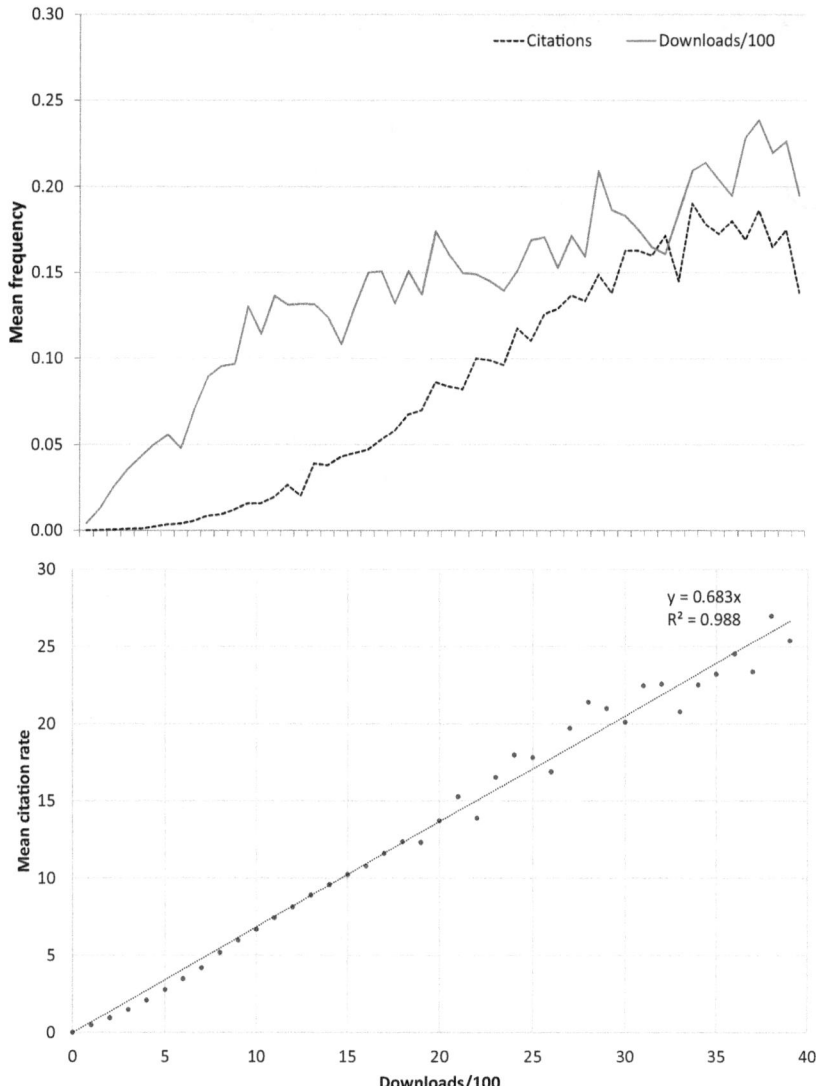

Figure 1: Monthly evolution of downloads versus citations (top) and conditional mean citation rates as a function of downloads five years after online availability (bottom) of the 80,000 documents of the Elsevier set according to Glänzel and Heeffer (2014).

Glänzel and Chi (2019) summarized the following findings: further studies focusing on WoS usage statistics and other PlumX metrics by the ECOOM team also showed that traditional concepts and methods can be integrated into the new metrics. A Journals Usage Index (Chi and Glänzel, 2018) was defined in analogy to the Garfield Impact Factor while the idea of relative citation indicators, and the Characteristic Scales and Scores (CSS; Glänzel and Schubert, 1988; Chi and Glänzel, 2018),

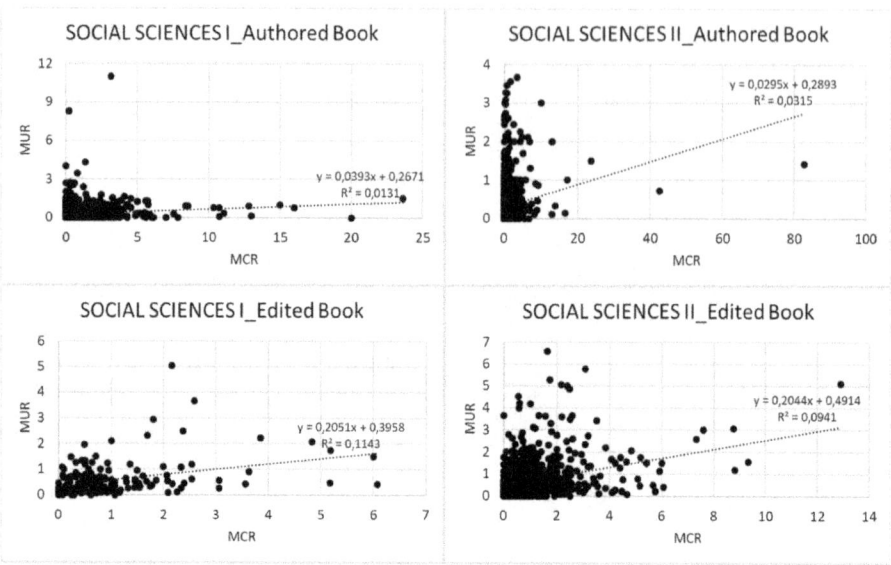

Figure 2: Scatter plots of MUR vs. MCR for two document types in two major fields according to Chi and Glänzel (2019).

proved to work for new metrics as well. In short, in these previous studies we could already make some specific observations. The most important one concerns the difference between the patterns of basic research in the Sciences and in SSH. In terms of WoS usage statistics of journal articles, social sciences displayed disproportionately higher "usage" than citation impact (Chi and Glänzel, 2018; 2019). This did not strike us unexpectedly because citations to periodicals play a less pronounced part in SSH than in the Sciences. All the more, we found it interesting that the usage of authored and edited books did not reflect the same patterns (Chi and Glänzel, 2019). Figure 2 gives the correlation between the mean usage rate (MUR) and the mean citation rate (MCR) of two document types of book publications, authored and edited books, as reflected by the 2013 volume of Clarivate Analytics Book Citation Index (BKCI).

Further Challenges and Limitations

Some (conceptual, methodological, and other) Scientometrics 2.0 assumptions are not yet validated and tested. On the conceptual part, metrics developers, indicator designers and users should guarantee replicability and robustness, guarantee commensurability, pay attention to the interpretation of metrics, and avoid arbitrariness in designing measures. In this context, the conceptual part is devoted to a critical view at the interpretation of impact and indicators, the identification, characterization, and role of users on the basis of the promises of "alternative metrics". Bookstein (1997) who has analyzed the problem of anchoring this ability in scientometrics noted three (out of other) demons to measurement that are challenges to quantitative approaches and become even more critical in the new altmetrics context, in particular: randomness, fuzziness, and ambiguity.

On the methodological part, indicator designers and users should avoid over-sophistication (cf. composite, all-in-one indicators), simplification that ignores essential data aspects and characteristics, arbitrariness in the selection of variables and their weighting, and error-proneness. For instance, multiple categories, namely, Usage, Captures, Mentions, Social Media, and Citations, were distinguished in the analysis section. In addition, Moed (2015) pointed to the question of acceptable error rates already in the context of traditional scientometrics. The classification of users proved highly error prone.

Furthermore, the growing effect of OA, i.e. Diamond, Gold, Bronze/Hybrid, Green, and Black, is insufficiently quantifiable end measurable. So far published studies are partially reporting contradictory observations (cf. Eysenbach, PLoS Biology, 2006; Davis et al., BMJ, 2008). The possible effect of "predatory OA" on future publication cultures is also not yet sufficiently known. (e.g., Xia et al., JASIST, 2015).

In a recent study (Glänzel and Chi, 2019), the example of the category "public, environmental & occupational health" has provided an interesting and assumingly typical insight in the properties of altmetrics. Above all, these properties determine the opportunities and limitations for their possible application in an evaluative context. Most strikingly, in this study, just like in our previous papers (e.g., Chi et al., 2019; Chi and Glänzel, 2019), we have found some lack of consistency in these measures. Adding, removing or just changing repositories or databases may result in dramatic changes and may turn local or regional effects into global phenomena. The database SciELO may just serve as an example for this effect. Just counting downloads, mentions, likes, tweeds and other social-media related measures without knowing the real purpose behind these actions certainly cannot provide unequivocally interpretable (quantitative) evidence. Significance and robustness of measures did not yet meet the standards of traditional bibliometric tools and the interpretability of altmetrics indicators requires even more context analysis than those of scholarly communication. At this moment, we find that the currently used altmetric metrics to measure the broader impact of research still fall short of the enormous expectations and the sometimes nonreflective enthusiasm in their use.

As far as science policy is concerned, the problem of the inappropriate use of scientometrics has been well documented and ranges from uninformed use, over selecting and collecting "most advantageous" indicators to the obvious and deliberate misuse of data. Uninformed use and misuse are not always beyond the responsibility of bibliometric research. Unfortunately, bibliometricians do not always resist the temptation to follow popular, even populist trends in order to meet the expectations and demands of customers or policymakers. Any kind of uninformed use or misuse of bibliometric methods and indicators involves the danger of bringing bibliometric research itself into disrepute. Scientometrics 2.0 or the next horizon in bibliometric research thus poses several challenges to scientometrics as a discipline and to its practitioners who should avoid the dangers of inappropriate use of novel indicators, the meaning and mathematical foundation of which are not fully understood neither sufficiently validated (Debackere, Glänzel, and Thijs, 2019).

To conclude, we refer to van Noorden's (2014, p. 129) statement: "Some analysts argue that despite their millions of users, massive social academic networking sites have not yet proven their essential worth." What the future will bring for Scientometrics 2.0 thus remains to be seen.

Acknowledgements

This article is based on previous works published in ISSI Newsletter (Glänzel and Chi, 2016) and presented at the 19th COLLNET meeting in Macau, China (Glänzel and Chi, 2018) and the 17th ISSI Conference in Rome, Italy (Glänzel and Chi, 2019). Figure 1 has been reproduced from Glänzel and Heeffer (2014), and Figure 2 from Chi and Glänzel (2019) with the permission of the authors.

References

Almind, TC & Ingwersen, P 1997, 'Informetric analyses on the world wide web: methodological approaches to 'webometrics'', *Journal of Documentation*, vol. 53, no. 4, pp. 404–26.

Bollen, J, de Sompel, HV, Smith, JA, Luce, R 2005, Toward alternative metrics of journal impact: A comparison of download and citation data, *Information Processing & Management*, vol. 41, no. 6, pp. 1419–1440.

Bookstein, A 1997, 'Informetric Distributions. III. Ambiguity and Randomness', *JASIST*, vol. 48, no. 1, pp. 2–10.

Bornmann, L & Haunschild, R 2018, 'Normalization of zero-inflated data: An empirical analysis of a new indicator family and its use with altmetrics data', *Journal of Informetrics*, vol. 12, no. 3, pp. 998–1011.

Brody, T, Harnad, S & Carr, L 2006, 'Earlier web usage statistics as predictors of later citation impact', *JASIST*, vol. 57, no. 8, pp. 1060–72.

Cave, R 2012, 'Overview of the Altmetrics Landscape', in *Proceedings of the Charleston Library Conference*, pp. 349–56, Purdue University Press.

Chi, P-S & Glänzel, W 2018, 'Comparison of citation and usage indicators in research assess-ment in scientific disciplines and journals', *Scientometrics*, vol. 116, no. 1, pp. 537–54.

Chi, P-S & Glänzel, W 2019, 'Citation and usage indicators for monographic literature in the Book Citation Index in the social sciences', *ISSI Newsletter*, vol. 14, no. 4, pp. 80–86.

Chi, P-S, Gorraiz, J & Glänzel, W 2019, 'Comparing capture, usage and citation indicators: an alt-metric analysis of journal papers in chemistry disciplines', *Scientometrics*, vol. 120, no. 3, pp. 1461–73.

Davis, PM, Lewenstein, BV, Simon, DH, Booth, JG, Connolly, MJL 2008, Open access publishing, article downloads, and citations: randomised controlled trial, *BMJ* vol. 337, no. 7665, article number: a568.

Debackere, K, Glänzel, W & Thijs, B 2019, 'Scientometrics Shaping Science Policy and vice versa, the ECOOM case', in W Glänzel, HF Moed, U Schmoch & M Thelwall (eds.), *Springer Handbook of Science and Technology Indicators*, pp. 449–66, Springer Verlag.

Eysenbach, G 2006, Citation advantage of open access articles, *PLoS Biology*, vol. 4, no. 5, pp. 692–698, article number: e157.
Glänzel, W & Debackere, K 2003, 'On the opportunities and limitations in using bibliometric indicators in a policy relevant context', in R Ball (ed.), *Bibliometric Analysis in Science and Research: Applications, Benefits and Limitations*, Jülich.
Glänzel, W 2006, 'The *'perspective shift'* in bibliometrics and its and its consequences. I. International Conference on Multidisciplinary Information Sciences and Technologies' (InScit2006), Mérida, Spain, October 25–28, 2006, http://de.slideshare.net/inscit2006/the-perspective-shift-in-bibliometrics-and-its-consequences (July 15, 2020).
Glänzel, W & Heeffer, S 2014, 'Cross-national preferences and similarities in downloads and citations of scientific articles: A pilot study', in E Noyons (ed.), *Context Counts: Pathways to Master Big and Little Data*, pp. 207–15, Proceedings of the STI Conference 2014, Leiden University.
Glänzel, W & Chi, P-S 2016, 'Scientometrics 2.0 – and beyond? Background, promises, challenges and limitations', *ISSI Newsletter*, vol. 12, no. 3, pp. 33–36.
Glänzel, W & Chi, P-S 2018, 'Research beyond scholarly communication – The big challenge of scientometrics 2.0', Proceedings of the 19th COLLNET meeting, pp. 116–25, Macau, December 5–8, 2018.
Glänzel, W & Chi, P-S 2019, 'Research beyond scholarly communication – The big challenge of scientometrics 2.0', in G Catalano, C Daraio, M Gregori, H Moed & G Ruocco (eds.), Proceedings of the ISSI Conference 2019, pp. 424–36, Rome, Italy.
Glänzel, W, Schoepflin, U 1994, Little Scientometrics – Big Scientometrics ... and Beyond, *Scientometrics*, vol. 30, no. 2–3, pp. 375–384.
Glänzel, W, Schubert, A 1988, Characteristic Scores and Scales in Assessing Citation Impact. *Journal of Information Science*, vol. 14, no. 2, pp. 123–127.
Gorraiz, J, Gumpenberger, C & Schloegl, C 2014, 'Usage versus citation behaviours in four subject areas', *Scientometrics*, vol. 101, no. 2, pp. 1077–95.
Gorraiz, J, Blahous, B & Wieland, M 2018, 'Monitoring the Broader Impact of the Journal Publication Output on Country Level: A Case Study for Austria', in M Erdt, A Sesagiri Raamkumar, E Rasmussen & YL Theng (eds.), *Altmetrics for Research Outputs Measurement and Scholarly Information Management*, AROSIM 2018, Communications in Computer and Information Science, vol. 856, Springer, Singapore.
Costas, R, Zahedi, Z & Wouters, P 2015, 'Do "altmetrics" correlate with citations? Extensive com-parison of altmetric indicators with citations from a multidisciplinary perspective', *JASIST*, vol. 66, no. 10, pp. 2003–19.
Gumpenberger, Ch, Glänzel, W & Gorraiz, J 2016, 'The ecstasy and the agony of the altmetric score', *Scientometrics*, vol. 108, no. 2, pp. 977–82, doi: https://doi.org/10.1007/s11192-016-1991-5.
Hoffman, ChP, Lutz, Ch & Meckel, M 2014, Impact Factor 2.0: Applying Social Network Analysis to Scientific Impact Assessment, SSRN.
Konkiel, S 2013, 'Altmetrics: a 21st Century Solution to Determining Research Quality', *Online Searcher*, vol. 37, no. 4, pp. 11–15.
Lewison, G 2000, Citations as a means to evaluate biomedical research. In: B. Cronin and H. Atkins (Eds.), *The Web of Knowledge. A Festschrift in honour of Dr. Eugene Garfield*, Information Today, Inc., Medford, New Jersey. ASIST Monograph Series, pp. 361–372.
Lewison, G 2004, 'Citations to papers from other documents. Evaluation of the Practical Ef-fects of Biomedical Research', in HF Moed et al. (eds.), *Handbook of Quantitative Science and Technology Research*, pp. 457–72.
Lewison, G 2008, 'The returns to society from medical research (in Spanish)', *Medicina Clínica*, vol. 131, Suppl. 5, pp. 42–47.

Moed, HF 2005, 'Statistical relationships between downloads and citations at the level of individual documents within a single journal', *JASIST*, vol. 56, no. 10, pp. 1088–97.

Moed, HF, Halevi, G 2015, Multidimensional assessment of scholarly research impact, *Journal of the Association for Information Science and Technology*, vol. 66, no. 10, pp. 1988–2002.

Persson, O, Glänzel, W, Danell, R 2004, Inflationary bibliometric values: The role of scientific collaboration and the need for relative indicators in evaluative studies. *Scientometrics*, vol. 60, no. 3, pp. 421–432.

PlumX (2020), PlumX Metrics. Plum Analytics, https://plumanalytics.com/learn/about-metrics/ (July 15, 2020).

Priem, J & Hemminger, BH 2010, 'Scientometrics 2.0: New metrics of scholarly impact on the social Web', *First Monday*, doi: https://doi.org/10.5210/fm.v15i7.2874.

Priem, J, Taraborelli, D, Groth, P & Neylon, C 2010, Altmetrics: A manifesto, http://altmetrics.org/manifesto/ (July 15, 2020).

Priem, J 2014, Altmetrics. In B Cronin & CR Sugimoto (eds.), *Beyond Bibliometrics: Harnessing multidimensional indicators of scholarly impact*, MIT Press, Cambridge, MA, pp. 263–287.

Pritchard, A 1969, Statistical bibliography or bibliometrics? *Journal of Documentation*, vol. 24, no. 4, pp. 348–349.

Sugimoto, C 2016, Unlocking social data for science indicators (White paper), NSF Workshop on Bibliometric Indicators, Arlington.

Thelwall, M 2012, 'Journal impact evaluation: a webometric perspective', *Scientometrics*, vol. 92, no. 2, pp. 429–41.

van Els, WP, Jansz, CNM, le Pair, C 1989, The citation gap between printed and instrumental output of technological research – The case of the electron-microscope, *Scientometrics*, vol. 17, no. 5–6, pp. 415–425.

Van Noorden, R 2014, 'Online collaboration: Scientists and the social network', *Nature*, vol. 512, pp. 126–29.

Wouters, P & Costas, R 2012, *Users, narcissism and control – tracking the impact of scholarly publications in the 21st century*, SURF.

Wouters, P, Glänzel, W, Gläser, J & Rafols, I 2013, 'The Dilemmas of Performance Indicators of Individual Researchers – An Urgent Debate in Bibliometrics', *ISSI Newsletter*, vol. 9, pp. 48–53.

Wouters, P., Zahedi, Z. & Costas, R 2019, 'Social media metrics for new research evaluation', in W Glänzel, H Moed, U Schmoch & M Thelwall (eds.), *Handbook of science and technol-ogy indicators*, pp. 687–714, Springer Berlin-Heidelberg.

Xia, JF, Harmon, JL, Connolly, KG, Donnelly, RM, Anderson, MR, Howard, HA 2015, Who publishes in "predatory" journals? *Journal of the Association for Information Science and Technology*, vol. 66, no. 7, pp. 1406–1417.

Zahedi, Z., Costas, R. & Wouters, P 2014, 'How well developed are altmetrics? A cross-disciplinary analysis of the presence of 'alternative metrics' in scientific publications', *Scientometrics*, vol. 101, no. 2, pp. 1491–1513.

3.2 From Simple Publication Figures to Complex Indicators: Bibliometrics and the Dilemma of Methodological Correctness, Significance, and Economic Necessity

Dirk Tunger, Heinz Ahn, Marcel Clermont, Johanna Krolak, and Andreas Meier

Abstract: Due to competition, scientific institutions are increasingly making use of concepts and instruments from business administration, in a way similar to New Public Management reforms, which advocate a business-like approach to the running of public service institutions. This study is concerned with the question of how bibliometric indicators would have to be defined in order to meet scientific and economic requirements. For this purpose, different types of bibliometric indicators, their way of functioning and their possible applications are considered.

Keywords: performance measurement; bibliometric indicators; scientific impact; business administration.

Scientific institutions increasingly find themselves encountering competition for the brightest minds, the most prestigious research projects, and the most impactful publications. In addition, "[e]very enterprise and almost every organization or corporation is confronted with the task to monitor and evaluate the performance [...] of its teams, or of the whole unit" (Wagner-Döbler, 2003, p. 23).

In this context, universities and non-university research establishments are faced with the task of making effective and efficient decisions that are both scientifically and economically sound. The present study is concerned with the question of how bibliometric indicators would have to be defined in order to meet scientific and economic requirements. In attempting to answer this fundamental question, we focus on determining how normalized indicators can be derived from discipline-specific pub-

---

Dirk Tunger, TH Köln, Faculty of Information Science and Communication Studies, Institute of Information Management & Forschungszentrum Jülich GmbH, Project Management Jülich, Center of Excellence "Analyses, Studies, Strategy", d.tunger@fz-juelich.de
Heinz Ahn, TU Braunschweig, Institute of Management Control & Accounting, Department of Business Sciences, hw.ahn@tu-braunschweig.de
Prof. Dr. **Marcel Clermont**, Duale Hochschule Gera-Eisenach, Fachbereich Wirtschaftswissenschaften, marcel.clermont@dhge.de
Johanna Krolak, Forschungszentrum Jülich GmbH, Central Library, j.krolak@fz-juelich.de
Andreas Meier, Forschungszentrum Jülich GmbH, Central Library, a.meier@fz-juelich.de

https://doi.org/10.1515/9783110646610-016

lication and citation habits that would permit complex cross-discipline comparisons in an interdisciplinary scientific community.

Due to the competition mentioned above, scientific institutions are increasingly making use of concepts and instruments from business administration, in a way similar to New Public Management reforms, which advocate a business-like approach to the running of public service institutions. As a result, elements such as performance assessments and impact comparisons between various scientific institutions are being promoted more and more – all in the interest of securing an effective and efficient allocation of resources. An institution acts effectively if the changes in state resulting from its actions correspond to the intended purposes. In contrast, efficiency refers to all objectives associated with an action that can be categorized into purposes, resources, and side effects as unintended characteristics of future states (Weber, 1976). An alternative course of action is deemed efficient if it causes a change of state which represents an improvement with regard to the objective without simultaneously leading to negative consequences for any other objective (Ahn, 2003, p. 92 ff.; for a concrete analysis taking bibliometric indicators into account, see for example Clermont, 2016).

The issues associated with efficiency assessments thus go beyond those associated with effectiveness assessments in two aspects: effectiveness refers solely to the purposes (or purpose-related objectives) included in an analysis – for example, the purpose of research is the generating of public knowledge (e.g. by means of publications) – whereas with regard to efficiency, the objectives, resources (e.g. scientists), and side effects (e.g. risks resulting from research findings) are relevant. Furthermore, the efficiency must always be assessed within the context of the alternative actions or units of comparison under consideration (e.g. all higher education institutions versus universities only). Thus, an assessment of whether or not a scientific institution uses its available resources efficiently, and to what degree, depends on what elements of service performance and what units of comparison are included in the analysis (Ahn, 2003, p. 99 f.).

What objectives are significant in a given assessment situation ultimately depends on the preferences of the individual observer. In principle, therefore, it is at the observer's discretion how individual aspects are interpreted – whether they represent purposes, desirable side effects, resources, or undesirable side effects (Ahn and Dyckhoff, 2004, p. 517 ff.). Assessments are thus intrinsically subjective (see for example Tappe, 2014). For example, the question of whether external funding represents an input or output of research is a subject of much critical discussion. To bring to light the subjectivity of a given assessment – which is influenced by numerous factors – any subjective elements need to be disclosed. This creates transparency for third parties and prevents any criticism concerning a lack of clarity of the published results, ultimately increasing acceptance of those results and any decisions based on them (Ahn and Clermont, 2018, p. 890).

When determining the relevant objective-related benchmarks, a number of requirements must be considered. On a pragmatic level, these primarily include data availability and the economic viability of data acquisition, and on a qualitative level, the validity and reliability of a benchmark (Kromrey, 2006, p. 179 ff.).

There are a number of possible solutions to obtaining valid and reliable findings for bibliometric analyses. Firstly, the scientific disciplines to be included in the analysis can be examined with regard to comparability. However, this frequently leads to relatively one-sided and partial investigations, since in this case only the effectiveness and efficiency of individual disciplines, for instance, are investigated (see for example Clermont, 2016). Secondly, the concept behind the indicators used can be carefully considered. For example, standardization or normalization in the definition and design of indicators can ensure comparability across disciplines by moving away from absolute numbers (e.g. number of publications, P, or number of citations, C) and relative numbers (e.g. number of citations per publication, CPP), instead adopting percentages of impact (e.g. journal or discipline normalization; cf. for example Ball, Mittermaier and Tunger, 2009).

The reason generally given for the use of bibliometric indicators to measure research effectiveness and efficiency is that research results are primarily communicated in the form of scientific publications (i.e. publications are the main output), which permits a quantification of research achievements and their impact on the scientific community. When using publication and citation indicators, these should be linked with other indicators because individual indicators are less meaningful than a set. As outlined above, when conducting comparisons, the fact that different disciplines have fundamentally different structures with respect to their publication culture must be taken into consideration. It is not only the basic indicators (number of publications and citations) that can exhibit vastly different characteristics: there are also differences concerning the type and medium of publication, the publication language, the number of co-authors, and the time between publication and first citation.

Another problem concerning the comparability of disciplines is the difference in coverage in publication and citation databases. These different degrees of coverage are depicted in Figure 1. The figure shows the distribution of one year's publications in Web of Science (WoS, publication year 2018, document type "Article") across different fields, based on the mapping of publications to fields and subsequent aggregation using the classification introduced by Archambault et al. (2011). In contrast to the WoS classification, this is free of overlaps and redundancies. The result shows that approximately 20% of all publications are produced in the field of clinical medicine, while mathematics only achieves a little more than a tenth of the number of medical publications.

Valid comparisons can only be made by taking discipline-specific differences into consideration when creating indicators and indicator tests. A general consideration for bibliometric analyses is that bibliometric data are not meaningful when used alone. Explanatory power is only generated through comparison with other units. But this is exactly where a problem arises: finding two identical, perfectly comparable units is almost impossible. For example, discipline-specific differences can be identified which make the use of absolute numbers or other basic bibliometric in-

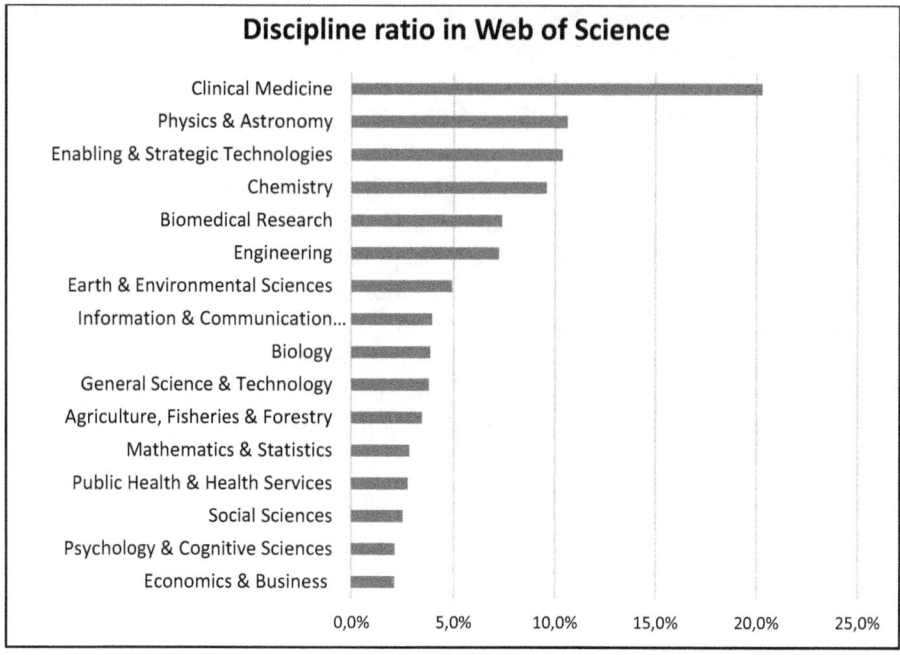

Figure 1: Ratio of publication numbers for different disciplines in Web of Science for 2018.

dicators impossible due to their limited significance. This is where the concept of normalized bibliometric indicators becomes relevant: including benchmarks (e.g. total number of journals used or associated scientific fields) creates a reference system that makes the classification of scientific output and impact much less dependent on a specific discipline. This makes interdisciplinary bibliometric comparisons meaningful.

With respect to citations, normalized citation indicators follow the same approach. In general, a distinction can be made between a posteriori and a priori normalization methods (Glänzel et al., 2011). A posteriori indicators or "cited-side" normalizations first calculate the usual citation rate for a given number of documents and subsequently compare it to the expected average value for all publications in the relevant discipline. A value of more than 1 indicates that the publication investigated is better received than the average publication in the same discipline, while a value of below 1 signals below-average citation performance. A disadvantage of a posteriori normalizations is that drawing a comparison with a discipline-specific expected value requires a (sometimes arbitrary) definition of the relevant disciplines. A change in the underlying classification can thus lead to changes in the results (Zitt et al., 2005). Examples of a posteriori normalized indicators include the mean normalized citation score (MNCS) (van Raan et al., 2010a), the normalized mean citation rate (NMCR) (Schubert and Braun, 1986), and the J-factor (Ball, Mittermaier, and Tunger, 2009). The above-mentioned disadvantage does not apply to the J-factor since this indicator is not based on a discipline classification, instead using as a reference the journal set of the institution to be investigated.

The a priori or "citing-side" method tries to avoid dependence on discipline definitions by normalizing citations before calculating a citation rate. Different citation frequencies between different disciplines are equalized here on the basis of the length of the reference lists on the citing side, i.e. how many citations the sources contain (Waltman and van Eck, 2010a; Zitt, 2010). The idea behind this is based on fractional counting of citations, a method introduced by Small et al. (1985) in the context of co-citation analysis. For discipline-specific normalization, citations in documents with short reference lists – and therefore disciplines with lower citation rates – carry more weight than citations in publications with large numbers of references, i.e. high citation rates. In contrast to a posteriori normalization, differences in citation behaviour are identified beforehand instead of using an expected value for comparison. Examples of such a priori normalizations include the audience factor (Zitt, 2010; Zitt and Small, 2008), the source normalized impact per paper (SNIP) (Moed, 2010), the fractional counted impact factor (Leydesdorff and Opthof, 2010), and the mean source normalized citation score (MSNCS) (Waltman and van Eck, 2010b).

The normalization methods described above can be applied to different disciplines and can also be used to compare different journals. In reference to this, these indicators are also referred to as field- or journal-normalized indicators. Table 1 lists frequently used indicators according to these criteria and shows their origin in the literature; a detailed and complete list of these indicators can be found at Krolak et al. (2020), available online as excel-file: http://hdl.handle.net/2128/24903 (July 15, 2020).

Table 1: Examples of field- and journal-normalized indicators (cf. Krolak et al., 2020)

Basic indicators		Normalized indicators			
		Field-normalized indicators		Journal-normalized indicators	
Indicator	Author	Indicator	Author	Indicator	Author
h-index	Hirsch (2005)	NMCR – normalized mean citation rate	Glänzel and Braun (1990)	AF – audience factor	Zitt and Small (2008)
P – number of publications		CPP/FCSm	De Bruin (1993) Moed (1995)	J-factor	Ball, Mittermaier, and Tunger (2009)
C – number of citations		MNCS – mean normalized citation score	van Raan et al. (2010a)	SNIP – source normalized impact per paper Revised SNIP	Moed (2010) Waltmann, van Eck, van Leuwen, and Visser (2013)

Table 1 *(Continued)*

Basic indicators	Normalized indicators	
	Field-normalized indicators	Journal-normalized indicators
CPP – citations per paper		MSNCS – mean source normalized citation score	Waltmann, and van Eck (2013)

With regard to the different concepts for normalized indicators and the associated significance, opinions differ even within the bibliometric scientific community. This is illustrated by the dispute between Opthof/ Leydesdorff and the Centre for Science and Technology Studies (CWTS) in Leiden, for instance. In a 2010 paper, the former criticized CWTS's established "crown indicator" as flawed, for example since it divides averages instead of averaging divided values (Opthof and Leydesdorff, 2010, p. 423). This was countered by van Raan et al. (2010b) from CWTS who argued that the criticism was mostly unfounded and that the order in which average values are calculated is irrelevant for the calculation and significance of indicators.

However, there was one criticism with which the authors from CWTS agreed: that all publications should be given the same weighting during normalization, which is not the case with the crown indicator. As a consequence of this criticism, the indicator was modified by CWTS shortly afterwards and introduced to the literature as the "new crown indicator" (Waltman et al., 2011a). In a further empirical study, the CWTS authors found that the difference between the two indicators (crown and new crown indicators) is very small on higher aggregation levels (institution or country). On lower levels (journal or working group), however, the difference was much more pronounced (Waltman et al., 2011b). In response to the modified indicator, Leydesdorff and Opthof (2011) criticized the WoS subject categories, which serve as one of the principles for calculating the indicator but which are, according to the authors, defined too vaguely.

Ultimately, it must be questioned whether it makes sense to call any one indicator a "crown indicator": the Leiden Manifesto for research metrics (Hicks et al., 2015), which was also developed at CWTS, makes clear that bibliometric conclusions should not be based on a single indicator. Instead, a set of indicators should always be used to assess science. This ultimately shows that there are currently no real standards in bibliometrics for impact measurement indicators, although the development of indicators – including complex ones – has quite a long history in some cases: Schubert and Glänzel (1983) pioneered normalized bibliometric indicators, using relative citation indicators (relative citation rate, RCR) and expected values (mean expected citation rate, MECR, and field expected citation rate, FECR) very early on as part of journal- or field-normalized studies. Since then, this type of representation of bibliometric results has been complemented by CSS classes (characteristics scores and scales) (Glänzel, 2011). With this method, a number of classes are formed into which publications are categorized based on their impact (e.g. four classes, with publications categorized from very low to very high). This approach has the advantage of making averaging unnecessary.

In summary, the sheer number of normalized citation indicators in use shows that although citation analyses can reflect various aspects of formal scientific communication, there is no "superindicator" that can definitively ascertain the quality of scientific work (Hornbostel, 1997, p. 326). An individual indicator or ranking is not capable of providing a complex overall picture; only a set of different indicators can achieve this. This corresponds to the above-mentioned economic requirements of representing effectiveness and/or efficiency in bibliometric studies, and once again illustrates the context dependence and subjectivity of such investigations.

And yet, it must be noted that precisely because of this complexity, many bibliometric indicators retain a purely academic character, while only a small number – that are frequently (too) simple – have found their way into application. The original h-index developed by Hirsch (2005), for example, has achieved considerable significance in university policy. Outside the bibliometric community, however, the criticism of either this index or the h-index variants developed as a result (see for example Niederklapfer, 2014; Bornmann et al., 2008; or Bornmann and Daniel, 2009) is not widely known.

References

Ahn, H 2003, Effektivitäts- und Effizienzsicherung: Controlling-Konzept und Balanced Scorecard, Frankfurt am Main et al.
Ahn, H & Dyckhoff, H 2004, 'Zum Kern des Controllings: Von der Rationalitätssicherung zur Effektivitäts- und Effizienzsicherung', in E Pietsch & G Scherm (Hrsg.), Controlling. Theorien und Konzeptionen, 501–25.
Ahn, H & Clermont, M 2018, 'Performance Management', in H Corsten, R Gössinger & T Spengler (Hrsg.), Handbuch Produktions- und Logistikmanagement in Wertschöpfungsnetzwerken, pp. 886–903.
Archambault, E, Beauchesne, OH, & Caruso, J 2011, 'Towards a Multilingual, Comprehensive and Open Scientific Journal Ontology', in *Proceedings of the 13th International Conference of the International Society for Scientometrics and Informetrics*, pp. 66-77.
Ball, R, Mittermaier, B & Tunger, D 2009, 'Creation of journal-based publication profiles of scientific institutions – a methodology for the interdisciplinary comparison of scientific research based on the J-factor', *Scientometrics*, vol. 81, pp. 381–92, doi: https://doi.org/10.1007/s11192-009-2120–5.
Bornmann, L, Mutz, R & Daniel, HD 2008, 'Are there better indices for evaluation purposes than the h index? A comparison of nine different variants of the h index using data from biomedicine', *Journal of the American Society for Information Science and Technology*, vol. 59, no. 5, pp. 830–37, doi: https://doi.org/10.1002/asi.20806.
Bornmann, L & Daniel, HD 2009, 'The state of h index research. Is the h index the ideal way to measure research performance?', *EMBO reports*, vol. 10, no. 1, pp. 2–6, doi: https://doi.org/10.1038/embor.2008.233.

Braun, T & Glänzel, W 1990, 'United Germany – The new scientific superpower', *Scientometrics*, vol. 19, no. 5–6, pp. 513–21.

Clermont, M 2016, 'Effectiveness and efficiency of research in Germany over time: An analysis of German business schools between 2001 and 2009', *Scientometrics*, vol. 108, no. 3, pp. 1347–81.

De Bruin, RE, Kint, A, Luwel, M & Moed, HF 1993, 'A study of research evaluation and planning: The University of Ghent', *Research Evaluation*, vol. 3, no. 1, pp. 25–41.

Glänzel, W, Schubert, A & Debackere, K 2011, 'A priori vs. a posteriori normalisation of citation indicators. The case of journal ranking', *Scientometrics*, vol. 87, no. 2, pp. 415–24, doi: https://doi.org/10.1007/s11192-011-0345-6.

Glänzel, W 2011, 'The application of characteristic scores and scales to the evaluation and ranking of scientific journals', *Journal of Information Science*, vol. 37, no. 1, pp. 40–48, doi: https://doi.org/10.1177/0165551510392316.

Hicks, D, Wouters, P & Rafols, I 2015, 'Bibliometrics: The Leiden Manifesto for research metrics', *Nature*, vol. 520, no. 7548, pp. 429–31, doi: https://doi.org/10.1038/520429a.

Hirsch, JE 2005, 'An index to quantify an individual's scientific research output', *Proceedings of the National Academy of Sciences of the United States of America*, vol. 102, no. 46, pp. 16569–72.

Hornbostel, S 1997, Wissenschaftsindikatoren – Bewertungen in der Wissenschaft, Westdeutscher Verlag, Opladen.

Krolak, J, Clermont, M & Tunger, D 2020, 'Collection of bibliometric indicators – consideration of established publication and citation indicators in terms of application, interpretation and consideration of advantages and disadvantages', http://hdl.handle.net/2128/24903 (July 15, 2020).

Kromrey, H 2006, Empirische Sozialforschung, 11, Auflage, Stuttgart.

Leydesdorff, L & Opthof, T 2010, 'Normalization at the field level: Fractional counting of citations', *Journal of Informetrics*, vol. 4, no. 4, pp. 644–46, doi: https://doi.org/10.1016/j.joi.2010.05.003.

Leydesdorff, L & Opthof, T 2011, 'Remaining problems with the "New Crown Indicator" (MNCS) of the CWTS', *Journal of Informetrics*, vol. 5, no. 1, doi: https://doi.org/10.1016/j.joi.2010.10.003.

Moed, HF, De Bruin, RE & van Leeuwen, TN 1995, 'New bibliometric tools for the assessment of national research performance: Database description, overview of indicators and first applications', *Scientometrics*, vol. 33, no. 3, pp. 381–422.

Moed, HF 2010, 'Measuring contextual citation impact of scientific journals', *Journal of Informetrics*, vol. 4, no. 3, pp. 265–77, doi: https://doi.org/10.1016/j.joi.2010.01.00.

Niederklapfer, T 2014, Der Hirsch-Index und seine Varianten, Masterthesis Universitätslehrgang Library and Information Studies MSc, Universität Innsbruck, http://diglib.uibk.ac.at/ulbtirolhs/download/pdf/216431?originalFilename=true (July 15, 2020).

Opthof, T & Leydesdorff, L 2010, 'Caveats for the journal and field normalizations in the CWTS ("Leiden") evaluations of research performance', *Journal of Informetrics*, vol. 4, no. 3, pp. 423–30, doi: https://doi.org/10.1016/j.joi.2010.02.003.

Schubert, A & Glänzel, W 1983, 'Statistical reliability of comparisons based on the citation impact of scientific publications', *Scientometrics*, vol. 5, no. 1, pp. 59–73, doi: https://doi.org/10.1007/BF02097178.

Schubert, A & Braun, T 1986, 'Relative indicators and relational charts for comparative assessment of publication output and citation impact', *Scientometrics*, vol. 9, no. 5–6, pp. 281–91, doi: https://doi.org/10.1007/BF02017249.

Small, H, Sweeney, E & Greenlee, E 1985, 'Clustering the science citation index using co-citations. II. Mapping science', *Scientometrics*, vol. 8, no. 5–6, pp. 321–40, doi: https://doi.org/10.1007/BF02018057.

Tappe, K 2014, 'Subjektivität in der Leistungsbeurteilung', Controlling, 26. Jg., pp. 509–12.

van Raan, AFJ, van Eck, NJ & Waltman, L 2010a, 'The new set of bibliometric indicators of CWTS. Book of Abstracts of the 11th International Conference on Science and Technology Indicators', pp. 291–93, Leiden, the Netherlands.

van Raan, AF, van Leeuwen, TN & Waltman, LJ 2010b, 'Rivals for the crown: Reply to Opthof and Leydesdorff', Journal of Informetrics, vol. 4, no. 3, pp. 431–35, doi: https://doi.org/10.1016/j.joi.2010.03.008.

Wagner-Döbler, R 2003, 'The system of research and development indicators: entry-points for information agents', in Bibliometric analysis in Science and Research – Applications, Benefits and Limitations, Forschungszentrum Jülich, Zentralbibliothek, p. 23.

Waltman, L & van Eck, NJ 2010a, 'A general source normalized approach to bibliometric research performance assessment', in Book of Abstracts of the 11th International Conference on Science and Technology Indicators, pp. 298–99, Leiden, the Netherlands.

Waltman, L & van Eck, NJ 2010b, 'The relation between eigenfactor, audience factor, and influence weight', Journal of the American Society for Information Science and Technology, vol. 61, no. 7, pp. 1476–86, doi: https://doi.org/10.1002/asi.21354.

Waltman, L, van Eck, NJ & van Raan, AF 2011a, 'Towards a new crown indicator: Some theoretical considerations', Journal of Informetrics, vol. 5, no. 1, pp. 37–47, doi: https://doi.org/10.1016/j.joi.2010.08.001.

Waltman, L, van Eck, NJ & van Raan, AF 2011b, 'Towards a new crown indicator: An empirical analysis', Scientometrics, vol. 87, no. 3, pp. 467–81, doi: https://doi.org/10.1007/s11192-011-0354-5.

Waltman, L, van Eck, NJ, van Leeuwen, TN & Visser, M 2013, 'Some modifications to the SNIP journal impact indicator', Journal of Informetrics, vol. 7, no. 2, pp. 272–85.

Waltman, L & van Eck, NJ 2013, 'A systematic empirical comparison of different approaches for normalizing citation impact indicators', paper presented at the Proceedings of SSI 2013–14th International Society of Scientometrics and Informetrics Conference.

Weber, M 1976, Wirtschaft und Gesellschaft, 1, Halbband, 5, Aufl., Tübingen.

Zitt, M, Ramanana-Rahary, S & Bassecoulard, E 2005, 'Relativity of citation performance and excellence measures: From cross-field to cross-scale effects of field-normalisation', Scientometrics, vol. 63, no. 2, pp. 373–401, doi: https://doi.org/10.1007/s11192-005-0218-y.

Zitt, M & Small, H 2008, 'Modifying the journal impact factor by fractional citation weighting: The audience factor', Journal of the American Society for Information Science and Technology, vol. 59, no. 11, pp. 1856–60, doi: https://doi.org/10.1002/asi.20880.

Zitt, M 2010, 'Citing-side normalization of journal impact: A robust variant of the Audience Factor', Journal of Informetrics, vol. 4, no. 3, pp. 392–406, doi: https://doi.org/10.1016/j.joi.2010.03.004.

3.3 The Journal Impact Factor: A Bibliometric Indicator with a Long Past

Dirk Tunger

Abstract: No bibliometric indicator in science is as well known, discussed, misused, hated and controversial as the Journal Impact Factor. Although it is polarized, it is still an important part of the development of bibliometric indicators (cf. Dong et al., 2005). This paper will briefly outline the development and importance of the Journal Impact Factor (JIF).

Keywords: Journal Impact Factor, JIF, bibliometric indicators, scientific impact, bibliometric methods, meaningful metrics.

The Journal Impact Factor as part of the Science Citation Index

It has always been the task of libraries to select single journals for their own stock out of all existing scientific journals. This is important not only because of the limitations of financial resources, but also because not all scientific journals have the same impact. Eugene Garfield, the developer of the Science Citation Index, already knew this and took advantage of it when he developed the Science Citation Index, which initially appeared in book form. Garfield stated that a citation is the reference in a scientific paper to a previous publication. It marks a flow of information and thus signals proximity in terms of content. Eugene Garfield's idea for a citation index to improve the information retrieval of scientific publications was based on this approach. A citation index "is an ordered list of cited articles each of which is accompanied by a list of citing articles" (Garfield, 1984a, p. 528). In a citation index not only are the pure bibliographic data listed, but also the footnotes referenced in an article. This is the basis for proving the connections between the individual scientific articles: "Any source citation may subsequently become a reference citation" (Garfield, 1984a, p. 528). The aim is therefore, "to find out the authors and documents, that have cited the given author or document" (Diodato, 1994, p. 35). When looking through the references in papers that are interesting for a particular research question, one can only find older publications on the same topic. However, when looking in a citation Index, one can find more recent publications on the same topic.

The Science Citation Index is an example of such an index. When Eugene Garfield developed the Science Citation Index, an online database was not yet conceivable. The original index was published in book form and consisted of different com-

---

Dirk Tunger, TH Köln, Faculty of Information Science and Communication Studies, Institute of Information Management & Forschungszentrum Jülich GmbH, Project Management Jülich, Center of Excellence "Analyses, Studies, Strategy", d.tunger@fz-juelich.de

ponents (Garfield, 1984b, pp. 546–550): on the one hand, it was possible to find an essay under the name of each author (Source Index), however, the citations were not listed in this part. In addition, papers could be found under keywords in the Permuterm Subject Index. The main component was the actual Citation Index, the part in which the publications (from all previous calendar years) cited by other scientists in the year under review were listed under the name of the first author, indicating the cited publication. The Journal Impact Factor, also referred to as impact factor in this publication, was also part of the Science Citation Index and part of a book that listed and described the covered sources.

In the meantime the Science Citation Index has become a database. However, many components can be traced back to the book form, including the impact factor. Due to its reputation and high profile, the Science Citation Index is currently one of the most frequently used sources for bibliometric evaluations. Comparisons with Scopus have led to a high rate of agreement in the results (Archambault et al., 2009; Ball and Tunger, 2006), although the number of covered journals in the Science Citation Index is higher. This confirms one of Garfield's basic assumptions that so-called core journals exist: a relatively small number of journals contain the majority of the literature published on a topic. This makes it possible to look at only a part of scientific literature and still cover the relevant publications. But this also means that not every journal has the same impact.

The influence of a journal is usually measured by the impact factor. The impact factor is a special form of a citation rate, with which citations per publication are measured. JIF thus provides information on how often an article of a journal is cited on average. It is an indicator that only works at journal level and not on the level of individual papers. This means that it is not possible with the JIF to obtain, through cumulation of JIF or something similar, an indicator that allows a valid statement about the real impact of single papers or individuals. This is a description of the principle and does not yet include any statement about its usefulness.

Calculation of the Impact Factor

The exact calculation of the impact factor is as follows:

The impact factor is an indicator for the number of articles published by a journal in two consecutive years (publication window) and the number of citations to these articles in the following year (citation window).

Or as a formula (fig. 1).

The example in Figure 1 shows the calculation of the impact factor of *Nature:* the citations in 2018 for the publications from 2016 and 2017 result in an impact factor of 43.070, which is due to the fact that the 880 publications from 2016 and the 837 publications from 2017 receive 41,183 citations (publications in 2016) and 32,769 citations (publications in 2017) in 2018. By ISI definition, only research articles, proceedings papers and reviews are "citable" items. Editorials, letters, news items, and meeting

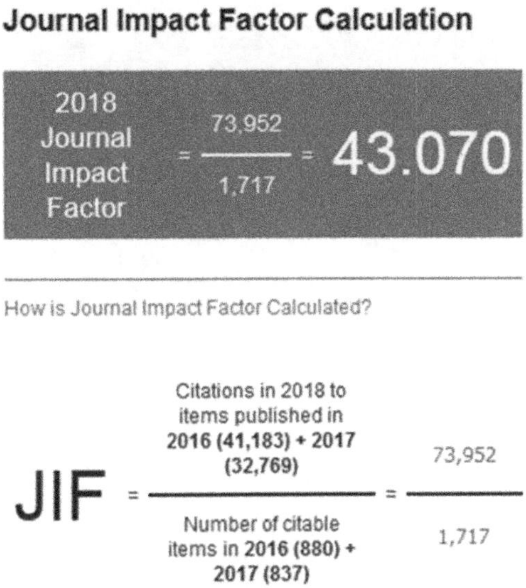

Journal Impact Factor Calculation

$$\text{2018 Journal Impact Factor} = \frac{73{,}952}{1{,}717} = 43.070$$

How is Journal Impact Factor Calculated?

$$\text{JIF} = \frac{\text{Citations in 2018 to items published in 2016 (41,183) + 2017 (32,769)}}{\text{Number of citable items in 2016 (880) + 2017 (837)}} = \frac{73{,}952}{1{,}717}$$

Figure 1: Example for calculating the impact factor of *Nature*.

abstracts are "non-citable items" for the purpose of calculating the denominator. All items, however, may be counted in the numerator during the calculation. An impact factor of 43.070 now means that an "average publication" with publication year 2016 or 2017 was cited 43 times on average in 2018. However, it should be noted that the distribution is skewed: there are *Nature* Papers that are still uncited after a few years and there are those that are cited much more than the average. Therefore, conclusions with the help of the impact factor can only be drawn in relation to the entire journal and not to the individual paper.

Publishers try to attract authors with high impact factors, which leads to a problem: publishers try to influence the impact factor. An example is seen as in 2016 we can find 2,807 publications in Web of Science for *Nature*:

# 1	2,807	so-"nature" and py=2016
		Indexes=SCI EXPANDED, SSCI, A&HCI, CPCI-S, CPCI-SSH, BKCI-S, BKCI-SSH, ESCI, CCR-EXPANDED, IC Timespan=All years

Figure 2: Search query with result for *Nature* in the Web of Science.

How can this be, when in Figure 1 for the calculation of the impact factor only 880 papers from 2016 were included in the calculation? This is due to the distribution of the papers across document types:

Select	Field: Document Types	Record Count	% of 2,807	Bar Chart
☐	EDITORIAL MATERIAL	962	34.271 %	▬▬▬
☐	ARTICLE	845	30.103 %	▬▬▬
☐	NEWS ITEM	388	13.823 %	▬
☐	LETTER	290	10.331 %	▬
☐	CORRECTION	159	5.664 %	▪
☐	BOOK REVIEW	102	3.634 %	▪
☐	REVIEW	36	1.283 %	ı
☐	BIOGRAPHICAL ITEM	22	0.784 %	ı
☐	RETRACTION	3	0.107 %	ı

Figure 3: Distribution of *Nature* papers from 2016 by document type.

Only 30 % of the *Nature* publications from 2016 are of the document type "Article". More than 60 % are "Editorial Material", "News Item", "Letter" or "Correction" and some other type. This is a completely atypical distribution. A typical distribution can be seen in Figure 4, also publication year 2016, for the journal *Physical Review Letters*:

# 1	2,478	so="physical review letters" and py=2016
		Indexes=SCI-EXPANDED, SSCI, A&HCI, CPCI-S, CPCI-SSH, BKCI-S, BKCI-SSH, ESCI, CCR-EXPANDED, IC Timespan=All years

Figure 4: Search query with result for *Physical Review Letters* in the Web of Science.

In *Physical Review Letters* in 2016 there are about the same number of papers as in *Nature*. However, the distribution in *Physical Review Letters* is completely different than in *Nature*:

Select	Field: Document Types	Record Count	% of 2,478	Bar Chart
☐	ARTICLE	2.343	94.552 %	▬▬▬▬
☐	CORRECTION	84	3.390 %	▪
☐	EDITORIAL MATERIAL	49	1.977 %	ı
☐	LETTER	2	0.081 %	ı

Figure 5: Distribution of *Physical Review Letters* from 2016 by document type.

Physical Review Letters shows a usual distribution of publications by document type: about 95 % of the publications are of the document type "Article", the rest being almost negligible.

What advantage does *Nature* have in calculating the impact factor from the atypical distribution of document types? The document types are divided into "Citable" and "Non-citable" items, with only the marked document types "Article" and "Review" used by the publications in Figure 3 for the calculation of the denominator.

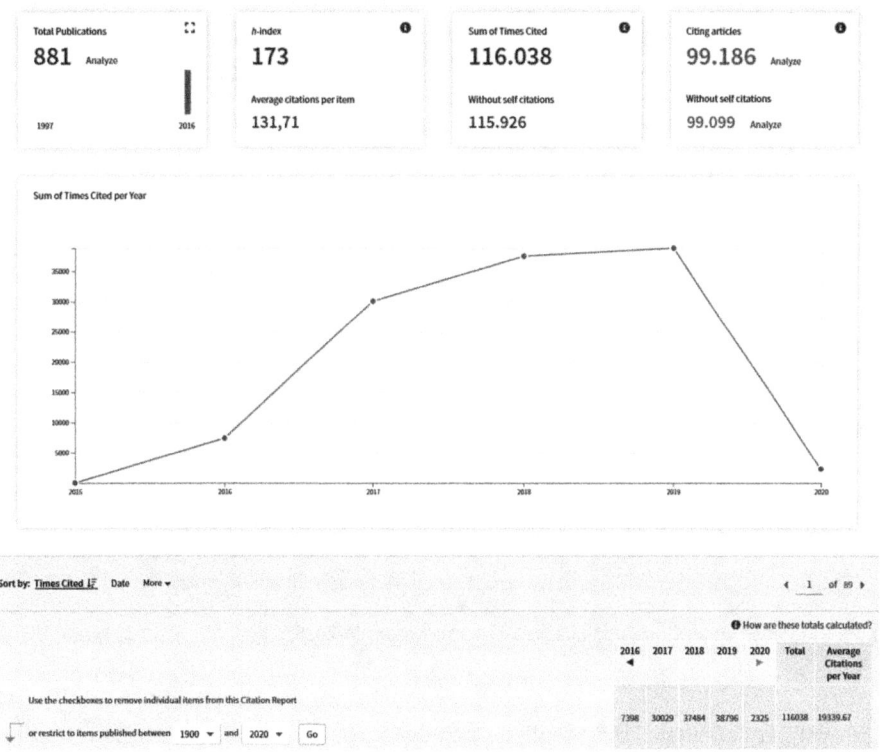

Figure 6: Citation Report for "citable" items in *Nature* in 2016.

If you now try to calculate the impact factor yourself, you will get 881 citable items for *Nature* in 2016, which is almost the same value as in the Journal Citation Report. These 881 documents lead to 37,484 citations in 2018. This is still almost 4,000 citations less than the number of citations given in the calculation of the impact factor in the Journal Citation Report. The rest of the citations come from the "non-citable" items, which is actually a contradiction in terms (fig.7).

The "non-citable" items, over 1,900 *Nature* publications from 2016, lead to 3751 citations in 2018. These are the missing citations in order to achieve the citation numbers on which the calculation of the impact factor is based. If you look at the Citation Report for all *Nature* publications in 2016, you can see how the citation numbers add up: all *Nature* publications from 2016 together achieve 41,235 citations. This corresponds to the value given in the Journal Citation Report for calculating the impact factor. Since almost 4,000 citations are not divided by 2,807 publications but only

Figure 7: Citation Report for "non-citable" items in *Nature* in 2016.

by the 881 citable items, this results in an advantage for *Nature* in the amount of the impact factor of about 3 citations per publication, i.e. a value that is three higher for just one of the two publication years (fig. 8).

The reason why one deals with "citable" and "non-citable" items goes back to the past, when the computing capacities were significantly lower than today and one wanted to reduce the data processing time by reducing the number of publications. At the same time, however, for technical reasons, the citations of the "non-citable" items could not be removed. Nowadays, the calculation would have to be adjusted to prevent publishers from gaining an advantage for their journals.

Further Criticism of the Impact Factor

Other points of criticism of the impact factor are:
- Manipulable by publishers
  See the previous example for influencing the impact factor based on the document types used.

3.3 The Journal Impact Factor: A Bibliometric Indicator with a Long Past — 165

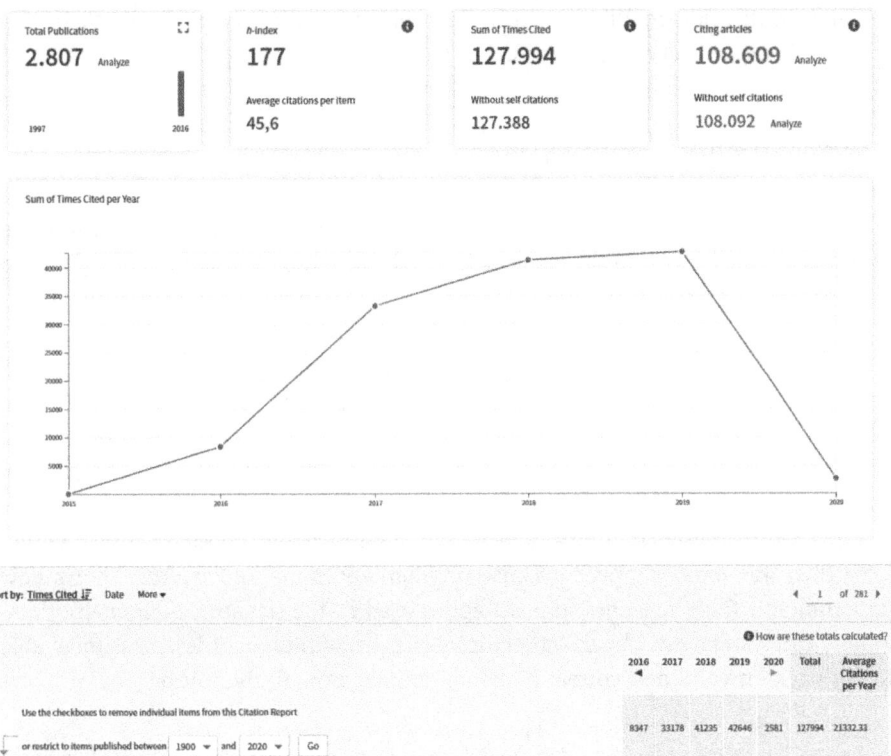

Figure 8: Citation Report for all *Nature* items in 2016.

- Journal measure
  The impact factor is a pure journal measure. It has no significance on the level of individual publications.
- Discipline dependent
  Like any form of citation rate, the impact factor is discipline-dependent. This means that comparisons across disciplines are not possible.
- Publication window versus citation window
  Publication windows and citation windows are of different sizes. This leads to distortions. In contrast to common citation windows in bibliometric analyses, both the publication and the citation window of the impact factor are particularly short. This means that only a low number of publications or citations are considered in the impact factor.
- Apparent accuracy
  The impact factor with its three digits after the comma suggests an accuracy that it cannot maintain (e.g. due to errors in the database, which occur during the processing of the data). To take this into account, no indicator should pretend an accuracy that does not exist in reality, as stated in the Leiden Manifesto (cf. e.g. Tunger 'On the Need for Accessability, Standardization, Regulation

and Verification in Bibliometrics: The Leiden Manifesto and Beyond', in this handbook or Hicks et al., 2015).

The Cumulative Impact Factor

The JIF is only meaningful in terms of the impact on a particular journal. It is not possible to calculate scientific impact for individual articles or on any aggregated level for authors or institutions. Thus, what is called cumulative impact factor and is often used in medicine is scientific nonsense.

Impact factors cannot be cumulated with each other and the impact of individual scientists cannot be calculated with the help of impact factors. The scientific bibliometric community has always tried to eliminate this misuse of the impact factor from science management. Unfortunately, this has not worked so far. Medicine in particular tends to use this erroneous use again and again. If the cumulative impact factor is wrongly used in a form that is forbidden in science because it has no validity, then this often happens because no alternatives are known. This shows how important it is that the technical possibilities used by the scientific bibliometric community can also be used by the community of users of bibliometrics, so as to be able to fall back on valid and correct bibliometric indicators in the future.

Use and Current Significance of the Impact Factor

The impact factor can be used to inform about journal impact. Thus, it can be used to answer questions such as:
- which journals have the greatest impact in a topic area
- whether a library has licensed the journals with the greatest impact for its user group
- how the journal impact of individual journals has changed over time
- whether a community publishes in the high-impact journals of the subject or in its low-impact journals

Outlook: Does the Impact Factor still have any Significance Today?

The impact factor was one of the first indicators that was available systematically and comprehensively in science. At the time of its introduction by Eugene Garfield, it was the first time that many scientific core journals, covered by the Science Citation Index, could be compared in terms of their impact. This was a new possibility to determine the significance of journals according to their impact, to select one's publication medium according to this, to subscribe to journals etc. Even if the impact factor is heavily criticized, erroneous, susceptible to manipulation, it remains an institution in science and is still used today by publishers. Its use is perhaps also an indication that there is a lack of clear alternatives in science management. Here it should be noted that the bibliometric community is divided into two groups: one part of the community has access to at least one local installation of one of the three major multidisciplinary databases, Web of Science, Scopus or Dimensions (cf. Tunger, 'On the Need for Accessability, Standardization, Regulation and Verification in Bibliometrics: The Leiden Manifesto and Beyond', in this handbook). For the group that has access to a local installation of a citation index there are completely different possibilities in the calculation of indicators and alternatives to the impact factor than for the group that depends on the web interface of the databases.

This does not mean that there are no alternatives. One is the Scimago Journal Rank (SCImago, 2020), developed by the Scimago research group in Spain and described as follows: "A new size-independent indicator of scientific journal prestige, the SJR2 indicator, is proposed. This indicator takes into account not only the prestige of the citing scientific journal but also its closeness to the cited journal using the cosine of the angle between the vectors of the two journals' cocitation profiles. To eliminate the size effect, the accumulated prestige is divided by the fraction of the journal's citable documents, thus eliminating the decreasing tendency of this type of indicator and giving meaning to the scores" (Guerrero-Bote and Moya-Anegón, 2012). The Scimago Journal Rank is publicly available on the website (SCImago, 2020) and as presented by Guerrero-Bote and Moya-Anegón (2012), it correlates with the JIF. In contrast to the JIF, the Scimago Journal Rank weights the different journals from which the citations come and does not evaluate all citations equally. It is comparable with the Google page rank. The impact factor will certainly continue to be used in science, hopefully with the understanding that journal impact is multidimensional (Haustein, 2012). However, this also shows how important it is to deal responsibly with metrics. It is very difficult to remove numbers or metrics from use once they have spread.

References

Archambault, E, Campbell, D, Gingras, Y & Larivière, V 2009, 'Comparing of science bibliometric statistics obtained from the web and Scopus', *Journal of the American Society for Information Science and Technology*, vol. 60, no. 7, pp. 1320–26.

Ball, R & Tunger, D 2006, 'Science indicators revisited – Science Citation Index versus SCOPUS: A bibliometric comparison of both citation databases', *Information Services and Use*, vol. 26, no. 4, pp. 293–301.

Diodato, V 1994, *Dictionary of Bibliometrics*, Harworth Press, New York.

Dong, P, Loh, M & Mondry, A 2005, 'The "impact factor" revisited', *Biomed Digit Libr*, vol. 2, no. 7, https://doi.org/10.1186/1742-5581-2-7.

Haustein, S 2012, *Multidimensional Journal Evaluation. Analyzing Scientific Periodicals Beyond the Impact Factor*, de Gruyter Saur, Berlin, Boston.

Hicks, D, Wouters, P, Waltman, L, de Rijcke, S & Rafols, I 2015, 'Bibliometrics: The Leiden Manifesto for research metrics', *Nature*, vol. 520, pp. 429–431, doi: https://doi.org/10.1038/520429a (last accessed 10.2.2020).

Garfield, E 1984a, 'Science Citation Index – A New Dimension in Indexing', *Essays of an Information Scientist*, vol. 7, pp. 525–35.

Garfield, E 1984b, 'Permuterm Subject Index: An autobiographical review', *Essays of an Information Scientist*, vol. 7, pp. 546–50.

Guerrero-Bote, VP & Moya-Anegón, F 2012, 'A further step forward in measuring journals' scientific prestige: The SJR2 indicator', *Journal of Informetrics*, vol. 6, no. 4, pp. 674–88.

SCImago 2020, https://www.scimagojr.com (July 15, 2020).

3.4 The *h*-index

Grischa Fraumann and Rüdiger Mutz

Abstract: The *h*-index is a mainstream bibliometric indicator, since it is widely used in academia, research management and research policy. While its advantages have been highlighted, such as its simple calculation, it has also received widespread criticism. The criticism is mainly based on the negative effects it may have on scholars, when the index is used to describe the quality of a scholar. The "h" means "highly-cited" and "high achievement", and should not be confused with the last name of its inventor, Hirsch. Put simply, the *h*-index combines a measure of quantity and impact in a single indicator. Several initiatives try to provide alternatives to the *h*-index to counter some of its shortcomings.

Keywords: *h*-index, metrics, author-level metrics, indicators, productivity, publications, citation impact.

Introduction

The *h*-index was developed by Jorge Hirsch, a physicist at the University of California at San Diego, who published the concept in the *Proceedings of the National Academy of Sciences of the USA* (Hirsch, 2005). The *h*-index was defined by Hirsch as follows: "A scientist has index h if h of his or her N_p papers have at least h citations each and the other $(N_p - h)$ papers have $\leq h$ citations each." (Hirsch, 2005) The "h" means "highly-cited" and "high achievement", and should not be confused with the last name of its inventor (Hirsch and Buela-Casal, 2014; Schubert and Schubert, 2019). Put simply, the *h*-index "combines a measure of quantity and impact in a single indicator" (Costas and Bordons, 2007).

While the *h*-index was proposed in 2005 and is considered a classical bibliometric indicator, there is still an ongoing debate on its value in bibliometrics and in the scholarly community in general. Due to its popularity, it has even been called a mainstream bibliometric indicator (Costas and Franssen, 2018). It is one of the most well-known indicators, but it has received negative and positive judgements alike.

The development of indicators was part of a shift from higher level entities (e.g., countries, institutions, journals) towards the bibliometrics of individual researchers

---

Grischa Fraumann, Research Assistant at the TIB Leibniz Information Centre for Science and Technology in the R&D Department, and PhD Fellow at the University of Copenhagen in the Department of Communication. He is also a Research Affiliate at the "CiMetrias: Research Group on Science and Technology Metrics" at the University of São Paulo (USP), grischa.fraumann@tib.eu

Rüdiger Mutz, Senior Researcher at Center for Higher Education and Science Studies (CHESS), University of Zurich, ruediger.mutz@uzh.ch

(Costas, van Leeuwen, and Bordons, 2010; Hicks et al., 2015). This shift was related to how single researchers' research outputs should be measured via quantitative indicators. How analyses should be conducted on an individual level was and still remains an open question in bibliometrics (Bornmann and Marx, 2014). The relatively simple *h*-index calculation has contributed to its widespread use (Sugimoto and Larivière, 2018), and it was promoted in several journals and news outlets in the beginning (Ball, 2005). Hirsch's original work from 2005, for example, has been cited 4,530 times according to the bibliographic databases *Scopus* (accessed October 25, 2019), 3,999 times according to *Web of Science* (accessed October 25, 2019) and 5,240 times according to *The Lens* (accessed September 23, 2019). Due to the high number of publications on the *h*-index (Waltman, 2016), this book chapter focuses on some central topics of *h*-index research and refers mostly to comprehensive literature reviews (Costas and Bordons, 2007).

h-index History

The quantitative distribution of scholarly works on the h-index over a period of 13 years may provide an insight into its historical development. Therefore, a bibliometric analysis was conducted based on the bibliographic database *The Lens* (Jefferson et al., 2018) to query all works for "*h*-index" in the title, abstract, keyword or field of study. All publications from January 1, 2005, the year of Hirsch's original h-index publication, to December 31, 2018 were retrieved (accessed September 22, 2019).

The total number of publications was 3,817, and the number increased more or less steadily each year until it dropped slightly in 2009 and once again in 2013 (Figure 1). The numbers from 2014 until 2018 are year by year almost the same, about 400 documents per year.

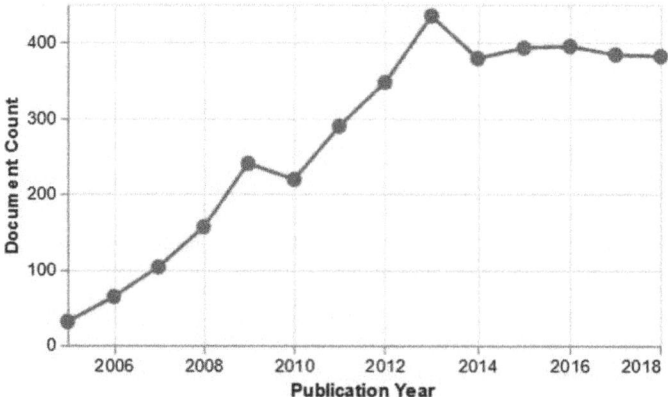

Figure 1: Scholarly works over time on the *h*-index (source: *The Lens*).

The *h*-index has been applied in several academic disciplines, such as physics, biomedicine, information science and business studies (Costas and Bordons, 2007). However, a comparison between disciplines by using the *h*-index is not recommended (Hirsch, 2005; van Leeuwen, 2008) because of different citation practices, among others. There are attempts to put the *h*-index in a common scale in order to make inter-field comparisons possible (Iglesias and Pecharromán, 2007).

Due to the ever increasing number of online sources that provide bibliometric data, the possibility to calculate and/or display the *h*-index has also changed dramatically (Costas and Franssen, 2018; Teixeira da Silva and Dobránszki, 2018). For example, the *h*-index is prominently placed on *Google Scholar* profiles (Costas and Wouters, 2012; Sugimoto and Larivière, 2018) and also in the *Web of Science* and *Scopus* (Leydesdorff, Bornmann, and Opthof, 2019).

The scope of application of the *h*-index has been extended, for instance, to journals (e.g., Braun, Glänzel, and Schubert, 2006) and to research groups (e.g., van Raan, 2006). Several variants of the *h*-index have been developed to address specific limitations of the *h*-index (see section 4), for example, the *g*-index as the most prominent one (Egghe, 2006).

h-index Concept

In order to enhance the understanding of the basic *h*-index concept, a graphical derivation of the index could be helpful (Alonso et al., 2009). In Figure 2 the so-called rank frequency distribution for a researcher is shown. His or her publications are sorted in descending order according to their citations. The publication with the highest citation is ranked first, then the publication with the second highest citation and so on. The *h*-index corresponds to intersection between the rank-frequency distribution and the 45° degree line, where the number of papers is equal to the number of publications. For the specific researcher the *h*-index amounts to 22. The *h*-core comprises 22 publications, which contribute to the *h*-index and are cited at least 22 times. Neither the number of citations the highly cited papers receive nor the papers outside the *h*-core are of importance.

Several advantages of the *h*-index were discussed in the literature (Alonso et al., 2009; Bornmann and Daniel, 2005; Bornmann and Daniel, 2007; Costas and Bordons, 2007). It is a robust indicator in the sense that it is rather insensitive to lowly cited papers. It is an objective indicator and might play a certain role together with other indicators and expert judgements during funding or promotion decisions. It claims to perform better than any single indicator. Hirsch himself postulated that the *h*-index has a predictive capacity for researchers' careers to a greater extent than conventional citation indicators (Alonso et al., 2009; Hirsch, 2007). Bornmann and Daniel (2005), for instance, found that the *h*-index for successful applicants for post-doctoral biomedicine fellowships was significantly higher than for non-successful applicants.

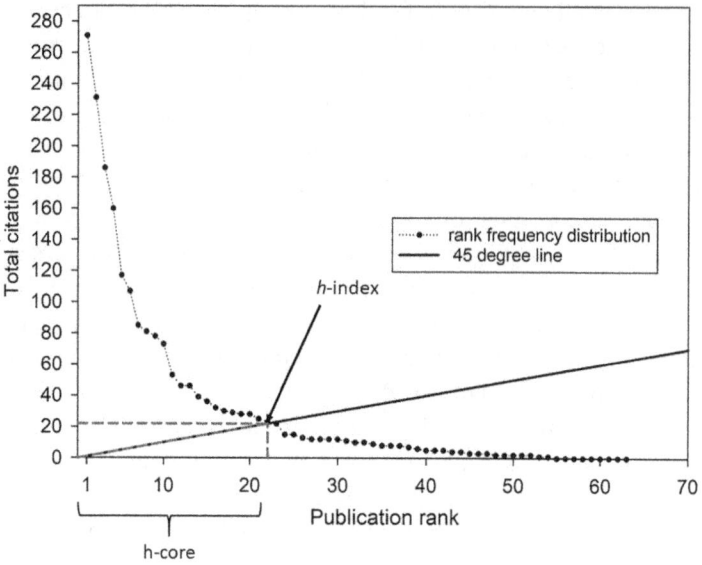

Figure 2: Graphical representation of the *h*-index.

h-index Problems and Alternatives

The *h*-index is widely used by researchers, for example in the medical sciences (Cronin and Sugimoto, 2014), but it has also been widely criticised (Bornmann, Mutz, and Daniel, 2010; Hauschke, 2019; Waltman and van Eck, 2012). The *h*-index's widespread availability online has the potential for problematic usage in research evaluation, which should never rely on a single indicator (Costas and Bordons, 2007). Conversely, this simplicity and objectivity is sometimes also seen as an advantage of the *h*-index (Alonso et al., 2009). However, the indicator could also lead to questionable self-citation practices carried out to increase the *h*-index (Costas and Bordons, 2007). For example, the *h*-index may be problematic due to the Matthew effect, whereby a high-profile researcher may attract more and more citations based on her or his displayed *h*-index (Alonso et al., 2009).

Costas and Bordons pointed out the problem of size dependency of the *h*-index. Imagine the following scenario:

> [S]cientist "A" with 10 documents cited 10 times each would have an h-index of 10; whereas scientist "B", with 5 documents which were cited 200 times each, would only achieve an h-index of 5. Scientist "B" publishes fewer documents, but their impact is much higher than the other's (i.e., a higher citation per document rate). Scientist "A" publishes many more documents, albeit with a lower impact. Despite this, according to the h-index, scientist A would be regarded as much more successful than "B" (Costas and Bordons, 2007).

The example above illustrates that researchers with a higher h-index might be those who have a high quantity of publications with average citations compared to researchers that publish less but have a few highly-cited publications (Costas and Franssen, 2018).

The h-index is also influenced by the length of a researcher's career or lifetime citedness (Alonso et al., 2009; Ball, 2017; Bornmann and Marx, 2011; Costas and Bordons, 2007; Hicks et al., 2015). It combines quantity as well as impact in one indicator or single number (Hirsch, 2005). Colloquially, this concept might also be called an all-in-one metric (Bornmann and Marx, 2011), while its value cannot decrease because it relies on the number of publications and citations (Gingras, 2016). Obviously, this focus on lifetime citedness may be disadvantageous to early career researchers. The merger of two concepts in one indicator has also been criticised (Sugimoto and Larivière, 2018), even if Hirsch's original proposal was to simplify "to [a] great extent the characterization of researchers' scientific output" (Alonso et al., 2009). Furthermore, the h-index might be manipulated, for example in *Google Scholar* (Costas and Wouters, 2012; Gingras, 2016). Additionally, it does not distinguish between negative or positive citations (Alonso et al., 2009), although such a distinction is difficult to achieve as it requires natural language processing (Teufel, Siddharthan, and Tidhar, 2006). A researcher could have a different h-index depending on the bibliographic database (Bar-Ilan, 2008; Hicks et al., 2015) and academic disciplines (Hicks et al., 2015). Lists of researchers that display their h-index[1] may be insightful, but the use of the h-index in hiring and promotion decisions might be problematic (Hicks et al., 2015). According to the Leiden Manifesto (Hicks et al., 2015, Principle 7), the San Francsico Declaration on Research Assessment (DORA) (Cagan, 2013, Principle 3), and the Hong Kong Principles (Moher et al., 2020, Principle 1), research assessment of individual researcher should consider a broad range of bibliometric measures, not only a single indicator, such as the h-index. In general, quantitative research assessment should support not replace qualitative judgements of experts (e. g., peer review) (Hicks et al., 2015).

Alternative types of indicators have been studied, such as the g-index (Costas and Bordons, 2008; Egghe, 2006), the hg-index, the A-index, and the m-index (Alonso et al., 2009). Meta-analyses have been carried out to study correlations between the h-index and its variants (Bornmann et al., 2011), such as the g-index. Strikingly, a 2011 meta-analysis concluded that 35 out of 37 variants seemed to duplicate the h-index, except for the modified impact index (*MII*) and m-index (Bornmann et al., 2011). This means that most variants are highly correlated with the h-index (Bornmann and Mutz et al., 2009). Bornmann et al. also categorised the variants into two groups, namely the "impact of the productive core" and the "quantity of the productive core". The productive core refers to the most received citations (Bornmann, Mutz, and Daniel, 2008). Studies have also concluded that the h-index and its var-

---

1 https://www.webometrics.info/en/hlargerthan100 (July 15, 2020).

iants are not needed compared to standard bibliometric measures, such as number of publications and total citation counts (Bornmann, Mutz, and Daniel, 2009). Due to these findings, some scholars suggested not developing new variants of the h-index any longer (Bornmann and Marx et al., 2009) but rather to complement or enrich the h-index with additional information (Bornmann, Mutz, and Daniel, 2010). Variants of the h-index, such as the ones mentioned above, are also regarded as superficial enhancements (Waltman, 2016). From a bibliometric perspective, the h-index seems to have no analytical value as such (Leydesdorff, Bornmann, and Opthof, 2019), despite its frequent use in academia, research management and policy. Initiatives are underway to employ indicators by involving the scholarly community (Hauschke, Cartellieri, and Heller, 2018), to overcome the evaluation gap between what is measured by indicators and what is valued by researchers (Heuritsch, 2018; Wouters, 2017).

Conclusions

This article has provided an overview of the h-index, described its applications, reviewed several studies that scrutinise the h-index and discussed its advantages and disadvantages. Developed by Hirsch in 2005 as an "index to quantify an individual's scientific output" (Hirsch, 2005), the h-index is still being debated almost 15 years later. A vast amount of literature on the h-index is available. As such, it is perhaps one of the most studied topics in bibliometrics and scientometrics, and it has had an influence on the scholarly community as a whole and even beyond on research management and policy. Several variants of the h-index have been developed over the years, but a significant improvement would be to provide additional information and indicators and explain the h-index context. The h-index certainly also has some advantages, such as its simple calculation and wide availability. A problem that remains is its isolated use in research evaluation, potential comparisons among academic disciplines and the fact that it is taken by some at face value to judge the quality of a researcher's work. Finally, the display of the h-index in bibliographic databases, such as *Google Scholar*, codifies this indicator (Sugimoto and Larivière, 2018) and normalises its perception. The future of the h-index is still being debated, but the negative assessments seem to be in the majority.

References

Alonso, S, Cabrerizo, FJ, Herrera-Viedma, E & Herrera, F 2009, 'h-Index: A Review Focused in Its Variants, Computation and Standardization for Different Scientific Fields', *Journal of Informetrics*, vol. 3, no. 4, pp. 273–89, https://doi.org/10.1016/j.joi.2009.04.001.
Ball, P 2005, 'Index Aims for Fair Ranking of Scientists', *Nature*, vol. 436, no. 7053, p. 900, https://doi.org/10.1038/436900a.
Ball, R 2017, *An Introduction to Bibliometrics: New Development and Trends*, Elsevier Science.

Bar-Ilan, J 2008, 'Which h-index? – A Comparison of WoS, Scopus and Google Scholar', *Scientometrics*, vol. 74, no. 2, pp. 257–71, https://doi.org/10.1007/s11192–008–0216-y.

Bornmann, L & Daniel, H-D 2005, 'Does the h-index for Ranking of Scientists Really Work?', *Scientometrics*, vol. 65, no. 3, pp. 391–92, https://doi.org/10.1007/s11192-005-0281–4.

Bornmann, L & Daniel, H-D 2007, 'What Do We Know About the h-index?', *Journal of the American Society for Information Science and Technology*, vol. 58, no. 9, pp. 1381–85, https://doi.org/10.1002/asi.20609.

Bornmann, L & Marx, W 2011, 'The h-index as a Research Performance Indicator', *European Science Editing*, vol. 37, no. 3, pp. 77–80.

Bornmann, L & Marx, W 2014, 'How to Evaluate Individual Researchers Working in the Natural and Life Sciences Meaningfully? A Proposal of Methods Based on Percentiles of Citations', *Scientometrics*, vol. 98, no. 1, pp. 487–509, https://doi.org/10.1007/s11192–013–1161-y.

Bornmann, L, Marx, M, Schier, H, Rahm, E, Thor, A & Daniel, H-D 2009, 'Convergent Validity of Bibliometric Google Scholar Data in the Field of Chemistry – Citation Counts for Papers That Were Accepted by Angewandte Chemie International Edition or Rejected but Published Elsewhere, Using Google Scholar, Science Citation Index, Scopus, and Chemical Abstracts', *Journal of Informetrics*, vol. 3, no. 1, pp. 27–35, https://doi.org/10.1016/j.joi.2008.11.001.

Bornmann, L, Mutz, R & Daniel, H-D 2008, 'Are There Better Indices for Evaluation Purposes Than the h-index? A Comparison of Nine Different Variants of The h-index Using Data from Biomedicine', *Journal of the American Society for Information Science and Technology*, vol. 59, no. 5, pp. 830–37, https://doi.org/10.1002/asi.20806.

Bornmann, L, Mutz, R & Daniel, H-D 2009, 'Do We Need the h-index and Its Variants in Addition to Standard Bibliometric Measures?', *Journal of the American Society for Information Science and Technology*, vol. 60, no. 6, pp. 1286–89, https://doi.org/10.1002/asi.21016.

Bornmann, L, Mutz, R & Daniel, H-D 2010, 'The h-index Research Output Measurement: Two Approaches to Enhance Its Accuracy', *Journal of Informetrics*, vol. 4, no. 3, pp. 407–14, accessed September 23, 2019, https://doi.org/10.1016/j.joi.2010.03.005.

Bornmann, L, Mutz, R, Daniel, H-D, Wallon, G & Ledin, A 2009, 'Are There Really Two Types of h-index Variants? A Validation Study by Using Molecular Life Sciences Data', *Research Evaluation*, vol. 18, no. 3, pp. 185–90, https://doi.org/10.3152/095820209X466883.

Bornmann, L, Mutz, R, Hug, SE & Daniel, H-D 2011, 'A Multilevel Meta-Analysis of Studies Reporting Correlations Between the h-index and 37 Different h-index Variants', *Journal of Informetrics*, vol. 5, no. 3, pp. 346–59, https://doi.org/10.1016/j.joi.2011.01.006.

Braun, T, Glänzel, W & Schubert, A 2006, 'A Hirsch-Type Index for Journals', *Scientometrics*, vol. 69, no. 1, pp. 169–73, https://doi.org/10.1007/s11192-006-0147–4.

Cagan, R 2013, 'The San Francisco Declaration on Research Assessment', *Disease models & mechanisms*, vol. 6, no. 4, pp. 869–70, https://doi.org/10.1242/dmm.012955.

Costas, R & Bordons, M 2007, 'The h-index: Advantages, Limitations and Its Relation with Other Bibliometric Indicators at the Micro Level', *Journal of Informetrics*, vol. 1, no. 3, pp. 193–203, https://doi.org/10.1016/j.joi.2007.02.001.

Costas, R & Bordons, M 2008, 'Is g-index Better Than h-index? An Exploratory Study at the Individual Level', *Scientometrics*, vol. 77, no. 2, pp. 267–88, https://doi.org/10.1007/s11192-007-1997–0.

Costas, R & Franssen, T 2018, 'Reflections Around 'the Cautionary Use' of the h-index: Response to Teixeira Da Silva and Dobránszki', *Scientometrics*, vol. 115, no. 2, pp. 1125–30, https://doi.org/10.1007/s11192-018-2683–0.

Costas, R, van Leeuwen, TN & Bordons, M 2010, 'A Bibliometric Classificatory Approach for the Study and Assessment of Research Performance at the Individual Level: The Effects of Age on Productivity and Impact', *Journal of the American Society for Information Science and Technology*, vol. 46, no. 2, https://doi.org/10.1002/asi.21348.

Costas, R & Wouters, P 2012, 'Users, Narcissism and Control – Tracking the Impact of Scholarly Publications in the 21st Century', SURFfoundation, Utrecht, http://research-acumen.eu/wp-content/uploads/Users-narcissism-and-control.pdf (July 15, 2020).

Cronin, B & Sugimoto, CR 2014, *Beyond Bibliometrics: Harnessing Multidimensional Indicators of Scholarly Impact*, The MIT Press.

Egghe, L 2006, 'Theory and Practise of the g-index, *Scientometrics*, vol. 69, no. 1, pp. 131–52, https://doi.org/10.1007/s11192-006-0144-7.

Gingras, Y 2016, *Bibliometrics and Research Evaluation: Uses and Abuses*, History and foundations of information science, The MIT Press, Cambridge, Massachusetts.

Hauschke, C 2019, 'Problematische Aspekte bibliometrie-basierter Forschungsevaluierung', *Informationspraxis*, bd. 5, nr. 1, https://doi.org/10.11588/ip.2019.1.49609.

Hauschke, C, Cartellieri, S & Heller, L 2018, 'Reference Implementation for Open Scientometric Indicators (ROSI)', *Research Ideas and Outcomes*, vol. 4, p. 59, https://doi.org/10.3897/rio.4.e31656.

Heuritsch, J (January 22) 2018, 'Insights into the Effects of Indicators on Knowledge Production in Astronomy', http://arxiv.org/pdf/1801.08033v1 (July 15, 2020).

Hicks, D, Wouters, P, Waltman, L, de Rijcke, S & Ràfols, I 2015, 'Bibliometrics: The Leiden Manifesto for Research Metrics', *Nature*, vol. 520, no. 7548, pp. 429–31, https://doi.org/10.1038/520429a.

Hirsch, JE 2005, 'An Index to Quantify an Individual's Scientific Research Output', *Proceedings of the National Academy of Sciences of the United States of America*, vol. 102, no. 46, pp. 16569–72, https://doi.org/10.1073/pnas.0507655102.

Hirsch, JE 2007, 'Does the h-index Have Predictive Power?', *Proceedings of the National Academy of Sciences of the United States of America*, vol. 104, no. 49, pp. 19193–98, https://doi.org/10.1073/pnas.0707962104.

Hirsch, JE & Buela-Casal, G 2014, 'The Meaning of the h-index', *International Journal of Clinical and Health Psychology*, vol. 14, no. 2, pp. 161–64, https://doi.org/10.1016/S1697-2600(14)70050-X.

Iglesias, JE & Pecharromán, C 2007, 'Scaling the h-index for Different Scientific ISI Fields', *Scientometrics*, vol. 73, no. 3, pp. 303–20, https://doi.org/10.1007/s11192-007-1805-x.

Jefferson, OA, Jaffe, A, Ashton, D, Warren, B, Koellhofer, D, Dulleck, U & Ballagh, A et al. 2018, 'Mapping the Global Influence of Published Research on Industry and Innovation', *Nature Biotechnology*, vol. 36, no. 1, pp. 31–39, https://doi.org/10.1038/nbt.4049.

Leydesdorff, L, Bornmann, L & Opthof, T 2019, '$h_α$: The Scientist as Chimpanzee or Bonobo', *Scientometrics*, vol. 118, no. 3, pp. 1163–66, https://doi.org/10.1007/s11192-019-03004-3.

Moher, D, Bouter, L, Kleinert, S, Glasziou, P, Sham, MH, Barbour, V, Coriat, A-M, Foeger, N, & Dirnagl, U 2020, The Hong Kong Principles for assessing researchers: Fostering research integrity. *PLOS Biology* 18(7): e3000737. https://doi.org/10.1371/journal.pbio.3000737.

Schubert, G & Schubert, A 2019, 'The Eponymic Use of Jorge E. Hirsch's Name', ISSI #59, vol. 15, no. 3.

Sugimoto, CR & Larivière, V 2018, *Measuring Research: What Everyone Needs to Know®*, Oxford University Press, New York.

Teixeira da Silva, JA & Dobránszki, J 2018, 'Multiple Versions of the h-Index: Cautionary Use for Formal Academic Purposes', *Scientometrics*, vol. 115, no. 2, pp. 1107–13, https://doi.org/10.1007/s11192-018-2680-3.

Teufel, S, Siddharthan, A & Tidhar, D 2006, 'Automatic Classification of Citation Function', in *Proceedings of the 2006 Conference on Empirical Methods in Natural Language Processing*, 103–10, EMNLP '06, Association for Computational Linguistics, Stroudsburg, PA, USA, http://dl.acm.org/citation.cfm?id=1610075.1610091 (July 15, 2020).

van Leeuwen, T 2008, 'Testing the Validity of the Hirsch-Index for Research Assessment Purposes', *Research Evaluation*, vol. 17, no. 2, pp. 157–60, https://doi.org/10.3152/095820208X319175.

van Raan, AFJ 2006, 'Comparison of the Hirsch-Index with Standard Bibliometric Indicators and with Peer Judgment for 147 Chemistry Research Groups', *Scientometrics*, vol. 67, no. 3, pp. 491–502, https://doi.org/10.1556/Scient.67.2006.3.10.

Waltman, L 2016, 'A Review of the Literature on Citation Impact Indicators', *Journal of Informetrics*, vol. 10, no. 2, pp. 365–91, https://doi.org/10.1016/j.joi.2016.02.007.

Waltman, L & van Eck, NJ 2012, 'The Inconsistency of the h-index', *Journal of the American Society for Information Science and Technology*, vol. 63, no. 2, pp. 406–15, https://doi.org/10.1002/asi.21678.

Wouters, P 2017, 'Bridging the Evaluation Gap', *Engaging Science, Technology, and Society*, vol. 3, p. 108, https://doi.org/10.17351/ests2017.115.

4 Alternative Metrics (Altmetrics)

4.1 The Future Has Already Begun: Origin, Classification, and Applications of Altmetrics in Scholarly Communication

Dirk Tunger and Andreas Meier

Abstract: Does bibliometrics still adequately capture the impact of scientific publications? New sources have been established in which scientific communication also takes place. Are these sources capable of generating a faster and more comprehensive picture of scientific output? This article presents the aim, methods and possibilities of altmetrics and puts it into a context of bibliometrics and foresight related processes.

Keywords: altmetrics, foresight process, scientific impact, social media.

The altmetrics approach is a controversial topic with respect to the communication of research findings within the scientific community and to society at large. The introduction of "alternative metrics" (altmetrics) is at the center of current discourse about whether or not the focus on classic bibliometric indicators still reflects the true impact of research work in the Internet age. During the course of this discussion, the term "altmetrics" was coined as a collective term for alternative indicators which account for perception of web-based communication beyond the conventional peer-review method:

> "I like the term #articlelevelmetrics, but it fails to imply *diversity* of measures. Lately, I'm liking #altmetrics."[1]

These indicators reveal who cites, discusses, or shares scientific publications in the national press, social media, policy documents, and other web-based sources, and who is concerned with publications both within the science system and beyond.[2]

---

[1] Jason Priem on Twitter on the origin of the term "altmetrics" in 2010: https://twitter.com/jasonpriem/status/25844968813?lang=en (July 15, 2020).
[2] Cf. Tunger, Meier and Hartmann, 2017.

Dirk Tunger, TH Köln, Faculty of Information Science and Communication Studies, Institute of Information Management & Forschungszentrum Jülich GmbH, Project Management Jülich, Center of Excellence "Analyses, Studies, Strategy", d.tunger@fz-juelich.de
Andreas Meier, Forschungszentrum Jülich GmbH, Central Library, a.meier@fz-juelich.de

https://doi.org/10.1515/9783110646610-019

Altmetrics Research

Since the introduction of the term "altmetrics" by Priem et al.[3] in 2010, the altmetrics community has conducted roughly ten years of research on this topic. On the one hand, the visibility and presence of altmetrics are quite impressive (Haustein, 2016a) for a number of reasons: many scientific publishers use them as marketing tools, several hundred publications on the subject have appeared, a dedicated journal has been established,[4] and there is now even a conference dedicated to the topic of altmetrics.[5] On the other hand, there is no uniform definition of the term, and therefore no consensus on what exactly altmetrics measure or on the conclusions that can be drawn from the results (Haustein, 2016b; Franzen, 2017; Butler et al., 2017).

The Altmetric Attention Score, in the form of the "Altmetric donut", is currently used by many scientific publishers and institutions as a marketing tool (see section on "Practical application of altmetrics in scientific institutions" below). The Altmetric donut has been implemented by several parties, including the websites of the jour-

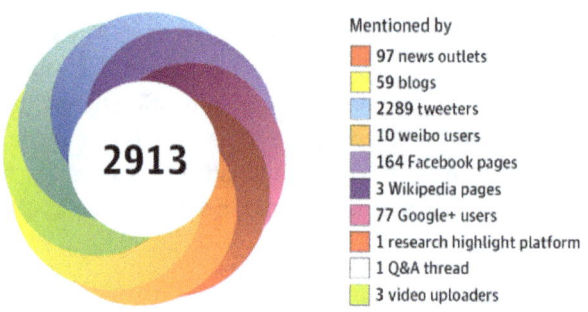

Figure 1: Example of an Altmetric donut and its composition.

nals *Nature* and *Science* and the repositories of the universities of Cambridge and Zurich. The composition of the attention score is based on an algorithm that adds up a weighted count of the attention received by scientific output in diverse sources.

This trend is regarded with some scepticism in science (Franzen, 2017). Simply adding up counts to create a single metric (composite indicator) is "problematic" (Tunger et al., 2017; European Commission, 2017a). The attention score does not represent the overall impact of scientific performance, but is instead suited to identifying the publications that have sparked a great deal of interest in the media (Warren et al., 2016; European Commission, 2017b).

---

3 Cf. Priem et al., 2010.
4 See https://www.journalofaltmetrics.org/ (July 15, 2020).
5 See http://www.altmetricsconference.com/ (July 15, 2020).

Tension between Bibliometrics and Altmetrics

There is a certain tension between bibliometrics and altmetrics in spite of the fact that altmetrics originated in the bibliometrics community. Both disciplines are intended to fulfil the same purpose, i.e. to generate a picture of scientific impact, but have a different basis.

Almost like a reflex, the two fields are often set in relation to each other, compared or viewed as an either/or choice. Bornmann and Haunschild (2016) investigated to what extent the Leiden Manifesto for Research Metrics, which was drawn up for metrics in research evaluation by Hicks et al. in 2015, can also be applied to altmetrics. The authors came to the conclusion that no normalized indicators have endured to date, that the data are often not openly accessible and not transparent, and that authors of scientific publications can manipulate their metrics by gaming. In this sense, we are still far from being able to apply the rules that apply to bibliometrics to altmetrics (cf. e.g. Tunger et al., 'From Simple Publication Figures to Complex Indicators: Bibliometrics and the Dilemma of Methodological Correctness, Significance, and Economic Necessity' in this handbook). The term "metrics" in the word "altmetrics" also often raises false expectations by suggesting that they generate "measurements" or "statistics". This does not apply to altmetrics, however. Instead, altmetrics determine absolute frequencies and correlate them in the form of the Altmetric donut. This can provide a new perspective on the communication by and about science in social media. The Expert Group on Altmetrics, which compiled a report on behalf of the European Commission in 2017, also argues that altmetrics and bibliometrics constitute "complementary approaches to evaluation". With regard to altmetrics, an obvious advantage is that a wider audience can be reached that is not necessarily part of the science system, and also that information can be gathered and processed much faster than is the case in classic bibliometrics. That the importance of altmetrics in the science system is completely different to that of bibliometrics is apparent in the simple fact that traditional scientific publications (as used by bibliometrics) are at the centre of the scientific reward system. In contrast, communication via social media is not part of this system – and this difference alone makes it much harder for altmetrics to become established.

But there is a parallel: Eugene Garfield made footnotes of scientific publications available as new and previously unused information. It quickly became apparent that not every publication has the same value: many papers are published in science, but they are not evenly distributed across the journals, as Bradford already stated many years earlier. Similarly, citations are not evenly distributed across publications, but equally skewed. This is how citations became a currency in science.

Through the Science Citation Index, scientists could for the first time systematically see which other scientists cited their papers. The realization that scientific impact is no longer only determined by classical scientific publications, but also by the perception of scientific publications in network media, has led to the need for bibliometrics to complement this.

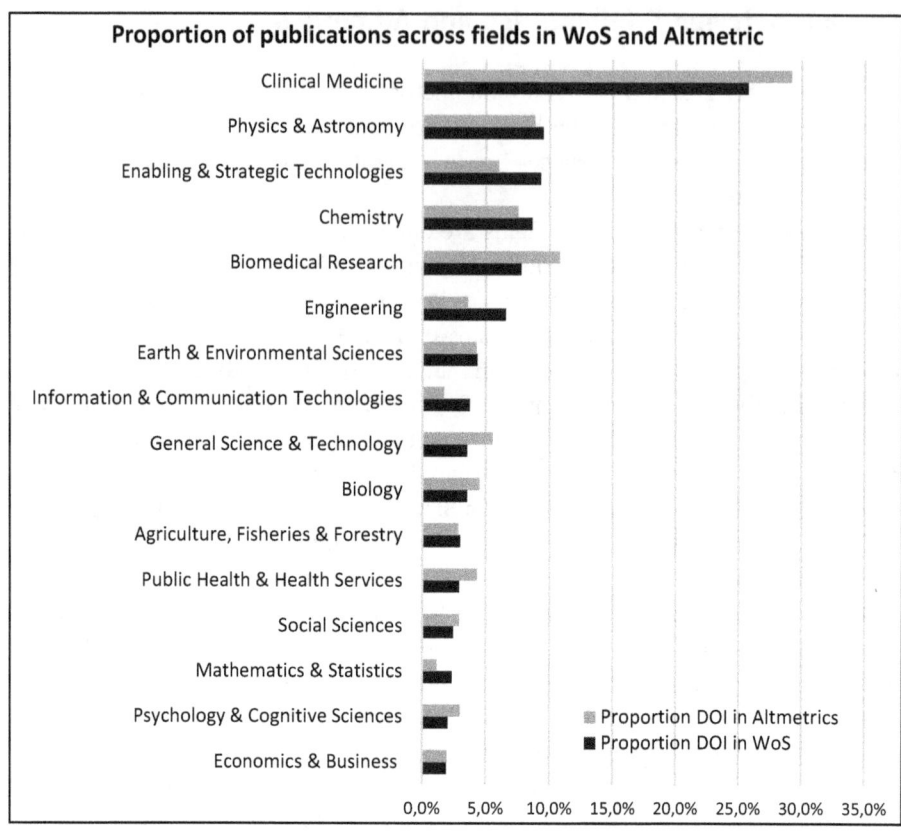

Figure 2: Comparison of the proportions of the fields in WoS Altmetrics.

With Altmetrics, impact becomes visible faster than with bibliometrics (e. g. Mendeley Readerships) and additional sources are added that go beyond classical science communication. Thus Altmerics can be compared to the introduction of the Science Citation Index, which now enables scientists to see where they are cited. These citations are now called Tweets, Posts, Likes or Mentions.

It is interesting to take a look at the distribution of papers across fields in Web of Science and Altmetrics. The distribution of DOIs in Web of Science for the year 2018 is shown in red, based on the mapping of publications to fields and subsequent aggregation using the classification introduced by Archambault et al. (2011). In contrast to the WoS classification, this is free of overlaps and redundancies. The respective proportions of resonance to these papers in altmetrics are depicted in blue. The disciplines are mapped according to the underlying scientific publication and the mapping is absolutely comparable between Web of Science and Altmetrics.

It becomes apparent that in Altmetrics, for example, there is more response to papers from clinical medicine than to engineering papers. This very clearly shows another difference between bibliometrics and Altmetrics and makes clear that these are two different systems. Altmetrics is not based on rules of science communication but on rules of mass communication (cf. Tunger et al. 2017).

Attention as the Currency of Science

It can be assumed that scientists publish not only to advance science but also to increase their reputation: they need not publish much, but the publications need to attract as much attention as possible in order to attain the best possible reputation. It is a sign of appreciation for any scientist when their work is noticed, viewed as relevant, and cited by a colleague.

This applies to both the traditional publication process and to online publications: "In the media society, it is no longer sufficient to simply be rich: you also need a high profile (own translation, Franck, 1996). Franck calls this the "economy of attention". Although this approach is not immediately transferable to science, many scientists also try to gain a certain degree of popularity or prominence within their specialist community to strengthen their own position. This concept can be described as "visibility": if you want to say something, you need to be visible. By using social media, an audience beyond the scientific community itself is addressed. The closer media society and science become, for example by using social media in science, the more easily the maxim described by Franck can be transferred to science.

Altmetrics Feasibility Study

To what extent and in what way does it make sense to use altmetrics in science policy and science management? This is the question at the centre of a feasibility study on altmetrics compiled at Jülich (Tunger, Meier, and Hartmann, 2017). In what way are altmetrics currently used, what conclusions can be drawn from them, and where do bottlenecks loom?

The feasibility study outlines the four different fields of application and explains their respective application of altmetrics.

Science Evaluation, Performance Assessment, and Measurement of Social Impact

In these sensitive areas, care must be taken with regard to the application of altmetrics, and validation represents an essential component. In the scientific discourse, a deeper understanding of the heterogeneity and significance of the data,[6] a meaning-

---

[6] In contrast to bibliometrics, there are a number of different types of sources in altmetrics (e.g.

ful indicator system, and benchmarks are all important. In the near future, altmetrics will be more of a complementary component than an independent indicator for the assessment of scientific performance. In addition, some research topics are more in the focus of society than others, without necessarily displaying a larger social impact.[7]

Public Relations, Visibility, and Promotion of Activities

The communication of science and its visibility in the public sphere is partly represented by altmetrics. In any case, it should be noted that there is a rising trend in social media activity measured according to the frequency of contributions and the number of people involved. There is thus an increased importance and potential of using social media platforms to proactively draw attention to research, i.e. promote it.

As an example in this context, institutional efforts such as those undertaken by universities or the European Commission can be observed, which strategically position their own publications and activities – in keeping with opening up the science system, expanding knowledge transfer, and addressing social challenges.

Science

Applying altmetrics in science can take a direction similar to that described in the section on public relations: for scientists, the visibility of their publications is essential. The reputation resulting from others using their scientific output in the form of ideas, statements, calculations, and findings or results is an essential part of the science system. Only when this output is used – whether in other scientific publications or in web-based communication, social media, news pieces, or policy documents – is a lasting benefit created for the scientist in question.

---

likes, tweets, posts, news pieces, mentions in policy papers), all of which have their own meaning and interpretation.

[7] In this context, attention should be drawn to the news values theory: it describes factors as to why some topics are likely to be reported while others are unlikely to become the object of journalistic reports in the mass media. The theory describes factors such as surprise, sensation, usefulness, and prominence, the different weighting of which influences the manner of reporting (cf. Galtung and Ruge, 1965).

Libraries

Kerstin Gimpl (2017) addressed altmetrics in libraries in depth. Academic libraries are usually where contacts can be found within a scientific institution for issues related to publication data and bibliometrics. They clean data, compile publication profiles, and collect data within the scope of evaluations. Librarians can thus be seen as specialists for handling data, particularly data related to publications, user statistics, and stock management. This is where altmetrics represent somewhat of a junction, as they illuminate the use of publications in social media. It is therefore plausible for libraries to be directly involved whenever the issue of altmetrics is addressed at an institution (Gimpl, 2017), similar to the situation at Forschungszentrum Jülich.

Practical Application of Altmetrics in Scientific Institutions

Jülich made the decision and began to implement altmetrics. The Altmetric Explorer provided by Altmetric (https://www.altmetric.com [July 15, 2020]) was licensed in 2017 and has been tested on the campus since. In order to simplify the compilation of Jülich's publications, all identifiers of Jülich's publications were sent to Altmetric and are immediately visible via the Altmetric Explorer (using the appropriate marking). Users can thus switch between the entire Altmetric database and Jülich's own publications with just a click. There is also a constant exchange of data between Jülich's JuSER publications portal and Altmetric: all identifiers of publications that are newly registered in JuSER[8] are sent to Altmetric via OAI Protocol for Metadata Harvesting (PMH) and are promptly available in the Altmetric Explorer. This guarantees that Jülich's latest publications can be identified as new.

The Altmetric donut or badge is also automatically updated in Jülich's JuSER publications portal. In addition to the bibliographic data on these publications, altmetric data can also be found here: the Altmetric Explorer can be accessed via the Altmetric badge. The latest mentions can be viewed in detail in the individual sources.

Altmetrics are also used by Forschungszentrum Jülich's Corporate Communications. Press releases are issued on particularly interesting Jülich publications. In these cases, social media reactions to the publication are also taken into consideration by integrating the Altmetric badge in the press release in a manner similar to the JuSER publications portal.

Many universities and institutions, such as the University of Helsinki, ETH Zurich, and École Polytechnique Fédérale de Lausanne (EPFL), also use altmetrics on their websites and in their repositories. The main incentive is that this enables

---

[8] http://juser.fz-juelich.de (July 15, 2020).

them to ascertain the range of their own publications beyond traditional citation metrics.[9] Duke University's communications team uses the system to quickly determine how, where, and when the university's publications are talked about on social media.[10] Cambridge University uses altmetrics to "assess early stage impact; as online activity around a paper is more likely to occur in the first few weeks after publication, in contrast to traditional metrics which take longer to accrue." Another aim is to "track attention for specific projects, groups or departments" as well as to "identify key influencers". It is also possible to "identify potential research collaborators" and measure the impact of other forms of scientific work such as reports or applications, which would not be possible by means of traditional bibliometrics.[11] This also applies to scientists who have yet to establish themselves in a field.

Application of Altmetrics in Foresight Processes

In addition to the application of altmetrics in scientific institutions, they can also be used as input in other contexts such as foresight or roadmapping processes. These data describe a form of attention and also permit conclusions to be drawn on trend developments over time. The following is an example: policy papers are one of the components of altmetrics and, as Figure 2 shows, one of the document types that are analyzed by the Altmetric platform. What topics are included in policy papers? This can be determined by analyzing the abstracts of scientific publications cited in the policy papers. To improve the presentation of the terms, a controlled vocabulary is used in addition to these abstracts. The same could be done with scientific publications and their use on Twitter or in news articles or other sources. In this way, contents can be visualized in altmetrics and can, for example, be incorporated into foresight processes (Tunger, 2019).

Conclusion

Altmetrics are still being developed and tested (cf. Tunger et al. 2020). But we should not overlook the fact that by citing a scientific publication, the author is already making a relevance decision which is reflected in bibliometrics. It could not be explained otherwise that there is e.g. a direct correlation between the citation of publications and their referencing to Mendeley, or between publications with intellectual relevance assessment and bibliometric or altmetric indicators (Breuer et al. 2020). Alt-

---

9 See https://www.altmetric.com/press/press-releases/european-institutions-increasingly-adopting-altmetrics-to-complement-existing-bibliometric-analysis/ (July 15, 2020).
10 See https://www.altmetric.com/case-studies/duke-university/ (July 15, 2020).
11 See https://www.research-information.admin.cam.ac.uk/what-information-available/altmetric-institutions (July 15, 2020).

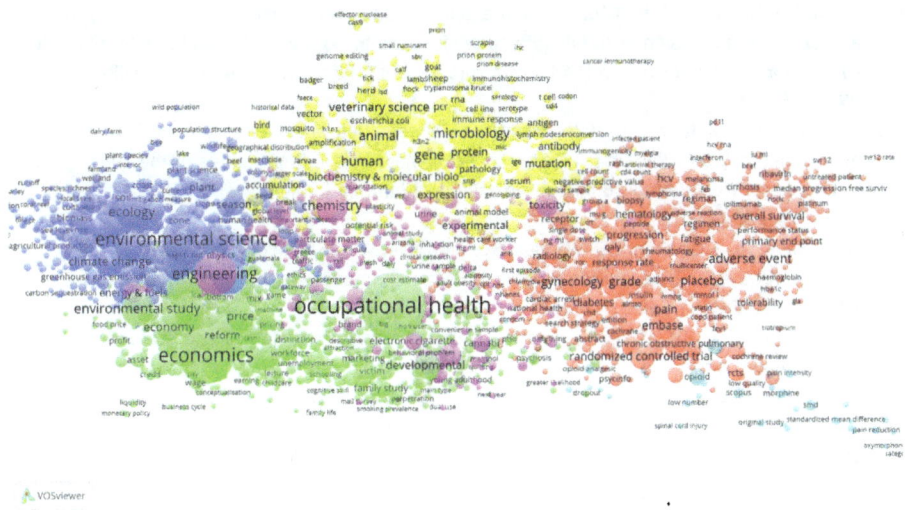

Figure 3: Example of using altmetrics in the foresight context.

metrics are far from making a regular contribution to quantitative research evaluations in the near future. However, altmetrics represent communication that is highly significant in science and is increasingly reaching beyond scientific journals. Capitalizing on this development and considering the creation of incentives to reward the use of new forms of communication, resulting in added value for science, is a pioneering approach. Which new communication forms will succeed in science and become established alongside traditional forms of publication remains to be clarified. This will apply to an even greater extent if incentives for carrying science into society via social media are increased and incorporated into the science reward system. As shown, there are further fields of application where the use of altmetrics would make sense. The next step could involve an intensive dialogue with science on which new communication forms are best suited to science and which would be best suited for a dialogue between science and society, for example within the context of the transfer from science to society or of the integration of civil society in science. These forms of scholarly communication will in future have both value and their place in the science system. Social media will change scholarly communication. We call this the digitization of scholarly communication – and we consider the future, which has already begun.

References

Archambault, E, Beauchesne, OH, & Caruso, J 2011, 'Towards a Multilingual, Comprehensive and Open Scientific Journal Ontology', in Proceedings of the 13th International Conference of the International Society for Scientometrics and Informetrics, pp. 66-77.

Bornmann, L & Haunschild, R 2016, 'To what extent does the Leiden manifesto also apply to altmetrics? A discussion of the manifesto against the background of research into altmetrics', *Online Information Review*, vol. 40, no. 4, pp. 529–43, https://doi.org/10.1108/OIR-09-2015-0314.

Breuer, T, Schaer, P & Tunger, D 2020, 'Relations Between Relevance Assessments, Bibliometrics and Altmetrics', in G Cabanac, I Frommholz & P Mayr (eds.), Proceedings of the 10th International Workshop on Bibliometric-enhanced Information Retrieval, S. 101–12, http://ceur-ws.org/Vol-2591/ (July 15, 2020).

Butler, JS, Kaye, ID, Sebastian, AS, Wagner, SC, Morrissey, PB, Schroeder, GD, Kepler, CK & Vaccaro, AR 2017, 'The Evolution of Current Research Impact Metrics: From Bibliometrics to Altmetrics?', *Clinical Spine Surgery*, vol. 30, no. 5.

European Commission 2017a, Next-generation metrics: Responsible metrics and evaluation for open science, https://doi.org/10.2777/337729.

European Commission 2017b, Mutual Learning Exercise: Open Science - Altmetrics and Rewards.

Franck, G 1996, 'Aufmerksamkeit – Die neue Währung', https://web.archive.org/web/20110501074409/http://www.heise.de/tp/artikel/2/2003/1.htm (July 15, 2020).

Franzen, M 2017, 'Digitale Resonanz. Neue Bewertungskulturen fordern die Wissenschaft heraus', *WZB Mitteilungen*, vol. 155, S. 30–33.

Galtung, J & Ruge, MH 1965, 'The Structure of Foreign News', *Journal of Peace Research*, vol. 2, no. 1, pp. 64–90, https://doi.org/10.1177/002234336500200104.

Gimpl, K 2017, Evaluation von ausgewählten Altmetrics-Diensten für den Einsatz an wissenschaftlichen Bibliotheken (engl. Evaluation of selected Altmetrics services for use in academic libraries); Master-Thesis MALIS (Master in Library and Information Science); Technische Hochschule Köln, Fakultät für Informations- und Kommunikationswissenschaften, urn:nbn:de:hbz:79pbc-opus-10341.

Haustein, S 2016a, 'Vier Tage für fünf Jahre Altmetrics', *Bericht über die Konferenz 2AM und den Workshop altmetrics15. b.i.t. online*, vol. 19, no. 1, pp. 110–12.

Haustein, S 2016b, 'Grand challenges in altmetrics: heterogeneity, data quality and dependencies', *Scientometrics*, doi: https://doi.org/10.1007/s11192-016-1910-9.

Hicks, D, Wouters, P, Waltman, L, de Rijcke, S, and Rafols, I 2015, 'Bibliometrics: The Leiden Manifesto for research metrics', *Nature*, vol. 520, no. 7548, pp. 429–31, https://doi.org/10.1038/520429a.

Priem, J, Taraborelli, D, Groth, P & Neylon, C 2010, Altmetrics: A Manifesto, http://altmetrics.org/manifesto (July 15, 2020).

Tunger, D, Meier, A & Hartmann D 2017, Altmetrics Feasibility Study, http://juser.fz-juelich.de/record/851696 (July 15, 2020).

Tunger, D 2019, 'Altmetrics – on the way to the "economy of attention"? Feasibility study Altmetrics for the German Ministry of Science and Research (BMBF)', in 17th International Conference on Scientometrics & Informetrics, Rome, Italy, pp. 2262–72, http://hdl.handle.net/2128/23974 (July 15, 2020).

Tunger, D, Ahn, H, Clermont, M, Krolak, J, Langner, J & Mittermaier, B 2020, 'Altmetrics as an indicator of performance measurement of universities? An analysis based on decision-theoretical concepts and empirical findings' (in preparation for submission to *Scientometrics*).

Warren, HR, Raison, N & Dasgupta, P 2016, 'The Rise of Altmetrics', *Journal of the American Medical Association*, vol. 317, no. 2, pp. 131–32.

4.2 History, Development and Conceptual Predecessors of Altmetrics

Clemens Blümel and Stephan Gauch

Abstract: The contribution by Blümel and Gauch engages with the history of altmetrics, or, more precisely, with the sociotechnical arrangements within the scientometric community that gave way to the conceptual and technical becoming of altmetrics. Rather than starting out with a general overview on the history of the scientometric community, the authors set their starting point in the mid-90s with the emergence of the World Wide Web. Based on a bibliometric analysis by tracing the citation structure of current altmetrics-related publications, they are able to identify three phases that relate to the discursive processing of the community. The first phase can be associated with the coining of the concept of online usage statistics, giving birth to cybermetrics or webometrics. In the second phase of "methodological scrutinization", scientometricians dealt with emerging quality issues that these new indicators produced vis-à-vis established scientometric practices, e.g. by engaging in cross-correlation studies and identifying systematic issues. The third phase is characterized by "conceptual scrutinization" where scientometricians re-conceptualize and re-organize concepts according to these new indicators. We argue that these patterns are repeating in the case of altmetrics, which currently leads to the opening up of disciplinary logics to other fields and conceptual approaches.

Keywords: bibliometrics, reflexivity, altmetrics, webometrics.

Introduction

Altmetrics is without a doubt a booming topic within scientometrics. Research on the topic has grown at a vast pace, providing the scientometrics research community with novel concepts, data sources, and analytic strategies (Costas et al., 2014; Weller, 2015). This article discusses the history, the development, and future trends of the field. The history we are unfolding in this chapter is a specific one. It is based on a corpus of 479 scientific articles identified within SCI, SSCI, AHCI, and CPCI that have been collected through a term-based search strategy as well as a traversal of the citation tree of those papers identified. It is therefore a history that is informed by the respective communities that operate with these metrics. This has been comple-

---

Dipl.-Soz. **Clemens Blümel,** German Centre for Higher Education Research and Science Studies (DZHW), Department Research System and Science Dynamics, Schützenstraße 6a, 10117 Berlin, Germany

Dr. **Stephan Gauch,** Nachwuchsgruppenleiter "Reflexive Metrics – Rückwirkungen und Praktiken quantifizierter Wertordnungen in der Wissenschaft", Humboldt-Universität zu Berlin, Institut für Sozialwissenschaften, Lehrbereich Wissenschaftsforschung, Germany

mented by interviews with selected practitioners, experts, proponents as well as critics. It therefore must be understood as a very specific perspective on the subject. We also focused on such articles that addressed subjects that stand in difference to altmetrics, i.e. in deconstructing the history of altmetrics we focused on papers that address concepts that preceded the concept of altmetrics, or, more precisely, concepts that have been employed to shape the idea of altmetrics.

The concept of altmetrics, as marked by a statement of difference to previous metrics, emerged roughly around the year 2010, when information scientist Jason Priem coined the term. Yet, although the term has been coined in 2010, the field has a prehistory that goes back to the 1990s. Some of these discussions back then have been re-articulated in altmetrics. Thus, there seems to be a recurring pattern of knowledge production which might also inform the self-characterization of scientometrics. Therefore, this chapter also aims at including the prehistory of altmetrics into the common story of the field. The patterns of argumentation which span these decades arguably may not only inform future trends, but also contribute to self-reflection of knowledge production within scientometrics.

Altmetrics Concept

The current debate on altmetrics goes back to Jason Priem, coining the term in 2010, proposing a diversity of metrics related to scholarly communication in the web. Despite its scholarly use there is, however, no common understanding, and hence no common definition of the term. According to the website of altmetric.com, an important provider of altmetrics data, altmetrics is defined as "metrics and qualitative data that are complementary to traditional, citation-based metrics."[1] Another account at the same website refers to altmetrics as "the creation and study of new metrics based on the Social Web for analyzing, and informing scholarship". According to Weller, altmetrics are primarily evaluation methods "that serve as alternatives to citation based metrics" (Weller, 2015). The emergence of altmetrics has led to a rich literature about the measurement of traces in the social web to scholarly documents, and the construction of various new indicators and metrics for usage of scholarly output other than based on citations.

Conceptual Predecessors of Altmetrics

To understand the current situation of Altmetrics and its position within the disciplinary discourse of scientometrics, it is beneficial to understand how and where ideas originated and which opportunities and challenges for further development may

---

1 https://www.altmetric.com/about-altmetrics/what-are-altmetrics/ (July 15, 2020).

eventually emerge in the near future. With the advent of the web and the establishment of web based services, it comes as no surprise that the informetric community took up the idea of the web as a relevant new source of information flows. In the following, we want to depict the road that led to the establishment and evolution of what may be best described as web-based information science. We do not attempt to focus on specific applications of these types of approaches.[2] Rather, we focus on the conceptual work which was involved in the evolution of the field. It should be noted that bibliometrics and scientometrics had been established as a consolidated field of research at that time, with core journals such as the Journal of the Association for Information Science and Technology (founded in 1950) and the more inter-disciplinary Scientometrics (founded in 1979) being in place for a substantial amount of time.

"Usage" as a Relevant Category of Importance

The first phase in the prehistory of altmetrics can be situated in the years after 1995 with Bossy, Bray, and Ingwersen being the most highly cited authors in that phase in our corpus. The emergence of the web and its reception by the information science community led to the coining of new terms to label metrics for web based communication, with "Netometrics" as the first concept (Bossy, 1995). Bossy (1995) heralded web-based indicators as early as 1995 to be "The new face of Scientometrics". She based her assessment on the ideas of the French science studies scholars Latour and Callon by arguing that "remote files retrieval counts" or "clients hypertext links" may give way to new forms of evaluation as they represent discourse that is closer to the laboratory and a Latourian "Science in Action" perspective (Latour and Woolgar, 1987). Conceptional scrutinization became a matter of urgency: "[W]e will have to decide what counts can be used as indicators ("of what?")" (Bossy, 1995). Attempts were made to establish a parallel infrastructure to the Science Citation Index but aimed at the web, dubbed the Open Text Index (Bray, 1996). Ideas of a global brain that would revolutionize scholarly information were introduced using the term "Webometry" (Abraham, 1997). In parallel, Almid and Ingwersen (1996) coined the phrase "Internetometrics" in a conference paper, which they rephrased to "Webometrics" just one year later for their journal publication (Almid and Ingwersen, 1996). A journal termed "Cybermetrics" was founded in 1997; in the first issue of this journal, references in the web became "sitations" (Rousseau, 1997).

With these new opportunities, scrutinization of the web and measuring with the web became an immediate and pressing topic (Bar-Ilan, 1999; Ingwersen, 1998; Snyder and Rosenbaum, 1999). In addition, the quality of web indexing services came into

---

[2] In a similar vein, Benoit Godin (2006) has provided a conceptual history of bibliometrics, focusing on the establishments that paved the way to its institutionalization.

question (Clarke and Willett, 1997). The usefulness and capabilities of indexing services was perceived to be inadequate for bibliometric types of analyses (Lawrence, 1998). "Polymorphous mentioning" that is, mentioning of an individual in multiple contexts, was expected to become a defining feature of web-based scholarly communication (Cronin et al., 1998). They also argued that web-based scholarly communication was not limited to scholarly discourse and formal communication, but also reflected informal communication among researchers. Attempts were made to enroll and adapt evaluative concepts from the realm of bibliometrics, such as the Journal Impact Factor (JIF) in terms of a Web Impact Factor (WIF) (Ingwersen, 1998). The same accounts for the concepts of explorative bibliometrics, such as bibliographic coupling and co-citation for the web (Kleinberg, 1999).

Reflection and Consolidation in Webometrics and Cybermetrics

Beginning with the year 2000, informetrics then entered a phase of further scrutinization and conceptual reflection. This period also featured a surge in "correlation studies", which aimed at assessing statistical correlations between established bibliometric and webometric indicators and concepts. These studies also furthered understanding of the relationship between bibliometric and cybermetric concepts. Thereby, they shifted the discussion about new indicators to the remaining advantages or disadvantages for each metric. If no such correlation or low levels of correlation are found, discourse shifts either towards further methodological scrutinizations and inclusion of further variables (or properties thereof), or towards arguments that such indicators may measure a different form of impact, which in turn can be a subject of subsequent debate.

Harter and Ford (2000) were the first to highlight systematic issues and challenges for web-based assessment of E-journal impacts. Odlyzko (2002) argued that with the advent of new forms of web-based communication, the need for traditional peer review would decrease, and by the same token, novel forms of scrutinization and communication would emerge outside traditional journals (ibid.). Broadening this argument, Cronin (2001) held that despite the rich potential of these new forms of web-based assessment, the need for conceptual scrutiny would prevail: "Undoubtedly, though, construct validity issues will continue to surface, as new forms of web-based invocation are factored into bibliometric evaluations and sociometric narratives of scientific communication" (Cronin, 2001).

Bar-Ilan (2001) introduced a first comprehensive review about the issue of data collection on the web, arguing that the web is by design a place of volatility. She also contended that search engines and tools available would have to be assessed as inadequate for informetric purposes. Prime et al. (2002) analyzed differences between co-citations and co-sitations and concluded that these should not be deemed as conceptual equivalents and analogies needed to be cautiously evaluated. Vaughan and Shaw (2003) made a similar point for bibliographic and web citation in general.

User motivation and user behaviour studies (Ke et al., 2002; Kim, 2000; Wilkinson et al., 2003;) as well as content-based analyses (Thelwall, 2003) emerged with the goal to understand hyperlinking behaviour.

Between 2003 and 2006 methodological scrutinizations reached a point that warranted extensive programmatic orientations through state-of-the-art reviews and framework concepts for webometrics and cybermetrics (Thelwall et al., 2005). Conceptual reflection extended towards early webometric concepts such as the Web Impact Factor (Noruzi, 2006), the need for understanding the use of new outlets of academic output such as online journals (McDonald, 2007) or the relationship between self-promotion and visibility (Dietrich, 2008), and underlying nature of web data in terms of its persistence over time (Bar-Ilan and Peritz, 2004; Koehler, 2004).

The Establishment and Development of the Altmetrics Movement

While there were many attempts to introduce new measures and motivations to utilize the web as a source for analysis and monitoring of scholarly activity (Almid and Ingwersen, 1996; Almind and Ingwersen, 1997; Bossy, 1995), no dedicated terminology has been created since 2012. It was in 2010 when the term "Altmetrics" was coined by the information scientist Jason Priem.[3] After the publication of a dedicated altmetric manifesto, publications related to the measurement of digital scholarly activity or social media use of scholars has significantly increased (Fenner, 2014; Gonzalez-Valiente et al., 2016; Priem, 2013).

In these literatures, we observe patterns of argumentation that show similarities to the phase between 1995 and the early 2000s. After the coining of the term, many different opportunities for quantitative analysis and the screening of data sources have been explored. In the scholarly publishing field, Article Level Metrics started with first providing data on the usage of scholarly media for its journals (Franzen, 2015; Lin and Fenner, 2013). Soon, other providers of data emerged that were also active in pushing forward scholarly literature on social media use (Adie and Roe, 2013; Liu and Adie, 2013). New channels of dissemination such as Twitter and Facebook have then been integrated in the quantitative assessment.

After this initial stage of exploration of opportunities, we can observe a strong increase in scrutinization and cross-validation studies. There are two dominant topics among these scrutinization studies: the first kind of are "coverage studies" of articles with mentions in social media platforms and their intensity (Cacciatore et al., 2012; Haustein et al., 2014; Onyancha, 2015). The second type are cross validation studies that employ comparisons of altmetric data sources with traditional measures of scholarly performance such as citations. As Costas, Zahedi and Wouters (2014)

---

[3] "I like the term #articlelevelmetrics, but it fails to imply diversity of measures. Lately, I'm liking #altmetrics".

point out, these studies have at least found some correlations "suggesting that these two approaches are somehow related but not the same". The studies differ, however, in the way that comparisons are accomplished. Some studies focus on a specific provider such as altmetric.com in order to compare different social media data with other bibliometric information consistently (Chamberlain, 2013; Costas et al., 2014; Das and Mishra, 2014). Other studies concentrate in their comparisons on a single (scholarly) social media data source such as Mendeley (Gunn, 2013; Thelwall and Sud, 2016), Facebook or Academia.edu (Thelwall and Kousha, 2014) in order to explore significant characteristics and structures of that media use and its (scholarly) audience. Finally, a third group of studies compares the relationships and or correlation between different social media or Altmetrics data sources (Gunn, 2013; Li et al., 2012). Particularly in the first two groups, altmetric data and social media use has been attributed predictive power, when correlations to citations are approved. In other cases, where such correlation could not be observed, scholars have argued that such metrics point at some other type of impact, that is, societal impact (Bornmann, 2014; 2016; Cress, 2014).

This enormous increase in scrutinization, cross validation, and indicator construction has finally led to a third phase where the different ways of data collection have been compared and systematically analyzed for consistency. In particular, this has led to the emergence of conceptual scrutinization. Motivated by the differences between the different data, Haustein et al. asked what the tracking of scholarly activities precisely means (Haustein et al., 2016). Increasingly, indicator construction of the different providers also became a relevant topic (Gumpenberger et al., 2016). Such patterns of evolution, we argue, show that historical patterns of argumentation reemerge in the existing discussion of Altmetrics. Contrary to previous analyses, however, these activities of redefining scholarly impact emerged in a different environment.

Discussion and Conclusion

In this paper, we have attempted to provide an overview of the history and pre-history of the altmetrics movement. Through the combination of bibliometric methods with qualitative analysis, we were able to identify dominant themes and patterns of argumentation that can be divided into three phases of intellectual development in the exploration of metrics for the scholarly web. We argue that the patterns of argumentation that have arisen in the first two phases with the emergence of terminological exploration, scrutinization, and conceptualization can be re-established in the current Altmetrics debate. However, different to the earlier decades, the metrics that have been developed in the scientometrics and informetrics field have found a much stronger resonance among the science policy field where the notion of societal impact has been strongly pushed (Blümel and Gauch, 2017). At the same time, new providers and platforms have developed that have integrated different data for scholarly social media use and are legitimized by scholarly debates on altmetrics. As scholars of scientometrics and informetrics, we therefore should be more careful about which data we use and what the use of these data signifies. That would imply the stronger theoretical conceptualization not only in the field of Altmetrics but for scientometrics in general. There have been recurring phases of criticism towards scientometrics about the low level of a coherent theoretical framing. With the uptake of alternative metrics, this discussion, fueled by an irritation of the scientometric communities and its practices, has been renewed and might also allow for the integration of new perspectives such as media theory. What might such a theoretical framework be based upon and what purpose may it serve? Currently, a specific type of questions seems to shape the discourse in the scientometric community vis-à-vis altmetrics. Why and how did altmetrics gain so much momentum compared to cybermetrics? What are the "relevant aspects" to measure, i.e. how should the development of indicators be organized? What facilitates a "responsible use" of indicators and what role does the scientometric community play in this? All these questions share the notion for a need of reflexivity of scientometrics that reach far beyond discussions of methodology or data quality. Such a framework would have to deviate from the notions of a stable identity of scientometrics that facilitate differences and effects. Rather, it might be more productive to reverse this notion and focus on how individuals, communities, and also indicators actualize their identities through process of relationalization, i.e. how they seek and integrate differences to define their identities in an interplay of meaning and relevance. If such a theoretical framework were to serve as a basis for such a notion of reflexivity, suitable candidates may be found in a closer integration of recent developments in the sociology of quantification and (e-)valuation as well as the sociology of critique and justification.

References

Abraham, Ralph H 1997, 'Webometry: Measuring the complexity of the world wide web', *World Futures*, vol. 50, no. 1–4, pp. 785–91, doi: https://doi.org/10.1080/02604027.1997.9972670.
Adie, E & Roe, W 2013, 'Altmetric: Enriching scholarly content with article-level discussion and metrics', *Learned Publishing*, vol. 26, no. 1, pp. 11–17, doi: https://doi.org/10.1087/20130103.
Almind, TC & Ingwersen, P 1997, 'Informetric analyses on the world wide web: Methodological approaches to 'webometrics'', *Journal of Documentation*, vol. 53, no. 4, pp. 404–26, doi: https://doi.org/10.1108/EUM0000000007205.
Bar-Ilan, J 1999, 'Search engine results over time: A case study on search engine stability', *Cybermetrics*, vol. 2/3, no. 1.
Bar-Ilan, J 2001, 'Data Collection Methods on the Web for Informetric Purposes: A Review and Analysis', *Scientometrics*, vol. 50, no. 1, pp. 7–32.
Bar-Ilan, J & Beritz, BC 2004, 'Evolution, continuity, and disappearance of documents on a specific topic on the Web: a longitudinal study of informetrics', *Journal of the American Society for Information Science and Technology*, vol. 55, no. 11, pp. 980–90.

Blümel, C & Gauch, S 2017, *The valuation of online science communication. A study into the scholarly discourses of Altmetrics and their reception*, Berlin.

Bornmann, L 2014, 'Validity of altmetrics data for measuring societal impact: A study using data from Altmetric and F1000Prime', *Journal of Informetrics*, vol. 8, no. 4, pp. 935–50, doi: https://doi.org/10.1016/j.joi.2014.09.007.

Bornmann, L 2016, 'Scientific Revolution in Scientometrics: the Broadening of Impact from Citation to Societal', in CR Sugimoto (ed.), *Theories of Informetrics and Scholarly Communication: A Festschrift in Honor of Blaise Cronin*, pp. 347–59, de Gruyter, Berlin.

Bossy, MJ 1995, 'The Last of the Litter: 'Netometrics'', *Solaris*, vol. 2).

Bray, T 1996, 'Measuring the Web', *Computer Networks and ISDN Systems*, vol. 28, no. 7–11, pp. 993–1005, doi: https://doi.org/10.1016/0169–7552(96)00061-X.

Cacciatore, MA, Anderson, AA, Choi, D-H, Brossard, D, Scheufele, DA, Liang, X, Ladwig, PJ, Xenos, M & Dudo A 2012, 'Coverage of emerging technologies: A comparison between print and online media', *New Media & Society*, vol. 14, no. 6, pp. 1039–59, doi: https://doi.org/10.1177/1461444812439061.

Chamberlain, S 2013, 'Consuming Article-Level Metrics: Observations and Lessons', *Information Standards Quarterly*, vol. 25, no. 2, p. 4, doi: https://doi.org/10.3789/isqv25no2.2013.02.

Clarke, SJ & Willett P 1997, 'Estimating the recall performance of Web search engines', *Aslib Proceedings*, vol. 49, no. 7, pp. 184–89, doi: https://doi.org/10.1108/eb051463.

Costas, R, Zahedi, Z & Wouters P 2014, 'Do "Altmetrics" correlate with Citations? Extensive Comparison of Altmetric Indicators with Citations from a multidisciplinary Perspective', *Journal of the Association for Information Science and Technology*, vol. 66, no. 10, pp. 2003–19.

Cress, PE 2014, 'Using altmetrics and social media to supplement impact factor: maximizing your article's academic and societal impact', *Aesthetic surgery journal*, vol. 34, no. 7, pp. 1123–26, doi: https://doi.org/10.1177/1090820X14542973.

Cronin, B 2001, Bibliometrics and beyond: some thoughts on web-based citation analysis.

Cronin, B, Snyder, HW, Rosenbaum, H, Martinson, A & Callahan E 1998, 'Invoked on the Web', *Journal of the American Society for Information Science*, vol. 49, no. 14, pp. 1319–28, doi: https://doi.org/10.1002/(SICI)1097–4571(1998)49:14<1319:AID-ASI9>3.0.CO;2-W.

Das, AK & Mishra S 2014, 'Genesis of Altmetrics or Article-Level Metrics for Measuring Efficacy of Scholarly Communications: Current Perspectives', *SSRN Electronic Journal*, doi: https://doi.org/10.2139/ssrn.2499467.

Dietrich, JP 2008, 'Disentangling Visibility and Self-Promotion Bias in the Arxiv: Astro-Ph Positional Citation Effect', *Publications of the Astronomical Society of the Pacific*, vol. 120, no. 869, pp. 801–04.

Fenner, M 2014 'Altmetrics and Other Novel Measures for Scientific Impact', in S Bartling & S Friesike (eds.), *Opening Science*, pp. 179–89, Springer International Publishing, Cham.

Franzen, M 2015. 'The Impact Factor had its day. Altmetrics and the Future of Science', *Soziale Welt – Zeitschrift für Sozialwissenschaftliche Forschung und Praxis*, vol. 66, no. 2, pp. 225–242.

Godin, B 2006, 'On the origins of bibliometrics', *Scientometrics*, vol. 68, no. 1, 109–33.

Gonzalez-Valiente, CL, Pacheco-Mendoza, J & Arencibia-Jorge, R 2016, 'A review of altmetrics as an emerging discipline for research evaluation', *Learned Publishing*, vol. 29, no. 4, pp. 229–38, doi: https://doi.org/10.1002/leap.1043.

Gumpenberger, C, Glanzel, W & Gorraiz J 2016, 'The ecstasy and the agony of the altmetric score', *Scientometrics*, no. 108, no. 2, pp. 977–82, doi: https://doi.org/10.1007/s11192-016-1991–5.

Gunn, W 2013, 'Social Signals Reflect Academic Impact: What it means when a scholar adds a paper to Mendeley', *Information Standards Quarterly*, vol. 25, no. 2.

Harter, SP & Ford, CH 2000, 'Web-Based Analysis of E-Journal Impact: Approaches, Problems, and Issues', *Journal of the American Society for Information Science*, vol. 51, no. 13, pp. 1159–76.

Haustein, S, Peters, I, Bar-Ilan, J, Priem, J, Shema, H & Terliesner, J 2014, 'Coverage and adoption of altmetrics sources in the bibliometric community', *Scientometrics*, vol. 101, no. 2, pp. 1145–63, doi: https://doi.org/10.1007/s11192-013-1221-3.

Haustein, S, Bowman, TD & Costas, R 2016, 'Interpreting "altmetrics": viewing acts on social media through the lens of citation and social theories', in CR Sugimoto (ed.), *Theories of Informetrics and Scholarly* Communication, pp. 372–405, de Gruyter Mouton, Berlin.

Ingwersen, P 1998, 'The calculation of web impact factors', *Journal of Documentation*, vol. 54, no. 2, pp. 236–43, doi: https://doi.org/10.1108/EUM0000000007167.

Ke, HR et al. 2002, 'Exploring behavior of e-journal users in science and technology: transaction log analysis of Elsevier's ScienceDirect OnSite in Taiwan', *Library & In-formation Science Research*, vol. 24, no. 3, pp. 265–91.

Kim, J 2000, 'Motivations for hyperlinking in scholarly electronic articles: A qualitative study', *Journal of the American Society for Information Science*, vol. 51, no. 10, pp. 887–99.

Kleinberg, JM 1999, 'Authoritative sources in a hyperlinked environment', *Journal of the ACM*, vol. 46, no. 5, pp. 604–32, doi: https://doi.org/10.1145/324133.324140.

Koehler, W 2004, 'A Longitudinal Study of Web Pages Continued: A Consideration of Document Persistence', *Information Research*, vol. 9, no. 2.

Latour, B & Woolgar, S 1987, *Science in Action*, Harvard University Press, Cambridge, Massachusetts.

Lawrence, S 1998, 'Searching the World Wide Web', *Science*, vol. 280, no. 5360, pp. 98–100, doi: https://doi.org/10.1126/science.280.5360.98.

Li, X, Thelwall, M & Giustini, D 2012, 'Validating online reference managers for scholarly impact measurement', *Scientometrics*, vol. 91, no. 2, pp. 461–71, doi: https://doi.org/10.1007/s11192-011-0580-x.

Lin, J & Fenner, M 2013, 'Altmetrics in Evolution: Defining and Redefining the Ontology of Article-Level Metrics', *ISQ*, vol. 25, pp. 20–26.

Liu, J & Adie, E 2013, 'Five challenges in altmetrics: A toolmaker's perspective', *Bulletin for the American Society for Information Science and Technology*, vol. 39, no. 4, pp. 31–34.

McDonald, J 2007, 'Understanding Online Journal Usage: A Statistical Analysis of Citation and Use', *Journal of the American Society for Information Science and Technology*, vol. 58, no. 1, pp. 39–50.

Noruzi, A 2006, 'The Web Impact Factor: A Critical Review', *The Electronic Library*, vol. 24, no. 4, pp. 490–500.

Odlyzko, A 2002, 'The rapid evolution of scholarly communication', *Learned Publishing*, vol. 15, no. 1, pp. 7–19, doi: https://doi.org/10.1087/095315102753303634.

Onyancha, OB 2015, 'Social media and research: an assessment of the coverage of South African universities in ResearchGate, Web of Science and the Webometrics Ranking of World Universities', *South African Journal of Libraries and Information Science*, vol. 81, no. 1, pp. 8–20.

Priem, J 2013, 'Beyond the Paper', *Nature*, vol. 495, pp. 437–40.

Prime, C, Bassecoulard, E & Zitt M 2002, 'Co-Citations and Co- Sitations: A Cautionary View on an Analogy', *Scientometrics*, vol. 54, no. 2, pp. 291–308.

Rousseau, R 1997, 'Sitations: An exploratory study', *Cybermetrics*, vol. 1, no. 1–7.

Snyder, H & Rosenbaum, H 1999, 'Can search engines be used as tools for web-link analysis?: A critical view', *Journal of Documentation*, vol. 55, no. 4, pp. 375–84, doi: https://doi.org/10.1108/EUM0000000007151.

Thelwall, M 2003, 'What Is This Link Doing Here? Beginning a Fine-Grained Process of Identifying Reasons for Academic Hyperlink Creation', *Information Research*, vol. 8, no. 3.

Thelwall, M & Kousha, K 2014, 'Academia.edu: Social network or Academic Network?', *Journal of the Association for Information Science and Technology*, vol. 65, no. 4, pp. 721–31, doi: https://doi.org/10.1002/asi.23038.

Thelwall, M & Sud P 2016, 'Mendeley readership counts: An investigation of temporal and disciplinary differences', *Journal of the Association for Information Science and Technology*, vol. 67, no. 12, pp. 3036–50, doi: https://doi.org/10.1002/asi.23559.

Thelwall, M, Vaughan, L & Björneborn L 2005, 'Webometrics', *Annual Review of Information Science and Technology*, vol. 39, pp. 81–135.

Vaughan, L & Shaw, X 2003, Bibliographic and Web Citations: What Is the Difference?

Weller, K 2015, 'Social media and altmetrics: An overview of current alternative approaches to measuring scholarly impact', *Incentives and Performance*, 261–76.

Wilkinson, D, Harries, G, Thelwall, M & Price, L 2003, 'Motivations for Academic Web Site Interlinking: Evidence for the Web as a Novel Source of Information on Informal Scholarly Communication', *Journal of Information Science*, vol. 29, no. 1, pp. 49–56.

4.3 Social Media and Altmetrics

Kaltrina Nuredini, Steffen Lemke, and Isabella Peters

Abstract: This chapter describes the relationship between social media and altmetrics. It briefly discusses how social media platforms' features can create altmetrics and why this is in line with the concept of "affordances". Since altmetrics are built on the data that is derived from user activities on social media platforms, the affordances of these platforms are important for the development of altmetrics. Affordances produce meaning and control the behavior of users that interact with such platforms. Although social media platforms are not necessarily targeted at researchers, the features of these platforms often support the research enterprise. Therefore, this chapter also explains researchers' social media engagement, such as the reasons some researchers use social media platforms on a daily basis. It also provides three classification approaches that aid the interpretation of altmetrics. Last but not least, it discusses the issues that influence the general adoption of altmetrics by focusing on the challenges social media platforms present to altmetrics.

Keywords: social media, academia, scholarly output, altmetric, affordances, heterogeneity, altmetrics classifications

Introduction

The development of altmetrics and social media is inseparably interlinked. Most of the altmetrics aggregators heavily use data provided by social media platforms. "Social media" comprises web-based platforms that allow for publishing user-generated content, communicating and networking, for example, social networking systems, discussion boards, multimedia platforms, instant messaging/chat, blogs, microblogs, podcasts, wikis, and tagging systems (Peters and Heise, 2014). Although these platforms are not necessarily targeted towards researchers and their work-related needs, the platforms' features often support the research enterprise so well that König and Nentwich (2017) argue that social media could be one-stop-shop like work environments for science. What is more, social media platforms have witnessed a constant rise in user numbers, including researchers who also increasingly subscribe to them, which reflects that social media fill a need researchers have. This and the growing critique on traditional bibliometrics and quantitative indicators used for assessment of scholarly work (as for example formulated in 2013 in the

---

Kaltrina Nuredini, ZBW – Leibniz Information Centre for Economics, Germany, kaltrina.nuredini@gmail.com
Steffen Lemke, member of the Web Science team at ZBW Leibniz Information Centre for Economics, S.Lemke@zbw.eu
Prof. Dr. **Isabella Peters**, ZBW Leibniz Information Centre for Economics & Kiel University, Düsternbrooker Weg 120, 24105 Kiel, Germany, i.peters@zbw.eu

San Francisco Declaration on Research Assessment "DORA[1]" or the Altmetrics Manifesto[2]) are the two major drivers behind the altmetrics movement. Moreover, the availability of data which can be used for altmetrics increased over time, which is strongly related to the rapid development of sophisticated application programming interfaces (APIs) provided by social media platforms.

Social media (Burgess, Marwick and Poell, 2017) allow, amongst others, for easy publishing of texts and other media on the web without any gatekeepers. This characteristic was inherited by altmetrics and has led to the formulation of four major arguments in favor of the utilization of altmetrics (Wouters and Costas, 2012): fast feedback; reflection of societal impact; diversity of scholarly products and assessment methods; and openness of data and acquisition. Whereas citations take years to accumulate (Brody, Harnad, and Carr, 2006), social media can provide almost instant feedback to scholarly works; feedback which can be quantified and summarized as altmetrics. In fact, most of the altmetrics appear within only a couple of days after the publication of a scholarly product (Shuai, Pepe, and Bollen, 2012). The maximum requirement for establishing an account on a social media platform is an email address, leading to an almost infinite amount of users that can populate social media and that can engage with scholarly products. Social media are also, most of the times, not restricted to academic users,[3] so there is a chance that altmetrics reflect engagement from users outside of the scholarly community. Social media platforms allow for the publication of a variety of research products, e.g., presentation slides, code, bibliographies, and therefore serve needs to present outcomes of scholarly work better than the traditional options to publish. Those social media-based scholarly products can again be shared, commented, and interacted with on social media platforms, which result in new altmetrics that reflect various forms of engagement with such products. As such, altmetrics reflect a broader diversity of research products and the signals they generate on social media platforms. Of course, these manifold social media-based publication options increase the amount of scholarly information available requiring advanced filtering systems. Priem and colleagues (2010) argue that altmetrics can serve as filters and may support users in finding relevant information. Finally, in contrast to the traditional bibliographic databases, such as Web of Science or Scopus, whose data has to be purchased, most social media data can be accessed via public APIs. Hence, the altmetrics' underlying data as well as the methods used for data gathering are open for all and can be scrutinized by third parties.

This fundamental change in scholarly publishing and engagement with scholarly outcomes, induced by social media, and the quantitative statements that can be derived from that, led the bibliometrics community to search for suitable terminology

---

1 https://sfdora.org/ (July 15, 2020).
2 http://altmetrics.org/manifesto/ (July 15, 2020).
3 Academia.edu and ResearchGate are exceptions since they require an email address from an academic institution.

to describe such kinds of metrics. Priem and Hemminger (2010) proposed "Scientometrics 2.0", whereas Haustein, Bowman, and Costas (2016) argued for "social media metrics" – which is similar to the concept of "webometrics" (Thelwall, Vaughan, and Björneborn, 2005) – to highlight from which data sources the metrics are derived from. "Social media metrics" was criticized because it would not include mentions of scholarly works in policy documents and newspapers, which some altmetrics aggregators count in for altmetrics (Holmberg, 2015). Other terms were "tweetations" to indicate that the citation was made on Twitter (Eysenbach, 2011), "complimentrics" as an alternative name of complementary metrics with the intention to complement traditional citation metrics (Adie, 2014), "influmetrics" as a new form of informetrics that measure only the influence of research output (Ronald and Ye, 2013; Bowman, 2015, p.17), or "article-level metrics" (Lin and Fenner, 2013a). However, the most popular term so far is "altmetrics", coined by Priem in 2010,[4] to emphasize that, in addition to traditional citations, social media-based metrics allow for an alternative assessment of scholarly works.

There are two ways in which social media substantially fuel altmetrics as quantified engagement with scholarly output on social media platforms, e. g. when users tweet about an article. This can be described as the "narrow approach to altmetrics" because only interactions with traditionally published scholarly works are considered;

as social media-content as a form of scholarly communication measured by altmetrics and other bibliometric indicators, e. g. if a dataset is cited in a journal article and tweeted on Twitter. This can be described as the "broad approach to altmetrics" because various publication types are considered as well as different types of indicators.

To elaborate on the relation between social media and altmetrics, we will first briefly explain how the social media platforms' features determine what can be fed into altmetrics or social media-based indicators and why this is in line with the concept of "affordances". Next, we will discuss how and for what reasons which researchers use social media in their daily practices to explain what meaning social media engagement can have. We will describe classifications that aid interpretation of altmetrics. We conclude the chapter by summarizing the issues that affect the broad adoption of altmetrics by focusing on the challenges social media platforms introduce to altmetrics.

---

[4] https://twitter.com/jasonpriem/status/25844968813 (July 15, 2020).

The Relationship between the Affordances of Social Media Platforms and Altmetrics

The concept "affordance" is often used in studies of design and human-computer interaction (Gaver, 1991) and describes "what material artifacts [...] allow people to do" (Bucher and Helmond, 2017). There is a multitude of definitions for this concept that have been well summarized by Bucher and Helmond (2017). All definitions highlight that features of, for example, social media platforms are not just features that enable particular actions by their users (e.g. posting a status update) but that affordances carry connotation, produce meanings, constrain and control behavior on platforms, and that they are used for communication, which, ultimately, affects how users use and interact with such platforms (Bowman, 2015). Moreover, platform use is also influenced by how users imagine and expect features to work as well as by the designers that envision, or better, allow the users to engage with the platforms' functionalities in particular ways.

Altmetrics build on the data that is derived from user actions on social media platforms. Hence, the affordances are crucial for the development of altmetrics. It is the producers of social media platforms who dictate via affordances what forms user interaction can (not) take and, ultimately, which data can be analyzed and used in altmetrics. For example, altmetric aggregators, such as PlumX or Altmetric.com, look for scholarly publications and whether and how often they appear in tweets (i.e. a posting on Twitter), are liked (e.g. an endorsement on Facebook) or are referenced (e.g. in Wikipedia or policy documents) because it is possible to do so, which means Twitter or Facebook allow for tracking this interaction and for third parties to access that data. However, altmetrics aggregators cannot aggregate any information on user engagement if it is not reflected in an affordance provided by the social media platform. Given the algorithmic structure of today's social media platforms there are also (for the user) hidden affordances[5] that, for example, influence how information is displayed, as in rankings, and along with it if and what type of interaction takes place.

On the other hand, users use affordances in a plethora of ways to express their intention, while there is even the chance that users use an affordance for goals that have not been intended by the designers of the platforms (e.g. if a researcher keeps all posts on Facebook private because (s)he uses the account for bookmarking). Such motivations, as well as the different environments in or the devices (e.g. access via an app or desktop version) via which interactions take place must be taken into account when interpreting altmetrics. This is similar to more traditional bibliometric

---

5 There are, however, approaches to address this issue and to increase transparency, e.g. NISO Altmetrics Data Quality Code of Conduct, https://www.niso.org/publications/rp-25-2016-altmetrics (July 15, 2020).

studies that also go beyond pure numbers when analyzing and explaining the impact of scientific work.

The high dependency of altmetrics on, most of the time, commercial data and platforms poses a severe challenge in altmetrics research, given that there is no way to ever learn about all affordances the platforms provide, how they work, and how they are used by all stakeholders. Therefore, in terms of interpretation altmetrics studies must be incomplete and will always leave questions unanswered.

This does not mean, however, that altmetrics research should not take an effort to increase the knowledge on social media's affordances, or any other data provider, to support the understanding and interpretation of altmetrics, to reveal the value of counted use of affordances and to learn about the motivation why the numbers were generated in the first place. The state of knowledge in this regard is summarized in the next paragraph.

Researchers and how they use Social Media

Social media aids researchers in the collaborative production and exchange of knowledge including stakeholders outside of academia, e.g. policymakers or the general public (Nentwich and König, 2014). Rowlands et al. (2011) confirm that almost 50 % of researchers use social media to communicate, share, and disseminate scholarly information and, along with it, make different research outputs (i.e., articles, slides, datasets, code) more transparent. Similar results were obtained by, amongst others,[6] Tenopir et al. (2013), Mehrazar et al. (2018), and Priem et al. (2012), which we will summarize in the following.

Academic researchers that use social media platforms are frequently coming from Europe and Africa, and less from Asia and North America (Rowlands et al., 2011) and the majority of academic users of social media are male (Sugimoto et al., 2017). Additionally to researchers, institutions from higher education, libraries, and organizations like publishers or journals use social media platforms. According to Rowlands et al. (2011), Earth Sciences is the discipline with the highest share of researchers active on social media, followed by Environmental Sciences, Physics, Life Sciences, Neurosciences, Social Sciences, Mathematics, and Computer Science etc. Besides the disciplines, the use of social media tools can also be influenced by the experience or the age of the researchers. Experienced researchers use social media platforms (i.e. Twitter, LinkedIn) primarily for sharing their research output with the public, while young researchers often use social media channels that provide questioning and answering features (e.g. StackExchange, StackOverflow) to

---

[6] For a more exhaustive overview on academic social media use please refer to Sugimoto et al. (2017).

search for information as well as platforms for publishing code (e.g. GitHub; Mehrazar et al., 2018).

The type of social media also significantly affects the purposes of scholarly work for which they are used. For example, platforms related to dissemination, consumption, communication, and promotion are extensively used in comparison with platforms related to building up scholarship (Sugimoto et al., 2017).

Facebook, LinkedIn, Academica.edu, and ResearchGate have a wide application in scholarly communication processes. These social networks allow researchers to create public profiles along with relations to other users, to disseminate research and to follow research outputs via postings. They are used for professional branding (Sugimoto et al., 2017). Facebook is popular among younger researchers (Rowlands et al., 2011). LinkedIn is a platform often used by (older generations of) academics (Rowlands et al., 2011). ResearchGate and Academia.edu are two popular academic networks allowing researchers to upload and discover new scholarly publications. Another motivation for using academic networks is tracking the impact of research as well as of those they follow (Melero, 2015).

Mendeley, Zotero, CiteULike, and BibSonomy are social bookmarking and reference management systems (Sugimoto et al., 2017). These platforms are used to organize literature, share, save or favorite publications. Mendeley has been heavily investigated especially because it delivers altmetric data, i.e. readership counts, that is used by all altmetrics aggregators (Costas, Zahedi, and Wouters 2015). Its core users are doctoral students followed by master students (Costas et al., 2015; Nuredini and Peters, 2015; Zahedi et al., 2013). Students usually use Mendeley to search for articles whereas professors use Mendeley to publish their research (Mohammadi et al., 2016).

Twitter is a microblogging tool used by 93 % of researchers and is identified as the source often used for self-promotion, communication, and discussions during scientific conferences (Rowlands et al., 2011). Twitter supports dissemination of scholarly information and is especially used by experienced researchers (Bowman, 2015). Twitter affordances such as tweets, retweets, and hashtags are used by researchers to communicate scientific messages (Letierce et al., 2010). Some researchers are using less RSS feeds to find information or write fewer blog posts and instead share information quickly by posting a tweet. Also, hashtags are used to alert peer researchers so that other Twitter users can follow the discussions.

WordPress and Blogger are the most used blogging services by researchers that blog about their scientific ideas (Rowlands et al., 2011). Scientific blogs allow researchers to share opinions with each other as well as test the quality of publications that are published online by peer-reviewing and discussing them (Shema et al., 2012).

SlideShare, FigShare, and GitHub are social data sharing services where researchers can share and reuse slides, code, figures, infographics, conference posters etc. YouTube is used for video sharing where online TED conferences are found to be among the most prominent contemporary scholarly communication initiatives (Sugimoto et al., 2017).

All these different actions that (different groups of) researchers (typically) perform on social media present different types of engagement evoked by affordances, leading to a multidimensional nature of altmetrics (Holmberg, 2015). Thus, several classifications have been suggested to better describe altmetrics, reflect their multidimensionality, make them comparable, and aid their interpretation.

Classifications of Social Media and Altmetrics

We will present three approaches that a) take into account the sources from which altmetrics are derived from, b) are based on the level of engagement with scholarly products that altmetrics may reflect, and c) are used by altmetrics aggregators.

Source-based Classifications of Altmetrics

Wouters et al. (2018) have classified social media platforms used for altmetrics into those with social media focus, those with scholarly focus, or both (see Figure 1). Platforms that have a strong social media focus are Twitter, Facebook, LinkedIn, and Stackexchange. They enable users to interact, share, communicate etc. Platforms with a strong scholarly focus are for example Scopus or Web of Science, Mendeley, F1000 Recommendations, as well as Wikipedia citations. ResearchGate and Academia.edu can be considered a mix of social media and scholarly focus. Wouters et al. (2018) suggest that in addition to traditional scholarly platforms (e.g. Web of Science), altmetrics derived from platforms with a scholarly focus can be used for research evaluation purposes. With that, they follow the traditional approach of bibliographic and citation databases that determine what is a countable item by assessing the source and labeling it as appropriate (i.e. citations from certain journals are counted while others are not).

Engagement-based Classifications of Altmetrics

Haustein, Bowman, and Costas (2016) propose a framework accounting for the different levels of engagement on social media that can happen between the users and research outputs. The framework is composed of three activities: access, appraise, and apply. Access captures activities such as "views" or "downloads", reflecting interest in research outputs. Appraise is associated with affordances such as "mentioning" of or "commenting" on research within different platforms. Apply captures "adoption" or "application" of (parts of) the research to create new research results, for example by re-using datasets, code etc. Another classification of altmetrics based on different

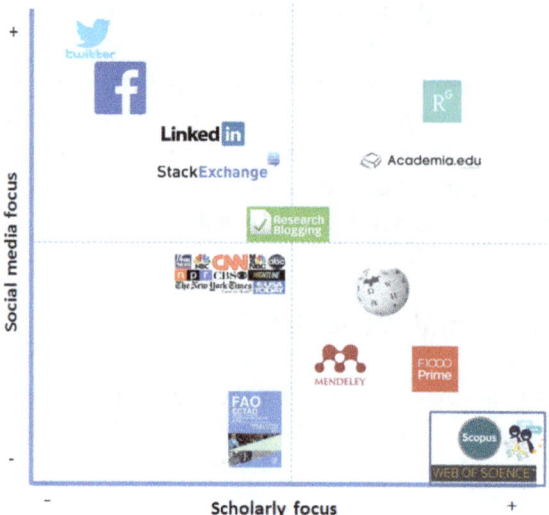

Figure 1: Classification of platforms used for collection of altmetrics data (Wouters et al., 2018).

levels of engagement has been presented by PLOS ALM. This classification is suggested to reflect the correlations between metrics, and to be expandable for future metrics (Lin and Fenner, 2013a).

Engagement-based classifications of altmetrics utilize the inherent "value" of a certain type of engagement with a scholarly product that can lead to a hierarchy of valuable engagements. The premise behind this structure is that access requires far less engagement, intellectual effort, or time than apply and that, therefore, they should be treated differently (Lemke et al., 2018). It is the engagement-based classifications which strongly take into account the affordances of social media. Wouters et al. (2018) identified the internal heterogeneity of altmetric indicators which is an important feature that one should be careful when using. They consider indicators that come from the same platforms but they imply different actions. For example, a tweet and retweet arguably have different roles and should be valued differently. Altmetrics that are accumulated from Mendeley or F1000 recommendations are conceptually near citations or peer review and those that come from Twitter or Facebook show another impact (believed as social impact). Mendeley readership information are being identified with a positive correlation to citations, meaning that these two metrics are related. On the other hand, F1000 recommendations known as metrics of quality face a low number of articles that are recommended on these services and the correlation between these counts with citations is weak, meaning that they are not related.

Altmetrics Aggregators-based Classifications

The following classifications stem from real-world applications and have been proposed by enterprises aiming at aggregating altmetrics information. They follow different approaches to reflect altmetrics' multidimensionality, often combining source-based and engagement-based classifications.

ImpactStory allows researchers to create personal profiles and track the online impact (via blogs, Wikipedia, Mendeley and more) of their scholarly outputs (Piwowar and Priem, 2013). The ImpactStory classification of altmetrics differentiates between impact on two types of users: a) scholars, to show the scientific impact of research outputs, and b) the public, to reflect the societal impact of research. According to this classification, scholars rather, for example, discuss research in scientific blogs and read PDFs, whereas public users often use Twitter or Facebook and read HTML documents. ImpactStory further divides all of its various altmetrics into five categories: viewed, saved, discussed, recommended, and cited.

PLOS uses a very similar scheme for its article-level metrics, as it was heavily inspired by ImpactStory's classification (Lin and Fenner, 2013b). According to Fenner (2013), the five categories inherited from ImpactStory represent different levels of engagement with a respective research article. Both ImpactStory's and PLOS ALM's classifications of social media and their altmetrics metrics are shown in Figure 2. Some discrepancies result from slight conceptual differences between the two approaches, e.g. on ImpactStory, "Wikipedia mentions" are categorized as cited, whereas PLOS classifies them as discussed.

PlumX is another altmetric provider that, just like PLOS and ImpactStory, uses five categories: citations, usage, captures, mentions, and social media. They reflect different kinds of attention a research product can receive. PlumX does not proclaim any kind of hierarchy to exist between these categories. For example, captures are assumed to be leading indicators of future citations, while social media is supposed to be a good measure of "how well a particular piece of research has been promoted".[7]

Altmetric.com uses a less explicit system as it does not assign all altmetrics to broad categories. It rather uses a source-based classification and differs between altmetrics stemming from News, Blog, Policy document, Patent, Peer review, and Syllabi. However, a particular classification of altmetrics takes place on Altmetric.com by applying weightings for the calculation of the Altmetric Attention Score. Individual altmet-

---

[7] https://plumanalytics.com/learn/about-metrics/ (July 15, 2020).

ric signals get weights[8] depending on their source (e. g. eight points for a "mention in the news", three points for a "citation on Wikipedia"). So, different altmetrics are implicitly classified based on their source's assumed "value" as a generator of attention.

Area	Scholars	Public
ImpactStory		
Viewed	PDF downloads	HTML downloads
Saved	CiteULike, Mendeley	Delicious
Discussed	Science blogs, journal comments	Blogs, Twitter, Facebook
Recommended	Citations by editorials	Press article
Cited	Citations, full-text mentions	Wikipedia mentions
PLOS	No distinction is made between scholars and public	
Viewed	HTML/ PDF (PLOS or PubMed Central), XML (PLOS)	
Saved	CiteULike, Mendeley	
Discussed	NatureBlogs, ScienceSeeker, ResearchBlogging, PLOS Comments, Wikipedia, Twitter, Facebook	
Recommended	F1000Prime	
Cited	CrossRef, PubMed Central, Web of Science, Scopus	

Figure 2: ImpactStory and PLOS classification (Bornmann, 2014, p. 7).

Altmetrics: Challenges Inherited from Social Media

Altmetrics are identified and suggested as new indicators that can complement citations and that would be suitable for evaluative purposes (Priem et al., 2010; Wouters et al., 2018). Although altmetrics come with the potential to evaluate research, they do have challenges. We will focus on the challenges that are introduced to altmetrics by typical characteristics of social media platforms rather than describing the more general problems altmetrics or altmetrics aggregators may have.

When using altmetrics data quality is an important criterion (Haustein, 2016). Here the APIs of social media introduce a severe bottleneck because it is the owners of social media platforms who decide which data is released and can be fed into altmetrics. Different access rights, that are also subject to change induced by the social media companies, allow download of different portions of social media (e. g. Twitter

---

[8] https://www.altmetric.com/about-our-data/the-donut-and-score/ (July 15, 2020).

Firehose vs. Twitter Streaming API vs. Twitter Search API)[9]. However, it is often unclear which data can be accessed via which API and whether any data is missing (Morstatter et al., 2013; Zahedi et al., 2014).

Furthermore, the users, or rather their usage routines, severely challenge the wide application of altmetrics. The first problem occurs while identifying scholarly works on social media platforms. The identification is the prerequisite for the collection of altmetrics and is most often done via persistent identifiers, such as DOIs, attached to scholarly products. If the metadata (usually DOIs) of research products is not available nor correct, either because the users have not mentioned it or because the social media platforms have not processed it properly, collected altmetric data may result in missing or wrong values. For instance, if an article does not have a DOI and the altmetric information is requested based on the article's title, it can happen that this article might not be found with altmetric information because the social media platform is not able to identify the paper based on its title only. This phenomenon is most evident for articles with missing metadata often originated from Mendeley (Zahedi et al., 2014; Nuredini and Peters, 2015).

The second problem for altmetrics, especially when used in research evaluation, derives from the social media affordances. Altmetrics can decrease over time because users might delete their social media accounts (and along with them all traces that reflect engagement on the platform) or remove single scholarly products from their account on reference management systems. Such, surely permitted, affordance use of social media has to lead to the elimination of certain altmetrics that have been accumulated for particular research products and which requests constant updating of altmetrics data, if not in real-time then at least on a regular basis, a pain-taking and time-consuming task for all users of altmetrics, indeed.

Conclusion

Broad and narrow approaches to altmetrics leave traces on the web: data that can be further analyzed and that can help understand how researchers and other stakeholders interact with scholarly works. Altmetrics particularly benefit from the speedy publication process provided by social media, its lack of gatekeepers, and the platforms' public APIs. However, user engagement is always enabled as well as constrained by the affordances the social media platforms provide. Hence, altmetrics can only reflect what was allowed to be done on the platform and not necessarily the real user intention.

To support the interpretation of altmetrics, several classifications have been proposed to group similar altmetrics. However, because of the affordances, the hetero-

---

[9] Twitter has in recent times introduced a new set of APIs: Standards APIs, Premium APIs, Enterprise APIs (https://developer.twitter.com/en/products/products-overview# [July 15, 2020]).

geneity of social media platforms, as well as the different users using social media, proposed classes are not disjunct and, as studies have shown, most often fail in accurately describing the meaning of aggregated user engagement.

The challenges that altmetrics inherit from social media make it difficult to apply altmetrics for research assessment but, despite that, altmetrics demonstrate some potential as a supplement to traditional bibliometrics because of their kinship to social media (i.e. diversity, speed, openness). It is for sure that social media and altmetrics pose a moving target as platforms and affordances will be invented or will disappear in the future. Continuous investigation of users, affordances, platforms, and motivations will ensure that researchers can identify those use cases, e.g. information filtering, that make the best of social media's and altmetrics' potential.

References

Adie, E 2014, 'Taking the alternative mainstream', *Profesional De La Informacion*, vol. 23, no. 4, pp. 349–51.

Bornmann, L 2014, 'Do altmetrics point to the broader impact of research? An overview of benefits and disadvantages of altmetrics', *Journal of informetrics*, vol. 8, no. 4, pp. 895–903.

Bowman, TD 2015, *Investigating the use of affordances and framing techniques by scholars to manage personal and professional impressions on Twitter*, Dissertation, Indiana University, http://www.tdbowman.com/pdf/2015_07_TDBowman_Dissertation.pdf (July 15, 2020).

Brody, T, Harnad, S & Carr, L 2006, 'Earlier web usage statistics as predictors of later citation impact', *Journal of the American Society for Information Science and Technology*, vol. 57, no. 8, pp. 1060–72.

Bucher, T & Helmond, A 2017, 'The affordances of social media platforms', in J Burgess, T Poell & A Marwick (eds.), *The SAGE Handbook of Social Media*, SAGE, London, New York.

Burgess, J, Marwick, A & Poell, T (eds.) 2017, *The SAGE handbook of social media*, SAGE, London, New York.

Costas, R, Zahedi, Z & Wouters, P 2015, 'Do "altmetrics" correlate with citations? Extensive comparison of altmetric indicators with citations from a multidisciplinary perspective', *Journal of the Association for Information Science and Technology*, vol. 66, no. 10, pp. 2003–19, doi: https://doi.org/10.1002/asi.2330.

Eysenbach, G 2011, 'Can tweets predict citations? Metrics of social impact based on Twitter and correlation with traditional metrics of scientific impact', *Journal of medical Internet research*, vol. 13, no. 4, p. e123, doi: https://doi.org/10.2196/jmir.2012.

Fenner, M 2013, 'What Can Article-Level Metrics Do For You?', *PLOS Biology*, vol. 11, no. 10, p. e1001687, doi: https://doi.org/10.1371/journal.pbio.1001687.

Gaver, WW 1991, 'Technology affordances', in *Proceedings of the SIGCHI conference on Human factors in computing systems*, New Orleans, Louisiana, USA, pp. 79–84, doi: https://doi.org/10.1145/108844.108856.

Haustein, S 2016, 'Grand challenges in altmetrics: heterogeneity, data quality and dependencies', *Scientometrics*, vol. 108, no. 1, pp. 413–23.

Haustein, S, Bowman, TD & Costas, R 2016, 'Interpreting "altmetrics": viewing acts on social media through the lens of citation and social theories', in CR Sugimoto (ed.), *Theories of Informetrics and Scholarly Communication. A Festschrift in Honor of Blaise Cronin*, De Gruyter, Berlin.

Holmberg, K 2015, 'Classifying altmetrics by level of impact', in AA Salah, Y Tonta, AAA Salah, C Sugimoto & U Al, Proceedings of the 15th International Society of Scientometrics and Informetrics Conference, pp. 101–02, Istanbul, Turkey.

König, R, & Nentwich, M 2017, 'Soziale Medien in der Wissenschaft' in JH Schmidt & M Taddicken (eds.), Handbuch Soziale Medien, pp. 169–88, Springer, Wiesbaden.

Lemke, S, Mehrazar, M, Mazarakis, A & Peters, I 2018, 'Are there different types of online research impact?', in Proceedings of the Association for Information Science and Technology, vol. 55, no. 1, pp. 282–89.

Letierce, J, Passant, A, Breslin, JG & Decker, S 2010, 'Understanding how Twitter is used to spread scientific messages', in Proceedings of the WebSci10: Extending the Frontiers of Society Online, April 26–27, Raleigh, NC, US.

Lin, J & Fenner, M 2013a, 'The many faces of article-level metrics', Bulletin of the American Society for Information Science and Technology, vol. 39, no. 4, pp. 27–30.

Lin, J & Fenner, M 2013b, 'Altmetrics in Evolution: Defining and Redefining the Ontology of Article-Level Metrics', Information Standards Quarterly, vol. 25, no. 2, pp. 20–26, doi: https://doi.org/10.3789/isqv25no2.2013.04.

Mehrazar, M, Kling, CC, Lemke, S, Mazarakis, A & Peters, I 2018, 'Can We Count on Social Media Metrics? First Insights into the Active Scholarly Use of Social Media', arXiv preprint, arXiv:1804.02751.

Melero, R 2015, 'Altmetrics–a complement to conventional metrics', Biochemia medica: Biochemia medica, vol. 25, no. 2, pp. 152–60.

Mohammadi, E, Thelwall, M & Kousha, K 2016, 'Can Mendeley bookmarks reflect readership? A survey of user motivations', Journal of the Association for Information Science and Technology, vol. 67, no. 5, pp. 1198–1209.

Morstatter, F, Pfeffer, J, Liu, H & Carley, KM 2013, 'Is the sample good enough? comparing data from twitter's streaming api with twitter's firehose', in Seventh International AAAI Conference on Weblogs and Social Media, Cambridge, USA, July 8–10, 2013, pp. 400–08, https://www.aaai.org/ocs/index.php/ICWSM/ICWSM13/paper/view/6071/6379 (July 15, 2020).

Nentwich, M & König, R 2014, 'Academia goes Facebook? The potential of social network sites in the scholarly realm', in S Bartling & S Friesike (eds.), Opening science, pp. 107–24, Springer, Cham.

Nuredini, K & Peters, I 2015, 'Economic and Business Studies Journals and Readership Information from Mendeley', in Re: inventing Information Science in the Networked Society, Proceedings of the 14th International Symposium on Information Science, Zadar/Croatia, 19th–21st May 2015 (ISI 2015), Glückstad, vwh Verlag Werner Hülsbusch, pp. 380–92.

Peters, I, & Heise, C 2014, Soziale Netzwerke für Forschende: Eine Einführung. CoScience – Gemeinsam forschen und publizieren mit dem Netz, https://osl.tib.eu/w/Handbuch_Co Science/Online-Profil-_und_Netzwerk-Dienste (July 15, 2020).

Piwowar, H & Priem, J 2013, 'The power of altmetrics on a CV', Bulletin of the American Society for Information Science and Technology, vol. 39, no. 4, pp. 10–13.

Priem, J, Taraborelli, D, Groth, P & Neylon, C 2010, Altmetrics: A manifesto, http://altmetrics.org/manifesto (July 15, 2020).

Priem, J & Hemminger, BH 2010, 'Scientometrics 2.0: New metrics of scholarly impact on the social Web', First Monday, vol. 15, no. 7, https://firstmonday.org/ojs/index.php/fm/article/view/2874 (July 15, 2020).

Priem, J, Piwowar, HA & Hemminger, BM 2012, 'Altmetrics in the wild: Using social media to explore scholarly impact', arXiv preprint arXiv:1203.4745 (July 15, 2020).

Ronald, R & Fred, YY 2013, 'A multi-metric approach for research evaluation', Chinese Science Bulletin, vol. 58, no. 26, pp. 3288–90.

Rowlands, I, Nicholas, D, Russell, B, Canty, N & Watkinson, A 2011, 'Social media use in the research workflow', *Learned Publishing*, vol. 24, no. 3, pp. 183–95.

Shema, H, Bar-Ilan, J & Thelwall, M 2012, 'Research blogs and the discussion of scholarly information', *PloS one*, vol. 7, no. 5, p. e35869.

Shuai, X, Pepe, A & Bollen, J 2012, 'How the scientific community reacts to newly submitted preprints: Article downloads, twitter mentions, and citations', *PloS one*, vol. 7, no. 11, p. e47523, https://journals.plos.org/plosone/article?id=10.1371/journal.pone.0047523 (July 15, 2020).

Sugimoto, CR, Work, S, Larivière, V & Haustein, S 2017, 'Scholarly use of social media and altmetrics: A review of the literature', *Journal of the Association for Information Science and Technology*, vol. 68, no. 9, pp. 2037–62.

Tenopir, C, Volentine, R & King, DW 2013, 'Social media and scholarly reading', *Online Information Review*, vol. 37, no. 2, pp. 193–216.

Thelwall, M, Vaughan, L & Björneborn, L 2005, 'Webometrics', *Annual review of information science and technology*, vol. 39, no. 1, pp. 81–135.

Wouters, P & Costas, R 2012, 'Users, narcissism and control: tracking the impact of scholarly publications in the 21st century', SURFfoundation, Utrecht, pp. 847–57, http://research-acumen.eu/wp-content/uploads/Users-narcissism-and-control.pdf (July 15, 2020).

Wouters, P, Zahedi, Z & Costas, R 2018, 'Social media metrics for new research evaluation', arXiv preprint arXiv:1806.10541.

Zahedi, Z, Costas, R & Wouters, PF 2013, 'What is the impact of the publications read by the different mendeley users? Could they help to identify alternative types of impact?', *PLoS ALM Workshop*, San Francisco.

Zahedi, Z, Haustein, S & Bowman, T 2014, 'Exploring data quality and retrieval strategies for Mendeley reader counts', in *SIG/MET workshop, ASIS&T 2014 annual meeting*, Seattle, www.asis.org/SIG/SIGMET/data/uploads/sigmet2014/zahedi.pdf.

4.4 Altmetric.com: A Brief History
Ben McLeish

Abstract: Shortly following the publication of the altmetrics manifesto, a number of small companies were founded to address the demand of services around metrics aggregation on scholarly outputs. This chapter endeavours to tell the story of the Altmetric service, a small company which now has its home at Digital Science.

Keywords: altmetric, history, metric aggregation, database, commercial.

A Brief History

Review the publications of any major publisher today, or use one of the many research portals or library search systems deployed online and you are more likely than not to bump into the ubiquitous Altmetric badge or "donut" graphic. This usually multicolored hollow disc, appearing with a score at its otherwise blank centre, displays how an article or other research output has been mentioned. If an article has been in the news, this donut displays a red portion, or is entirely red if the item in question has been mentioned exclusively in the news. If the article has been linked to on Twitter, that recognizable Twitter-like light blue color also appears on the donut. All in all, this donut displaying different types of attention for the item you are looking at could have one, or several, of 18 different types of attention, from blogs, news, social media and references on Wikipedia through to references in patents and mentions in policy documents.

The ubiquity of these badges across the web has made Altmetric in all senses synonymous with the wider altmetrics movement, with its attempts to bring into the mainstream the consideration of the value of research attention outside of purely article citations. Given that there are millions of these badges around the web, displaying tens of millions of references they have aggregated from the world's leading news and discussion platforms, it might be tempting to think that Altmetric must be some enormous company; in fact, as of mid 2019, the company numbers a mere 25, and at its founding in 2011 and in its early days actually consisted of only one person, founder Euan Adie. Whilst working as a researcher, Adie had already begun working on an aggregator platform for scientific blogs, the now defunct Postgenomic.com. Recognizing that researchers should have the ability to take all the available credit for the impact resulting from their works, and that this is immensely hard and time-consuming to do by hand, Adie decided to diversify the tracking of blogs into a wider effort to detect, capture, and store the records of as many venues of discussion about research as one could reasonably and relevantly include.

Ben McLeish, Director of Engagement & Advocacy of dimensions.ai and altmetric.com, ben@altmetric.com

https://doi.org/10.1515/9783110646610-022

Thus, the mission of the service at the outset was to collate and organise the world's detectable and linkable online attention and discussion about research items[1]. "To allow researchers to take credit where credit is due" was the common tagline, as Adie presented the concept of Altmetric during public presentations. A simple bookmarklet, sitting in your browser's bookmarks bar, could with one click drop down the Altmetric donut for any item which had a scholarly identifier, like a DOI, present on the page. This donut could be clicked, and the viewer would be navigated to a tabbed Details Page view, where every tweet, every public Facebook Page post or policy document was organized and linked to. Comparative scores showed how this item's attention compared to other items of the same age, or from the same publication, or indeed how the volume and nature of the attention compared to the full corpus of research items for which attention had been found online. There was no longer a need to attempt to tease out the tweets which referenced the work of a researcher, or vanity googling the title of a publication to see what pages on the Internet refer to it by name. Researchers could now easily see where online news or blogs referred to their published articles, even if they were not themselves named in the coverage, or if all relevant keywords were absent, or even if the publication itself was not referred to except via a link to the original article. Soon after developing the early version of this service, Adie submitted the concept and the service to Elsevier's Apps for Science Competition, where it won first prize, and gave Adie enough capital to develop what is now known as the Altmetric Explorer.[2]

The Altmetric Explorer delivered a global view of the attention which research has received, searchable and filterable by attention source, time frame, keyword and, from the 2018 period onwards, by research organisation affiliation, Fields of Research subject area, funder, publisher, and by Open Access status of the research. Additionally, institutional clients could ask Altmetric to import the publication profile of the organisation into a private instance of the Explorer, along with the institutional hierarchy of the institution, right down to the publication footprint of individual researchers. This importing was achieved by a connector between either the institutional repository or the Current Research Information System deployed by the institution. For customers without such research infrastructure, a spreadsheet could be uploaded manually which would populate the client's custom view of the Explorer as well. In this manner, not only were customers able to see their own publications and the current as well as historical trends in research attention they had been receiving, but were able to toggle to the full database as well, to compare their attention with any timeframe, any other automatically detected affiliation, or any other manner of filtering or facetting the attention they chose to employ.

---

[1] Liu J & Adie E, 'New perspectives on article-level metrics: developing ways to assess research uptake and impact online', https://insights.uksg.org/articles/10.1629/2048–7754.79/ (July 15, 2020).
[2] Adie, E & Roe, W 2013, 'Altmetric: enriching scholarly content with article-level discussion and metrics', *Learned Publishing*, vol. 12, no. 3, pp. 11–17.

Foundational Approaches to the Tracking Attention to Research

A database of research attention, allowing for a summary view of the world's attention to the world's research, navigable by, for example, keyword, date, publisher, or type of attention seems, in hindsight, to be an extremely obvious idea. Just as Internet search engines began with indexing the entire web so as to provide a basic comprehensive service which matched its subject, so Altmetric decided that it would attempt to collate the global reach and engagement around all research, whether they came from a particular publisher, institution, country, or potential institution wishing to access the research interactions of their online audience.

In order to supply a meaningful database which would allow for trustworthy reporting, several decisions were made as to what data should be included as well as excluded. The datapoint about online engagement most widely and most frequently raised was that of usage statistics received by research, which Altmetric chose from the outset not to include in its database. There are many reasons for this. Most prevalently, despite many years and valuable efforts by the scholarly community to standardize download statistics in the form of the COUNTER framework (now in its fifth Code of Practise iteration[3]), it is still impossible to get a centralized and reliably maintained store of all usage statistics worldwide for the publishing community. This would be critical if Altmetric were to be able to offer usage stats one-to-one per item. Additionally, the rise of institutional repositories and third-party non-publisher platforms such as ResearchGate, Academia.edu, and other repositories of publications has meant a proliferation of decentralized usage which cannot be aggregated successfully by any provider of altmetrics data.

To complicate matters further, databases of aggregated content by suppliers other than the original publisher produce additional decentralization of usage statistics. These platforms are often subject to embargo period by the original publisher. This means that if an altmetrics provider is able to obtain download statistics from the database provider, yet cannot collect statistics from the original publisher, a large chunk of usage data would be missing; precisely the usage expected to be among the highest in the early stages after publication. As Altmetric wanted to be able to evenly and fairly measure the attention sources, usage statistics, which are also anonymized by nature and therefore would provide limited information about the nature of the audience, was decided against as an attention source.

Another key decision early on, which affects clearly what sources can be considered, was whether or not the sources in question would be openly accessible for members of the public to visit and review themselves. Closed, private or otherwise publicly inaccessible sources were chosen by and large to be excluded from the Altmetric service's tracking for several reasons. The first was technical. Private Twitter

---

[3] Project COUNTER, The COUNTER Code of Practice for Release 5 https://www.projectcounter.org/code-of-practice-five-sections/abstract/ (July 15, 2020).

accounts, or policy organizations who do not make their briefings public for financial or political reasons, are sources of data which are technically not able to be reviewed by the Altmetric tracking service, as access to the data itself is restricted. A further reason for excluding these inaccessible sources is that Altmetric wanted to ensure that the attention data that are made available are what is termed "auditable." If a particular piece of research has had a great amount of attention, the user should have the ability to witness, audit or review the attention itself, rather than being presented with a data point which cannot be viewed or accessed. This is particularly important not just because the inability to access a source of attention presents a lower quality user experience, but because the potential positive or negative attention an item might receive presently has to be adjudicated by the person reviewing the attention data. Altmetric can only inform its users of the level of attention something has received, and direct them to the source of this attention. When it comes to the semantic implications of the material, this is left up to the users themselves to collate and sort.

Altmetric's Sources of Attention

Having explained some of the data exclusions from the Altmetric service, it is now worth listing what is tracked by the service. At time of writing, Altmetric tracks any public linking to research on the Twitter platform, public posts on Facebook pages (not from individual users), 3,000 separate news sites, 15,200 blogs, 249 YouTube channels (whose mentions we discover via links in the video description field), references to research found in the English, Swedish, and Finnish versions of Wikipedia, recommendations of articles on the Faculty of 1000 Prime platform, any mention of research within a half a million policy documents from 70 policy organizations across the world, references within 40 million patents, references from post-publication peer review platforms Publons and PubPeer, posts on Reddit, and on Q&A sites Stackoverflow and StackExchange.

Additionally, some sources have been tracked in the past which have either been deprecated due to technical limitations, or have gone offline. In the case of the latter, Google's "Google+" service was ended formally in April 2019. In the case of the former, LinkedIn, Weibo, and Pinterest all became technically untrackable in mid-2015. Where historical data exists, this has been kept in the database.

These combined sources total some 107 million references to 13 million items of research. While Altmetric benchmarks January 2012 as the date at which sources are considered to have begun, there are mentions in the service dating back to the late 1940s, where policy documents from the Food and Agricultural Organisation of the United Nations referenced an item which have since been given digital metadata (such as a DOI), and thus have been found via Altmetric's text mining technology. This means when a new institution implements the Altmetric service, the institution sees a full view of their research attention.

The Altmetric Attention Score

Such a massive dataset requires waypoints and indicators to provide contextual information which is otherwise lost in the sheer volume of data points. To address this, a critical component to making Altmetric's large database of attention usable is the presence of an integrated scoring system for contextualizing how much or how little relative attention an item has received. This takes the form of a singular numeric indicator, the Altmetric Attention Score, placed in the centre of the donut that each item with attention receives. Each piece of research is given a ranking based on how much attention has been received relative to other items from the same journal, from the same time frame of publication to a combination of these two prior positions, and finally compared to everything else the Altmetric service has tracked since its inception.

As a rule, the higher the score is, the more interaction an item has received. The score is weighted so that social media posts, being brief, quick to produce, and easy to repost or retweet, score lower than the appearance of a mention in a blog, which requires a lot more editorial work and authorship, and constitutes a deeper impact with the source of the mention. Further still, appearances in news sites are weighed even higher than blogs, as these sites are often the most prominent aggregators of research news, attract a large audience, and signify real value for researchers in their quest for research promotion.

However, not all of Altmetric's sources aggregate in this fashion. Appearances of research within patent literature as citations and references to research within policy documents are not scored by volume, as this sort of attention is less "public" facing; instead, patent references are scored by patent office count, and policy sources are scored by policy organisation. Forty references by the World Health Organisation therefore do not get a factor of 40 applied to a baseline score, but count as a score of three, awarded for the policy body itself. However, every mention is still collected and linked, as are all mentions in Altmetric.[4]

Shortlinks

Tracking links to scholarly attention is the primary method by which Altmetric picks up references to research, with the exception of news and policy sources, which are also treated with text-mining, so that article titles, author names, publication years, and journal names can be detected and resolved to a DOI. The main challenge with link tracking is that while it is possible to curate a library of known scholarly sources of data (including publisher websites, lists of repository sources, academic platforms

---

4 Davies, F, 'Numbers behind Numbers: The Altmetric Attention Score and Sources Explained', https://www.altmetric.com/blog/scoreanddonut/ (July 15, 2020).

etc.) the nature of online media, especially blogs, Facebook and Twitter, is to shorten all links to shared items for the sake of brevity and the platform's own user and content tracking and analytics requirements. Hence, every link to research is disguised as an unrecognized short link. Facebook uses the prefix fb.me, Twitter uses t.co and so on. To solve this, Altmetric developed a short link-resolving software process known internally as "Embiggen",[5] which reverse-engineers the links back to their original form and then captures the item. As of July 2019, the time of writing, more than 8,400 unique short linking services are supported natively in the Altmetric service. If a user shares a piece of research and shortens it, or shares it via a service which shortens the link automatically, most likely Altmetric will be able to track it.

Serving as a Dataset for Altmetrics Research

It is worth ending the foregoing with a note on how Altmetric's data is made available for the research community. While the service itself is offered commercially to all sectors and has by any measure been successful in that regard, Altmetric has from its inception maintained a strict and vital mandate to make its data available to third parties and researchers in order to promote and enable research around altmetrics as a discipline itself. As we maintain the largest and most auditable dataset around research engagement, the value of the service is fundamentally linked to its service to the research community. We have always made available either parts or all of the data to research-minded individuals and projects; in the years leading up to 2018, this was done upon request, while since 2018 Altmetric has offered a Research Data Access Program complete with a registration form for researchers to fill in. After a review, no-cost licenses are issued along with the data for non-commercial re-use in research projects and other efforts. It is our hope that these efforts, along with those of similar organizations in the discipline, help to cement the rightful place of the standing of the public's attention to research, how it is interacted with online, and perhaps improve and refine the methods of communication of that research for better understanding and education of the greater part of the populace who are not engaged directly in an academic field. In an age where mistrust of experts and active anti-science bias are rife and having a direct impact upon policies concerning the environment and the social fabric of the world, such efforts are perhaps as important as the research itself.

---

5 Mucur, P, 'A Ruby library to expand shortened URLs', Github.com (July 15, 2020).

4.5 PlumX Metrics (Plum Analytics) in Practice

Juan Gorraiz and Christian Gumpenberger

Abstract: Academic libraries are predestined to embrace usage metrics and altmetrics in order to provide innovative research support services. These new metrics should not be reduced to evaluative purposes only, but rather be appealing for researchers to promote their research outputs, enhance their visibility and increase the likeliness to be cited. This paper demonstrates two practical applications of altmetrics by means of PlumX: first, monitoring altmetrics data at the national and institutional level; and second, providing altmetrics as complementary data in bibliometric reports for research assessment.

In the first case, monitoring analyses helped in revealing new trends and assessing to what extent usage and altmetrics data are already available and applicable. Altmetrics are still in their infancy and acceptance and uptake among researchers is slow, particularly in the humanities. However, our study hints at an increasing use of social media within the scholarly community in Austria.

In the second case, our study corroborates that altmetrics provide additional information on the bigger picture concerning the broader impact of research output. Faculty-wide application is yet a scarce procedure with limited added-value, but their inclusion in the assessment of individual researchers is a service with an increasing demand, which can be particularly valuable in disciplines where traditional metrics are scarce and problematic. However, inclusion always requires preceding researcher's consent and according education on the known shortcomings and restrictions. PlumX has proven to be a very useful tool in order to monitor the broader impact of the publication output, either at national, institutional or individual level. Its multidimensional aspect is explicitly noteworthy and useful.

Keywords: altmetrics, PlumX, bibliometrics, research output, monitoring, individual assessment.

Introduction

The early twenty-first century was affected by two major developments (Gorraiz, Wieland, and Gumpenberger, 2017). First was the swift adoption of digital information on the Internet, specifically available from e-journals (Kraemer, 2006; Gorraiz, Gumpenberger, and Schlögl, 2014), which resulted in an increased tracking of usage data

---

Dr. **Juan Gorraiz**, Department for Bibliometrics and Publication Strategies, University of Vienna, Boltzmanngasse 5, 1090 Vienna, Austria, juan.gorraiz@univie.ac.at
Christian Gumpenberger, Department for Bibliometrics and Publication Strategies, University of Vienna, Boltzmanngasse 5, 1090 Vienna, Austria, christian.gumpenberger@univie.ac.at

https://doi.org/10.1515/9783110646610-023

(e.g. views and downloads) and a renaissance of usage metrics beyond the scope of librarian collection management complementary to citation metrics for scientometric purposes (Glänzel and Gorraiz, 2015). Second, was the social media revolution and all subsequent Web 2.0 practices, which have also gained momentum in the scholarly realm (Procter et al., 2010; Kietzmann et al., 2011; Wouters and Costas, 2012; Haustein et al., 2014).

Usage metrics and new social media-based metrics now exist alongside traditional metrics. The term "altmetrics" (for alternative metrics) was coined by Priem et al. (2010). This broader scope now facilitates a more diverse assessment of research outputs on different levels. They are not meant to replace citations, but rather serve as additional means for a more comprehensive resonance of research output, now often called "broader impact" (Bornmann, 2014).

However, the use of these new metrics for evaluative purposes is still very controversial and challenging. Unresolved issues such as standardization, stability, reliability, completeness, interrelationship, scalability, and normalization of the collected data are still to be tackled. Several studies have so far addressed the crucial question of what altmetrics actually measure (e.g. Rasmussen and Andersen, 2013; Haustein, Bowman, and Costas, 2016; Haustein, 2016; Repiso, Castillo-Esparcia, and Torres-Salinas, 2019; Gorraiz, 2018). Bornmann, Haunschild, and Adams (2019) recently investigated the validity of altmetrics by using two REF datasets and came to the conclusion that "they may capture a different aspect of societal impact (which can be called unknown attention) to that seen by reviewers (who are interested in the causal link between research and action in society)".

Moreover, these new metrics should not be reduced to evaluative purposes only, but rather should be appealing for researchers to promote their research outputs, enhance their visibility, and increase the likeliness to be cited. Academic libraries are predestined to embrace these new metrics and provide innovative research support services specifically tailored to their different target groups from academia and research administration (Gumpenberger, Wieland, and Gorraiz, 2012).

Altmetrics are still in their infancy and acceptance, and uptake among researchers is slow, particularly in the humanities. It is mainly the young and digital-borne researchers who show more interest and require respective support services for ideal use.

There are currently two major altmetrics aggregators, namely Altmetric.com[1] and PlumX[2].

Altmetric.com has become popular in the publishing world and is already well-implemented in many e-journals websites. It is also notorious for its debatable composite indicator "altmetric attention score" (Gumpenberger, Glänzel, and Gorraiz,

---

[1] https://www.altmetric.com/ (July 15, 2020).
[2] https://plumanalytics.com/ (July 15, 2020).

2016), better known as the so-called donut, which tries to reflect the mere attention that a work has received in the digital world in a single number.

PlumX is the second major altmetrics aggregator, which was recently acquired by Elsevier and incorporated in their Scopus platform. It is promoted as an ideal tool for tracking ALL metrics (a deliberate move from "alt-metrics" to "all metrics") by distinguishing between five categories: quotations, use, captures, mentions, and social media, which are represented by the so-called "plum print". This multidimensional approach is a big advantage, since all data are provided separately and can be interpreted by anyone as they see fit.

A recent study by Bar-Ilan et al. (2019) showed that there are differences in the altmetric counts reported by these two altmetric aggregators.

This paper demonstrates two practical applications of altmetrics by means of PlumX: first, monitoring altmetrics data at the national and institutional level (distinguished between micro-, meso-, and macro-level analyses (Vinkler, 1988); second, providing altmetrics as complementary data in bibliometric reports for individual researcher assessment.

The reader will be informed to what extent PlumX can contribute meaningfully to sound bibliometric analyses provided at universities.

Methodology

For the national monitoring exercise, all Web of Science Core Collection (WoS CC) publications containing "Austria" at least once in their affiliation data and with available DOIs were retrieved for the last four complete publication years (2014, 2015, 2016, and 2017) and entered into the PlumX altmetrics dashboard. The resulting dataset includes the scores of all measures according to their origin and are categorised into five dimensions: Usage, Captures, Mentions, Social Media, and Citations.

In order to analyze the differences between knowledge areas, all publications retrieved in WoS Core Collection have been reclassified according to the field "research areas" in six main knowledge areas: 1) Life Sciences, 2) Physical Sciences, 3) Engineering & Technology, 4) Health Sciences, 5) Social Sciences, and 6) Arts & Humanities.

The most relevant indicators for the assessment of the new metrics are:
Data availability = number of data records traced in PlumX;
Data with scores = number of data records traced in PlumX with at least one score (≥1);
Coverage = data with scores (%) = number of data records traced in PlumX with at least one score (≥1) in relation to the number of the WoS CC records searched;
Intensity = sum of all signals or scores;
Density = sum of all signals or scores in relation to the number of all WoS records traced

Effective density = sum of all signals or scores in relation to the number of all WoS records traced with at least one score (≥1).

Including altmetrics data in bibliometric reports for individual researcher assessment is a regular and ongoing task. However, it always depends on the consent of the assessed person. The procedure is the same as described beforehand for the national monitoring exercise, except for an accordingly variable time interval. A general example is demonstrated in the results section.

Last but not least, PlumX was used as a case study for one faculty at the University of Vienna in order to demonstrate impact beyond the scholarly citation realm. The obtained exploratory altmetrics data (2007–2019) were complemented by retrieved records from APA and NEXIS mass media databases.

Results

Part 1 – National Level

Our monitoring exercise shows that a large diversity of signals can be traced for each measure in each dimension by means of PlumX, however, actually only very few of them achieve a certain degree of significance. Their occurrence is either merely accidental or very specific for some particular publications. The most relevant measures are represented in Figures 1 and 2. The highly skewed distribution of the collected signals or scores for each measure is noteworthy in addition.

Table 1 and Table 2 reflect the different indicator values for each publication year. Table 1 shows that the percentage of publications with readers in Mendeley, the citations in Scopus, and all three usage data in EBSCO decrease with each more recent publication year due to the shorter window for measurement, as expected. Publications require some years to be cited or used depending on the specific habits in each research field. The opposite phenomenon can be observed for the percentage of publications with data for the mentions in news and the number of tweets. Here we see increased values for more recent publication years. The percentage of publications with social media has been steadily increasing from ~28% in 2014 to ~42% in 2017. The percentage of publications with mentions in the media has only slightly increased and remains under 8%. Our results hint at an increasing use of social media within the scholarly community in general and a particular increase of Twitter usage in Austria.

Furthermore, a rising number of publications are tweeted or mentioned very shortly after they have been made available and even sometimes before their official publication.

Table 1: Percentage of publications with data for each indicator and tool.

Publication Year	2014	2015	2016	2017
Readers Mendeley	87.52%	86.64%	85.94%	84.21%
Citations Scopus	88.04%	85.64%	81.17%	74.60%
Citations Wikipedia	3.09%	2.80%	2.22%	1.96%
Tweets Twitter	29.23%	33.57%	39.48%	44.21%
Mentions News	1.86%	3.85%	4.84%	5.93%
Abstract Views EBSCO	88.50%	82.98%	80.67%	71.52%
Full Text Views EBSCO	27.15%	25.98%	17.16%	6.16%
Export-Saves Ebsco	58.26%	40.46%	32.23%	18.53%

Table 2: Effective density of each indicator per publication year.

Publication Year	2014	2015	2016	2017
Readers Mendeley	43.40	37.88	33.11	27.20
Citations Scopus	22.00	16.52	12.13	7.18
Citations Wikipedia	1.74	2.41	2.21	1.51
Tweets Twitter	7.04	9.09	8.23	12.58
Mentions News	4.40	4.85	3.75	5.25
Abstract Views EBSCO	148.10	118.88	91.94	55.25
Full Text Views EBSCO	77.07	54.04	54.65	81.92
Export-Saves Ebsco	13.36	13.70	10.23	6.30

Concerning the effective density (number of scores/number of publications with at least one score), the values of all indicators again decrease with each more recent publication year (according to the reduced time window) except for the density of tweets, a fact that corroborates the assumption of an increasing Twitter usage within the scholarly community. Noteworthy is also the increase of the density of news mentions in 2017: each publication gets on average five mentions in the news. These values can help as reference points for estimating whether a publication has a high or low resonance for each indicator.

Furthermore, usage indicators, and particularly abstracts and full text views, are responsible for the highest values, followed by the number of readers in Mendeley. These are still significantly higher than the number of citations in Scopus, especially with a decreasing citation window.

The behavior of the six selected main knowledge areas is reflected in the results, which are summarized in Tables 3 and 4. Table 3 reveals the coverage (percentage of data with scores) in total and for each dimension for the publications from each year (2014, 2015, and 2016). Table 4 represents the absolute number of items with scores and the effective density for the publications from each year and for each area. In this case, we used the most representative measures of each dimension instead of the total sum of signals due to the heterogeneity of the data collected in each tool: number of readers in Mendeley (captures), citations from Scopus, number of tweets in Twitter (social media) and number of views of abstracts, PDF views, and HTML views in EBSCO.

Table 3: Coverage in PlumX for each measure, publication year, and main knowledgearea.

PY	Subject category	Total number of items	% of items with scores	% of items with scores in Captures	% of items with scores in Citations	% of items with scores in Social Media	% of items with scores in Mentions	% of items with scores in Usage
2014	Arts & Humanities	143	91.6%	65.0%	35.7%	7.0%	2.1%	91.6%
	Engineering & Technology	3163	97.7%	94.0%	88.5%	20.9%	5.2%	80.7%
	Health Sciences	4896	97.7%	95.0%	86.4%	37.1%	5.8%	94.1%
	Life Sciences	3493	98.9%	96.5%	92.5%	36.4%	6.1%	92.0%
	Physical Sciences	3560	99.0%	94.2%	90.5%	14.7%	2.4%	86.0%
	Social Sciences	1260	95.2%	92.5%	79.2%	33.7%	4.9%	90.6%
	Not available	1	100.0%	100.0%	100.0%	0.0%	0.0%	0.0%
	Total	16516	98.0%	94.5%	88.0%	28.5%	4.9%	89.0%
2015	Arts & Humanities	168	85.1%	61.9%	26.8%	7.1%	1.8%	79.2%
	Engineering & Technology	3964	96.0%	90.3%	81.0%	23.8%	6.3%	69.2%
	Health Sciences	5288	97.3%	92.9%	82.5%	44.5%	6.9%	92.0%

Table 3 *(Continued)*

PY	Subject category	Total number of items	% of items with scores	% of items with scores in Captures	% of items with scores in Citations	% of items with scores in Social Media	% of items with scores in Mentions	% of items with scores in Usage
	Life Sciences	3616	98.9%	96.2%	90.7%	45.9%	10.0%	91.8%
	Physical Sciences	3820	97.9%	90.3%	85.9%	16.5%	3.1%	76.9%
	Social Sciences	1574	96.1%	91.4%	72.4%	33.2%	5.5%	88.1%
	Not available	22	100.0%	95.5%	81.8%	0.0%	0.0%	86.4%
	Total	18452	97.3%	92.1%	83.1%	33.1%	6.4%	83.5%
2016	Arts & Humanities	218	85.8%	46.8%	16.1%	9.2%	2.8%	81.2%
	Engineering & Technology	4529	94.7%	89.2%	65.2%	27.8%	6.8%	70.2%
	Health Sciences	5724	96.1%	88.6%	68.8%	50.5%	7.6%	88.0%
	Life Sciences	4103	98.3%	93.9%	78.2%	54.1%	10.6%	88.2%
	Physical Sciences	3991	96.2%	86.5%	74.8%	19.9%	3.9%	72.2%
	Social Sciences	1696	92.5%	85.5%	57.4%	35.3%	4.5%	86.3%
	Not available	122	91.0%	75.4%	24.6%	15.6%	0.8%	47.5%
	Total	20383	95.8%	88.6%	69.3%	38.3%	6.9%	80.5%

Table 4: Density of the most representative measures traced in PlumX for each publication year and main knowledge area.

PY	Subject area	# items with Readers in Mendeley	Density: Readers in Mendeley	# items with Citations in Scopus	Density: Citations in Scopus	# items with Tweets in Twitter	Density: Tweets in Twitter	# items with Abstract Views in EBSCO	Density: Abstract Views in EBSCO
2014	Arts & Humanities	68	8.47	46	2.63	10	2.20	130	264.16
	Eng & Technol	2936	25.36	2706	13.32	563	21.06	2540	166.16
	Health Sciences	4554	20.99	4103	17.82	1588	7.34	4590	101.85
	Life Sciences	3346	29.65	3137	13.82	1182	8.72	3197	106.49
	Physical Sciences	3261	13.07	3115	12.76	471	2.66	3038	61.21
	Social Sciences	1116	26.98	937	9.61	377	8.05	1140	524.16
2015	Arts & Humanities	71	5.61	43	2.44	12	2.92	133	195.46
	Eng & Technol	3546	19.20	3038	8.24	845	32.69	2715	126.63
	Health Sciences	4854	17.34	4168	11.61	2174	9.34	4848	84.52
	Life Sciences	3450	23.98	3137	8.96	1599	6.34	3299	105.19
	Physical Sciences	3423	11.50	3095	8.46	584	5.07	2904	44.88
	Social Sciences	1385	18.57	1017	5.57	500	7.10	1377	320.83
2016	Arts & Humanities	66	3.09	32	1.31	16	8.13	177	101.19
	Eng & Technol	4009	14.61	2675	4.49	1176	15.34	3147	100.91
	Health Sciences	4978	12.66	3558	5.77	2782	9.39	4985	57.84
	Life Sciences	3820	17.31	2975	4.78	2168	9.34	3593	79.23

Table 4 *(Continued)*

PY	Subject area	# items with Readers in Mendeley	Density: Readers in Mendeley	# items with Citations in Scopus	Density: Citations in Scopus	# items with Tweets in Twitter	Density: Tweets in Twitter	# items with Abstract Views in EBSCO	Density: Abstract Views in EBSCO
	Physical Sciences	3434	9.11	2766	5.30	746	3.58	2827	38.27
	Social Sciences	1400	14.10	796	2.85	574	7.68	1454	234.86

The major results of this analysis can be summarized as follows:
- The highest coverage is reported by the number of readers in Mendeley independent from the area.
- The lowest coverage is reported by the area Arts & Humanities. Nevertheless, the percentage of usage data is higher than in the other four dimensions. The percentage of uncited data in this area is twice or three times higher than in the other four considered areas. This is due to the longer cited half-life and the lower reference densities characteristic for this discipline.
- The behavior of the four hard sciences (Engineering & Technology, Health Sciences, Life Sciences, and Physical Sciences) is very similar in all dimensions, except for social media, where Health and Life Sciences account for the highest percentage of coverage, followed very closed by the Social Sciences.
- The percentage values for the Social Sciences in the other three dimensions (captures, citations, and mentions) lie in-between the ones obtained for the hard sciences and those for Arts & Humanities.
- Concerning social media, a low coverage is reported for the Physical Sciences and a relative insignificance has been observed in the Arts & Humanities.
- The results obtained for the effective density correspond very well with the ones concerning data coverage.
- All effective densities are decreasing according to the reduced measuring window except for tweets, where the effective density has even increased within recent years despite the reduced time window in all areas. The only exception is Engineering & Technology, where a maximum was reached in 2015 probably due to an outlier.
- High usage density values are reported in the Arts & Humanities and Social Sciences, and lower ones for the Physical Sciences in comparison to the other hard sciences.
- According to the results of our national monitoring exercise, besides articles and reviews, guidelines are the document type with the highest coverage and effective densities in all measures. Conference proceedings are hardly traced in PlumX. It is noteworthy that corrections and retractions are comparably often

viewed, tweeted, and mentioned in the news, despite usually remaining almost uncited.
- Concerning journals, PLoS One, Scientific Reports, Physical Review B, Nature Communications, and Physical Review Letters are the most frequently traced in PlumX, which is in good agreement with the Austrian publication frequency in WoS Core Collection. For Lecture Notes in Computer Science (including subseries Lecture Notes in Artificial Intelligence and Lecture Notes in Bioinformatics) significant usage and citation densities but a rather insignificant presence in the social or mass media is observed. As a marginal note, fewer than 20% of the publications of the most frequently used journal by Austrian scientists (*Wiener Klinische Wochenschrift*) are traced in PlumX. This is probably due to the fact that the journal has not yet been including new metrics in its web portal, which seriously affects its visibility on the web. Another reason is the incompleteness of the data traced by the tool itself (Gumpenberger, Glänzel, and Gorraiz, 2016), especially usage data, exclusively collected via EBSCO.

Part 2 – Individual Level

The individual assessment at the University of Vienna comprises of an interview with the researcher under evaluation, the elaboration of a bibliometric report of the researcher's publication output, the discussion and validation of the obtained results with the researcher as well as further optional analyses. The produced bibliometric reports are provided to the researchers themselves and inform them about the quantitative aspects of their research output. They also serve as a basis for further discussion concerning their publication strategies. These reports are eventually intended for informed peer review practices. The most important feature of the generated bibliometric report is its multidimensional and individual character. It relies on a variety of basic indicators and further control parameters in order to foster comprehensibility.

The structure of the bibliometric report generally comprises following parts:
- Activity, i.e. the number of publications along a timeline and with differentiation of document types to reflect the productivity and coverage analysis in the used data sources
- Visibility, i.e. assessment of publication sources (number of articles in peer reviewed journals, Impact Factor or alternative journal impact measures like SJR and SNIP) to reflect the editorial barrier and to unveil publication strategies
- Impact, i.e. the number of citations including several citation indicators to reflect the citation impact in the publish or perish scientific community
- Collaboration, i.e. the number of co-authors/co-affiliations to reflect national and international networking
- Focus or Scope, i.e. disciplinary versus cross-disciplinary versus interdisciplinary

- State-of-the-art, i.e. determination of the knowledge base according to the analysis of the references

Figure 1 shows an example of an individual profile or report. In recent years, we have also introduced a new facet by including a measure of the attention that the publication output has attracted on the web. This analysis includes the most important features of the results obtained in PlumX (see Web attention).

To this end, all the publication identifiers (DOI, ISBN etc.) available have been ingested in PlumX.

The beforehand mentioned interview with the researcher under evaluation already addresses relevant questions concerning this topic: 1. Do you maintain a personal website? An entry in Wikipedia? A Google Scholar Citations profile? 2. Do you use a reference manager system? If yes, which one? Why do you think it is helpful? 3. Do you actively engage in mailing lists or blogs? If yes, which ones? 4. Do you use other Social Media tools? If yes, which ones? 5. What do you think about usage metrics (downloads) and altmetrics? 6. Do you generate research data? If yes, how do you manage and archive them?

After performing the altmetrics analysis in PlumX, the results are discussed with the scientist, and the most relevant features are picked up and included in the report.

Part 3 – Faculty Level

Up to now, faculty research achievements for the more recent years have been predominantly determined by the number of publications in Q1 journals due to the short citation window, which is almost insignificant in some sub-disciplines of the Social Sciences and the Humanities. It was hoped that altmetrics could help to demonstrate impact beyond the scholarly citation realm in some of these fields. To this purpose, a case study was performed for a selected faculty, but there was no clear perceived added value at least in this analysis.

Our case study resulted in a low proportion of publications with data and showed low relevance. Apart from citations and (always incomplete) usage data, only the number of readers and tweets reached some significance. However, these two indicators lack applicable value for academic evaluation practices according to the opinion of the members of the analyzed faculty. Only the mentions in news were considered to be somehow meaningful as an indicator. However, it became evident from the comparison of altmetrics results with the ones obtained from mass media databases (APA and NEXIS) that the latter focus on researcher names rather than on the actual research outputs themselves. Some researchers of the faculty are actually quite well represented in the media in a broader context, which is however not reflected by altmetrics, since they primarily rely on specific research outputs identified by DOIs and other output-related permanent identifiers.

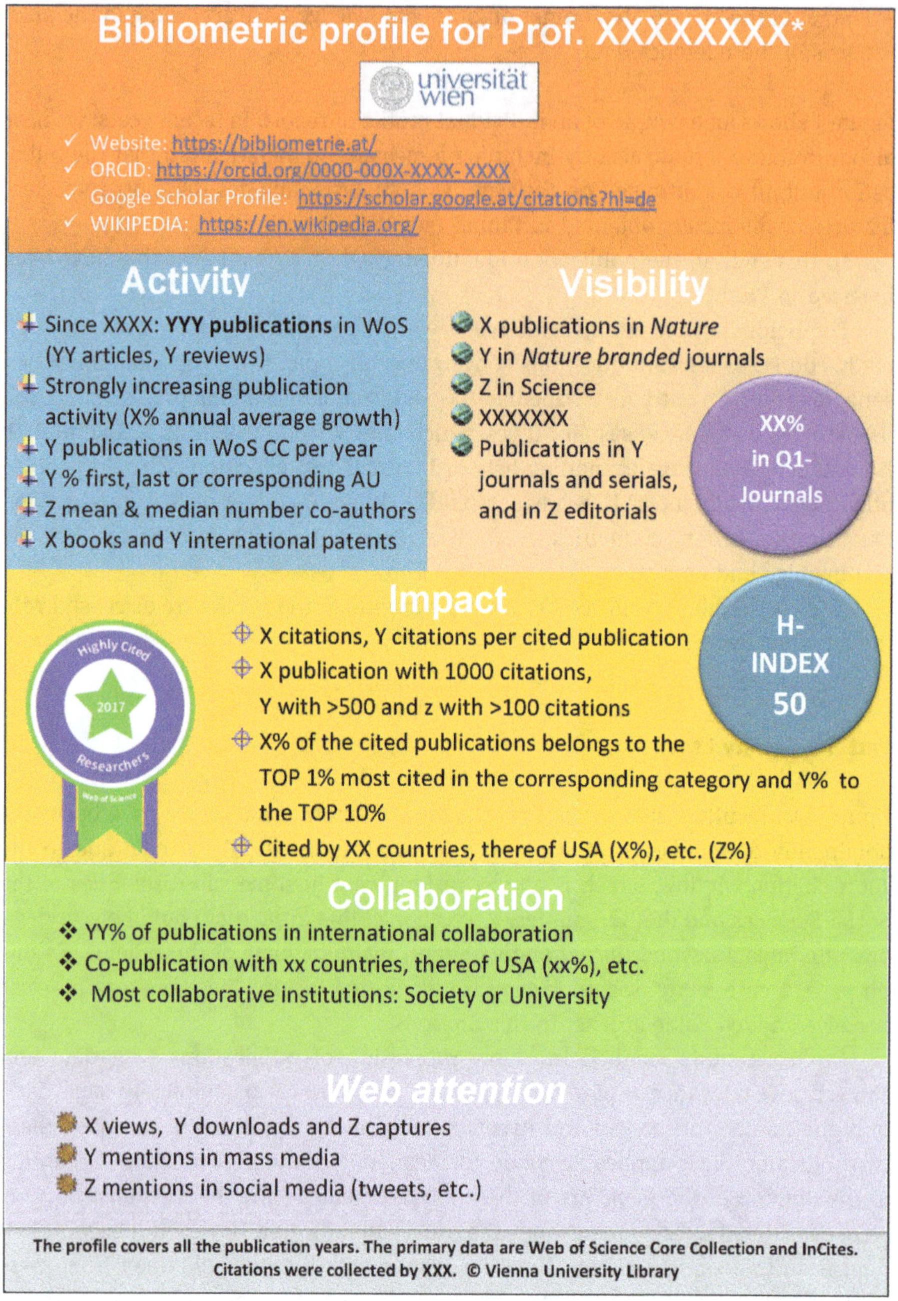

Bibliometric profile for Prof. XXXXXXXX*

universität wien

- Website: https://bibliometrie.at/
- ORCID: https://orcid.org/0000-000X-XXXX-XXXX
- Google Scholar Profile: https://scholar.google.at/citations?hl=de
- WIKIPEDIA: https://en.wikipedia.org/

Activity

- Since XXXX: **YYY publications** in WoS (YY articles, Y reviews)
- Strongly increasing publication activity (X% annual average growth)
- Y publications in WoS CC per year
- Y % first, last or corresponding AU
- Z mean & median number co-authors
- X books and Y international patents

Visibility

- X publications in *Nature*
- Y in *Nature branded* journals
- Z in Science
- XXXXXXX
- Publications in Y journals and serials, and in Z editorials

XX% in Q1-Journals

Impact

- X citations, Y citations per cited publication
- X publication with 1000 citations, Y with >500 and z with >100 citations
- X% of the cited publications belongs to the TOP 1% most cited in the corresponding category and Y% to the TOP 10%
- Cited by XX countries, thereof USA (X%), etc. (Z%)

Highly Cited 2017 Researchers Web of Science

H-INDEX 50

Collaboration

- YY% of publications in international collaboration
- Co-publication with xx countries, thereof USA (xx%), etc.
- Most collaborative institutions: Society or University

Web attention

- X views, Y downloads and Z captures
- Y mentions in mass media
- Z mentions in social media (tweets, etc.)

The profile covers all the publication years. The primary data are Web of Science Core Collection and InCites. Citations were collected by XXX. © Vienna University Library

Figure 1: Bibliometric report for an individual evaluation.

Conclusions

Altmetrics provide additional information on the bigger picture concerning the broader impact of research output. PlumX has proven to be a very useful tool in order to monitor the broader impact of the publication output, either at national, institutional or individual level. Its multidimensional aspect is explicitly noteworthy and useful.

Monitoring studies help in revealing new trends and furthermore allow one to assess to what extent altmetrics data are already available and applicable. Our study hints at an increasing use of social media within the scholarly community in general and an increase of Twitter usage in Austria in particular. Certainly, similar studies in more countries are desirable to come to a better understanding.

Two main groups of indicators or measures can be distinguished in general: long-term indicators (citations) and short-term indicators (usage, mentions, social media).

Faculty-wide application of altmetrics is yet a scarce procedure with limited added value, but their inclusion in the assessment of individual researchers is a service with an increasing demand, which can be particularly valuable in disciplines where traditional metrics are scarce and problematic. However, inclusion always requires preceding researcher's consent and according education on the known shortcomings and restrictions.

The stability and reproducibility of altmetrics data is an issue yet to be solved by PlumX (as well as by competitor altmetrics aggregators). Technically, there is room for improvement regarding the possibility to select different measuring windows. Periodical monitoring exercises currently only work on the basis of archiving already obtained results and later comparison with other results from different time intervals.

References

Bar-Ilan, J, Halevi, G & Milojević, S 2019, 'Differences between Altmetric Data Sources–A Case Study', *Journal of Altmetrics*, vol. 2, no. 1.

Bornmann, L 2014, 'Do altmetrics point to the broader impact of research? An overview of benefits and disadvantages of altmetrics', *Journal of informetrics*, vol. 8, no. 4, pp. 895–903.

Bornmann, L, Haunschild, R & Adams, J 2019, 'Do altmetrics assess societal impact in a comparable way to case studies? An empirical test of the convergent validity of altmetrics based on data from the UK research excellence framework (REF)', *Journal of Informetrics*, vol. 13, no. 1, pp. 325–40.

Glänzel, W & Gorraiz, J 2015, 'Usage metrics versus altmetrics: confusing terminology?', *Scientometrics*, vol. 102, no. 3, pp. 2161–64.

Gorraiz, J, Gumpenberger, C & Schlögl, C 2014, 'Usage versus citation behaviours in four subject areas', *Scientometrics*, vol. 101, no. 2, pp. 1077–95.

Gorraiz, J, Wieland, M & Gumpenberger, C 2017, 'To be visible, or not to be, that is the question', *Int. J. Soc. Sci. Humanity*, vol. 7, no. 7, pp. 467–71.

Gorraiz, J 2018, 'A Thousand and one reflections of the publications in the mirrors' labyrinth of the new metrics', *El Professional Información*, vol. 27, pp. 231–36, doi: https://doi.org/10.3145/epi.2018.mar.01.

Gumpenberger, C, Glänzel, W & Gorraiz, J 2016, 'The ecstasy and the agony of the altmetric score', *Scientometrics* vol. 108, no. 2, pp. 977–82.

Gumpenberger, C, Wieland, M & Gorraiz, J 2012, 'Bibliometric practices and activities at the University of Vienna', *Library management*, vol. 33, no. 3, pp. 174–83.

Haustein, S 2016, 'Grand challenges in altmetrics: heterogeneity, data quality and dependencies', *Scientometrics*, vol. 108, no. 1, pp. 413–23.

Haustein, S, Bowman, TD & Costas, R 2016, 'Interpreting "altmetrics": viewing acts on social media through the lens of citation and social theories', in CR Sugimoto (ed.), *Theories of informetrics and scholarly communication. A Festschrift in Honor of Blaise Cronin*, pp. 372–405, De Gruyter, Berlin, http://arxiv.org/abs/1502.05701 (July 15, 2020), doi: https://doi.org/10.1515/9783110308464-022.

Haustein, S, Peters, I, Bar-Ilan, J, Priem, J, Shema, H & Terliesner, J 2014, 'Coverage and adoption of altmetrics sources in the bibliometric community', *Scientometrics*, vol. 101, no. 2, pp. 1145–63.

Kietzmann, JH, Hermkens, K, McCarthy, IP & Silvestre, BS 2011, 'Social media? Get serious! Understanding the functional building blocks of social media', *Business horizons*, vol. 54, no. 3, pp. 241–51.

Kraemer, A 2006, 'Ensuring consistent usage statistics, part 2: working with use data for electronic journals', *The Serials Librarian*, vol. 50, no. 1–2, pp. 163–72.

Priem, J, Taraborelli, D, Groth, P & Neylon, C 2010, 'Altmetrics: a manifesto, 26 October 2010', accessed July 9, 2019, http://altmetrics.org/manifesto (July 15, 2020).

Procter, R, Williams, R, Stewart, J, Poschen, M, Snee, H, Voss, A & Asgari-Targhi, M 2010, 'Adoption and use of Web 2.0 in scholarly communications', *Philosophical Transactions of the Royal Society A: Mathematical, Physical and Engineering Sciences*, vol. 368, no. 1926, pp. 4039–56.

Rasmussen, PG & Andersen, JP 2013, 'Altmetrics: an alternate perspective on research evaluation', *Sciecom info*, vol. 9, no. 2, https://journals.lub.lu.se/index.php/sciecominfo/article/view/7292/6102 (July 15, 2020).

Repiso, R, Castillo, A & Torres-Salinas, D 2019, 'Altmetrics, alternative indicators for Web of Science Communication journals', accessed July 9, 2019, https://doi.org/10.1007/s1192-019-03070.

Vinkler, P 1988, 'An attempt of surveying and classifying bibliometric indicators for scientometric purposes', *Scientometrics*, vol. 13, no. 5–6, pp. 239–59.

Wouters, P & Costas, R 2012, *Users, narcissism and control: tracking the impact of scholarly publications in the 21st century*, pp. 847–57, SURFfoundation, Utrecht.

4.6 PLOS Article-Level Metrics

Steffen Lemke, Kaltrina Nuredini, and Isabella Peters

Abstract: Since 2009, the *Public Library of Science* (PLOS) has provided comprehensive article-level metrics for all publications in its PLOS journals. These PLOS article-level metrics (PLOS ALM) reflect the attention an individual article has received from the scientific community and other parties online and include citations, social media mentions, usage statistics, bookmarks and recommendations. Conceptually, in PLOS ALM all metrics are divided into the five categories of *Viewed*, *Saved*, *Discussed*, *Recommended*, and *Cited*, which represent different levels of engagement with respective articles.

The Public Library of Science offers three essential ways for accessing their PLOS ALM data: visualizations on articles' landing pages, raw metrics data via an API, and via the reporting tool *PLOS ALM Reports*. Moreover, the Open Source application used for collecting PLOS ALM, called *Lagotto*, can be installed and customized to flexibly retrieve metrics data from a large variety of sources and thus create ALM datasets. This makes PLOS ALM an interesting starting point for users who aim to establish an ALM database for their own publication corpora.

Comparisons of PLOS ALM to metrics from other providers, e.g. Altmetric.com, CrossRef, or Plum Analytics, have shown that conceptual and technological differences between providers can lead to very different metrics values for the same articles across them. Hence, increased caution is necessary when using ALM from different providers side by side.

Keywords: Public Library of Science, PLOS, Lagotto, article-level metrics, ALM, altmetrics, citations, usage metrics, metrics aggregators.

History and Background

In 2003 *PLOS Biology*, the first journal of the *Public Library of Science*, was launched to serve as an Open Access outlet for "the very best in biology research" (Parthasarathy, 2005, p. e296), to then be followed by its sister journal *PLOS Medicine* in 2004.[1] Already shortly after these launches, both journals' editors repeatedly voiced their concerns regarding the reasonableness of *Thomson ISI*'s (nowadays *Clarivate Analyt-*

---

[1] https://www.plos.org/history (July 15, 2020).

Steffen Lemke, ZBW Leibniz Information Center for Economics, Kiel, Germany, s.lemke@zbw.eu
Kaltrina Nuredini, ZBW Leibniz Information Center for Economics, Kiel, Germany, kaltrina.nuredini@gmail.com
Prof. Dr. **Isabella Peters,** ZBW Leibniz Information Center for Economics & Kiel University, Kiel, Germany, Düsternbrooker Weg 120, 24105 Kiel, Germany, i.peters@zbw.eu

https://doi.org/10.1515/9783110646610-024

ics') impact factor as a performance measure, pointing towards the promising alternative of measuring the uptake of each article individually by counting the times it has been downloaded (Parthasarathy, 2005, p. e296; The PLOS Medicine Editors, 2006, p. e291). A number of years later, in 2009, the comprehensive provision of such article-level impact metrics for all publications in PLOS journals was realized through the introduction of *PLOS Article-Level Metrics* (from here on referred to as *PLOS ALM*). Article-level metrics (ALM) provide coverage of the attention an article has received from the scientific community (Fenner, 2013, p. 1) as well as other parties online. These metrics include different indicators such as citations, social media mentions, usage statistics, bookmarks and recommendations (Fenner, 2013, p. 1) and are considered to be an extension of citations (see section "Included Sources").

PLOS Article-Level Metrics' Technological Foundation: Lagotto

The technological backbone of PLOS ALM is called *Lagotto*. Started in March 2009, *Lagotto* is the Open Source application developed by PLOS that handles the collection of PLOS ALM from their various online sources by individually querying their APIs. Its latest release, version 5.0.1, was published on April 12, 2016 with an MIT license.[2] Although that version's release notes hint at plans for further releases in the future, at the time of writing (July 2019) new commits to *Lagotto*'s official GitHub project last occurred a little over three years ago, so, currently, regular new releases are not to be expected.

The software as well as detailed information on its installation, deployment, and setup can be obtained online.[3] Following these guidelines, interested users can install (and customize) their own instances of *Lagotto* to create individual datasets of ALM. The minimum inputs required by *Lagotto* to collect metrics for an article are its DOI, title, and publication date. *Lagotto* can be configured to retrieve data from a large variety of different sources, some of which may pose additional requirements on input data, such as API keys or other means of authentication. The data retrieval from each source is carried out by individual software agents (of which there are more than 50). Therefore, the exact parameters used to reference articles in outgoing API calls vary depending on the respective source; on most sources, articles are referenced by either DOI and/or journal landing page URL (see also Zahedi and Costas [2018, p. 12] for examples).

In the following, when referring to *Lagotto*, we mean the software application that is used by PLOS (and by other users) to collect ALM. PLOS ALM on the other hand refers to the specific corpus of metrics data and the directly related services provided by PLOS. Or to put it differently: PLOS ALM are a publicly accessible dataset

---

2 https://github.com/lagotto/lagotto/releases (July 15, 2020).
3 http://alm.plos.org/docs, http://www.lagotto.io/ (July 15, 2020).

created and updated by using a specific instance of *Lagotto*, which fetches metrics data for all articles that have been published in PLOS journals (and only PLOS journals). Besides PLOS, several other organizations have used *Lagotto* for their own applications, e.g. *Copernicus Publications*, the *Public Knowledge Project*, the *Making Data Count* project, or the **metrics* project.[4]

Included Sources

PLOS ALM are comprised of a variety of data sources which are divided into the five categories of *Viewed*, *Saved*, *Discussed*, *Recommended*, and *Cited* (see also Figure 1). These categories were conceptualized to be coherent in themselves and between each other, to reflect shared correlations between metrics, and to be scalable in respect of the introduction of future metrics (Lin and Fenner, 2013, p. 24). Lin and Fenner (2013, p. 24), who developed this categorization system for PLOS ALM, mention the ontology of metrics used by ImpactStory[5] (now part of *Our Research*) back then as a large influence. ImpactStory's concept for distinguishing between types of metrics included five identically labeled categories such as those used by PLOS ALM, but further divided all categories along a second axis of user types to differentiate between attention among *Public* and *Scholars* (Piwowar, 2012; Lin and Fenner, 2013, p. 25).

Together, the indicators included in PLOS ALM comprise bibliometrics (*Cited*), usage metrics (*Viewed*), and altmetrics (*Saved*, *Discussed*, and *Recommended*). So in addition to being a more direct impact metric for individual research articles than the journal-based impact factor, the ability of PLOS ALM to incorporate other indicators than citations leads to further benefits over mere bibliometrics. First, the included web-based indicators can accumulate much sooner after an article's publication than citations (see also Wouters and Costas [2012, p. 38]). Second, the included usage statistics might provide a better reflection of impact in more practical fields of research. And third, they may be better at highlighting articles of general interest other than citations (Fenner, 2013, p. 1). In addition to their relative speed, Chamberlain (2013, p. 5) mentions their high degree of openness as well as their diversity of sources as two main advantages of ALM over journal-based metrics.

Fenner (2013, p. 1), who from 2012 to 2015 served as technical lead for the PLOS ALM project, suggests that the five categories of metrics represent different levels of engagement with a respective article, as is shown in Figure 1. And even different metrics from the same category might represent varying ways of users interacting with scientific articles: while HTML views might reflect how often an article was browsed

---

[4] The **metrics* project initially approached its aim of providing a highly transparent solution for the collection of ALM by developing its own extension to *Lagotto*. Later on, a standalone application was developed instead, though conceptually still drawing heavily from *Lagotto*. A link for downloading said software can be found at https://metrics-project.net/en/about/results/ (July 15, 2020).
[5] https://our-research.org/ (July 15, 2020).

and read online, a download (i.e. a PDF view) might reflect a reader's desire to revisit an article more often in the future (Fenner, 2013, p. 1).

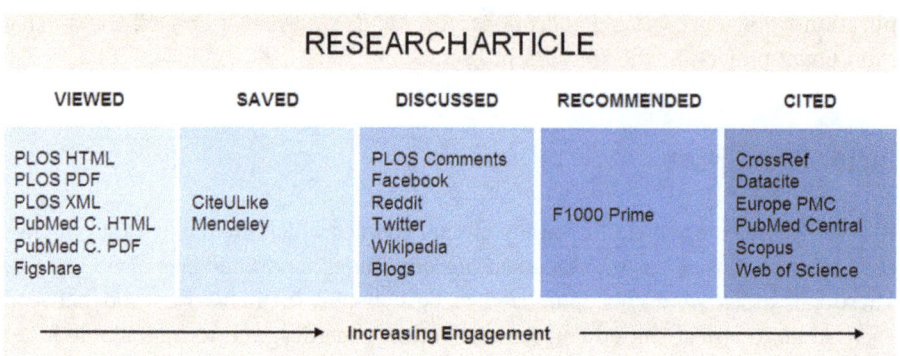

Figure 1: Included data sources (based on Fenner [2013, p. 2] and PLOS [2019]).

Taking PLOS Biology as an example, nearly all published research articles will be viewed, downloaded, bookmarked, and also cited at least once sooner or later, while for the categories in-between (*Discussed* and *Recommended*) the shares of articles receiving these kinds of treatments are much smaller (Fenner, 2013, p. 2).

It should be noted that not all sources included in PLOS ALM nowadays have been available since their first implementation in 2009, but accumulated over time. For example, the collection of tweets for PLOS articles only started on June 1, 2012, hence PLOS ALM Twitter counts do not contain data from before this date. Also, the frequency with which articles' metrics are updated varies between sources. According to PLOS, for some of them there can be lags of up to one month between a metric's change and the according update in PLOS ALM. The currentness of individual metrics therefore cannot be guaranteed. A detailed list of all sources included in PLOS ALM right now can be found online.[6] An informative overview of the five categories of sources as well as relevant considerations regarding their interpretation is available on *Lagotto*'s website.[7]

PLOS ALM on Article Landing Pages

For every PLOS article, an overview about its article-level metrics is displayed on its landing page within the PLOS ecosystem (Figure 2). This overview only shows a restricted number of metrics, aggregated into the four groups *Save*, *Citation*, *View*, and *Share* (which reflects a part of the category *Discussed* from Figure 1). More detailed

---

[6] http://alm.plos.org/docs/sources (July 15, 2020).
[7] http://www.lagotto.io/plos/#usageInfo (July 15, 2020).

information for each article can be accessed by clicking on one of the four categories or the "Metrics" tab.

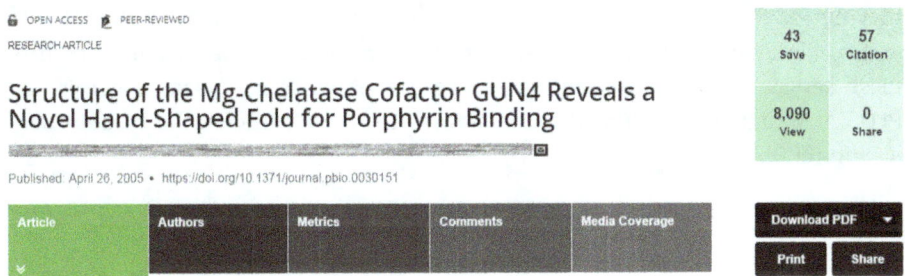

Figure 2: Excerpt from a PLOS article landing page with aggregated article-level metrics.

The Metrics tab offers a detailed table of the article's views and downloads separated by their sources, as well as a temporal view on the accumulation of views since the article's publication (Figure 3). Hovering over the tiles representing specific sources in some cases unveils more fine-grained information about what the respective metric consists of, e.g. for Mendeley readerships the separate shares of individual and group bookmarks are shown. By clicking on a tile, the user can retrieve the individual objects behind the counted references. For example, a click on *Scopus* leads the user to a list of documents citing the respective article on the Scopus website.[8] This feature is not available for all sources though.

Figure 3: Detailed article-level metric data
(left: article's detailed views statistics; right: article's source-specific statistics).

---

8 https://www.scopus.com/home.uri (July 15, 2020).

Ways of Accessing PLOS ALM

Apart from the landing pages of articles on PLOS, there are two direct ways for retrieving PLOS ALM data for individual (or sets of) articles: a) the PLOS ALM API, and b) PLOS ALM Reports. Despite differences in the data's presentation, both of these services access the same shared corpus of PLOS ALM data. Licensing of PLOS ALM data is under Creative Commons Zero 1.0 Universal Public Domain Dedication (CC0).[9]

The PLOS ALM API[10]

PLOS offers an open application programming interface (API) for ALM data. Since the release of *Lagotto* version 3.12.7 in January 2015, almost all article-related data is available without the necessity of an API key. API keys now only serve the purpose of authenticating users with admin privileges, who wish to perform administrative actions like creating, deleting, or updating articles in the corpus.

The API supports queries for up to 50 articles at a time, which can be specified by comma-separated lists of publication identifiers in the API call. Accepted types of identifiers are DOIs, PubMed IDs, PubMed Central IDs, arXiv IDs, Scopus IDs, Web of Science IDs, arks, and publisher URLs. If no identifier type is specified in the query, by default PubMed IDs are used. The PLOS ALM API does not provide search functionalities; instead one of the mentioned identifiers needs to be provided to refer to an article and to retrieve the ALM.

The default format of return values from the API is JSON. PLOS invites software developers to make use of data returned from their APIs, but asks them to indicate that said data originated from PLOS. Over the past, wrappers for the PLOS API have been published for the programming languages Python[11] and R[12] (the original package maintainers' support for the latter, however, has been discontinued in 2018).

Further documentation of the PLOS ALM API is available online.[13]

---

9 http://www.lagotto.io/plos/ (July 15, 2020).
10 http://alm.plos.org/api (July 15, 2020).
11 https://github.com/lagotto/pyalm (July 15, 2020).
12 https://github.com/ropensci/alm (July 15, 2020).
13 http://alm.plos.org/docs/api (July 15, 2020).

PLOS ALM Reports[14]

PLOS ALM Reports is a reporting tool that allows users to retrieve current article-level metrics without having to engage in programming, as the reports can be created by simply navigating through a series of HTML forms.

Unlike the API, PLOS ALM Reports provides a search functionality that can be used to add articles to the report that match a specified query to the PLOS publication corpus. Like in the API, articles can also be referred to via publication identifiers, although only DOIs and PubMed IDs are accepted. Sets of up to 500 articles at a time can be added as comma-separated CSV-files. Once the list of articles to include in the report is submitted, metrics for the individual articles are displayed alongside their metadata. Additionally, three types of interactive visualizations are offered: a bubble chart reflecting articles' page views, downloads, article age, as well as one additional metric of choice; a sunburst graph reflecting articles' usage, Scopus citations and subject areas; and a geographical map displaying the locations of the articles' authors' affiliations.

Reports remain accessible via unique URLs. Their full summaries can be downloaded in CSV format, the visualizations in PNG format. Furthermore, the curated set of articles included in a report can be saved for later reference by downloading a list of their DOIs, which is also offered in CSV format.

While the two options explained above represent two ways of directly accessing the data corpus of PLOS ALM, for a small particular subset of them, there is another, "indirect", way to do so: PLOS- and PubMed-view counts from PLOS ALM are also included in the suite of metrics presented by Plum Analytics, where they form a part of the subcategory *Full-Text Views* from the category of *Usage Metrics*.[15]

PLOS ALM Compared to Other Article-level Metrics Providers

The field of ALM has been vibrant over the past decade, with several competitors launching their own metrics collection- and aggregation services (Jobmann et al., 2014, pp. 2–16; Zahedi, 2018, pp. 51–88). Besides PLOS, providers such as Plum Analytics, Altmetric.com, or CrossRef all provide their own ranges of ALM, sharing some common data sources while also providing some unique features.

Even for the same type of ALM, several options to collect it for an article often exist, all of which can lead to differing results. For example, while *Lagotto* uses the Twitter Search API[16] to capture mentions of scientific articles in tweets, one could also use Twitter's real time streaming API[17] or one of its fee-based tweet ar-

---

14 http://almreports.plos.org/ (July 15, 2020).
15 https://plumanalytics.com/learn/about-metrics/usage-metrics/ (July 15, 2020).
16 https://developer.twitter.com/en/docs/tweets/search/overview (July 15, 2020).
17 https://developer.twitter.com/en/docs/tweets/filter-realtime/overview (July 15, 2020).

chives[18] for this instead. Furthermore, a data collector's decisions regarding which identifiers, URLs, or types of scholarly objects to include in queries will all influence their results (Zahedi and Costas, 2018, p. 11). Moreover, the frequencies with which an article's metrics get updated are also up to the collector and can have a significant effect on that article's score at a given point in time. And even beyond such mostly technical considerations, sometimes conceptual decisions about what should actually qualify as an occurrence of a respective metric-related event have to be made. For example, if we want to count the number of times articles have been mentioned in tweets, should "retweets" in this count be treated exactly like original tweets? Or when counting readerships on Mendeley, should only individual users' bookmarks be considered (as Altmetric.com does it), or should group bookmarks be added to the total count as well (as *Lagotto* does it)?

The variance of possibilities for collecting ALM considered, it is no surprise that metrics data provided by different aggregators is not necessarily consistent across them. Bearing in mind that such inconsistencies will often be the result of deliberate conceptual or technology-related decisions, it should be clear that comparatively high degrees of coverage or intensity for a metric do not necessarily mean that an aggregator provides a more "comprehensive" or "realistic" picture of the attention surrounding articles. Instead, providers' differing approaches of measuring metrics just mean that they often provide answers to slightly different questions, and thus will be of varied utility depending on the use case at hand.[19]

Chamberlain (2013, pp. 7–9) set out to evaluate the consistency between PLOS ALM and data from three other aggregators, namely Altmetric.com, Plum Analytics, and ImpactStory. Comparing the values that these four services provide for a sample of 565 journal articles regarding seven different ALM, he revealed varying and sometimes considerable differences regarding individual metrics' intensity. While for example results obtained for PMC citations were for many articles very different across providers, most social media-based metrics (mentions on Facebook and Twitter, as well as readerships on Mendeley) showed less variability. Chamberlain (2013, p. 9) concludes from this that "casual users, and especially those conducting article-level metrics research, should use caution when using ALM data from different providers".

Zahedi and Costas (2018) more recently compared PLOS ALM (referring to them as *Lagotto*) to Altmetric.com, Plum Analytics, and CrossRef Event Data by examining altmetric counts provided by these four services (as well as by the Mendeley REST API) for a set of 31,437 PLOS ONE articles. Using Pearson correlation analysis to de-

---

18 https://developer.twitter.com/en/docs/tutorials/choosing-historical-api.html (July 15, 2020).
19 In 2016, the *NISO Alternative Assessment Metrics Project* passed a "code of conduct" that should obligate data aggregators and providers to increase the data quality of their metrics by disclosing their methods of collecting, aggregating, and updating data, among other things. An example for how to comply with this code of conduct is given by *CrossRef Event Data* at https://www.eventdata.crossref.org/guide/app-niso/ (July 15, 2020).

termine degrees of agreement between pairwise combinations of the four aggregators, they found Mendeley readership counts to be relatively consistent across all pairings of data providers (with correlation coefficients ranging between r = 0.87 and 0.99), followed by Twitter counts with moderate to high correlations (r = 0.49 to 0.98). Correlations between Wikipedia counts reported by the aggregators were mostly weak to moderate (r = 0.28 to 0.87), while the overall lowest pairwise correlations (r = 0.11 to 0.39) were found for Facebook counts (Zahedi and Costas, 2018, pp. 9–11).

With regard to article coverage, compared to their alternatives PLOS ALM reached high coverage with respect to Wikipedia mentions, average coverage regarding Twitter mentions and Mendeley readerships, and relatively low coverage regarding Facebook counts (Zahedi and Costas, 2018, pp. 5–6). In terms of reported metrics' intensity, measured as the mean average of counts for a metric across all articles included in the study, PLOS ALM reached the highest mean score of all providers for Mendeley readership counts and the second highest mean scores for Twitter mentions, Facebook counts, and Wikipedia mentions (Zahedi and Costas, 2018, p. 6). As noted before, aggregators providing higher degrees of coverage or intensity for a metric cannot easily be interpreted as "better" than their competitors, as the reasons for these differences can be manifold (see also Zahedi and Costas [2018, pp. 11–22] for detailed explanations of possible reasons for the differences they found across the aggregators).

Acknowledgments

This chapter was supported by the DFG-funded research project *metrics* (project number: 314727790). We wish to thank Astrid Orth for her valuable feedback during this chapter's creation. Furthermore, we wish to thank all contributors to *Lagotto*'s development and documentation for providing the indispensable foundation this chapter is based on.

References

Chamberlain, S 2013, 'Consuming Article-Level Metrics: Observations and Lessons', *Information Standards Quarterly*, vol. 25, no. 2, pp. 5–13, doi: https://doi.org/10.3789/isqv25no2.2013.02.

Fenner, M 2013, 'What Can Article-Level Metrics Do For You?', *PLOS Biology*, vol. 11, no. 10, e1001687, doi: https://doi.org/10.1371/journal.pbio.1001687.

Jobmann A, Hoffmann, CP, Künne, S, Peters, I, Schmitz, J & Wollnik-Korn, G 2014, 'Altmetrics for large, multidisciplinary research groups: Comparison of current tools', *Bibliometrie – Praxis und Forschung*, vol. 3, https://doi.org/10.5283/bpf.205 and http://www.bibliometrie-pf.de/article/view/205/258 (July 15, 2020).

Lin, J & Fenner, M 2013, 'Altmetrics in Evolution: Defining and Redefining the Ontology of Article-Level Metrics', *Information Standards Quarterly*, vol. 25, no. 2, pp. 20–26, doi: https://doi.org/10.3789/isqv25no2.2013.04.

Parthasarathy, H 2005, 'Measures of Impact', *PLOS Biology*, vol. 3, no. 8, e296, doi: https://doi.org/10.1371/journal.pbio.0030296.

Piwowar, H 2012, *A new framework for altmetrics. Impactstory blog* [online], accessed July 4, 2019, http://blog.impactstory.org/31524247207/ (July 15, 2020).

PLOS 2019, *Track Impact with ALMs* [online], https://www.plos.org/article-level-metrics (July 15, 2020).

The PLOS Medicine Editors 2006, 'The Impact Factor Game', *PLOS Medicine*, vol. 3, no. 6, p. e291, doi: https://doi.org/10.1371/journal.pmed.0030291.

Wouters, P & Costas, R 2012, 'Users, narcissism and control – tracking the impact of scholarly publications in the 21st century', 1st edn., Stitching Surf, Utrecht.

Zahedi, Z 2018, *Understanding the Value of Social Media Metrics for Research Evaluation*, Leiden, http://hdl.handle.net/1887/67131 (July 15, 2020).

Zahedi, Z & Costas, R 2018, 'General discussion of data quality challenges in social media metrics: Extensive comparison of four major altmetric data aggregators', *PLOS ONE*, vol. 13, no. 5, pp. 1–27, doi: https://doi.org/10.1371/journal.pone.0197326.

4.7 Eigenfactor

Grischa Fraumann, Jennifer D'Souza, and Kim Holmberg

Abstract: The Eigenfactor™ is a journal metric, which was developed by Bergstrom and his colleagues at the University of Washington. They invented the Eigenfactor as a response to the criticism against the use of simple citation counts. The Eigenfactor makes use of the network structure of citations, i.e. citations between journals, and establishes the importance, influence or impact of a journal based on its location in a network of journals. The importance is defined based on the number of citations between journals. As such, the Eigenfactor algorithm is based on Eigenvector centrality. While journal based metrics have been criticized, the Eigenfactor has also been suggested as an alternative in the widely used San Francisco Declaration on Research Assessment (DORA).

Keywords: Eigenfactor, alternative metrics, metrics, journals, bibliometrics, Journal Impact Factor, citations, rating.

Introduction

This chapter provides an overview on the Eigenfactor™, a journal metric, which was developed by Bergstrom (2007) and his colleagues at the University of Washington. They invented the Eigenfactor as a response to the criticism against the use of simple citation counts (Bergstrom, 2007). They also claimed a need for alternative metrics (West, Bergstrom and Bergstrom, 2010), which in this case should not be confused with altmetrics, which are metrics to track mentions of scholarly articles online (Priem et al., 2010).

The Eigenfactor makes use of the network structure of citations, i.e. citations between journals (Bergstrom, 2007). The citations are retrieved from Journal Citation Reports (JCR), which is a part of Clarivate Analytics' Web of Science (West, Bergstrom, and Bergstrom, 2010). The Eigenfactor is defined as a flow-based journal ranking, because it simulates the workflow of a researcher searching through journals using citation links (Bohlin et al., 2016). By doing so, it is "interpreted as a proxy for how often a researcher who randomly navigates the citation landscape accesses content from the journal" (Bohlin et al., 2016). These navigational traces, i.e. citations between journals, can be used to calculate a journal's influence (Chang, McAl-

---

Grischa Fraumann, Research Assistant at the TIB Leibniz Information Centre for Science and Technology in the Open Science Lab, Research Affiliate at the "CiMetrias: Research Group on Science and Technology Metrics" at the University of São Paulo (USP), gfr@hum.ku.dk
Jennifer D'Souza, Postdoctoral Researcher at the TIB Leibniz Information Centre for Science and Technology in the Data Sciences and Digital Libraries group, Jennifer.DSouza@tib.eu
Kim Holmberg, Senior Researcher at the Research Unit for the Sociology of Education (RUSE) at the University of Turku, kim.holmberg@abo.fi

eer, and Oxley, 2013), importance of a journal to the scientific community (Bergstrom, West, and Wiseman, 2008) or even impact of a journal (Ball, 2017), in which "important journals are those that are highly cited by important journals" (Bohlin et al., 2016). The Eigenfactor algorithm (West, Bergstrom, and Bergstrom, 2010) is based on Eigenvector centrality, which is a commonly used measure to calculate centrality in network analyses (Martin, Zhang, and Newman, 2014).

Bergstrom (2007) describes the approach of ranking journals as similar to the way Google's PageRank algorithm works. Google ranks websites based on the number of hyperlinks between different websites, but all hyperlinks are not considered as equal, as a hyperlink from a website that already receives a significant number of links is more valuable than a hyperlink from a website with only a few links. The Eigenfactor ranks journals in a similar manner by using citations between journals. Bergstrom describes the approach as follows: "We measure the importance of a citation by the influence of the citing journal divided by the total number of citations appearing in that journal" (Bergstrom, 2007). Bergstrom also argues that this approach corrects the differences between journals and disciplines. That is to say, the "Eigenfactor measures the total influence of a journal on the scholarly literature or, comparably, the total value provided by all of the articles published in that journal in a year" (Bergstrom, 2007). Furthermore, Bergstrom developed an article influence rank which "is proportional to the Eigenfactor divided by the number of articles" (Bergstrom, 2007). This rank is comparable to the Journal Impact Factor (Bergstrom, West, and Wiseman, 2008).

Bergstrom (2007) also proposed a way to measure research impact outside the scientific community. This was proposed to be done by calculating references to scholarly articles from a curated list of major newspapers, such as *New York Times*, *The Guardian*, *Wall Street Journal*, *Washington Post*, *London Times*, *Miami Herald*, *Financial Times*, *Le Monde*, *Boston Globe*, and *Los Angeles Times*.

Role of the Eigenfactor within the Scientific Community

Scientific journals have been an important communication channel for scientific discoveries (Gingras, 2016), ever since the first scientific journal was established in 1665 (Mack, 2015). While there are differences between academic disciplines, such as the social sciences and humanities that have a stronger tradition in publishing books (Hicks, 2005), journals can be found across the range of scientific research. With the introduction of the Internet and the World Wide Web, the importance of scientific journals as a communication and distribution channel has diminished. However, the scientific journal as a publication venue has not changed much since its earliest beginnings (Auer et al., 2018; Wouters et al., 2019). Auer et al. (2018), for example, highlight that journal publications which are mainly based on PDFs could be changed to an interoperable format. This could be done by providing the text in XML (Structured Markup Language). By doing so, the text would provide an improved machine readability and linkage between different documents. The final goal with this move could be to interlink this content in a comprehensive knowledge graph. Further initiatives explore the possibility to decentralize the journal publication system by applying blockchain technology (Blocher, Sadeghi, and Sandner, 2019).

Citations have for a long time been considered as recognition of the value of earlier work, i.e. that researchers acknowledge that they have used or found value in the works that they reference. With that, citations have become part of the academic reward system, with highly cited researchers considered to have made a greater impact (Merton, 1973). Citations take, however, a long time to accumulate, as the scientific publishing process can take years. To counter this time delay, journal-based metrics have been developed (Fersht, 2009). The assumption with journal-based impact metrics is that "better" journals have a more rigorous peer review process and that only the "best" research will be published in them. With that, in which journals researchers publish is sometimes even seen as a quality indicator of their work (Chang, McAleer, and Oxley, 2013), which in turn may have consequences on their academic careers (Bohlin et al., 2016; Brembs, Button, and Munafò, 2013) or even generate questionable financial rewards (Quan, Chen, and Shu, 2017). Furthermore, national journal rankings are developed in several countries (Quan, Chen, and Shu, 2017; Huang, 2019). Journal based metrics, such as the Journal Impact Factor, may also be heavily influenced by a small number of articles that receive the majority of citations (Seglen, 1992). Lariviére and Sugimoto (2018), for instance, provided an extensive review of the critique on Journal Impact Factors. Rankings of journals are, thus, a highly-debated topic because they might also affect research assessments (Tüselmann, Sinkovics, and Pishchulov, 2015). On the one hand, journal rankings are oftentimes also accepted by researchers as part of the publishing process (Brembs, Button, and Munafò, 2013), while on the other hand, it has been argued that journals with a higher impact factor seem to be more likely to publish fraudulent work than low-ranked journals (Brembs, Button, and Munafò, 2013; Fang and Casadevall, 2011). Metrics were developed to classify and understand the journal system better (Garfield, 1972), and journal metrics have been developed in several contexts. Furthermore, journal-based metrics can provide a deeper insight into the similarity of journals (D'Souza and Smalheiser, 2014). The first study that tried to develop objective criteria on journals based on citation counts was published in 1927, and focused on the main U.S. chemistry journals for the year 1926. The authors concluded that the majority of journals receive a relatively low number of citations (Gingras, 2016).

As briefly mentioned above, the Eigenfactor was developed as part of a research project at the University of Washington, and the concept is available on a public website. Bergstrom and colleagues tried to serve the needs of various stakeholders, among others the library community, for example, to support librarians' decision-making on journal subscriptions (Kurtz, 2011). One of the goals of the Eigenfactor is to help academic librarians identify the most important journals when deciding which journals to subscribe to. With the constantly increasing subscription prices it is important to know which journals are the most important and that will be used by scholars. This also relates to the fact that with an ever increasing amount of journals (Bohlin et al., 2016; van Gerestein, 2015) a comprehensive overview without rankings and metrics seems impossible. Even if the quality of a journal can only be assessed objectively by human reading of the published articles (Bergstrom, West, and Wiseman, 2008), rankings and metrics to classify journals are a common practice (Bohlin et al., 2016).

Compared to other journal-based metrics, the Eigenfactor has been proposed as an alternative by the San Francisco Declaration on Research Assessment (DORA) (Cagan, 2013). In turn, the Eigenfactor also supports the Initiative for Open Citations (I4OC). The exact extent to which the Eigenfactor is used in the scientific community and research evaluations is unknown. Nevertheless, studies on hiring and tenure promotion provide a glimpse into the use of metrics. Alperin et al. (2018), for example, concluded that metrics, such as the Journal Impact Factor, are used as a measure by hiring and promotion committees in Canada and the United States. The Journal Impact Factor, for example, is used in several decision-making processes in national research systems (Bohlin et al., 2016), and instead of evaluating journals it is also used to evaluate researchers, which is a highly controversial topic (Fersht, 2009; West, Bergstrom, and Bergstrom, 2010; Wouters et al., 2019).

Critical Perspectives on Journal-based Metrics and Comparison to the Impact Factor

While the Eigenfactor provides some advantages that have been described above, just like any indicator, it does not come without limitations. The Journal Impact Factor was first described in 1972, and is one of the most common journal rankings (Bohlin et al., 2016; Guédon, 2019). It is defined as follows: "The impact factor of a journal in a given year measures the average number of citations to recent articles from articles published in the given year" (Bohlin et al., 2016). The Eigenfactor is also referred to as a rival of the Journal Impact Factor (Reider, 2017) that addresses some of the shortcomings of the former (Tüselmann, Sinkovics, and Pishchulov, 2015). A criticism of the Journal Impact Factor refers to the fact that all citations are assigned the same weight, without taking into account their origin, the journal where the citations occur (Bohlin et al., 2016).

A major difference between the Eigenfactor and the Journal Impact Factor is that the former uses a five-year time window and the latter a two-year window for citations. The broader window should account for citations that appear at a later stage after the research has been published (Bohlin et al., 2016). While a Journal Impact Factor with a five-year time window was also introduced, it seems to be less common than the Journal Impact Factor with a two-year time window (Chang, McAleer, and Oxley, 2013). Another advantage of the Eigenfactor is that self-citations are excluded, which removes score inflations from journal opportunistic self-citations (Bohlin et al., 2016; Chang, McAleer, and Oxley, 2013).

Likewise to the use of any other bibliometric or scientometric indicator, the Eigenfactor should not be used in isolation, and should be supported, for example, by qualitative expert judgements, something that has been emphasised by the Leiden Manifesto for Research Metrics, among others (Hicks et al., 2015). Finally, Bohlin et al. (2016) postulate the most important criterion for evaluating journal-based metrics is the robustness of the method regarding the selection of journals.

Calculating the Eigenfactor™ Score

The Eigenfactor score is intended to measure the importance of a journal to the scientific community by considering the origin of the incoming citations, and is thought to reflect how frequently an average researcher would access content from that journal. The Eigenfactor for a journal is arrived at by a series of steps (eigenfactor.org). These are elicited below.

First, a five-year cross-citation matrix Z is extracted from the Journal Citation Report (JCR) (clarivate.com).[1]

$Z_{(ij,Y_6)}$ = Citations from journal j in year Y_6 to articles published in journal i during the five years Y_1 to Y_5

For instance, given the 2019 JCR, the entries of the cross-citation matrix would be: Z_{ij} = Citations from journal j in 2019 to articles published in journal i during the 2014 to 2018 five-year period. A longer five-year citation window allows taking into account that certain fields do not have as rapid citation trends as others and only begin a few years after the articles are published. For instance, the average article in a leading cell biology journal might receive 10–30 citations within the two first years after publishing, while, in contrast, the average article in a leading mathematics journal would do very well to receive two citations over the same period. In this regard, measures that only look at citations in the first two years after publication (e. g., Journal Impact Factor) can be misleading (if disciplinary differences are not accounted for).

Note that in Z, its diagonal elements are set to 0, thereby omitting journal self-citations. This handles over-inflating journals that engage in the practice of opportunistic self-citation.

In the second step, Z is normalized by the column sums (i.e., by the total number of outgoing citations from each journal) to obtain citation probabilities for each journal

---

[1] Each year more journals from the Sciences and Social Sciences are indexed in the Journal Citation Report. For the sake of comparison, in 2016, 7611 "source" journals were indexed versus 11,877 in 2019. https://clarivate.com/webofsciencegroup/solutions/journal-citation-reports/ (July 21, 2020).

column-wise to other journals represented by the matrix rows. The resulting matrix is the column-stochastic matrix H, such that

$$H_{ij} = \frac{Z_{(ij,Y_6)}}{\sum_k Z_{(kj,Y_6)}}$$

However, not all the journals listed in H are cited by other journals. These journals will all have 0 entries in their corresponding column j. For such journals, an article vector a with entries a_j for each source journal J is computed as follows:

$$a_j = \frac{|J_{Y_1 to Y_5}|}{\sum_k |K_{Y_1 to Y_5}|}$$

where $|J_{Y_1 to Y_5}|$ is the number of articles published by J in the preceding five-year window and the denominator is the number of articles published by all source journals in the JCR over the same five-year window. Thus all journals with no citation links are uniformly populated with a, transforming H into H'.

Third, a stochastic traversal matrix P is defined following Google's Page-Rank approach, as follows:

$$P = \alpha H' + (1 - \alpha)\alpha.e^T$$

Here, e^T is a row vector of 1s, where T is the transpose function, and thus $A = \alpha.e^T$ is a matrix with identical columns each equal to the article vector a.

Under a stochastic process interpretation,[2] the traversal matrix P defines a random walk on the journal citation network that is either a transition with probability α weighted by the entries in H', i.e. the journal citation probabilities, or is a jump to an arbitrary journal with probability $(1 - \alpha)$ weighted by the entries in a, i.e. the proportion of articles published by each journal. Note that without α the traversal will be confined only to the nodes with high H' values. Thus α makes allowance for arbitrary citations not contained in the actual data. At each time instant in the random process P modelling a random walk from journal J to journal K, the random variables correspond to matrix values based on the intermediate traversals between journals. Additionally, since P possesses the Markov property[3] whereby traversals to K depend only on knowing the present journal J it came from and no prior history, P is a Markov random process.

---

[2] A stochastic or random process is defined as a collection of random variables indexed at unique time instances.

[3] The Markov property, when applied to stochastic processes, restricts the conditional probability distribution of future states to depend only upon the present state, and not on the entire sequence of states that preceded it, thereby limiting the considered state sequence history.

In the fourth and last step, the Eigenfactor score of each journal is computed. Formally, the Eigenfactor score EF_i of journal i is defined as the percentage of the total weighted citations that journal i receives from source journals. Thus the vector of Eigenfactor scores is written as

$$EF = 100 \frac{H\pi^*}{\sum_i [H\pi^*]_i}$$

where vector π^* is extracted from the stochastic traversal matrix P as its leading Eigenvector. Under the stochastic process interpretation the π^* vector corresponds to the maximum (also known as steady-state) fraction of time spent at each journal represented in P. In the Eigenfactor score, this translates as the measure of the journal influence for weighting citations.

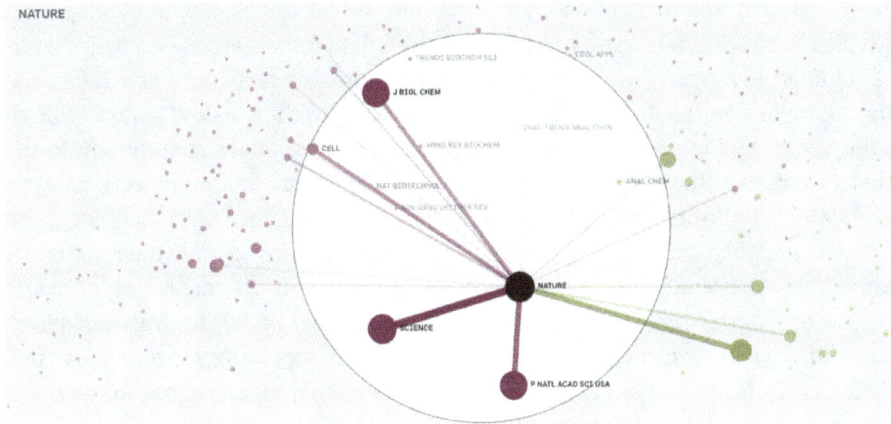

Figure 1: A magnified view (within the white circle lens) of a map visualization (well-formed.eigenfactor.org [July 21, 2020]) of Eigenfactor scores (reflected by the node sizes) as a citation network of journals focusing on the journal *Nature* (black node) computed on a subset of journals in the citation data from Thomson Reuters' Journal Citation Reports. For all nodes connected to *Nature*, the edge thicknesses represent the relative amount of citation flow (incoming and outgoing) with respect to it; color-codes correspond to different domains found in the data subset.

Consider in Figure 1 an illustration of the resulting Eigenfactor scores for journals within a citation network. In the figure, the nodes correspond to journals and the nodes sizes reflect their scaled Eigenfactor scores. The calculations presented above recall two aspects involved in computing the Eigenfactor score for the selected journal *Nature* in the figure: (1) citation probabilities from other journals to the journal *Nature* (contained in matrix H' described above); and relying on it, (2) a stochastic traversal pattern defined by P to *Nature*. The figure vaguely depicts this via the edges between *Nature* and other journals and from the edge thicknesses reflecting the citation inflow and outflow. In general, for each journal found in the JCR data, the Eigenfactor score algorithm uses the structure of the entire network to evaluate the importance of each journal, cutting across all disciplines with self-citations excluded. This corresponds to a simple model of research in which readers follow chains of citations as they move from journal to journal. Consequently, journals are considered to be influential if they are cited often by other influential journals.

Conclusions

As defined by the inventors of the Eigenfactor, "[s]cholarly references join journals together in a vast network of citations" (eigenfactor.org [July 21, 2020]). Given the sheer amount of journals that have emerged over time, this citation data has been measured and analyzed to sort and classify journals.

In this article, one such metric, namely the Eigenfactor, has been presented. Apart from that, the role of this indicator within the scientific community in general has also been addressed. Leveraging the citation data from Clarivate Analytics' Journal Citation Reports (JCR), the Eigenfactor rates journals of science and social science according to the number of incoming citations over a five-year period, with citations from highly ranked journals weighted to make a larger contribution to the Eigenfactor than those from poorly ranked journals via a citation network analysis method inspired from Google's PageRank. Different disciplines have different citing practices and different time scales on which citations occur, therefore the Eigenfactor with its five-year citation window overcomes limitations of its contemporary metric the Journal Impact Factor. This is because the latter kind of metrics with smaller citation time windows can err on the side of assigning higher ratings to journals in disciplines with faster citation patterns rather than creating an allowance for all disciplines and their unique citation patterns.

While metrics might be useful to sort and classify large amounts of data, the concept of a journal's importance also raised criticism. For example, journal-based metrics might have unintended effects on the research system and individual researchers if evaluations are based on metrics without taking into account qualitative expert judgement. There are also initiatives being carried out that try to visualize research outputs beyond journals, and try to acknowledge several forms of impact (e.g., Hauschke, Cartellieri, and Heller, 2018). This article described the Eigenfactor, and mentioned some examples of its role in research systems.

References

Alperin, JP, Muñoz Nieves, C, Schimanski, L, Fischman, GE, Niles, MT & McKiernan, EC 2018, 'How significant are the public dimensions of faculty work in review, promotion, and tenure documents?', *Humanities Commons.* https://doi.org/10.7554/eLife.42254

Auer, S, Kovtun, V, Prinz, M, Kasprzik, A, Stocker, M & Vidal, ME 2018, 'Towards a knowledge graph for science', in R Akerkar, M Ivanović, S-W Kim, Y Manolopoulos, R Rosati, M Savić, C

Badica & M Radovanović (eds.), *Proceedings of the 8th International Conference on Web Intelligence, Mining and Semantics – WIMS '18, New York, New York, USA*, pp. 1–6, ACM Press. https://doi.org/10.1145/3227609.3227689

Ball, R 2017, *An Introduction to Bibliometrics: New Development and Trends*, Elsevier Science. https://doi.org/10.1016/C2016-0-03695-1

Bergstrom, C 2007, 'Eigenfactor: Measuring the value and prestige of scholarly journals', *College & Research Libraries News*, vol. 68, no. 5, pp. 314–316. https://doi.org/10.5860/crln.68.5.7804

Bergstrom, CT, West, JD & Wiseman, MA 2008, 'The Eigenfactor metrics', *The Journal of Neuroscience: The Official Journal of the Society for Neuroscience*, vol. 28, no. 45, pp. 11433–11434. https://doi.org/10.1523/JNEUROSCI.0003-08.2008

Blocher, W, Sadeghi, AR & Sandner, P 2019, 'Blockchain and the future of publishing', in C Draude, M Lange & B Sick (eds.), *INFORMATIK 2019: 50 Jahre Gesellschaft für Informatik – Informatik für Gesellschaft (Workshop-Beiträge)*, pp. 587–588, Gesellschaft für Informatik e.V, Bonn. https://dx.doi.org/10.18420/inf2019_ws61

Bohlin, L, Viamontes Esquivel, A, Lancichinetti, A & Rosvall, M 2016, 'Robustness of journal rankings by network flows with different amounts of memory', *Journal of the Association for Information Science and Technology*, vol. 67, no. 10, pp. 2527–2535. https://doi.org/10.1002/asi.23582

Brembs, B, Button, K & Munafò, M 2013, 'Deep impact: unintended consequences of journal rank', *Frontiers in Human Neuroscience*, vol. 7, p. 291. https://doi.org/10.3389/fnhum.2013.00291

Cagan, R 2013, 'The San Francisco declaration on research assessment', *Disease Models & Mechanisms*, vol. 6, no. 4, pp. 869–870. https://doi.org/10.1242/dmm.012955

Chang, C-L, McAleer, M & Oxley, L 2013, 'Coercive journal self citations, impact factor, journal influence and article influence', *Mathematics and Computers in Simulation*, vol. 93, pp. 190–197. https://doi.org/10.1016/j.matcom.2013.04.006

D'Souza, J & Smalheiser, NR 2014, 'Three journal similarity metrics and their application to biomedical journals', *PloS One*, vol. 9, no. 12, e115681. https://doi.org/10.1371/journal.pone.0115681

Fang, FC & Casadevall, A 2011, 'Retracted science and the retraction index', *Infection and immunity*, vol. 79, no. 10, pp. 3855–3859. http://doi.org/10.1128/IAI.05661-11

Fersht, A 2009, 'The most influential journals: Impact factor and Eigenfactor', *Proceedings of the National Academy of Sciences of the United States of America*, vol. 106, no. 17, pp. 6883–6884. https://doi.org/10.1073/pnas.0903307106

Garfield, E 1972, 'Citation analysis as a tool in journal evaluation', *Science (New York, N.Y.)*, vol. 178, no. 4060, pp. 471–479.

Gingras, Y 2016, *Bibliometrics and Research Evaluation: Uses and Abuses. History and Foundations of Information Science*, The MIT Press, Cambridge, Massachusetts. https://mitpress.mit.edu/books/bibliometrics-and-research-evaluation

Guédon, J-C, Jubb, M, Kramer, B, Laakso, M, Schmidt, B, Šimukovič, E, Hansen, J, Kiley, R, Kitson, A, van der Stelt, W, Markram, K & Patterson, M 2019, *Future of Scholarly Publishing and Scholarly Communication: Report of the Expert Group to the European Commission*, European Commission, Brussels. https://doi.org/10.2777/836532

Hauschke, C, Cartellieri, S & Heller, L 2018, 'Reference implementation for open scientometric indicators (rosi)', *Research Ideas and Outcomes*, vol. 4, e31656. https://doi.org/10.3897/rio.4.e31656

Hicks, D 2005, 'The four literatures of social science', in HF Moed, W Glänzel, & U Schmoch (eds.), *Handbook of Quantitative Science and Technology Research*, vol. 23, pp. 473–496, Kluwer Academic Publishers, Dordrecht. https://doi.org/10.1007/1-4020-2755-9_22

Hicks, D, Wouters, P, Waltman, L, de Rijcke, S & Rafols, I 2015, 'Bibliometrics: The Leiden manifesto for research metrics', *Nature*, vol. 520, no. 7548, pp. 429–431. https://doi.org/10.1038/520429a

Huang, Y 2019, 'Monitoring of research output in China', *3rd ENRESSH Training School*, October 23, Poznań, Poland.

Kurtz, MJ 2011, 'The emerging scholarly brain', in A Accomazzi (ed.), *Future Professional Communication in Astronomy II, Volume 1 of Astrophysics and Space Science Proceedings*, pp. 23–35, Springer New York. https://doi.org/10.1007/978-1-4419-8369-5_3

Larivière, V & Sugimoto, CR 2018, 'The journal impact factor: A brief history, critique, and discussion of adverse effects', *CoRR abs/1801.08992*. https://doi.org/10.1007/978-3-030-02511-3_1

Mack, C 2015, '350 years of scientific journals', *Journal of Micro/Nanolithography, MEMS, and MOEMS*, vol. 14, no. 1. https://doi.org/10.1117/1.JMM.14.1.010101

Martin, T, Zhang, X & Newman, MEJ 2014, 'Localization and centrality in networks', *Physical Review*, vol. 90, no. 5, p. 211. https://doi.org/10.1103/PhysRevE.90.052808

Merton, RK 1973, *The Sociology of Science: Theoretical and Empirical Investigations*, University of Chicago Press. https://press.uchicago.edu/ucp/books/book/chicago/S/bo28451565.html

Priem, J, Taraborelli, D, Groth, P & Neylon, C 2010, *Altmetrics: A Manifesto*. https://www.altmetrics.org/manifesto

Quan, W, Chen, B & Shu, F 2017, 'Publish or impoverish: An investigation of the monetary reward system of science in China (1999–2016)', *Aslib Journal of Information Management*, vol. 69, no. 5, pp. 486–502. https://doi.org/10.1108/AJIM-01-2017-0014

Reider, B 2017, 'Brace for impact', *The American Journal of Sports Medicine*, vol. 45, no. 10, pp. 2213–2216. https://doi.org/10.1177/0363546517721707

Seglen, PO 1992, 'The skewness of science', *Journal of the American Society for Information Science*, vol. 43, no. 9, pp. 628–638. https://doi.org/10.1002/(SICI)1097–4571(199210)43:9<628::AID-ASI5>3.0.CO;2–0

Tüselmann, H, Sinkovics, RR & Pishchulov, G 2015, 'Towards a consolidation of worldwide journal rankings – a classification using random forests and aggregate rating via data envelopment analysis', *Omega*, vol. 51, pp. 11–23. https://doi.org/10.1016/j.omega.2014.08.002

van Gerestein, D 2015, 'Quality open access market and other initiatives: a comparative analysis', *LIBER Quarterly*, vol. 24, no. 4, p. 162. http://doi.org/10.18352/lq.9911

West, JD, Bergstrom, TC & Bergstrom, CT 2010, 'The Eigenfactor metrics: A network approach to assessing scholarly journals', *College & Research Libraries*, vol. 71, no. 3, pp. 236–244. https://doi.org/10.5860/0710236

Wouters, P, Sugimoto, CR, Larivière, V, McVeigh, ME, Pulverer, B, de Rijcke, S & Waltman, L 2019, 'Rethinking impact factors: better ways to judge a journal', *Nature*, vol. 569, no. 7758, pp. 621–623. https://doi.org/10.1038/d41586-019-01643-3

4.8 Academic Social Networks and Bibliometrics
Clemens Blümel

Abstract: This contribution deals with Academic Social Network Sites (ASNS) as a resource for bibliometricians and informetricians. ASNS are a rather novel medium for scholarly communication, but they have reached a broad userbase and gained attention by novel information aggregators (such as PlumX), publishers and data providers. Based on a short sketch of basic characteristics and services of ASNS, this chapter provides an overview of existing research devoted to ASNS and its uses. In particular, the contribution deals with how metrics relying on data from ASNS are constructed and what problems and challenges arise in dealing with these metrics. I argue that more conceptual and theoretical work is to be done in order to understand the meanings of ASNS usage.

Keywords: academic social network sites, digital platforms, disciplinary differences, alternative metrics.

Introduction

The exchange of ideas through formal and informal channels has always been a key element of the scholarly communication system and a relevant part of academics' daily practice (Kronick, 2001; Guedon, 2001). With the advent of the Internet, scholars have rapidly begun to discover various sites for the exchange of ideas and material. Nowadays, special academic social networking sites (hereafter, ASNS) are among those online sites which are used most frequently by scientists (Jeng, He, and Jiang, 2015; Nández and Borrego, 2013; Ortega, 2015). Since their inception, some of these networks such as ResearchGate have reached high numbers of users (van Noorden, 2014). They are now part of what has been termed innovative forms of scholarly dissemination (Görögh et al., 2017).

Due to their position between the formal and the informal, ASNS have not only attracted academic users; they have also been subject to expectations towards changes of the scholarly communication system. For instance, it has been envisioned that with the advent of social networking sites, scholarly communication will become more collaborative and inclusive than within the current regime (Megwalu, 2015; Nielsen, 2012). Research into the uses and the meaning of academic social networking sites has therefore often focused on in what ways and to what extent academic social networking sites have spurred collaborative activity or to which extent they

---

Dipl.-Soz. **Clemens Blümel**, German Centre for Higher Education Research and Science Studies (DZHW), Department Research System and Science Dynamics, Schützenstraße 6a, 10117 Berlin, Germany

have changed the current culture of appreciation for scholarly output. This transformative aspect of academic social networking sites will also be dealt with within this chapter.

Academic social networks have attracted broad interest among researchers, research managers and other stakeholders in science, and they are increasingly studied within the bibliometric community (Erdt et al., 2016). Bibliometric research devoted to ASNS has been spurred by the availability of process generated data, provided by novel aggregators of altmetric data, such as altmetric.com or PlumX.

Bibliometricians have particularly studied characteristics and effects of ASNS, the strategies of individuals (Nentwich and König, 2014), institutions (Mansour, 2015), and organizations across disciplines (Ortega, 2015) and different academic positions using these sites (Nández and Borrego, 2013). To a large extent, however, research into the uses of ASNS has been conducted in order to generate, construct or criticize novel indicators based on data of academic social networking sites (Copiello and Bonifaci, 2019; Orduna-Malea et al., 2017; Thelwall and Kousha, 2015), as part of what is currently termed alternative metrics (Priem and Hemminger, 2010).

Against this background, this chapter provides an overview of bibliometric research devoted to ASNS. Based on such analysis, it is attempted to generate more general propositions of ASNS and to what extent they have changed scholarly communication and reputation management. The chapter is organized as follows: In the first part, I provide an overview of existing services at different forms of ASNS. I then proceed by reporting from current research how these features are used. Thirdly, I will report in which ways new metrics and indicators based on or related to ASNS have been constructed and how those metrics have been receipted within the community of bibliometricians. Finally, I will conclude by outlining the meanings of ASNS for the current scholarly communication and a future outlook.

The Landscape of Social Networking Sites in the Academic Sphere

Scholars started using social networking sites from the very beginning of the Internet. To this end, they have used existing services for private or professional online networking. After its foundation in 2004, Facebook soon became the most important site for researchers not only because of its global presence (Bar-Ilan et al., 2012; Nentwich and König, 2014; Thelwall and Kousha, 2015c), but also because it allowed individuals to bridge professional and private dissemination (Procter et al. 2010).

Since 2008, however, several dedicated academic social networking services with novel functions and services for academics have been founded, among which, in terms of users, Academia.edu and ResearchGate are now the largest providers. As by today, ResearchGate has 15 million and Academia.edu more than 75 million members. In addition, there are other, smaller academic social networking services which focus on a specific aspect of scholarly knowledge production and which provide social networking functions in addition to their basic service. Examples for the latter are Mendeley or CiteUlike. Given their tailored services, academic social networks appear to be more suited for scholarly communication than the more generic networking sites such as LinkedIn and Facebook, although the latter are still also widely used (van Noorden, 2014). Hence, scholars have now a broad landscape of different social networks from which they can choose and which they can use for networking with their peers and for disseminating their research: first, there are still the large generic sites like LinkedIn, second, there are genuine academic social networking sites, and, third, there are digital sites with other main functionalities. It is no exaggeration to say that academic social networking has now been established as a professional practice within the scholarly realm. Yet, what makes ASNS specific, particularly in comparison to their generic counterparts in the commercial and the private world?

Characteristics of Social Networks within the Scholarly Realm

In order to account for what ASNS are, one needs to firstly understand the more general characteristics of online social networking sites and which services they typically provide to their users. Boyd and Ellison (2007) have outlined that most social networks provide services for a) a profile, b) a service for the articulation of users to which they are connected, and c) affordances to interact with others. These characteristics are relevant for ASNS as well. Yet, there are some services which are particularly relevant for their scholarly audience, which make them different from other generic sites.

One of the most defining features of ASNS is that they allow for generating a differentiated user profile. It appears that such a service is particularly appreciated among scholars (Nentwich and König, 2014). In order to keep their communities informed, researchers use social networks to provide more information about them as academic beings, highlighting what topics they are interested in and what their research is for. Thus, academic social networking sites have responded to the general trend of self-marketization of scientists (van Noorden, 2014). Nentwich and König (2014) have called this phenomenon the "digital calling card function" (Nentwich and König, 2014, p. 113) of ASNS. Second, academic social networking sites offer services for sharing publications. Scholars can easily upload their publications and provide information about these papers. This is what distinguishes them most from more general social networking sites, because the indexing of publications on ASNS is quite advanced.

Following the path towards Open Access, many scholars are requested to provide access to their papers. The dissemination of publication via social networks is understood as a means to comply with these principles. A study by Piwowar et al. (2017) has shown that ASNS have the biggest share within the sites providing green open access.[1] A third characteristic of ASNS is that they provide services for collaboration: there are tools for following other's activities as well as tailored question and answer sections for academic needs, but there are also services for establishing groups or collaborative projects on specific research or methodological topics (Jeng, He, and Jiang, 2015). Finally, ASNS also allow for focusing attention on research outputs. Again, this feature is particularly specific for the usage of ASNS: online acts of appraisal or endorsement such as views, likes or followings allow for making specific research more visible across the social networking sites. Similar to other novel data sources for altmetrics, these are among the features of ASNS which have received most attention within the realm of bibliometrics (Bardakcı, Arslan, and Ünver, 2018).

User Studies of Academic SNS

Intensity and Frequency of ASNS Usage

As has been established in the preceding section, academic social networking sites provide a wide range of different services. Given such diversity of services, however, it was unclear how these online sites were being used and perceived. Yet, there were expectations raised that ASNS increase collaboration and inclusion among the scholarly community, particularly younger and more unexperienced scholars (Mansour et al., 2015). In order to establish to what extent these services have changed communicative behavior and the stances of academics, research into academic social networks has focused on exploring users' characteristics, their perceptions, and their behaviors towards ASNS, mostly by conducting large surveys (Procter et al., 2010; van Noorden, 2014; Nández and Borrego, 2013).

A large scale survey of the nature group in 2014 (van Noorden, 2014) found that many scholars are aware of the biggest providers in ASNS (ResearchGate, Academia.edu, Mendeley). However, the first quantitative user studies (Procter et al., 2010) revealed that expectations of increased collaboration through academic social networking sites appeared to be far-fetched: frequent and stable interaction on Academic Social Networking Sites does not take place. Instead, findings show that usage of ASNS is not very intense: according to Procter et al. (2010, p. 4043), only 13% of those signing up to these sites can be considered as frequent users (visiting the sites once a week or more).

Similarly, a study conducted by Nandez and Borrego (2013) found that most respondents were using ASNS passively (35%) or even sporadically (34%), while only 18% can be considered as frequent users, using the platform on a weekly (13%) or

---

[1] Yet, researchers have to make sure that intellectual property rights are not infringed. Recently, Academic Social Network Sites came into play of commercial scholarly publishers. In 2017, ResearchGate was accused of violating copyright infringement by Elsevier Ltd. (Else 2018). Academia.edu was issued in 2013 with a takedown notice of its services for similar reasons (Else, 2018; Clarke, 2013).

daily (5%) basis and in a more collaborative and intense way (Nández and Borrego 2013, p. 786). These observations seem to contradict what users reported about their motivations to use such sites. Thus, Nandez and Borrego (2013) concluded there would be a "lack of coincidence between stated reason" and observed or reported behaviour (frequency of interaction, upload of documents). These findings were confirmed by other studies. Based on a small scale study of a Library and Information Science faculty in Kuwait, Mansour et al. (2015) found that the stated reasons for user participation were mostly linked to a desire to "communicate with others" (95.2%), but that actual communication appeared to be moderate (Mansour, 2015, p. 540).

Another expectation related to the emergence of social networks was that they might contribute substantially to the inclusion of younger scientists in scholarly communication outside the realm of scholarly journals. Although in general there are some indications that novel dissemination channels are more frequently used by younger researchers and PhD students, there are mixed results specifically for the use of ASNS: Mansour et al. (2015) studied the educational level of users and non-users of ASNS for the faculty of Library and Information Science and found no significant differences between users and non-users of ASNS (Mansour, 2015, p. 531). Van Noorden (2014) revealed that ASNS were merely used for generating collaborations among established researchers (van Noorden, 2014). Yet, Megwalu (2015) found that most registered users of Academial.edu were graduate students, while the most frequent users were associate professors and postdocs. Thus, there is no clear indication that ASNS would serve as a corrective to the existing journal world; instead it appears that in terms of user demography, they appear to reproduce existing academic hierarchies.

Even more discouraging are the findings regarding propositions related to increased collaboration of scholars through ASNS. By surveying open group users on Mendely, Jeng et al. (2015) found that it was difficult to motivate scholars to use these collaborative tools. According to gender aspects, it appeared easier to motivate female researchers than their male counterparts to take part in these settings (Megwalu, 2015). From the research conducted so far, there are some indications that for many of the respondents, it may simply be enough to be present on the academic social networking site, a phenomenon which Nentwich and Koenig (Nentwich and König, 2014, p. 113) have called "a me too presence", investing particularly time in boosting their academic profiles. Bik and Goldstein (2013) therefore concluded ASNS may be perceived as sites in which academics compete for "future recognition".

Disciplinary Differences in ASNS Usage

The intensity of ASNS usage among scholars, however, cannot be generalized. There are important differences in using these sites across disciplines. Such disciplinary differences are an important aspect for bibliometric research evaluation (Ortega

2015, p. 520). Often these differences are limiting quantitative comparisons and indicator development.[2] It comes therefore as no surprise that disciplinary differences are also intensely studied for social networking sites. As Ortega (2015) has outlined, the "tools" provided by ASNS "need to be analysed in order to validate whether they are representative of the entire scholarly community or if only specific types of disciplines are using them" (Ortega, 2015, p. 520).

Disciplinary differences were particularly apparent regarding the choice and usage intensity of these sites. Surveys and user studies have shown that the two biggest ASNS sites showed enormous differences regarding the disciplinary background of their users. While Academia.edu users are to a large extent scholars from the social sciences and the humanities (Megwalu, 2015; Thelwall and Kousha, 2014), registrations on ResearchGate initially were dominated by biomedical researchers and natural scientists (Thelwall and Kousha, 2015).

Different research has shown that there are not only disciplinary differences in the choice of providers but also in usage intensity. Ortega (2015), exploring profiles, affiliations, co-authorships, follower data, and publication lists from the Spanish extra university research organization Consejo Superior de Investigaciones Cientificas (CSIC) for ResearchGate, Academia.edu and Google Scholar Citations, has found large disciplinary differences regarding the use of these social networking sites.[3] He found that social scientists and humanities scholars were not only more present on the aforementioned sites (Ortega, 2015, p. 524), but they were also more active than their counterparts from biomedicine (Ortega, 2015, p. 525).

Jamali et al. (2016) argue that the different expectations towards reputational value of academic social networking sites may explain why sociologists tend to use these platforms more frequently than their colleagues from the natural sciences (Jamali, Nicholas, and Herman, 2016). In addition, applying Whitley's framework of mutual dependency and task uncertainty, Megwalu (2015) argued that the presence and activity of sociologists and linguists on Academia.edu may be explained by the cultural practices of these disciplines with a high degree of diversity for research topics (Megwalu, 2015, p. 198) while a relative low degree of uncertainty regarding the methods used assures that sociologists can advise each other.

---

[2] For instance, scholars in the social sciences and the humanities are not publishing their research to a similar extent in the journal literature, thereby limiting the applicability of bibliometric measures based on indices within this literature.

[3] Yet, it appears questionable to what extent Google Scholar Citations can be considered an academic social network site, since one of the defining characteristics of social network sites is missing on GSC, a list of contacts with which the user can traverse links and get in contact on the site. It is just the citing publications which can be easily accessed through the interface.

Indicator Development

Bibliometric research into the usage and usage metrics of ASNS is to a significant extent driven by the interest of constructing new indicators for online activity. ASNS are a substantial part of scholarly online activity (Manca, 2018) and data derived from these platforms provide new perspectives of the "social nature of science" (Ortega, 2015, p. 520). Hence, most research on ASNS has been devoted to the discussion, development, and evaluation of indicators based on data from ASNS or, more specifically, on specific indicators generated by providers of ASNS themselves (Copiello and Bonifaci, 2019; Nicholas, Clark, and Herman, 2016; Orduna-Malea, Martin-Martin, and Lopez-Cozar, 2016; Orduna-Malea et al., 2017; Kraker and Lex, 2015; Jordan, 2015).

Several researchers have discussed the suitability of ASNS data as a means for measuring attention or impact, referring particularly to what is currently rather vaguely defined as other or novel types of impact (Priem and Hemminger, 2010). Based on studies of Mendeley, Jeng et al. (2015) have found that ASNS are relevant for measuring scholarly activity and communication and support processes, e. g. answering questions in Q&A forums. The quest for indicators for alternative impact is prevalent in studies on ASNS metrics. Hoffmann et al. (2016), for instance, contend network centrality measures are a substantial complementary source for measuring reputation (Hoffmann, Lutz, and Meckel, 2016). Yet, the various inhomogeneous and disparately distributed usage patterns as well as the aforementioned disciplinary differences suggest that scholars should devise some caution to the use of ASNS data for research evaluation.

Even more contested is the value of indicators generated and aggregated by providers of ASNS themselves, which aim at providing new metrics and measures for reputation. Most research in the realm of ASNS has been directed to exploring the ResearchGate Score, investigating its advantages and weaknesses (Copiello and Bonifaci, 2019; Orduna-Malea et al., 2017; Kraker and Lex, 2015; Jordan, 2015), particularly compared to existing indicators known to the community, but also based on principles on indicator development which have been proclaimed within the realm of Open Science (Priem and Hemminger, 2010). The ResearchGate score is a composite indicator which allows users to compare themselves with others on the platform, putting together different information generated from the

platform and supporting services. Up to now, however, the calculation of the score is unpublished. Some research has been undertaken to study the score and its suitability for measuring scholarly impact or reputation. Thelwall and Kousha (2015) have found that on the institutional level, correlations with existing rankings are only moderate, but that they may be more useful as alternative measures for distribution of social and reputational capital. Contrary to that, Yu et al. (2016) have found high correlations to rankings based on institutional as well as on individual levels (data retrieved from REF). Other research on the score established that it may be unsuited as a "measure of reputation". Based on a study of their own account, Kraker and Lex (2015), argued that the main shortcomings are: its intransparency, its reliance on the disputed Journal Impact Factor, and its volatility in how the indicator is calculated.[4] Jordan (2015) confirmed that JIF based measures appeared to contribute substantially to the RG score, while at the same time these metrics were considered inappropriate for measuring individual contributions on the platform. Thus, although the idea of the score appears to be innovative, in its current form, it appears to fail in applying existing metrics while hiding relevant information about its calculation.

Conclusion

Academic Social Networking Sites are considered to be a particularly visible part of digital scholarship. Driven by the opportunities to generate contacts among their peers (Procter et al., 2010), these sites have grown steadily in terms of registrations. Yet, what is more, their establishment was accompanied with expectations of bridging the gaps between established and younger researchers, and, in more general terms, contributing to increased collaboration among the scholarly community. With their specific role between formal and informal scholarly communication, these sites were envisioned to overcome some of the limitations of generic social networking sites. Scholars from bibliometrics have shown that these expectations may be exaggerated (Jeng, He, and Jiang, 2015; Nández and Borrego, 2013; Mansour, 2015), and that ASNS may serve different functions, such as what is considered the digital calling card (Nentwich and König, 2014). Most research, however, was undertaken to explore the potentials of ASNS as alternative providers of measures for scholarly reputation. This contribution aimed to point out that such attempts have, generally speaking, not succeeded so far. Neither are process generated data from ASNS a good proxy for either informal or formal communication exchange (Orduna-Malea et al., 2017), because online acts such as views or downloads are only poorly understood; nor do novel indicators provided by some of the ASNS themselves function as alternatives to existing indicators due to their intransparency (Ortega, 2015; Kraker and Lex, 2015). Yet, the analysis of data generated by academic social networking sites can yield some interesting insights into the structure (Mansour, 2016) and dynamics of science (Megwalu, 2016). More conceptual and theoretical work is to be done in order to understand the meanings of ASNS usage (Manca, 2018).

---

4 For instance, they observed changes of the ResearchGate Score for their profile, without a significant change in the data.

References

Bardakcı, S, Arslan Ö & Ünver, TK 2018, 'How Scholars Use Academic Social Networking Services', *Information Development*, vol. 34, no. 4, pp. 334–45, doi: https://doi.org/10.1177/0266666917712108.

Bik, HM & Goldstein, MC 2013, 'An Introduction to Social Media for Scientists', *PLoS biology*, vol. 11, no. 4, e1001535.

Clarke, M 2013, 'The End of an Era for Academia.Edu and Other Academic Networks?', https://scholarlykitchen.sspnet.org/2013/12/11/has-elsevier-signaled-a-new-era-for-academia-edu-and-other-professional-networks/ (July 15, 2020).

Copiello, S & Bonifaci, P 2019, 'ResearchGate Score, Full-Text Research Items, and Full-Text Reads: A Follow-up Study', *Scientometrics*, vol. 119, no. 2, pp. 1255–62, doi: https://doi.org/10.1007/s11192-019-03063-6.

Else, H 2018, 'Major Publishers Sue ResearchGate over Copyright Infringement', *Nature*, vol. 112, p. 241. doi: https://doi.org/10.1038/d41586-018-06945-6.

Erdt, M, Nagarajan, A, Sin, S-CJ & Theng, Y-L 2016, 'Altmetrics: An Analysis of the State-of-the-Art in Measuring Research Impact on Social Media', *Scientometrics*, vol. 109, no. 2, pp. 1117–66, doi: https://doi.org/10.1007/s11192-016-2077-0.

Görögh, E, Sifacaki, E, Vignoli, M, Gauch, S, Blümel, C, Kraker, P, Hasani-Mavriqi, I, Luzi, D, Walker, M & Toli, E 2017, 'Opening up New Channels for Scholarly Review, Dissemination, and Assessment', in L Morgan (ed.), *The 13th International Symposium*, pp. 1–11, ACM Publishers.

Guedon, J-C 2001, *In Oldenburg's Long Shadow: Librarians, Research Scientists, Publishers and the Control of Scientific Publishing*, ARL, Washington D.C.

Hoffmann, CP, Lutz, C & Meckel, M 2016, 'A Relational Altmetric? Network Centrality on ResearchGate as an Indicator of Scientific Impact', *J Assn Inf Sci Tec*, vol. 67, no. 4, pp. 765–75, doi: https://doi.org/10.1002/asi.23423.

Jamali, HR, Nicholas, D & Herman, E 2016, 'Scholarly Reputation in the Digital Age and the Role of Emerging Platforms and Mechanisms', *Research Evaluation*, vol. 25, no. 1, pp. 37–49, doi: https://doi.org/10.1093/reseval/rvv032.

Jeng, W, He, D & Jiang, J 2015, 'User Participation in an Academic Social Networking Service: A Survey of Open Group Users on Mendeley', *J Assn Inf Sci Tec*, vol. 66, no. 5, pp. 890–904, doi: https://doi.org/10.1002/asi.23225.

Jordan, K, 2015, 'Exploring the ResearchGate Score as an Academic Metric: Reflections and Implications for Practice, Quantifying and Analysing Scholarly Communication on the Web (ASCW'15)', http://ascw.know-center.tugraz.at/wp-content/uploads/2015/06/ASCW15_jordan_response_kraker-lex.pdf (July 15, 2020).

Kraker, P & Lex, E, eds. 2015, *A Critical Look at the ResearchGate Score as a Measure of Scientific Reputation*, Zenodo.

Kronick, D 2001, 'The Commerce of Letters: Networks and "Invisible Colleges" in Seventeenth- and Eighteenth-Century Europe', *Library Quarterly*, vol. 71, pp. 28–43.

Manca, S 2018, 'ResearchGate and Academia.Edu as Networked Socio-Technical Systems for Scholarly Communication: A Literature Review', *Research in Learning Technology*, vol. 26, doi: https://doi.org/10.25304/rlt.v26.2008.

Mansour, EAH 2015, 'The Use of Social Networking Sites (SNSs) by the Faculty Members of the School of Library & Information Science, PAAET, Kuwait', *The Electronic Library*, vol. 33, no. 3, pp. 524–46, doi: https://doi.org/10.1108/EL-06-2013-0110.

Megwalu, A 2015, 'Academic Social Networking: A Case Study on Users' Information Behavior', in Woodsworth A & Penniman D (eds.), *Current Issues in Libraries, Information Science and*

Related Fields, vol. 39, pp. 185–214, Advances in Librarianship, Emerald Group Publishing Limited.

Nández, G & Borrego, Á 2013, 'Use of Social Networks for Academic Purposes: A Case Study', The Electronic Library, vol. 31, no. 6, pp. 781–91, doi: https://doi.org/10.1108/EL-03-2012-0031.

Nentwich, M & König, R 2014, 'Academia Goes Facebook? The Potential of Social Network Sites in the Scholarly Realm', in S Bartling & S Friesike (eds.), Opening Science, e107–24, Springer International Publishing, Cham.

Nicholas, D, Clark, D & Herman, E 2016, 'ResearchGate: Reputation Uncovered', Learned Publishing, vol. 29, no. 3, pp. 173–82, doi: https://doi.org/10.1002/leap.1035.

Nielsen, M 2012, Reinventing Discovery: The New Era of Networked Science, Princeton: Princeton University Press, Princeton University Press, Princeton, NJ.

Orduna-Malea, E, Martin-Martin, A & Lopez-Cozar, ED 2016, 'ResearchGate as a Source for Scientific Evaluation: Revealing Its Bibliometric Applications', Profesional De La Informacion, vol. 25, no. 2, pp. 303–10, doi: https://doi.org/10.3145/epi.2016.mar.18.

Orduna-Malea, E, Martín-Martín, A, Thelwall, M & Delgado López-Cózar, E 2017, 'Do ResearchGate Scores Create Ghost Academic Reputations?', Scientometrics, vol. 112, no. 1, pp. 443–60, doi: https://doi.org/10.1007/s11192-017-2396-9.

Ortega, JL 2015, 'Disciplinary Differences in the Use of Academic Social Networking Sites', Online Information Review, vol. 39, no. 4, pp. 520–36.

Piwowar, H, Priem, J, Larivière, V, Alperin, JP, Matthias, L, Norlander, B, Farley, A, West, J & Haustein, S 2017, 'The State of OA: A Large-Scale Analysis of the Prevalence and Impact of Open Access Articles', doi: https://doi.org/10.7287/peerj.preprints.3119v1.

Priem, J & Hemminger, BM 2010, 'Scientometrics 2.0. Toward New Metrics of Scholarly Impact on the Social Web', First Monday, vol. 15, no. 7.

Procter, R, Williams, R, Stewart, J, Poschen, M, Snee, H, Voss, A & Asgari-Targhi, M 2010, 'Adoption and Use of Web 2.0 in Scholarly Communications', Philosophical transactions. Series A, Mathematical, physical, and engineering sciences, vol. 368, no. 1926, pp. 4039–56, doi: https://doi.org/10.1098/rsta.2010.0155.

Thelwall, M & Kousha, K 2014, 'Academia.Edu: Social Network or Academic Network?', J Assn Inf Sci Tec, vol. 65, no. 4, pp. 721–31, doi: https://doi.org/10.1002/asi.23038.

Thelwall, M & Kousha, K 2015, 'ResearchGate: Disseminating, Communicating, and Measuring Scholarship?', J Assn Inf Sci Tec, vol. 66, no. 5, pp. 876–89, doi: https://doi.org/10.1002/asi.23236.

van Noorden, R 2014, 'Online Collaboration: Scientists and the Social Network', Nature, vol. 512, no. 7513, pp. 126–29. doi: https://doi.org/10.1038/512126a.

Yu, MC, Wu, YCJ, Alhalabi, W, Kao, HY & Wu, WH 2016, 'Research Gate: An Effective Altmetric Indicator for Active Researchers?', Computers in Human Behavior, vol. 55, no. 1001–6, doi: https://doi.org/10.1016/j.chb.2015.11.007.

4.9 ResearchGate and the Academic Social Network Sites: New Environments for New Bibliometrics?

Enrique Orduña-Malea and Emilio Delgado López-Cózar

Abstract: The objective of this work is to identify the main features of ResearchGate as an academic social network and its potential for research evaluation. To do this, first the birth of academic social networks in general, and ResearchGate in particular, are described. Next, a literature review about ResearchGate is carried out, showing the main topics covered by literature. Then, the general features of ResearchGate are identified and categorized, as well as all the metrics and indicators provided, broken down by entity. Finally, the main limitations and shortcomings of Research-Gate to be used as a bibliometric tool are synthetized. As a conclusion, our findings show potential of ResearchGate as a database (great coverage of documents, growing number of active users, and a wide variety of metrics). Nevertheless, it cannot be currently used for research evaluation due to several shortcomings (irreproducible indicators or lack of professional search/export features). These limitations are mainly derived from the ResearchGate business model, which is intended to be employed as a tool to enhance worldwide connectedness among researchers on the one hand and as a marketing tool to disseminate research-related ads and events on the other.

Keywords: academic social networks, bibliometrics, scientometrics, bibliographic databases, online academic profiles, scholarly communication, research evaluation, Altmetrics, social media metrics, ResearchGate.

Birth of Academic Social Networks (ASN)

The most widely accepted definition of social network is that provided by Boyd and Ellison (2007). These authors define social network sites as "web-based services that allow individuals to (1) construct a public or semi-public profile within a bounded system, (2) articulate a list of other users with whom they share a connection, and (3) view and traverse their list of connections and those made by others within the system".

Under the lens of this definition, SixDegrees (http://www.sixdegrees.com [July 15, 2020]), launched in 1997, is generally considered the first recognizable social network. Notwithstanding, Classmates (https://www.classmates.com [July 15, 2020]), a platform created in 1995 originally oriented to help users find class members and col-

---

Enrique Orduña-Malea, Universitat Politècnica de València, Spain, enorma@upv.es
Emilio Delgado López-Cózar, Universidad de Granada, Spain, edelgado@ugr.es

https://doi.org/10.1515/9783110646610-027

leagues from kindergarten, primary school, high school, college, workplaces, and the U.S. military, stands as one of the first social network services in history, with a reasonable resemblance in its nature to the later Facebook (https://en.wikipedia.org/wiki/Classmates.com [July 15, 2020]).

Since its inception in the 1990s, a plethora of social network platforms has been launched to date. Some of them experienced a short life while others are surviving with varying degrees of success. Just as social networks have evolved over time, along with available web technology, definitions have also done so.

In this way, Ellison and Boyd (2013) updated their view, defining a social networking site as an "online environment where users, besides creating personal profiles and establishing contact among themselves, they can also produce and insert content at disposal of their contacts or the entire community". Beyond connectivity among users, this definition emphasizes a content publishing oriented view of social platforms, which precisely emerges as one of the essential features of academic social networks.

Academic social networks constitute a subcategory of social networks especially suited for the scholarly community. However, these online platforms are not exclusively restricted to researchers, but directed additionally to a broader audience (mainly practitioners and students). Their potential to connect academics across the globe is the most important contribution of these networking platforms to higher education.

The mixture of audience and networking capabilities has fostered the emergence of many denominations. Ortega (2016) compiles a non-exhaustive list of the most frequently used terms (academic social sites, academic social networking sites, academic social networks, academic social networking services, social media for academics).

The amalgam of terms casts shadows of uncertainty about the main goal of academic social networks. This issue drives Jordan (2019) to express doubts about whether academic social networks are primarily oriented to social networking or alternative publishing. In line with this argument, Jordan (2019) divides academic social networks into two main categories: on the one hand, those that have been developed primarily to facilitate profile creation and user connectivity (e.g. Academic.edu and ResearchGate); on the other hand, those with a primary focus on posting and sharing academic-related content (e.g. Mendeley). However, the boundaries between these two categories are blurred, and the question of which comes first, the chicken (connectivity) or the egg (content), is not so easy to answer.

With all this, it is not surprising that academic social network definitions have mushroomed. The most complete definition to date is that provided by Ortega (2016). A slightly adapted definition is proposed below:

An Academic Social Network is a bounded online space that allows users to create and customize an author profile, to publish and disseminate academic-related content, to connect with other users through a wide variety of networking features, and to obtain a battery of metrics (both at the profile-level, content-level and affiliation-level) about the activity of its members within the platform.

The most currently widely used academic social networks are Academia.edu, Mendeley, and ResearchGate. Coincidentally, all three were launched in the same year, 2008. Other platforms, such as Loop (https://loop.frontiersin.org [July 15, 2020]) or Scholarlyhub (https://www.scholarlyhub.org [July 15, 2020]), have been recently released, although with a limited audience to date.

Among the three major academic social networks, Mendeley deserves a special mention. Even though it is provided with networking tools and allows users to create academic profiles enhanced with metrics, Mendeley's main function is to serve as a bibliographic references manager, while its use as an academic profile remains low. All features related to the dissemination of publications and metrics are supervening. They are added by its owner Elsevier, as part of its business strategy to compete in the field of bibliographic profiles, taking advantage of the users registered in Mendeley and the wide dissemination of this platform.

If we focus our attention to the remaining two academic social network giants, Academia.edu claims to have 79,227,014 registered users providing up to 22 million documents (https://www.academia.edu/about [July 15, 2020]). On its part, ResearchGate claims to have over 15 million users and 100 million documents (https://www.researchgate.net/press [July 15, 2020]). This higher coverage with fewer documents achieved by ResearchGate may be due to the demography of users (more oriented towards humanities in Academia.edu) as well as to the automatic indexing of documents from full text repositories.

This greater number of academic documents, along with the availability of free features, may explain the higher web traffic on ResearchGate (157 million users monthly) compared to Academia.edu (96 million users a month), according to the Similarweb analytic tool (https://www.similarweb.com [July 15, 2020]), making ResearchGate the most popular academic social network today.

This chapter will be focused on ResearchGate. First, a brief review on the topics covered by the literature will be introduced. Then, the general and bibliometric features of the platform will be identified and synthetized. Finally, the use of ResearchGate as a source of data for research evaluation will be discussed.

ResearchGate: Sharing and Discovering Research Worldwide

Virology and computer scientist Dr. Ijad Madisch was working at Massachusetts General Hospital in Boston on an interdisciplinary project when he ran into a problem in the lab. He tried to find an expert who could help him but this quest was unfortunately in vain, and it was at that time he had the idea of ResearchGate.

The academic social network was founded together with Dr. Sören Hofmayer, and Horst Fickenscher in 2008. Since then, the company has completed four rounds of financing and investors (Benchmark Capital Series, Founders Fund, Bill Gates, Tenaya Capital, Goldman Sachs Investment Partners, Wellcome Trust, and Four Rivers Group) with a clear business strategy focused on highly targeted advertising based on analysis of the activities of users.

After a decade, academic literature about ResearchGate has flourished covering a wide spectrum of complementary topics. Jordan (2019) synthesizes the following five main themes about academic social networks in general, which can be applied to ResearchGate in particular: (1) open access publishing; (2) user interactions; (3) user perspectives; (4) platform demographics and social structure; and (5) metrics.

Besides the general studies on academic social networks covering ResearchGate (Ovadia, 2014; Bhardwaj, 2017; Jordan and Weller, 2018; Manca, 2018), there are standout contributions about specific issues of the platform. We can thus highlight its use as a repository (Borrego, 2017; Jamali, 2017; Lee et al., 2019), the operating of the questions and answers tool (Li et al., 2015; Jeng et al., 2017), and the analysis of user patterns (Muscanell and Utz, 2017; Liu and Fang, 2018; Meier and Tunger, 2018).

Other studies have focused on platform demography (Ortega, 2015a; 2016; 2017) and the use of metrics for research evaluation (Kraker and Lex, 2015; Orduna-Malea, Martin-Martin, and Delgado Lopez-Cozar, 2016; Yu et al., 2016; Orduna-Malea et al., 2017; Copiello and Bonifaci, 2018; Delgado López-Cózar and Orduña-Malea, 2019). The quantitative analysis of different units, such as articles (Thelwall and Kousha, 2017a; 2017b), authors (Mikki et al., 2015; Ortega, 2015b; Orduna-Malea and Delgado López-Cózar, 2017; Martín-Martín, Orduna-Malea, and Delgado López-Cózar, 2018), and universities (Thelwall and Kousha, 2015; Lepori, Thelwall, and Hoorani, 2018; Yan and Zhang, 2018; Yan, Zhang, and Bromfield, 2018) have also been studied. Finally, its use in building an academic online reputation (Nicholas, Herman, and Clark, 2016; Nicholas, Clark, and Herman, 2016), and the application of gamification techniques to hook users (Hammarfelt, Rijcke, and Rushforth, 2016) have been also covered by literature.

Literature related either directly (analyzing different aspects of the platform) or indirectly (using the platform as a tool to solve other goals) to ResearchGate is highly concentrated from 2015 onwards. A search in Scopus database looking for documents containing the term "ResearchGate" in the title, abstract or keywords (query 1) yields 362 documents as of March 20, 2019 (from 2008 to 2018), of which 39.95% (159 documents) have been published in 2018. When the query is expanded to include additional terms (query 2), the results amount to 557 related documents, which receive 3,470 citations (Table 1).

Table 1: Academic literature about ResearchGate: number of publications and accumulated citations in Scopus.
Query 1: TITLE-ABS-KEY ("ResearchGate").
Query 2: TITLE-ABS-KEY ("academic social networks" OR "academic social networking" or "academic social sites" OR "ResearchGate" OR "Academia.edu").

YEAR	Query 1		Query 2	
	Publications	Accumulated citations	Publications	Accumulated citations
2008	0	1	5	2
2009	0	2	4	16
2010	1	0	11	49
2011	1	2	17	65
2012	5	4	17	95
2013	5	7	21	105
2014	19	38	39	196
2015	44	106	62	311
2016	46	292	83	518
2017	82	549	108	837
2018	159	894	190	1276
TOTAL	362	1895	557	3470

Considering all 557 documents yielded by query 2, all terms co-appearing in the title, abstract, and keywords of these contributions provide a panoramic view of the main topics in which ResearchGate has gained interest over the years (Figure 1). As we can observe, four different clusters are identified. The first cluster (red) is related to social media, the second (green) to databases and bibliographic reviews, especially in medicine, the third (yellow) to publishing, while the fourth (blue) represents a miscellaneous collection of terms, mainly case studies.

Figure 2 shows the co-occurrence of author keywords considering the 557 articles collected. This map provides a complementary view showing a block of terms related to social media (other academic social networks, metrics, meta-research etc.) on the one hand, and another block of terms related to web design (human centred design, user experience, design education etc.) on the other.

General Features of ResearchGate

The general features offered by ResearchGate have changed over the years, showing today a platform quite different from the one that existed a few years ago. Some tools are new (for example, the creation of projects, research labs or the author/document research interest metric), others have been modified (for example, the Q&A service or the stats history display), and others have disappeared (such as the impact points, the social validation of author skills and the in-text comment tool).

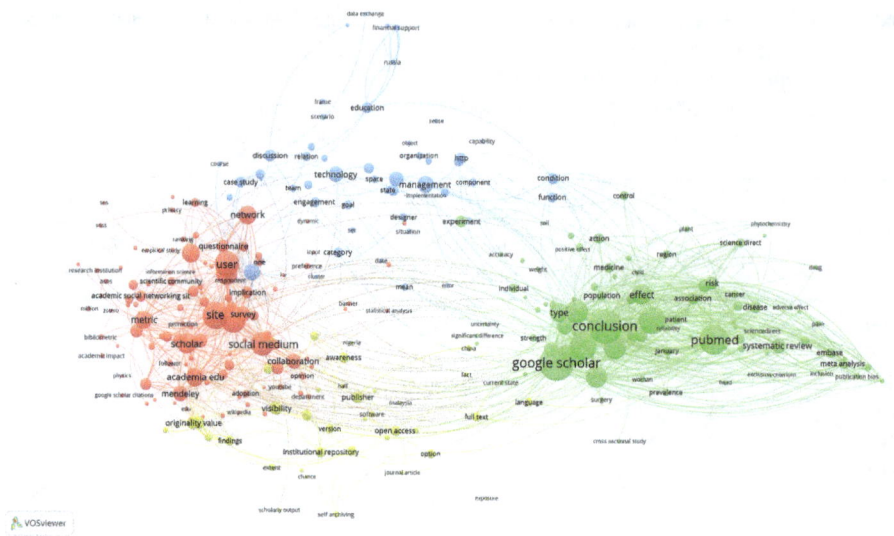

Figure 1: Topics related with ResearchGate: terms appearing in the Title, Abstract, and Keywords (n=557 articles). Source: Scopus; visualization: VOSViewer.
Query: TITLE-ABS-KEY ("academic social networks" OR "academic social networking" or "academic social sites" OR "ResearchGate" OR "Academia.edu").

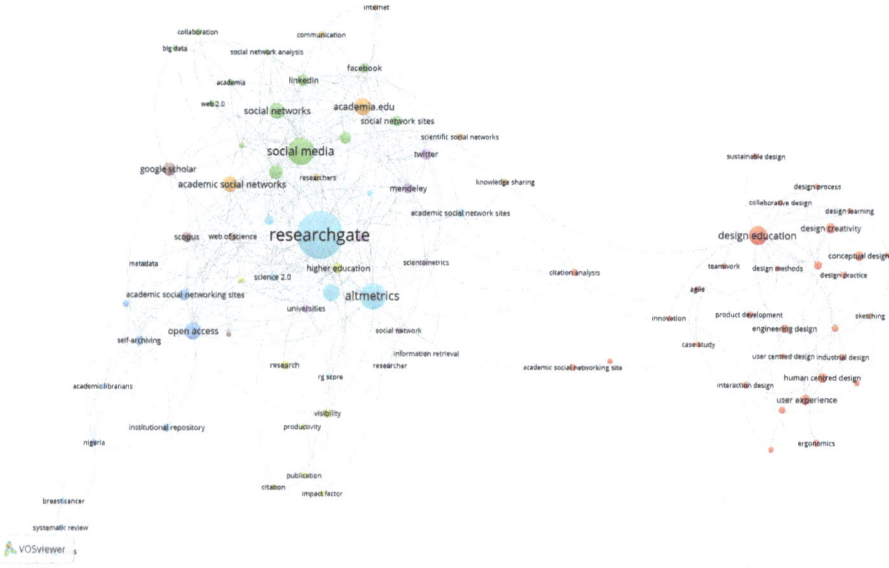

Figure 2: Topics related with ResearchGate: Author keywords. Source: Scopus; visualization: VOS-Viewer.
Query: TITLE-ABS-KEY ("academic social networks" OR "academic social networking" or "academic social sites" OR "ResearchGate" OR "Academia.edu").

All features currently available have been compiled and classified in different categories (account, publications, connectivity, information, and working). As we can see, ResearchGate is not only a social network but also an immersive work environment for academic-related professionals (Table 2).

Table 2: ResearchGate general features by category and level of application (as of May 2019).

CATEGORY	LEVEL	FEATURE
ACCOUNT	Settings	Account
		Ads
		Connection with external services
		Notifications
		Privacy
		Profile
		Security
	Profile	Authority stats
		CV export/import
		CV Info
		User preferences
PUBLICATIONS	Author contributions	Categorize
		Citation in context
		Creative Commons inclusion
		Delete
		Documents upload
		Edit
		Figures upload
		Private storage
		Publication identification (DOIs)
		Publication stats
		Supplementary resources upload
	Other contributions	Comment
		Download
		Read
		References stats
CONNECTIVITY	Author	Answer
		Author mention
		Author request
		Authorship suggestions
		Co-authors invitation
		Group authors (in projects and labs)
		Contributors adding
		Discussion
		Follow
		Private Message
		Question
		Reply

Table 2 *(Continued)*

CATEGORY	LEVEL	FEATURE
INFORMATION	Document	Document Request Feedback Follow Recommend Share
	Authors & Documents	Author updates Personalized alerts Recommendation system Stats achievements Timeline Weekly reports
	Projects	Updates
	Q&A	Weekly Q&A digest
	System	Search
WORKING	Employee	Job bookmark Job post
	Employer	Ad display Job recruit

Bibliometric Features of ResearchGate

The great coverage of documents (more than 100 million) and users (more than 15 millions) make ResearchGate a suitable source to be applied in bibliometric studies.

Ortega (2016) provides the most complete overview on ResearchGate coverage to date. As regards documents, the most used typologies are journal articles and conference papers, mainly from Health Sciences, Physical Sciences and Life Sciences. Otherwise, profile users have been also categorized by discipline (Medicine, Biology, and Engineering), user positions (PhD Student, Professor and Postdoc Researcher), and affiliation (more than 44,183 universities covered as of June 2015).

ResearchGate provides a wide variety of metrics related to the different entities of the database (e.g. authors, documents, projects, institutions), which make the platform a complex and unique showcase of indicators showing the use of the social network by users as well as their consumption of information.

An exhaustive list of metrics per entity is available in Table 3, where up to 40 metrics have been identified over 13 different entities.

Table 3: Metrics available in ResearchGate broken down by entity type.

METRIC	RESEARCHGATE ENTITIES													
	Author	Publication	Request	Journal	Comment	Project	Lab	Department	Institution	Question	Answer	Discussion	Reply	Jobs
Answer										YES				
Article Influence				YES										
Bookmark														X
Citation	YES	YES												
Cited Half-Life				YES										
Comment		YES												
Eigenfactor				YES										
External h-index	YES													
Follower	YES	X				YES				YES		YES		
Following	YES													
Immediacy Index				YES										
Members							YES	YES	YES					
Non-member Full Text Read		YES												
Non-member Other Reads		YES												
Non-member Read		YES												
Open Requests			YES											
Publications	YES						YES	YES	YES					
Question						YES								
Recommendation	YES	YES			YES	YES				YES	YES	YES	YES	
References						YES								
Reply					YES					YES		YES		
Research Interest	YES	YES												
Research Interest Percentile (Date Publication)	YES	YES												
Research Interest Percentile (Field)	YES	YES												
Research Interest Percentile (Platform)	YES	YES												

METRIC	RESEARCHGATE ENTITIES													
	Author	Publication	Request	Journal	Comment	Project	Lab	Department	Institution	Question	Answer	Discussion	Reply	Jobs
Research you received			YES											
Research you requested			YES											
Research you sent			YES											
RG Journal Impact				YES										
RG Member Total Full Text Read	YES	YES												
RG Member Total Other Reads	YES	YES												
RG Member Total Read	YES	YES												
RG Members Selective Full Text Read	YES	YES												
RG Members Selective Other Read	YES	YES												
RG Members Selective Read	YES	YES												
RG Score	YES								YES					
RG Score Percentile	YES													
Share		X			X	X			X	X	X	X	X	
Total Full Text Read	YES	YES (Weekly)												
Total h-index	YES													
Total Other Reads	YES													
Total Read	YES	YES				YES		YES (Weekly)	YES (Weekly)	YES		YES		
Updates						YES								
Views														YES

As we can see in Table 3, in some cases one element can be both a metric linked to one entity (comments received by one document) and an entity itself (a comment may receive a number of replies).

We can also find features (such as following a document or sharing a document with another user) whose corresponding metrics are not publicly available (marked "x" in Table 3). This may be due to the low usage of such features. For example, Ortega (2016) evidences that only 0.6% of documents sampled had received a follow.

ResearchGate provides other features in addition to these metrics, both at the author level (shared publications with top collaborators, top citing researchers per document, top weekly reads by country and institution) and at the institution level (top publications in the previous week, weekly popular members, number of reads in the previous week, top reads by country, top collaborating institutions, RG Score distribution).

ResearchGate as a Source Data for Research Evaluation

All features provided by ResearchGate, as well as its demography of users, publications coverage, and indicators available beyond citation-based metrics, make this academic social network a platform of interest, to be used as a source in bibliometric studies and, in some cases, even for research evaluation.

Nonetheless, ResearchGate was not conceived as a bibliometric tool, and its operating and terms of service jeopardize its use for those purposes. The main limitations of RG to be used for bibliometric analyses and research evaluation are summarized in the Table 4.

Table 4: ResearchGate evaluation sheet.

A. COVERAGE	
Transparency	Official data about platform coverage is not accurate ("+100 million documents"; "+15 million users"). Help Desk is available with information about publications, stats, and scores. However, composed indicators (especially RG Score) are not fully transparent and cannot be calculated with the information provided. This issue infringes the Leiden Manifesto. Moreover, ResearchGate does not declare how the platform works, i.e. how its crawlers identify and download documents.
Master list	A directory of publications and profiles are available. However, its degree of exhaustiveness is not explicitly indicated. https://www.researchgate.net/directory/publications https://www.researchgate.net/directory/profiles (July 15, 2020)
Indexing policies	Manual procedure: Authors upload contributions themselves. Automatic procedure: ResearchGate collects data from repositories that contain publications with a Creative Commons license, including PubMed. A master list of repositories harvested is not provided.

Copyrighted content	ResearchGate can automatically delete full text contents, without any prior notice to the authors, if publishers' copyright infringement is detected, such as for selected publishers that have reported against RG in the court, such as Elsevier or Wiley. Creative commons can be added to preprints by the authors to control how these publications can be reused.
Citing documents	Citing documents can only be accessed directly from the cited document page (citations feature).
Citing journals	Citing journals can only be accessed directly from the citing document metadata.

B. SEARCH INTERFACE

Search options	My contributions search: Users can filter by document type (all, full-text, article, book, chapter, conference paper, data, presentation, poster, etc.). Advanced search is not available. Users can only insert free text in the search box. General search: Users can search by entity (researchers, projects, questions, publications, jobs, institutions, departments). Advanced search is not available. Users can only insert free text in the search box.
Search results	My contributions search and General search: Each result corresponds with a card that includes entity descriptive metadata, impact metrics, connectivity features, and a hyperlink, which provides access to the entity page. For example, the entity "Publications" includes the document type (article, book chapter, poster etc.), if it belongs to a project, if a full text is available, some impact metrics (reads, citations received), and social buttons (Recommend, Follow, Share).
Results page	My contributions search and General search: Results are not split in result pages. Instead of this, there is a dynamic charge of results. The initial charge corresponds with 10 results.
Ranking options	My contributions search: Results can be sorted by title, date of publication (newest and oldest), and date of upload in the platform (recently added). General search: Default option seems to operate by relevance, according to the string inserted in the search box (especially in concordance with the title of the entity). There are no additional options for ordering results.
Language	All interface is only available in English

C. DATA QUALITY

Duplicate documents	There are a significant number of duplicated documents, due to the automatic capture of publications from repositories. ResearchGate automatically merges items where all information is identical (including title, date of publication, author list, and journal). It can take up to 72 hours for the publications to be merged. However, this operation only occurs when documents have been uploaded by the author. This implies that users cannot eliminate a great quantity of existing duplicates in their profiles.

Bibliographic data	There is no control quality. It depends completely on the author. In the case of documents that have been automatically included in author profiles from repositories, the bibliographic data is inherited from the repositories metadata. Once included in the author profile, metadata can be edited by the authors directly.
Citation data	Errors in citations have been detected, both false negatives (absence of a real citation) and false positives (inclusion of a citation that does not exist). ResearchGate officially states that they regularly import citation data from different sources. Unfortunately, these sources are not declared. In addition, ResearchGate indicates that citations using standard citation styles are usually extracted accurately. However, there are some cases where this can be difficult: When citations have incomplete metadata (e.g. publication date, journal, abstract) When the citing paper is not on ResearchGate When full-text PDFs are created by scanning a hard copy, meaning citations cannot be extracted
Metrics volatility	Citation data can fluctuate depending on the ability to cite documents within the platform. Therefore, citations can drop. Reads can fluctuate when publications are merged or eliminated. RG Score fluctuates in an unpredictable way due to continuous changes in its methodology. This value can drop as it measures profiles' reputation in the platform with respect to the remaining profiles.
Author affiliation	Only one affiliation is allowed. Currently, the only way to add multiple affiliations to the profile is by listing them as part of your research experience.

D. DATA EXPORTING

Data export	No API is available. It is not even possible to export/download/reuse all the data for one's own publications. The use of robots, spiders, scrapers, data mining tools, data gathering and extraction tools, or other automated means to access ResearchGate for any purpose is not permitted, except with the prior express permission of ResearchGate in writing.

E. DATA VISUALIZATION

Data access	The degree of accessibility to the information (mainly available metrics) varies according to the relationship with the platform: registered/unregistered user, author/non-author, follower/non-follower, and member/non-member of projects or laboratories.

Final Remarks

This work evidences the potential of ResearchGate as a database (great coverage of documents, growing number of profiles and active users, and a wide variety of citation-based metrics and altmetrics at the author level, article level, and institution level.

Nevertheless, it cannot be currently used for research evaluation due to several shortcomings (irreproducible indicators, continuous changes without warning users, or lack of professional search/export features). These limitations are mainly derived from the ResearchGate business model, which is intended to be employed as a tool to enhance worldwide connectedness among researchers on the one hand and as a marketing tool to disseminate research-related ads and events on the other.

References

Bhardwaj, RK 2017, 'Academic social networking sites: Comparative analysis of ResearchGate, Academia.edu, Mendeley and Zotero', *Information and Learning Science*, vol. 118, no. 5/6, pp. 298–316.

Borrego, Á 2017, 'Institutional repositories versus ResearchGate: The depositing habits of Spanish researchers', *Learned Publishing*, vol. 30, no. 3, pp. 185–92.

Copiello, S & Bonifaci, P 2018, 'A few remarks on ResearchGate score and academic reputation', *Scientometrics*, vol. 114, no. 1, pp. 301–06.

Delgado López-Cózar, E & Orduna-Malea E 2019, Research interest score: el nuevo indicador bibliométrico que mide la influencia de las publicaciones de un autor en ResearchGate, https://doi.org/10.13140/RG.2.2.16342.50249.

Hammarfelt, BMS, Rijcke, SD & Rushforth, AD 2016, 'Quantified academic selves: The gamification of science through social networking services.' *Information research*, vol. 21.

Jamali, HR 2017, 'Copyright compliance and infringement in ResearchGate full-text journal articles', *Scientometrics*, vol. 112, no. 1, pp. 241–54.

Jeng, W, DesAutels, S, He, D & Li, L 2017, 'Information exchange on an academic social networking site: A multidiscipline comparison on Researchgate Q&A', *Journal of the Association for Information Science and Technology*, vol. 68, no. 3, pp. 638–52.

Jordan, K 2019, 'From social networks to publishing platforms: A review of the history and scholarship of academic social network sites', *Frontiers in Digital Humanities*, vol. 6, no. 5.

Jordan, K & Weller, M 2018, 'Academics and social networking sites: Benefits, problems and tensions in professional engagement with online networking', *Journal of Interactive Media in Education*, no. 1.

Kraker, P & Lex, E 2015 (June), 'A critical look at the ResearchGate score as a measure of scientific reputation', in *Proceedings of the quantifying and analysing scholarly communication on the web workshop (ASCW'15), Web Science conference*.

Lee, J, Oh, S, Dong, H, Wang, F & Burnett, G 2019, 'Motivations for self-archiving on an academic social networking site: A study on researchgate', *Journal of the Association for Information Science and Technology*.

Lepori, B, Thelwall, M & Hoorani, BH 2018, 'Which US and European Higher Education Institutions are visible in ResearchGate and what affects their RG score?', *Journal of Informetrics*, vol, 12, no. 3, pp. 806–18.

Li, L, He, D, Jeng, W, Goodwin, S & Zhang, C 2015 (May), 'Answer quality characteristics and prediction on an academic Q&A Site: A case study on ResearchGate', in *Proceedings of the 24th international conference on world wide web*, pp. 1453–58, ACM.

Liu, XZ & Fang, H 2018, Which academic papers do researchers tend to feature on ResearchGate? *Information Research*, vol. 23, no. 1, http://www.informationr.net/ir/23-1/paper785.html (July 15, 2020).

Manca, S 2018, 'ResearchGate and Academia.edu as networked socio-technical systems for scholarly communication: A literature review', *Research in Learning Technology*, vol. 26.

Martín-Martín, A, Orduna-Malea, E & Delgado López-Cózar, E 2018, 'Author-level metrics in the new academic profile platforms: The online behaviour of the Bibliometrics community', *Journal of Informetrics*, vol. 12, no. 2, pp. 494–509.

Meier, A & Tunger, D 2018, 'Survey on opinions and usage patterns for the ResearchGate platform', *PloS one*, vol. 13, no. 10, e0204945.

Mikki, S, Zygmuntowska, M, Gjesdal, ØL & Al Ruwehy, HA 2015, 'Digital presence of Norwegian scholars on academic network sites – where and who are they?', *PloS one*, vol. 10, no. 11, e0142709.

Muscanell, N & Utz, S 2017, 'Social networking for scientists: An analysis on how and why academics use ResearchGate', *Online information review*, vol. 41, no. 5, pp. 744–59.

Nicholas, D, Clark, D & Herman, E 2016, 'ResearchGate: Reputation uncovered', *Learned Publishing*, vol. 29, no. 3, pp. 173–82.

Nicholas, D, Herman, E & Clark, D 2016, 'Scholarly reputation building: How does ResearchGate Fare?', *International Journal of Knowledge Content Development & Technology*, vol. 6, no. 2, p. 67.

Orduna-Malea, E & Delgado López-Cózar, E 2017, 'Performance behavior patterns in author-level metrics: A disciplinary comparison of Google Scholar Citations, ResearchGate, and ImpactStory', *Frontiers in Research Metrics and Analytics*, vol. 2, p. 14.

Orduna-Malea, E, Martin-Martin, A & Delgado López-Cózar, E 2016, 'ResearchGate as a source for scientific evaluation: Revealing its bibliometric applications', *Profesional de la Informacion*, vol. 25, no. 2, pp. 303–10.

Orduna-Malea, E, Martín-Martín, A, Thelwall, M & Delgado López-Cózar, E 2017, 'Do ResearchGate Scores create ghost academic reputations?', *Scientometrics*, vol. 112, no. 1, pp. 443–60.

Ortega, JL 2015a, 'Disciplinary differences in the use of academic social networking sites', *Online Inform. Review*, vol. 39, no. 4, pp. 520–36, doi: https://doi.org/10.1108/OIR-03–2015–0093.

Ortega, JL 2015b, 'Relationship between altmetric and bibliometric indicators across academic social sites: The case of CSIC's members', *Journal of informetrics*, vol. 9, no. 1, pp. 39–49.

Ortega, JL 2016, *Social network sites for scientists: A quantitative survey*, Chandos Publishing.

Ortega, JL 2017, 'Toward a homogenization of academic social sites: A longitudinal study of profiles in Academia.edu, Google Scholar Citations and ResearchGate,' *Online Information Review*, vol. 41, no. 6, pp. 812–25.

Ovadia, S 2014, 'ResearchGate and Academia.edu: Academic social networks', *Behavioral & social sciences librarian*, vol. 33, no. 3, pp. 165–69.

Thelwall, M & Kousha, K 2015, 'ResearchGate: Disseminating, communicating, and measuring Scholarship?', *Journal of the Association for Information Science and Technology*, vol. 66, no. 5, pp. 876–89.

Thelwall, M & Kousha, K 2017a, 'ResearchGate articles: Age, discipline, audience size, and impact', *Journal of the Association for Information Science and Technology*, vol. 68, no. 2, pp. 468–79.

Thelwall, M & Kousha, K 2017b, 'ResearchGate versus Google Scholar: Which finds more early citations?', *Scientometrics*, vol. 112, no. 2, pp. 1125–31.

Yan, W & Zhang, Y 2018, 'Research universities on the ResearchGate social networking site: An examination of institutional differences, research activity level, and social networks formed', *Journal of Informetrics*, vol. 12, no. 1, pp. 385–400.

Yan, W, Zhang, Y & Bromfield, W 2018, 'Analyzing the follower–followee ratio to determine user characteristics and institutional participation differences among research universities on ResearchGate', *Scientometrics*, vol. 115, no. 1, pp. 299–316.

Yu, MC, Wu, YCJ, Alhalabi, W, Kao, HY & Wu, WH 2016, 'ResearchGate: An effective altmetric indicator for active researchers?', *Computers in human behavior*, vol. 55, pp. 1001–06.

4.10 Mendeley

Robin Haunschild

Abstract: Reference manager Mendeley was founded in 2007 and bought by Elsevier in 2013. This article examines the use of the reference manager Mendeley as a citation database. It analyses the literature in which different citation indices are compared with the Mendeley citation count. The Mendeley ciation count is primarily an altmetric citation index, which takes its data from various sources and considers books, book contributions and conference papers in addition to well covered journal articles. Citation measurement is still the gold standard, but information from the Mendeley citation count is increasingly being taken into account.

Keywords: Mendeley, Online Reference Manager, research evaluation, altmetrics, reader impact, directed impact, academic status groups.

Introduction

Mendeley is a free online reference manager with a desktop and a mobile application besides the online version. Mendeley can be used to bookmark publications and cite them while writing one's own manuscripts. Publications can be read using Mendeley and comments and notes can be added. Metadata can be extracted from PDF files of publications using the desktop version of Mendeley. Mendeley provides anonymous data about the readership of a publication, e.g. how often a publication has been read; how the readership distributes across (user-assigned) academic status groups, academic disciplines, and countries. However, Mendeley readership information regarding academic status and academic discipline are more often available than information regarding the reader's countries (Haunschild et al., 2015a; Haunschild et al., 2015b). Besides Mendeley's features regarding reference management, Mendeley is also a data repository and a social networking community. This chapter will only refer in the following to Mendeley as an online reference manager.

Mendeley was founded in November 2007 by three German PhD students who named it after the biologist Gregor Mendel and the chemist Dmitri Mendeleyev. Already in 2008, publications regarding Mendeley had appeared (Henning and Reichelt, 2008; Hull et al., 2008). Both publications described the core features of Mendeley. In 2013, Elsevier (2013) purchased Mendeley.

Traditional bibliometrics use citation counts of publications for research evaluation and impact assessment. It is well known that citations need time to be observed. Usually, before publications are cited, several steps have to take place: (i) the publications have to be read by other researchers who have to conduct their

---

Robin Haunschild, Max Planck Institute for Solid State Research, Heisenbergstr. 1, 70569 Stuttgart, Germany, R.Haunschild@fkf.mpg.de

own research based on the read publications; (ii) these researchers have to write their own manuscripts and submit them to a suitable journal; (iii) after a successful peer review process, the new publication citing older publications has to be indexed by indexing services. These steps can take several months or even years depending on the scientific field. As Mendeley is located in the very early part of this process (reading or citing publications), many bibliometricians hope that research evaluation and impact assessment can be supplemented by Mendeley reader count analyses. This hope has been substantiated by a survey conducted by Mohammadi et al. (2016) who reported that "[a]bout 85% of the respondents across all disciplines bookmarked papers in Mendeley to cite them in their publications" (p. 1202), and "82% of the Mendeley users had read or intended to read at least half of the bookmarked publications in their personal libraries" (p. 1203). Furthermore, D'Angelo and Di Russo (2019) reported that distributions of Mendeley reader counts and citation counts "for publications in different fields share some common fundamental characteristics and similarities" (pp. 735–736).

Mendeley belongs to the sources of altmetrics but is different from all other altmetrics in several aspects. Mendeley readership counts are more numerous than the counts in any other altmetrics source (Zahedi et al., 2014; Repiso et al., 2019). The audience is of predominantly scholarly character (Bornmann and Haunschild, 2017; Haunschild et al., 2015a; Kousha and Thelwall, 2019; Bornmann and Haunschild, 2015). The impact measured using Mendeley reader counts is rather well understood in contrast to most (maybe even all) of the other altmetrics. These differences point out that Mendeley occupies a unique position within the colorful umbrella of altmetrics.

Sources and Collection of Mendeley Readership Data

Mendeley readership information can be gathered from different sources: (i) directly from Mendeley (from the web interface or from the application programming interface, API, see for example https://dev.mendeley.com/methods); or (ii) altmetrics aggregators such as Altmetric.com (see https://www.altmetric.com), Plum Analytics (PlumX, see https://plumanalytics.com), or Impact Story (see https://www.impactstory.org [all July 15, 2020]). Bar-Ilan et al. (2019) compared Mendeley reader counts gathered from Mendeley directly, from Altmetric.com and from PlumX. Most queried publications (more than 95%) were found at Mendeley, while approximately 60–90% were found at PlumX and only about 40% at Altmetric.com. Altmetric.com uses certain social media platforms (e.g. Twitter and Facebook) as primary sources. Publications found in these primary sources are also queried at Mendeley. As fewer publications are mentioned in Tweets or Facebook posts, Mendeley readership information from Altmetric.com is often incomplete. PlumX was able to significantly increase its coverage of Mendeley readership information since Elsevier purchased PlumX in 2017 (Michalek, 2017) and thereby owned both Mendeley and PlumX.

Correlation between Mendeley Reader Counts and Citation Counts

One of the first studies to explore the suitability of online reference managers for scholarly impact measurement has been presented by Li et al. (2011) and Li et al. (2012). They analyzed the correlation between Mendeley reader counts and citation counts using a sample of 1,613 papers published in Nature and Science in 2007. They found Spearman correlations between 0.54 and 0.60 between both metrics. This result indicates that Mendeley reader counts convey in part similar information as citation counts but also in part different information. This result is based on a very small data set from a single publication year and only two different journals, but it has been validated by later studies using multiple publication years (Schlogl et al., 2014; Schlogl et al., 2013), different journals (Haustein et al., 2014; Haustein et al., 2013; Zahedi et al., 2014; Zahedi et al., 2013), a large sample from medicine-related disciplines (Thelwall and Wilson, 2016), and a full Web of Science (WoS) publication year (Mohammadi et al., 2015).

A meta-analysis by Bornmann (2015) showed a pooled correlation of 0.51 between Mendeley reader counts and citation counts. Somewhat lower correlations were reported for social sciences and humanities (Mohammadi and Thelwall, 2014). Overall, correlations between Mendeley reader counts and citation counts tend to be higher for older publications (Thelwall and Sud, 2016). One possible explanation would be that Mendeley reader counts occur more quickly than citation counts. Therefore, highest correlations can be expected when a publication's life is coming to an end and most citations and readers are accumulated. A comparison with F1000Prime recommendation scores showed a significant relationship between quality of publications and Mendeley reader counts (Bornmann and Haunschild, 2018).

Normalization of Mendeley Reader Counts

Like citation counts, Mendeley reader counts show a skewed distribution across scientific disciplines and publication years (see for example Mohammadi et al., 2015; Bornmann and Haunschild, 2017; Maflahi and Thelwall, 2016). Furthermore, without a proper frame of reference, it is impossible to say if 50 Mendeley readers for a paper published in 2013 in computational chemistry is more than can be expected or not. Therefore, normalization procedures are indispensable when Mendeley reader counts are compared across scientific fields and publication years.

Haunschild and Bornmann (2016a), Haunschild and Bornmann (2016b), Bornmann and Haunschild (2016a), and Fairclough and Thelwall (2015) proposed mean-based normalization procedures. One proposed kind of field-normalization procedure uses the discipline assigned from the database provider to the publication. This is in the spirit of the mean normalized citation score (MNCS) for citations

(Waltman et al., 2011a; Waltman et al., 2011b), i.e. normalization on the cited-side or paper-side. Similar to the spirit of the citing-side indicators (Waltman and van Eck, 2013), Mendeley reader counts can be normalized on the reader-side (Bornmann and Haunschild, 2016a). In this case, the user-assigned discipline from Mendeley is used for normalization and no external classification system is needed. Besides normalization purposes, disciplinary information of Mendeley readers were used to construct overlay maps for journals and universities (Bornmann and Haunschild, 2016b).

Academic status information were used for visualization purposes, network analyses (Haunschild et al., 2015a), and field-normalized impact assessments regarding specific societal groups (Bornmann and Haunschild, 2017). Bornmann and Haunschild (2017) have measured the Mendeley reader impact regarding two societal groups in an explorative study: (i) educational sector and (ii) bachelor students. The results are promising and show that it seems to be possible to perform target-oriented field-normalized impact assessment with Mendeley readership information. Using such assessment strategies, it becomes possible to judge other aspects of paper quality than those measurable using citation counts, e.g. how well are publications from different universities received by students? However, it is often problematic to unambiguously define groups. For example, should professors be included in the educational sector, another sector (e.g. research sector), or both sectors?

Mendeley Readership Information for Impact Assessment of Non-journal Publications

Journal publications are usually well covered by popular citation indices. This is different for other publication types, such as books, book sections, and conference papers. Mendeley readership information may be used to assess the impact of sparsely indexed document types.

Kousha and Thelwall (2019) analyzed the Mendeley reader counts of dissertations and compared them with Google Scholar citation counts. Only low correlations were found between both metrics which might be due to the overall low counts. The authors also analyzed the Mendeley readership information regarding the academic status of the readers. About two thirds of the reader counts originate from students (PhD, doctoral, post-graduate, master, and bachelor). This proportion agrees quite well with the Mendeley readership distribution found by Bornmann and Haunschild (2017) and Haunschild et al. (2015a) for journal publications. This indicates that a similar Mendeley readership distribution across academic status information can be expected for journal publications and dissertations.

Aduku et al. (2016) reported moderate to high correlations between Mendeley readership counts and citation counts for conference proceedings in two computer science disciplines. However, they also reported low correlations for two construction and engineering disciplines while moderate to high correlations were found for journal publications in all four disciplines. This supports usage of Mendeley readers for impact assessment of conference papers in computer sciences but questions its application in the case of conference papers in building and construction disciplines.

Summary

Overall, many different aspects of Mendeley readership information were studied in the scientific literature. Most studies about Mendeley analyze the correlation of Mendeley reader counts with citation counts. This indicates that the scientific community is still in the process of evaluating if Mendeley reader counts can replace or supplement citation counts for research evaluation. Most studies provided a positive answer to this question, at least regarding supplementing citation counts. Despite many advantages of Mendeley, citation counts are still the gold standard for impact assessments on a large scale. In contrast to citation counts, Mendeley reader counts can decrease when users remove a publication from their library. Furthermore, it should be kept in mind that not every reader will become a citer.

References

Aduku, KJ, Thelwall, M & Kousha, K 2016, 'Do Mendeley reader counts reflect the scholarly impact of conference papers? An investigation of Computer Science and Engineering fields', in I Rafols, J Molasgallart, E Castromartinez & R Woolley (eds.), *21st International Conference on Science and Technology Indicators*, Univ Politecnica Valencia, Valencia.

Bar-Ilan, J, Halevi, G & Milojević, S 2019, 'Differences between Altmetric Data Sources – A Case Study', *Journal of Altmetrics*, vol. 2, p. 8.

Bornmann, L 2015, 'Alternative metrics in scientometrics: a meta-analysis of research into three altmetrics', *Scientometrics*, vol. 103, pp. 1123–44.

Bornmann, L & Haunschild, R 2015, 'Which people use which scientific papers? An evaluation of data from F1000 and Mendeley, *Journal of Informetrics*, vol. 9, pp. 477–87.

Bornmann, L & Haunschild, R 2016a, 'Normalization of Mendeley reader impact on the reader- and paper-side: A comparison of the mean discipline normalized reader score (MDNRS) with the mean normalized reader score (MNRS) and bare reader counts', *Journal of Informetrics*, vol. 10, pp. 776–88.

Bornmann, L & Haunschild, R 2016b, 'Overlay maps based on Mendeley data: The use of altmetrics for readership networks', *Journal of the Association for Information Science and Technology*, vol. 67, pp. 3064–72.

Bornmann, L & Haunschild, R 2017, 'Measuring field-normalized impact of papers on specific societal groups: An altmetrics study based on Mendeley Data', *Research Evaluation*, vol. 26, pp. 230–41.

Bornmann, L & Haunschild, R 2018, 'Do altmetrics correlate with the quality of papers? A large-scale empirical study based on F1000Prime data', *Plos One*, vol. 13, p. 12.

D'Angelo, CA & di Russo, S 2019, 'Testing for universality of Mendeley readership distributions', *Journal of Informetrics*, vol. 13, pp. 726–37.

Elsevier 2013, *Elsevier acquires Mendeley, an innovative, cloud-based research management and social collaboration* platform, https://www.elsevier.com/about/press-releases/corporate/elsev

ier-acquires-mendeley,-an-innovative,-cloud-based-research-management-and-social-collaboration-platform (July 15, 2020).

Fairclough, R & Thelwall, M 2015, 'National research impact indicators from Mendeley readers', *Journal of Informetrics*, vol. 9, pp. 845–59.

Haunschild, R & Bornmann, L 2016a, 'Normalization of Mendeley reader counts for impact assessment', *Journal of Informetrics*, 10, pp. 62–73.

Haunschild, R & Bornmann, L 2016b, 'Normalization of Mendeley reader impact on the reader-and paper-side', in I Rafols, J Molasgallart, E Castromartinez & R Woolley (eds.), *21st International Conference on Science and Technology Indicators*, Univ Politecnica Valencia, Valencia.

Haunschild, R, Bornmann, L & Leydesdorff, L 2015a, 'Networks of reader and country status: an analysis of Mendeley reader statistics', *Peerj Computer Science*, vol. 1, e32.

Haunschild, R, Stefaner, M & Bornmann, L 2015b, 'Who Publishes, Reads, and Cites Papers? An Analysis of Country Information', in AA Salah, Y Tonta, C Sugimoto & U Al (eds.), *Proceedings of Issi 2015 Istanbul: 15th International Society of Scientometrics and Informetrics Conference*, Int Soc Scientometrics & Informetrics-Issi, Leuven.

Haustein, S, Peters, I, Bar-Ilan, J, Priem, J, Shema, H & Terliesner, J 2013, 'Coverage and adoption of altmetrics sources in the bibliometric community', in J Gorraiz, E Schiebel, C Gumpenberger, M Horlesberger & H Moed (eds.), *14th International Society of Scientometrics and Informetrics Conference*, Int Soc Scientometrics & Informetrics-Issi, Leuven.

Haustein, S, Peters, I, Bar-Ilan, J, Priem, J, Shema, H & Terliesner, J 2014, 'Coverage and adoption of altmetrics sources in the bibliometric community', *Scientometrics*, vol. 101, pp. 1145–63.

Henning, V & Reichelt, J 2008, 'Mendeley – A Last.fm For Research?', *2008 IEEE Fourth International Conference on eScience*, pp. 327–28.

Hull, D, Pettifer, SR, Kell, DB 2008, 'Defrosting the Digital Library: Bibliographic Tools for the Next Generation Web', *Plos Computational Biology*, vol. 4, p. 14.

Kousha, K & Thelwall, M 2019, 'Can Google Scholar and Mendeley help to assess the scholarly impacts of dissertations?' *Journal of Informetrics*, vol. 13, pp. 467–84.

Li, XM, Thelwall, M & Giustini, D 2011, 'Validating Online Reference Managers for Scholarly Impact Measurement', in E Noyons, P Ngulube & J Leta (eds.), *Proceedings of Issi 2011: The 13th Conference of the International Society for Scientometrics and Informetrics, Vols 1 and 2*, Int Soc Scientometrics & Informetrics-Issi, Leuven.

Li, XM, Thelwall, M & Giustini, D 2012, 'Validating online reference managers for scholarly impact measurement', *Scientometrics*, vol. 91, pp. 461–71.

Maflahi, N & Thelwall, M 2016, 'When are readership counts as useful as citation counts? Scopus versus Mendeley for LIS journals', *Journal of the Association for Information Science and Technology*, vol. 67, pp. 191–99.

Michalek, A 2017, *Plum Analytics Joins Elsevier* [Online], https://plumanalytics.com/plum-analytics-joins-elsevier (July 15, 2020).

Mohammadi, E & Thelwall, M 2014, 'Mendeley Readership Altmetrics for the Social Sciences and Humanities: Research Evaluation and Knowledge Flows', *Journal of the Association for Information Science and Technology*, vol. 65, pp. 1627–38.

Mohammadi, E, Thelwall, M, Haustein, S & Lariviere, V 2015, 'Who Reads Research Articles? An Altmetrics Analysis of Mendeley User Categories', *Journal of the Association for Information Science and Technology*, vol. 66, pp. 1832–46.

Mohammadi, E, Thelwall, M & Kousha, K 2016, 'Can Mendeley bookmarks reflect readership? A survey of user motivations', *Journal of the Association for Information Science and Technology*, vol. 67, pp. 1198–1209.

Repiso, R, Castillo-Esparcia, A & Torres-Salinas, D 2019, 'Altmetrics, alternative indicators for Web of Science Communication studies journals', *Scientometrics*, vol. 119, pp. 941–58.

Schlogl, C, Gorraiz, J, Gumpenberger, C, Jack, K & Kraker, P 2013, 'Download vs. citation vs. readership data: the case of an information systems journal', in J Gorraiz, E Schiebel, C Gumpenberger, M Horlesberger & H Moed (eds.), *14th International Society of Scientometrics and Informetrics Conference*, Int Soc Scientometrics & Informetrics-Issi, Leuven.

Schlogl, C, Gorraiz, J, Gumpenberger, C, Jack, K & Kraker, P 2014, 'Comparison of downloads, citations and readership data for two information systems journals', *Scientometrics*, vol. 101, pp. 1113–28.

Thelwall, M & Sud, P 2016, 'Mendeley readership counts: An investigation of temporal and disciplinary differences', *Journal of the Association for Information Science and Technology*, vol. 67, 3036–50.

Thelwall, M & Wilson, P 2016, 'Mendeley Readership Altmetrics for Medical Articles: An Analysis of 45 Fields', *Journal of the Association for Information Science and Technology*, vol. 67, pp. 1962–72.

Waltman, L & van Eck, NJ 2013, 'Source normalized indicators of citation impact: an overview of different approaches and an empirical comparison', *Scientometrics*, vol. 96, pp. 699–716.

Waltman, L, van Eck, NJ, van Leeuwen, TN, Visser, MS & van Raan, AFJ 2011a, 'Towards a new crown indicator: an empirical analysis', *Scientometrics*, vol. 87, pp. 467–81.

Waltman, L, van Eck, NJ, van Leeuwen, TN, Visser, MS & van Raan, AFJ 2011b, 'Towards a new crown indicator: Some theoretical considerations', *Journal of Informetrics*, vol. 5, pp. 37–47.

Zahedi, Z, Costas, R & Wouters, P 2013, 'How well developed are altmetrics? Cross-disciplinary analysis of the presence of 'alternative metrics' in scientific publications (RIP)', in J Gorraiz, E Schiebel, C Gumpenberger, M Horlesberger & H Moed (eds.), *14th International Society of Scientometrics and Informetrics Conference*, Int Soc Scientometrics & Informetrics-Issi, Leuven.

Zahedi, Z, Costas, R & Wouters, P 2014, 'How well developed are altmetrics? A cross-disciplinary analysis of the presence of 'alternative metrics' in scientific publications', *Scientometrics*, vol. 101, pp. 1491–1513.

5 Applications, Practice and Special Issues in Bibliometrics

5.1 An Ecology of Measures and Indicators: Bibliometrics in Resource Allocation

Björn Hammarfelt and Fredrik Åström

Abstract: This chapter briefly reviews how bibliometric indicators are used for allocating resources in academia. How these measures can be understood in relation to different evaluation systems is discussed, and various types of applications – including individual level use – are outlined. Furthermore, attention is given to the effect of evaluation in terms of incentives and possible adverse effects. The importance of contextualizing the influence of metrics is emphasised, as individuals and fields are likely to react differently to performance-based assessments. In conclusion, bibliometric measures are perhaps best understood as part of a larger "ecology" in which different types of assessment procedures, funding arrangements and allocation systems interact.

Keywords: bibliometrics, indicators, funding, research evaluation systems, performance, effects

Introduction

It has become increasingly important for publicly funded institutions to be able to account for how their finances are used, and to demonstrate their efficiency by showing how their activities can be measured using performance indicators. Academic research is no exception in this case. Increased demands for accountability in academia can be related to general societal trends described under headings such as "the audit society" (Power, 1997) and "the evaluation society" (Dahler-Larsen, 2011). The monitoring of scientific endeavours through performance indicators permeates the whole academic system, from national governments using statistics on publications and citations to allocate funds for research and higher education institutions (HEIs) to individual scholars feeling an increasing pressure to publish.

Many authors connect the use of metrics to larger developments in the organization of science, where "neoliberalism" and the commercialization of research and higher education are the most prominent (Mirowski, 2011; Stephan, 2012).

In this chapter we provide a brief overview of how bibliometrics are applied in allocating resources and positions in contemporary academia. A short summary of possible effects of indicator use is provided, and the chapter concludes by outlining some ideas on research assessment and metric use.

Björn Hammarfelt, Swedish School of Library and Information Science, University of Borås, Sweden, bjorn.hammarfelt@hb.se
Fredrik Åström, Lund University Library, Lund University, Sweden, fredrik.astrom@lub.lu.se

https://doi.org/10.1515/9783110646610-029

Evaluation Systems

Publicly funded science is usually either subjected to *ex ante* evaluation, often in the form of evaluation of projects for funding, or *ex post evaluation* of outcomes and impact through national or local research evaluation systems. Project funding decisions are often, but not always, foremost reliant on peer review in various forms, while ex post assessments more commonly involve bibliometrics. The remainder of this chapter focuses primarily on various forms of ex post evaluation, yet it is important to emphasize the importance of project funding for how research is organized more generally (Franssen et al., 2018; Whitley et al., 2018).

An important distinction in the literature on ex post systems of evaluation is the one between *strong* research evaluation systems (RES) and *weak* ones (Whitley, 2007). Strong RES are institutionalised assessments which are performed regularly and publicized widely. Moreover, such assessments allow for rankings of the institutions involved, and they influence decisions regarding the allocation of resources. Overall, these RES have significant influence on how universities are managed (Whitley, 2007). Weak systems on the other hand are more informally organized, and results from such evaluations are seldom published. Moreover, the purpose of assessments is usually to improve organizations rather than to reach general judgments, and rankings. Generally, while weak systems might provide incentive for changes, these are likely to be "...incremental rather than radical" (Whitley, 2007, p. 9).

It has also been suggested that strong systems of evaluation influence research fields differently depending on the structure of the field in question. For example, fields in which researchers can obtain resources from a diverse set of funders, and where audiences and reputational control are dispersed, are less likely to be profoundly affected. In contrast, the impact of such systems will be greater in fields where a scientific elite has considerable influence over resources, and where systematic assessment rarely has been conducted before (Whitley, 2007, p. 21)

Performance-based Research Funding

Strong RES, in the form of "performance-based research funding systems" (PRFS) has been implemented in many countries since the mid-80s, with the UK's Research Assessment Exercise, launched in 1986, often being seen as the first example of such. Later, Australia became one of the first nations to introduce a system for resource allocation based on bibliometric measures. Since then, a range of countries has implemented similar systems using either, or both, publication and citation counts. The rationale for such systems is basically to reward institutions (and individuals) that perform according to the criteria of quality as defined in the system.

In an overview, Hicks (2012) defines PRFS using five criteria: (1) research is the primary activity evaluated (hence, teaching and other activities are excluded); (2) research outputs are evaluated (systems focusing solely on grants received or numbers of PhD students are excluded); (3) research evaluation is done ex post (not ex ante as in the case of project funding); (4) the distribution of government funds must depend on the results of evaluation; and (5) PRFS are applied on the national level. Following this definition, Hicks (2012) found 14 OECD countries that had implemented or were preparing to introduce PRFS in 2010. A more recent study by Zacharewicz and colleagues (2019) found that 10 EU member states deployed bibliometrics in some form in their performance-based funding scheme.

The use of bibliometric indicators on the national level for allocation of resources is perhaps the most visible and debated use. Starting with Butler's (2003) critical assessment of the Australian system for research evaluation, this has also been the most commonly studied activity in terms of consequences and effects. Similar studies regarding the effect of national systems for resource allocation have since been performed in, for example, Denmark, Norway, and Flanders (Aagaard et al., 2015; Engels et al., 2012; Ingwersen and Larsen, 2014). While changes in publication patterns have been found – especially in terms of increasing amounts of English language publications – it has still been difficult to isolate the effects of PRFS from other contextualized factors (for example funding and internationalization) that influence research practices. Indeed, it has been argued that the possible effects of bibliometric models are less dependent on the exact amounts being re-allocated, and that rather it is the effects on the reputation of researchers that is important (Hicks, 2012).

Levels of Application: From Macro to Individual Use

Typically, in terms of levels of application, bibliometric analyses are categorized through the size of the unit of analysis. Analyses of individual persons or research groups are considered as micro-level analysis. If the unit of analysis is for instance a department at a university, the analysis is considered to be on the meso-level. And if the unit is a higher education institution (HEI) such as a university, or even larger units such as countries or other geopolitical regions, the analysis is considered to be on the macro-level (Vinkler, 1988). This categorization covers all kinds of bibliometric analyses, whether performed for evaluating the outcomes of a research project or the performance of a university, or if performed for the purpose of allocating funds between departments at a local faculty or between HEIs in a country based on previous performance.

As covered above, the use of bibliometrics on national levels is perhaps most visible, yet indicators are also used locally for distributing funds within universities. Such models are often local variants of national models of evaluation which have "trickled down" to the local level (Aagaard, 2015). Many local allocation systems share similar features, as shown by Hammarfelt and colleagues (Hammarfelt et al., 2016) in their study of Swedish academia, yet they often contain distinguishing features which makes each system unique. Moreover, it is not uncommon that larger universities apply different models for each faculty. The purpose of these systems, which in many cases allocate relatively small shares of all funds, is often not very well described. However, when explicitly stated, the rationale of these systems resembles goals defined on a national level, which is to enhance competitiveness and productivity by incentivising publications in certain, highly regarded, channels.

Notably, however, output statistics and indicators, in the form of publication numbers, citation scores, and various journal ratings and rankings, are commonly used for assessing careers when making decisions regarding appointments and promotions. While often informally, and together with traditional peer review, metrics do play a major role in these high-stake situations. Hence, this less visible use of bibliometric indicators is important to study if we want to understand how knowledge production and the organization of research is shaped by these measures.

Generally, researchers are ambivalent towards bibliometric indicators and citation counts (Aksnes and Rip, 2009), and while many acknowledge that citations say something about the standing of research, there is considerable concern that such measures are inadequate for measuring societal relevance and scientific impact. The usefulness of such bibliometric indicators also differs substantially between fields, with the social sciences and humanities being especially difficult to assess. Still, well known and criticised indicators, such as the Journal Impact Factor and the h-index, do play an important role in the assessment of individual researchers in many disciplines. This is despite vocal concerns, for example expressed in the *Leiden manifesto on research metrics* (Hicks et al., 2015) regarding the use of such measures on the individual level.

Taking the much-debated journal impact factor (JIF) as an example, it is evident that it is used as shorthand for evaluating research. As shown by Rushforth and de Rijcke (2015), the JIF is used to assess research even before it is published, as it comes to influence the goals and strategies of research groups in biomedicine. Publishing in journals with a high impact factor is of key importance, both for the continued success of the group and for the ability of individual researchers to find a job. The importance of the JIF is most pronounced in medicine and natural sciences, yet other "judgment devices" for assessing quality – such as journal rankings and ratings – take on similar roles in other disciplines such as economics (Hammarfelt and Rushforth, 2017). Overall, the well-established use of metrics in allocating resources to individuals in terms of funding and positions is of great importance for understanding how metrics come to influence research. That measures are enmeshed with field specific and local evaluation procedures makes them even more persuasive as they come to be part of established disciplinary norms of assessment.

Displacement, Reduction, and Gaming: Effects of Evaluation

A recent overview regarding the effects of bibliometric measurement outlines several possible consequences of indicator use (Rijcke et al., 2016). First, indicator use might lead to goal displacement where scoring high according to the assessment criteria becomes a goal in itself rather than a way of measuring if certain goals are meet. Second, criteria for measuring research quality often puts a limit on activities that count, which in turn might lead to task reduction among researchers. Certain types of work (e.g. book publishing, societal engagement) might be abandoned for activities that are recognized as valuable in evaluation systems (for example by publishing in purely academic journals in the medical field instead of journals directed towards "practitioners"). Such task reduction is especially worrisome in research fields that are heterogeneous when it comes to methods and dissemination channels. Third, higher education institutions are also deeply affected by evaluation systems and indicators. Research assessment systems on the national level have helped to establish a "transfer market for scientists", and to form a "champions league" of universities (Collini, 2012). Thus, institutional effects where universities increasingly are forced to take part in assessment systems and university rankings contribute to a further emphasis on performance measures also within these organizations. In addition to these larger structural effects, we see lower level responses to the use of metrics, ranging from salami-publishing and the gaming of indicators to "citation cartels" (Martin, 2013). Central to this issue are questions of authorship, what it means to be an author both ethically and practically, and how an increasing focus on evaluation affects attribution of authorship across disciplines (Biagioli and Galison, 2014). Even more importantly, systematic research evaluation systems may "...discourage scientists from investing in long term, highly risky and interdisciplinary research, and from changing current orthodoxies..." (Whitley, 2007, p. 8). Finally, the demands of evaluation systems may be particularly demanding for fields in the social sciences and humanities, while another group identified as particularly sensitive to these measures are young researchers, who have not yet established themselves in academia (Haddow and Hammarfelt, 2019; Müller, 2014)

Conclusions: The Uncertainty of Research and the Future of Academic Assessment

Research is an inherently uncertain activity, and its outcomes and effects are exceedingly hard to capture, especially in the short term. Moreover, indicators, especially in performance-based evaluation systems, are always part of a larger context. In fact, they can be seen as included in a larger "ecology of measures" and assessments procedures, or, as expressed by Brandtner (2017), these can be viewed as part of an evaluative landscape. In this landscape, researchers need to navigate in a complex setting where various assessment procedures and indicators interact (Åström and Hammarfelt, 2019). The degree of project funding in a system is, for example, a factor which in combination with a strong RES based on bibliometrics may further competition, and ultimately reduce risk-taking and innovativeness. A specific tension facing researchers in many fields is the meeting of institutional systems of evaluation (for example PRFS on the national level) and disciplined collegial norms and practices which, for example, play a role in assessment for academic positions and research grants. Furthermore, a researcher's or institution's position within this landscape may have considerable influence on the effects of indicator-based evaluation. For example, an established professor might respond differently compared to a young postdoc on a temporary contract. Similarly, a prominent university might have greater ability to ignore various rankings and measures, while less recognized institutions have less room to manoeuvre. Overall, evaluations on individual, organizational, and national levels, as well as between institutional and reputational assessments, interact in forming a multifaceted and complex landscape of academic evaluation.

Traditionally, bibliometric measures have been ill-equipped to capture the various and multifaceted ways through which academic performance is expressed. Looking towards the future, it is therefore likely that established criteria and indicators will be challenged and supplemented by other types of assessment procedures; at the time of writing there is currently a discussion in both Sweden and Norway on discontinuing the use of bibliometric indicators in the national PRFS (Styr- och resursutredningen, 2019; Svarstad, 2019). Calls for societal impact and the development of ways of evaluating how research influence society, in combination with a strong movement towards "open science", are developments that point to a broadening of assessment methods and process. Development of so called "alternative metrics", and the establishment of new and partly more open citation databases, is likely to further accentuate the movement towards an even richer, and ever more complex, landscape of (bibliometric) evaluation.

Acknowledgments

This chapter was supported by *The Swedish Foundation for the Social Sciences and Humanities* (SGO14–1153–1).

References

Aagaard, K 2015, 'How incentives trickle down: Local use of a national bibliometric indicator system', *Science and Public Policy*, vol. 42, pp. 725–37.

Aagaard, K, Bloch, C & Schneider, JW 2015, 'Impacts of performance-based research funding systems: The case of the Norwegian Publication Indicator', *Research Evaluation*, vol. 24, pp. 106–17.

Aksnes, DW, Rip, A 2009, 'Researchers' perceptions of citations', *Research Policy* vol. 38, pp. 895–905.

Åström, F & Hammarfelt, B 2019, 'Conceptualising dimensions of bibliometric assessment: From resource allocation systems to evaluative landscapes'. In Giuseppe Catalano, Cinzia Daraio, Martina Gregori, Henk F. Moed, Giancarlo Ruocco (eds.), *Proceedings of the 17th International Conference on Scientometrics and Informetrics* (ISSI 2019), September 2–5, 2019, Rome, Italy, pp. 1256–1261.

Biagioli, M & Galison, P (eds.) 2014, *Scientific authorship: Credit and intellectual property in science*, Routledge, New York.

Brandtner, C 2017, 'Putting the world in orders: Plurality in organizational evaluation', *Sociological Theory*, vol. 35, pp. 200–27.

Butler, L 2003, 'Explaining Australia's increased share of ISI publications – the effects of a funding formula based on publication counts', *Research Policy*, vol. 32, pp. 143–55.

Collini, S 2012, *What are universities for?*, Penguin, London.

Dahler-Larsen, P 2011, *The evaluation society*, Stanford University Press, Stanford.

Engels, TC, Ossenblok, TL & Spruyt, EH 2012, 'Changing publication patterns in the social sciences and humanities, 2000–2009', *Scientometrics* vol. 93, pp. 373–90.

Franssen, T, Scholten, W, Hessels, LK & de Rijcke, S 2018, 'The drawbacks of project funding for epistemic innovation: Comparing institutional affordances and constraints of different types of research funding', *Minerva*, vol. 56, pp. 11–33.

Haddow, G & Hammarfelt, B 2019, 'Early career academics and evaluative metrics: Ambivalence, resistance and strategies', in F Cannizzo & N Osbaldiston (eds.), *Social structures of global academia*, pp. 125–43, Routledge, London.

Hammarfelt, B, Nelhans, G, Eklund, P & Åström, F 2016, 'The heterogeneous landscape of bibliometric indicators: Evaluating models for allocating resources at Swedish universities', *Research Evaluation*, vol. 25, 292–305.

Hammarfelt, B & Rushforth, AD 2017, 'Indicators as judgment devices: An empirical study of citizen bibliometrics in research evaluation', *Research Evaluation*, vol. 26, pp. 169–80.

Hicks, D 2012, 'Performance-based university research funding systems', *Research Policy*, vol. 41, pp. 251–61.

Hicks, D, Wouters, P, Waltman, L, de Rijcke, S & Rafols, I 2015, 'Bibliometrics: The Leiden manifesto for research metrics', *Nature*, vol. 520, pp. 429–31.

Ingwersen, P & Larsen, B 2014, 'Influence of a performance indicator on Danish research production and citation impact 2000–12', *Scientometrics*, vol. 101, pp. 1325–44.

Martin, BR 2013, 'Whither research integrity? Plagiarism, self-plagiarism and coercive citation in an age of research assessment', *Research Policy*, vol. 42, pp. 1005–14.

Mirowski, P 2011, *Science-mart*, Harvard University Press, Cambridge, MA.

Müller, R 2014, 'Racing for what? Anticipation and acceleration in the work and career practices of academic life science postdocs', *Forum Qualitative Sozialforschung / Forum: Qualitative Social Research*, vol. 15.

Power, M 1997, *The audit society: Rituals of verification*, Oxford University Press, Oxford.

Rijcke, S de, Wouters, PF, Rushforth, AD, Franssen, TP & Hammarfelt, B 2016, 'Evaluation practices and effects of indicator use – a literature review', *Research Evaluation*, vol. 25, pp. 161–69.

Rushforth, A & Rijcke, S de 2015, 'Accounting for impact? The journal impact factor and the making of biomedical research in the Netherlands', *Minerva*, vol. 53, pp. 117–39.

Stephan, PE 2012, *How economics shapes science*, Harvard University Press, Cambridge, MA.

Styr- och resursutredningen 2019, *En långsiktig, samordnad och dialogbaserad styrning av högskolan*, Utbildningsdepartementet, Stockholm.

Svarstad, J 2019, 'Publiseringsindikatoren: Kunnskapsdepartementet vurderer å fjerne belønning for publisering', Forskerforum, January 31, 2019, https://www.forskerforum.no/vurderer-a-fjerne-belonning-for-publisering (July 15, 2020).

Vinkler, P 1988, 'An attempt of surveying and classifying bibliometric indicators for scientometric purposes', *Scientometrics*, vol. 13, pp. 239–59.

Whitley, R 2007, 'Changing governance of the public sciences', in R Whitley & J Gläser (eds.), *The changing governance of the sciences*, pp. 3–27, Springer, Heidelberg.

Whitley, R, Gläser, J & Laudel, G 2018, 'The impact of changing funding and authority relationships on scientific innovations', *Minerva*, vol. 56, pp. 109–34.

Zacharewicz, T, Lepori, B, Reale, E & Jonkers, K 2019, 'Performance-based funding in EU member states – a comparative assessment', *Science and Public Policy*, vol. 46, pp. 105–15.

5.2 Benchmarkings and Rankings
Ronald Rousseau

Abstract: This chapter contains a short review about "benchmarking" and "ranking". Examples, such as university rankings and their underlying philosophy, illustrate this review.

Keywords: benchmarking in bibliometric evaluation, university rankings.

Introduction: Benchmarking and Rankings

Benchmarking

In practice, the terms benchmark and benchmarking are used with slightly different meanings, namely:
a: something that serves as a standard by which others or other things may be measured or judged;
b: a point of reference from which measurements may be made;
c: a reference group with whom measurements are compared;
d: a standardized problem or test that serves as a basis for evaluation or comparison, often used to measure computer system performance, (Lewis and Crews, 1985).

The difference between points a and b is that point a refers to what is used for comparison, while b refers to any point of measurement: this could be the best possible, a gold standard, but also, and often, the least acceptable one, or any situation in-between.

In business management, to benchmark often means to study a competitor's product or business practices, in order to improve the performance of one's own company. As such, benchmarking is one aspect of total quality management. From a similar point of view, benchmarking has been discussed in a library context as a library management tool (Pritchard, 1995; Garrod and Kinnell, 1997). As this contribution is meant to be used within a bibliometric context we will not consider the computer system and business management meanings of "benchmarking" anymore, instead focusing on the use of benchmarking in a bibliometric context.

Ronald Rousseau, Centre for R&D Monitoring (ECOOM) and Dept. MSI, KU Leuven, Belgium, ronald.rousseau@kuleuven.be and University of Antwerp, Faculty of Social Sciences, B-2020 Antwerpen, Belgium, ronald.rousseau@uantwerpen.be

Rankings

Based on the work of Glänzel and Debackere (2009) we define ranking as positioning comparable objects from a given set S on an ordinal scale. In bibliometrics, ranking objects from a set S is usually based on indicator values, or a combination of indicator values associated with the objects in S.

Use of the Term Benchmarking in Bibliometric Research

Next we review some instances of uses of the term benchmark(ing) in a bibliometric context. We begin by observing that an original study of a new topic forms by itself a benchmark for all follow-up studies on this topic (Porter and Rafols, 2009). Manganote et al. (2014) wrote that research impact, internationalization, and leadership indicators have become benchmarks in a worldwide discussion about research quality and impact policies for universities. Clearly, these colleagues refer to meaning a) of the term benchmarking. They propose visualization maps at the institutional level as benchmarks for institutional strategies. This suggestion follows from Rafols et al. (2010) who introduced overlay maps for comparative purposes in benchmarking, investigating collaborative activities and their temporal change. We recall that in an overlay map, the original map of science – referred to as the base map – provides the location of each item of interest, e. g. all publications of one research unit, placed on top (overlay) the base map. Rafols et al. (2010) pointed out that several choices must be made regarding the data to be displayed in the two maps. First, should these maps display an input, an output or an outcome? Second, should the overlay data be normalized or not?

When it comes to journals in which research is published, those "with an impact factor" are often preferred above those without. Practically, this means that journals included in Clarivate's Journal Citation Reports (JCR) form a benchmark set. Yet, it has rightly been pointed out that this set cannot be used for all purposes. In particular, the social sciences and humanities pose a problem here because the JCR is clearly biased in favour of English language publications (Archambault et al., 2006). In order to counter this bias, many countries such as China, Brazil, Norway, and other European countries designed and constructed local databases and current research information systems, often to provide data for a performance-based funding system. The *Journal of Data and Information Science* (2018) devoted a complete issue on the so-called Norwegian Model and its influence on other countries (Sivertsen, 2018).

Frenken et al. (2017) rightly pointed out that in many cases global benchmarking, i.e. with respect to the whole world, can be misleading. For universities, as an example, benchmarking is most meaningful between universities of a similar size, supplemented with information on a university's specific mission and orientation. This would lead to more specific and more meaningful peer groups of universities. Somewhat in the same vein, Haddawy et al. (2017) state that since few universities can afford to be excellent in all subject areas, university administrators face the difficult decision of selecting areas for strategic investment. To support strategic decision-making, universities require research benchmarking data that is sufficiently fine-grained to show variation among specific research areas and identify focused areas of excellence. In their article they propose a Global Research Benchmarking System (GRBS) which provides fine-grained data to internationally benchmark university research performance in over 250 areas of science and technology. The authors provided a comparison of their GRBS results with those of three well-known ranking systems (Academic Ranking of World Universities (ARWU), Times Higher Education World University Ranking (THE-WUR), and QS World University Ranking, (QS-WUR)) showing how GRBS was able to identify pockets of excellence within universities that are overlooked by these aggregate level approaches.

Rousseau et al. (2017) claim that in comparing evaluation panels with the groups they must evaluate, distance based on cognitive similarity must be taken into account to reach an optimal choice. These authors provide several options and compare with a baseline model which does not take cognitive distance into account. They show that, based on a real assessment exercise at the University of Antwerp (Belgium), the benchmark model scores poorest, illustrating that taking cognitive similarity into account is important when composing evaluation panels.

When it comes to article citations, the world's top 1% and top 10% most highly cited research papers are often considered as benchmark groups (Tijssen et al., 2002).

Rankings in Bibliometrics

Ranking objects might be considered a natural human endeavour. Already in the nineteenth century, de Candolle (1873), a forerunner of modern scientometrics and the science of science, had published a relative ranking, by ranking countries by the number of international scientific society members per inhabitant. We note that the question if rankings should be based on absolute numbers (favouring large entities) or relative ones (e.g. with respect to inhabitants, or to number of scientists) is still very much alive.

With respect to the question "Which units can be ranked in the information sciences?" we first note that any set of indicators for any type of item leads to a ranking according to this indicator, depending moreover on the used database and probably the time frame used. Consequently, it is no surprise to find e.g. rankings of countries depending on the number of publications, of journals based on their impact factor (Garfield, 1972), scientists based on the h-index (Hirsch, 2005), and articles based on their citations (Garfield, 1986; Sanz-Casado et al., 2016), to mention just a few examples.

As ranking journals based on their impact factor has received many criticisms (Vanclay, 2012), more refined approaches have been proposed. An interesting one can be found in Stringer et al. (2008). The main idea of their work is to maximize the efficiency of locating high-impact research.

Other rankings such as university rankings are usually based on a composite indicator: a weighted average of several stand-alone indicators. However, besides rankings based on indicators, one may also construct rankings based on a consensus among peers (Aledo et al., 2018). Moreover, rankings are necessary in the peer review process for funding research projects (Marsh et al., 2008). Next we pay special attention to university rankings.

University Rankings

A special phenomenon related to university evaluation is the occurrence of worldwide university rankings and the related phenomenon of world-class universities (van Parijs, 2009). Ranking universities and research institutions, and this on a worldwide scale, is a rather recent phenomenon. Moreover, one may rightly ask if it is really possible to measure "the quality of universities". Yet, nowadays such rankings have captured the whole scientific world. In 2003, the Institute of Higher Education of Shanghai Jiao Tong University in China was the first to publish such a ranking. Soon others followed. Such lists have given rise to so-called world-class universities, namely those universities topping these lists. In the next sections we will briefly discuss the methods used to derive these rankings and present the Van Parijs typology of worldwide university rankings (van Parijs, 2009). Before going into details, we recall the main annually published worldwide university rankings:
- The Academic Ranking of World Universities (ARWU), informally known as the Shanghai ranking. This is the ranking drawn by the Institute of Higher Education of Shanghai Jiao Tong University. It can be found at http://www.arwu.org/ (July 15, 2020).
- The World University Ranking of the Times Higher Education (THE-WUR), formerly the Times Higher Education Supplement, (THES), drawn from 2004 to November 2009 in collaboration with a private company, QS Quacquarelli Symonds. Since then THE-WUR collaborated with Thomson Reuters, but switched to Scopus in 2015. This ranking can be found at: https://www.timeshighereducation.com/world-university-rankings (July 15, 2020). Quacquarelli Symonds now has its own QS World University Rankings (QS-WUR), found at https://www.topuniversities.com/ (July 15, 2020).
- The Leiden Ranking: CWTS' rankings (note the plural) available since 2008 at http://www.cwts.nl/ranking/ (July 15, 2020).
- Since 2009 the SIR (SCImago Institutions Ranking) has joined the set of worldwide university rankings, which can be seen at http://www.scimagoir.com/ (July 15, 2020). This report ranks nowadays, i.e. in 2019, more than 6,400 re-

search institutions and organizations and in different ways. It takes research performance, innovation, and web presence into account and provides sectorial rankings such as universities, hospitals, government institutions, and private institutions.

Finally, Reuters' ranking of the World's Most Innovative Universities is noted as a special type of university ranking.

Using different criteria leads to different rankings. Most university rankings use a composite indicator: different indicators are weighted and added, leading to a final ranking. The Shanghai Jiao Tong University ranking (ARWU) takes into account all universities with top researchers (Nobel laureates, Fields medallists, or highly cited researchers according to the Web of Science databases) or papers in *Nature* or *Science*. It is based on the following indicators: quality of education, measured by the number of alumni that received a Nobel Prize or a Fields Medal; quality of faculty, measured by the number of university members that have been granted a Nobel Prize or Fields medal and the number of highly cited researchers in 21 large fields; research output, measured by the number of articles published in the journals *Science* and *Nature* over the latest five years, accounting for author order, and the total number of publications (article type) included in the Web of Science. For institutions specializing in the social sciences or humanities, articles in *Science* and *Nature* are not taken into account and the weight of this indicator is spread over the other indicators.

THE-WUR uses a set of 13 indicators, grouped into the following five categories: teaching, research, citations, international outlook, and industry income. QS-WUR is based on six indicators: academic reputation, employer reputation, student-to-faculty ratio, citations per faculty, international faculty ratio, and international student ratio. QS-WUR provides rankings for 48 subjects. THE-WUR, moreover, assesses universities against the United Nations' Sustainable Development Goals. Calibrated indicators provide comparisons across three broad areas: research, outreach, and stewardship are taken into account.

The CWTS Leiden Rankings are focused on research and do not include teaching or reputation. No composite indicator is provided; instead, users choose themselves which indicators fit best for their own purposes. In the 2019 edition, four types of indicators are provided: indicators of research impact, indicators of research collaboration, information about open access, and gender-related information. A choice is offered between fractional counting and whole counting of contributions.

Compared with other university rankings, the Leiden Ranking offers more advanced indicators of scientific impact and collaboration and uses a more transparent methodology. The Leiden Ranking does not rely on subjective data obtained from reputational surveys or on data provided by universities themselves. Moreover, it refrains from aggregating different dimensions of university performance into a single overall indicator.

The SCImago Institutional Ranking provides a composite indicator, which combines 12 indicators from three domains: research, innovation, and societal impact.

Once these lists became known and started attracting the attention of scientists, research policymakers, and even newspapers, discussions emerged about the feasibility of such lists: do there really exist indicators that lead to a meaningful ranking of universities? Clearly, no single indicator can lead to a ranking that takes all aspects of university education and research into account. Hence a better question might be: which indicators may contribute to an accurate measurement of the quality of universities? Which methodology should be used to attain the goals of such rankings? And what precisely are these goals? The idea itself that such a ranking might be feasible can be considered as a consequence of the globalization of university and higher education. We note that these questions can also be formulated for rankings of most other items.

The Van Parijs Typology of University Rankings

In an elegantly argued essay, Van Parijs (2009) makes a distinction between three models related to university rankings.

A. The Market Model

According to this model, the purpose of this type of list is to support the market for higher education. This was, indeed, the original purpose of the ARWU ranking. Its creators wanted to inform Chinese students about which universities were the best places for going abroad to study. In this model, universities are ranked for the benefit of students, considered as consumers of educational services provided by universities and institutes of higher education. The market model type of list wants to fill an information gap. Clearly a "one-size-fits-all" approach can never succeed. A solution for this problem is an interactive ranking in which customers (students) may adapt weights of different indicators. For some students the price of a university education must receive the highest weight, for others the standing of the physics (or any other) department. Of course, the language in which the education is provided may be a factor used to exclude certain universities. All this leads to a phenomenon referred to by Van Parijs as "my rankings", where each ranking corresponds to the personal preference of one person.

B. The Podium Model

In this model, ranking is the result of a yearly "World Championship". The "best university in the world" features at the top. This approach is in an essential way different from the market model. Even if students had no choice at all, this model would still exist as university leaders want their university to be the best in the world. Of course, as in reality, students do have a choice (be it a restricted one), the podium value can be used as a sales argument for attracting prospective students. Obviously, no university leader can ignore this function of university rankings.

C. The Input-output Model

Yet, those responsible for the resources devoted to universities and institutes of higher education need another type of list. They are not only interested in an absolute scale of accomplishments but in the efficiency with which universities handle the means entrusted to them. Not all universities start on an equal footing: some have more supporting staff; some are situated in a more attractive part of the country (or of the world), and so on. Policymakers want to know how a university transforms means into relevant accomplishments. Allocating money to the best performers in this sense will lead to a better attainment of the objectives of educational authorities. Moreover, if one university performs significantly better than another, and this using the same amount of, or even fewer resources, there might be good reasons to imitate the methods of the better performing one.

Rankings and the Ideal University

Constructing (better) rankings is not just a bibliometric question: it is also an ethical question. When university policymakers have defined what they see as an ideal university (and their opinions may differ), universities can be ranked according to different views on this ideal. Moreover, it is better not to rank whole universities but disciplines, specialized research institutes or departments (including those especially fostering multidisciplinary research). This was actually done by the Leiden and the SCImago ranking, with most other rankings following suit.

Criticism on University Rankings

Using detailed rankings, an impression of differences can be generated, whereas equality may prevail (Waltman, 2016). Moreover, this may be a violation of one of the principles of the Leiden Manifesto, namely, providing misplaced precision (Hicks et al., 2015). This impression was confirmed in Leydesdorff et al. (2019), which concluded that at the country level distinctions between more than three (high, middle, low level) or maybe four groups of universities may not be meaningful. For this reason, completely ordered rankings must be used very carefully (if at all) and classifications consisting of different levels are to be preferred. This can, for example, be obtained by rankings based on the $h^{(3)}$-index as shown for journals in Fassin and Rousseau (2019). A more refined solution is offered by using Data Envelopment Analysis. This method can deal with multiple inputs (such as number of researchers and monetary input) and multiple outputs (such as publications and citations) and leads to different grades or levels of the objects under study (Yang et al., 2016).

Ranking systems often select universities based on overall institutional performance and thus have a bias toward the most comprehensively strong universities. Such an approach can miss world-class programs or centres of excellence that exist in universities that do not as a whole rank among the worldwide top. It is, indeed, well recognized that great differences exist in performance among researchers and programs within individual institutions (Haddawy et al., 2017). A criticism specific to the ARWU ranking is its heavy reliance on Nobel Prizes and alumni with Nobel Prizes as proxies for research and teaching excellence. Since the Nobel Prize is typically given toward the end of a researcher's career, it is clear that use of these indicators provides at best a historical perspective on university performance that may not relate much to current performance (Billaut et al., 2010; Enserink, 2007; van Raan, 2005). It has also been argued that use of these indicators tends to downplay social sciences and humanities as well as other fields in which the Nobel Prize is not awarded (Billaut et al., 2010).

Discussion

Before serious ranking or grading can begin, thorough data cleaning must be performed as databases have many shortcomings: names of authors and institutions are spelled differently from one article to the next, or university affiliations are omitted altogether. The true number of papers from a university can be much higher than found by a simple search. Are work, money, and time involved in this data cleaning process worth doing?

Aguillo et al. (2010) have tried to compare some rankings. As the main rankings use different criteria they tend to differ considerably. Only top universities, such as Harvard, stay as top universities in each ranking. However, one may say that we do not need dedicated rankings to know that such institutions are top universities. For most other universities these rankings entail a huge reproducibility problem.

Some lists regularly change their methodology. For instance, they adapt the weights given to different indicators. Although there is nothing wrong with a change in methodology, on the condition that the new approach is a real improvement, it makes comparisons over time difficult or even impossible.

In terms of predictions about rankings it is of importance to study the dynamics or stability of the ranking in which one is interested (García-Zorita et al., 2018). If a particular ranking is highly dynamic then a better ranking in one particular year is probably meaningless. Yet, if a ranking is very stable, then a better ranking might be highly significant.

We further note that the so-called bibliometric laws connected to the names of Lotka, Zipf, and Bradford in their rank-frequency form start from ranking sources such as authors or words, according to the number of items they "produce", such as articles or occurrences in a text, over a given period of time (Egghe, 2005).

Conclusion

Bibliometricians have studied journal rankings for decades. Recently, however, other types of rankings have come to the fore, in particular (world) university rankings. Although such rankings may be condemned as a kind of race based on narrowly defined parameters, making "big" even "bigger", this does not necessarily have to be the case. According to Van Parijs (2009), university rankings must be redesigned so that they provide institutions and policymakers the incentives to honour the highest intellectual and social values. Again, a similar remark holds for most other rankings.

Although most attention still goes to rankings of universities as a whole, most providers of such rankings nowadays provide – more sensible – rankings per large field.

Rankings may lead to increased competition, which in turn may lead researchers to shy away from the really hard research questions. In as far as this happens, a policy focusing on rankings may lead to the opposite results of what was originally intended.

References

Aguillo, Isidro F, Bar-Ilan, J, Levene, M & Ortega JL, 2010, 'Comparing University Rankings', *Scientometrics*, vol. 85, no. 1, pp. 243–56.
Aledo, JA, Gámez, JA, Molina, D & Rosete, A 2018, 'Consensus-based Journal Rankings: A Complementary Tool for Bibliometric Evaluation', *Journal of the Association for Information Science and Technology*, vol. 69, no. 7, pp. 936–48.
Archambault, É, Vignola-Gagné, É, Côté, G, Larivière, V & Gingras, Y 2006, 'Benchmarking Scientific Output in the Social Sciences and Humanities: The Limits of Existing Databases', *Scientometrics*, vol. 68, no. 3, pp. 329–42.
Billaut, J-C, Bouyssou, D & Vincke, P 2010, 'Should You Believe in the Shanghai Ranking? An MCDM View', *Scientometrics*, vol. 84, no. 1, pp. 237–63.
de Candolle, A 1873, *Histoire des Sciences et des Savants depuis Deux Siècles*, Georg, Genève.
Egghe, L 2005, *Power Laws in the Information Production Process: Lotkaian Informetrics*, Elsevier.
Enserink, M 2007, 'Who Ranks the University Rankers?', *Science*, vol. 317, no. 5841, pp. 1026–28.
Fassin, Y & Rousseau, R 2019, 'The H(^{3}) – Index of Academic Journals', *Malaysian Journal of Library and Information Science*, vol. 24, no. 2, pp. 41–53.

Frenken, K, Heimeriks, GJ & Hoekman, J 2017, 'What Drives University Research Performance? An Analysis Using the CWTS Leiden Ranking Data', *Journal of Informetrics*, vol. 11, no. 3, pp. 859–72.

García-Zorita, C, Rousseau, R, Marugan-Lazaro, S & Sanz-Casado, E 2018, 'Ranking Dynamics and Volatility', *Journal of Informetrics*, vol. 12, no. 3, pp. 567–78.

Garfield, E 1972, 'Citation Analysis as a Tool in Journal Evaluation – Journals Can Be Ranked by Frequency and Impact of Citations for Science Policy Studies', *Science*, vol. 178, no. 4060, pp. 471–79.

Garfield, E 1986, 'The 250 Most-cited Primary Authors in the 1984 SCI. 1. Names, Ranks, and Citation Numbers', *Current Contents*, vol. 45, pp. 3–11.

Garrod, P & Kinnell, M 1997, 'Benchmarking Development Needs in the LIS Sector', *Journal of Information Science*, vol. 23, no. 2, pp. 111–18.

Glänzel, W & Debackere, K 2009, 'On the "Multi-Dimensionality" of Ranking and the Role of Bibliometrics in University Assessment', in C Dehon, D Jacobs & C Vermandele, *Ranking Universities*, pp. 65–75, Editions de l' Université de Bruxelles, Bruxelles, ISBN: 978-2-8004-1441-6.

Haddawy, P, Hassan, S-U, Abbey, CW & Beng Lee, I 2017, 'Uncovering Fine-Grained Research Excellence: The Global Research Benchmarking System', *Journal of Informetrics*, vol. 11, no. 2, pp. 389–406.

Hicks, D, Wouters, P, Waltman, L, de Rijcke, S & Rafols, I 2015, 'The Leiden Manifesto for Research Metrics', *Nature*, vol. 520, no. 7548, pp. 429–31.

Hirsch, JE 2005, 'An Index to Quantify an Individual's Scientific Research Output', *Proceedings of the National Academy of Sciences of the United States of America*, vol. 102, no. 46, pp. 16569–72.

Lewis, BC & Crews, AE 1985, 'The Evolution of Benchmarking as a Computer Performance Evaluation Technique', *MIS Quarterly*, vol. 9, no. 1, pp. 7–16.

Leydesdorff, L, Bornmann L & Mingers, J 2019, 'Statistical Significance and Effect Sizes of Differences among Research Universities at the Level of Nations and Worldwide Based on the Leiden Rankings', *Journal of the Association for Information Science and Technology*, vol. 70, no. 5, pp. 509–25.

Manganote, EJT, Araujo, MS & Schulz, PA 2014, 'Visualization of Ranking Data: Geographical Signatures in International Collaboration, Leadership and Research Impact', *Journal of Informetrics*, vol. 8, no. 3, pp. 642–49.

Marsh, HW, Jayasinghe, UW & Bond, NW 2008, 'Improving the Peer-Review Process for Grant Applications – Reliability, Validity, Bias, and Generalizability', *American Psychologist*, vol. 63, no. 3, pp. 160–68.

Porter, AL & Rafols, I 2009, 'Measuring and Mapping Six Research Fields over Time', *Scientometrics*, vol. 81, no. 3, pp. 719–45.

Pritchard, SM 1995, 'Library Benchmarking: Old Wine in New Bottles?', *Journal of Academic Libraries*, November, pp. 491–95.

Rafols, I, Porter, AL & Leydesdorff, L 2010, 'Science Overlay Maps: A New Tool for Research Policy and Library Management', *Journal of the American Society for Information Science*, vol. 61, no. 9, pp. 1871–87.

Rousseau, R, Guns, R, Jakaria Rahman, AIM & Engels, TCE 2017, 'Measuring Cognitive Distance between Publication Portfolios', *Journal of Informetrics*, vol. 11, no. 2, pp. 583–94.

Sanz-Casado, E, García-Zorita, C & Rousseau, R 2016, 'Using H-Cores to Study the Most-Cited Articles of the 21st Century', *Scientometrics*, vol. 108, no. 1, pp. 243–61.

Sivertsen, G 2018 (guest editor), Special Issue on Applications of the Norwegian Model, *Journal of Data and Information Science*, vol. 3, no. 4.

Stringer, MJ, Sales-Pardo, M & Nunes Amaral, LA 2008, 'Effectiveness of Journal Ranking Schemes as a Tool for Locating Information', *PLoS ONE*, vol. 3, no. 2, e1683.

Tijssen, RJW, Visser, MS & van Leeuwen, TN 2002, 'Benchmarking International Scientific Excellence: Are Highly Cited Research Papers an Appropriate Frame of Reference?', *Scientometrics*, vol. 54, no. 3, pp. 381–97.

Van Parijs, P 2009, 'European higher education under the spell of university rankings', *Ethical Perspectives*, vol. 16, no. 2, pp.189–206.

van Raan, AFJ 2005, 'Fatal Attraction: Conceptual and Methodological Problems in the Ranking of Universities by Bibliometric Methods', *Scientometrics*, vol. 62, no. 1, pp. 133–43.

Vanclay, JK 2012, 'Impact Factor: Outdated Artifact or Stepping-Stone to Journal Certification?', *Scientometrics*, vol. 92, no.2, pp. 211–38.

Waltman, L 2016, 'Conceptual Difficulties in the Use of Statistical Inference in Citation Analysis', *Journal of Informetrics*, vol. 10, no. 4, pp. 1249–52.

Yang, G, Ahlgren, P, Yang, L, Rousseau, R & Ding, J 2016, 'Using Multi-Level Frontiers in DEA Models to Grade Countries/Territories', *Journal of Informetrics*, vol. 10, no. 1, pp. 238–53.

5.3 Technological Trend Analysis

Miloš Jovanović

Abstract: The present review gives a short introduction to the background of TTA and its methods in the context of bibliometrics, with a focus on the literature from the past 15 years (i.e. 2005–2019) but also including some important older publications. It deals with quantitative TTA (where bibliometrics and patentometrics are employed) and qualitative TTA (which uses e.g. expert interviews, historical reviews or questionnaires) and then finishes with a discussion of the methods and a conclusion.

Keywords: bibliometrics, scientometrics, Technological Trend Analysis, technological forecasting, technology forecasting, patentometrics, patent analysis, horizon scanning, visualization.

Introduction

A popular quote used in the context of technological trend analysis (for the purpose of this paper abbreviated as TTA) says "I'm more interested in the future than in the past, because the future is where I intend to live." The source of this quote is not clear; it is often attributed to Albert Einstein but no written source is provided along with the quote. However, the content of the quote sums up the reason why scientists are pursuing research in the field of TTA: everyone is interested in the future. TTA has many different aspects, some of which are tightly interwoven with the field of bibliometrics. The present review, as part of a handbook on bibliometrics, wishes to give a short introduction to the background of TTA and its methods in the context of bibliometrics, with a focus on the literature from the past 15 years (i.e. 2005–2019) but also including some important older publications.

First of all, a definition of the term TTA and its background will help put it into context and provide a backdrop for its use in bibliometrics. Historically speaking, TTA is part of future research in general, which has its roots in the military sector of post-WW2 USA. Back then, same as today, the reason for doing future research was to be prepared for future trends and especially future technologies (Grüne, 2013). An example can be found in the industry, because product developers and manufacturers need to know where to invest their future resources and how to plan new facilities or what new equipment to buy. Another example is governments, which need to know where and how to allocate funds toward their research institutions. In its most extreme example, the failure to correctly anticipate a military technology and make the appropriate investments beforehand can lead to serious reper-

---

Dr. **Miloš Jovanović**, Fraunhofer Institute for Technological Trend Analysis INT, Euskirchen, Germany, Milos.Jovanovic@int.fraunhofer.de

cussions for a country's security (Kott and Perconti, 2018). Taking this into account, TTA is often a tool for strategic decision support.

Future research and TTA are just two examples of terms that describe a field of research, along with its methods, that deal with trends and the future in general. Others are for example "technological/technology forecasting", "technology monitoring" or "technology/horizon scanning". The terms are loosely defined and have a certain overlap. For example "environmental scanning" is defined as the "systematic process of picking up weak signals and trends […]" and is also referred to as "horizon scanning" (Centre for Strategic Futures & Civil Service College, 2012). Applied to technologies, this can then be described as "technological forecasting" or "technology monitoring". An important distinction is the one between "scanning" (which describes the search for new trends or technologies) and "monitoring" (which describes the monitoring of already found trends or technologies to stay up to date) (Grüne, 2013).

Looking at technologies also means that TTA is not evaluating research per se. For example, a multitude of bibliometric analyses exists that looks at the research output of individual journals, authors, institutions or countries. TTA normally is a variant of a topic analysis where each topic consists of a technology, a group of technologies or a research topic in general. However, an analysis can also deal with non-technological topics.

Thus, a simple and pragmatic definition of TTA for the present paper is that TTA is an "analysis of past and present information about a certain technology which seeks to identify past, present and future trends of the development of said technology through the usage of qualitative and quantitative methods." Since the present paper focuses on TTA in the context of bibliometrics, the "information" in definition normally refers to research publications and in extension to patents.

Of course, comparable to other research fields, TTA involves certain challenges. For example, in the absence of a magical crystal ball that can actually display the future, one must rely on different methods that are used in TTA. From its very beginning, both qualitative and quantitative methods have been used. The following will give a short overview of the different methods, with a focus on the quantitative bibliometric methods and studies.

Quantitative Technological Trend Analyses

Bibliometric Technological Trend Analysis

The vast majority of studies that deal with quantitative TTA can be found in the bibliometric field. Often, they complement qualitative studies of different technologies (Grüne, 2013). Reasons for studying technologies, or scientific topics in general, range from a historical perspective (taking into account past developments) to a glance at possible future developments, for example via extrapolation of the past.

The sources of these studies very often are databases that are used in many bibliometric studies, i.e. mostly the Web of Science and Scopus, while some also use Google Scholar, dimensions.ai or similar databases.

Not all studies explicitly link their methods to TTA or use that term. Above mentioned terms like "technological forecasting" are also often used. The methods used in these studies are often simply referred to as "bibliometrics" and combined with more general methods like "text mining" or other statistical methods. In addition to that, methods like "keyword co-occurrence analysis", citation and co-citation analysis (which are considered to be a part of bibliometrics), and different kinds of clustering methods are mentioned and applied to the titles and author keywords of publications (e.g. in Daim et al., 2006; Konstantinidis et al., 2017, Pinto et al., 2019). Going even further into the content of research articles, methods based on semantics are employed to gain a deeper understand of the analysed texts (Yang et al., 2015). These kinds of methods can also be seen as being a part of text mining methods. Another method which is applied in TTA is the attempt to identify and extrapolate typical growth patterns in the publication data, one popular example being the "double boom cycle" described by Schmoch (2007). In short, a double boom exists if high publication numbers for a technology are followed by a similarly high number of patents. If identified correctly, a pattern like this can help to better assess the future development of a technology (see also Adamuthe and Thampi (2019) for a more recent example of trend line analyses). Finally, network analysis and different kinds of visualizations of the research landscape are used in the context of TTA (for example co-authorship networks and co-word networks in Li et al. (2018) or country co-authorship networks in Romero and Portillo-Salido (2019)). Here, one can also note that, through advances in computational power, the possibilities for new visualization methods have improved very much in the past 15 years. Further recent additions to methods for TTA are machine learning and the use of big data (see for example Gao et al., 2019).

The technologies studied via TTA are often just as diverse as the methods employed, for example "perovskite solar cell technology" (Li et al., 2019), "dye-sensitized solar cell" (Gao et al., 2019), "Internet of things in health" (Konstantinidis et al., 2017), "optical sensing and imaging technologies and applications" (Chen et al., 2018), "fuel cell, food safety and optical storage" (Daim et al., 2006), "radio frequency identification (RFID)" (Chao et al., 2007), "solid waste reuse and recycling" (Li et al., 2018), "sigma-1 receptor research" (Romero and Portillo-Salido, 2019), "global stem cell research" (Li et al., 2009), "graphene research" (Lv et al., 2011), "paraquat intoxication research" (Zyoud, 2018) or "proteomics" (Tan et al., 2014).

As noted above, trend analyses can also deal with non-technological topics like "Entrepreneurship research" (Ferreira et al., 2019) or "Webometrics in Libraries" (Udartseva, 2018). From a bibliometric point of view, these analyses are similar to TTA, but the extrapolations are based on different assumptions and patentometric analyses are normally not part of them.

Patentometric Technology Analysis

Patentometrics analysis is in many ways similar to bibliometric analysis (for the present author, it is a subset of bibliometrics; see Jovanovic, 2011, p. 16). The main and obvious difference is the use of patents instead of scientific journal publications as the basis of an analysis. The content of a patent is, of course, very different in comparison to a research article. A research article wishes to report on new findings or methods while a patent wants to secure a claim on an invention and is a possible prerequisite for a product. Thus, the reason for conducting patentometric analyses is often the attempt to measure the success of a company via their patenting activity or the link between patents and research, since patents normally include citations to other patents and non-patent literature (see for example Sampat and Ziedonis, 2005).

Some methods used in patentometry have already been mentioned above, e.g. "text mining", statistical methods etc. (see for example Lee et al., 2009). An example of patentometric methods applied for TTA can be found in Rodriguez Salvador and La Mancilla de Cruz (2018) where "additive manufacturing patents in the Industry 4.0 context" are analyzed.

TTA can involve both bibliometric and patentometric analyses as can be seen in some of the above mentioned studies, e.g. Li et al. (2019) and Lv et al. (2011).

Qualitative Technological Trend Analyses and Combination of Methods

Qualitative TTA is very often conducted by technology experts who use desktop research to achieve a certain level of expertise in a technology they wish to analyze. This desktop research can be complemented with other qualitative methods like expert interviews, historical reviews or questionnaires (e.g. through Delphi studies, see Jiang et al. (2017) for one study where this method was utilized). For a good overview on the methods of qualitative TTA see Grüne (2013).

Apart from the examples of quantitative and qualitative TTA described above, there also exist studies that combine methods from both classes of analyses. For example, Zhang et al. (2016) combine topic analysis and clustering with expert knowledge via a panel, while Chao et al. (2007) use a combination of bibliometric analysis and historical review of the literature. Depending on the time and effort one can spend on a TTA, it is the opinion of the author that a combination of a number of both quantitative and qualitative methods is always better than employing singular methods.

Discussion and Conclusion

There are studies trying to evaluate the accuracies of technology trend analyses, e. g. to answer the question of how well a forecast stood up to the test of time. They however do not deal with technologies that were developed but not forecast (e. g. Kott and Perconti (2018) who found a high accuracy of forecasts in certain fields like Cyber Warfare). But the question of whether the accuracy of technological forecasts should be evaluated ex post at all is still an open one. An argument against such a practice, from the point of view of this author, is the fact that the forecast by itself already has an influence on the future. An argument in favor of this practice can be found, e. g. in Lerner et al. (2015), who analyzed forecasts from the health sector (forecasts done by expert panels, not through bibliometric analysis) and found factors to improve their quality (e. g. through cyclical revision).

Earlier publications noted the importance to acknowledge the limitations that a pure bibliometric and/or patentometric approach can have on TTA. For example, not all important research institutions or companies actually publish their results in journals or keep their results secret. This will always lead to incomplete pictures of the past and present with regard to a technology's research. Also, time lags between the writing and publication of articles and their citation can lead to a blurred picture. Because of this, Watts and Porter (1997) argued for a combination of methods that are both qualitative (e. g. expert interviews) and quantitative in nature. They also noted that such a complimentary approach "should be standard practice". As has been seen above, most studies in the field of TTA chose such an approach, one recent example being Li et al. (2019).

To conclude, the methods employed in TTA are varied and often combined in different ways, which is in alignment with recommendations by experts (see paragraph above). The topics in TTA range from concrete technologies to research themes from all disciplines. The field is very active, with studies coming out nearly every month and at least two journals that deal with these kinds of studies, i. e. "Scientometrics" (with a focus on bibliometric and patentometric methods) and "Technological forecasting and social change" (with a focus on the technologies). TTA represents a valuable set of methods that can be used to obtain a picture of a technology's (or, more generally speaking, a research topic's) situation in the research landscape. Recent progress in visualization techniques has led to improved ways of depicting the results of bibliometric and patentometric analyses, thus enhancing the possibility to convey complicated results to a broader public. This is true for all bibliometric and patentometric analyses, not only those conducted in the field of TTA. Also, the introduction of new methods like machine learning and their possible application to "big data" (even though the definition of "big data" in the context of bibliometrics is not always clear) shows that TTA is evolving with new possibilities. It remains to be seen how well these new methods will fit into the existing ones, but their first applications are promising.

References

Adamuthe, AC & Thampi, GT 2019, 'Technology forecasting: A case study of computational technologies', *Technological Forecasting and Social Change*, vol. 143, pp. 181–89.

Centre for Strategic Futures & Civil Service College 2012, *Foresight: A glossary* [Online], Singapore, https://www.csf.gov.sg/media-centre/publications/foresight-glossary (July 15, 2020).

Chao, C-C, Yang, JM & Jen, WY 2007, 'Determining technology trends and forecasts of RFID by a historical review and bibliometric analysis from 1991 to 2005', *Technovation*, vol. 27, no. 5, pp. 268–79.

Chen, S, Wang, Y & Qiu, S 2018, 'Bibliometric trend analysis on global image processing research', *Optical Sensing and Imaging Technologies and Applications*, p. 134, SPIE, Beijing, China.

Daim, TU, Rueda, G, Martin, H & Gerdsri, P 2006, 'Forecasting emerging technologies: Use of bibliometrics and patent analysis', *Technological Forecasting and Social Change*, vol. 73, no. 8, pp. 981–1012.

Ferreira, JJM, Fernandes, CI & Kraus, S 2019, 'Entrepreneurship research: mapping intellectual structures and research trends', *Review of Managerial Science*, vol. 13, no. 1, pp. 181–205.

Gao, H, Gui, L & Luo, W 2019, 'Scientific Literature based Big Data Analysis for Technology Insight', *Journal of Physics: Conference Series*, vol. 1168, p. 32007.

Grüne, M 2013, 'Technologiefrühaufklärung im Verteidigungsbereich', in A Zweck & R Popp (eds.), *Zukunftsforschung im Praxistest*, pp. 195–230, Springer, Wiesbaden.

Jiang, R, Kleer, R & Piller, FT 2017, 'Predicting the future of additive manufacturing: A Delphi study on economic and societal implications of 3D printing for 2030', *Technological Forecasting and Social Change*, vol. 117, pp. 84–97.

Jovanovic, M 2011, *Fußspuren in der Publikationslandschaft: Einordnung wissenschaftlicher Themen und Technologien in grundlagen-und anwendungsorientierte Forschung mithilfe bibliometrischer Methoden*, Fraunhofer Verlag, Euskirchen.

Konstantinidis, ST, Billis, A, Wharrad, H & Bamidis, PD 2017, 'Internet of Things in Health Trends Through Bibliometrics and Text Mining', in R Randell, R Cornet, C McCowan, N Peek & PJ Scott (eds.), *Informatics for health: Connected citizen-led wellness and population health*, pp. 73–77, IOS Press, Amsterdam, Washington DC.

Kott, A & Perconti, P 2018, 'Long-term forecasts of military technologies for a 20–30 year horizon: An empirical assessment of accuracy', *Technological Forecasting and Social Change*, vol. 137, pp. 272–279.

Lee, S, Yoon, B & Park, Y 2009, 'An approach to discovering new technology opportunities: Keyword-based patent map approach', *Technovation*, vol. 29, no. 6–7, pp. 481–97.

Lerner, JC, Robertson, DC & Goldstein, SM 2015, 'Case studies on forecasting for innovative technologies: frequent revisions improve accuracy', *Health affairs (Project Hope)*, vol. 34, no. 2, pp. 311–18.

Li, L-L, Ding, G, Feng, N, Wang, M-H & Ho, Y-S 2009, 'Global stem cell research trend: Bibliometric analysis as a tool for mapping of trends from 1991 to 2006', *Scientometrics*, vol. 80, no. 1, pp. 39–58.

Li, N, Han, R & Lu, X 2018, 'Bibliometric analysis of research trends on solid waste reuse and recycling during 1992–2016', *Resources, Conservation and Recycling*, vol. 130, pp. 109–17.

Li, X, Xie, Q, Daim, T & Huang, L 2019, 'Forecasting technology trends using text mining of the gaps between science and technology: The case of perovskite solar cell technology', *Technological Forecasting and Social Change*, vol. 146, pp. 432–49.

Lv, PH, Wang, G-F, Wan, Y, Liu, J, Liu, Q & Ma, F-C 2011, 'Bibliometric trend analysis on global graphene research', *Scientometrics*, vol. 88, no. 2, pp. 399–419.

Pinto, M, Fernández-Pascual, R, Caballero-Mariscal, D, Sales, D, Guerrero, D & Uribe, A 2019, 'Scientific production on mobile information literacy in higher education: a bibliometric analysis (2006–2017)', *Scientometrics*, vol. 120, no. 1, pp. 57–85.

Rodriguez Salvador, M & La Mancilla de Cruz, J 2018, 'Presence of Industry 4.0 in Additive Manufacturing: Technological Trend Analysis', *Dynall (Dyna Inegnieria e Industria)*, vol. 93, no. 1, pp. 597–601.

Romero, L & Portillo-Salido, E 2019, 'Trends in Sigma-1 Receptor Research: A 25-Year Bibliometric Analysis', *Frontiers in pharmacology*, vol. 10, p. 564.

Sampat, BN & Ziedonis, AA 2005, 'Patent Citations and the Economic Value of Patents', in HF Moed, W Glänzel & U Schmoch (eds.), *Handbook of Quantitative Science and Technology Research*, pp. 277–98, Kluwer Academic Publishers, Dordrecht.

Schmoch, U 2007, 'Double-boom cycles and the comeback of science-push and market-pull', *Research Policy*, vol. 36, no. 7, pp. 1000–15.

Tan, J, Fu, HZ & Ho, Y-S 2014, 'A bibliometric analysis of research on proteomics in Science Citation Index Expanded', *Scientometrics*, vol. 98, no. 2, pp. 1473–90.

Udartseva, OM 2018, 'An Overview of Webometrics in Libraries: History and Modern Development Tendencies', *Scientific and Technical Information Processing*, vol. 45, no. 3, pp. 174–81.

Watts, RJ & Porter, AL 1997, 'Innovation Forecasting', *Technological Forecasting and Social Change*, no. 56, pp. 25–47.

Yang, C, Zhu, D & Zhang, G 2015, 'Semantic-Based Technology Trend Analysis', *2015 10th International Conference on Intelligent Systems and Knowledge Engineering (ISKE)*, pp. 222–28, IEEE, Taipei, Taiwan.

Zhang, Y, Zhang, G, Chen, H, Porter, AL, Zhu, D & Lu, J 2016, 'Topic analysis and forecasting for science, technology and innovation: Methodology with a case study focusing on big data research', *Technological Forecasting and Social Change*, vol. 105, pp. 179–91.

Zyoud, S'eH 2018, 'Investigating global trends in paraquat intoxication research from 1962 to 2015 using bibliometric analysis', *American journal of industrial medicine*, vol. 61, no. 6, pp. 462–70.

5.4 Research Collaboration and Bibliometric Performance

Tindaro Cicero and Marco Malgarini

Abstract: In this chapter, we evaluate the effects of research collaborations on scientific impact, as measured by the Field Weighted Citation Impact indicator. We distinguish collaborations according to their geographic origin (national, international, institutional) and to the affiliation of the researchers (academic and corporate collaborations) and evaluate the importance of each in terms of citation impact. Our main result is that international collaborations significantly improve scientific impact regardless of the research field under consideration. On the other hand, national collaborations positively affect impact only in some fields, while institutional collaborations are found to be either insignificant or detrimental (limited to Health Sciences) to scientific performance. We also find that corporate collaborations are relevant and that their effect grows the higher their share with respect to total publications.

Keywords: academic collaborations, corporate collaborations, scientific impact, bibliometrics, panel data, Feasible Generalised Least Squares.

Introduction

Research collaborations can be classified in terms of their geographic and organizational characteristics (Sonnenwald, 2007): geographically, we can distinguish among local, national, and international collaborations. On the other hand, inter-sectoral collaborations arise when scholars from universities or research centres interact with professionals working in the industry sector in their research activities; on the basis of this definition, we distinguish among corporate and academic collaborations, characterized respectively by collaboration with a co-author operating in the corporate or academic sector. Interdisciplinary and complexity of modern science is leading to growing collaboration among researchers involved in scientific activities (Lee and Bozeman, 2005); however, different types of collaborations may have fairly different impact in terms of bibliometric performances. International collaborations favor an increase in the number of citations received (Schmoch and Schubert, 2008; Goldfinch et al., 2003); moreover they have a positive effect on the quality of publications (Lissoni et al., 2011; He et al. 2009; Smeby and Try, 2005) and are also positively correlated to a scientist's future research output (He et al., 2009). As a conse-

---
Tindaro Cicero, Italian National Agency for the Evaluation of Universities and Research Institutes (ANVUR), Responsable for National Scientific Habilitation, Via Ippolito Nievo, 35 00153 Roma, C.F. e P.I. 97653310587, Italy, tindaro.cicero@anvur.it
Marco Malgarini, Head of National Scientific Habilitation, Italy, marco.malgarini@anvur.it

quence, and especially in the hard sciences, collaboration activity with other countries is usually considered to produce the most successful research (Adams, 2013; Frenken et al., 2010). Another line of research supports the opposite causal relationship: in this case, it is possible that research productivity has a positive effect on international collaborations (Kato and Ando, 2013; Abramo et al., 2011).

Looking at individual data at the author level, national collaborations could take an important role in influencing research productivity (Abramo et al., 2017) to the detriment of international collaborations. This phenomenon could be explained by the individual huge cost to collaborate internationally in some scientific fields. On the other hand, inter-sectoral collaborations are considered as very relevant in stimulating economic growth and are deemed to have a positive effect on research production; their effect on impact is however more questionable, since this kind of collaboration may prevalently target empirical or practical applications rather than scientific impact (Mowery, 2007). Anyhow, there are many reasons for industry-universities collaborations (Rybnicek and Königsgruber, 2019): among other things, a relevant share of new products or processes based on the contribution of academic research (Bekkers and Bodas Freitas, 2008).The goal of this chapter is to study the recent evolution of the different kind of collaborations, trying also to understand their influence on research impact, considering data referred to the period 2001–2018 (see also Cicero and Malgarini, 2017). In the following, we first introduce the dataset and then run a simple panel data model relating the sector-specific Field Weighted Citation Impact (FWCI) of 35 OECD and developing countries to the share of collaborative papers. Some consideration on the results obtained concludes the analysis.

Recent Trends in Research Collaborations

Data for the analysis derive from SCIVAL-Scopus database and concerns articles, reviews, and conference papers produced by six OECD countries[1] and China, published in the period 2001 to 2018. Data are disaggregated by Fields of Science and Technology (FoS), a scientific classification elaborated by the OECD; more specifically we focus on STEM areas, classified in four main sectors, namely Agricultural sciences, Engineering and Technology, Medical and Health Sciences, and Natural Sciences. We first gather information about the composition of scientific production, in terms of types of research collaboration: in particular, we first distinguish among academic and corporate collaborations, and then look at different kind of collaborations distinguished on a geographical basis, hence considering institutional, national, and international collaborations. First of all, looking at the data (Figure 1) we observe that between 2001 and 2018 the share of collaborative publications has globally

---

[1] France, Germany, Italy, Netherlands, United Kingdom, US.

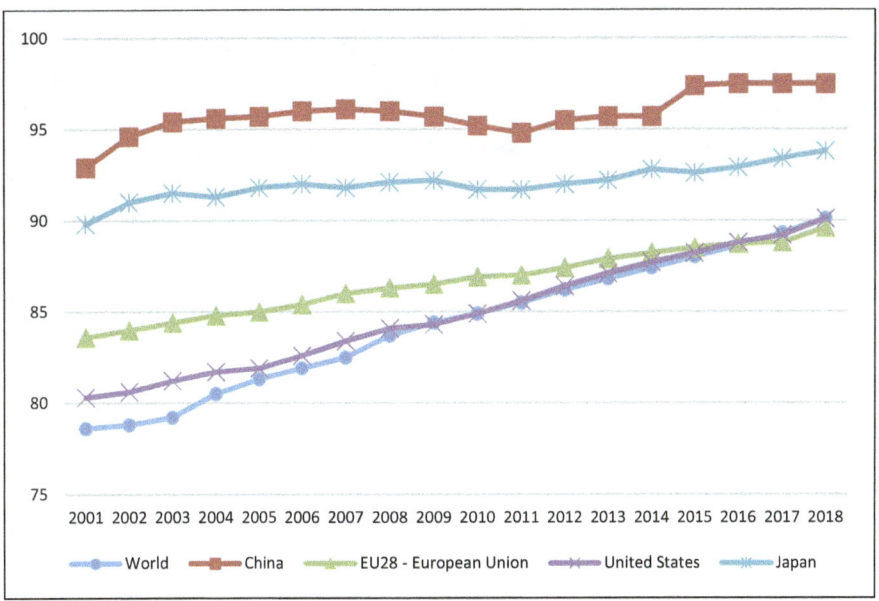

Figure 1: Research Collaborations, 2001–2018 (as a share of total publications in STEM fields). Source: authors' elaboration on Scival data.

increased from 78.6 to 90.1%. The growth has been particularly strong in the US and in the European Union, even if the higher share of collaborative papers is observed in the two Asian countries considered in our analysis. In fact, in 2018 over 95% of Chinese scientific production is collaborative research, while Italy and Japan are only slightly behind (93.8 and 93% respectively); on the other hand, the lowest share of collaborative research is found in the UK and in the EU EU28. More specifically, in the last 20 years, national and international collaborations have remarkably increased (see also Adams et al., 2007), while inter-institutional collaborations (i.e. collaborations within the same university/research centre) have been losing ground, while remaining on average the most used form of collaborative research at the global level (Figure 2). According to the literature, various factors have facilitated international collaborations in recent years, including development of information and communication technologies, the decline in transportation costs (Katz and Martin, 1997) and increasing international mobility of researchers.

However, collaborations types may vary remarkably across countries (Figure 3): considering the year 2018, international collaborations are largely prevalent in the UK and in the EU, and are also very important in the US, while in the Asian countries and in the world average institutional collaborations do still prevail.

Finally, Figure 4 shows how corporate collaborations have evolved in recent years: after a remarkable increase from 2.1 to 2.7% in the period 2001–2007, they started to decline again, being equal to 2.2% in 2018. Relevant differences emerge, however, at the country level: corporate collaborations are equal in 2018 to 5.1%

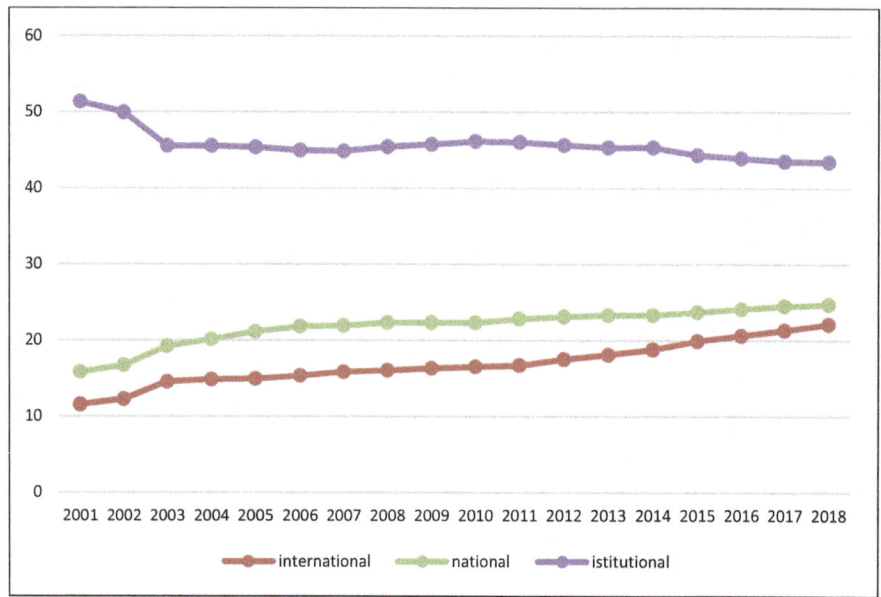

Figure 2: Collaboration types, 2001–2018 (as a share of total publications in STEM fields). Source: authors' elaboration on Scival data.

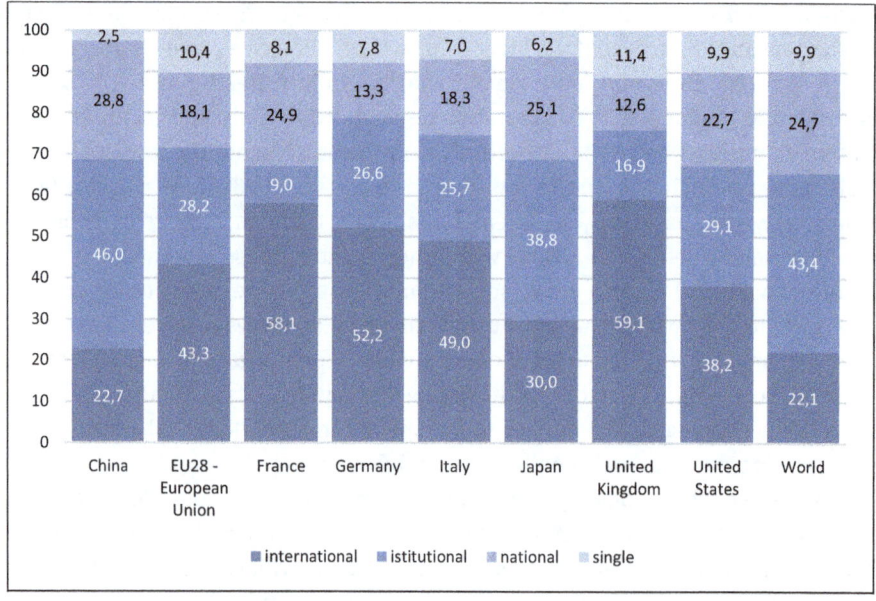

Figure 3: Collaboration types by country, 2018 (as a share of total publications in STEM fields). Source: authors' elaboration on Scival data.

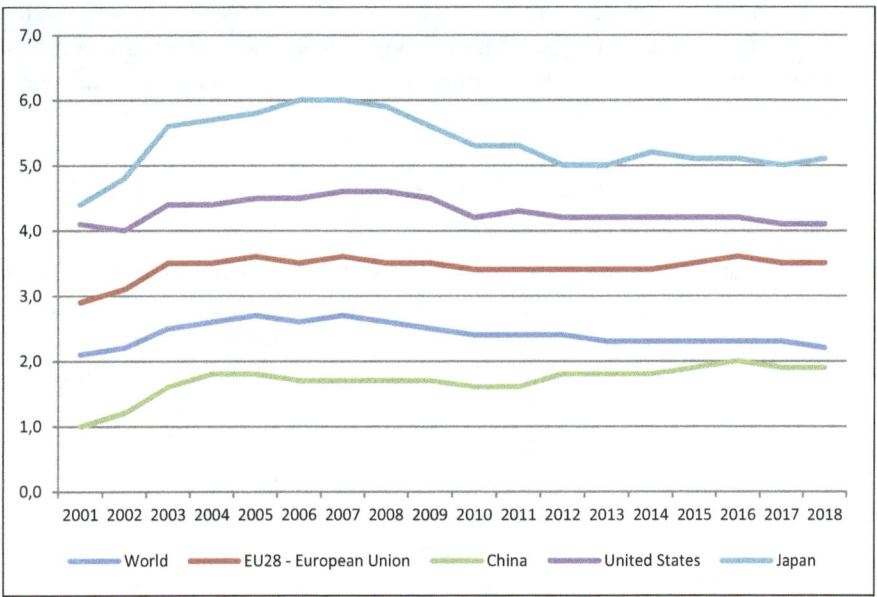

Figure 4: Corporate Collaboration by country, 2001–2018 (as a share of total publications in STEM fields). Source: authors' elaboration on Scival data.

of total publications in Japan and 4.1% in the United States, being stable at around 3% in Europe. On the other hand, they remain quite low in China (1.9%) and in other developing countries (0.9% in India, 1.8% in Russia, 2% in Brazil, among others). University-industry collaborations have indeed been favoured in recent years by technological transfer policies aiming at boosting economic growth (see Lillywhite et al., 2005), even if the actual influence of university-industry collaborations is not clear-cut.

Research Collaborations and Bibliometric Impact

In order to study the bibliometric impact of research collaboration, we consider for each country scientific area and year as well as the citation impact, measured by the Field-Weighed Citation Impact (FWCI, see Research Intelligence, 2019), which takes into account differences in research behaviours across disciplines. FWCI is defined as the ratio of the total citations received at a certain data by the publications, and the total citations that would be expected based on the average of the subject field. Therefore, a Field-Weighted Citation Impact greater than 1 indicates that publications in that particular country/field/year have been cited more than what would be expected based on the world average for similar publications. The indicator has shown a positive trend in recent years in almost all of the countries considered in our analysis; the increase is partly attributable to actual growth of the scientific impact and partly to the general expansion of the Scopus database. Our working hypothesis is that the Field Weighted Citation impact is influenced by different type of collaborations. In doing so, we started by the Fixed effects regression model that can be specified as follows:

$$fwci_{ijt} = \alpha + collaborations^z_{ijt} * \beta^z_{i,j} + year_t * \gamma_t + v_{i,j} + \varepsilon_{ij} \qquad (1)$$

In (1), α is the constant term, $v_{i,j}$ are country and sector specific fixed effects and $\varepsilon_{i,j}$ is the error term. Collaborations include the various forms of co-authorship introduced above: more specifically, we first estimate a model in which we consider the effect of academic and corporate collaborations and then a second model in which we include institutional, national, and international collaborations. In both cases, the sign and magnitude of the β coefficients associated with a z-specific collaboration type should be interpreted as the differential effect with respect to the case of single-author papers. Fixed effect models remove the effect of those time-invariant characteristics that are unique to the country and the sector; they are designed to allow studying the net effect of the predictors (in our case, different kind of collaborations) on the outcome (in our case, the Field Weighted Citation Index). Having rejected the null hypothesis that coefficients for all years are jointly equal to zero, we also include a set of time dummies in order to take into account the time trend in citation impact observed in the period considered. The use of fixed effects versus the random effects model is confirmed by the Hausman test.[2]

In estimating the models, we extend our original dataset, considering 35 countries[3] including all G7 and most of the major new and old industrial countries. According to the literature, we do expect that research collaborations in general, and international collaborations in particular, have a positive effect on research impact, since they allow a larger access to scientific publications and may generate research of higher quality with respect to those that are single-author. The effects of inter-sectoral collaboration are in principle less clear-cut, since corporate collaborations may also be considered to be potentially detrimental to citations in some fields, as a possible consequence of the fact that this kind of collaboration does not pursue scientific impact as its primary target.

However, the residuals of the fixed effects estimation of model 1 are correlated across countries (Pesaran test)[4]; moreover, the overall estimation is affected by heteroscedasticity (Wald test)[5] and by autocorrelation of first order (LM test)[6]. In order to

---

[2] Test di Hausman: Chi-square: 122.62; Prob.>Chi-square: 0.000.
[3] Countries considered are: Australia; Austria; Belgium; Brazil; Canada; China; Czech Republic; Denmark; Finland; France; Germany; Greece; Hungary; India; Ireland; Israel; Italy; Japan; Netherlands; New Zeeland; Norway; Poland; Portugal; Romania; Russian Federation; Slovak Republic; Slovenia; South Africa, South Korea, Spain; Sweden; Switzerland; Turkey; United Kingdom; and United States.
[4] Pesaran's test of cross-sectional independence: -2.353; Prob.:0.0186.
[5] Wald's test for heteroscedasticity: Chi-square: 1028.49; Prob.>Chi-square: 0.000.

overcome the problems mentioned above, we fit a panel-data linear model with fixed effects using the Feasible Generalized Least Squares method (FGLS). It allows controlling in the estimation for the presence of AR(1) autocorrelation within panels and cross-sectional correlation and heteroscedasticity across panels. Table 1 presents the results of the estimation of model 1 estimated with FGLS, considering as predictor the ratio between corporate and academic collaborations, where data on collaboration are expressed as a share of total publications. In this sense, a greater ratio means a greater weight of corporate versus academic collaborations. In the regression model, this ratio may be interpreted as an estimate of the differential effect in terms of citation impact of publishing a corporate collaborative paper with respect to the publication with the academy. We also add the square root[7] of the ratio to evaluate the effect of greater weight of corporate collaborations: this variable is intended to capture a possible non-linear effect of corporate collaborations, in the sense that their impact on normalized citation may differ according to weight of corporate collaborations. Large percentages of corporate collaborations are always significant in all the fields; remarkably, in Engineering they have a negative effect on impact for lower levels of corporate collaborations, having instead a strong positive influence when corporate collaborations are an important share of total publications. On the other hand, the effect of corporate collaborations in Health Sciences is stronger the lower the share of corporate collaborations.

Table 1: Academic and corporate collaborations and bibliometric performance.
    ***: p-value < 0.01; **p-value<0.05; *p-value <0.10
    Source: authors' elaboration on Scival data.

	Overall	Agricultural Sciences	Engineering and Technology	Health Sciences	Natural Sciences
Observations	630	630	630	630	630
Countries	35	35	35	35	35
Years	18	18	18	18	18
Corporate/Academic	1.892	1.774**	-3.476***	5.072***	-0.544
(Corporate/Academic)^0.5	2.463***	2.594***	4.006***	1.294***	3.143***
Constant	0.544***	0.718***	0.573	1.751***	-0.746***

---

6 LM test: F(1,34): 20.853; Prob.>F:0.000.
7 We consider the square root and not the exponential because the ratio is a number between zero and one.

Table 2 presents the results of the estimation over the period 2001–2018 when considering different types of collaborations according to geographical location; again, estimates are performed both at the aggregate level and for each scientific field using FGLS. Also, in this case, data on collaboration are expressed as a share of total publications: coefficients for the various types of collaborations may be interpreted as an estimate of the differential effect in terms of citation impact of publishing a collaborative paper with respect to the publication of a single-author paper. At the aggregate level, only international collaborations have a significant positive effect on scientific impact, whilst institutional collaborations have a negative effect. National collaborations do not play a relevant role. Similar results emerge at the level of each scientific field: international collaborations always have a significant positive effect. At the level of individual scientific sectors, national collaborations have a low positive role in Agricultural Sciences and in Natural Sciences; the effect is negative in Health Sciences. The effect of institutional collaborations is only significant in Health Sciences with a negative influence; in the other fields, no effects are evident.

Table 2: Research collaborations and bibliometric performance.
***: p-value < 0.01; **p-value<0.05; *p-value <0.10
Source: authors' elaboration on Scival data.

	Overall	Agricultural Sciences	Engineering and Technology	Health Sciences	Natural Sciences
Observations	630	630	630	630	630
Countries	35	35	35	35	35
Years	18	18	18	18	18
International collaborations	0.021* **	0.022 ***	0.019*** *	0.008**	0.0208***
Institutional collaborations	-0.011***	-0.002	0.004	-0.034***	0.004
National collaborations	0.002	0.006**	0.005	-0.014*****	0.006**
Constant	0.613***	0.130***	0.468	-2.107***	0.174

Concluding Remarks

Our results confirm the precious role of international collaboration on the scientific impact at country level. The statistical methodology, the dataset, and the presence of small countries are determinant on the obtained results and could influence the statistically significance of covariates. Anyhow, national and institutional collaborations are marginal. Collaborating with the industries carrying out research and development activities rewards scientific impact, with different magnitude, in every field of STEM.

References

Abramo, G, D'Angelo, AC & Murgia, G 2017, 'The relationship among research productivity, research collaboration, and their determinants', *Journal of Informetrics*, vol. 11, no. 4, pp. 1016–30.

Abramo, G, D'Angelo, CA & Solazzi, M 2011, 'The relationship between scientists' research performance and the degree of internationalization of their research', *Scientometrics*, vol. 86, no. 3, pp. 629–43.

Adams, J 2013, 'Collaborations: the fourth age of research', *Nature*, vol. 497, no. 7451, pp. 557–60.

Adams, J, Gurney, K & Marshall, S 2007, Patterns of international collaboration for the UK and leading partners. Report commissioned by the UK Office of Science and Innovation, Evidence Ltd., June.

Bekkers, R & Freitas, IMB 2008, 'Analysing knowledge transfer channels between universities and industry: To what degree do sectors also matter?', *Research policy*, vol. 37, no. 10, pp. 1837–53.

Cicero T & Malgarini, M 2017, 'The effect of research collaboration on citation impact: a dynamic panel data analysis', *Science, Technology and Innovation (STI) Conference*, Paris, September 6, 2017.

Frenken, K, Ponds, R & Van Oort, F 2010, 'The citation impact of research collaboration in science-based industries: A spatial-institutional analysis', *Papers in Regional Science*, vol. 89, no. 2, pp. 351–71.

Goldfinch, S, Dale, T & DeRouen Jr., K 2003, 'Science from the periphery: 25 collaboration, networks and 'periphery effects' in the citation of New Zealand Crown Research Institutes articles, 1995–2000', *Scientometrics*, vol. 57, no. 3, pp. 321–37.

Hausman, JA 1978, 'Specification tests in econometrics', *Econometrica: Journal of the econometric society*, pp. 1251–71.

He, ZL, Geng, XS & Campbell-Hunt, C 2009, 'Research collaboration and research output: A longitudinal study of 65 biomedical scientists in a New Zealand university', *Research Policy*, vol. 38, no. 2, pp. 306–17.

Kato, M & Ando, A 2013, 'The relationship between research performance and international collaboration in Chemistry', *Scientometrics*, vol. 97, no. 3, pp. 535–53.

Katz, JS & Martin, BR 1997, 'What is research collaboration?', *Research policy*, vol. 26, no. 1, pp. 1–18.

Lee, S & Bozeman, B 2005, 'The Impact of Research Collaboration on Scientific Productivity', *Social Studies of Science*, vol. 35, no. 5, pp. 673–702, https://doi.org/10.1177/0306312705052359.

Lillywhite, JM, Jawkes, J & Libbin, J 2005, 'Measuring net benefit resulting from university-industry collaboration. An example from the New Mexico Chile task force', *Western Economics Forum*, 4.

Lissoni, F, Mairesse, J, Montobbio, F & Pezzoni, M 2011, 'Scientific productivity and academic promotion: A study on French and Italian physicists', *Industrial and Corporate Change*, vol. 20, no. 1, pp. 253–94.

Mowery, DC 2007, 'University-industry research collaboration and technology transfer in the United States since 1980', *How universities promote economic growth*, 163.

Pesaran, MH 2007, 'A simple panel unit root test in the presence of cross-section dependence', *Journal of applied econometrics*, 22, no. 2, pp. 265–312.

Research Intelligence 2019, *Research Metrics Guidebook*, Elsevier.

Rybnicek, R & Königsgruber, R 2019, 'What makes industry–university collaboration succeed? A systematic review of the literature', *Journal of Business Economics*, vol. 89, no. 2, pp. 221–50.

Schmoch, U & Schubert, T 2008, 'Are international co-publications an indicator for quality of scientific research?', *Scientometrics*, vol. 74, no. 3, pp. 361–77.

Smeby, J & Try, S 2005, 'Departmental contexts and faculty research activity in Norway', *Research in Higher Education*, vol. 46, no. 6, pp. 593–619.

Sonnenwald, DH 2007, 'Scientific collaboration', in B Cronin (ed.), *Annual Review of Information Science and Technology*, vol. 41, pp. 643–81, Information Today, Medford, NJ.

5.5 On the Need for Accessibility, Standardization, Regulation, and Verification in Bibliometrics: The Leiden Manifesto and Beyond

Dirk Tunger

Abstract: The Leiden Manifesto addresses many points that have crystallized over the years as the majority opinion of the bibliometric community, summarized and bundled in one publication. The 10 bullet points of the manifesto are considered in detail, commented on and put into an overall context of the bibliometric community.

Keywords: Leiden Manifesto, bibliometric community, standardization, bibliometric methods, methods discussion.

Bibliometric analysis has been of increasing importance for science for years, not only with the number of publications in the core journals of the scientific discipline but also as the number of scientific publications in which bibliometrics are used as an application is increasing (cf. e. g. Tunger and Wilhelm, 2013). They are used, for example, for the description of trend developments in science, for benchmarking processes in scientific institutions, in the allocation of third-party funding, and in appointment procedures of scientists. A large number of possible indicators exist which describes the publication behavior and the reception of publications of individual scientists, institutions, countries, publishers or journals. In addition to absolute publication and citation figures, the most prominent examples of this are the h-Index, the Journal Impact Factor (cf. e. g. Tunger, 'The Journal Impact Factor: a bibliometric indicator with a long past', in this handbook) and the positions in rankings usually derived from several indicators.

"Bibliometric analyses will establish themselves in the coming years as an integral part of any scientific assessment" (Ball and Tunger, 2005, p. 51). This statement from 2005 describes relatively precisely the development of the significance of bibliometrics and the bibliometric community in the scientific system in recent years. It may seem very ambitious at first glance, but it has been confirmed in many places in the meantime: examples include the interest in bibliometric methods and results at scientific conferences or publications, the evaluation guidelines of the BMBF (German research ministry) or the development of the bibliometric community (cf. e. g. Tunger and Wilhelm, 2013).

Dirk Tunger, TH Köln, Faculty of Information Science and Communication Studies, Institute of Information Management & Forschungszentrum Jülich GmbH, Project Management Jülich, Center of Excellence "Analyses, Studies, Strategy", d.tunger@fz-juelich.de

Who carries out bibliometric analyses? It can be said that bibliometrics is an interdisciplinary discipline. Mathematicians, sociologists and natural scientists have been joined by information scientists who have developed bibliometrics as a business field in libraries (Ball and Tunger, 2006):

> Information specialists are today at the focus of enormous volumes of data made available worldwide from science and its output. As information professionals they are basically in a position to handle these volumes of data and to distil reliable information from them (Ball and Tunger, 2006, p. 565).

Bibliometrics received a big boost when publication data became available in larger quantities, around 2000. At that time, the Web of Science, which had previously only been available as a CD-ROM edition (but which was already a significant improvement to the book version from the time period before), became available in a flat-rate licensable Internet version. In comparison to the time before the turn of the millennium, when online databases were billed according to the time they were switched on and the amount of data downloaded, the online version was able to do unlimited research on the Web and download data with no additional cost. This led to an exponential development of publications in which bibliometrics was used as a method from 2000 onwards, while the purely scientific publications in the core journals of the bibliometric community recorded only a slight linear increase, approximately proportional to the development of the total volume of publications in Web of Science (Tunger and Wilhelm, 2013, p. 94).

This brief introduction is intended to outline the development of bibliometrics in order to better understand the resulting needs for standardization and regulation. After the turn of the millennium, the use of bibliometrics had entered a major boom phase – parallel to the New Public Management with its performance orientation and benchmarking, which also affected science – which in part led to bibliometrics losing confidence and falling into disrepute (cf e.g: Bild der Wissenschaft, 1993 or Weingart, 1984).

The result was a discussion in the community for a long time, which focused on the framework conditions under which bibliometric analyses should be applied, which restrictions should be observed, and how to deal with indicators (cf. e. g. Tunger et al., 'From Simple Publication Figures to Complex Indicators: Bibliometrics and the Dilemma of Methodological Correctness, Significance, and Economic Necessity', in this handbook).

A major problem that ultimately divides the community is the question of data access. There are few groups that have access to a local installation of a citation database, either to one, two or all of the three big ones (Web of Science, Scopus or Dimensions); this is how they have unlimited access to bibliometric data. Most groups that deal with bibliometrics have to live with the limitations of Web access: in the online version, you can do unlimited research and download data at no extra cost, but this is not unlimited: Web of Science allows 500 publications per download,

Scopus several thousand. This is sufficient for bibliographic applications, but not for bibliometric applications. Especially for the calculation of complex bibliometric indicators, such as field or journal normalizations, the Web interface is not sufficient because the number of required data sets is in the millions.

In the context of the outlined development of the community and the reception of bibliometric analyses, statements over years and decades have manifested themselves among scientists of the bibliometric community, which were later summarized and published as the "Leiden Manifesto" (Hicks et al., 2015) and to which a commentary and explanation by the author of this article is given below:

1. **Quantitative evaluation should support qualitative, expert assessment.**
   Bibliometrics can be an input to discuss and deepen a particular research question with experts and to merge it with information from other data sources.

2. **Measure performance against the research missions of the institution, group or researcher.**
   The indicators used should match the objectives pursued by the scientists and address these objectives.

3. **Protect excellence in locally relevant research.**
   Especially in the humanities and social sciences, journal publications (and even more so in English) are of subordinate importance because the topics dealt with have a local character (e.g. urban studies in a large German city). Here it makes no sense to go only on the basis of bibliometric metrics into journals, for whose readers the topic is not relevant.

4. **Keep data collection and analytical processes open, transparent, and simple.**
   For bibliometric evaluations, it is important that their realization is comprehensible and thus follows scientific principles. This is where one of the problems mentioned above comes into play: since only very few scientists in the bibliometric community have access to a local installation of the Web of Science, only very few scientists are able to verify evaluations with meaningful normalized indicators.

5. **Allow those evaluated to verify data and analysis.**
   In order to be able to check the completeness of the underlying data sets and their accuracy, the scientist or unit under investigation in the focus of the study should be informed before publication or dissemination of the results and should have the possibility to check the data.

6. **Account for variation by field in publication and citation practices.**
   Field-specific publication and citation habits should always be taken into account in all bibliometric evaluations. An important question here is whether the

field studied belongs to those that publish a sufficiently high proportion in sources covered in the selected database.

7. Base assessment of individual researchers on a qualitative judgement of their portfolio.

One has to be very careful with bibliometric evaluations of individuals: due to the small number of cases, results for individuals are always subject to high fluctuations.

A minimum number of publications should be available, otherwise statistics would not work. It should also be noted that individuals can have very different publication frequencies due to very individual curricula vitae, different positions in the scientific system and different practices in institutes, and thus also very different impact. However, this may only be due, for example, to the fact that in some institutions the head of the institute is on nearly every publication and in others not.

8. Avoid misplaced concreteness and false precision.

To specify the Journal Impact Factor to three digits after the comma is nonsense (Clarivate, 2019; Tunger, 'The Journal Impact Factor: a bibliometric indicator with a long past', in this handbook). There are too many errors in the Web of Science databases for that. This must also be stated accordingly in the presentation of results of bibliometric analyses.

9. Recognize the systemic effects of assessment and indicators.

Never create incentives for unintended effects with quantitative evaluations. You want to measure something and that should not be based on what is measured. The best way to achieve this is to always work with a set of indicators and not to highlight individual indicators. Thus there is no crown indicator, even if such a designation is tempting (Hornbostel, 1997).

10. Scrutinize indicators regularly and update them.

The system of science indicators is changing because opportunities are changing and because science policy objectives are changing. Own evaluations and indicators used should always be adapted and updated so that they always reflect the state of the art.

The Leiden Manifesto addresses many points that have crystallized over the years as the majority opinion of the bibliometric community, summarized and bundled in one publication. Only one point was not considered in the Leiden Manifesto: the discussion about the fact that bibliometrics does not measure research quality, but the visibility, perception or resonance of the underlying publications in the scientific world.

Practical experience has shown that it is the visibility and the resonance achieved that can be measured. This is also due to the fact that these terms are much easier to grasp than the concept term "quality", which rightly also has to take into account teaching, third-party funding, honors received and other aspects (cf. Hornbostel, 1997, p. 180; Moed, 2002, p. 731 ff). The errors and the behavior of indicators in the event of errors in existing databases must not be underestimated either (Schmidt, 2018).

For many popular newspapers there is no difference between quality and perception of a scientific work, but when one thinks, for example, about the publications of the geneticist Hwang in the journal *Science* (Hwang et al., 2004, pp. 1669–1674; Hwang et al., 2005, pp. 1777–1783), which were later retracted as fakes (Hwang, 2006a, p. 335; Hwang, 2006b, p. 335), it is not possible to automatically deduce high quality even if the original works are often cited. Ohly also sees this when he asks: "Is scientific quality measured or rather only scientific visibility and resonance?" (Ohly, 2004, p. 106). In information science, the term "perception" is more appropriate, as is the experience at Forschungszentrum Jülich in discussions with scientists. The term "perception", as has often become clear in personal conversations, is also much more easily accepted by scientists.

Stefan Hornbostel is of the opinion that there is no single indicator for quality in research: "There is no 'super indicator' that would provide the ultimate answer to the question of the quality of scientific work" (Hornbostel, 1997, p. 326).

There are also other aspects that could have been dealt with more intensively in the Leiden Manifesto: these include in any case the discussion of the impact factor and its partly wrong use as an impact metric for persons or institutions (so-called cumulative impact factor), on which the impact factor is not oriented at all and about which it therefore cannot make any statement. The impact factor is a pure journal measure and is only applicable on the level of journal impact.

The Leiden Manifesto is, however, a step into the right direction to agree on a minimum basis that is accepted and applied by all as the basis of their own work on research metrics. This discussion must go on and provide further standards in the bibliometric community, so that the question does not have to be "which h-index"? (Bar-Ilan, 2007) So, in the medium term, real standards should be discussed and introduced into the bibliometric community, e. g. on selection criteria for indicators used in research evaluation, as well as standards in the data basis and its correction. In order to achieve this, an important next step would be to allow more people or institutions of the bibliometric community access to a local installation of one of the large publication and citation databases.

References

Ball, R & Tunger, D 2005, Bibliometrische Analysen – Daten, Fakten und Methoden: Grundwissen Bibliometrie für Wissenschaftler, Wissenschaftsmanager, Forschungseinrichtungen und Hochschulen (engl.: Bibliometric Analysis – Data, Facts and Methods: Basic Knowledge about Bibliometrics for Scientists, Science Managers, Research Institutions and Universities), Eigenverlag Forschungszentrum Jülich GmbH, Jülich, ISBN: 978-3-89336-383-4.

Ball, R & Tunger, D 2006, 'Bibliometric analysis – A new business area for information professionals in libraries? Support for scientific research by perception and trend analysis', *Scientometrics*, vol. 66, no. 3, pp. 561–77.

Bar-Ilan, J 2007, 'Which h-index? – A comparison of WoS, Scopus and Google Scholar', *Scientometrics*, vol. 74, no. 2, pp. 257–71.

Bild der Wissenschaft 1993, 'Der Forschungsindex. Eine Messlatte für die Wissenschaft (engl.: The research index. A yardstick for science)', no. 5, pp. 32–39.

Clarivate 2019, A closer look at the Journal Impact Factor numerator. Hrsg. Von Clarivate Analytics, https://clarivate.com/blog/science-research connect/closer-look-journal-impact-factor-numerator/ (July 15, 2020).

Hicks, D, Wouters, P, Waltman, L, de Rijcke, S & Rafols, I 2015, 'Bibliometrics: The Leiden Manifesto for research metrics', *Nature*, vol. 520, pp. 429–31, accessed August 6, 2019, doi: https://doi.org/10.1038/520429a.

Hornbostel, S 1997, Wissenschaftsindikatoren – Bewertungen in der Wissenschaft (engl.: Science Indicators – Assessments in Science), Opladen, Westdeutscher Verlag.

Hwang, WS 2006a, 'Patient-specific embryonic stem cells derived from human SCNT blastocysts (Retraction of Vol. 308, pg. 1777–1783)', *Science*, vol. 311, no. 5759, p. 335.

Hwang, WS 2006b, 'Evidence of a pluripotent human embryonic stem cell line derived from a cloned blastocyst (Retraction of Vol. 303, pg. 1669–1674)', *Science*, vol. 311, no. 5759, p. 335.

Hwang, W, Ryu, Y, Park, J, Park, E, Lee, E, Koo, J, Jeon, H, Lee, B, Kang, S, Kim, S, Ahn, C, Hwang, J, Park, K, Cibelli, J & Moon, S 2004, 'Evidence of a pluripotent human embryonic stem cell line derived from a cloned blastocyst', *Science*, vol. 303, no. 5664, pp 1669–74.

Hwang, W, Roh, S, Lee, B, Kang, S, Kwon, D, Kim, S, Kim, S, Park, S, Kwon, H, Lee, C, Lee, J, Kim, J, Ahn, C, Paek, S, Chang, S, Koo, J, Yoon, H, Hwang, J, Hwang, Y, Park, Y, Oh, S, Kim, H, Park, J, Moon S & Schatten, G 2005, 'Patientspecific embryonic stem cells derived from human SCNT blastocysts', *Science*, vol 308, no. 5729, pp. 1777–83.

Moed, HF 2002, 'The impact-factors debate: the ISI's uses and limits – Towards a critical, informative, accurate and policy-relevant bibliometrics', *Nature*, vol. 415, pp. 731–32.

Ohly, P 2004, Bibliometrie in der Postmoderne. Wissensorganisation und Verantwortung: Gesellschaftliche, ökonomische und technische Aspekte (engl.: Bibliometrics in Postmodernism. Knowledge organisation and responsibility: social, economic and technical aspects.), Proceedings of the 9th Conference of the German Section of the International Society for Knowledge Organization, Duisburg, pp. 103–14.

Schmidt, F 2018, Fehlerabschätzungen bei bibliometrischen Analysen (engl.: Error estimation in bibliometric analyses), Master thesis for the academic degree 'Master of Library and Information Science' at Technische Hochschule Köln, https://publiscologne.thkoeln.de/frontdoor/index/index/start/6/rows/10/sortfield/score/sortorder/desc/searchtype/simple/query/felix/docId/1312 (July 15, 2020).

Tunger, D & Wilhelm, J 2013, 'The bibliometric community as reflected by its own methodology', *J. Sci. Res.*, vol. 2, pp. 92–101.

Weingart, P & Winterhager, M 1984, Die Vermessung der Forschung – Theorie und Praxis der Wissenschaftsindikatoren (engl. The Measurement of Research – Theory and practice of science indicators), Campus Verlag, Frankfurt am Main.

5.6 Gender and Bibliometrics: A Review

Tahereh Dehdarirad

Abstract: This study provides a comprehensive review of the literature regarding the main bibliometric indicators in relation to gender and the underlying factors which have an effect on the research productivity and impact of female and male scholars. The main indicators studied in the literature were the number of publications, the number of citations, self-citations, Journal Impact Factor, h-Index, authorship positions, and collaboration patterns. The literature on the visibility of scholars from the point of social media metrics has also been appraised. Underlying factors have a complex and inconclusive impact on productivity. The literature was divided into two groups, based on personal and structural factors.

Keywords: academia, bibliometrics, bibliometric indicators, causing factors, gender differences.

Introduction

Gender inequality is a persistent feature in all modern societies. It is a global problem that hinders development, productivity, and economic growth (World Bank, 2012; Bandiera and Natraj, 2013; Thelwall et al., 2018). While progress has been made to reduce gender inequality, changes can be slow and are subject to significant variation in relation to factors such as country and research field (LERU, 2012). Within academia, gender imbalance amongst researchers still remains. In 2015, only one third of researchers in the EU were women. Women are also underrepresented in high academic positions; in 2017, women made up only 27% of the members of boards of research organisations (European Commission, 2019).

These gender gaps have prompted numerous studies to look at various aspects of gender inequality in Science and Technology, using different bibliometric indicators. Various studies have sought to identify the factors causing these inequalities, especially in relation to scientific performance and impact. Studying women's contribution to Science and higher education can provide an insight into the gender gap in scientific activities and the resulting gender imbalance (Leahey, 2006). This can assist us in the understanding the factors behind these inequalities (Fox, 2005).

The aim is to provide a comprehensive review of the literature, from different disciplines, time periods, and diverse national and international settings. This study has two main objectives:
i) Understanding the main bibliometric indicators being studied regarding gender

---

Tahereh Dehdarirad, Chalmers University of Technology, Department of Communication and Learning in Science, Göteborg, Sweden, Tahereh.Dehdarirad@chalmers.se

ii) Understanding the underlying factors and variables which have had an effect on the research productivity and impact female and male scholars

Methodology

For both objectives, scientific papers related to bibliometric indicators and gender were identified. This was done by conducting a search of electronic databases such as Google Scholar, Medline, Springer, PubMed, Science Direct, Scopus, and Web of Science, using a combination of relevant key terms. The proceedings of relevant conferences such as ISSI, STI, and Nordic Workshop were checked manually where they were not indexed in bibliographical databases. Additionally, to ensure that recent research trends in this subject area were captured, the references of the most recent papers were checked. Although this literature review aims to be as comprehensive as possible, it should be considered that some studies may not have been included.

The key terms used for gender and each bibliometric indicator (first objective) are shown in Table 1. Wildcards and truncation were used in the search strategy. Furthermore, the search was not limited to a specific time period.

Table 1: Bibliometric indicators studied in relation to gender and a summary of the most common key terms used in the search queries.

Indicator	Search key terms
Gender	Gender, women, men, female, male, sex, gender equality, gender difference, gender equity
Bibliometrics	Bibliometrics, scientometrics, informetrics, webometrics
Publication productivity	(Scientific) productivity, publication productivity, number of publications, productivity puzzle, research productivity, publication
Research impact and visibility (traditional metrics)	(normalized, field weighted) Citation, Impact factor, H-index, (scientific, research) impact, Hirsch index, self-citation
Social media visibility (altmetrics)	Social media, Altmetrics, alternative metrics
Collaboration	(national/international/cross-gender) collaboration, co-authorship, number of collaborators, homophily in collaboration
Authorship positions and author by-line order	authorship, author(ship) order (position), first, last, corresponding authorship

For the second objective, the results of the studies were divided into two main categories, individual and structural factors. This was done as per studies by Zainab

(1999) and Abramo, D'Angelo and Caprasecca (2009a). Table 2 provides a summary of the main variables studied in each group of factors in relation to the literature.

Table 2: Two main factors and their corresponding variables studied in relation to gender and bibliometrics literature.

Individual	Structural
Academic and physical age	
Rank	
Discipline	Climate (Culture)
Marriage and marital status	Workload (teaching load)
Presence and number of children	Access to resources and funding
Marriage and marital status	
Scholars' level of specialization and research topic of an article	

Bibliometric Indicators Studied with Regard to Gender

This section provides an overview of the literature regarding the bibliometric indictors which have been studied in relation to gender.

Number of Publications

In terms of the number of publications characterized by Cole and Zuckerman (1984) as a productivity puzzle, the literature generally supports the view that women have lower publication rates compared to men (Cole and Zuckerman, 1984; Xie and Shauman, 1998; Prpić,, 2002; Sax et al., 2002; Bordons et al., 2003; Fox, 2005; Gallivan and Benbunan-Fich, 2006; Mauleón and Bordons, 2006; Symonds et al., 2006; Abramo, et al., 2009a, 2009b; Puuska, 2010; D'Amico, Vermigli, and Canetto, 2011; Larivière et al., 2013; Rørstad and Aksnes, 2015; Cameron, White, and Gray, 2016; Bendels et al., 2018). A small number of studies have found no significant publication gaps between men and women (Gupta, Kumar, and Aggarwa, 1999; Lewison, 2001; Bordons et al., 2003; Tower, Plummer, and Ridgewell, 2007; Mauleón, Bordons, and Oppenheim, 2008; Borrego et al., 2010; Sotudeh and Khoshian, 2014). Some studies have shown that the gap seems to decrease or can disappear over time (Abramo et al., 2009b; van Arensbergen, van der Weijden, and van den Besselaar, 2012).

Research Impact and Visibility

The research impact and visibility of female and male scholars has been evaluated in different studies and using various indicators such as the number of citations, self-citations/citing behaviour, journal impact factor, h-index, and social media metrics.

Number of Received Citations

Regarding the number of received citations, the literature in different countries and fields has shown mixed results.

Some research suggests that women's publications are cited at lower rates than those of men. In their study on a sample of tenure-track and tenured linguists and sociologists, Hunter and Leahy (2010) found that women were at a disadvantage in terms of the number of received citations, even after controlling for children. The results of a large-scale study of 8,500 Norwegian researchers in different fields showed that the publications of female researchers were cited less than men (Aksnes et al., 2011). Pudovkin et al. (2012) concluded that male scientists were more prolific and cited more often than females in their study on 313 papers of research staff at the Deutsche Rheuma-Forschungszentrum. The results of a study on some prestigious geography journals also showed that citation rates were highest for articles either singly or collaboratively authored by males (Rigg, McCarragher, and Krmenec, 2012). In the field of International Relations (IR), Maliniak, Powers, and Walter (2013) found that women were systematically less cited than men, after controlling for factors such as year and location of publication, tenure status, and institutional affiliation. They concluded this is because women generally cite themselves less than men, and men, who make up a disproportionate share of IR scholars, tend to cite men more than women. In a large-scale global and cross-disciplinary study, Larivière et al. (2013) discovered that when a woman was in first or last authorship position, the paper attracted fewer citations than when a man was in one of these positions. Caplar, Tacchella, and Birrer's (2017) study of 200,000 publications in five major Astronomy journals during the period of 1950–2015 showed that male first authored articles received more citations than female. The result of a more recent study on a set of articles in 54 journals listed in Nature Index showed that articles with female key (first or last) authors were cited less frequently than articles with male key authors (Bendels et al., 2018).

In contrast, some researchers have found that women receive more citations per paper than men. Long (1992)'s pioneering study on the productivity of biochemists in the United States (US) concluded that the average number of citations per publication for women was higher than that of men. In a study of 721 PhDs holders from Spanish universities (1990–2002), Borrego et al. (2010) found that articles authored by female PhD holders were cited significantly more often, even when self-citations were excluded. In another study on research staff at the Deutsche Rheuma-Forschungszentrum, Kretschmer, Pudovkin, and Stegmann (2012) classified the staff in two sub-groups of "high-end (star)" (25% of the population) scientists and the complementary (75% of the population). The results revealed that female researchers performed slightly better than their male counterparts in the large complementary subgroup, although this was not the case with the star scientists. According to a study on a global sample of 26,783 publications in the field of Management, marginal difference in citation impact was found in favour of female scholars. Women were also slightly more likely than men to publish the top 10% most cited papers (Nielsen, 2017). A more recent study on publications from core Neurosurgery journals demonstrated that female neurosurgery scientists were slightly less prolific in terms of scientific productivity. However, women were slightly more visible regarding citations (Sotudeh, Dehdarirad, and Freer, 2018). Card et al. (2019) found that female authored papers received about 25% more citations than observably similar male authored papers in their study on 53 Economics journals.

In addition, some studies found no difference in citation rates between males and females. In the field of Library and Information Science, Peñas and Willett (2006) found that male academics published significantly more papers on average than female authors, but there was no significant difference in the numbers of citations. Symond et al. (2006) found no difference in the median number of citations per paper for males and females in a study on the publication records of 168 life scientists in the fields of Ecology and Evolutionary Biology at British and Australian universities. The result of a study on surgical research found no significant gender difference in the mean number of citations per publication (Housri et al., 2008). Studying gender differences in citation rates for dendrochronologists, Copenheaver et al. (2010) found no effect of gender on a paper's probability to be cited. They suggested that the high productivity of female dendrochronologists and co-authoring with male colleagues makes male scholars aware of their work, thus eliminating citation gender bias. The results of a systematic evaluation of articles published in the *Journal of Peace Research* for the period of 1983–2008 found no evidence of gender bias in terms of citation counts (Østby et al., 2013). Sotudeh and Khoshian's (2014) study in the field of Nanoscience showed no significant differences between the mean impacts of male and female researchers.

Self-citation

The literature on self-citation generally tends to agree on the lower propensity of women to self-cite. The results of a study of 12 International Relations journals between 1980 and 2006 found that women cited their own work significantly less often than men (Maliniak et al., 2013). In a study of 12,725,171 articles from different disciplines, Ghiasi, Larivière, and Sugimoto (2016a) found that men received citations from their own papers at a higher rate than women. Men also tend to give more citations to their own publications. The result of a study on the publications of 1,512 scholars in the field of Ecology found that 8.5% of women's and 10.5% of men's citations were self-citations. The difference in self-citations resulted in higher h-index scores for men (Cameron et al., 2016). Using a data set of 1.5 million research papers from JSTOR between 1779 and 2011, King et al. (2017) found that overall men cited their own papers 56% more than women, and in the last two decades, men self-cited 70% more than women.

However, there are a few studies that have found no gender differences in self-citation. A study of papers in five Archaeology journals found that men tend to cite themselves slightly more often than women. However, this trend was not statistically significant, leading the author to conclude that there was no gender difference in self-citation (Hutson, 2006). The results of a more recent study using 1.6 million papers from PubMed demonstrated that gender had the lowest effect on the probability of self-citation, amongst an extensive set of factors. The authors concluded that productive authors self-cited, regardless of their gender (Mishra et al., 2018).

Journal Impact Factor

Studies on journal impact factor have produced mixed findings. While some have highlighted the similarity of the journals in which women and men published (Lewison, 2001; Bordons et al., 2003; Mauleón, Bordons, and Oppenheim, 2008; Barrios, Villarroya, and Borrego, 2013; Dehdarirad and Nasini, 2017), some have shown higher impact factor for journals in which men published (Nielsen, 2016; Mihaljević-Brandt, Santamaría, and Tullney, 2016; Bendels et al., 2018). In a study of 3,293 male and female researchers in all fields at Aarhus University, Nielsen (2016) found that except for the natural sciences, men tend to publish in journals with a slightly higher impact factor than women. Analyzing the scholarly output of ~150,000 mathematicians from 1970–2010, Mihaljević-Brandt et al. (2016) found that female authors published significantly less in the top journals compared to their male counterparts. Analyzing the publications of all full professors in Psychology in Germany, Mayer and Rathmann (2018) found that on average men published 0.9 more articles in top journals than women. In their study on 293,557 research articles from 54 journals listed in the Nature Index, Bendels et al. (2018) found a large negative correlation between the 5-Year-Impact-Factor of a journal and female representation in first and last authorship positions. Analyzing publications in Biology and Computational Biology from the PubMed and arXiv databases, Bonham and Stefan (2017) found a significant negative correlation between impact factor and the proportion of female authors for the Biology dataset. By contrast, no significant correlation was found in Computational Biology.

There are studies that have shown that women tend to publish in higher impact journals. An analysis of publications of 333 Spanish scientists (1996–2000) in Materials Science showed that women in the research scientist category, on average, publish in higher impact factor journals than men in the same rank (Mauleón and Bordons, 2006). In a study on Surgery publications, Housri et al. (2008) found that the average impact factor of journals in which women published was significantly higher than men. Studying the scientific output of 731 PhD holders in Spain, Borrego et al. (2010) demonstrated that the journals where female PhD holders had published had a significantly higher median impact factor than those in which male PhD holders had published. Similarly, in their study on female engineers, Ghiasi, Larivière, and Sugimoto (2016) found that women published papers in journals with higher impact factors than their male peers.

h-index

The results of some studies in different fields have suggested that women have an overall lower h-index compared with men. Studying Otolaryngology faculty members' publications in the US, Eloy et al. (2013) found that men had significantly higher h-indices than women. The results of Holiday's (214) study among US academic radiation oncology faculty members showed that men have higher H-indices overall than their female counterparts. Carter's et al. (2017) study in the field of Social Science showed that men had higher h-Index scores than women. Analyzing the publications of 1,712 academic neurologists from top-ranked US neurology programs, McDermott et al. (2018) demonstrated that men had a higher log Scopus h-index than women, after adjustment for years since medical school graduation.

Some studies have found no overall gender differences (Diamond et al., 2016) or differences after accounting for certain variables such as self-citations and non-research active years (Cameron et al., 2016). Several studies on gender differences in h-index have also investigated these differences based on academic rank of scholars. The results of these studies are reported in the section *Individual factors and characteristics, Rank.*

Social Media Metrics

Some studies have addressed gender disparities in social media metrics. These studies do not seem to be conclusive. Some have found that females showed a higher visibility in terms of Web citations (Kretschmer and Aguillo, 2005), average Mendeley readers (Bar-Ilan and Van der Weijden, 2015; Sotudeh et al., 2018), profile views on Academia.Edu in certain disciplines (Thelwall and Kousha, 2014), or event counts from Twitter (Paul-Hus et al., 2015; Sotudeh et al., 2018), blogs, and news (Paul-Hus et al., 2015). In contrast, some others showed higher visibility for male authors in terms of average Mendeley readers (Sotudeh, Dehdarirad, and Pooladian, 2016), or even similar visibility as males in blogs, news, on Facebook, or LinkedIn (Sotudeh et al., 2018). A recent study by Thelwall (2018) found that the number of readers was different for female scholars in different countries. For example, female authored research had fewer Mendeley readers in India, but more in Spain, Turkey, the UK, and the USA.

Collaboration Patterns

The literature on gender differences in scientific collaboration mainly focuses on three topics. These are studies related to the impact of gender on the number of collaborators, cross-gender or single gender collaboration, and international collaboration.

Impact of Gender on Collaboration and the Number of Collaborators

The literature generally agrees that men collaborate more than women (Bozeman and Corley, 2004; Lee and Bozeman, 2005; Özel, Kretschmer and Kretschmer, 2013). Additionally, women tend to have fewer collaborators than men (Bozeman and Corley, 2004; Lee and Bozeman, 2005). In a study on Turkish publications in Social Science, Özel, et al. (2013) found that male authors are in general keener to collaborate than females. By analyzing publication records of 3,980 faculty members in six Science, Technology, Engineering, and Mathematical (STEM) disciplines at US research universities, Zeng et al. (2016) found that female faculty members have significantly fewer co-authors during their careers than males. They associated this difference to females' lower publication rate and shorter career lengths. Analyzing articles published between 1970 and 2011 in 1,627 Economics journals indexed in the EconLit database, Ductor, Goyal, and Prummer (2018) found that women have fewer collaborators.

Some studies have found that women are more likely to collaborate (Bozeman and Gaughan, 2011; Abramo, D'Angelo and Murgia, 2013). Using data from an NSF-funded Survey of Academic Researchers conducted in the United States in 2004 to 2005, Bozeman and Gaughan (2011) found that men and women differ relatively little with respect to research collaborations. They also found that women have more collaborators, especially when controlling for structural and climate factors. Similarly, in a study on the scientific publications of Italian professors from 11 subject areas, Abramo et al. (2013) demonstrated that female researchers are generally more likely to collaborate than their male colleagues. They linked this finding to women's higher percentage of co-authored publications.

In contrast some studies have shown no gender differences in collaboration or number of collaborators (Hunter and Leahy, 2008; Savic et al., 2018). Studying a sample of articles in two leading Sociology journals between 1935 and 2005, Hunter and Leahey (2008) found no significant gender differences in rates of collaboration. They attributed this finding to the progress of women within this field. Analyzing the publications of researchers employed in the Faculty of Sciences at the University of Novi

Sad in Serbia, Savic et al. (2018) found that female and male researchers have a similar number of collaborators.

Cross-gender Collaboration and Homophily in Collaboration

In terms of homophily in collaboration, some studies have suggested that women are involved in same gender collaborations more than men. Additionally, women have more female collaborators than male (McDowell and Smith, 1992; Bozeman and Corley, 2004; Boschini and Sjogren, 2007). In one of the first studies on this topic, McDowell and Smith's (1992) study examined the publications of a sample of 178 PhD holders from the top 20 United States institutions between 1969 and 1986. They found that women were over five times more likely than men to have female co-authors. Examining data from 451 scientists and engineers at academic research centres in the United States, Bozeman and Corley (2004) found that female scientists had a higher percentage (36%) of female collaborators than males (24%). However, they found that there are great differences, according to rank, with non-tenure track females having 84% of their collaborations with females, whereas for tenured females the figure was 34%. Boschini and Sjogren (2007) found that women are more than twice as likely as men to have a female co-author in their analysis of articles published in three Economics journals. The results of a slightly more recent study in the fields of Criminology and Criminal Justice have also indicated that females are more likely to publish with other female authors (Crow and Smykla, 2015). The results of another study in the same fields between 1974 and 2014 also demonstrated that women are more likely to publish papers with other females (Zettler, Cardwell, and Craig, 2017).

By contrast, other studies have found a higher propensity for women to partake in cross-sex collaboration (Fisher et al, 1998; Zawacki-Richter and von Prümmer, 2010) or a higher propensity of men in homophily and inter-gender collaboration (Fisher et al., 1998; Farrell and Smyth, 2014; Araújo et al., 2017). Fisher et al. (1998) found in a study of three leading journals in Political Science that over half of the articles published by women resulted from cross-sex collaboration. In contrast, men appear more likely to author articles on their own or co-author with other men. The results of Zawacki-Richter and von Prümmer's (2010) study on papers published in five prominent Distance Education journals indicated that more women than men collaborate with members of the opposite sex. In their study on articles published in the Group of Eight (Go8) Law Reviews in Australia, Farrell and Smyth (2014) showed that men collaborate with other men much more often than women collaborate with other women. They postulated that a reason for this might be the existence of "old boy networks" in male dominated professions, which women find difficult to access. By analyzing a unique dataset of more than 270,000 scientists in different fields in Brazil, Araújo et al. (2017) discovered that while men were more likely to collaborate with other men, women were open to collaborate with either sex.

In contrast, some studies found a similar tendency for female and male scholars for inter-sex collaboration (Holman and Morandin, 2019) or to collaborate with men (Ghiasi, Larivière, and Sugimoto, 2016b). For example, the results of Holman and Morandin's (2019) study on 9.15 million articles indexed on PubMed and arXiv demonstrated that both female and male researchers preferentially collaborate with colleagues of the same gender across Life Sciences. Ghiasi et al. (2016b) found that engineers, regardless of their gender, generally collaborate with men, due to the male dominated nature of the field.

International Collaboration

Regarding gender differences in terms of international collaboration, published data suggests that women on average have lower rates of international collaboration than men. This finding has been consistent in different countries such as the US (Frehill and Zippel, 2011), Canada (Larivière et al., 2011), Italy (Abramo et al., 2013) and Norway (Aksnes, Piro, and Rørstad, 2019). Similarly, the results of a bibliometric analysis at a global level by Elsevier (2017) demonstrated that women were less likely than men to collaborate internationally. In contrast, the results of the *She Figures* report by the European Commission (2015) reported only marginal gender differences in international collaboration, with women having almost equal propensity to publish articles with international co-authors.

Authorship Positions and Author By-line Order

Some studies have found that women are underrepresented in first and or last authorship positions. In a global scale analysis of scientific publication from different disciplines, Larivière et al. (2013) found that women were underrepresented as first authors. Additionally, for every article with a female first author, there were nearly two (1.93) articles first-authored by men. Studying the manuscripts submitted to the *Journal of Evolutionary Biology* (*JEB*) between 2012 and 2016, Edwards, Schroeder, and Dugdale (2018) found an underrepresentation of female authors in first and last positions. They linked this finding to the lower publication rate of women compared with men. In a study on articles published in clinical and basic Science journals with high-impact factors between 2005 and 2014, Aakhus et al. (2018) found that women were less likely than men to be listed as first author in articles published in clinical journals.

Another group of studies has found that women are more likely to appear at first authorship position and less at last authorship position, which is associated with seniority. Analysing Clinical Ophthalmology literature published between 2000 and 2009, Shah et al. (2013) found an increasing trend in the percentage of female first and last authorship positions. However, there were fewer female last authors compared to female first authors. Studying female authorship in prominent General Radiology journals between 1993 and 2013, Liang et al. (2015) found that women continued to remain a minority, especially in last (senior) authorship positions. Furthermore, when comparing female representation in different authorship positions, female senior authorship consistently remained significantly lower than first authorship during this period. Schisterman et al. (2017) found that females were more likely to be first authors, but less likely to be last authors in a study conducted in the field of Epidemiology between 2008 and 2012. Similar results were also reported by Fox, Ritchey, and Paine (2018) when studying two data sets in the field of Ecology between 2009 and 2015. In an analysis of 9.15 million academic papers in STEMM (Science, Technology, Engineering, Mathematics, and Medicine) published since 2002 and indexed in PubMed and arXiv, Holman, Stuart-Fox, and Hauser (2018) found that in almost all disciplines women were substantially underrepresented as last (senior) authors and overrepresented as first (junior) authors. Similar results have been also found in the fields of Internal Medicine (Gayet-Ageron, Poncet, and Perneger, 2019), Contemporary Psychology (González-Álvarez and Cervera-Crespo, 2019) and Psychiatry (Hart, Frangou, and Perlis, 2019).

Despite the existence of gender gap, some studies have found improvement in the gender gap and an increase in the presence of women in key authorship positions over time. In a study of JSTOR papers published between 1990–2012, West et al. (2013) found that prior to 1990 women were significantly underrepresented in the first author position. However, since 1990, this gap has almost been closed. Analyzing publications in the *Journal of Bone and Mineral Research (JBMR)* between 1986 and 2015, Wininger et al. (2017) found a significant increase in the percentage of female first authors over time, from 35.8% in 1986 to 47.7% in 2015. Studying authorship patterns in the *Journal of Orthopaedic Research (JOR)*, Seetharam et al. (2018) found an increase in both female first and corresponding authorship positions between 1983 and 2015. They concluded that this may have been due to an increase in the number of women entering the field and the percentage of women on the JOR editorial board and in leadership positions. Analyzing papers published in the *Annals of Biomedical Engineering* from 1986 to 2016, Aguilar et al. (2019) showed that the percentage of both female first and corresponding authors increased over the past 30 years and have almost become equal. Similarly, in their study on papers published in four major Musculoskeletal Science journals between 1985 and 2015, Russel et al. (2019) found an increase in women as both first and corresponding authors.

Factors

Analyzing gender difference in scientific productivity without controlling for all relevant variables may lead to biased results, as some of these underlying variables may be the cause of differences observed (Mayer and Rathmann, 2018). As a result of this, some studies have analyzed the gender gap in publication productivity and impact when controlling for different factors. These factors can be categorized in two different groups, individual and structural or environmental. The following sections will provide an overview of these studies and the main factors that have an effect on publication and impact. However, it should be considered that the main focus will be on factors in relation to scientific productivity.

Individual Factors

Regarding individual factors, the literature has mainly focused on age, discipline, the presence of children, and marital status, amongst others.

Academic and Physical Age

Considering career length, Long (1992) and Symonds et al. (2006) found that women produce fewer publications than men during the first decade of their career, but by the later stages of their career they have a similar number of publications as male researchers. Similarly, in a study conducted on academic psychologists in United States, Joy (2006) found that men tend to publish more than women during their initial push for tenure, but not thereafter, whereas women tend to publish more as they mature professionally. The difference between publication productivity and citation impact between female and male researchers in Germany was also smaller for senior[1] researchers compared to that of junior[2] and mid-career[3] researchers (Pan and Kalinaki, 2015). In a survey of young researchers from the main research institutions in Thailand and Malaysia, Beaudry and St-Pierre (2016) found that young women produced fewer publications in their early career but were more productive as they grew older. In a study on the scholarly output of ~150,000 mathematicians, Mihaljević-Brandt, Santamaría, and Tullney (2016) found that women published less than men at the beginning of their careers. Their findings showed that men were shown to publish on average 9% and 13% more papers than women within their first five and 10 years as authors, respectively.

In contrast, some researchers have found no differences between genders in their early career (van Arensbergen et al., 2012) and others have found differences in their late career (Mauleón et al., 2008; van den Besselaar and Sandström, 2016). In their study of life scientists at the Spanish National Research Council (CSIC), Mauleón et al. (2008) found that women with intermediate levels of seniority

---

[1] Scholars with more than 10 years since first publication.
[2] Scholars with more than 10 years since first publication.
[3] Scholars with 5–10 years since their first publications.

(11–20 and 21–30 years of working life) had lower productivity than their male counterparts. In a study of 852 Dutch social scientists, van Arensbergen et al. (2012), found that scientific productivity differences between the sexes were small to non-existent among young researchers.[4] Using the same sample, van den Besselaar and Sandström (2016) compared the performance levels of female and male scholars over a 10-year period, starting from three years after the completion of their PhD. They found male researchers were more productive during this period and that the productivity gap increased during the 10-year period. Regarding physical age, studying data on research output from the University of Iceland, Zoega (2017) found that men tend to produce more publications than women in their thirties and forties but less in their fifties and sixties.

Rank

Regarding academic rank, a number of studies agree that the performance gap between the sexes seems to decline with career progress. Eloy et al. (2013)'s study on Otolaryngology in the US indicated that women produce less research output earlier in their careers than men, but at senior levels they equal or exceed the research productivity of men. Studying gender differences among radiation oncologists at U.S. academic institutions, Holliday et al. (2014) found that men had a higher number of publications and a higher median h-index compared to women. However, after controlling for rank, these differences were largely non-significant. They concluded that women who achieved senior status had productivity metrics comparable to their male counterparts. The results of a study among Gynaecologic Oncology faculty members in the United States demonstrated that men had significantly higher H-indices at the Assistant Professor level. However, this difference disappeared at higher professional levels (Hill et al., 2015). Diamond et al. (2016) found that female gastroenterologists holding senior faculty positions were equally as productive as their male counterparts. Similarly, in a more recent study of the faculty members from top-ranked US Neurology programmes, McDermott et al. (2018) found that men had more publications than women at all academic ranks, but the disparity in publication number decreased with advancing rank.

In contrast to the previously mentioned studies, others have reported better performance for women in the earlier stages of their career (Battaglia et al., 2019) or a bigger gender gap in performance at senior positions (Valsangkar et al., 2016; Carter et al., 2017). For example, in a study in the field of Emergency Radiology, Battaglia et al. (2019) found that academic productivity at the rank of assistant professor was significantly higher for women than men. Valsangkar et al. (2016) found that in all academic ranks in science or research divisions, the numbers of publications and cita-

---

[4] Having finished their PhD studies within the last 3 years.

tions among female surgical faculty members were lower than men. This difference was more pronounced at senior academic ranks. Similarly, in a study of Social Work faculty members in doctoral programmes in the United States, Carter et al. (2017) found that the gender gap in productivity, measured as h-index, was the largest at the full professor level and smallest at the associate professor level, where women's h-Index scores were close to those of men.

Some other studies have reported mixed results in relation to academic ranks. Carleton, Parkerson, and Horswill (2012) found that in Clinical Psychology men published significantly more than women at assistant and full professorial ranks, but not at the associate rank. Choi, Fuller, and Thomas' (2009) study among Radiation Oncology faculty members at U.S. academic institutions found an overall lower h-index for female radiation oncologists. However, when stratified by academic rank, the gender differences disappeared. Similarly, Tomei's et al. (2014) study of neurological surgeons' publications found no statistical differences in h-index at assistant, associate, and full professor ranks.

Discipline

Some studies have investigated gender differences in productivity based on academic rank of scholars and discipline.

When studying publication rate by gender and rank in different disciplines among Norwegian university researchers, the results were different for each discipline (Rørstad and Aksnes, 2015). In Natural Sciences, Engineering & Technology and Social Sciences, on average, female scientists tended to have lower publication rates than their male colleagues for all positions. In Medicine, female professors and associate professors were slightly more productive than their male colleagues, whereas in Humanities male professors and male PhD students had higher publication rates. In a study of 33,000 Italian research scientists from Technology and Science disciplines, Abramo et al. (2009b) found that men had an overall higher performance than women. However, in Physical and Chemical Sciences, female full and associate professors published more than their male counterparts. In Earth Sciences, female assistant professors had higher outputs than their male colleagues. When comparing publication rate by discipline only, van Arensbergen et al. (2012) found that in Economics, performance differences existed between female and male young Dutch scholars, whereas in Psychology, the differences were not statistically significant. Similarly, in a study on peer-reviewed articles by Social Scientists in the U.K., Bird (2011) found that within certain disciplines such as Social Policy and Psychology that have relatively high proportions of female academics, publication productivity was almost equal. It was concluded that the number of women within a discipline might be important, as a "critical mass" of women may facilitate career progression, including publication productivity. A large-scale study on seven Science, Technology, Engineering, and Mathematics (STEM) disciplines conducted by Duch et al. (2012)

showed that for disciplines such as Molecular Biology, where research expenditures were high, females consistently published at a rate significantly lower than males. However, in Industrial Engineering, no significant difference between the genders was observed. In their study on a large sample of articles in STEMM disciplines, Holman and Stuart-Fox (2018) found that the gender gap in authorship appears to persist for STEMM fields, particularly Surgery, Computer Science, Physics, and Mathematics. However, in Social Sciences and Speech-Language Pathology, women publish more than 50% of the papers.

Presence and Number of Children

Regarding children and faculty members' role as parents, several authors have underlined the fact that having children has an adverse impact on publication productivity. As indicated in Hargens et al. (1978)'s study on research chemists in the United States, rearing children potentially reduces the amount of time for writing papers, which could reduce professional performance in terms of productivity or visibility. In a study on a sample of full-time academic Medical School faculty members in USA, Carr et al. (1998) found that compared to men with children, women with children had fewer publications. However, there were no significant differences between the sexes for faculty members without children. Hunter and Leahey (2010) analyzed the effects of children on the entire careers of female and male academics in Linguistics and Sociology in research universities in the United States. Their findings suggest that having children accounts for part of the productivity gender gap in these academic disciplines and attributed this to typical division of labor in the home. Beaudry and St-Pierre (2016) found that women who had children were less productive in comparison to their male counterparts with children.

Some studies have found that having children may or may not reduce research productivity, when the age of children is taken into account (Kyvik, 1990; Kyvik and Teigen, 1996; Stack, 2004; Fox, 2005; Abramo et al., 2009b; Krapf, Ursprung, and Zimmermann, 2014). This is because children of different ages demand different amounts of attention from their parents (Hunter and Leahy, 2010). In a sample of all academic fields, Kyvik (1990) found that women who have children are more productive than women without children, but the age of the children has an effect on productivity. In comparison with men, women with young children are less productive than their male counterparts, but women whose children are aged 10 years or older are just as productive as men in the same family situation and academic position (Kyvik, 1990; Kyvik and Teigen, 1996). The authors suggested women may take more responsibility than men for preschool and early school-age children. Similarly, in a sample of PhD recipients in Science (including Social Science) and Engineering, Stack (2004) found that female scientists with pre-school children were less productive than other scientists, even when compared to women with multiple children in other age ranges. The author suggested this was due to the fact that young children require more parental attention.

In contrast to previous studies, Fox (2005) found that women engineers and scientists with pre-school children were more productive than their childless counterparts or women with school age children. Fox suggested that women scientists with pre-school children allocate their time better for research. In a more recent study, Krapf et al. (2017) conducted research on the effect of pregnancy and parenthood on the research productivity of nearly 10,000 Economists registered in the RePEc (Research Papers in Economics) database. Their findings revealed that mothers of at least two children are on average more productive than mothers of only one child, and that mothers in general are more productive than childless women. They linked this finding to planned motherhood.

Marriage and Marital Status

Regarding marital status, mixed results have been reported. The positive effect of marriage on the scientific and academic performance of both female and male academics has been reported in studies by Luukkonen-Gronow and Stolte-Heiskanen (1983) and Long (1990). However, other studies reported the positive effect of marriage only on female academics (Aiston and Jung, 2015; Juraqulova, Byington, and Kmec, 2015). Juraqulova et al. (2015) found that women in STEM and non-STEM fields believed they were more productive as a result of marriage compared to their male counterparts.

Nevertheless, some other studies have found a positive relation between marriage and scientific impact for only male academics (Prpić, 2002; Hancock and Baum, 2010). Studying a sample of 840 young scientists in Croatia, Prpić (2002) showed that men were more productive when married. Similarly, in their survey of roughly 5,000 assistant professors from 80 countries, Hancock and Baum (2010) found that marriage provides a greater productivity boost to men than women. The results of Sax et al. (2002)'s study of 8,544 full-time teaching faculty members in the United States indicated that marital status appeared not to have an effect on women's level of research productivity.

Scholars' Level of Specialization and Research Topic of an Article

Some research suggests that the selection of research topics and the level of specialization may account for the gap between male and female researchers' performance (Leahy, 2006; Pan and Kalinaki, 2015). As women specialize less than men and choose different research topics, they might be less productive (Leahey, 2006; Pan and Kalinaki, 2015). However, Abramo, D'Angelo, Flavia, and Di Costa (2018) recommended caution in making this conclusion. This is because specialization and topic choice of the sexes seems to vary between fields and disciplines. Elsewhere, Abramo et al. (2017) demonstrated that males tend to diversify research activity more than females. However, this seems mainly due to higher publication intensity. When controlled for individual output, gender differences appeared significant in only two disciplines of Mathematics and Biology.

Structural and Environmental Factors

These factors refer to those practices, policies, and conditions that have a role in the success or failure of both female and male academics' career within a university setting (National Academy of Sciences, 2007; Robinson, 2012). These include institutional culture, workload, teaching load, and access to resources and funding.

Climate (Culture)

According to Smeby and Try (2005), organization culture has a great impact on the number of published scientific articles. It is commonly believed that good scientific environments stimulate productivity (Aksnes, 2012). In the scientific literature, there is some evidence which suggests the existence of a normative masculinist culture that puts women at a disadvantage, especially within certain academic fields (Wolffensperger, 1993; Willemsen, 2002; Riley et al., 2006; Bagilhole et al., 2008). For example, according to a report by the National Academies of Science, Engineering, and Medicine (US) (2006), it was concluded that the deficit of women in STEMM[5] is not because too few women enter the field, but because of departmental cultures that systematically impede the career advancement of women in Academic Medicine, Science, and Engineering. Engineering cultures in both academia and industry seem to favor men (Sarathchandra et al., 2018). In their literature review on the cultures of Science, Engineering, and Technology (SET) in the United Kingdom, Bagilhole et al. (2008) indicated that SET cultures make it difficult for women to succeed in their career. The authors believe this is due to the lack of suitable policies to support working mothers, and that success in SET is measured against traditionally masculine norms. Thelwall et al. (2019) suggest that the imbalances in the fields of Science, Technology, Engineering, and Mathematics may be partly due to off-putting masculine cultures. Due to the absence of a supportive culture, women tend to be more focused on teaching as opposed to research. This results in women being less productive and receiving less scholarly recognition (Buckley et al., 2000; Ioannidou and Rosania, 2015). Riley et al. (2006) suggested that the reason for low number of female authors in *The Psychologist Journal* is due to the sexist cultures in academia and Psy-

---

5 STEMM (Science, Technology, Engineering, Mathematics and Medicine).

chology. In meta-analysis carried out by Astegiano, Sebastián-González, and de Toledo Castanho (2019), culture was found to be one of the factors influencing gender differences in productivity.

Workload (Teaching Load)

Certain studies agree that women faculty members spend a greater proportion of their time teaching than men (Gander, 1999). Teaching and service activities are often seen as more "feminine" (Social Sciences Feminist Network Research, 2017). Xie and Shauman (2003) revealed that even though the difference in teaching load between the sexes was on the decline, women continued to favor teaching activity more than men and devoted less time to research. In a survey of 11,013 full and part-time faculty members in 450 US colleges and universities, Russell (1991) found that men on average spent a higher percentage of time on research activities, whilst women spent a higher percentage of time on teaching and service activities. Similarly, a study by the Association of University Teachers (AUT) (2004) in the United Kingdom argued that "institutionalized sexism" denies female academics recognition for their research activity. A survey of 3,080 Life Science faculty members at 50 universities in the United States demonstrated that female full professors worked more hours overall and spent significantly more time in administrative and professional activities and less in research than men (DesRoches et al., 2010). Olinto and Leta (2011)'s study in Brazilian universities showed that women receive a larger share of teaching assignments, which might jeopardize their involvement with research. According to a survey of UK university staff in Science-based subjects, female academics reported spending more time on teaching and public engagement tasks, and less time on research than their male counterparts (Aldercotte et al., 2017). Albert, Davia, and Legazpe (2016) suggested that women's increased focus on teaching and public engagement might make them less scientifically productive.

Access to Resources and Funding

Access to funding and resources is important for both men and women, as it provides essential support for research and publications (Husu and de Cheveigné, 2010), while the distribution of resources drives patterns of publication (Duch et al., 2012). According to a report by the US National Academy of Sciences (2010), access to institutional resources has given female Science and Engineering faculty members the opportunity to be more productive between 1980 and 2010. Ceci and Williams (2011) indicated that women are as successful at publishing as men, when comparisons are made between men and women with similar resources and characteristics (e. g. type of institution, access to funding and resources, tenure, teaching load). In a study of seven STEM fields in top research institutions in the U.S., Duch et al. (2012)

indicated that the lower publication rates of female scholars might be explained by the lower level of institutional support and resources received by females. In a study in Health Sciences, the results indicated that not having access to enough public funding may have a slightly negative effect on women's relative citation rate (Beaudry and Larivière, 2016).

Regarding funding and gender, several studies have reported that men receive more funding (Stack, 2004; Head et al., 2013; Eloy et al., 2013) and are more successful in acquiring grant funding (Bailyn, 2008; van der Lee and Ellemers, 2015). However, when controlling for factors that correlate with grant success such as discipline, institution (Hosek et al., 2005), academic rank (Waisbren et al., 2008; Svider et al., 2014), and percentage of female applicants (Pohlhause et al., 2011), no gender differences have been found. Ranga, Gupta, and Etzkowitz (2012)'s literature review on funding and gender found that studies generally address certain issues. These are tendency to apply for grant funding, number of grants applied for, and the amount of funding requested. Most studies in these areas agree that women are less likely to apply for grants (Hosek et al., 2005; Pohlhaus et al., 2011; Boyle, 2015), and request smaller amounts of money (Blake and La Valle, 2000; Waisbren et al., 2008; Bedi, Van Dam, and Munafo, 2012).

Conclusions

This study has provided an overview of the literature on gender and bibliometrics from two points of view: i) bibliometrics indictors and ii) factors causing gender differences in these bibliometrics indicators, with a special focus on scientific productivity and impact.

Regarding the indicators, the review has shown that the most common indictors which have been studied in the literature were the number of publications, the number of citations, self-citations, Journal Impact Factor, h-Index, authorship positions, and collaboration patterns. The visibility of scholars from the point of social media metrics has also been studied. h-index was found to be a common indicator, studied mainly in Medical and Life Sciences (Oncology, Neurology, Surgery, Emergency Radiology, Otolaryngology, etc.) and used for productivity and assessing the impact of female and male scholars.

Regarding the number of publications and authorships, the literature is generally consistent regarding the lower scientific productivity of female scholars. This gap seems to be wider in STEM fields. These imbalances in Science, Technology, Engineering, and Mathematics fields have been associated with the masculine cultures of these disciplines and the lower levels of institutional support and funding for women in these fields (Duch et al, 2012; Thelwall et al., 2019). The productivity gap between the sexes seems to decline with career progress and at senior levels. Within certain disciplines such as Social Policy and Psychology that have a relatively high proportion of female academics, publication productivity was found to be almost equal. The number of women within a discipline might be important as a "critical mass" of women may facilitate women's career progression, including their publication productivity (Bird, 2011). Furthermore, in disciplines where research expenditures were high, such as Molecular Biology, females consistently published at a rate significantly lower than males (Duch et al., 2012).

The review of citation showed some disciplines where the citation gap is large and favors men (Linguistics, Sociology, Geography, International Relations, Astronomy), some where the gap is negligible (Library and Information Science, Nanoscience, Surgery, Life Sciences, Dendrochronology), and others where it is in favor of women (Biochemistry, Management, Economics, Neurosurgery). It seems that in disciplines such as Social Sciences and Life Sciences where there are more female scholars, women receive a similar or a higher number of citations. This might mean a reduction of the "Matthew effect" where men's research is viewed as the most central and important in a field (Dion, Sumner, and Mitchell, 2018). However, the relationship between the proportion of female scholars in a field and the number of citations seems not to be direct. This is because a variety of other factors might explain this gender gap. For example, men's willingness to self-cite at higher rates has been suggested as a reason for this (Maliniak et al., 2013; Ghiasi et al., 2016a). The difference in self-citations has resulted in higher h-index scores for men (Cameron et al., 2016). Dion et al. (2018) associated this gender gap in citation to the "Matilde effect" and implicit biases in citation practices. According to Dion et al. (2018), women's research may be cited more frequently in disciplines with higher gender diversity, but men's research may still be treated as more important.

The effect of factors on productivity and impact is complex and inconclusive. As discussed in this literature review, there were many interacting factors that contributed to gender differences in research productivity. These factors were divided into two groups of personal (individual) and structural (environmental) in the literature.

Overall, by studying the literature on gender and bibliometrics, this review has provided an overview of the literature on gender differences in scientific productivity and impact. This is important as these gender differences might result in gender imbalances in career progression of female and male scholars. As indicated by Thelwall (2018), research impact is an important dimension of gender differences. If female authored research is undervalued, then women have less opportunities for career progression. In fact, the gender productivity gap has often been used as the important reason for women's underrepresentation (Astegiano et al., 2019). In nearly every discipline and type of institution, research impact and publication productivity are the decisive factors in tenure, promotion, and salary decisions (Hancock and Baum, 2010).

This literature review has provided an overview of the underlying causing factors. This is important, because analyzing gender differences in scientific productivity and impact without controlling for all relevant variables may lead to biased results and decisions. Thus, this study may create awareness on this topic for concerned parties and provide a starting point for identifying actions required to overcome the gender gap.

References

Aakhus, E, Mitra, N, Lautenbach, E & Joffe, S 2018, 'Gender and byline placement of co-first authors in clinical and basic science journals with high impact factorsbyline placement of co-first authors by gender in journals with high impact factorsletters', *Jama*, vol. 319, pp. 610–11.

Abramo, G, D'Angelo, CA & Caprasecca, A 2009a, 'The contribution of star scientists to overall sex differences in research productivity', *Scientometrics*, vol. 81, p. 137.

Abramo, G, D'Angelo, CA & Caprasecca, A 2009b, 'Gender differences in research productivity: A bibliometric analysis of the Italian academic system', *Scientometrics*, vol. 79, pp. 517–39.

Abramo, G, D'Angelo, CA & Di Costa, F 2017, 'Specialization versus diversification in research activities: the extent, intensity and relatedness of field diversification by individual scientists', *Scientometrics*, vol. 112, pp. 1403–18.

Abramo, G, D'Angelo, CA & Di Costa, F 2018, 'The effects of gender, age and academic rank on research diversification', *Scientometrics*, vol. 114, pp. 373–87.

Abramo, G., D'Angelo, CA & Murgia, G 2013, 'Gender differences in research collaboration', *Journal of Informetrics*, vol. 7, pp. 811–22.

Aguilar, IN, Ganesh, V, Mannfeld, R, Gorden, R, Hatch, JM, Lunsford, S, Whipple, EC, Loder, RT & Kacena, MA 2019, 'Authorship Trends Over the Past 30-Years in the Annals of Biomedical Engineering', *Annals of Biomedical Engineering*, vol. 47, pp. 1171–80.

Aiston, SJ & Jung, J 2015, 'Women academics and research productivity: an international comparison', *Gender and Education*, vol. 27, pp. 205–20.

Aksnes, DW 2012, Review of literature on scientists' research productivity, Kungl. Ingenjörsvetenskapsakademien, Stockholm.

Aksnes, DW, Piro, FN & Rørstad, K 2019, 'Gender gaps in international research collaboration: a bibliometric approach', *Scientometrics*.

Aksnes, DW, Rorstad, K, Piro, F & Sivertsen, G 2011, 'Are female researchers less cited? A large-scale study of Norwegian scientists', *Journal of the American Society for Information Science and Technology*, vol. 62, pp. 628–36.

Albert, C, Davia, MA & Legazpe, N 2016, 'Determinants of Research Productivity in Spanish Academia', *European Journal of Education*, vol. 51, pp. 535–49.

Aldercotte, A, Guyan, K, Lawson, J, Neave, S & Altorjai, S 2017, *ASSET 2016: experiences of gender equality in STEMM academia and their intersections with ethnicity, sexual orientation, disability and age*, Equality Challenge Unit (ECU), London.

Araújo, EB, Araújo, NAM, Moreira, AA, Herrmann, HJ & Andrade, JS, Jr 2017, 'Gender differences in scientific collaborations: Women are more egalitarian than men', *PLOS ONE*, vol. 12, e0176791.

Association Of University Teachers 2004, The Unequal: Academy UK Academic Staff 1995/6 to 2002/3, AUT, London.

Astegiano, J, Sebastián-González, E & de Toledo Castanho, C 2019, 'Unravelling the gender productivity gap in science: a meta-analytical review', *Royal Society Open Science*, vol. 6, 181566.

Bagilhole, B, Powell, A, Barnard, S & Dainty, A 2008, Researching Cultures in Science, Engineering and Technology: An analysis of current and past literature. Research Report

Series for UKRC No.7. Engineering and Technology, Bradford, UK, Resource Centre for Women in Science.

Bailyn, L 2008, 'Comment on "gender differences in research grant applications and funding outcomes for medical school faculty"', *J Womens Health (Larchmt)*, vol. 17, pp. 303–04.

Bandiera, O & Natraj, A 2013, 'Does Gender Inequality Hinder Development and Economic Growth? Evidence and Policy Implications', The World Bank, Washington, DC.

Bar-Ilan, J & van der Weijden, I 2015, 'Altmetric Gender Bias? – An Exploratory Study', *International Journal of Computer Science: Theory and Application*, vol. 4, pp. 16–22.

Barrios, M, Villarroya, A & Borrego, Á 2013, 'Scientific production in psychology: a gender analysis', *Scientometrics*, vol. 95, pp. 15–23.

Battaglia, F, Shah, S, Jalal, S, Khurshid, K, Verma, N, Nicolaou, S, Reddy, S, John, S & Khosa, F 2019, 'Gender disparity in academic emergency radiology', *Emerg Radiol*, vol. 26, pp. 21–28.

Beaudry, C & Larivière, V 2016, 'Which gender gap? Factors affecting researchers' scientific impact in science and medicine', *Research Policy*, vol. 45, pp. 1790–1817.

Beaudry, C & St-Pierre, C 2016, What factors influence scientific and technological output: The case of Thailand and Malaysia, 21st International Conference on Science and Technology Indicators – STI 2016, Editorial Universitat Politecnica de Valencia, Valencia, Spain.

Bedi, G, van Dam, NT & Munafo, M 2012, 'Gender inequality in awarded research grants', *The Lancet*, vol. 380, p. 474.

Bendels, MHK, Müller, R, Brueggmann, D & Groneberg, DA 2018, 'Gender disparities in high-quality research revealed by Nature Index journals', *PLOS ONE*, vol. 13, e0189136.

Bird, KS 2011, 'Do women publish fewer journal articles than men? Sex differences in publication productivity in the social sciences', *British Journal of Sociology of Education*, vol. 32, pp. 921–37.

Blake, M & la Valle, I 2000, 'Who applies for research funding?: key factors shaping funding application behaviour among women and men in British higher education institutions', National Centre for Social Research, London.

Bonham, KS & Stefan, MI 2017, 'Women are underrepresented in computational biology: An analysis of the scholarly literature in biology, computer science and computational biology', *PLOS Computational Biology*, vol. 13, e1005134.

Bordons, M, Morillo, F, Fernández, MT & Gómez, I 2003, 'One step further in the production of bibliometric indicators at the micro level: Differences by gender and professional category of scientists', *Scientometrics*, vol. 57, pp. 159–73.

Borrego, Á, Barrios, M, Villarroya, A & Ollé, C 2010, 'Scientific output and impact of postdoctoral scientists: a gender perspective', *Scientometrics*, vol. 83, pp. 93–101.

Boschini, A, Sj, XF & Gren, A 2007, 'Is Team Formation Gender Neutral? Evidence from Coauthorship Patterns', *Journal of Labor Economics*, vol. 25, pp. 325–65.

Boyle, PJ, Smith, LK, Cooper, NJ, Williams, KS & O'Connor, H 2015, 'Gender balance: Women are funded more fairly in social science', *Nature*, vol. 525, pp. 181–83.

Bozeman, B & Corley, E 2004, 'Scientists' collaboration strategies: implications for scientific and technical human capital', *Research Policy*, vol. 33, pp. 599–616.

Bozeman, B & Gaughan, M 2011, 'How do men and women differ in research collaborations? An analysis of the collaborative motives and strategies of academic researchers', *Research Policy*, vol. 40, pp. 1393–1402.

Buckley, LM, Sanders, K, Shih, M & Hampton, CL 2000, 'Attitudes of clinical faculty about career progress, career success and recognition, and commitment to academic medicine. Results of a survey', *Arch Intern Med*, vol. 160, pp. 2625–29.

Cameron, EZ, White, AM & Gray, ME 2016, 'Solving the Productivity and Impact Puzzle: Do Men Outperform Women, or are Metrics Biased?', *BioScience*, vol. 66, pp. 245–52.

Caplar, N, Tacchella, S & Birrer, S 2017, 'Quantitative evaluation of gender bias in astronomical publications from citation counts', *Nature Astronomy*, vol. 1, 0141.

Card, D, Dellavigna, S, Funk, P & Iriberri, N 2019, *Are Referees and Editors in Economics Gender Neutral?* NBER, US.

Carleton, RN, Parkerson, HA & Horswill, SC 2012, 'Assessing the publication productivity of clinical psychology professors in Canadian Psychological Association-accredited Canadian psychology departments', *Canadian Psychology/Psychologie canadienne*, vol. 53, pp. 226–37.

Carr, PL, Ash, AS, Friedman, RH, Scaramucci, A, Barnett, RC, Szalacha, L, Palepu, A & Moskowitz, MA 1998, 'Relation of family responsibilities and gender to the productivity and career satisfaction of medical faculty', *Ann Intern Med*, vol. 129, pp. 532–38.

Carter, TE, Smith, TE. & Osteen, PJ 2017, 'Gender comparisons of social work faculty using h-Index scores', *Scientometrics*, vol. 111, pp. 1547–57.

Ceci, SJ & Williams, WM 2011, 'Understanding current causes of women's underrepresentation in science', *Proceedings of the National Academy of Sciences*, vol. 108, pp. 3157–62.

Choi, M, Fuller, CD & Thomas, CR. Jr. 2009, 'Estimation of citation-based scholarly activity among radiation oncology faculty at domestic residency-training institutions: 1996–2007', *Int J Radiat Oncol Biol Phys*, vol. 74, pp. 172–78.

Cole, JR & Zuckerman, H 1984, 'The Productivity Puzzle: Persistence and Change in Patterns of Publication of Men and Women Scientists', *Advances in Motivation and Achievement*, vol. 2, pp. 217–258.

Copenheaver, CA, Goldbeck, K & Cherubini, P 2010, 'Lack of Gender Bias in Citation Rates of Publications by Dendrochronologists: What is Unique about this Discipline?', *Tree-Ring Research*, vol. 66, pp. 127–33.

Crow, MS & Smykla, JO 2015, 'An Examination of Author Characteristics in National and Regional Criminology and Criminal Justice Journals, 2008–2010: Are Female Scholars Changing the Nature of Publishing in Criminology and Criminal Justice?', *American Journal of Criminal Justice*, vol. 40, pp. 441–55.

D'Amico, R, Vermigli, P & Canetto, SS 2011, 'Publication productivity and career advancement by female and male psychology faculty: The case of Italy', *Journal of Diversity in Higher Education*, vol. 4, pp. 175–84.

Dehdarirad, T & Nasini, S 2017, 'Research impact in co-authorship networks: a two-mode analysis', *Journal of Informetrics*, vol. 11, pp. 371–88.

DesRoches, CM, Zinner, DE, Rao, SR, Iezzoni, LI & Campbell, EG 2010, 'Activities, productivity, and compensation of men and women in the life sciences', *Acad Med*, vol. 85, pp. 631–39.

Diamond, SJ, Thomas, CR., Jr., Desai, S, Holliday, EB, Jagsi, R, Schmitt, C & Enestvedt, BK 2016, 'Gender Differences in Publication Productivity, Academic Rank, and Career Duration Among U.S. Academic Gastroenterology Faculty', *Acad Med*, vol. 91, pp. 1158–63.

Dion, ML, Sumner, JL & Mitchell, SM 2018, 'Gendered Citation Patterns across Political Science and Social Science Methodology Fields', *Political Analysis*, vol. 26, pp. 312–27.

Duch, J, Zeng, XHT, Sales-Pardo, M, Radicchi, F, Otis, S, Woodruff, TK & Nunes Amaral, LA 2012, 'The Possible Role of Resource Requirements and Academic Career-Choice Risk on Gender Differences in Publication Rate and Impact', *PLOS ONE*, vol. 7, e51332.

Ductor, L, Goyal, S & Prummer, A 2018, *Gender & Collaboration*. Faculty of Economics, University of Cambridge.

Edwards, HA, Schroeder, J & Dugdale, HL 2018, 'Gender differences in authorships are not associated with publication bias in an evolutionary journal', *PLOS ONE*, vol. 13, e0201725.

Eloy, JA, Svider, P, Chandrasekhar, SS, Husain, Q, Mauro, KM, Setzen, M & Baredes, S 2013, 'Gender disparities in scholarly productivity within academic otolaryngology departments', *Otolaryngol Head Neck Surg*, vol. 148, pp. 215–22.

Elsevier 2017, Gender in the Global Research Landscape, https://www.elsevier.com/research-intelligence/campaigns/gender-17 (July 15, 2020).

European Commission 2015, *She Figures 2015. Gender in Research and Innovation Statistics and Indicators*, Directorate-General for Research and Innovation, Brussels.

European Commission 2019, She Figures 2018, Directorate-General for Research and Innovation, Brussels.

Farrell, J & Smyth, R 2014, 'Trends in co-authorship in the Australian group of eight law reviews', *Monash University Law Review*, vol. 39.

Fisher, BS, Cobane, CT, Thomas, MVV & Cullen, FT 1998, 'How Many Authors Does It Take to Publish an Article? Trends and Patterns in Political Science', *PS: Political Science and Politics*, vol. 31, pp. 847–56.

Fox, CW, Ritchey, JP & Paine, CET 2018, 'Patterns of authorship in ecology and evolution: First, last, and corresponding authorship vary with gender and geography', *Ecology and Evolution*, vol. 8, pp. 11492–507.

Fox, MF 2005, 'Gender, Family Characteristics, and Publication Productivity among Scientists', *Social Studies of Science*, pp. 35131–150.

Frehill, LM & Zippel, K 2011, 'Gender and international collaborations of academic scientists and engineers: Findings from the survey of doctorate recipients, 2006', *Journal of the Washington Academy of Sciences*, vol. 97, pp. 49–69.

Gallivan, MJ & Benbunan-Fich, R 2006, 'Examining the relationship between gender and the research productivity of IS faculty', *ACM SIGMIS CPR conference on computer personnel research: Forty four years of computer personnel research: achievements, challenges & the future*, California, USA

Gander, JP 1999, 'Faculty Gender Effects On Academic Research And Teaching', *Research in Higher Education*, vol. 40, pp. 171–84.

Gayet-Ageron, A, Poncet, A & Perneger, T 2019, 'Comparison of the contributions of female and male authors to medical research in 2000 and 2015: a cross-sectional study', *BMJ Open*, vol. 9, e024436.

Ghiasi, G, Larivière, V & Sugimoto, CR 2016a, 'Gender Differences in Synchronous and Diachronous Self-citations', in I Ràfols, J Molas-Gallart, E Castro-Martínez & R Woolley (eds.), The 21st International Conference on Science and Technology Indicators, Universitat Politècnica de València, Valencia, Spain.

Ghiasi, G, Larivière, V & Sugimoto, CR 2016b, 'On the Compliance of Women Engineers with a Gendered Scientific System', *PLOS ONE*, vol. 10, e0145931.

González-Álvarez, J & Cervera-Crespo, T 2019, 'Contemporary psychology and women: A gender analysis of the scientific production', *Int J Psychol*, vol. 54, pp. 135–43.

Gupta, BM, Kumar, S & Aggarwal, BS 1999, 'A comparision of productivity of male and female scientists of CSIR', *Scientometrics*, vol. 45, pp. 269–89, doi: https://doi.org/10.1007/bf02458437.

Hancock, KJ & Baum, M 2010, 'Women and Academic Publishing: Preliminary Results from a Survey of the ISA Membership', *International Studies Association annual convention*, New Orleans.

Hargens, LL, Mccann, JC & Reskin, BF 1978, 'Productivity and Reproductivity: Fertility and Professional Achievement among Research Scientists', *Social Forces*, vol. 57, pp. 154–63.

Hart, KL, Frangou, S & Perlis, RH 2019, 'Gender Trends in Authorship in Psychiatry Journals From 2008 to 2018', *Biol Psychiatry*.

Head, MG, Fitchett, JR, Cooke, MK, Wurie, FB & Atun, R 2013, 'Sex discrepancies in infectious disease research funding 1997–2010: a systematic analysis', *The Lancet*, vol. 382, S44.

Hill, EK, Blake, RA, Emerson, JB, Svider, P, Eloy, JA, Raker, C, Robison, K & Stuckey, A 2015, 'Gender Differences in Scholarly Productivity Within Academic Gynecologic Oncology Departments', *Obstetrics and gynecology*, vol. 126, pp. 1279–84.

Holliday, EB, Jagsi, R, Wilson, LD, Choi, M, Thomas, CR., Jr. & Fuller, CD 2014, 'Gender differences in publication productivity, academic position, career duration, and funding among U.S. academic radiation oncology faculty', *Acad Med*, vol. 89, pp. 767–73.

Holman, L & Morandin, C 2019, 'Researchers collaborate with same-gendered colleagues more often than expected across the life sciences', *PLOS ONE*, vol.14, e0216128.

Holman, L, Stuart-Fox, D & Hauser, CE 2018, 'The gender gap in science: How long until women are equally represented?', *PLOS Biology*, vol. 16, e2004956.

Hosek, SD, Cox, AG, Ghosh-Dastidar, B, Kofner, A, Ramphal, NR, Scott, J & Berry, SH 2005, Gender Differences in Major Federal External Grant Programs, RAND Corporation, Santa Monica, CA, https://www.rand.org/pubs/technical_reports/TR307.html (July 15, 2020).

Housri, N, Cheung, MC, Koniaris, LG & Zimmers, TA 2008, 'Scientific impact of women in academic surgery', *J Surg Res*, vol. 148, pp. 13–16.

Hunter, L & Leahey, E 2008, 'Collaborative Research in Sociology: Trends and Contributing Factors', *The American Sociologist*, vol. 39, pp. 290–306.

Hunter, LA & Leahey, E 2010, 'Parenting and research productivity: New evidence and methods', *Social Studies of Science*, vol. 40, pp. 433–51.

Husu, L & de Cheveigné, S 2010, 'Gender and gatekeeping of excellence in research funding: European perspectives', in B Riegraf,, E Kirsch-Auwärter & U Müller (eds.), *Gender Change in Academia*, Verlag für Sozialwissenschaften.

Hutson, SR 2006, 'Self-Citation in Archaeology: Age, Gender, Prestige, and the Self', *Journal of Archaeological Method and Theory*, vol. 13, pp. 1–18.

Ioannidou, E & Rosania, A 2015, 'Under-Representation of Women on Dental Journal Editorial Boards', *PLOS ONE*, vol. 10, e0116630.

Juraqulova, ZH, Byington, TC & Kmec, JA 2015, 'The Impacts of Marriage on Perceived Academic Career Success: Differences by Gender and Discipline', *International Journal of Gender, Science and* Technology, vol. 7, no. 3.

King, MM, Bergstrom, CT, Correll, SJ, Jacquet, J & West, JD 2017, 'Men Set Their Own Cites High: Gender and Self-citation across Fields and over Time', *Socius*, vol. 3, 2378023117738903.

Krapf, M, Ursprung, HW & Zimmermann, C 2014, 'Parenthood and Productivity of Highly Skilled Labor: Evidence from the Groves of Academe', CESifo Working Paper Series No. 4641.

Krapf, M, Ursprung, HW & Zimmermann, C 2017, 'Parenthood and productivity of highly skilled labor: Evidence from the groves of academe', *Journal of Economic Behavior & Organization*, vol. 140, pp. 147–75.

Kretschmer, H & Aguillo, IF 2005, 'New indicators for gender studies in Web networks', *Information Processing & Management*, vol. 41, pp. 1481–94.

Kretschmer, H, Pudovkin, A & Stegmann J 2012, 'Research evaluation. Part II: gender effects of evaluation: are men more productive and more cited than women?', *Scientometrics*, vol. 93, pp. 17–30.

Kyvik, S 1990, 'Motherhood and Scientific Productivity', *Social Studies of Science*, vol. 20, pp. 149–60.

Kyvik, S & Teigen, M 1996, 'Child Care, Research Collaboration, and Gender Differences in Scientific Productivity', *Science, Technology, & Human Values*, vol. 21, pp. 54–71.

Larivière, V, Ni, C, Gingras, Y, Cronin, B & Sugimoto, CR 2013, 'Bibliometrics: global gender disparities in science', *Nature*, vol. 504, pp. 211–13.

Larivière, V, Vignola-Gagné, E, Villeneuve, C, Gélinas, P & Gingras, Y 2011, 'Sex differences in research funding, productivity and impact: an analysis of Québec university professors', *Scientometrics*, vol. 87, pp. 483–98.

League Of European Research Universities (LERU) 2012, Women, research and universities: excellence without gender bias Universities, League of European Research, Leuven, Belgium.

Leahey, E 2006, 'Gender Differences in Productivity: Research Specialization as a Missing Link', *Gender & Society*, vol. 20, pp. 754–80, doi: https://doi.org/10.1177/0891243206293030.

Lee, S & Bozeman, B 2005, 'The Impact of Research Collaboration on Scientific Productivity', *Social Studies of Science*, vol. 35, pp. 673–702.

Lewison, G 2001, 'The quantity and quality of female researchers: A bibliometric study of Iceland. *Scientometrics*, vol. 52, pp. 29–43.

Liang, T, Zhang, C, Khara, RM & Harris, AC, 2015, 'Assessing the Gap in Female Authorship in Radiology: Trends Over the Past Two Decades', *Journal of the American College of Radiology*, vol. 12, pp. 735–41.

Long, JS 1992, 'Measures of Sex Differences in Scientific Productivity', *Social Forces*, vol. 71, pp. 159–78.

Luukkonen-Gronow, T & Stolte-Heiskanen, V 1983, 'Myths and Realities of Role Incompatibility of Women Scientists', *Acta Sociologica*, vol. 26, pp. 267–80.

Maliniak, D, Powers, R & Walter, BF 2013, 'The Gender Citation Gap in International Relations', *International Organization*, vol. 67, pp. 889–922.

Mauleón, E & Bordons, M 2006, 'Productivity, impact and publication habits by gender in the area of Materials Science', *Scientometrics*, vol. 66, pp. 199–218.

Mauleón, E, Bordons, M & Oppenheim, C 2008, 'The effect of gender on research staff success in life sciences in the Spanish National Research Council', *Research Evaluation*, vol. 17, pp. 213–25.

Mayer, SJ & Rathmann, JMK 2018, 'How does research productivity relate to gender? Analyzing gender differences for multiple publication dimensions', *Scientometrics*, vol. 117, pp. 1663–93.

McDermott, M, Gelb, DJ, Wilson, K, Pawloski, M, Burke, JF, Shelgikar, AV & London, ZN 2018, 'Sex Differences in Academic Rank and Publication Rate at Top-Ranked US Neurology Programs', *JAMA Neurol*, vol. 75, pp. 956–61.

McDowell, JM & Smith, JK 1992, 'The Effect Of Gender-Sorting On Propensity To Coauthor: Implications For Academic Promotion', *Economic Inquiry*, vol. 30, pp. 68–82.

Mihaljević-Brandt, H, Santamaría, L & Tullney, M 2016, 'The Effect of Gender in the Publication Patterns in Mathematics', *PLOS ONE*, vol. 11, e0165367.

Mishra, S, Fegley, BD, Diesner, J & Torvik, VI 2018, 'Self-citation is the hallmark of productive authors, of any gender', *PLOS ONE*, vol. 13, e0195773.

National Academy Of Sciences 2007, *Beyond Bias and Barriers: Fulfilling and Potential of Women in Academic Science and Engineering*, National Academies Press, Washington DC.

Nielsen, MW 2016, 'Gender inequality and research performance: moving beyond individual-meritocratic explanations of academic advancement', *Studies in Higher Education*, vol. 41, pp. 2044–60.

Nielsen, MW 2017, 'Gender and citation impact in management research', *Journal of Informetrics*, vol. 11, pp. 1213–28.

Olinto, G & Leta, J 2011, 'Gender (im)balances in teaching and research activities in Brazil', *Conference of the international society for scientometrics and informetrics*, University of Zululand, South Africa, Durban.

Özel, B, Kretschmer, H & Kretschmer, T 2014, 'Co-authorship pair distribution patterns by gender', *Scientometrics*, vol. 98, pp. 703–23.

Pan, L & Kalinaki, E 2015, Mapping Gender in the German Research Arena, Elsevier, https://www.elsevier.com/research-intelligence/resource-library/gender-2015 (July 15, 2020).

Paul-Hus, A, Sugimoto, CR, Haustein, S & Larivière, V 2015, 'Is there a gender gap in social media metrics?', *ISSI 2015–15th International conference of the International Society for Scientometrics and Informetrics*, Bogazici University Printhouse, Istanbul.

Peñas, CS & Willett, P 2006, 'Brief communication: Gender differences in publication and citation counts in librarianship and information science research', *Journal of Information Science*, vol. 32, pp. 480–85.

Pohlhaus, JR, Jiang, H, Wagner, RM, Schaffer, WT & Pinn, VW 2011, 'Sex differences in application, success, and funding rates for NIH extramural programs', *Acad Med*, vol. 86, pp. 759–67.

Prpić, K 2002, 'Gender and productivity differentials in science', *Scientometrics*, vol. 55, pp. 27–58, doi: https://doi.org/10.1023/A:1016046819457.

Pudovkin, A, Kretschmer, H, Stegmann, J & Garfield, E 2012, 'Research evaluation. Part I: productivity and citedness of a German medical research institution', *Scientometrics*, vol. 93, pp. 3–16.

Puuska, H-M 2010, 'Effects of scholar's gender and professional position on publishing productivity in different publication types. Analysis of a Finnish university', *Scientometrics*, vol. 82, pp. 419–37.

Ranga, M, Gupta, N & Etzkowitz, H 2012, 'Gender effects in research funding', Deutsche Forschungsgemeinschaft, Bonn.

Rigg, LS, McCarragher, S & Krmenec, A 2012, 'Authorship, Collaboration, and Gender: Fifteen Years of Publication Productivity in Selected Geography Journals', *The Professional Geographer*, vol. 64, pp. 491–502.

Riley, S, Frith, H, Archer, L & Veseley, L 2006, 'Institutional sexism in academia', *The Psychologist*, vol. 19, pp. 94–97.

Robinson, KA 2012, *Institutional Factors Contributing to the Under-representation of African American Women in Higher Education: Perceptions of Women in Leadership Positions*, Doctoral thesis, Georgia Southern University.

Russell, SH 1991, 'The Status of Women and Minorities in Higher Education: Findings from the 1988 National Survey of Postsecondary Faculty', *CUPA Journal*, vol. 42, pp. 1–11.

Rørstad, K & Aksnes, DW 2015, 'Publication rate expressed by age, gender and academic position – A large-scale analysis of Norwegian academic staff', *Journal of Informetrics*, vol. 9, pp. 317–33.

Savic, M, Ivanovic, M, Radovanovic, M & Surla, BD 2018, 'Gender-Based Analysis of Intra-Institutional Research Productivity and Collaboration', *Fundamenta Informaticae*, vol. 162, pp. 237–58.

Sax, LJ, Hagedorn, LS, Arredondo, M & Dicrisi, FA 2002, 'Faculty Research Productivity: Exploring the Role of Gender and Family-Related Factors', *Research in Higher Education*, vol. 43, pp. 423–46.

Schisterman, EF, Swanson, CW, Lu, YL & Mumford, SL 2017, 'The Changing Face of Epidemiology: Gender Disparities in Citations?', *Epidemiology*, vol. 28, pp. 159–68.

Seetharam, A, Ali, MT, Wang, CY, Schultz, KE, Fischer, JP, Lunsford, S, Whipple, EC, Loder, RT & Kacena, MA 2018, 'Authorship trends in the Journal of Orthopaedic Research: A bibliometric analysis', *J Orthop Res*, vol. 36, pp. 3071–80.

Shah, DN, Huang, J, Ying, GS, Pietrobon, R & O' Brien, JM 2013, 'Trends in female representation in published ophthalmology literature, 2000–2009', *Digit J Ophthalmol*, vol. 19, pp. 50–55.

Smeby, J-C & Try, S 2005, 'Departmental Contexts and Faculty Research Activity in Norway', *Research in Higher Education*, vol. 46, pp. 593–619.

Social Sciences Feminist Network Research Interest Group 2017, 'The Burden of Invisible Work in Academia Social Inequalities and Time Use in Five University Departments', *Humboldt Journal of Social Relations*, vol. 39, pp. 228–45.

Sotudeh, H, Dehdarirad, T & Freer, J 2018, 'Gender differences in scientific productivity and visibility in core neurosurgery journals: Citations and social media metrics', *Research Evaluation*, vol. 27, pp. 262–69.

Sotudeh, H, Dehdarirad, T & Pooladian, A 2016, 'Scientific productivity and the impact of neurosurgery scientists in WOS and Mendeley: a gender study', in I Rafols (ed.), *21st International Conference on Science and Technology Indicators*, 470–473, Universitat Politecnica de Valencia, Valencia.

Sotudeh, H & Khoshian, N 2014, 'Gender differences in science: the case of scientific productivity in Nano Science & Technology during 2005–2007', *Scientometrics*, vol. 98, pp. 457–72.

Stack, S 2004, 'Gender, Children and Research Productivity', *Research in Higher Education*, vol. 45, pp. 891–920.

Svider, PF, D'aguillo, CM, White, PE, Pashkova, AA, Bhagat, N, Langer, PD & Eloy, JA 2014, 'Gender differences in successful National Institutes of Health funding in ophthalmology', *J Surg Educ*, vol. 71, pp. 680–88.

Symonds, MRE, Gemmell, NJ, Braisher, TL, Gorringe, KL & Elgar, MA 2006, 'Gender Differences in Publication Output: Towards an Unbiased Metric of Research Performance', *PLOS ONE*, vol. 1, e127.

Thelwall, M 2018, 'Do females create higher impact research? Scopus citations and Mendeley readers for articles from five countries', *Journal of Informetrics*, vol. 12, pp. 1031–41.

Thelwall, M, Bailey, C, Tobin, C & Bradshaw, N-A 2019, 'Gender differences in research areas, methods and topics: Can people and thing orientations explain the results?', *Journal of Informetrics*, vol. 13, pp. 149–69.

Thelwall, M & Kousha, K 2014, 'Academia.edu: Social network or Academic Network?', *Journal of the Association for Information Science and Technology*, vol. 65, pp. 721–31.

Tomei, KL, Nahass, MM, Husain, Q, Agarwal, N, Patel, SK, Svider, PF, Eloy, JA & Liu, JK 2014, 'A gender-based comparison of academic rank and scholarly productivity in academic neurological surgery', *J Clin Neurosci*, vol. 21, pp. 1102–05.

Tower, G, Plummer, J & Ridgewell, B 2007, 'A Multidisciplinary Study Of Gender-Based Research Productivity In The Worlds Best Journals', *Journal of Diversity Management (JDM)*, vol. 2, pp. 23–32, doi: https://doi.org/10.19030/jdm.v2i4.5020.

Waisbren, SE, Bowles, H, Hasan, T, Zou, KH, Emans, SJ, Goldberg, C, Gould, S, Levine, D, Lieberman, E, Loeken, M, Longtine, J, Nadelson, C, Patenaude, AF, Quinn, D, Randolph, AG, Solet, JM, Ullrich, N, Walensky, R, Weitzman, P & Christou, H 2008, 'Gender differences in research grant applications and funding outcomes for medical school faculty', *J Womens Health (Larchmt)*, vol. 17, pp. 207–14.

Valsangkar, N, Fecher, AM, Rozycki, GS, Blanton, C, Bell, TM, Freischlag, J, Ahuja, N, Zimmers, TA & Koniaris, LG 2016, 'Understanding the Barriers to Hiring and Promoting Women in Surgical Subspecialties', *Journal of the American College of Surgeons*, vol. 223, pp. 387–398.e2.

van Arensbergen, P, van der Weijden, I & van den Besselaar, P 2012, 'Gender differences in scientific productivity: a persisting phenomenon?', *Scientometrics*, vol. 93, pp. 857–68.

van den Besselaar, P & Sandström, U 2016, 'Gender differences in research performance and its impact on careers: a longitudinal case study', *Scientometrics*, vol. 106, pp. 143–62.

van der Lee, R & Ellemers, N 2015, 'Gender contributes to personal research funding success in The Netherlands', *Proceedings of the National Academy of Sciences*, vol. 112, pp. 12349–353.

West, JD, Jacquet, J, King, MM, Correll, SJ & Bergstrom, CT 2013, 'The Role of Gender in Scholarly Authorship', *PLOS ONE*, vol. 8, e66212.

Willemsen, TM 2002, 'Gender Typing of the Successful Manager – A Stereotype Reconsidered', *Sex Roles*, vol. 46, pp. 385–91.

Wininger, AE, Fischer, JP, Likine, EF, Gudeman, AS, Brinker, AR, Ryu, J, Maupin, KA, Lunsford, S, Whipple, EC, Loder, RT & Kacena, MA 2017, 'Bibliometric Analysis of Female Authorship

Trends and Collaboration Dynamics Over JBMR's 30-Year History', *Journal of Bone and Mineral Research*, vol. 32, pp. 2405–14.

Wolffensperger, J 1993, 'Science Is Truly a Male World: The Interconnectedness of Knowledge, Gender and Power within University Education', *Gender and Education*, vol. 5, pp. 37–54.

World Bank 2012, The World Development Report 2012: Gender Equality and Development, The World Bank, Washington, DC.

Xie, Y & Shauman, KA 1998, 'Sex Differences in Research Productivity: New Evidence about an Old Puzzle', *American Sociological Review*, vol. 63, pp. 847–70.

Xie Y, & Shauman, KA 2003, *Women in Science: career processes and outcomes*, Harvard University Press, Cambridge.

Zainab, AN 1999, 'Personal, Academic And Departmental Correlates Of Research Productivity: a Review Of Literature', *Malaysian Journal of Library & Information Science*, vol. 4, pp. 73–110.

Zawacki-Richter, O & von Prümmer, C 2010, 'Gender and collaboration patterns in distance education research', *Open Learning: The Journal of Open, Distance and e-Learning*, vol. 25, pp. 95–114.

Zeng, XHT, Duch, J, Sales-Pardo, M, Moreira, JAG, Radicchi, F, Ribeiro, HV, Woodruff, TK & Amaral, LAN 2016, 'Differences in Collaboration Patterns across Discipline, Career Stage, and Gender', *PLOS Biology*, vol. 14, e1002573.

Zettler, HR, Cardwell, SM & Craig, JM 2017, 'The gendering effects of co-authorship in criminology & criminal justice research', *Criminal Justice Studies*, vol. 30, pp. 30–44.

Zoega, G 2017, 'Does research activity decline with age?', *Icelandic Review of Politics and Administration*, vol. 3, pp. 103–18.

Østby, G, Strand, H, Nordås, R. & Gleditsch, NP 2013, 'Gender Gap or Gender Bias in Peace Research? Publication Patterns and Citation Rates for Journal of Peace Research, 1983–20081', *International Studies Perspectives*, vol. 14, pp. 493–506.

5.7 Visualization of Research Metrics

Hélène Draux

Abstract: Research metrics, closely related to statistics and network analysis, benefit greatly from visualizations. This chapter introduces briefly some guidelines for visualizations (design or color selections) before describing the visualizations frequently used. We first introduce the Chart Chooser, which starts from the type of analysis required and then considers the characteristics of the data. This includes either static or interactive graphs that are common in statistics, which we complement with advanced graphs more able to represent the links between scholarly objects (be it publications, universities, researchers, funders and so on). These flow diagrams (heatmaps, chord diagrams and networks) are the opportunity to get an overview of the problem and dig deeper in it. The chapter finally mentions the tools and software most often used in bibliometrics visualization.

Keywords: visualisation, graphs, bibliometrics, design.

Introduction

Research metrics are used in research assessment and evaluation and aim at measuring impact. Graphics, on the other hand, reveal data (Tufte, 2001). Kirk (2016) defines visualization as "the representation and presentation of data to facilitate understanding". As such, visualizations are used in multiple environments for: showing context; supporting answering a question; decision making; analyzing and discovering patterns; or communicating. These multi purposes mean that the same data could be visualized in different ways depending on its use. In bibliometrics, the core data measures research projects, universities, a field of research or researchers themselves. Metrics visualization, relying primarily on quantitative data, is a close parent to quantitative visualization.

The most frequent objects of research metrics visualization are metadata and research indicators related to projects, scholarly items (e.g. publications, grants, patents), and people. Most of these research items are linked, either by citation or ownership (researchers' own publications). This quantitative data can be enhanced with textual information related to scholarly items, such as titles and abstracts.

Static graphs provide precomposed views of the data – although sometimes required due to the format of the presentation, interactive visualizations can empower the users to explore the data for themselves. Interactive visualizations have the benefits of presenting multiple dimensions, allowing to give a wider perspective, but also addressing different level of users – from users new to the subject or those more familiar with the data – as users can select what they see. Contrary to what is often

---

Hélène Draux, Research Data Scientist at Digital Science, h.draux@digital-science.com

expected, interactive visualizations are not restricted to the web – they can also be html files delivered to the user and seen through a web browser, with data either stored locally or in the cloud. That said, static graphs can also depict multi-dimensional data, as will be shown later. The choice of format – static or interactive – depends largely on the mode of distribution and the intention of use.

The following steps should be considered when creating a graphical visualization:
1. Consider the purpose of the visual: visualizations can for instance show context, support answering a question, making decisions, analyzing and discovering patterns, or communicating a message. The purpose of the visual is essentially to decide what type of support is most adapted.
2. Understand your audience: their knowledge of the field or visuals. This is critical to the amount of information that is required on the visualization and the onboarding required to the visualization.
3. Availability and quality of the data: most data are imperfect, and bibliometric data is no exception – there is missing or interpreted data. This is important to first understand it, and if possible to annotate the data with relevant explanations.
4. Static or interactive: depending on the format of delivery, this can restrict possibilities. Static graphs are more adapted to printed/presented material, while interactive graphs are either shared via the Internet or in a digital format.

A large part of research metrics visualization is akin to quantitative data visualization, and as such the present chapter initially introduces the visualization types, first the classic representations, and then presents some more advanced visualizations. Once the visualization types are introduced, we can look into tools and software available to create these visualizations.

Design

Design is paramount in visualization; it is the first thing that users will see of the visualization. Here are a few seminal concepts of data visualization design, adapted from classical work in the field of data visualization.

Rules

Tufte (2001) drew some rules for graphical displays, which should be seen as guidelines for clear, precise, and efficient data visualization:
- Show the data
- Induce the viewer to think about the substance rather than about methodology, graphic design, the technology of graphic production or something else

- Avoid distorting what the data have to say
- Present many numbers in a small space
- Make large data sets coherent
- Encourage the eye to compare different pieces of data
- Reveal the data as several levels of detail, from a broad overview of the fine structure
- Serve a reasonably clear purpose: description, exploration, tabulation or decoration
- Be closely integrated with the statistical and verbal descriptions of a data set.

These guidelines have been further condensed by Cairo (2016) into five principles: truthful, functional, beautiful, insightful, and enlightening.

Tufte also coined a few terms that address issues and principles of graphical display: "chartjunk" and "data-ink ratio" (Tufte, 2001). Chartjunk refers to parts of the chart that are not useful to the message and distract from understanding the graph. It is related to what Tufte calls "data-ink ratio", which is the proportion of ink that is used to represent the data compared to the overall graph. Clear messages are achieved with the lowest data-ink ratio, leading to minimalist looking graphs.

Colors

Colors in a graph should encode some dimensions of the data, so as to avoid cluttering the graph. The choice of colour is an art in itself, but guidelines – inspired by the cartographers – can help decide which color(s) to select. Guidelines written by Brewer (1994) are the most widely used, and can be found as default in many data visualization packages, as well as at http://colorbrewer2.org (July 15, 2020).

Visualization Types

Basic Visualizations

Regardless of the format – static or interactive – a graph needs to be selected to present the story of the data. The selection will depend on the data and what story needs to be told. A useful tool designed by Andrew Abela at ExtremePresentation is the Chart Chooser (Abela, 2006), as pictured in Figure 1. This classifies visualizations into four categories: Comparison, Relationship, Distribution, and Composition.

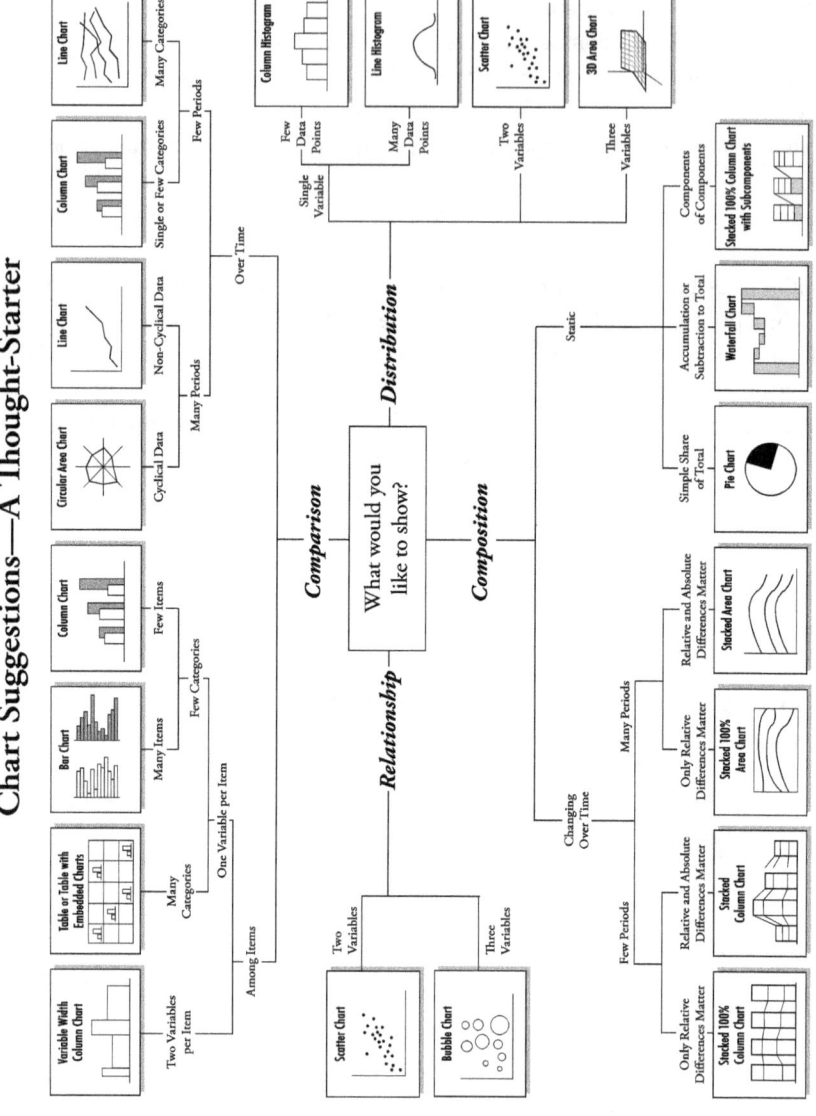

Figure 1: Chart Chooser.

Advanced Visualizations

The Chart Chooser, as a hierarchical decision-making tool, supports thoughtful decisions, considering the purpose first, then the data. This very simple Chart Chooser was, from the words of the author, meant to open discussions (FlowingData, 2009). A few modifications could be suggested here. For instance, the Comparison > Over time > Many Categories suggest creating an overlap of line charts. This can be useful when comparing two variables across multiple items – e.g. publication over time in multiple research institutions, journals, and so on. However, this graph, that is called a spaghetti graph, can become overwhelming. The example below, Figure 2, was published in a peer-reviewed article (Filardo et al., 2016). The number of lines, and similar colours, means it is hard to compare the lines.

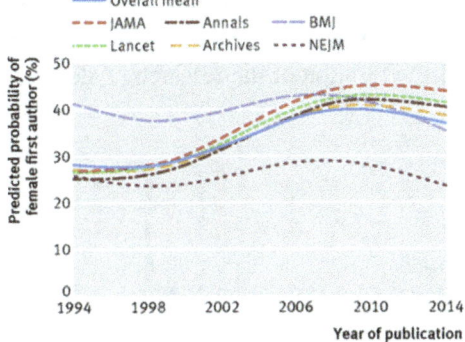

Figure 2: Adjusted association between female first author and time of publication by journal (February 1994 to June 2014).

In this case, small multiples (similar to faceting), introduced by Tufte (1990), can solve the problem by adding a dimension. It shows multiple times the same graph for each item – institution, journals, and so on. A better design would have one small graph for each of the six journals, showing all the lines greyed for each graph and coloring only the relevant line. A good rule of thumb is that spaghetti graphs are acceptable when lines can be distinguished from one another.

Representing Relationships

Other graphs not present in the Chart Chooser are graphs that can represent relationship data. However, research data, at its core, is linked: publications cite other publications, policy documents or patents; they are supported by grants; and are mentioned by members of the general public on social media. Therefore, visualizations that can show these relationships can tell powerful stories. It is then possible to extract from these networks other metrics to further comprehend a phenomenon. Flow charts and network graphs are then effective ways to convey the links between these items.

Flow Charts

Flow charts show links between multiple items (e.g. articles, clinical trials or patents). Often, this will be aggregated data, such as the number of publications in a group (e.g. university or field of research). The aim of the flow chart will be to show a process: where do the items go towards or away from.

The most appropriate flow charts in quantitative studies are Sankey diagrams and alluvial diagrams. Sankey diagrams show the flow of resources between nodes in a network with line width representing flow magnitude (Börner, 2015). Alluvial diagrams, a specific type of Sankey diagram, show changes over time; each node is a year for instance. Figure 3 is such an example; it shows the relationship between the location of the researcher and the location of the research (Tydecks et al., 2018).

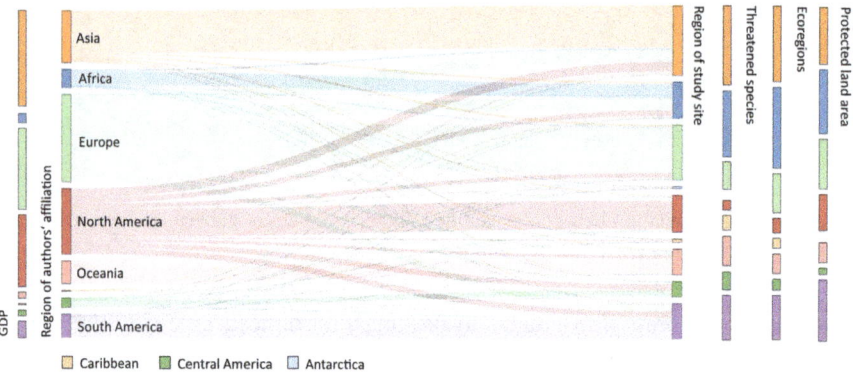

Figure 3: Sankey diagram quantifying research flows from the region of author affiliation to the region of research conductance. From Tydecks et al (2018).

Chord diagrams

Chord diagrams will show relationships through connections between and within category items (Kirk, 2016). The advantage of the chord diagram is that it links between and within categories. Nguyen Quang et al. (2019) used this to show a flow of citations between clusters.

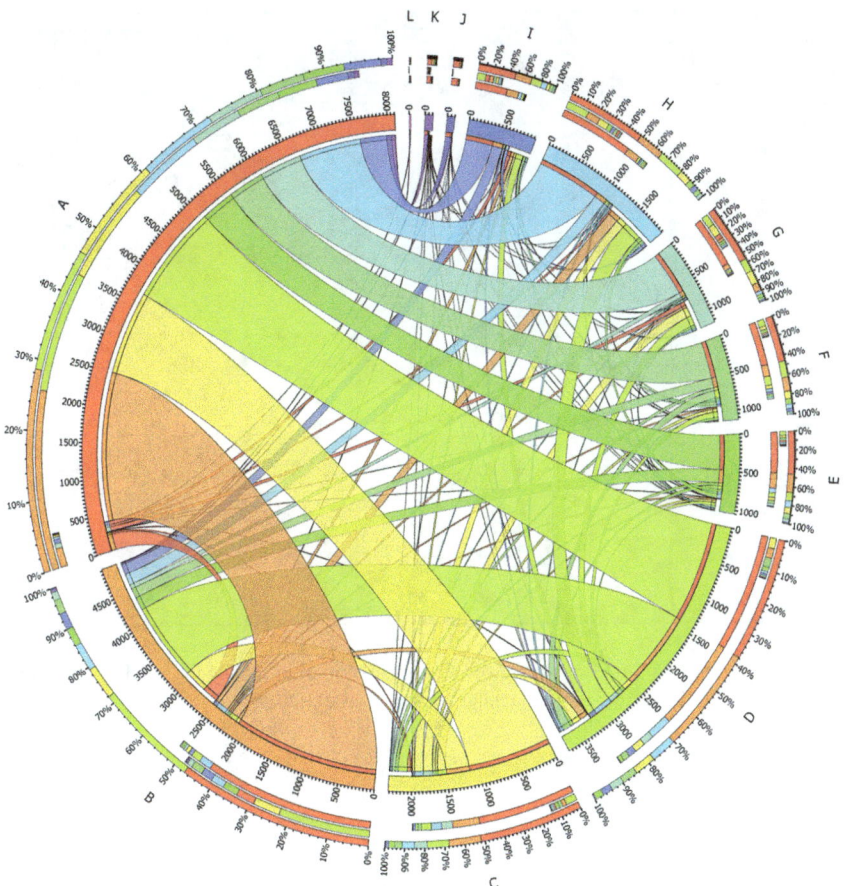

Figure 4: Chord diagram of the flow of citations between the identified clusters, excluding intra-cluster citations. From Nguyen Quang et al. (2019).

Heatmaps

Another way to represent the quantitative values between two categories is to use a heatmap. These graphs allow for the comparison of values across two categories, using often a coloring scheme, and can be annotated with the number. Figure 5, from Chinchilla-Rodríguez et al. (2019), shows such an example, with country of first author in row, and country of the other authors in column, with the Mean Normalized Citation Score in the value of the cell. This shows outliers, such as Argentina (bottom row of the third square) with a large portion of red coloured squares comparatively to its neighbours; it shows it reaches high quality papers when written with these countries.

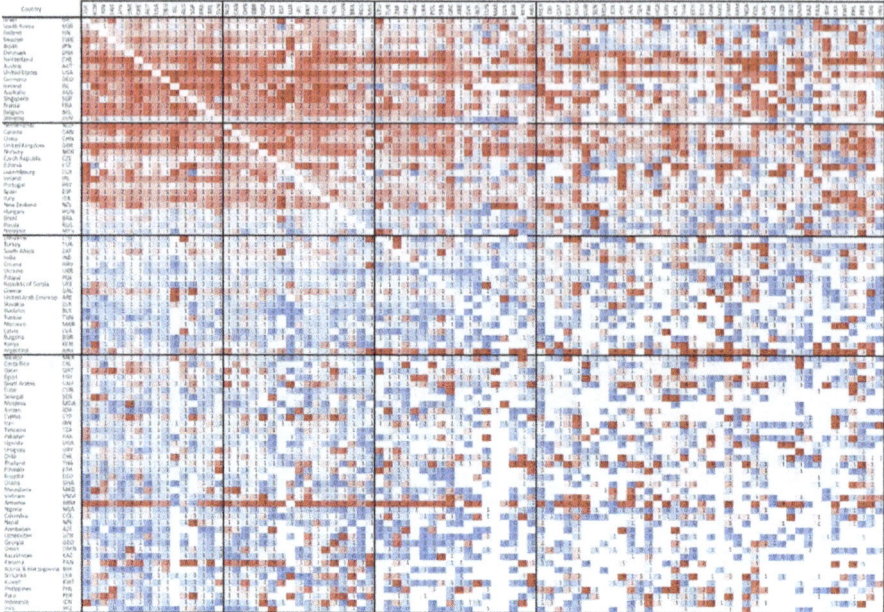

Figure 5: Matrix of the MNCS (Mean Normalized Citation Score) of international collaboration ties between countries, 2000–2016. From Chinchilla-Rodríguez et al. (2019).

Networks

There are two main types of networks used in bibliometrics: networks dealing with the context of the document (authors or references) and networks dealing with the text of the document (often titles and abstracts, but sometimes limited to titles or expanded to full text). Bibliometric networks are used as social networks or as topic mapping. Social networks are interested in finding patterns of relations between authors, for example using co-authorship. Topic mapping are similarity-based networks, which attempt to identify research topics or disciplines. This can be done through citation analyses – an article that cites another one is roughly in the same topic – or natural language processing analyses – articles using the same language will be in a roughly similar topic.

Yan and Ding (2012) distinguish also six types of bibliometric network: citation, co-authorship, co-citation, bibliographic coupling, co-word, or topical network. See Table 1 for the nodes and relationship used for these networks.

Table 1: Bibliometric network types.

	Nodes	Relationship
Citation	Documents	Citations
Co-authorship	Authors	Published together
Co-citation	Documents	Cited by the same documents
Bibliographic coupling	Documents	Documents that reference the same documents
Co-word	Words	Appear in the same document
Topical	Documents	Same topic

Networks are built using a list of relationships (the links), their respective weights (strength of the links), and nodes. Once laid out, the networks reveal clusters of similarity; either social clusters or give an insight into a group of universities or fields.

Porter and Watts (2019) created a static network of what a university looks like, which they complemented with an interactive version (https://wdaull.ds-innovation-experiments.com/ [July 15, 2020]). The static version is made of a small multiple network graph, using coloring to represent the fields of research. Figure 6 shows the collaboration networks of two universities; for each university the external collaboration (on the left) and the internal collaboration (on the right). From a broad overview of the network, it is apparent that Cornell University is strong externally in the blue and beige subjects (respectively medical and environmental sciences) while Virginia Tech's external collaboration is less dense and with a large component of beige, blue, and brown (medical, environmental sciences, and physical sciences). The poster they designed creates a visual comparison of the universities, while the online tool empowers the user to dig deeper into the data behind the network.

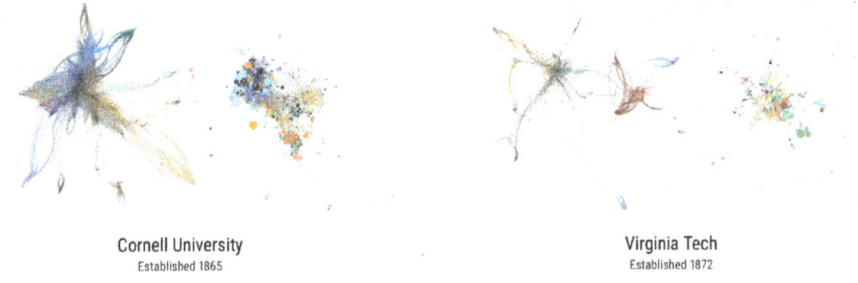

Cornell University
Established 1865

Virginia Tech
Established 1872

Figure 6: Extract from the poster "What Does a University Look Like?" (Porter and Watts, 2019).

Visualization formats

Static

Static graphs represent one state of the data only; the user can only read what was selected by the author of the graph. This has the advantage for the author to focus on the message to be delivered and can be shared in multiple venues – be it printed or online. Since it restricts the amount of information that can be shared, it can make it more difficult to share more complex stories.

Interactive

Interactive graphs allow authors to show more data, as the user is not a passive receiver of the information but can potentially select, pan, zoom, and filter it. Although this is a powerful advantage, this comes with the drawback of relying on software (a browser, with possibly an Internet connection and potentially the right plugin, software, and environment) and skills to explore the visualization.

Tools and software

Basic Static Infographics

Although Excel is able to produce most of the graphs on the Chart Chooser, it cannot produce the most advanced graphs and is usually difficult to customize basic details and produce high definition graphs. Instead, bibliometricians use python or R, two programming languages which allow for more reusability and fine tuning. The learning curve is steeper, but the applications are endless. The most common graphic libraries used are ggplot2 (in R) and matplotlib/seaborn (in python).

Interactive Graphs

There are a few open source tools for interactive graphs, with the most widely used d3.js and its derived libraries. It is coded in JavaScript, and so is available in every browser – online or not. Although d3.js is greatly customizable, it is famous for its complexity; therefore, many libraries work on top of d3.js, some in JavaScript, and others in python like plot.ly.

Network Graphics

Gephi or Cytoscape are open source software used for general purposes and can be used with data prepared in python or R. More specialized software, such as CiteSpace, VOSviewer, and CitNetExplorer, can also create bibliometric networks. Van Eck and Waltman have reviewed the latter two in their chapter, "Visualizing Bibliometric Networks" (van Eck and Waltman, 2014). Although highly technical, networks can easily be created in VOSViewer using data exported from Crossref, Dimensions, Europe PMC, OpenCitations, Semantic Scholar, and Wikidata (CWTS, 2019).

Networks can be difficult to handle in a static format. They require a lot of careful labelling in order to be easy to interpret, but because of that are more often used as a communication tool rather than an investigation tool. When using an interactive format, the user is allowed more freedom to explore. Gephi graphs for instance can easily be exported into a JavaScript library.

Conclusion

Bibliometrics gravitates around the fields of statistics and network analysis. It is therefore not surprising that most visualizations take from these fields. We have briefly reviewed here the foundations of data visualization, which are often overlooked and yet essential to efficient visual communication. Based on the review of data visualizations conducted for writing this chapter, it seems there is a positive trend towards more advanced charts and interactive network graphs in published scientific articles.

References

Abela, A 2006, 'Choosing a good chart – The Extreme Presentation(tm) Method', https://extremepresentation.typepad.com/blog/2006/09/choosing_a_good.html (July 15, 2020).
Börner, K 2015, *Atlas of Knowledge: Anyone Can Map*, MIT Press, Cambridge, Massachusetts.
Brewer, CA 1994, 'Color use guidelines for mapping', in *Visualization in modern cartography*, pp. 123–48.
Cairo, A 2016, *The Truthful Art: Data, Charts, and Maps for Communication*, New Riders.
Chinchilla-Rodríguez, Z, Sugimoto, CR, & Larivière, V 2019, 'Follow the leader: On the relationship between leadership and scholarly impact in international collaborations', *PLOS ONE*, vol. 14, e0218309, https://doi.org/10.1371/journal.pone.0218309.
CWTS 2019, 'VOSviewer supports large number of new data sources', CWTS, https://www.cwts.nl:443/blog?article=n-r2v284 (July 15, 2020).
Filardo, G, da Graca, B, Sass, DM, Pollock, BD, Smith, EB, & Martinez, MA-M 2016, 'Trends and comparison of female first authorship in high impact medical journals: observational study (1994–2014)', *BMJ*, i847, https://doi.org/10.1136/bmj.i847.

FlowingData 2009, Flow Chart Shows You What Chart to Use, FlowingData, accessed September 26, 2019, https://flowingdata.com/2009/01/15/flow-chart-shows-you-what-chart-to-use/ (July 15, 2020).

Kirk, A 2016, *Data Visualization: A Handbook for Data Driven Design, First edition*, SAGE Publications Ltd., Los Angeles.

Porter, S & Watts, J 2019, What Does a University Look Like?, https://doi.org/10.6084/m9.figshare.9742055.v2.

Quang, MN, Rogers, T, Hofman, J & Lanham, AB 2019, 'New framework for automated article selection applied to a literature review of Enhanced Biological Phosphorus Removal', *PLOS ONE*, vol. 14, e0216126, https://doi.org/10.1371/journal.pone.0216126.

Tufte, ER 2001, *The visual display of quantitative information*.

Tufte, ER 1990, *Envisioning Information*, Graphics Press USA.

Tydecks, L, Jeschke, JM, Wolf, M, Singer, G & Tockner, K 2018, 'Spatial and topical imbalances in biodiversity research', *PLOS ONE*, vol. 13, e0199327, https://doi.org/10.1371/journal.pone.0199327.

van Eck, NJ & Waltman, L 2014, 'Visualizing Bibliometric Networks', in Y Ding, R Rousseau & D Wolfram (eds.), *Measuring Scholarly Impact: Methods and Practice*, pp. 285–320, Springer International Publishing, Cham, https://doi.org/10.1007/978-3-319-10377-8_13.

Yan, E & Ding, Y 2012, 'Scholarly network similarities: How bibliographic coupling networks, citation networks, cocitation networks, topical networks, coauthorship networks, and coword networks relate to each other', *Journal of the American Society for Information Science and Technology*, vol. 63, pp. 1313–26, https://doi.org/10.1002/asi.22680.

5.8 Regional Distribution of Research: The Spatial Polarization in Question

Marion Maisonobe

Abstract: The objective of this chapter is threefold: showing how research activity is spatially organized in the contemporary world at different scales, what are the different means and datasets available to measure its spatial distribution, and what can explain the degree of polarization of this activity. The chapter adopts a critical view on the literature that stresses the spatial polarization of this activity as if it was a necessary feature of it. First, the chapter demonstrates that contrary to most expectations, this polarization has globally diminished since the second part of the twentieth century. Second, taking the example of the regional distribution of research in Europe, it insists on the various means and sources used to study this distribution and its evolution through time. To finish, it highlights an overlooked dimension of research activity: the fact that the institutional geography (authors' affiliations) does not reflect where research is actually done, especially in the case of field ground-based research; and it gives some direction for future research.

Keywords: geography of science, spatial scientometrics, regional economics, urban geography, spatial polarization.

Introduction

Scholars from distinct fields with different research questions are working at studying the geography of scientific production. We currently observe three main reasons and three main types of scholars interested to this aim:

- The first reason relates to the research of indicators to monitor scientific activity and to the will to relate scientific policies to the spatial organization of science. It interests in priority scientometricians and more specifically among them spatial scientometricians. Apart from the construction of indicators, this approach targets a better understanding of the "growth of science" as it is measurable through the growing publication of academic papers.
- The second reason relates to the attempt to link indicators of territorial development, innovation, and economic growth to indicators related to research activity (investment in R&D as well as research output). It interests in priority scholars specialized in regional economics that are keen to understand the mechanisms allowing transferring knowledge into innovation that can be useful for civil so-

---

Marion Maisonobe, UMR Géographie-cités, CNRS – Université Panthéon-Sorbonne – Université de Paris – EHESS, Campus Condorcet, Bâtiment de recherche Sud, 5, cours des Humanités, 93322 Aubervilliers, France, marion.maisonobe@cnrs.fr

ciety either through the commercialization of new products or through radical changes in people's lives and believes.
- The third reason relates to the ambition of understanding spatial mechanisms leading to the contemporary distribution of men and activities and their connections through material infrastructures (roads, railways, etc.) and immaterial exchanges of information and knowledge. The will of understanding certain territorial arrangement in particular also enters into this line of research: spatial dynamics of certain national systems, macro-regions, and linguistic areas. This approach interests in priority scholars belonging to the field of geography, but also historians and sociologists.

Historically, Joseph Ben-David was one of the first scholars who tried to elaborate a theory to explain the changing geography of scientific production by analyzing a move of the world science's center of gravity from Germany to the United-States between the mid-nineteenth century and the early 1970s. Ben-David was not only interested in scientific power, but by the entanglement between systems of higher education and the organization of scientific research, which explains why he sometimes referred to the nations he was focussing on as "centers of learning" or as "scientific centers" (Ben-David, 1991). His work falls within the stream of institutionalist sociology of science, which subsequently has lost ground since the 1970s. Later, most studies focussing on science production at the world level were performed by scientometricians using the Web of Science database to analyze the growth of science. As a result, the precise question of the spatial distribution of scientific production and its global evolution has more to do with spatial scientometrics nowadays, as can be seen from the presence of this chapter hereby.

This chapter begins by a review of the literature on the spatial distribution of contemporary research. It then shows that my group's observations on this point – obtained from analyses conducted on the Web of Science – diverge significantly from several published works on the subject in regional economics and urban geography as well as from political discourses on the spatial organization of research. Beyond my group's observations, the chapter takes the example of the regional distribution of research in Europe to stress the limits of what is measurable with bibliographic sources and of the means used to measure it. To finish, I insist on the advisability of using new sources to study the geography of research, taking into account not only the institutional geography of science but also sources that make it possible to locate the concrete place where research is carried out. To this aim, I give the example of the Research in Svalbard (RIS) database, which allows localising precisely the sites where researchers go to perform their field ground research on this arctic territory.

On the Spatial Polarization of Research

On the Spatial Polarization of Research before the 2000s

Research as we understand it today is an activity that was practised only in a very limited number of places until the mid-twentieth century. As mentioned by Jean Gottmann in the conclusion of his discourse on the "The need of an international policy for the sciences" at the Nobel Symposium in 1973: "the apparent order which existed after 1945, owing to the high concentration of science and technology in a very small number of countries and centres, has now been eroded. If any international policy for science has been operating in the last 20 years, it has certainly been one of geographic decentralization. It has borne results; one consequence of it is precisely the need for more common moorings" (Gottmann, 1973). The spatial diffusion of research is a phenomenon that can be related to an increase in the number of countries developing a system of higher education and investing in science during the second part of the twentieth century. The effects of this phenomenon are also observed within countries by Herbert Inhaber in an article published in 1977 in *Research Policy*, "Changes in centralization of science" (Inhaber, 1977). By retrieving data from the Institute for Scientific Information (ISI) on scientists' affiliations, Inhaber reckons that "When the relative change in concentration from 1967 to 1972 was considered, almost all of the countries considered had a fairly strong decrease. For most, the change was of the order of 2% a year". For Inhaber, "this dispersion of scientists may be due to less reliance on a small centralized corps of scientists once a nation reaches a "take-off" point in science". Together with an increasing spatial dispersion of scientists within countries, referring to 1990's UNESCO data, Thomas Schott reports an increasing participation in the world of science by a growing number of countries: "In recent decades, expenditure on research and development has increased nearly everywhere in absolute amounts and in most places also as a percentage of the gross national product. Scientists and engineers engaged in research and development have also increased nearly everywhere, both in absolute numbers and as a fraction of the population of their respective countries. All these measures indicate a growth in scientific activity in nearly every country in recent decades" (Schott, 1991). Despite these evolutions, Schott insists on the growing concentration of scientific activity in the wealthiest countries as measured by the growth in the global share of high-standard publications per country (+1.61 for the wealthiest countries against +0.96 for the poorest countries and -2.58 for communist countries between 1973 and 1986). This analysis focusses on the scientific domination of liberal democracies over communist countries following the collapse of the USSR. The classification Schott uses to group countries is very much influenced by this context and helps him to demonstrate the drop of Soviet science, which is of course very significant during the period under study. If we look into more details of the data computed by Schott (Table 1), we can observe that actually, among the "liberal democracies", it is only Japan and "the rest of Western Europe" that have registered considerable increases in their global share of publication. When normalizing by countries' population growth, the picture is interestingly different, suggesting a spatial diffusion of the scientific activity within countries, which has been faster within the wealthiest countries than within the poorest countries between 1973 and 1986. In the post-2000s literature on the spatial polarization of research, as shown in the next sub-section, the issues of data standardization and aggregation continue to play an important role in defining what is meant by "spatial polarization" and thus explain that even empirical analyses can disagree on the matter.

On the Spatial Polarization of Research after the 2000s

In 2005, confirming the diffusion trends identified earlier, Evan Schofer and John W. Meyer published in the *American Sociological Review* the result of an extensive research on "The Worldwide Expansion of Higher Education in the Twentieth Century" (Schofer and Meyer, 2005). Their research shows that a growing enrolment of the population in higher education and the development of university systems happened in every region of the world during the twentieth century. The authors analyze the institutional processes that led to what they call "a new model of society" including scientization, democratization and the expansion of human rights, the rise of development planning, and the structuration of the world polity. According to them, "the result is a highly expanded, and essentially global, system of higher education". However, if the global growth in the population of students, in the number of universities, and R&D institutions is a shared observation among academics, there is more debate regarding changes in the geography of research output.

Table 1: Changes in Production of Scientific Papers, 1973–1986. After Schott, 1991.

Scientific Community	Percentage of scientific papers*			Ratio of percentage papers to percentage population		
	1973	1986	Change	1973	1986	Change
Liberal Democracies:	81.77	83.38	+1.61	4.29	4.90	+0.61
United States	38.23	36.53	-1.70	7.12	7.49	+0.37
Canada	4.39	4.38	-0.01	7.84	8.45	+0.61
Japan	5.26	7.92	+2.66	1.92	3.23	+1.31
United Kingdom	9.21	7.97	-1.24	6.46	6.95	+0.49
West Germany	6.04	5.99	-0.05	3.85	4.87	+1.02
France	5.56	4.99	-0.57	4.21	4.45	+0.24
Rest of Western Europe	9.74	12.17	+2.44	1.67	2.34	+0.67
Australia, New Zealand	2.38	2.41	+0.03	5.75	6.18	+0.43
Israel	0.96	1.02	+0.06	11.53	11.75	+0.22
Communist Countries:	13.18	10.59	-2.58	1.25	1.14	-0.11
Soviet Union	9.00	7.39	-1.60	1.15	1.07	-0.09
Eastern Europe	4.18	3.20	-0.98	1.54	1.38	-0.16

Poor Countries:	5.06	6.02	+0.96	0.07	0.08	+0.01
North Africa, Near East	0.43	0.56	+0.14	0.12	0.13	+0.01
South Africa	0.45	0.53	+0.08	0.73	0.79	+0.06
Rest of Africa	0.35	0.31	-0.04	0.05	0.04	-0.01
India	2.53	2.35	-0.19	0.17	0.15	-0.02
Rest of Asia	0.33	1.07	+0.74	0.01	0.03	+0.02
Latin America	0.97	1.20	+0.23	0.13	0.15	+0.02

*Note: Articles by authors in each country and region in a year as percentage of total papers produced worldwide. Change is difference in that percentage 1973–86.
Sources: Number of papers: National Science Foundations SP # 1 Science Literature Indicators Database, Indicator Ib (1973-journal set), from CHI Research, derived from *Science Citation Index*.
Population: *World Tables Compressed Data Diskettes (DEK), op. cit.; Demographic Yearbook 1975* (New York: United Nations, 1979), and *Demographic Yearbook 1987, op. cit.*

According to certain scholars, research is an activity that is intrinsically concentrated and tends to become more and more polarized though time. Empirically, this vision is being nurtured by the gap between the distribution of the world population and the distribution of research output and impact. For instance, in the early 2000s, Michael Batty used the ISI's HighlyCited database composed of the top 100 or so cited individuals in 14 scientific fields to compute a level of spatial concentration of these individuals. He comments: "The pattern of concentration that this analysis reveals is remarkable: 1222 scientists work in 429 institutions which are located in 232 places in 27 countries. Almost half these scientists are in 50 institutions in 5 countries, most being in the United States" (Batty, 2003). In 2005, Richard Florida also relies on this source to observe: "Scientific advance is even more concentrated than patent production. Most occurs not just in a handful of countries but in a handful of cities – primarily in the United States and Europe. Chinese and Indian cities do not even register. As far as global innovation is concerned, perhaps a few dozen places worldwide really compete at the cutting edge" (Florida, 2005). In both cases, the spatial distribution of the top cited scientists is analyzed only for a given year, which does not allow identifying a spatial trend. However, Florida links his observation to a dynamic theory. According to him, the concentration of creative talents in a few hotspots able to connect to the global system of cities is intensifying from the 1990s. This theory borrows from regional economics the principles according to which innovating activities tend to cluster in a few centers because of "the powerful productivity advantages, economies of scale, and knowledge spillovers such density brings". In 2010, the bibliometric analyses of Christian W. Matthiessen, Annette W. Schwartz, and Soren Find offered a more precise and longitudinal analysis on the geography of research output encompassing the world's most publishing urban areas (Matthiessen et al., 2010). Instead of a reinforcing domination of the traditional centres, they observe that "Clearly, the position of European and North American research is under challenge from new high-producing centres outside these continents", which suggests a geographical expansion at the world level. However, measuring the evolution of the number of publications retrieved in the Science Citation Index (SCI) between 1996 and 2006, they remark: "Total growth has been 28 per cent and growth in the top 30 cities has been 34 per cent, which demonstrates a concentration process". In 2013, Michel Grossetti, Denis Eckert, Yves Gingras, Laurent Jégou, Vincent Larivière, and Béatrice Milard explored the same issue but offered an analysis more in line with pre 2000s observations (Grossetti et al., 2013). Instead of focussing on the most publishing places, their analysis encompasses all the publishing places retrieved in the SCI-Expanded. They demonstrate a deconcentration trend in the distribution of the scientific production happening both within most countries and between countries at the world level. First, they show that "the number of countries needed to account for 80% of world publications was 7 in 1978, 10 in 1988 (including the USSR), 13 in 1998 (with a united Germany and Russia separated from other former USSR countries), and 16 in 2008" (Table 2).

Table 2: Evolution between 1987 and 2007 of the 30 most productive countries in world publications. After Grossetti et al., 2013.

Country	Country/world share in 1987[a]	Country/world share in 1997[a]	Country/world share in 2007[a]	1987 rank	1997 rank	2007 rank
USA	34.3	29.8	24.5	1	1	1
China	0.9	2.4	8.6	18	12	2
Japan	7.3	9.0	7.8	4	2	3
Germany	7.4	7.4	5.9	3	3	4
UK	7.8	7.4	5.4	2	4	5
France	5.3	5.5	4.3	5	5	6
Italy	2.5	3.4	3.5	9	8	7
Canada	4.3	3.7	3.4	7	6	8
India	2.6	2.2	3.0	8	11	9
Spain	1.3	2.3	2.7	13	9	10
South Korea	0.1	1.1	2.7	42	16	11
Russia	5.1	3.5	2.2	6	7	12
Australia	2.1	2.2	2.1	10	10	13
Brazil	0.5	0.9	2.1	27	21	14
The Netherlands	1.8	2.0	1.7	11	13	15
Turkey	0.1	0.5	1.6	44	26	16
Taiwan	0.3	1.0	1.6	33	18	17
Poland	1.0	0.9	1.4	17	20	18
Sweden	1.6	1.6	1.2	12	14	19

Table 2 *(Continued)*

Country	Country/world share in 1987[a]	Country/world share in 1997[a]	Country/world share in 2007[a]	1987 rank	1997 rank	2007 rank
Switzerland	1.2	1.3	1.2	14	15	20
Belgium	0.9	1.0	0.9	19	17	21
Iran	0.0	0.1	0.8	73	51	22
Israel	1.0	0.9	0.8	16	19	23
Greece	0.3	0.5	0.7	31	28	24
Austria	0.6	0.7	0.6	23	24	25
Denmark	0.8	0.8	0.6	20	22	26
Finland	0.6	0.7	0.6	21	23	27
Mexico	0.2	0.4	0.6	35	32	28
Czech Republic	0.5	0.4	0.5	24	29	29
Singapore	0.1	0.3	0.5	45	35	30

Fractional counting of publications, with 3-year moving average.

Second, they show that: "The proportion of world publications by the 25 cities ranked among the top 30 in both 1997 and 2007 regressed by 3.7 percentage points. Unsurprisingly, the share of newcomers (absent from the top 30 in 1997 and present in 2007) increased by 1.1 percentage points. The share of the five other agglomerations (present in 1997 and absent in 2007) regressed by 0.7 percentage points during the same period". It thus emerges that a twofold process was at work during the 2000s: the rise of new players in the global game, including China, and a continuation of the spatial deconcentration of scientific production observed within countries since the 1970s. This work therefore calls into question the assimilation of the research activity of an activity that is intrinsically polarized. More recent studies show that this deconcentration has been going on during the 2010s and is also measurable when focussing on the spatial distribution of collaboration (Maisonobe et al., 2016), of citations (Maisonobe et al., 2017), and of the 10% top cited publications in the world (Maisonobe et al., 2018). Despite these global and comprehensive analyses, a series of publications in regional economics and urban geography still consider the spatial concentration of scientific activities as an ongoing or intensifying phenomenon. In the next section, we attempt to explain this apparent contradiction.

How to Measure a (De)concentration Process?

Different Methods and Scales, Different Observations?

As noted by Susanne A. Frick and Andrés Rodríguez-Pose for the measure of urban concentration of the population (Frick and Rodríguez-Pose, 2018), there exists an important variety of methods that can be used to measure a degree of spatial polarization and its evolution. Regarding the spatial concentration of research, the literature relies either on the evolution of the Gini index (Dolores León et al., 2011; Zitt et al., 1999), on the share of the top centers in research intensity (Grossetti et al., 2013; Maisonobe et al., 2018), or on the scaling parameter (called "beta") in urban scaling laws (Nomaler et al., 2014; Pumain et al., 2006). In addition, we observe a growing number of studies relying on network analysis metrics to measure the spatial distribution of knowledge exchanges and the evolving centrality of certain places in R&D networks (Bergé et al., 2017; Hong, 2008). Both the territorial units of analysis and the scale of analysis vary across studies.

Among all this literature, urban scaling studies are those emphasizing the most the concentrated and metropolitan nature of research activity. Unlike other methods of measuring spatial concentration of an activity, urban scaling laws measure a degree of urban concentration by taking into account the distribution of the activity in relation to the population of the cities in which the activity is distributed (see subsection III.2). In addition to being an index of concentration, the scaling parameter therefore makes it possible to know in which part of the urban hierarchy the activity under study is concentrated. Consequently, this methodology contributes to a better understanding of varying distribution patterns across countries. As shown by Grossetti et al. (2013), the geography of research depends on historical processes and planning choices that have been made throughout history and still have effects nowadays. This may explain why, in urban scaling studies, the degree of adjustment of research activities to the urban hierarchy ($R2$ value of the regression model) is generally lower than that of jobs in sales and public administration, or of employment in general. By focussing on England and Wales, Arcaute et al. notice this specificity in the spatial distribution of patents: "In addition to economic hubs, one also encounters knowledge hubs, which also present dragon-king-like qualities and which are not necessarily correlated with size. These hubs are the outcome of path-dependencies that give rise to emergent properties that are not present in all cities as is the case of patents. This is most dramatically demonstrated by the dominance of patent production in Cambridge, UK" (Arcaute et al., 2015). Despite their poorer fit to the urban hierarchy, and despite the variety of spatial boundaries and methods available to measure scaling coefficients, R&D activities generally appear more concentrated in the most populated territories (beta index greater than 1). However, among the authors highlighting these clear superlinear relationships between the distribution of R&D activity and urban population, there are two opposing interpretations. First, Bettencourt et al. rely on Florida's theory and consider super-linear regimes of scaling as the result of increasing returns to network interactions in the most populated places (Bettencourt et al., 2007). Second, Pumain et al. (2006) offer an evolutionary theory for interpreting urban scaling laws. According to them, human sectors characterized by a super-linear regime are innovative sectors concentrated in the top of the urban hierarchy at the time of their emergence. Their subsequent diffusion in the urban hierarchy transforms the scaling regime into a linear one (when the activity becomes common) and then into a sub-linear one (when it becomes mature).

This second interpretation seems adequate to describe the gradual deconcentration of research described in part II. Universities and research centers used to be rare institutions located in only a few places. With decentralization policies and the massification of students, these institutions have become much more common and located in an increasing number of cities. The spatial diffusion of these institutions has led to the world deconcentration of research results.

Yet, two recent counter examples deserve to be mentioned that highlight the limits of urban scaling to measure the spatial polarization of research activity. First, the study of Arcaute et al. shows that the beta index computed on 2000–2011 patents' distribution is very sensitive to the boundary definition used to delineate cities and that, for England and Wales, its relation with the urban population can be either linear or superlinear. Second, Leitão et al. discuss the classical use of OLS regressions for urban scaling laws, and, using different regression methods on multiple datasets, show that the relation of UK-patents [2000–2011] and OECD-patents [2008] to the population distribution is linear (Leitão et al., 2016). Their result questions the relevance of studies arguing that R&D activity naturally tends to concentrate in the most populated areas.

As the concentration index, the territory, and the method used to measure spatial polarization can lead to various observations, we consider it important to take into account geographical variations and avoid generalizations. Indeed the existing literature suggests that in some countries, R&D activity remains concentrated in the most populated areas, while other countries have a less centralized research system. There is also strong evidence that at the global level, the number of countries and cities involved in R&D activity have increased since the mid-twentieth century. Focusing on the European territory, the following sub-section highlights the sensitivity of observations to methodological choices.

The Regional Distribution of Research in Europe

In this sub-section, we examine the evolution of the geography of research at the European level between 2001 and 2012 using normalized publication outputs from the Web of Science database, as well as demographic, general employment and R&D data from Eurostat. R&D data from Eurostat include R&D expenditure (GERD), R&D employment, and patent applications to the EPO. Our goal is to compare the results obtained using different indicators and different methods. In order to relate

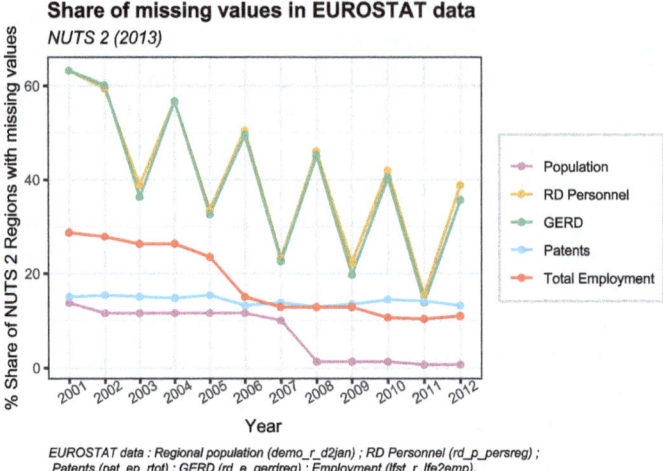

Figure 1: Share of missing values in Eurostat data at the NUTS 2 level.

the publication data to demographic data from Eurostat and to compare their spatial polarization to that of other R&D indicators, we mainly aggregate the publication data at the NUTS 2 level (which corresponds to national sub-regions). As a result, we conduct this analysis at a less precise spatial resolution than that of previous studies on the world geography of science.

We have chosen to start the analysis in 2001 because of the amount of missing data before this year in the Eurostat database and to stop the analysis in 2012 because patent data have stopped being registered after this date. In addition, post-2013 reforms in countries such as France and Poland have modified the administrative level of collect of R&D data, creating a discontinuity in the time series and making it difficult to follow a geographical evolution from 2001 to 2020 at the NUTS 2 level. The frequency of collection of R&D data following the recommendations of the Frascati Manual varies across country. As shown in Figure 1, certain countries such as Germany only collect these data biannually. For this reason, we have applied an interpolation method to estimate the missing values when the number of missing values for one region was strictly inferior to 11.

In order to include all the countries of the EU-28 perimeter together with Iceland, Norway, and Switzerland in the analysis, we have chosen to make other specific adjustments. As reflected by the important share of missing values at the NUTS 2 level (Figure 1), some countries report Eurostat data only at national level, such as Switzerland and Denmark (before 2007). In certain areas, the data are only available at an intermediate level (NUTS1), such as for Lithuania, Slovenia, Belgium, and the Southern Finland region, but also for the regions of Sachsen and Bavaria in Germany, as well as for Scotland and North-West England in the UK. In order to make the London area and the Budapest region comparable with other capital regions, we have also chosen to consider the NUTS1 level for these specific territories.

5.8 Regional Distribution of Research: The Spatial Polarization in Question

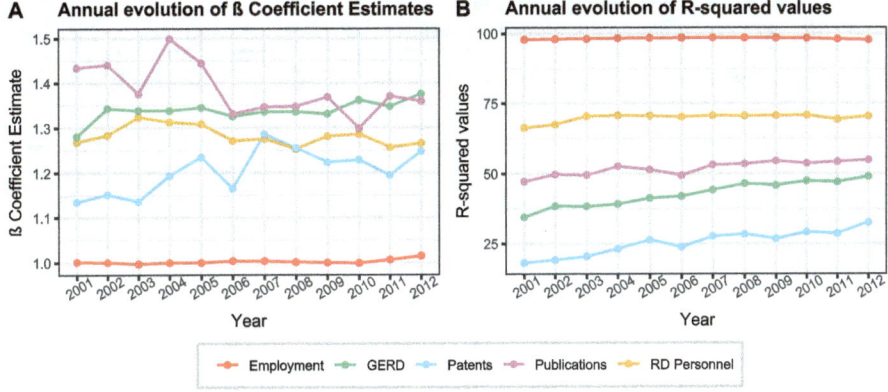

Figure 2: Annual evolution of the scaling parameters and of R-squared values.

By making these adjustments and by interpolating the data, we succeeded in removing all the missing values and covering 241 territories in our analysis.

This analysis is organized in three steps. First, we monitor the evolution of the scaling coefficient (beta) for all the three R&D indicators (R&D personnel, GERD, and patent applications) as well as for the spatial distribution of publication data. As a reference indicator, we consider the spatial distribution of employment data (all human sectors of activity combined) knowing that employment is expected to be less concentrated than R&D activity (in red on the figures). In the following steps, we compare the results of the first analysis with the results obtained by computing the Gini coefficient and the evolution of the percentage share of the top 30 European regions. To estimate the scaling coefficient, we use a classical Ordinary Least Square regression method between the considered variables and the number of inhabitants by regions (regional population).

As expected, employment exhibits a linear regime of scaling (beta equals to one) whereas R&D activity appears more concentrated in the most populated regions at the European scale (beta superior to one). However, the scaling parameter of R&D personnel and publication outputs has decreased over the period (Figure 2 A). While it appears the scaling parameter of R&D expenditure and patents has increased over the period, this information is subject to caution since the goodness of fit (R^2) is inferior to 50% for both indicators (Figure 2 B), meaning that these indicators poorly fit to population data. When, following the advice of Finance and Swerts regarding the interpretation of scaling parameters (Finance and Swerts, 2020), we consider their 95% confidence intervals (Figure 3) and note that the observed changes over the years have been too limited to be interpreted as changes in spatial polarization.

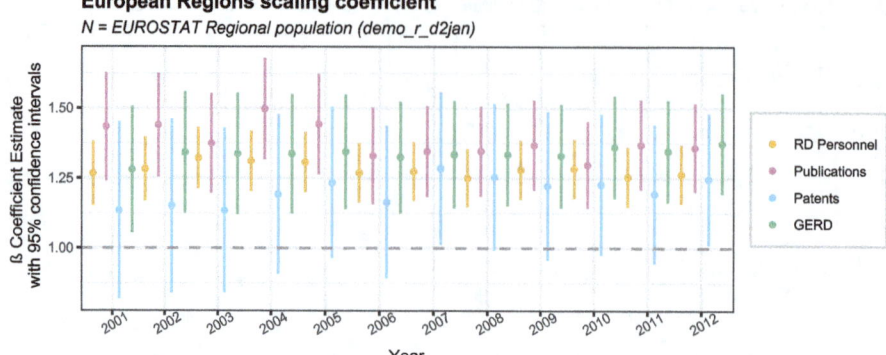

Figure 3: Annual evolution of the scaling parameters and of R-squared values.

Even if the measured changes are limited, the value of the Gini coefficient (Figure 3 A) as well as the one of the Gini coefficient weighted by the number of inhabitants (Figure 3 B) both exhibit a decrease of concentration for all indicators except the reference indicator (total employment). This analysis suggests a movement of greater convergence of European regions in terms of R&D activity consistent with the one measured by Zitt et al. (1999) for the 1990s and by Dolores Leon et al. (2011) for the 2000s relying on the evolution of the Gini index. While R&D outputs and expenditures still appear more concentrated than R&D personnel this gap appears to be narrowing over the period, especially in terms of publications. After 2008, the implementation of excellence policies have developed across European countries leading to a growing concentration of research funds in certain areas, which could explain that the concentration of R&D expenditures remains stable after this date.

As these polices tend to increase geographical inequalities among scientists, several authors have pointed out their effects in recent years. Indeed, it seems that if a process of dispersal of R&D activity is at work, it is important that the allocation of funding can accompany this process (Aagaard et al., 2019; Langfeldt et al., 2015; Larivière et al., 2010). When analyzing the evolution of the per cent share of the top 30 European regions the gap between the distribution of R&D expenditure and that of R&D personnel appears even wider (Figure 4 A). While the top 30 European regions concentrate about 60% of the total R&D expenditures, they only represent about 50% of the R&D personnel. Considering the ratio between the percentage share in R&D activity and the population share (Figure 4.B) does not make this difference less important.

5.8 Regional Distribution of Research: The Spatial Polarization in Question — 389

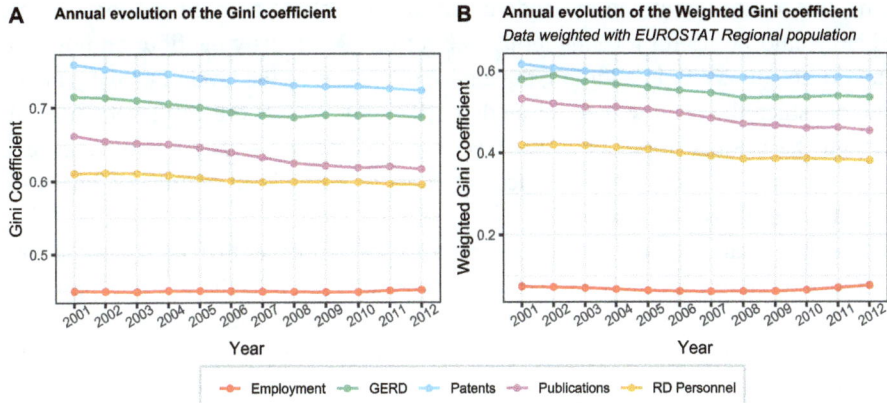

Figure 4: Annual evolution of the Gini coefficient and of the Weighted Gini coefficient.

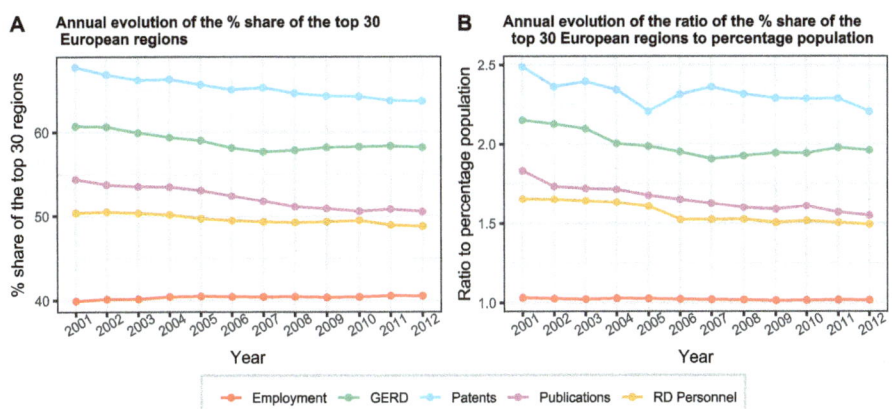

Figure 5: Annual evolution of the activity share and ratio of the top 30 European regions.

The results obtained when comparing the Gini coefficient with the evolving share of the top 30 regions are equivalent. Weighting and normalizing these indicators with the regional population does not modify the observations. The evolution of the scaling parameter, on the other hand, exhibits interesting differences. The scaling parameter for patents and R&D expenditures is smaller than that of publication activity, which is the opposite of what we measure with the value of the Gini coefficient and that of the top regions' percentage share. Since the goodness of fit is very low for these two indicators, it is possible that another model will better adjust to their distribution and thus better describe their spatial polarization (Leitão et al., 2016). Beyond this, other regression methods could also enable to account for zero values, which would be useful for long-term analyses of R&D activity distribution (Finance and Cottineau, 2018). In addition, the choice of regions as the level of analysis is disputable since the scaling method lends itself to analysis at the city level. Thus, although the scaling approach can be very interesting, especially at the level of a given national system, it requires accurate data at a fine level of analysis and a lot of caution in interpretation.

Despite these limitations, the three approaches show that R&D activities are geographically more concentrated than the active population at the level of the EU28. The Gini and activity share approaches indicate a gradual convergence between regions with a lower level of concentration at the end of the period. In particular, the gap between publishing activity and the distribution of research staff tends to narrow. The script and datasets used for this analysis are available at the following repository: https://framagit.org/MarionMai/the-regional-distribution-of-research-in-europe (July 15, 2020).

New Prospects for the Geography of Science

Beyond an Institutional Geography

Previous sections have highlighted the existence of several methods and numerous indicators to measure the degree of polarization of research activities. Depending on the territories, data are unevenly available, and, in the case of bibliographic sources such as the Web of Science or Scopus to measure publishing activity, there are representation biases related to the completeness of the databases and the evolution of their coverage over time (Basu, 2010; Zitt et al., 2003). On the administrative data side, although OECD countries are encouraged to follow the recommendations of the Frascati manual, there are significant differences in the pace of collection and in territorial divisions that complicate comparisons between countries. To our view, the geography of science literature should more systematically take into account and discuss these different limitations in the future. To improve the reproducibility of research in this still emerging field, our team shared the dataset of urban areas used to produce analyses at the world level and launched a geospatial application called NETSCITY that can geocode, cluster, and map any bibliographical dataset at the urban area and country level (Maisonobe et al., 2019).

However, both when studying the distribution of scientific personnel and production, the available data only reflect an institutional geography in the sense that these are the reported locations of the activity: the location of the laboratory where the researcher is attached and, in the case of company research, possibly the location of the company's head office. Thus, a field study financed by the Occitania Region in France has shown that researchers working in the Institutes of Technology of the small-sized town of Figeac signed their publications from Toulouse,

5.8 Regional Distribution of Research: The Spatial Polarization in Question

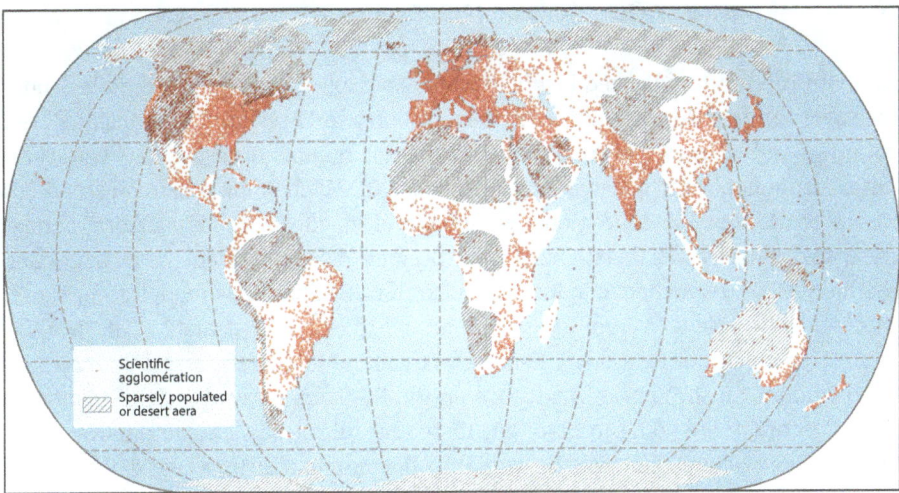

Map 1: Places from which at least one publication has been published between 1999 and 2014 (by Laurent Jégou).

where the headquarters of their lab is located (Chauvac and Naverau, 2019). Moreover, an important part of the scientific activity is not conducted within laboratory sites: applied sciences require fieldwork to be performed; history, archaeology, and humanities require the conducting of archival research and/or excavations; and many scientists, whatever their disciplines, praise the virtue of literary retreats and summer schools for writing and exchanging ideas. As a result, the geography obtained though administrative data and authors' affiliations only reflects partially the actual distribution of research.

Nevertheless, when mapping all the places where at least one publication registered in the Web of Science has been signed during the 2000s according to authors' affiliations, we can observe that this covers some very remote areas (Map 1). If this is the case, it is because certain scientists sign from the actual place where they have done their research, but this is not often the norm, in particular because of the competition between universities to appear well ranked at world level. Since authors' affiliations might not be the best indicator of where research is actually done, other approaches could be used such as retrieving the name of the places mentioned by the authors in the title, the abstract or even the full text of their publications. Another possibility is to refer to other available sources, such as databases registering the activity of scientists on their field ground. In the next subsection, we give the example of the Research in Svalbard (RIS) database.

The Case of the Research in Svalbard (RIS) Database

Svalbard is a territory located just below the exact location of the North Pole. Under the sovereignty of Norway, this archipelago is home to 13 scientific stations of eleven countries and welcomes every year a considerable number of researchers who carry out measurements and observations (Strouk, 2020). Much of the research carried out in this territory is related to global warming and its effects on fauna, flora, permafrost, and glaciers. As these topics have become more important in recent years, the number of researchers conducting research in Svalbard has tended to increase. In order to be able to control the situation, and to ensure the safety of all, Norway has set up a monitoring system. Researchers coming to do their research at Ny-Ålesund stations must indicate in advance on the Research in Svalbard (RIS) platform the project they are going to carry out there and fill in the GPS coordinates of the specific sites where they will be working, the number of times, and the period they will visit them. Researchers visiting other localities in Svalbard are also invited to detail their project on the platform so that RIS can also be a tool for coordination and possibly convergence between similar projects. However, it is likely that the database obtained does not cover all the projects carried out in the area. Nevertheless, this source appears well built and interesting enough to give an overview of a rarely considered aspect of the geography of research.

The map below highlights the sites visited by all scientists who have recorded a project in the platform before January 2020 and the number of fieldworks carried out and ongoing in these sites. To improve the readability of the map, the points located within a radius of one kilometer from each other have been aggregated. It can be observed that the stations located in Ny-Ålesund, Longyearbyen, Barentsburg, and Hornsund regularly feature in the list of places mentioned because they serve as stopover points for the majority of missions. They can be the place where boats are refuelling and where the scientists rest for a few days before moving on. In addition, a large number of sites declared by scientists are located near these towns. For example, the Kongsfjorden setting with the Kronebreen and Kongsvegen glaciers near Ny-Ålesund on the one hand and the Adventdalen valley near Longyerbyen, which is home to the University of Svalbard, on the other, are two natural areas most visited by scientists who have registered projects on the platform. While it is obvious, for logistic reasons, that the geography of the stations influences the distribution of research carried out in such a remote territory, it is also observed that a very large number of ad hoc missions are carried out at greater distances from the stations as well as at sea (small blue dots on the map). Thus, even in the northernmost part of our world, it is possible to find mechanisms for the polarization of research activities with zones of attraction around research stations and less frequented areas. This being said, the occupation of this territory by researchers of an increasingly diverse number of nationalities is a good indication of the increasingly globalized nature of research and its presence even in very remote lands, at a distance from major urban centers. Yet, this activity would not have been visible through traditional spatial bibliometrics approaches.

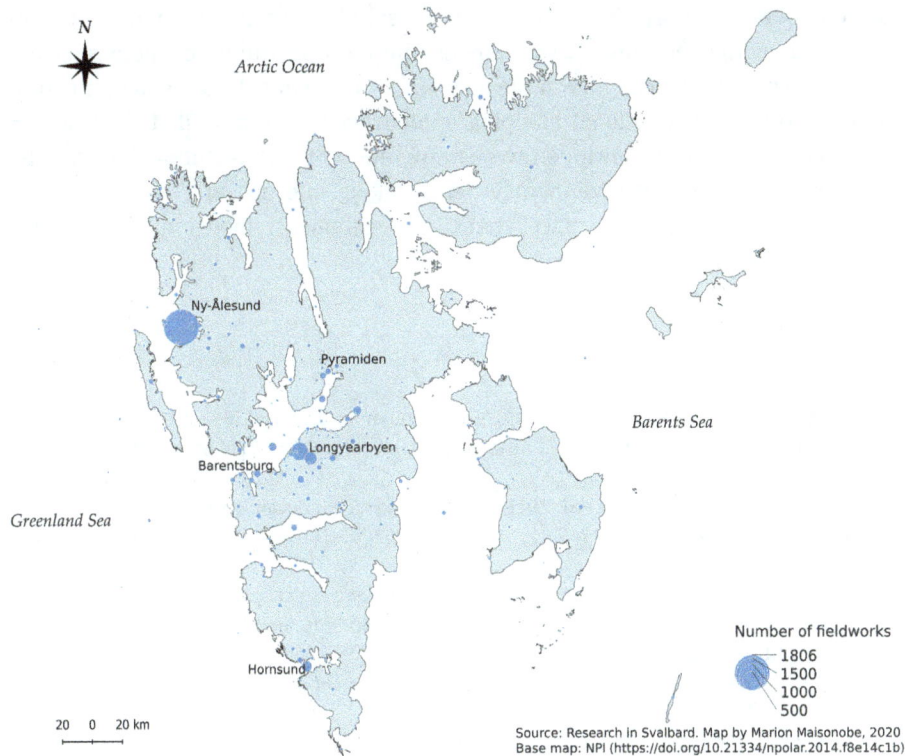

Map 2: Number of fieldworks per site registered in the Research in Svalbard database.

Conclusion

In this chapter, we have returned to the apparent paradox between the literature showing a continuous movement of spatial deconcentration of research activity, between and within countries, since the mid-twentieth century, and the literature stressing the metropolitan and naturally concentrated nature of research activities. We have shown that the latter, inspired by regional economics, was mainly based on observations made at a given date but not on longitudinal analyses. In order to overcome the apparent contradictions between these approaches, we have highlighted the different methods available to measure the spatial concentration of research activities and the different indicators available. An application of these different methods to the case of European data indicates that even at the European level, where research systems are mature, there has continued to be a slight devolution of research activity between 2001 and 2012. Thus, although universities and research centers are obviously not as dispersed as some community-based services, and thus continue to be more highly developed in some cities, regions, and countries, their polarization is not as great as it once was. Beyond the variety of methods, the question of data accessibility, the level of spatial resolution of the data, and their completeness is addressed. Finally, we demonstrate the opportunity of increasing the number of sources that can inform the geography of research. In particular, it is proposed to go beyond traditional mapping approaches based on affiliation data and public statistics, to work towards investigating not only an institutional geography of research but also a geography of science taking into account the very places where research is carried out, places that can be extremely remote and at a distance from urban centers.

References

Aagaard, K, Kladakis, A & Nielsen, MW 2019, 'Concentration or dispersal of research funding?', *Quantitative Science Studies*, vol. 1, no. 1, pp. 117–49, doi: https://doi.org/10.1162/qss_a_00002.

Arcaute, E, Hatna, E, Ferguson, P et al. 2015, 'Constructing cities, deconstructing scaling laws', *Journal of The Royal Society Interface*, vol. 12, no. 102, doi: https://doi.org/10.1098/rsif.2014.0745.

Basu, A 2010, 'Does a country's scientific 'productivity' depend critically on the number of country journals indexed?', *Scientometrics*, vol. 82, no. 3, pp. 507–16, doi: https://doi.org/10.1007/s11192-010-0186-8.

Batty, M 2003, 'The geography of scientific citation', *Environment and Planning A* 35, pp. 761–70, doi: https://doi.org/10.1068/a3505com.

Ben-David, J 1991, *Scientific Growth: Essays on the Social Organization and Ethos of Science*, in G Freudenthal (ed.), Los Angeles: Univ. of California Press.

Bergé, LR, Wanzenböck, I & Scherngell, T 2017, 'Centrality of regions in R&D networks: a new measurement approach using the concept of bridging paths', *Regional Studies*, vol. 51, no. 8, pp. 1165–78, doi: https://doi.org/10.1080/00343404.2016.1269885.

Bettencourt, LMA, Lobo, J, Helbing, D et al. 2007, 'Growth, innovation, scaling, and the pace of life in cities', *Proceedings of the National Academy of Sciences*, vol. 104, no. 17, p. 7301, doi: https://doi.org/10.1073/pnas.0610172104.

Chauvac, N & Naverau, B 2019, *Localisation Géographique de la Production Scientifique en Occitanie*, Rapport intermédiaire, Toulouse, CCRRDT OCCITANIE.

Dolores León, M, Fernández, AM & Flores, E 2011, 'Scientific and Technological Knowledge of Universities in the EU-15: Implications for Convergence', *European Planning Studies*, vol. 19, no. 4, pp. 683–703, doi: https://doi.org/10.1080/09654313.2011.548468.

Finance, O & Cottineau, C 2018, 'Are the absent always wrong? Dealing with zero values in urban scaling', *Environment and Planning B: Urban Analytics and City Science*, vol. 46, no. 9, pp. 1663–77, doi: https://doi.org/10.1177/2399808318785634.

Finance, O & Swerts, E 2020, 'Scaling Laws in Urban Geography. Linkages with Urban Theories, Challenges and Limitations', in D Pumain (ed.), *Theories and Models of Urbanization: Geography, Economics and Computing Sciences*, pp. 67–96, Springer International Publishing, Cham, doi: https://doi.org/10.1007/978-3-030-36656-8_5.

Florida, RL 2005, 'The world is spiky', *The Atlantic*, vol. 296, no. 3, pp. 48–51.

Frick, SA & Rodríguez-Pose, A 2018, 'Change in urban concentration and economic growth', *World Development*, vol 105, pp. 156–70, doi: https://doi.org/10.1016/j.worlddev.2017.12.034.

Gottmann, J 1973, 'The need of an international policy for the sciences', in *Nobel Symposium No. 26*, pp. 7–13, Oslo.

Grossetti, M, Eckert, D, Gingras, Y et al. 2013, 'Cities and the geographical deconcentration of scientific activity: A multilevel analysis of publications (1987–2007)', *Urban Studies*, doi: https://doi.org/10.1177/0042098013506047.

Hong, W 2008, 'Decline of the center: The decentralizing process of knowledge transfer of Chinese universities from 1985 to 2004', *Research Policy*, vol. 37, no. 4, pp. 580–95, doi: https://doi.org/10.1016/j.respol.2007.12.008.

Inhaber, H 1977, 'Changes in centralization of science', *Research Policy*, vol. 6, pp. 178–93, doi: https://doi.org/10.1016/0048-7333(77)90024-5.

Langfeldt, L, Benner, M, Siverstsen, G et al. 2015, 'Excellence and growth dynamics: A comparative study of the Matthew effect', *Science and Public Policy*, vol. 42, no. 5, pp. 661–75.

Larivière, V, Macaluso, B, Archambault, É et al. 2010, 'Which scientific elites? On the concentration of research funds, publications and citations', *Research Evaluation*, vol. 19, no. 1, pp. 45–53, doi: https://doi.org/10.3152/095820210X492495.

Leitão, JC, Miotto, JM, Gerlach, M & Altmann, EG 2016, 'Is this scaling nonlinear?', *Royal Society Open Science*, vol. 3, no. 7, 150649, https://doi.org/10.1098/rsos.150649.

Maisonobe, M, Grossetti, M, Milard, B et al. 2016, 'The global evolution of scientific collaboration networks between cities (1999–2014): multiple scales', *Revue française de sociologie*, vol. 57, no. 3, pp. 417–41, doi: https://doi.org/10.3917/rfs.573.0417.

Maisonobe, M, Grossetti, M, Milard, B et al. 2017, 'The global geography of scientific visibility: a deconcentration process (1999–2011)', *Scientometrics*, vol. 113, no. 1, pp. 479–93.

Maisonobe, M, Jégou, L & Cabanac, G 2018, 'Peripheral Forces', *Nature Index*, no. 563, S18-S19.

Maisonobe, M, Jégou, L, Yakimovich, N et al. 2019, 'NETSCITY: a geospatial application to analyse and map world scale production and collaboration data between cities', in *ISSI'19: 17th International Conference on Scientometrics and Informetrics*, Rome.

Matthiessen, CW, Schwarz, AW & Find, S 2010, 'World Cities of Scientific Knowledge: Systems, Networks and Potential Dynamics. An Analysis Based on Bibliometric Indicators', *Urban Studies*, vol. 47, no. 9, pp. 1879–97, doi: https://doi.org/10.1177/0042098010372683.

Nomaler, Ö, Frenken, K & Heimeriks, G 2014, 'On Scaling of Scientific Knowledge Production in U.S. Metropolitan Areas', *PLOS ONE*, vol. 9, no. 10: e110805, doi: https://doi.org/10.1371/journal.pone.0110805.

Pumain, D, Paulus, F, Vacchiani-Marcuzzo, C et al. 2006, 'An evolutionary theory for interpreting urban scaling laws', *Cybergeo: European Journal of Geography*, no. 343, doi: https://doi-org.inshs.bib.cnrs.fr/10.4000/cybergeo.2519.

Schofer, E & Meyer, JW 2005, 'The Worldwide Expansion of Higher Education in the Twentieth Century', *American Sociological Review*, vol. 70, no. 6, pp. 898–920, doi: https://doi.org/10.1177/000312240507000602.

Schott, T 1991, 'The world scientific community: Globality and globalisation', *Minerva*, vol. 29, no. 4, pp. 440–62.

Strouk, M, 2020, 'Science en puissances : la recherche scientifique, porte d'entrée vers la gouvernance arctique pour les États observateurs', to be published.

Zitt, M, Barré, R, Sigogneau, A et al. 1999, 'Territorial concentration and evolution of science and technology activities in the European Union: a descriptive analysis', *Research Policy*, vol. 28, no. 5, pp. 545–62, doi: https://doi.org/10.1016/S0048-7333(99)00012-8.

Zitt, M, Ramanana-Rahary, S & Bassecoulard, E 2003, 'Correcting glasses help fair comparisons in international science landscape: Country indicators as a function of ISI database delineation', *Scientometrics*, vol. 56, no. 2, pp. 259–82.

5.9 Bibliometrics and Co-Authorship

Dorte Drongstrup

Abstract: This chapter reviews co-authorship in relation to bibliometrics studies. It presents what co-authorship means in bibliometric studies, how co-authoring relates to research productivity, and how the methodological decision effects whether co-authoring increases productivity. The chapter presents different aspects of author order decisions and to what extent the author order is useful to interpret researchers' contribution to a publication. It discusses the methodological issues of assigning and counting co-authorship credit.

Keywords: bibliometrics, co-authorship, counting methods, co-authorship credit.

Bibliometrics and Co-authorship

Authorship in bibliometric studies is the link between the researcher and the publication. It is assumed that the researcher in the role as an author is responsible for all the content of the publication, and for this responsibility will receive authorship credit for their contribution to research. Some refer to authorship credit as "the coin of the realm" (Wilcox, 1998; Biagioli, 1999), since it helps researchers build a reputation which translates into additional benefits such as job security (tenure), promotions, higher salaries, and research funding (Haeussler and Sauermann, 2013; Merton, 1973).

This seemly uncomplicated author link between researcher and research or responsibility and credit is true if we are dealing with single authorship. However, the picture becomes more blurred when dealing with co-authorship, especially as the number of authors rises, making it increasingly difficult to assess who should have authorship credit and responsibility for a publication. Furthermore, multiple studies show that the criteria for being a co-author differ between fields (Du and Tang, 2013; Geelhoed et al., 2007, Lariviere et al., 2016; Birnholtz, 2006). The extent of a contribution to research will perhaps give you a co-authorship in physics, an acknowledgement in economics, and sometimes nothing in political science (Henriksen, 2018a; Birnholtz, 2006; Lariviere et al., 2016).

Authorship and responsible conduct of research guidelines have been introduced to secure similar co-author requirements across disciplines and research groups. However, these guidelines often have the loophole with the requirement that all authors should have contributed substantially (ICMJE, 2010; CSE, 2012) without further defining what significantly or substantially means. Furthermore, studies

---

Dorte Drongstrup, Research Librarian, PhD, University Library of Southern Denmark, University of Southern Denmark, Campusvej 55, 5230 Odense, Denmarkt, dh@bib.sdu.dk

show that these guidelines are often ignored or interpreted selectively (Smith et al., 2019; Pignatelli et al., 2005).

This lack of uniform co-authorship criteria also means that the extent to which co-authorship represents research collaboration differs extensively between disciplines and research groups (Katz and Martin, 1997; Laudel, 2001; Biagioli, 1999). However, it is common practice to use co-authorship as a method to investigate research collaboration in bibliometric based studies. Still, one should be careful in bibliometric studies to use co-authorship as a proxy for research collaboration, because of the lack of information about what co-author entails in the various disciplines and the great variance in co-authorship criteria (Ponomariov and Boardman, 2016).

Co-authorship and Productivity

Studies of co-authorship shows that the average number of authors has risen across most science branches during the last century (Henriksen, 2016; Lariviere et al., 2015; Price, 1963; Wuchty et al., 2007). This increase has led some researchers to predict the demise of single authorship (Price, 1963; Greene, 2007). On the other hand, Abt (2007) emphasizes that single authorship in the sciences is decreasing exponentially, so its complete demise is very unlikely.

In some science branches, such as life, health, and natural sciences, co-authoring is the norm, and has been for some time (e.g. Geminiani et al., 2014; Baek et al., 2015; Baerlocher et al., 2009; Cronin et al., 2004; Pritychenko 2016). In the social sciences, the picture is more unclear, since the tendency to co-author greatly differs depending on disciplines (e.g. Ossenblok et al., 2014; Endersby, 1996; Hollis, 2001; Tewksbury and Mustaine, 2011; Henriksen, 2018b).

Network analysis has been a useful tool to explore the different research communities co-authoring practices, and to examine the degree to which researchers choose to solely single author or co-author. For example, Uddin et al. (2012) investigated the co-authorship network of research publications about "steel structure" and found a decreasing trend towards publishing solely alone. Thus, most authors always co-author or do a mixture of single and co-authoring. In political science it depends on the subdiscipline and in some areas the majority still solely single-author, while others display a co-authoring trend similar to the physical sciences (Metz and Jäckle, 2017).

It is highly debated whether co-authorship increases productivity among researchers. The individual researcher who co-authors will often have a higher productivity measured in the total number of publications (Cainelli et al., 2012; Sugimoto and Cronin, 2012). However, if one fractionalizes each publication with the number of authors in the byline, the productivity of the individual researcher does not increase as the average number of authors rises (Pritychenko, 2016; Plume and van Weije, 2014; McKercher and Tung, 2016). Thus, as the section "Authorship credit" will highlight, it is not uncomplicated how you count and measure research productivity and performance.

Authorship Credit

Author Order

When publications have two or more authors in the byline, the researchers must decide who goes first. So, what should the author order be? This is not always an easy task and can sometimes create tensions among researchers. Overall, researchers have different ways of deciding on the author order, and it often depends on the culture of their field. The most common is contribution author order, where the order of the authors are decided based on how they have contributed to the paper. The first author is typically the most significant contributor, who often does most of the writing and empirical work, while the last author conceives the study, supervises, and provides funding. The middle authors tend to do more empirical work than writing and conceptualizing the study (Sauermann and Haeussler, 2017; Baerlocher et al., 2007). Thus, Lariviere et al. (2016) describe it as u-shaped relationship between author order and extent of contribution.

Another frequently used author order method is alphabetic author order, though according to Waltman (2012) only 4% of all publications from 2011 registered in Web of Science (Science Citation Index Expanded, the Social Sciences Citation Index, and the Arts & Humanities Citation Index) use alphabetic author order, and it has been decreasing the last couple of decades. Fields like mathematics, economics, and high-energy physics (HEP) are well known for using alphabetic author order, with over 50% of the publications intentionally in alphabetic order (Waltman, 2012; Henriksen, 2019). Alphabetic author order is based on the notion that everyone contributes, and a publication is a result of the all the authors' contribution. However, there are great differences in what constitutes a contribution.

Publications from mathematics and economics typically have on average only two to three authors, and the author is usually part of all aspects of the research. The division of labor among the researchers are therefore low. The application of alphabetic author order is for economists a method to prevent "free-riders", as well as to prevent disagreements (Henriksen, 2019). Mathematics partly explain it by the Hardy-Littlewoods rules, which state that it stays a joint work even if the contribution is not of the same proportion (Teixeira da Silva and Dobránszki, 2016), and in most areas of mathematics, joint research is a sharing of ideas and skills that cannot be attributed to the individuals separately (AMS, 2004).

HEP is infamous for author bylines longer than their actual publications (Castelvecchi, 2015), and it has a mean number of authors at 18 (Waltman, 2012). HEP researchers have been at the forefront of conducting large-scale, collaborative research (Birnholtz, 2006). Over 17,500 people from more than 70 countries are in 2017 part of research projects at CERN (CERN, 2017). These enormous collaborative projects involve numerous researchers and technicians, and it has been decided from the beginning that all involved should receive credit for the results, which takes years to create, analyze, and publish. Thus, the HEP research requires both intellectual and labor contributions (Biagioli, 2003). These large author groups also make it difficult to assign credit and impossible to assess who has performed the different research tasks.

Less popular approaches to decide the author order are by flipping a coin (Miller and Ballard, 1992), brownie bake-off (Young and Young, 1992) or other imaginative ways. Nevertheless, researchers using these kind of author order methods often include a disclaimer of the author order having any meaning. These different approaches and cultures concerning author order means that is difficult in a bibliometric analysis to know whether some authors should receive more credit than others. Even asking the individual authors could mean different interpretations of each contribution (Vinkler, 1993).

Methodological Issues: how do you Determine Credit of a Co-authored Publication

A central issue in studying co-authorship is how do you assign credit for a co-authored publication and measure productivity? In bibliometrics there is a continuing debate, since the different methods have their advantages and disadvantages; so far, no consensus has been reached (Gauffriau et al., 2007; Larsen, 2008). Should all authors get full credit (whole count), should it be fractionalized (fractional count), or should it only be the first author who receives credit (straight count)?

When you apply straight counting you assign all the credit to the first author and none to the co-authors, therefore, emphasizing the first author's contribution while ignoring the remaining authors. This can be highly problematic because of the lack of recognition of most authors (Lange, 2001), and straight count is today the least popular method. But, when Eugene Garfield created his Science Citation Index in 1962, it was the only conceivable method if the researcher did or could not obtain the physical publication. The decision to only include the first author of the publications in the Science Citation Index records was because of practical and economic reasons, and Garfield later on warned against the possible bias of using straight count (Garfield, 1977). The citation index was created to be a tool to search for similar research by seeing who has cited and been cited by others. But to create this link, each bibliographic post only contained the absolute necessary information to be able to look up the references and citations (Wouters, 1999). Therefore, all the citations would be allocated to the first author.

A common approach is whole, normal, or complete counting, which gives full credit to all authors. Each author of a three-authored paper gets as much credit as if they had written it as a single author. Thus, no matter the number of authors or the rank in the author order, all will receive equal credit. This method encourages co-authoring since everyone will get credit (Gauffriau et al., 2008). But, it also creates negative incentives to add non-contributing researchers, since the amount of credit each author receives is the same. This tendency is often referred to as honorary or guest authorship and will be further reviewed in the section "Contributorship". Another issue with using this counting method is the risk of overestimating the productivity or performance of researchers, thus creating an inflationary bias (Piro et al., 2013; Gauffriau et al., 2008; Hagen, 2008).

Fractional, adjusted, or complete-normalized counting gives a fraction of credit to each author (Gauffriau et al., 2008; Cronin and Overfelt, 1994; Lee and Bozeman, 2005), meaning each author of a three-authored paper will get a third of credit. As with whole count, the idea is that everyone has contributed equally to the research, so everyone should get the same amount of credit. Furthermore, the traditional idea behind authorship is that everyone contributes equally, meaning in the case of a co-authored publication, they give a fractional contribution. However, as mentioned in the "Author order" section, the extent to which the individual co-author contributes differs extensively. Thus, this generates an equalizing bias since it uniformly gives equal credit to all co-authors no matter the extent of their contribution (Hagen, 2009; Hagen, 2008; Hodge et al., 1981).

Harmonic counting has been suggested as a method to prevent this equalizing bias, since it assign authors credit based on their position in the author order. Hodge et al. (1981) propose the following formula for the ith author out of N authors:

$$\text{ith author credit} = \frac{\frac{1}{i}}{\left[1 + \frac{1}{2} + \cdots + \frac{1}{N}\right]}$$

This means the first author gets most of the credit and the following authors receive declining credit. Thus, for a three-authored paper, the first author will receive 55%, the second author will receive 27%, and the third author will receive 18% of credit. However, as mentioned in the author order section, in some disciplines it is the first and last author who contributes most. In these cases Hagen (2008) suggests using approximate equality, so the first and last author receive equal credit. Still, this counting method requires some insights into how the author order has been decided. For example, a two-authored publication would give 67% credit to the first author and only 33% to the second author, even though they might have contributed equally. Hence, no matter what counting method is applied, one should be aware of the different possible counting biases.

Contributorship

The issues of interpreting co-authors' contribution to research have brought suggestions of abandoning authorship and moving towards a contributorship model instead (Bates et al., 2004; Rennie, 1997; Davey Smith et al., 2018; Smith, 2012). Thus, a contributorship model would involve each contributor stating what their role was in creating the research publication. The argument is a contributorship model would better reflect the many and varied contributions researchers make in the process of creating a publication, especially in the health, life, and physical sciences (Davey Smith et al., 2018).

A less drastic approach is supplementing research publication with contribution statements, so each co-author must define how they have contributed to the research. However, few journals have adopted this praxis (Lariviere et al., 2016; Wager, 2007). Studies of these contribution statements show how the type of contribution by co-authors differ (Bates et al., 2004; Marusic et al., 2006), and in some fields this relates to the place in the author order (Lariviere et al., 2016; Sauermann and Haeussler, 2017). Furthermore, the procedures for describing the authors' contributions seem to influence how much and the type of contribution the individual co-authors have done (Bates et al., 2004). The contribution statements are an improvement in making it more transparent who has contributed and how to the research publications, but the lack of detail in some statements as well as disciplinary conventions means more research about the contribution statements are needed. Besides, it is not yet possible to obtain the contribution statements directly from the large citation or bibliographic databases.

Conclusion

Co-authoring is the norm in many disciplines and some funding agencies and policymakers see it as a success criterion that enhances the quality of research and visibility. However, as this review demonstrates, it is not uncomplicated to examine co-authorship or measure co-authoring researchers' productivity and performance. The limitations of the different counting methods and our insights into co-authorship decisions should be taken into consideration when performing bibliometric analysis of co-authored publications.

References

Abt, HA 2007, 'The future of single-authored papers', *Scientometrics*, vol. 73, pp. 353–58.
AMS 2004, *The Culture of Research and Scholarship in Mathematics: Joint Research and Its Publication* [online], American Mathematic Society, http://www.ams.org/profession/leaders/culture/CultureStatement04.pdf (July 15, 2020).

Baek, S, Yoon, DY, Cho, YK, Yun, EJ, Seo, YL, Lim, KJ & Choi, CS 2015, 'Trend Toward an Increase in Authorship for Leading Radiology Journals', *American Journal of Roentgenology*, vol. 205, pp. 924–28.

Baerlocher, MO, Gautam, T, Newton, M & Tomlinson, G 2009, 'Changing author counts in five major general medicine journals: effect of author contribution forms', *Journal of Clinical Epidemiology*, vol. 62, pp. 875–77.

Baerlocher, MO, Newton, M, Gautam, T, Tomlinson, G & Detsky, AS 2007, 'The meaning of author order in medical research', *Journal of Investigative Medicine*, vol. 55, pp. 174–80.

Bates, T, Anic, A, Marusic, M & Marusic, A 2004, 'Authorship criteria and disclosure of contributions – Comparison of 3 general medical journals with different author contribution forms', *Jama-Journal of the American Medical Association*, vol. 292, pp. 86–88.

Biagioli, M 1999, 'Aporias of Scientific Authorship: Credit and Responsibility in Contemporary Biomedicine', in M. Bagioli (ed.), *The science studies reader*, Routledge, New York.

Biagioli, M 2003, 'Rights or Rewards? Changing Frameworks of Scientific Authorship', in M Biagioli & P Galison (eds.), *Scientific authorship: credit and intellectual property in science*, Routledge, New York.

Birnholtz, JP 2006, 'What does it mean to be an author? The intersection of credit, contribution, and collaboration in science', *Journal of the American Society for Information Science and Technology*, vol. 57, pp. 1758–70.

Cainelli, G, Maggioni, MA, Uberti, TE & de Felice, A 2012, 'Co-authorship and productivity among Italian economists', *Applied Economics Letters*, vol. 19, pp. 1609–13.

Castelvecchi, D 2015 'Physics paper sets record with more than 5000 authors', *Nature*.

CERN 2017, *Our People* [online], CERN, accessed June 4, 2019, https://home.cern/about/who-we-are/our-people (July 15, 2020).

Cronin, B & Overfelt, K 1994, 'Citation-based auditing of Academic Performance', *Journal of the American Society for Information Science*, vol. 45, pp. 61–72.

Cronin, B, Shaw, D & Barre, KL 2004, 'Visible, less visible, and invisible work: Patterns of collaboration in 20th century chemistry', *Journal of the American Society for Information Science and Technology*, vol. 55, pp. 160–68.

CSE 2012, *White Paper on Publication Ethics. CSE's White Paper on Promoting Integrity in Scientific Journal Publications* [online], Council of Science Editors, accessed July 12, 2019, http://www.councilscienceeditors.org/i4a/pages/index.cfm?pageid=3331 (July 15, 2020).

Davey Smith, G, Munafò, M & Kivimäki, M 2018, 'Swap outdated authorship listings for contributorship credit', *Nature*, vol. 561, p. 464.

Du, J & Tang, XL 2013, 'Perceptions of author order versus contribution among researchers with different professional ranks and the potential of harmonic counts for encouraging ethical co-authorship practices', *Scientometrics*, vol. 96, pp. 277–95.

Endersby, JW 1996, 'Collaborative research in the social sciences: Multiple authorship and publication credit', *Social Science Quarterly*, vol. 77, pp. 375–92.

Garfield, E 1977, 'The 250 most-cited primary authors, 1961–1975. Part III. Each author's most-cited publication', *Current Contents*, vol. 51, pp. 5–20.

Gauffriau, M, Larsen, PO, Maye, I, Roulin-Perriard, A & von Ins, M 2007, *40 years discussion on the counting of publications*.

Gauffriau, M, Larsen, PO, Maye, I, Roulin-Perriard, A & von Ins, M 2008, 'Comparisons of results of publication counting using different methods', *Scientometrics*, vol. 77, pp. 147–76.

Geelhoed, RJ, Phillips, JC, Fischer, AR, Shpungin, E & Gong, YJ 2007, 'Authorship decision making: An empirical investigation', *Ethics & Behavior*, vol. 17, pp. 95–115.

Geminiani, A, Ercoli, C, Feng, CY & Caton, JG 2014, 'Bibliometrics Study on Authorship Trends in Periodontal Literature From 1995 to 2010', *Journal of Periodontology*, vol. 85, E136-E143.

Greene, M 2007, 'The demise of the lone author', *Nature*, vol. 450, p. 1165.

Haeussler, C & Sauermann, H 2013, 'Credit where credit is due? The impact of project contributions and social factors on authorship and inventorship', *Research Policy*, vol. 42, pp. 688–703.

Hagen, NT 2008, 'Harmonic Allocation of Authorship Credit: Source-Level Correction of Bibliometric Bias Assures Accurate Publication and Citation Analysis', *Plos One*, vol. 3.

Hagen, NT 2009, 'Credit for Coauthors', *Science*, vol. 323, p. 583.

Henriksen, D 2016, 'The rise in co-authorship in the social sciences (1980–2013)', *Scientometrics*, vol. 107, pp. 455–76.

Henriksen, D 2018a, *Research Collaboration and Co-authorship in the Social Sciences*, Ph.D. Dissertation, Aarhus University.

Henriksen, D 2018b, 'What factors are associated with increasing co-authorship in the social sciences? A case study of Danish Economics and Political Science', *Scientometrics*, vol. 114, pp. 1395–1421.

Henriksen, D 2019, 'Alphabetic or Contributor Author Order. What Is the Norm in Danish Economics and Political Science and Why?', *Journal of the Association for Information Science and Technology*, vol. 70, pp. 607–18.

Hodge, SE, Greenberg, DA & Challice, CE 1981, 'Publication Credit', *Science*, vol. 213, pp. 950–52.

Hollis, A 2001, 'Co-authorship and the output of academic economists', *Labour Economics*, vol. 8, pp. 503–30.

ICMJE 2010, 'Uniform Requirements for Manuscripts Submitted to Biomedical Journals: Writing and Editing for Biomedical Publication', *Publication Ethics: Sponsorship, Authorship, and Accountability*, International Committee of Medical Journal Editors.

Katz, JS & Martin, BR 1997, 'What is research collaboration?', *Research Policy*, vol. 26, pp. 1–18.

Lange, LL 2001, 'Citation Counts of Multi-Authored Papers – First-named Authors and Further Authors', *Scientometrics*, vol. 52, pp. 457–70.

Lariviere, V, Desrochers, N, Macaluso, B, Mongeon, P, Paul-Hus, A & Sugimoto, CR 2016, 'Contributorship and division of labor in knowledge production', *Social Studies of Science*, vol. 46, pp. 417–35.

Lariviere, V, Gingras, Y, Sugimoto, CR & Tsou, A 2015, 'Team size matters: Collaboration and scientific impact since 1900', *Journal of the Association for Information Science and Technology*, vol. 66, pp. 1323–32.

Larsen, PO 2008, 'The state of the art in publication counting', *Scientometrics*, vol. 77, p. 235.

Laudel, G 2001, 'Collaboration, creativity and rewards: why and how scientists collaborate', *International Journal of Technology Management*, vol. 22, pp. 762–81.

Lee, S & Bozeman, B 2005, 'The impact of research collaboration on scientific productivity', *Social Studies of Science*, vol. 35, 673–702.

Marusic, A, Bates, T, Anic, A & Marusic, M 2006, 'How the structure of contribution disclosure statements affects validity of authorship: a randomized study in a general medical journal', *Current Medical Research and Opinion*, vol. 22, pp. 1035–44.

McKercher, B & Tung, V 2016, 'The rise of fractional authors', *Annals of Tourism Research*, vol. 61, pp. 213–15.

Merton, RK 1973, *The sociology of science: theoretical and empirical investigations*, The University of Chicago Press, Chicago.

Metz, T & Jäckle, S 2017, 'Patterns of Publishing in Political Science Journals: An Overview of Our Profession Using Bibliographic Data and a Co-Authorship Network', *PS: Political Science & Politics*, vol. 50, pp. 157–65.

Miller, SD & Ballard, WB 1992, 'In My Experience: Analysis of an Effort to Increase Moose Calf Survivorship by Increased Hunting of Brown Bears in South-Central Alaska', *Wildlife Society Bulletin (1973–2006)*, vol. 20, pp. 445–54.

Ossenblok, TLB, Verleysen, FT & Engels, TCE 2014, 'Coauthorship of journal articles and book chapters in the social sciences and humanities (2000–2010)', *Journal of the Association for Information Science and Technology*, vol. 65, pp. 882–97.

Pignatelli, B, Maisonneuve, H & Chapuis, F 2005, 'Authorship ignorance: views of researchers in French clinical settings', *Journal of Medical Ethics*, vol. 31, pp. 578–81.

Piro, FN, Aksnes, DW & Rørstad, K 2013, 'A macro analysis of productivity differences across fields: Challenges in the measurement of scientific publishing', *Journal of the American Society for Information Science and Technology*, vol. 64, pp. 307–20.

Plume, A & van Weijen, D 2014, 'Publish or Perish? The rise of the fractional author', *Research Trends*, pp. 1–3.

Ponomariov, B & Boardman, C 2016, 'What is co-authorship?', *Scientometrics*, vol. 109, pp. 1939–63.

Price, DJDS 1963, *Little science, big science*, Columbia University Press, New York and London.

Pritychenko, B 2016, 'Fractional authorship in nuclear physics', *Scientometrics*, vol. 106, pp. 461–68.

Rennie, D 1997, 'Authorship credits', *Lancet*, vol. 350, p. 1035.

Sauermann, H & Haeussler, C 2017, 'Authorship and contribution disclosures', *Science Advances*, vol. 3, no. 11.

Smith, E, Williams-Jones, B, Master, Z, Larivière, V, Sugimoto, CR, Paul-Hus, A, Shi, M, Diller, E, Caudle, K & Resnik, DB 2019, 'Researchers' Perceptions of Ethical Authorship Distribution in Collaborative Research Teams', *Science and Engineering Ethics*, 1–28.

Smith, R 2012, 'Let's simply scrap authorship and move to contributorship', *BMJ (Online)*, 344.

Sugimoto, CR & Cronin, B 2012, 'Biobibliometric Profiling: An Examination of Multifaceted Approaches to Scholarship', *Journal of the American Society for Information Science and Technology*, vol. 63, pp. 450–68.

Teixeira da Silva, JA & Dobránszki, J 2016, 'Multiple Authorship in Scientific Manuscripts: Ethical Challenges, Ghost and Guest/Gift Authorship, and the Cultural/Disciplinary Perspective', *Science and Engineering Ethics*, vol. 22, pp. 1457–72.

Tewksbury, R & Mustaine, EE 2011, 'How many authors does it take to write an article? An assessment of criminology and criminal justice research article author composition', *Journal of Criminal Justice Education*, vol. 22, pp. 12–23.

Uddin, S, Hossain, L, Abbasi, A & Rasmussen, K 2012, 'Trend and efficiency analysis of co-authorship network', *Scientometrics*, 90, pp. 687–99.

Vinkler, P 1993, 'Research Contribution, Authorship and Team Cooperativeness', *Scientometrics*, vol. 26, pp. 213–30.

Wager, E 2007, 'Do medical journals provide clear and consistent guidelines on authorship?', *MedGenMed: Medscape general medicine*, vol. 9, p. 16.

Waltman, L 2012, 'An empirical analysis of the use of alphabetical authorship in scientific publishing', *Journal of Informetrics*, vol. 6, pp. 700–11.

Wilcox, LJ 1998, 'Authorship – The coin of the realm, the source of complaints', *Jama-Journal of the American Medical Association*, vol. 280, pp. 216–17.

Wouters, PF 1999, *The citation culture*, Universiteit van Amsterdam.

Wuchty, S, Jones, BF & Uzzi, B 2007, 'The increasing dominance of teams in production of knowledge', *Science*, vol. 316, pp. 1036–39.

Young, HJ & Young, TP 1992, 'Alternative Outcomes of Natural and Experimental High Pollen Loads', *Ecology*, vol. 73, pp. 639–47.

6 The Data Basis in Bibliometrics

6.1 Web of Science, Scopus and Further Citation Databases

Ingrid Bauer

Abstract: The aim of this chapter is to give an overview of the most important databases on the market that make bibliometric analysis possible: Web of Science, Scopus, Google Scholar, and Dimensions. This overview includes the historical background, the information about the owner of the database, the coverage (philosophy), and thus the selection procedure concerning publications and the most important metrics used and developed in those databases. Most of the information has been taken from the databases themselves as well as from their webpages. Having said that, this chapter is not a scientific in-depth analysis, but should give practical knowledge about the databases mentioned.

Keywords: Web of Science, Scopus, Google Scholar, Dimensions.

For decades, the SCI was the only database on the market that made bibliometric analysis possible. It goes back to Eugene Garfield, the founder of ISI (Institute for Scientific Information) and was established in the nineties as "Web of Science". It took more than 40 years until two other competitive databases were launched: "Scopus", a product from Elsevier, and "Google Scholar", a Google product as obvious by the name. Both databases were launched in the year 2004 (Hane, 2004; Butler, 2004, p. 423). Since then Scopus has found its place as a well-accepted product for citation analysis, while Google Scholar has turned out, due to its policy, to be more relevant as a search engine with some extra features for scientists to present their publication output.

Other companies such as Microsoft also started in this business: Microsoft developed an academic search engine called Microsoft Academic Search, which retired in 2012 but was relaunched as "Microsoft Academic" in 2016 (Harzing, 2016). In addition, some subject related databases such as zbMATH database in the field of mathematics (which is hosted by FIZ Karlsruhe and is part of Zentralblatt MATH), PubMed in the field of medical/pharmaceutical research and the social networking site for scientists and researchers ResearchGate (Ortega, 2016) also started to add bibliometric features.

The latest product, which could be a competitive database to Web of Science and Scopus, is the new "Dimensions" database, which was launched in 2018 (Harzing, 2019). Dimensions is a new scholarly search database that nails its colours to focus on the broader set of use cases that academics now face. By including awarded grants, patents, and clinical trials alongside publication and Altmetric attention

---

Ingrid Bauer, TU Wien, Team Universitätsentwicklung und Qualitätsmanagement, Austria

data, Dimensions states that it goes beyond the standard publication-citation ecosystem to give the user a much greater sense of context of a piece of research.

Table 1: Keydata of the most important Citation Databases

Database name	Launched in	Access free	Company owner	Web address
Web of Science	1964	No	Clarivate Analytics	webofknowledge.com
Scopus	2004	No	Elsevier	scopus.com
Google Scholar	2004	Yes	Google LLC	scholar.google.com
Dimensions	2018	Yes (policy will change)	Digital Science	dimensions.ai

Web of Science

Eugene Garfield (born 1925 in N.Y., USA; died 2017), by 1963, had already made his first release of the SCI (Science Citation Index), which focussed on natural and medical sciences exclusively at this time and covered about 613 journals (Garfield and Sher, 1963, p. 195; Garfield, 1964).

It should be stated that Eugen Garfield is probably the most prominent representative of the bibliometric community to date (Cronin and Atkins call him the "undisputed patriarch of citation indexing" (Cronin and Barsky Atkins, 2000)), with a degree in chemistry and library science as a background.

Significantly, Garfield's intention to start with an extensive citation analysis was not the evaluation of the research output itself, but the evaluation of the most interesting journals with those articles, which are of major interest to the specific scientific community. Eugene Garfield, who was working in the pharmaceutic area at that time, was simply very much interested in not wasting too much money on buying the wrong journals.

History and Databases

Garfield founded the Institute for Scientific Information (ISI) in 1960, which was located in Philadelphia, Pennsylvania. The first Science Citation Index was produced in 1963, nine years after he published the concept of citation indexing for the sciences in 1955 (Garfield, 1955, p. 68). In 1973 the Social Science Citation Index (SSCI) was created, and in 1975 the Arts & Humanities Citation Index was created to cover all kinds of research areas. In 1992 Garfield, at the age of 67, sold ISI to Thomson, a Canadian multinational media conglomerate based in Toronto.

In 2008, Thomson purchased the Reuters Group (a British multinational media and financial information company headquartered in London, United Kingdom) to form Thomson Reuters. In October 2016, Thomson Reuters Intellectual Property and Science business became independent and what is now known as Clarivate Analytics. In 2015 a new citation index was included, the ESCI (Emerging Source Citation Index) (Web of Science, 2020). Elsewhere, ISI was re-established in 2018 and now serves as a home for analytic expertise, guided by Garfield's legacy and adapted to respond to technological advancements.

Coverage

By 2019 the number of journals within the **Web of Science Core Collection** (Web of Science, 2020) (the premier resource on the platform and important citation index for scientific and scholarly research in all kinds of research fields), which includes the SCI, the SSCI, the AHCI and the ESCI, had very much expanded:

Table 2: Key data of the Web of Science Core Collection

	Release [year]	Release [nr. of journals]	2000 more than [nr. of journals]	2019 more than [nr. of journals]
Science Citation Index (SCI, since 2015 Expanded SCIE)	1963	613	6,200	9,200
Social Science Citation Index (SSCI)	1973	1,400 (appr.)	1,700	3,400
Arts & Humanities Citation Index (AHCI)	1978	1,000 (appr.)	1,000	1,800
Emerging Source Citation Index (ESCI)	2015	3,000	-	7,800

SCIE, created as SCI in 1964, is the Science Citation Index Expanded, which now indexes over 9,200 impactful journals across 178 scientific disciplines (Physics, Chemistry, Mathematics, Engineering, Computer science, Natural Science etc.) dating from 1900 to present.

SSCI contains over 3,400 journals across 58 social sciences disciplines (Anthropology, Law, Philosophy, Political Science, Psychology, Urban studies, and Women's studies etc.) dating from 1900 to present.

AHCI includes over 1,800 journals across 28 arts & humanities disciplines (Archaeology, Architecture, Art, Classics, History, Language and linguistics, Literature and poetry, Music, theatre & film, Religion etc.) dating from 1975 to present.

ESCI should extend the universe of publications in Web of Science to include high-quality, peer-reviewed publications of regional importance and in emerging scientific fields. Journals in ESCI have passed an initial editorial evaluation and can continue to be considered for inclusion in SCIE, SSCI and AHCI, which have rigorous evaluation processes and selection criteria. The ESCI is multidisciplinary and dates back from 2005 to present.

Table 3: Sources of the Web of Science Core Collection

Including	SCIE	SSCI	AHCI	ESCI
Journals [number]	9,200	3,400	1,800	7,800
Records [number]	53 Mio.	9,4 Mio.	4,9 Mio.	3 Mio.
Cited references [number]	1,180 Mio.	122 Mio.	33 Mio.	74 Mio.

Besides rating journals, books and conference proceedings also started to be included, which led to a citation index for books and conference proceedings being created: the Book Citation Index (BKCI) with more than 100,000 editorially selected books to date (adding about 10,000 books per year since 2005), and the Conference Proceedings Citation Index (CPCI) with over 200,000 conference proceedings to date, covering the period 1990 to present.

Web of Science offers in addition further specialty collections in various research areas (such as the Biological Abstracts, the Zoological Records, Medline in the area of medicine, the BIOSIS Citation Index in the area of Life Science etc.) and databases highlighting special regions around the world, e. g. the RSCI – Russian Science Citation Index (provided by the Russian Academy of Science), KCI Korean Journal Database (provided by the Korean Academy of Science), and the CSCD – Chinese Science Citation Index (provided by the Chinese Academy of Science).

The Web of Science Core Collection (SCIE, SSCI, AHCI, ESCI, BKCI, and CPCI) includes (as of August 2019) in total:
- about 22,000 peer-reviewed scholarly journals published worldwide (including about 5,000 Open Access journals)
- over 200,000 conference proceedings
- over 100,000 editorially selected books
- which results in about 75 million records and 1,400 Mio. cited references

Selection Process

To be added in one of the Indexes, a new journal has to undergo an extensive process. Web of Science uses a single set of 28 criteria to evaluate journals. The selection procedure itself is conducted by the Web of Science expert in-house editors who have no affiliations to publishing houses or research institutes, thus removing any potential bias or conflict of interest. The journal acceptance rate is about 10–12% for the three core indices (SCIE, SSCI and AHCI).

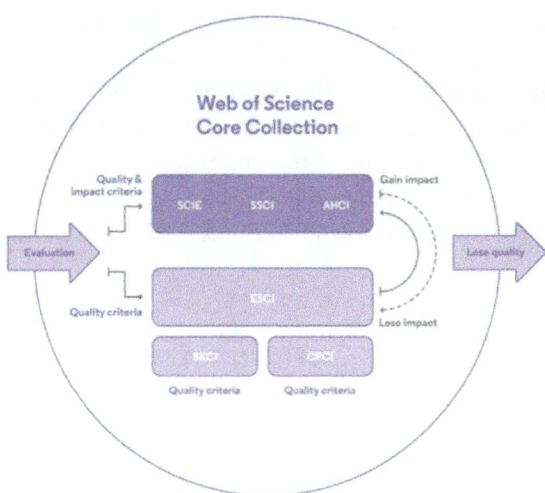

Figure 1: Selection Process for new Journals (Web of Science, 2020)

Metrics

Author, Institution and Field Performance is described by the Citation Report provided.

Concerning metrics (InCites Benchmarking & Analytics, 2020) characterizing a Researcher or Affiliations, Web of Science uses citation tracking, citation counts and author h-index calculations (which can be also applied for affiliations). "Hot" and "Highly Cited" articles per researcher/affiliation (top performing by citation comparison) are also available.

"Hot" papers are per definition "Papers which are recognized very soon after publication, reflected by rapid and significant numbers of citations". These papers are often key papers in their fields.

"Highly Cited Papers" are "Papers which continue to be cited for many years and are therefore key papers in the specific research field as the methods diffuse throughout the community and prove their utility".

Concerning metrics characterizing a journal, Journal Impact Factors and Journal Performance Quartiles are available via Journal Citation Reports Integration. The Journal Impact Factor gives information about citations in a specific year in relation to citable items published in the previous two years, dived by the number of items (e.g. articles) in these two years. Information about the trend of the Journal Impact Factors and the citation distribution is also available.

In addition to the classic Journal Impact Factor variations exist, such as the 5-year Impact Factor, the Immediacy Index (which measures how topical and urgent scientific articles are), the journal cited half-life factor and various normalized factors, taking into account that the publication and citation habits differ in different research areas.

Web of Science has also integrated the figures of the "Eigenfactor score," (Eigenfactor Metrics, 2020) an additional factor rating the importance of a scientific journal, which has been developed by a research group of the University of Washington (they have also developed an article influence score). The Eigenfactor score is available for free at its webpage (http://www.eigenfactor.org/ [July 15, 2020]).

Scopus

Scopus is Elsevier's abstract and citation database launched in 2004. Elsevier is one of the world's major providers of scientific, technical, and medical information, based in Amsterdam (Netherlands) and established in 1880. It is famous for its company logo, a tree entwined with a vine and the words Non Solus, which is Latin for not alone. The history of the Elzevier family's connection to publishing goes back to the sixteenth century, when the Protestant bookbinder Louis Elzevier settled in Leiden (Wikipedia, 2020). In 1931 Elsevier started international scientific publishing and in 1947 launched Biochemica et Biophysica Acta, their first English language journal (Reed Elsevier, 2020). In 1992 Elsevier merged with Reed and was called Reed Elsevier from then on.

Nowadays the Elsevier business is – as RELX's Scientific – part of RELX plc, a British corporate group comprising companies that publish scientific, technical, and medical material, as well as legal textbooks, with headquarters in London. Besides Scopus, Science Direct and Mendeley are also part of RELX Scientific.

Selection Process

From the beginning – in order to prevent any discredit – a Content Selection & Advisory Board (CSAB) was established in 2005 to promote an open and transparent content coverage policy, since Elsevier is the owner of Scopus and is also one of the main international publishers of scientific journals, which is a marked difference to Web of Science. To show transparency, the list of members of the CSAB can be found on the Scopus Webpage (Scopus Content Selection and Advisory Board, Elsevier 2020). Only about 500 – 600 new titles are accepted by the board per year and included in the database, going through an internal procedure similar to within Web of Science. A journal could also be downgraded when losing impact, similar to how Web of Science does.

Coverage

Scopus indexes serial publications (journals, trade journals, book series, and conference materials) that have been assigned an ISSN, non-serial source, such as books (with an ISBN unless it is a report) and patents (Elsevier, 2020). This is different to Web of Science as only one database exists.

At the moment Scopus covers almost 25,000 titles, including around 23,500 peer-reviewed high-quality scholarly journals (with over 4,000 full Open Access Journals) from more than 5,000 publishers and over 740 book series. In addition, it covers more almost 200,000 books with 20,000 added every year (books are indexed on both a book and chapter level).

Conference material enters Scopus in two different ways: as a special issue of a regular journal or as a dedicated proceeding conference. Over 10% of the Scopus database is comprised of conference papers (over 8.3 million conference papers from over 100,000 worldwide events), of which 2.3 million are published in journals, book series, and other sources. The remaining 5.7 million are published in conference proceedings.

In addition, Scopus includes over 39 million patent records derived from five patent offices (World Intellectual Property Organization, European Patent Office, US Patent Office, Japanese Patent Office, UK Intellectual Property Office).

Metrics

Concerning metrics characterizing a Researcher of an Affiliation, Scopus uses a Citation overview tracker, analyzing the author by various terms and giving information about the h-Index (Hirsch-Index) with or without self-citation.

Concerning metrics characterizing a journal, Scopus uses the CiteScore metrics, SCImago Journal Rank (SJR), and Source Normalized Impact per Paper (SNIP) (Roldan-Valadez et al., n.d.). CiteScore is a "modified Journal impact Factor". In contrast to Web of Science, Scopus refers to a three year period: citations in a specific year in relation to citable items published in the previous three years, dived by the amount of items – in most of the cases articles – in these three years.

The **Source Normalized Impact per Paper (SNIP)** measures actual citations received relative to citations expected for the serial's subject field. The SNIP indicator is calculated by CWTS (Centre for Science and Technology Studies), Leiden (CWTS, 2020). Another factor is the **SCImago Journal Rank (SJR)**, which measures weighted citations received by the serial. SJR accounts for both the number of citations received by a title and the importance or prestige of the titles where such citations come from.

At article level Scopus offers article-level metrics data from **PlumX Metrics** (Torres-Salinas, Gumpenberger, and Gorraiz, 2017; PlumX Metrics, 2020), which gives information about the impact of one specific article. It uses the so-called

"Plum Print", showing "Usage" (e.g. clicks, downloads, views), "Captures" (e.g. bookmarks, code forks, favorites), "Mentions" (e.g. blog posts, comments, reviews), reaction in "Social media" (tweets, Facebook likes, etc.), and "Citations" of the specific article.

Google Scholar

Google Scholar is a freely accessible web search engine that indexes the full text or metadata of scholarly literature across an array of publishing formats and disciplines. Released in beta in November 2004, the Google Scholar index includes most peer-reviewed online academic journals and books, conference papers, theses and dissertations, preprints, abstracts, technical reports, and other scholarly literature, including court opinions and patents.

Selection Process

Contrary to Web of Science and Scopus, who both stress their exclusivity and selection procedures for any kind of scholarly literature included in their coverage basket, Google Scholar adopts a different strategy: as individual scholars are able to create their personal "Scholar Citations profiles", it is up to the individual scholar to revamp their profile independently.

In addition, the most important difference is the fact that Google Scholar is freely available on the web. This makes a sizable difference to Web of Science and Scopus.

Coverage

Google Scholar covers full-text journal articles, technical reports, preprints, theses, books, and other documents, including selected webpages that are deemed to be scholarly. The disadvantage often noted by the bibliometric community is the fact that Google Scholar does not publish a list of journals crawled or publishers included, and the frequency of its updates is uncertain. Researchers even demonstrated about ten years ago that citation counts on Google Scholar can be manipulated and completely nonsense articles created with SCIgen were indexed from Google Scholar (Beel and Gipp, 2010). This makes it still an uncertain basis for bibliometric analyses, especially as Google Scholar does not display or export Digital Object Identifiers (DOIs), even though it is worthwhile for comparison with the bibliometric analysis on the basis of data from Web of Science of Scopus.

Features and Metrics

Google Scholar has gained a range of features over time, starting in 2006 with implementing a collection of bibliography managers, such as EndNote. In 2012 the personal "Scholar Citations profiles" were implemented, which are editable by authors themselves and give information about individual bibliometric factors, such as the h-index and i10-index (which is a specific Google Scholar metric and gives information about the number of publications with at least 10 citations).

Dimensions

The Dimensions database was launched in 2018 aiming to bring more transparency concerning data usage and complexity of research data.

One of the original constraints was that existing solutions sought to understand the research landscape solely through the lens of publication and citation data, with another constraint that existing solutions didn't expose in detail what data they did have. These constraints were reason enough to include more than 100 partners (funding agencies, research institutions etc.) to start this new database, which also includes publications also grants, clinical trials, patents, policy documents, and data sets.

Dimensions is run by Digital Science, a technology company with its headquarters in London, United Kingdom, founded in 2010. Digital Science belongs to the Holtzbrinck Publishing Group, a privately-held Stuttgart-based company which owns publishing companies worldwide, and also owns Altmetric, Figshare, Global Research Identifier Database (GRID), ReadCube, and many other companies.

Coverage

Dimensions gives access to data from 5,2 Mio. grants, 110 Mio. publications, about 550,000 clinical tests, 40 Mio. patents and about 470,000 policy papers. In addition, about 110 Mio. altmetric data sets are available (Dimensions, 2020).

So far, access for individual researchers is free, but Dimensions offers product versions (Dimensions Analytics, Dimensions Plus and Dimensions Profiles), which have to be paid for.

Metrics

Concerning the free and available version, Dimensions offers citation information with a short summary about the overall impression of an article, total citations, and recent citations.

At article level it has included the Relative Citation Ratio (RCR), which indicates the relative citation performance of a publication when comparing its citation rate to that of other publications in its area of research. A value of more than 1.0 shows a citation rate above average. In addition, there exists the Field Citation Ratio (FCR), which indicates the relative citation performance of a publication when compared to similarly-aged articles in its subject area.

At article level Dimensions has included the Altmetric Attention Score, which is a weighted count of all online attention.

At author level one can rank by RCR (Relative Citation Ratio), by Field Citation Ratio (FCR), by Altmetric Attention Score, by citations and relevance, which offers a very good overview about the most important publications of each author.

References

Beel, J & Gipp, B 2010, 'Academic Search Engine Spam and Google Scholar's Resilience Against it', *The Journal of Electronic Publishing*, vol. 13, no. 3.

Cronin, B & Barsky Atkins, H 2000, 'The scholar's spoor', in B Cronin & H Barsky Atkins (eds.), *The web of knowledge: a festschrift in honor of Eugen Garfield*, pp. 1–7, Information Today, Medford, N.Y.

CWTS, Welcome to CWTS Journal Indicators, [online], https://www.journalindicators.com/ (July 15, 2020).

Declan, B 2004, 'Science searches shift up a gear as Google starts Scholar engine', *Nature*, vol. 432, no. 7016, p. 423.

Eigenfactor Metrics, Eigenfactor [online], http://www.eigenfactor.org/ (July 15, 2020).

Garfield, E 1955, 'The preparation of printed indexes by automatic punched-card techniques', *American Documentation (pre-1986)*, vol. 6, no. 2, p. 68.

Garfield, E & Sher, I 1963, 'New Factors in the Evaluation of Scientific Literature Through Citation Indexing', *American Documentation (pre-1986)*, vol. 14, no. 3, p. 195.

Garfield, E 1964, 'Citation Indexing: A Natural Science Literature Retrieval System for the Social Sciences', *The American Behavioral Scientist (pre-1986)*, vol. 7, no. 10, pp. 58–61.

Hane, Paula J 2004, Elsevier Announces Scopus Service, http://newsbreaks.infotoday.com/nbreader.asp?ArticleID=16494 (July 15, 2020).

Harzing, A 2016, 'Microsoft Academic (Search): A Phoenix arisen from the ashes?', *Scientometrics*, vol. 108, no. 3, pp. 1637–47.

Harzing, A 2019, 'Two new kids on the block: How do Crossref and Dimensions compare with Google Scholar, Microsoft Academic, Scopus and the Web of Science?', *Scientometrics*, vol. 120, no. 1, pp. 341–49.

How Scopus works, Elsevier [online], https://www.elsevier.com/solutions/scopus/how-scopus-works (July 15, 2020).

InCites Benchmarking & Analytics: Alphabetical List of InCites Metrics. Clarivate, http://clarivate.libguides.com/incites_ba/alpha-indicators (July 15, 2020).

Lodewijk Elzevir, Wikipedia [online], https://en.wikipedia.org/wiki/Lodewijk_Elzevir (July 15, 2020).

Ortega, JL 2016, 'Social Network Sites for Scientists: A Quantitative Survey (Chandos information professional series)', Elsevier Science, Kent.

PlumX Metrics, Plumanalytics [online], https://plumanalytics.com/learn/about-metrics/ (July 15, 2020).

Publications, Dimensions [online], https://app.dimensions.ai/discover/publication (July 15, 2020).

Reed Elsevier, Internet Archive, https://web.archive.org/web/20081204103242/http://www.ulib.niu.edu/publishers/ReedElsevier.htm (July 15, 2020).

Roldan-Valadez, E, Salazar-Ruiz, S, Ibarra-Contreras, Y & Rios, R n.d., 'Current concepts on bibliometrics: A brief review about impact factor, Eigenfactor score, CiteScore, SCImago Journal Rank, Source-Normalised Impact per Paper, H -index, and alternative metrics', *Irish Journal of Medical Science (1971–)*, vol. 188, no. 3, pp. 939–51.

Scopus Content Selection and Advisory Board, Elsevier [online], https://www.elsevier.com/solutions/scopus/how-scopus-works/content/scopus-content-selection-and-advisory-board (July 15, 2020).

Torres-Salinas, D, Gumpenberger, Ch & Gorraiz, J 2017, 'PlumX As a Potential Tool to Assess the Macroscopic Multidimensional Impact of Books', Frontiers in Research Metrics and Analytics, 2, Frontiers in Research Metrics and Analytics, July 1, 2017.

Web of Science, Emerging Sources Citation Index [online], https://clarivate.com/webofsciencegroup/solutions/webofscience-esci/ (July 15, 2020).

Web of Science, Web of Science Core Collection [online], https://clarivate.com/webofsciencegroup/solutions/web-of-science/ (July 15, 2020).

Web of Science, Web of Science Journal Evaluation Process and Selection Criteria [online], https://clarivate.com/webofsciencegroup/journal-evaluation-process-and-selection-criteria/ (July 15, 2020).

6.2 Expanding Dimensions: A New Source in the Bibliometrician's Toolbox

Juergen Wastl

Abstract: Developed by Digital Science in collaboration with over 100 leading research organisations around the world, Dimensions is a unique platform combining data about publications, data sets, grants, patents, clinical trials, and policy documents. This database spans the broader global scientific landscape to enable individual researchers as well as research funders, research organizations, and publishers to discover, analyse, and understand multiple aspects of the research life cycle.

This chapter introduces the development and deployment of the Dimensions platform and describes the breadth of available functionality with focus on bibliometric applications and question sets that can be applied to the academic and broader outcomes of research, and gather insights to inform future strategy.

Keywords: linked data sets, interconnectivity, research trajectory, research classification systems, research evaluation, machine Learning, rcr (relative citation ratio), FOR (Field of Research), UoA (Unit of Assessment), SDG (Sustainable Development Goal).

Introduction

January 16, 2018 saw the launch of Dimensions, a new database in the space of bibliometric analysis (Digital Science, 2018). With Dimensions, Digital Science and its portfolio companies launched a product that distinguishes itself in a variety of aspects from other data providers and services in the scientometric community space. Digital Science aimed to take a different approach with Dimensions and applied a different take to its development. Early on in the conceptional phase, the relevant community of users, including researchers, institutions, funding bodies, and libraries, were invited to take part in developing the structure and functionality of Dimensions in order to make sure the product would suit the sector and its participants' needs: over 100 institutions collaborated with Digital Science on the specifications to be delivered (Hook, 2018).

There were various reasons for launching this new form of a database with a focus on bibliometric research. Fundamentally, the Dimensions project team identified the non-accessibility of publication and citation data for bibliometric research as a crucial factor, stalling, and even inhibiting, research on research. Efforts on providing publication and citation data are increasing, and Digital Science created with Dimensions a powerful tool that is increasingly recognized as a valuable, high-quality alternative that is free of charge for bibliometric research. Further broadening the ac-

---

Dr. **Juergen Wastl**, Director Academic Relations and Consultancy, Digital Science, j.wastl@digital-science.com

cess, Dimensions and ISSI announced in September 2019 the free access to Dimensions for its members (Dimensions, 2019). In this setting, Digital Science will follow the ISSI recommendation for individual access and reduce the involvement of Digital Science into the access decision process.

Dimensions also forms an integral part of the recently established Research on Research Institute (RoRI) launched on September 30, 2019 (Digital Science, 2019) in which the founding partners Wellcome Trust, University of Sheffield, CWTS Leiden, and Digital Science pool resources to instigate and reinvigorate research on research itself.

Although brief in its existence, comparisons of bibliometric data sources, particularly their coverage and comprehensiveness, were published by the bibliometric community (e.g. Harzing, 2019; Orduña-Malea and López-Cózar, 2018) including critical assessment e.g. on normalisation of publication types (Thelwall, 2018). Forthcoming publications using the breadth and depth of Dimensions data not only focus on publications and citations data and analysis, but also use other data sources for large scale analysis, e.g. the use of Dimensions grants data were a fundamental part of the methodology in a funding analysis for Mental Health related research (Woelbert et al., 2019)

Due to its nature of an agglomeration of multiple data sources and therefore not being restricted to publications and citations, Dimensions provides a richer and more encompassing picture of research and the context in which research occurs (Bode et al., 2018). Covering specific areas of the research process, it paves the way to analyze research impact over the entire research trajectory/life cycle (see Figure 1 for the scaffold of data sources in Dimensions)

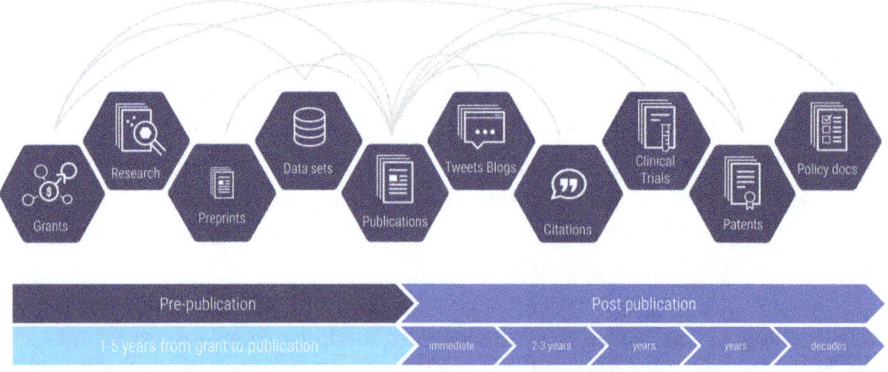

Figure 1: Research trajectory.

It is important to highlight another aspect that formed part of the conception of Dimensions. With the users in mind, Dimensions was not developed as a predefined data set but as a platform empowering users to make their own decisions regarding underpinning data use. It provides all available content without any pre-settings on what data is included or excluded. It is the users' decision to slice and dice and filter for the relevant set of data in Dimensions for relevant analyses e.g. provision of publication and citation data.

About Dimensions Data: the Challenge, the Community, and the Context

Dimensions combines data about publications, grants, patents, clinical trials, and policy documents that spans the global scientific landscape. To achieve this, there was a triad of challenges to overcome. The provision of the data in a shared platform, the interoperability and the connectivity between the different data sets needed to be addressed in order to enable discovery, analysis and to further the understanding of the multiple aspects of the research life cycle.

In order to provide and bring together a thoroughly comprehensive data set, Digital Science acquires the data from as "close to the source" as possible by working directly with publishers and funding bodies, with agreements with over 100 publishers in place to augment publication records with searchable full-text data. Patent data are sourced directly from national patent authorities that are established providers of global patent data such as the United States Patent and Trademark Office. Digital Science augments these sources with industry standard open data sources such as CrossRef. Each data record in Dimensions has a detailed record screen that provides a link to the original source record for the data (see Figure 3 for an example of the context of a publication details page).

As of February 2020, Dimensions contains five major blocks of data sources:
- **Publications:** the meta data backbone contains over 105 million records, covering articles, preprints, books, chapters, monographs, and more. About 76 million include full-text indexing. Rather than taking a selective approach to indexing specific journals, Dimensions' approach is inclusive, indexing records from multiple sources, and then providing tools to allow users to limit their searches. As a result of this inclusive approach, the Dimensions dataset is global and covers all disciplines of research in all regions of the world, and extends back as far as publishers have assigned DOIs to their articles (including the full digitized backfiles of most major publishers, e.g. back to 1665 for The Royal Society, 1832 for Springer Nature, and 1823 for Elsevier).
- **Data sets:** more than 1.4 million data sets sourced from figshare including datasets uploaded on figshare, as well as from other repositories such as Dryad, Zenodo, Pangea and Figshare hosted repositories including ACS and NIH. Datasets are defined as items shared on repositories which are categorised as datasets – this excludes posters, images and software. The datasets will be updated daily and more repositories will be added following the initial release.
- **Grants:** almost 5 million awarded grant records from over 430 funders in almost 40 countries, representing over $1.6 trillion of funded research. Grants data is

obtained from a number of public sources, from Gateway to Research and Europe PMC as well as directly from funder organizations.

- **Patents:** over 39 million records from 15 jurisdictions: USPTO, EPO, Germany, WIPO, Australia, UK, Canada, Russia, France, India, Netherlands, Hong Kong, New Zealand, Switzerland, and Ireland. Additional jurisdictions are in the process of being added.
- **Clinical Trials:** almost 500,000 clinical trials from 11 registries, covering the US, UK, Australia and New Zealand, Iran, Japan, India, Netherlands, Germany, China, South Korea, and the European Union.
- **Policy Documents:** over 430,00 full-text-indexed grey literature reports etc. from more than 70 bodies, including the UK Government, WHO, FAO, etc. The policy document data includes sources that are designed to change or otherwise influence guidelines, policy, or practice.

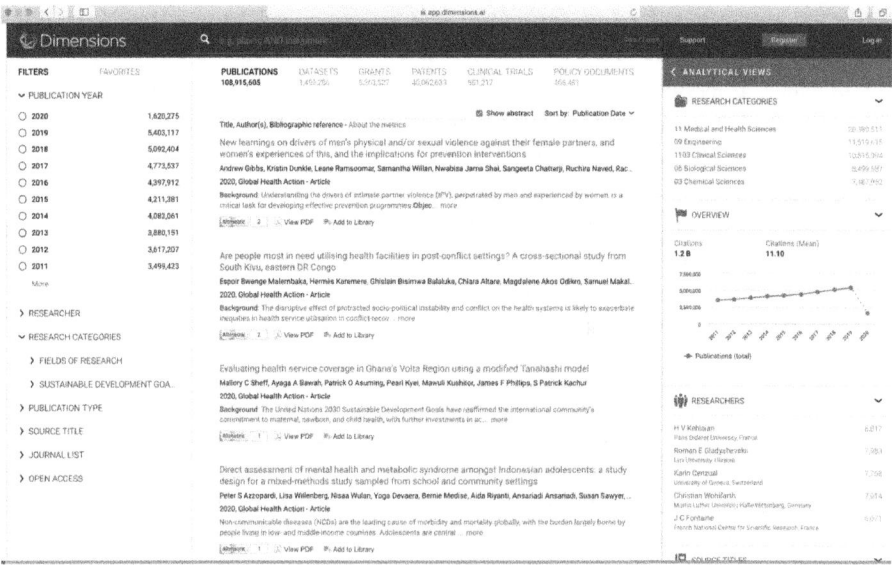

Figure 2: The User Interface of the free version of Dimensions.

The Dimensions data set is global, covering all disciplines in all regions of the world. As part of the data processing pipeline, non-English records are translated into English. For example, awarded grants from Japan are presented in Dimensions with the original abstract in Japanese as well as with an English translation (using automated methods).

Dimensions Data Enhancements

Dimensions has made substantial investments into collecting, compiling, and curating the data it provides, but also in its enrichment. By linking and contextualizing the records through data enrichment, Dimensions expands the discovery of research insights and analytical possibilities, particularly for bibliometric analysis.

By surfacing these links and enrichments, Digital Science provides enhanced and rich metadata such as standardized organization data and researcher disambiguation.

In the case of institutional affiliation, the Global Research Identifier Database (GRID) system is used to create a standardized, consistent view of an organization both within one content source and across different content sources. This GRID database has been established by Digital Science and is freely available and downloadable (https://www.grid.ac/).

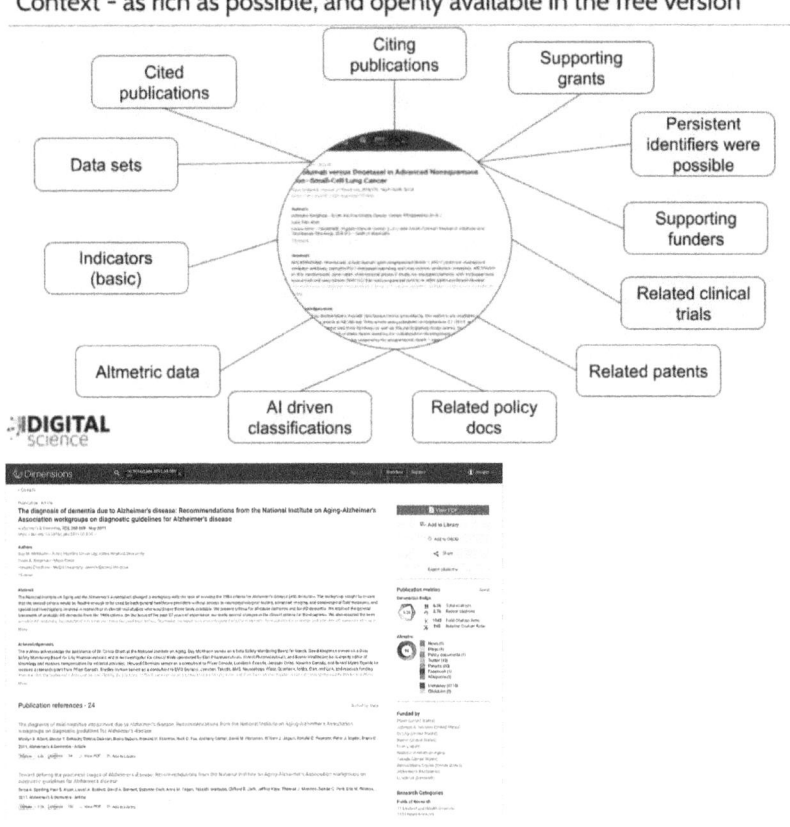

Figure 3: A Context and 3B Example page view of the context page.

In order to identify and disambiguate researchers, an algorithmic approach has been applied to name disambiguation by using affiliation data, co-authorship, and citation patterns as well as subject area traits.

All these enhancements allow users to efficiently digest and compare information in order to quickly analyze information. All content types – publications, grants, policy documents, and patents – share a suite of common data enrichments, which enables analysts to focus on drawing insights from data rather than aligning disparate sources.

The identification of references and the links between the different content sources are key to Dimensions as these provide users with a superior understanding of the context of a piece of research (such as linking publications to grants). In total, more than 1.3 billion direct connections between document records have been identified with more than 1 billion between publication records alone. This number is continually growing due to integration of more content (e.g. data sets and their link to the publications).

Further data enrichment is achieved by using artificial intelligence in the form of machine learning to maximize the utility of the information for search and analysis.

By extracting funding acknowledgements from full text publications, Dimensions can specifically address the questions and needs of funders, in particular on grants and research theme portfolios and their outputs and impact. Another relevant field of high importance, not only for funders but for researchers too, is the application of the categories of research and its outputs. Dimensions has so far implemented nine contemporary categorization schemes by leveraging the fields of natural language processing, machine learning, and artificial intelligence:

- Fields of Research (FOR) (ANZSRC)
- Research, Condition, and Disease Categorisation (RCDC)
- Health Category – Health Research Classification System (HRCS)
- Research Activity Codes - Health Research Classification System (HRCS)
- Broad Research Areas (ANZSRC)
- Health Research Areas
- ICRP Cancer Types
- CRP Common Scientific Outline (CSO)
- Units of Assessment (UoA) (UK REF2021)
- Sustainable Development Goals (SDG)

These categorizations are carried out and applied on an article-level basis. The latest, most recent additions of categorization schemes are based on the Sustainable Development goals (SDG; based on the 17 goals defined by the United Nation's Sustainability Agenda) and the UK national research evaluation process (Research Excellence Framework, REF), in which all areas of research are distributed across 34 disciplines, each called "Unit of Assessment". Next to its particular use in the UK for REF, this latest addition to the categorization schemes will have implications and use cases beyond this national assessment exercise (see example Porter et al., 2019) and may open new ways of comparing broad, all-encompassing discipline categorization schemes.

Dimensions User Interfaces

Dimensions can be used in a variety of ways suited to the individual's needs. The web based User Interface (UI) comes equipped with search, filter, and analytical views: a Search can be initiated and tailored to either title and abstract or carried out searching in full data (i.e. in the full-text of about 76 million publications) or by DOI (for publications) directly. Alternatively, a similarity search for a pasted abstract or other body of text can be instigated to retrieve results that are similar to the text applied to the search. This type of search examines the contents of the abstract/ body of text and extracts its key terms and phrases, in order to create a search concept from these. This search concept is then used to search the database for similar documents.

Search results can be narrowed down by the use of Filters, or combinations thereof. Many filters apply to all data sources (e.g. country, category) whereas some are source specific (publication type, Open Access, source title for publications only).

Users can switch to Analytical Views for rapid analysis of search results and trends at any stage of the search process and progress:
- Publications: Categories, Metrics Overview, Researchers, Source Titles, Funders, Research Organisations, Places
- Grants: Categories, Metrics Overview, Researchers, Funders, Research Organisations, Places
- Patents: Categories, Metrics Overview, Funders, Assignees, Places
- Clinical Trials: Categories, Metrics Overview, Funders, Sponsor, Places
- Policy Documents: Categories, Metrics Overview, Publishing Organization
- Compare the research footprint (using any of the Categories schemes) of two Research Organisations or Funders

Dimensions users can export results and save searches for future re-use and create email alerts for saved searches. In addition, users can define groups using multiple selections from any one filter in the user interface. Results of such searches can be easily exported to CSV or Excel (up to 50,000 records at a time) and publication records can be exported pre-formatted to be available for bibliometric analysis tools e.g. VOSviewer (CWTS, 2019).

Further workflow tools in dedicated instances are available to user specific needs. For example, research funders can make use of reviewer identification functionality and have access to coding support for instant automated classification of grants and other texts.

In addition to the Dimensions web UI, Digital Science provides a Dimensions API to enable programmatic access to the Dimensions data, queried through a Domain-

Specific Language documented at https://docs.dimensions.ai/dsl/. The API is designed to allow more powerful and more flexible access to the Dimensions data, without the constraints that a web interface inevitably applies. API are available in two forms of an Analytics API and a Metrics API, the former to search programmatically across the Dimensions database and the latter to retrieve citation based indicators for bibliometric research work (free for non-commercial use, see above).

Metrics: Publication Impact and Indicators

Dimensions was created to support diversity in metrics, not to create metrics in isolation from the community. The aim is to ensure that data is made available to the research community to create an increased diversity of open, reproducible community-owned metrics (Hook et al., 2018). For the provision of metrics and metrics-related data in Dimensions, Digital Science keeps the metrics close to the data whilst at the same time reaching out to the bibliometric community to do research on innovative metrics on the Dimensions data platform. Digital Science avoids imposing new metrics and includes article-level metrics instead of journal impact factors.

For publication metrics Digital Science have derived a new citation graph containing over one billion links between publications. Using this publication citation graph, Dimensions includes a variety of publications metrics such as citations, recent citations, relative citation ratio, and field citation rate (citations normalized by field and year), and Altmetric attention scores (an aggregate metric indicating the overall level of online attention for an article, see chapter 4.4). These are displayed in the Dimensions user interface by default.

Digital Science supported the development of new metrics (e.g. the NIH developed relative citation ratio (rcr) (Hutchins et al., 2016) which subsequently was implemented into Dimensions. Since the launch a variety of improvements with respect to filter and display of metrics were implemented into Dimensions and more additions are planned for future release.

The Dimensions platform has a growing use and user community. Its data now underpins the Nature index, highlighting research undertaken by institutions and countries in the natural sciences. For its annual tables the articles in natural sciences are drawn from 3.88 million articles tracked in 2018 based on the Dimensions platform (Armitage, 2019).

Summary

The Dimensions database is a new scholarly database that distinguishes itself by including the broader research life cycle, as displayed by awarded grants, patents, clinical trials, policy documents, and altmetric information, hence giving the user a much greater sense of context of a piece of research that goes beyond the standard publication-citation ecosystem.

Bibliography

Armitage, C 2019, 'In rankings, size is not the whole story', *Nature*, vol. 570, S1, https://www.nature.com/articles/d41586-019-01919-8 (July 15, 2020).

Bode, C, Herzog, C, Hook, D, McGrath, R 2018, A Guide to the Dimensions Data Approach, https://doi.org/10.6084/m9.figshare.5783094.v7.

CWTS 2019, VOSviewer supports large number of new data sources [WWW Document], CWTS, https://www.cwts.nl:443/blog?article=n-r2v284 (July 15, 2020).

Digital Science 2018, *Digital Science Launches Dimensions: a Next-generation Research and Discovery Platform Linking 124 Million Documents, Providing Free Search and Citation Data Across 86 Million Articles* [press release], January 15, https://www.digital-science.com/press-releases/digital-science-launches-dimensions-next-generation-research-discovery-platform-linking-124-million-documents-providing-free-search-citation-data-across-86-million-articles/ (July 15, 2020).

Digital Science 2019, *Research on Research Institute (RoRI) launches to enable more strategic, open, diverse, and inclusive research* [press release], September 30, https://www.digital-science.com/press-releases/research-on-research-institute-launches/ (July 15, 2020).

Dimensions 2019, 'Dimensions and the International Society for Scientometrics and Informetrics join forces to provide ISSI members with free access to Dimensions and Altmetric Data', *Dimensions News*, September 3, https://www.dimensions.ai/news/dimensions-issi-partnership/ (July 15, 2020).

Harzing, AW 2019, 'Two new kids on the block: How do Crossref and Dimensions compare with Google Scholar, Microsoft Academic, Scopus and the Web of Science?', *Scientometrics*, vol. 120, pp. 341–49, https://doi.org/10.1007/s11192-019-03114-y.

Hook, DW, Porter, SJ & Herzog, C 2018, Dimensions: Building Context for Search and Evaluation, https://doi.org/10.3389/frma.2018.00023.

Hutchins BI, Yuan X, Anderson, JM & Santangelo, GM 2016, 'Relative Citation Ratio (RCR): A New Metric That Uses Citation Rates to Measure Influence at the Article Level', *PLoS Biol*, vol. 14, no. 9, e1002541, https://doi.org/10.1371/journal.pbio.100254.

Orduña-Malea, E & Delgado López-Cózar, E 2018, 'Dimensions: re-discovering the ecosystem of scientific information', *El Profesional de la Información*, vol. 27, no. 2, pp. 420–31, https://doi.org/10.3145/epi.2018.mar.21.

Porter, S, Watts, J, Wastl, J & Draux, H 2019, What Does Research Look Like Based on REF 2021 UoAs?, https://doi.org/10.6084/m9.figshare.9926492.v1.

Thelwall, M 2018, 'Dimensions: a competitor to scopus and the web of science?' *J. Informetr.*, vol. 12, pp. 430–35, https://doi.org/10.1016/j.joi.2018.03.006.

Woelbert, E, Kirtley, A, Balmer, N & Dix, S 2019, 'How much is spent on mental health research: developing a system for categorising grant funding in the UK', *The Lancet Psychiatry*, vol. 6, pp. 445–52, https://doi.org/10.1016/S2215-0366(19)30033-1.

6.3 The Islamic World Science Citation Center (ISC): The Construction and Application

Jafar Mehrad and Mohammad Reza Ghane

Abstract: National citation indexing systems are as important as global systems for research policymakers, researchers, and journals in each country. The evaluation of scientific activities in national higher education institutes (HEIs) helps the decision-making process become more realistic. In this chapter we introduce ISC, its historical construction, and application. This study includes an overview of global attention to national tools for evaluating scientific performances: ISC historical background, policies, departments, and products.

Keywords: Islamic World Science Citation Center (ISC), national citation indexing systems.

Introduction

The right management of science needs the established assessment of science and researchers performance. Measuring incentives have been very effective in encouraging policymakers to invest globally and locally more on the research outputs, quality, and impact. From scientometrics' point of view we have experienced Clarivate Analytics (formerly ISI) and Scopus since early 1960s and 2000s at international level, respectively. At these times, "in many countries attention is being directed towards research assessment and the development of procedures for assessment both in universities and at a national level." (Key Perspectives Ltd., 2009, p. 5). Despite the usefulness of global research assessment systems, i.e. Clarivate Analytics and Scopus, policymakers need access to local systems. Local systems enable them to manage the procedures of scientific research performance and assess the results based on internal indicators (Tret'yakova, 2015, p. 231) that fit more to a country's researchers' behavior. It is noteworthy that setting up a national assessment system does not mean bypassing the international systems. Moreover, they can act as a supplementary tool for both internal and external objective and accurate assessment of research performance. The indications of domestic endeavors are China Scientific and Technical Papers and Citation Database (CSTPS), SciELO Citation Index, Russian Science

---

Jafar Mehrad, Prof. in Library and Information Science, Department of Knowledge & Information Sciences, Faculty of Education & Psychology, Shiraz University, Shiraz, Iran, mehrad@ricest.ac.ir
Mohammad Reza Ghane, Associate Prof. in Library and Information Science, Research Department of Evaluation and Collection Development, Regional Information Center for Science and Technology, Shiraz University, Shiraz, Iran, ghane@ricest.ac.ir

Citation Index, and KCI-Korean Journal database. The indexation of the local citation systems in ISI Web of Knowledge shows the worthiness of the projects.

There are plenty of initiatives regarding domestic citation indices. Historically, the domestic citation systems date back to 1987 when Chinese Science and Technology Paper and Citation Database (CSTPCD) was initiated to evaluate Chinese scientists' research performance using S & T journals. There are several national citation indexes in China (Moskaleva et al., 2018, p. 450) for evaluating national scientific performances. Chinese Science Citation Database (CDCD), which evaluated outputs in natural sciences, started in 1989 (Jin and Wang, 1999, p. 325). After this, the Chinese Social Sciences Citation index (CSSCI) began to evaluate social sciences disciplines journals. In the early twenty-first century, in 2002, Chinese Humanities and Social Sciences Citation Database (CHSSCD) was established (Su, Deng, and Shen, 2014, p. 1568): "National institute of Informatics (NII), formerly National Center for Science Information Systems (NACSIS), started to construct the Citation Database for Japanese Papers (CJP) in 1995, and release the service from January 2000" (Negishi, Sun, and Shigi, 2004, p. 333). The beginning of the 2000s has witnessed global tendencies toward national citation indexes. Iran is a pioneered country in research publications at international level (Moed 2016, p. 309). In this regard, a project was implemented to design and implement a national citation index. This project brought about the existence of the Islamic World Science Citation Center (ISC) that we introduce in this chapter. ISC came to being as a means to evaluate Iranian researchers' outputs in 2002, followed by the Russian Index of Science Citation (RISC), founded in 2005 (Moskaleva et al., 2018, p. 450). The government has agreed to allocate funds for RISC. This national citation index makes accessible Russian scholarly journals contents as well as their references to improve research findings quality based on bibliometric indicators. Now, scientific outputs of Russian Higher Education Institutes (HEIs) are not only available locally but also internationally by agreement with Clarivate Analytics. RISC is a part of the Web of Science platform known as the Russian Science Citation Index. In Europe, Serbian Citation Index (SCIndeks) was a pioneer in local assessment of journals, released in the 2000s but not overly successful. SCIndeks aimed at increasing visibility and improving quality of local journals through public access to the contents (Pajić, 2015, p. 604). Thanks to a financial decision in 2014, accessibility, the most important aspect of citation analysis systems, to a large amount of online data ceased in 2015 (ibid., p. 605). The Indian Citation Index (ICI) was later created in New Delhi and launched in 2009. The first goal of ICI was to provide more visibility for research outputs of researchers and HEIs throughout India. The second was free access to journal contents and the third was to measure the journal articles in the sciences, social sciences, arts, and humanities (Yadav and Yadav, 2014, p. 21). At present, ICI covers 1,173 top Indian scholarly journals with 14,067,190 references. ASEAN Citation Index (ACI) dated to 2011 organized scholarly journals published in the member countries of the ACI, i.e. Brunei Darussalam, Cambodia, Indonesia, Lao PDR, Malaysia, Myanmar, the Philippines, Singapore, Thailand, and Vietnam and was supported financially by the Thai's Office of the Higher Education Commission (OHEC) (Sombatsompop et al., 2011, p. 217).

In national scientific communities everyone contributes to the success of the visibility of research outputs to world science (Popovic, Antonic, and Stolic, 2011, p. 44). Accordingly, researchers claim that the international contributions are not the real scientific performance of a country; a comprehensive evaluation includes both international and national scientific efforts. In this sense, a database of this level of comprehensiveness does not exist. However, national citation indexing may be the only form of evidence available and can be considered necessary by policymakers for comprehensive research analysis alongside global evaluation systems. To this end, Iranian research policymakers involved the president of Regional Information Center for Science and Technology (RICeST), Prof. Jafar Mehrad, in the development and implementation of the national research evaluation program. RICeST and Ministry of Science, Research and Technology (MSRT) have been working together in a spirit of collaboration to develop new solutions. It was a real team effort, with everyone contributing something to the success of the project. The result was the implementation and operation of the Islamic World Science Citation Center (ISC). In this chapter we introduce ISC, its development, and products.

ISC Historical Background

General Information

Ideas behind establishing a qualitative and quantitative native tool for assessing scientific outputs of Iranian researchers and HEIs have developed at MSRT since 2001. It is noteworthy that the rise and fall of the economy is crucial in policymaking for journal acquisition in academic libraries. Oil prices fell around 2001, which formed a centralized decision on the acquisition of scientific journals by MSRT. MRST provided scholarly journals for all universities using a "big deal" model. A Document Delivery Service (DDS) met the researches' information needs from three focal points, i. e. University of Tehran, Tarbiat Modares University, and Regional Information Center for Science and Technology (RICeST). However, in spite of these focal points' best endeavors, the initiative ceased, since universities could not afford journal prices, university libraries based journal selection on Journal Impact Factor (JIF), and journal acquisitions paid special attention to JIF to make better collection management decisions around core journals (Mehrad, 2014, p. 1). It was a turning point in making collection development decisions alongside traditional approaches. The new attitude, using scientometric indicators, prevailed among the research policymakers. At the same time, a research project was set up by Prof. Jafar Mehrad (president of RICeST) and Roya Maqsoudi (senior researcher) with help from the Regional Information Center for Science and Technology (RICeST). The project aimed at providing an evaluation of Iranian scientific journals based upon scientometrics indicators

(Mehrad and Naseri, 2010, p. 6). The project managers wanted to promote equal opportunity for all national journals similar to the Institute for Scientific Information (ISI, now Clarivate Analytics). The project proposal was approved by RICeST Scientific committee in 2002, after which the executive team members started system designing. Alongside this work, a broad and varied framework of support has been set up in RICeST in response to the needs of the executive team. The president of RICeST exerted considerable effort to develop this national citation index. In this regard, he started a new round of negotiations with MSRT. The two sides finally reached an agreement to take various steps to try to boost the domestic research evaluation system. System design and data organization were soon developed simultaneously. In its early stage ISC journal coverage included 70 and 81 titles in 2001 and 2002, respectively. At present ISC covers 1,825 Iranian peer reviewed journals, with journals published in the Organization of Islamic Cooperation (OIC) member states expanding to 3,400 titles. Between 2002 and 2019 more than one million and five hundred records have been indexed in ISC, with more than 40 million references and one million citations.

ISC's vision was to develop in the future and to plan in a suitable way. To this end, the MSRT's policy was achieving ISC's objectives at national and international level. The OIC is the target of the ISC. OIC includes 57 states spread over four continents which was established in Rabat, Kingdom of Morocco, on September 25, 1969 (more information is available at https://www.oic-oci.org/page/?p_id=52&p_ref=26&lan=en [July 15, 2020]). The Third Islamic Conference of Ministers of Higher Education and Scientific Research was held in Kuwait on November 19–21, 2006. There were several important items on the agenda regarding scientific issues in OIC states, such as the subjects of "Science and Technology in the OIC Member Countries" and "Ranking of Universities Worldwide and Its Implications for Universities in the OIC Member Countries" proposed by Iran (SESRIC, 2006). It was stipulated that Iran would strengthen its two proposals and, in cooperation with ICESCO in Rabat, Morocco, would present at the Fourth Islamic Conference of Higher Education and Scientific Research in Baku, Republic of Azerbaijan, on October 6–8, 2008 (Mehrad, 2014, p. 4). At the conference, establishment of the ISC was approved and the statute and its organizational structure were prepared and approved by the Iran Ministry of Science, Research and Technology, called Islamic World Science Citation Center (ISC) (ibid, p. 4). The ISC was created from the RICeST and became an independent organization to evaluate OIC scientific production based on scientometric indicators. The Steering Council based on the charter of ISC was now responsible for the programming and evaluation process of scientific performance of OIC 57 Islamic countries. To achieve its objective, the first meeting of the ISC Executive Committee members was held on Saturday, April 25, 2009. The delegations from Iraq for Arabic countries, Sudan for African countries, and Malaysia for South East Asian countries, ISESCO and Ministry of Science, and Research and Technology, I. R. of Iran attended the meeting at the Regional Information Center for Science and Technology.

To introduce ISC to OIC member states, the ISC Executive Committee decided to hold conferences in Iran and 56 other Islamic countries. The first conference was held on December 20–21, 2008 in Tehran. The delegates from Morocco, Iraq, Lebanon, Malaysia, Bangladesh, Syria, Oman, Kuwait, Sudan, Pakistan, Ivory Coast, and Tunisia attended the two-day conference (ibid., p. 7). For the success of a larger conference with the hosting of Malaysia, a pre-con meeting was held in Shiraz in 2009. This meeting was known as the ISC second conference (pre-con meeting). The third conference was held in Malaysia for Asian South East Islamic countries on June 6–7, 2009. Participants included delegations from Malaysia, Indonesia, Brunei, Maldives, Bangladesh, and Malaysian library and Information Science specialists and librarians. There were several important items on the agenda. A special report from the ISC president was high on the agenda for the opening session. The next items were the introduction to the ISC and its objectives, policies, responsibilities, and products to the Asian South East Islamic countries, enhancing communications with ISC, improving executive committee productivity, and experiencing advanced and close collaboration with each other. The Press Festival was an opportunity to hold the fourth seminar. This event took place in Tehran on October 26–28, 2010 with the Ministry of Culture and Islamic Guidance co-hosting the seminar. The seminar attendees included the university chancellors, scientific journal editors from Iran and those countries that did not attend the previous seminars, and ISC representatives in the Islamic countries. OIC member states participants were from Pakistan, Malaysia, Azerbaijan, Iraq, Kyrgyzstan, Kuwait, Sudan, Jordan, Syria, Turkey, Afghanistan, Oman, and Egypt. The fifth Islamic Conference of the Ministers of Higher Education and Scientific Research on "Enculturation of Quality in Academia, Research and Innovation Towards Prosperity of Ummah" was held on October 18–21, 2010 in Kuala Lumpur, Malaysia. In this meeting, the ISC reported on its past two-year performance. The conference declaration lauded "the role of the Islamic Citation Centre in providing access to current and retrospective scientometrics and bibliographic database as well as citation indexing and analysis covering scientific journals from the member states, including journals in their national languages and suggests research journals publishing institutes to coordinate with ISC to accord better recognition to their research performances at international level" (Kuala Lumpur Declaration – ISESCO, 2010, p. 5). The ISC moved ahead in its activities from then on. The series of workshops and conferences of the ISC, while introducing its services and products, encouraged publications and countries to bring their scientific products into this citation system. Consequently, by April 2013 about 1,119 Arabic, 1,056 English, 887 Persian and 403 Scientific Journals in other languages had been registered and indexed in ISC. It is noteworthy that based on the ongoing rigorous selection criteria, journals add and delete throughout the year. The conferences and workshops have achieved significant success in introducing ISC products as a citation system to evaluate peer reviewed journal articles, researchers, and ultimately scientific performance of researchers from Iran and other Islamic countries. The ISC provided an XML journal submission system which speeds up data entry and makes it easier.

The XML system managed to boost journals submission. In addition to the OIC member states, non-Islamic countries such as India, Germany, England, and Poland have expressed a desire to submit their publications to ISC. The activities accelerated the introduction of ISC and helped develop it and strengthen its position. Thus, ISC transcends OIC countries and acts as an international citation system with an emphasis on Islamic countries. The scientific journals from different countries have, in recent times, established a good working relationship with the ISC.

ISC Policies

The ISC has to collect and process both local and all OIC prestigious journals. A collection policy is needed to address issues such as the selection, acquisition, evaluation, and maintenance of journals. The primary goal is feeding information to the ISC to enable the assessment of OIC journals. In the early stage the ISC is focused on local journals to be indexed in citation database. The most prevalent issue was with selecting and acquiring the OIC journals, as it was a time-consuming process, a problem that still exists. In Iran, MSRT governs journals evaluation and selection with a well-established set of criteria that have been applied for several years.

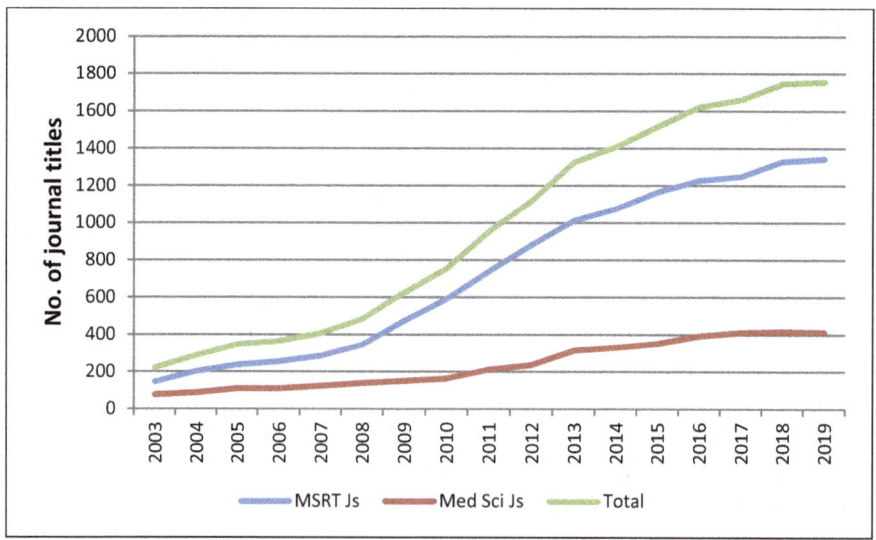

Figure 1: Farsi source journals distribution.

Over time, the number of accredited journals has grown (Figure 1) in sciences (S), technology (T), medical science (M), and humanities (H).

In total, ISC covers 1,756 Iranian titles in STM&H journals. Over the course of 17 years, journals grew from 221 to 1,756, with a 12.97% compound annual growth rate. There is no such clear information about peer reviewed journals in other OIC member states. For selecting and acquiring journals from 56 other OIC countries, ISC hired a broker to collect scholarly journals in Arabic, English, and French languages from 2005. We witnessed a remarkable increase in Arabic journals from four titles to 263 titles. In this regard, the mean annual growth rate of journals during 2006 to 2016 is 46.31%. The status of English journals also was on the increase over this period. The ISC indexing process shows 36 English journals were indexed in 2006, a number which has increased dramatically since it began. The titles growth in ISC would be helpful to have access to also, i.e. 1,834 titles in 2016 with the mean annual growth rate as 42.95% over the course of 11 periods. Figure 2 shows more breakdowns.

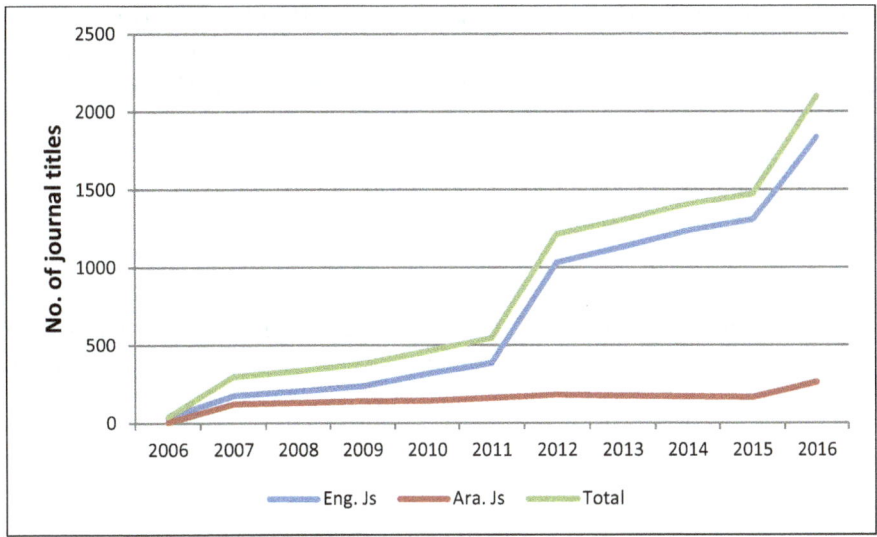

Figure 2: English and Arabic source journals distribution.

In 2002 the source journals of OIC member states were 15 titles in ISI's JCR, accounting for 0.2% of the total journals (7,530). At present JCR covers 12,298 titles, with the share of OIC 1.4% (171). The new figures from ISC are noteworthy alongside the above ones. In total, ISC covers 3,400 journal titles. Out of this 3,400 the share of English journals is about 54% (1,834), Farsi journals second with 38.3%, and Arabic journals third with 7.7% (263). In comparison with ISI's JCR, the OIC journals indexed in ISC are far more JCR. The facts and figures prove that all indexed in international citation indexes such as WoS and Scopus are not the entire picture of the scientific performance of a country or a region. The local research evaluation systems make the research assessment as inclusive as possible and cover deficiencies in the international citation indexing systems for "non-English countries" (Jin and Wang, 1999, pp. 325–326).

The collection policy is part of an ongoing effort to develop the ISC. ISC was soon recognized as a journal evaluation tool beyond the OIC member states and transcended the boundaries. Consequently, ISC policy welcomes journals around the world based on its journal selection criteria. There has been an increasing number of peer reviewed journals of different countries indexed in ISC, e.g. India, Germany, England, and Poland.

ISC Departments

The Vice-chancellor for Research Affairs' goal is to improve conformity with high standards of research performance assessment. It consists of four departments: the Department of Citation Programming (DCP), Department of Analysis of Resources (DAR), Department of Citation Analysis (DCA), and Department of Universities Ranking (DUR).

Department of Citation Programming

Originally, the DCP was the backbone of this project. The ISC is trying to develop the programs that will meet objectives. Regarding this, the program planning should support indexing, assessment, and monitoring of all prestigious journals of OIC member states.

Department of Analysis of Resources

Appropriate journal selection policy ensures the wise use of indicators and how to apply these indicators in practice. Collection development is at the heart of the ISC to establish priorities and plan for indexing journals from 57 OIC member states. To this end, source journals are reviewed by subject specialist librarians based on selection criteria, hence they involve the identification, selection, acquisition, and evaluation of source journals. This is where products of ISC, i.e. English Journal Citation Reports (EJCR), Islamic Countries SCI, ISC Master Journals List, English Current Contents (ECC), Journal Performance Indicators (JPI), Fast XML Uploading System, originate. Due to basic functions, Persian, Arabic, and English divisions were developed to meet the objectives. In each division the research experts monitor source journals that are identified as core to the disciplines. They keep watch of the new journals created in support of emerging research areas and remove those that do not meet the ISC selection policy criteria. The experts are continuously supervising the selection process.

Department of Citation Analysis

Identifying and evaluating the Iranian accredited journals is a continuous task at DCA. Titles from OIC member states and other countries have to be verified by experts. The DCA transparent selection process enables experts to decide journal eligibility for indexing in ISC. Using both quantitative and qualitative measures, journals are categorized into master journals, waiting list journals, and Core journals. Master journals include all Persian, English, Arabic, and French journals indexed in ISC, and journal impact factor (JIF) has been assigned to them. After submitting a journal to ISC, it undergoes the selection process. If the title meets the criteria such as academic credibility, publisher's reputation, internal and external geographical distribution of authors as well as editorial boards, bibliographic and citation information, publishing regularity, strict adherence to journal policy and scope, peer-review process, editorial board citation rate, and online journal content availability, it will be included in the ISC, otherwise the title will be removed from ISC databases.

Department of Universities Ranking

University rankings provide important information for university applicants and policymakers at national and international levels (Çakır, Acartürk and Alaşehir, 2015, p. 814). Prospective students use university rankings to find the appropriate destination for intra and extra country higher education. Policymakers, on the other hand, employ university rankings information to evaluate the university scientific performances (Bornmann and Glänzel, 2018, p. 1101) against competitors. At local level, all universities should be benchmarked against the best. To determine higher education quality, ISC has been evaluating and ranking Iranian higher education institutes since 2010. The evaluation process is based on 26 indicators in five general criteria of research (58%), education (15%), international reputation (9%), facilities (2%), and social, economic, and industrial activities (16%). The OIC mission is also to evaluate OIC universities. ISC ranks universities at local level for Iranian higher education institutes (HEIs) and international level for 57 ISC member states. To this end, the Iranian HEIs ranking were launched in 2010, with the first local ranking released in 2012, with the ISC Ranking of Islamic Countries Universities and Research Institutions released in 2013. Local ranking categorizes organizations from HEIs to comprehensive universities that offer a wide range of disciplines, universities of technologies, research institutes, universities of art, and medical sciences universities. The universities and research institutes are assessed and ranked based on aforementioned criteria in respective categories. For ISC University performance, the system provides tables regarding agricultural sciences, engineering and technology, medical and health sciences, natural sciences, and social sciences. It is also feasible to find best universities based on regions (i.e. Asiatic Region, Central Africa, Eastern Europe, Middle East, Northern Africa, and Southern Africa) or any country. More information is available through the ISC ranking website (https://iur.isc.gov.ir/ [July 15, 2020]).

Products of ISC

The ISC, with thousands of academic journals, provides databases for assessing performance of HEIs, researchers, countries, and journals. The products of ISC include English Journal Citation Reports (EJCR), Islamic Countries SCI, ISC Master Journals List, English Current Contents (ECC), and Journal Performance Indicators (JPI).

English Journal Citation Reports (EJCR)

English Journal Citation Reports (EJCR) assesses and compares journals in ISC after undergoing a rigorous evaluation. EJCR provides journal metrics such as JIF, immediacy index, and a journal's quartile ranking (assigned as quality) as well as features including journal title, total citations, and number of articles for librarians, researchers, publishers, and policymakers. There are three categories in EJCR: Master Journals, Waiting Journals, and Core journals. Each journal in EJCR is assigned to one category. Master journals are all journals covered in ISC databases; a journal must acquire the necessary score to be included in the Master journal list. A periodic evaluation will determine the journals' fate. Waiting journals are those that seem to thrive on the challenges of quality to be included in core journals. The reassessment proves that they meet international reputation, publisher's reputation, editorial scientific popularity, publishing standing, XML systems, self-citation rates, and JIF Quartile. Core journals are a collection of top-tier journals in various subject areas that has been thoroughly analyzed by an expert team of in-house ISC Editors. The criteria used in this evaluation ensure the high quality of the journals in terms of their scientific content. The ISC Core Collection uses a set of criteria for evaluating that ensures the high quality of the journals in terms of their scientific content and allows users to search with confidence and explore the deep citation connections in various subject areas. In this regard, indicators such as cutting-edge research topics, applicability of findings, readability and scientific quality, accurate methodology, understandable data presentation, rational discussion, rigorous reasoning, and conclusions are all considered in the selection of publications. Journals that are listed in the core journals of the Islamic World Science Citation Database are re-evaluated annually and transferred to the Waiting list journals or Master journals list if they do not satisfy the necessary conditions.

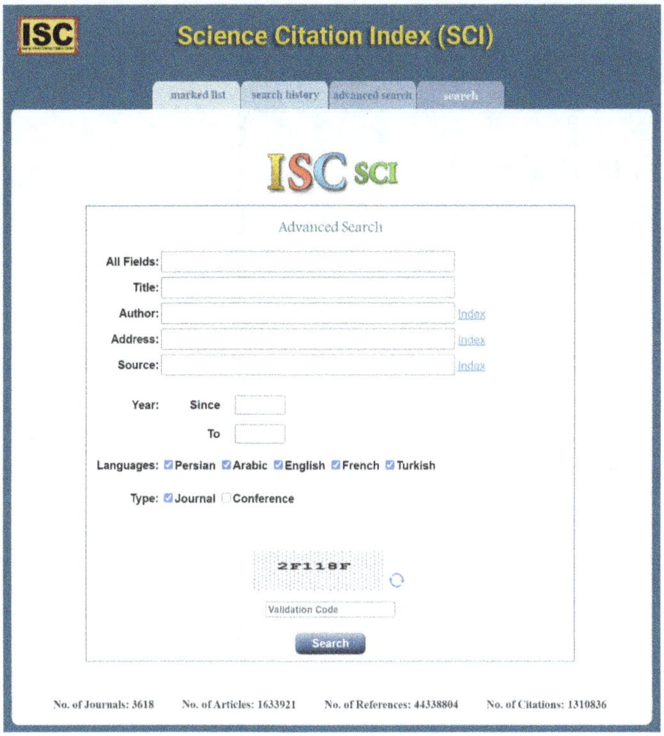

Figure 3: Advanced search tips for Islamic Countries Science Citation Index.

Islamic Countries Science Citation Index

Islamic Countries SCI or ISC SCI is another useful product of ISC that measures universities, researchers, and source journals with information from over 3,286 STM&H journals. This is a tool for retrieving and evaluating scientific literature from 57 OIC member countries by using citations. The SCI, which was created by Eugene Garfield and launched by Institute for Scientific Information (ISI) in 1964, is a "tool to facilitate the dissemination and retrieval of scientific literature" (Garfield, 2007, p. 65). But it is a language-bias tool (Van Leeuwent et al., 2001, p. 336) and ignores the most prestigious local journals from countries including OIC member states. There are more than 1,300,000 journal articles from 57 OIC countries in the ISC. Islamic Countries SCI evaluates scientific productivity of OIC members and is used alongside existing citation indexing systems such as SCI (ISI) and Scopus. Consequently, policymakers in each country can use it to effectively evaluate domestic scientific activities of HEIs. Using Islamic Countries SCI advanced search tips enables users to enter search queries using Boolean and proximity operators to narrow the scope of their search. Field tags can be seen in Figure 3. When one limits their search by All Fields, they retrieve only those records that contain the search term(s) entered in the search

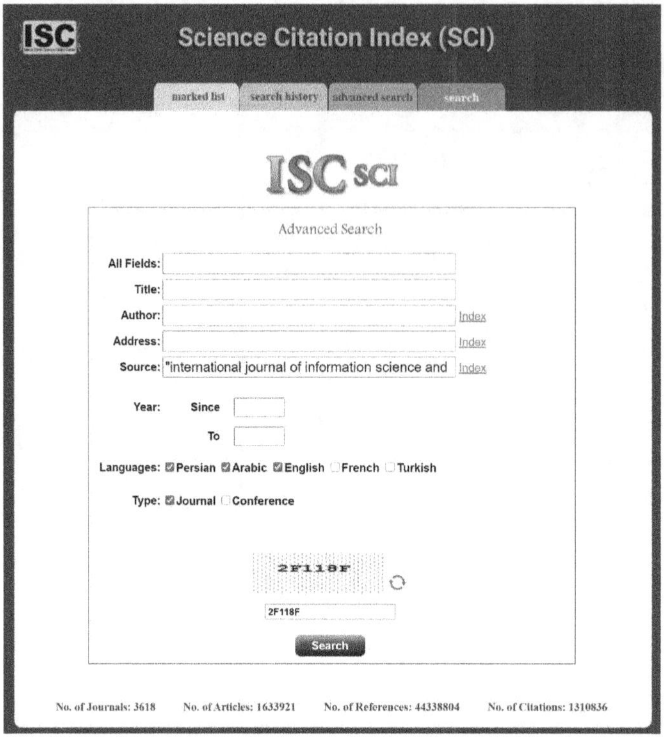

Figure 4: Journal source search.

field. All Fields approves a keyword search that appears for words anywhere in the record. Keyword searches are a precise replacement for a challenging search when you no longer know the standard subject heading. Author index helps users to find the authors for adding to the query. This is also true for the address and source index.

Islamic Countries SCI provides analysis for authors, HEIs, and journal sources. Using journal source index, suppose "International Journal of Information Science and Management" is searched (Figure 4). The system will retrieve published articles for all years, but the user can refine his/her search to year range through the "Since" box and "To" box.

The search result in this case shows 287 records for the journal source (Figure 5). One can sort the results by "relevance", "Recent Articles", "Most Cited", "former Articles", and "References" at the top of the search result.

One can analyze the results by the "Analyze" icon at the bottom of the page (Figure 6). Clicking the icon enables the user to analyze research results by items such as "Institution", "Publication Year", "Author", "Source", "Main Subjects", and "Sub Subjects" (Figure 7).

In another search we decided to find the publications affiliated to the "University of Malaya", one of the top-ranked universities in Malaysia. Using the address index,

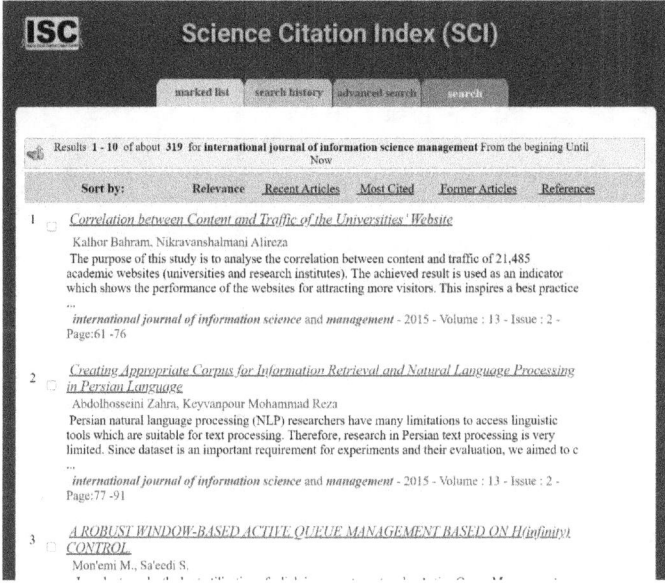

Figure 5: Search results.

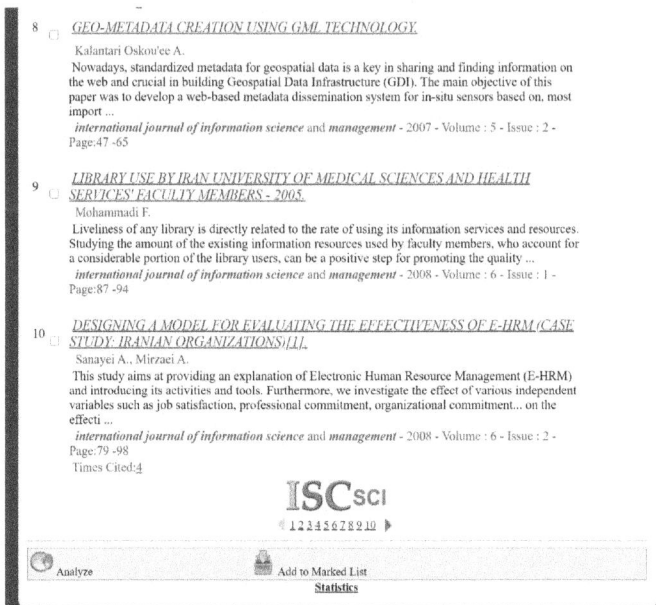

Figure 6: Showing "Analyze" icon at the bottom of the page.

the "University of Malaya" is selected (Figure 8). The search results retrieved 4,326 records that we sorted by "Most Cited" (Figure 9).

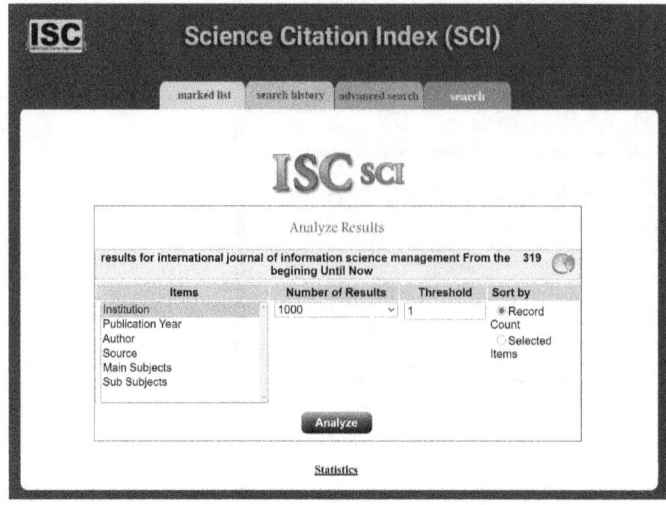

Figure 7: How to analyze results using different items.

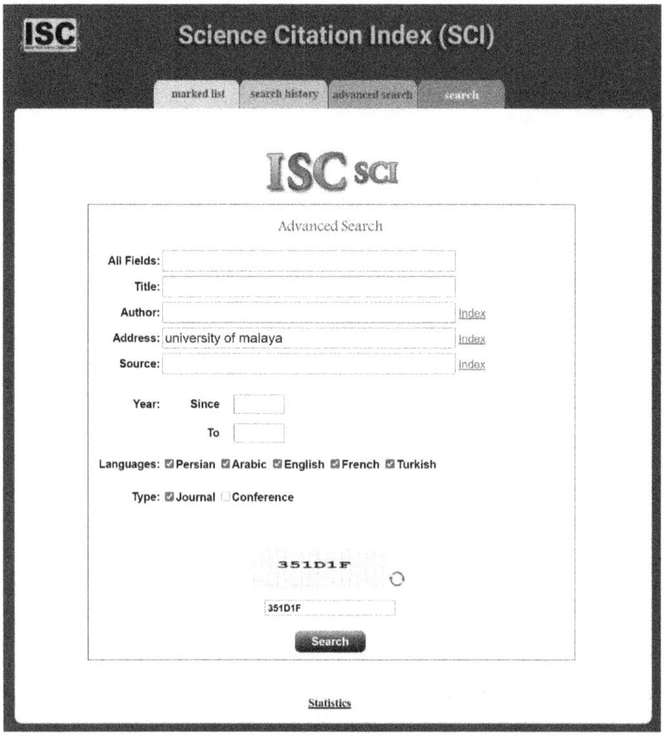

Figure 8: How to search publication of a certain university by address index.

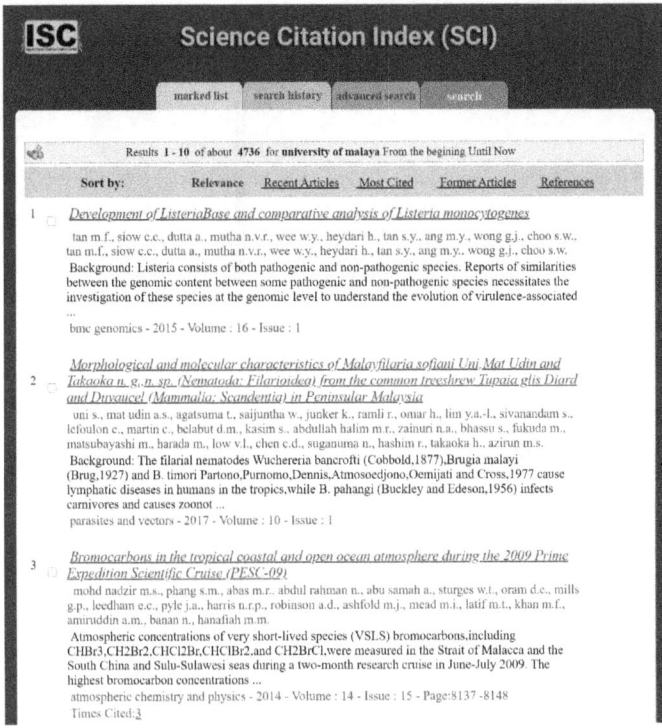

Figure 9: Publications affiliated to the "University of Malaya" sorted by most cited.

After analyzing the research results using "Main Subjects", the share of different subject areas is depicted, as shown in Figure 10.

English Current Contents

The rapid awareness of latest discoveries will be a crucial factor in the success of the new knowledge. English Current Contents keeps well-informed scientists and researchers of developments in their interested area of research (Current Contents, 1993, p. 173). English Current Contents is a current awareness service that provides tables of contents (ToC) and bibliographic information from the most recently published articles of journals indexed in bibliographic databases. English Current Contents (ECC) is a product of ISC and provides access to complete ToC, abstracts, and bibliographic information of leading journals in eight main subject areas, i.e. agriculture, art and architecture, basic sciences, engineering, environment and natural resources, humanities, medical sciences, and veterinary (Figure 11). Using ECC that is connected to SCI saves time on searching and allows for easy access to core researches through prestigious journals (Mehrad, 2014, p. 28).

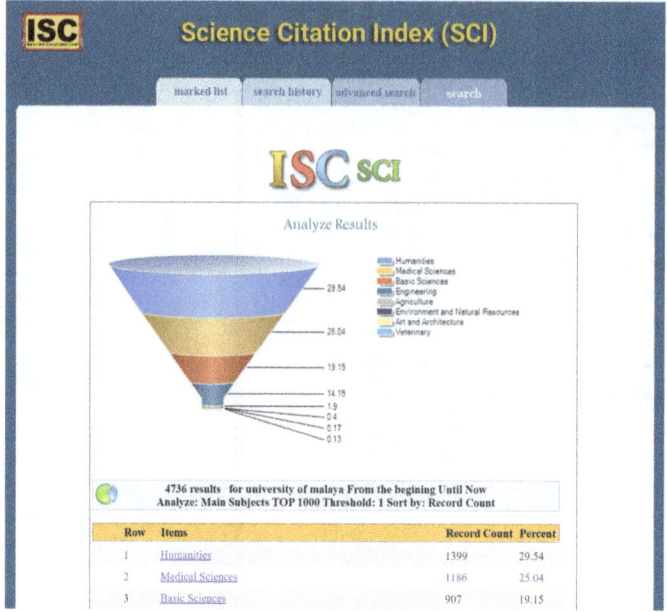

Figure 10: Search results for "University of Malaya" publications in main subjects.

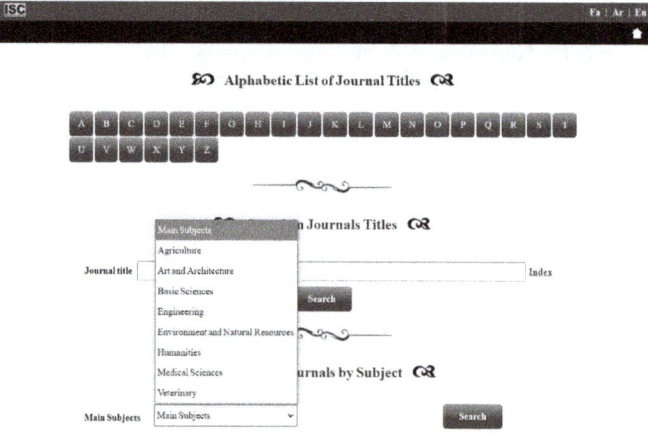

Figure 11: English Current Contents in eight main subjects.

Journals Performance Indicators

ISC Journals Performance Indicators (JPI) analyzes journals' performance based on eight indicators including citations impact, citations impact of cited articles, total number of citations, total number of articles, percentage of cited documents, relative citations impact of journals in ISC, percentage of ISC documents, and percentage of

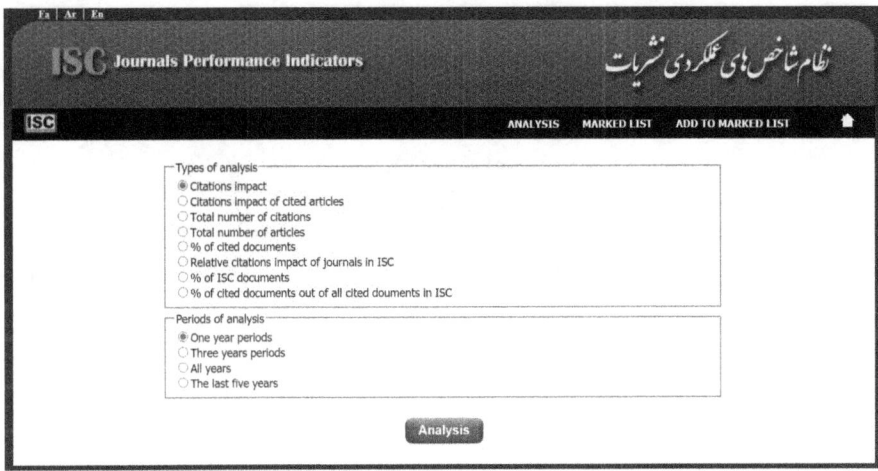

Figure 12: ISC Journal Performance Indicators.

cited documents out of all cited documents in ISC using a different timespan (Figure 12).

JPI provides journals analysis in eight subject categories, i.e. agriculture, art and architecture, basic sciences, engineering, environment and natural resources, humanities, medical sciences, and veterinary. One can compare journal performance using an indicator and restrict the search results to custom year range. Shown below (Figure 13) is when two journals from Turkey were selected, e.g. *the Turkish Journal of Pediatrics* and *Turkish Journal of Anesthesiology and Reanimation*, with their performances compared using "citations impact of cited articles".

ISC Master Journal List

The ISC Master Journal List enables users to find all journal titles covered in the ISC. One can find the right journal with respect to his/her research area. To find a certain journal one can search using ISSN or journal title. For title search one can insert the full title of the journal or parts of the journal's title (Figure 14). The journals are curated by a team of experts in journals evaluation. Through the ISC Master Journal List one can access both all ISC accredited journals and excluded journals.

ISC Conference Registration System

Academic conference papers are as important as top tier journal articles. Some post presented articles were published in peer-reviewed journals; for example "most than a quarter presentations at the three ISSI biennial meetings" received citations after

Title	ISSN	Year	Value
the turkish journal of pediatrics	00414301	2010	0.7010
the turkish journal of pediatrics	00414301	2011	0.59
the turkish journal of pediatrics	00414301	2012	0.57
the turkish journal of pediatrics	00414301	2013	0.3330
the turkish journal of pediatrics	00414301	2014	0.0720
turkish journal of anaesthesiology and reanimation	10165150	2010	0.0960
turkish journal of anaesthesiology and reanimation	10165150	2011	0.1540
turkish journal of anaesthesiology and reanimation	10165150	2012	0.0520
turkish journal of anaesthesiology and reanimation	10165150	2013	0.07
turkish journal of anaesthesiology and reanimation	10165150	2014	0.0390
turkish journal of anaesthesiology and reanimation	10165150	2015	0.0220

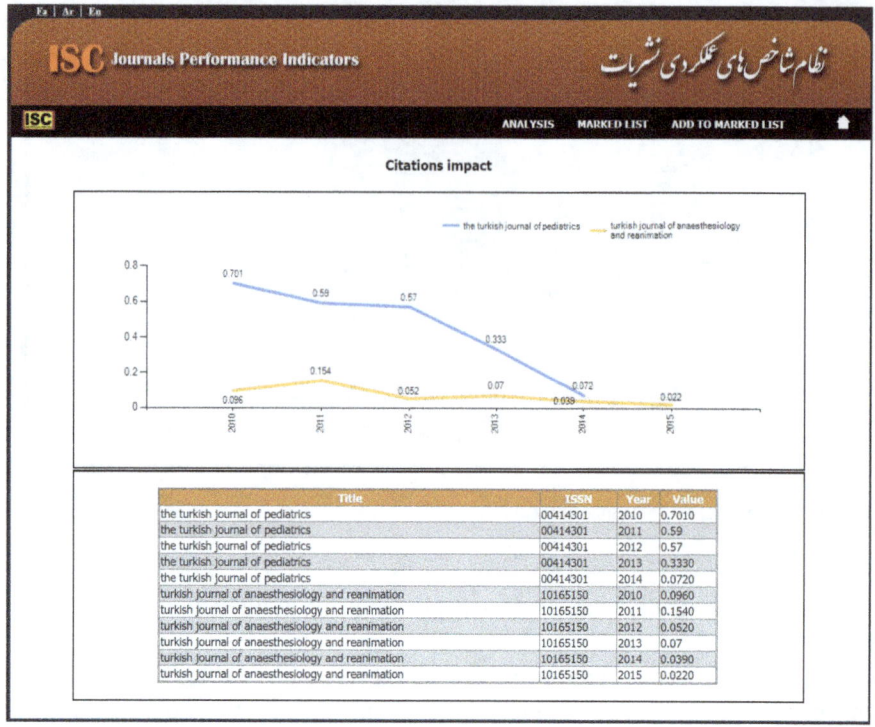

Figure 13: Results for comparison of two Turkish journals using citations impact of cited articles.

Row	Journal Title	ISSN	E_ISSN
1	3L The Southeast Asian Journal Of English Language Studies	01285157	
2	Abant Izzet Baysal University Graduate School Of Social Sciences Journal Of Social Sciences	13030035	21473064
3	Abant Izzet Baysal University Journal Of Faculty Of Education	13030493	21484929
4	Abstract And Applied Analysis	10853375	16870409
5	Academia- Revista Latinoamericana De Administracion	10128255	20565127
6	Academic Psychiatry	10429670	15457230
7	Acs Central Science	23747943	23747951
8	Acs Macro Letters		21611653
9	Acs Sensors	23793694	23793694
10	Acta Adriatica	00015113	18460453
11	Acta Agriculturae Slovenica	15819175	18541941
12	Acta Bioquimica Clinica Latinoamericana	03252957	18516114
13	Acta Botanica Brasilica	01023306	1677941X
14	Acta Botanica Croatica	03650588	18478476
15	Acta Botanica Mexicana	01877151	24487589

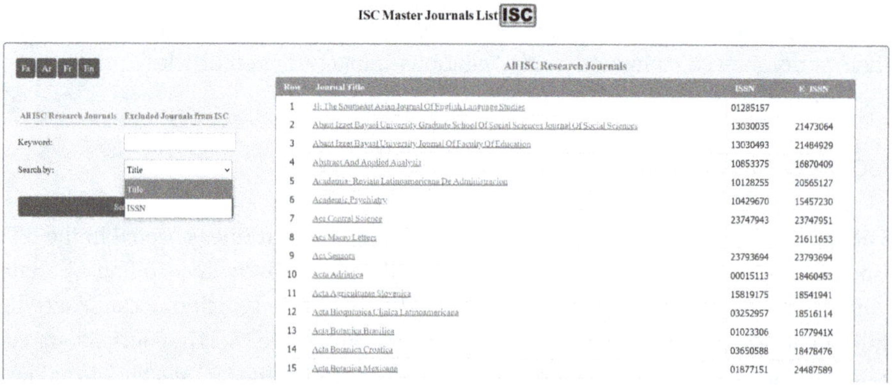

Figure 14: ISC Master Journal List.

publishing in a prestigious journal (Aleixandre-Benavent et al., 2009, p. 417). The ISC conference registration system has a robust evaluation for supporting conferences as well as submitting conference papers to the ISC database. It shows that the ISC takes into careful consideration the quality of conferences. In that regard, the quality of conference organizers, participants (Stević, et al., 2019, p. 2), and the reputation of sponsoring institutions are important. There are 2,720 registered conferences at the moment. The conferences include seven main subject categories. The number of conferences for humanities is 1,477, engineering 859, agriculture 515, basic sciences 493, art and architecture 299, medical sciences 135, and veterinary 50. The total number of conferences regarding main subject categories is 3,828. The difference between 2,720 registered conferences and numbers in subject categories is due to the degree of dependence or application of different subjects to each conference. The ISC conference registration system indicates 213 subcategories and a list of subcategories appears by clicking on the subcategories icon. One can search this database based on conference title, organizer, main category, subcategory, conference URLs, and assigned code and also sort the results through recently added, date of conference, and conference title. ISC evaluates registered conferences based on its regulation. The database provides comprehensive coverage of all conference articles. Hence, the policy is to cover the collective accredited conference.

Ranking of Universities

Research policymakers and universities are interested in university ranking at international, regional, and local levels. Accordingly, the establishment and operation of university ranking systems at three levels is welcomed by different stakeholders (Çakır et al., 2015, p. 814). It is true for Iranian policymakers and university administrators. To this end, ISC first established and operated a local ranking (Ranking of Universities and Research institutes of Iran) based on five criteria and 26 indicators in 2010 (Figure 15). It is noteworthy that the datasets are extracted from WoS and ISC in a five-year timespan. The university administrators also have to make a self-declaration through a questionnaire. The criteria include research, education, international reputation, facilities, and socio-economic and industrial activities.

Three years later, the regional ranking of universities i.e. Ranking of Islamic Countries Universities and Research Institutes, was released in 2013 (Figure 16). The regional ranking, which includes OIC member states, evaluates universities using research, education, international activity, and innovation criteria with 12 indicators. The 2018 version of ranking includes 187 universities that had indexed at least 800 documents in WoS during the four previous years to the ranking year and also registered their products in USPTO.

The ISC World University Ranking is the third ranking of ISC ranking systems (Figure 17). The universities with at least 1,500 documents recorded in WoS in the past four years are eligible for undergoing the evaluation process. University selection is based on this assumption that shows 1,603 universities in the 2018 ranking. The criteria and indicators for this ranking are the same as the Ranking of Islamic Countries Universities and Research Institutes.

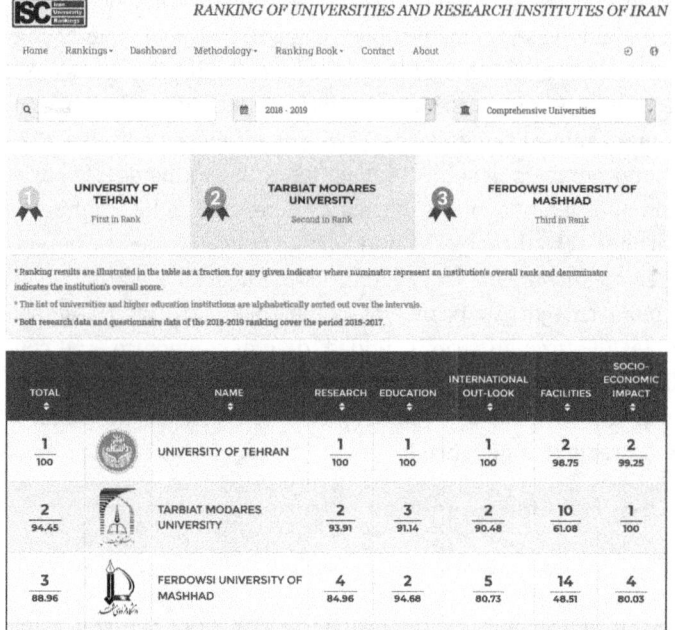

Figure 15: Ranking of Universities and Research institutes of Iran.

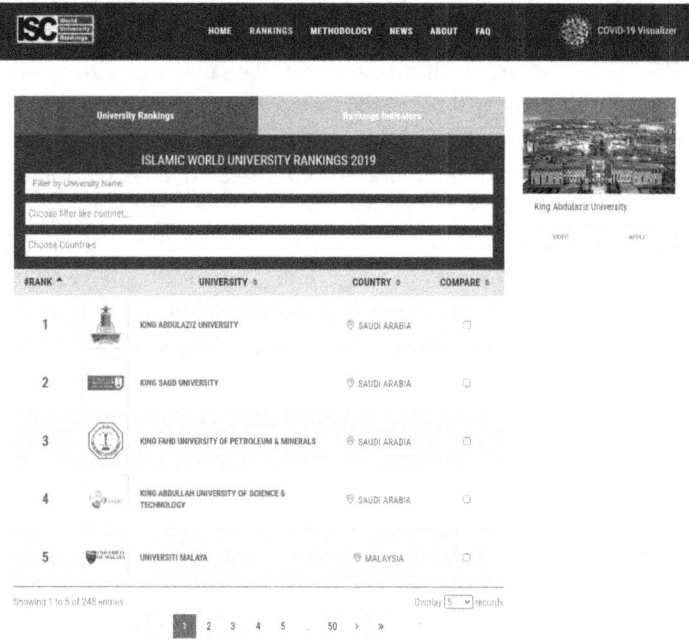

Figure 16: Islamic World University Ranking.

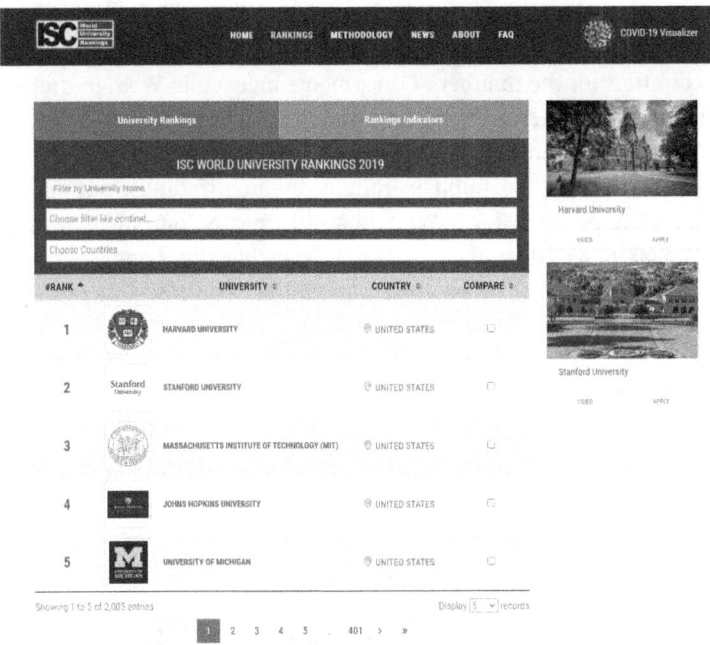

Figure 17: ISC World University Ranking.

Conclusion

Scientific performance of HEIs is essential for policymakers at intra- and inter-evaluation levels. Benchmarking will make greater improvements in the HEIs' services. Without governmental or private benchmarking, policymakers, university administrators, researchers, scientific journal owners, and customers can't be sure of the truth of the claims. Regarding scientific performance at international level, language bias accounts for one of the major pitfalls of global university rankings (van Raan, 2005, p. 139), which creates the incentive to establish, operate, and develop national evaluation systems. Another reason for development of national evaluation systems is local indicators (Çakır et al., 2015, p. 814) that depict a comprehensive performance of HEIs alongside with global evaluation systems and increasing incentives to do so. It is noteworthy that national evaluation systems were launched first and then international ones started to evaluate HEIs, researchers, and journals (Alaşehir et al., 2014, p. 174). Regarding scientific performance evaluation we therefore confronted the question of how to deal with the problem of language in scientific performance. International citation indexing systems cover journals in the English language. The total number of all documents in WoS is 66,375,914 from 1900 till November 4, 2019. Out of this number, 60,880,383 documents are in English language (91.7%), with the share of other languages 5,492,361 documents (8.3%). The figures prove that at least ISI is a language-biased system. Another figure shows that Persian and Arabic language documents are 394 and 895, respectively. It can be said that Iran is among the top 20 countries for the number of documents indexed in WoS. In this regard the important issue is that they are written in non-Persian languages, i.e. mostly in English. This is not all the scientific productions of Iranian researchers. There are about 1,700 prestigious journals that publish Iranian research findings; out of this number 42 journals are indexed in ISI JCR. What about the rest of journals that publish articles in Persian language? It is true for other OIC member states and even non-English language countries. In such cases, international citation indexing systems are a necessary but not sufficient justification for evaluating a country's scientific performance. Consequently, the facts induced research policymakers to establish and operate a national citation system, i.e. the ISC. In addition to the global tools that provide datafiles for evaluating scientific performance of all stakeholders, the ISC has a crucial role in the carrying out of bibliometric studies in relation to national and regional performances. The OIC member states' population is about 1.82 billion people, 24% of the world population. Accordingly, researchers in 57 Islamic countries will, no doubt, contribute to world science. Their national contributions are a comprehensive source and should be monitored. That is why ISC was created and launched. ISC is growing rapidly and is closely monitoring the scientific output of the Muslim world. Due to its growth among Islamic countries, non-Islamic countries around the world tend to index their peer reviewed journals to ISC. ISC, along with global citation databases and university rankings, provides a comprehensive picture of the scientific performance of researchers in their native language productions. The inclusion of national citation data for OIC member states makes this a unique tool for benchmarking countries' scientific performances, which will make greater improvements in HEIs' scientific impact. ISC acts as a dual purpose database which could also be used for carrying out individual researchers and journals citation analyses and also ranking universities based on accredited indicators extracted from ISC JCR and SCI.

References

Alaşehir, O, Çakır, MP, Acartürk, C, Baykal, N & Akbulut, U, 2014, 'URAP-TR: a national ranking for Turkish universities based on academic performance', *Scientometrics*, vol. 101, no. 1, pp. 159–78.

Aleixandre-Benavent, R, González-Alcaide, G, Miguel-Dasit, A, Navarro-Molina, C & Valderrama-Zurián, J 2009, 'Full-text publications in peer-reviewed journals derived from presentations at three ISSI conferences', *Scientometrics*, vol. 80, no. 2, pp. 407–18.

Bornmann, L & Glänzel, W 2018, 'Which differences can be expected when two universities in the Leiden Ranking are compared? Some benchmarks for institutional research evaluations', *Scientometrics*, vol. 115, no. 2, pp. 1101–05.

Çakır, MP, Acartürk, C, Alaşehir, O & Çilingir, C 2015, 'A comparative analysis of global and national university ranking systems', *Scientometrics*, vol. 103, no. 3, pp. 813–48.

"Current Contents", 1993, *Historical Social Research / Historische Sozialforschung*, vol. 18, no. 1, pp. 173–75, http://www.jstor.org/stable/20755730 (July 15, 2020).

Garfield, E 2007, 'The evolution of the science citation index', *International Microbiology*, vol. 10, no. 1, pp. 65–69.

Jin, B & Wang, B 1999, 'Chinese Science Citation Database: its construction and application', *Scientometrics*, vol. 45, no. 2, pp. 325–32.

Key Perspectives Ltd. 2009, 'A Comparative Review of Research Assessment Regimes in Five Countries and the Role of Libraries in the Research Assessment Process. Report commissioned by OCLC Research', http://www.oclc.org/research/publications/library/2009/2009-09.pdf (July 15, 2020).

Kuala Lumpur Declaration – ISESCO, 2010, https://www.isesco.org.ma/wp-content/uploads/2015/05/Declaration-Kuala-lumpur-Ang.pdf (July 15, 2020).

Mehrad, J & Naseri, M 2010, 'The Islamic World Science Citation Center: A new scientometrics system for evaluating research performance in OIC region', *International Journal of Information Science and Management (IJISM)*, vol. 8, no. 2, pp. 1–10.

Mehrad, J 2014, *The introduction to Islamic World Science Citation Center*, Takht-E-jamshid publishing, Shiraz.

Moed, HF 2016, 'Iran's scientific dominance and the emergence of South-East Asian countries as scientific collaborators in the Persian Gulf Region', *Scientometrics*, vol. 108, no. 1, pp. 305–314.

Moskaleva, O, Pislyakov, V, Sterligov, I, Akoev, M & Shabanova, S 2018, 'Russian index of Science citation: Overview and review', *Scientometrics*, vol. 116, no. 1, pp. 449–462.

Negishi, M, Sun, Y & Shigi, K 2004, 'Citation database for Japanese Papers: A new bibliometric tool for Japanese academic society', *Scientometrics*, vol. 60, no. 3, pp. 333–51.

Pajić, D 2015, 'The Serbian Citation Index: Contest and Collapse', in *Proceedings of ISSI conference 2015*, pp. 604–05.

Popovic, A, Antonic, S & Stolic, D 2011, 'The Role of National Citation Index in the Evaluation of National Science', in C Billenness et al. (eds), 3rd International Conference The Future of Information Sciences (INFuture) November 9–11, pp. 43–49, University of Zagreb, Zagreb.

SESRIC, The Third Islamic Conference of Ministers of Higher Education and Scientific Research 2006, http://www.sesric.org/event-detail.php?id=32 (July 15, 2020).

Sombatsompop, N, Premkamolnetr, N, Markpin, T, Ittiritmeechai, S, Wongkaew, C, Yochai, W, Ratchatahirun, P & Beng, LI 2011, 'Viewpoints on synergising ASEAN academic visibilities through research collaboration and the establishment of an ASEAN Citation Index Database 1', *Asia Pacific Viewpoint*, vol. 52, no. 2, pp. 207–18.

Stević, Ž, Đalić, I, Pamučar, D, Nunić, Z, Vesković, S, Vasiljević, M & Tanackov, I 2019, 'A new hybrid model for quality assessment of scientific conferences based on Rough BWM and SERVQUAL', *Scientometrics*, vol. 119, no. 1, pp. 1–30.

Su, X, Deng, S & Shen, S 2014, 'The design and application value of the Chinese Social Science Citation Index', *Scientometrics*, vol. 98, no. 3, pp. 1567–82.

Tret'yakova, OG 2015, 'Development of national citation index as a condition for the formation of a system to evaluate scientific research performance', *Economic and social changes: facts, trends, forecast*, no. 1, pp. 230–45.

Van Leeuwen, TN, Moed, HF, Tijssen, RJ, Visser, MS & Van Raan, AF 2001, 'Language biases in the coverage of the Science Citation Index and its consequences for international comparisons of national research performance', *Scientometrics*, vol. 51, no. 1, pp. 335–46.

Van Raan, AF 2005, 'Fatal attraction: Conceptual and methodological problems in the ranking of universities by bibliometric methods', *Scientometrics*, vol. 62, no. 1, pp. 133–43.

Yadav, B & Yadav, M 2014, 'Resources, facilities and services of the Indian citation index (ICI)', *Library Hi Tech News*, vol. 31, no. 4, pp. 21–29.

6.4 Institutional Repositories and Bibliometrics

Valeria Aman

Abstract: Institutional repositories are information systems that are institutionally defined and which make scholarly material widely accessible to the community. Repositories are a key service in supporting the mission and goals of their institution and can be seen as a digital embodiment of research activity. However, institutional repositories should be viewed as supplements and not as primary venues for scholarly publishing. To be successful, institutional repositories must be filled with scholarly work that can be searched and cited. This chapter describes the advent of institutional repositories, their role in scholarly communication and how they changed the profession of librarians. The main focus is on examining institutional repositories as instruments of monitoring research performance by discussing the metrics that repositories currently offer. Most commonly measured repository metrics are the number of items, item downloads, item uploads and citation-based metrics. These metrics are either platform-generated or result from interlinked databases to retrieve citations. Institutional repositories and bibliometrics as a method of research evaluation have gone through a redefinition of their role and tasks in recent decades. As there is no established standard of performance indicators, repository managers should be careful with interpretation of metrics.

Keywords: altmetrics, citation impact, institutional repositories, librarians, open access, research assessment, usage statistics.

Since the advent of the Internet, academics have recognized the information and communication technologies as efficient means to share results and to improve the hitherto slow turnaround of traditional publishing (Ramalho Correia and de Castro Neto, 2002). This led to the creation of repositories as digital collections and archives of research communities. Institutional repositories (IR) are a subset of digital repositories that are supposed to capture the research output of academic institutions rather than disciplines (Arlitsch and O'Brien, 2012). IR reformed the scholarly communication and increased the visibility of universities' output (Crow, 2002). Their mission is to disseminate without barriers research results and to function as directories of publications produced by its members. Previous research in the UK suggested that IR may play a crucial role in measuring research output and may affect university rankings (Key Perspectives Ltd., 2009). IR hold two types of metadata,

---

Valeria Aman, Deutsches Zentrum für Hochschul- und Wissenschaftsforschung GmbH, Abteilung 2 "Forschungssystem und Wissenschaftsdynamik", Außenstelle Berlin, Schützenstraße 6a, 10117 Berlin, Germany, aman@dzhw.eu

https://doi.org/10.1515/9783110646610-041

bibliographic and administrative information (attribution of publications to author or research units), making IR particularly interesting for bibliometric use. While some institutional repositories began as ad hoc vehicles for dissemination of research results, many of them have become efficient instruments to evaluate a university's scientific performance through bibliometric analyses (Iriarte et al., 2011). This chapter describes the advent of institutional repositories, their role in scholarly communication, and how they changed the profession of librarians. The main focus is on examining institutional repositories as instruments of monitoring research performance by discussing the metrics that repositories currently deliver.

The Role of Institutional Repositories in Scholarly Communication

The earliest successful repositories were e-print services developed to support the scholarly communication in disciplines with an existing tradition of sharing preprints or working papers, e.g. in high-energy physics, computer science, and economics (Day, 2004). One of the earliest and most popular preprint repositories in the world is arXiv, that was originally set up for the communication of preprints in high-energy physics. Since its inception in 1991, the arXiv allows physicists, mathematicians, biologists, and computer scientists to freely share their papers prior to formal peer review. To supplement discipline-based repositories, institutional repositories have been established to collect, to manage, to disseminate, and to preserve digital material produced by the research staff of institutes (Crow, 2002). IR have a much wider remit than preprint repositories, collecting all types of digital materials including research and teaching materials, students' theses, dissertations, and scientific data created by the institution and its members. IR are information systems that are institutionally defined and which make scholarly material widely accessible to the community. These repositories use descriptive metadata and run on web server technologies. IR are often seen as competition for traditional publishing or as a supplement to traditional publishing. IR could provide all of the functions of traditional publishing (registration, certification, dissemination, and archiving), placing the role of scholarly publishing back in the hands of institutions (Davis and Connolly, 2007). On the other hand, IR serve to disseminate so-called "grey literature", i.e. reports, working papers, visual presentations, and other materials that are ignored by traditional publishers (ibid.). Thus, IR provide a valuable supplement to the existing scholarly publishing model and can be seen as a strategic response to systematic problems in the scholarly journal system.

Increasing the access to literature is one main goal of institutional repositories. Their mission is directed at open access and they are harvested and indexed by internet search engines. The best de facto search engine for IR content is Google Scholar. IR contain a high share of grey literature that is not published elsewhere and yield a high indexing ratio in Google Scholar (Arlitsch and O'Brien, 2012). The Registry of

Open Access Repositories (ROAR) is an international database indexing the setup, location, and growth of IR, and their contents. OpenDOAR is a quality-assured global Directory of Open Access Repositories that enables the search for repositories based on a range of features, such as location, software, or content. The statistics feature in OpenDOAR informs about the number of repositories per country, the most common languages of content or the most common IR software platforms. There are more than 4,000 repositories listed, most of which are located in the US, followed by the UK and Germany. According to OpenDOAR, DSpace (43%) and EPrints (13%) are the most popular software platforms. Unlike many other software platforms, both DSpace and EPrints are open source and were launched in the early 2000s. DSpace was developed by MIT Libraries in collaboration with Hewlett-Packard to capture, describe, and preserve digital content which could be downloaded and installed with minimal configuration (Smith et al., 2004). Since its launch in 2002, DSpace has undergone widespread adoption in several communities (ibid.).

From Librarians to IR Managers

IR were created to boost open access to scholarship but continue to be seen primarily as the province of libraries (Thomas, 2007). Over the years, librarians have taken a more active role in scholarly publishing and have become responsible for the development and implementation of software for institutional repositories and their management. The increase in systematic evaluations of institutions and the allocation of research funds opened up new possibilities for academic libraries. Librarians started bibliometric activities to redefine and widen their professional role within the wider university organization (Åström, Hansson, and Olsson, 2011). It is not by chance that the expansion of the role of academic libraries and the profession of librarians is concurrent with the general trend that bibliometrics has been developed to a large extent by scholars from library and information science. Librarians can handle bibliographic data and electronic databases, whereas neither science managers nor scientists themselves have the know-how and tools to perform bibliometric analyses (Ball and Tunger, 2006). Moreover, librarians can provide immediate access to important data for research evaluation and thus reach a strong position in a university's organizational structure (Åström, and Hansson, 2012). To subsist as a central pillar in the university organization, librarians need to prove the value of their repositories continuously. To do so, librarians collect and interpret platform provided or in-house created metrics to assess the services of their universities or research institutions. Thus, librarians support research assessment by offering not only the full-text of documents but also accurate metadata on researchers producing the content and the audience of repositories (Day, 2004). The profession of librarians providing IR services has evolved in recent years and nowadays requires IT skills and specific knowledge about copyright conditions and information security. It is therefore better referred to as institutional repository managers.

Institutional Repositories and Bibliometric Measures for Research Assessment

The most commonly measured repository metrics are the number of items, item downloads, item uploads, and citation-based metrics. Most of the metrics are platform-generated or result from interlinked databases, e.g. to retrieve citations. The number of items in IR is an indicator of the scholarly output of an institution. Breaking the number of items into categories can provide an overview of faculties, fields, or other dimensions. Institutional repositories enable the measuring of productivity through the analysis of publication frequencies of authors or departments. Item uploads inform about the number of items uploaded to a repository in a specific time period. It can be tracked across time and reflects the growth of the repository. This metric also measures the scholarly output of an institution and can be segmented by campus units or by publication type to meet the needs of the audience. Upload numbers demonstrate the vitality of IR and sustained growth (Bruns and Inefuku, 2015).

Downloads demonstrate the usage of documents in repositories and are useful to encourage authors and repository managers to continue to deposit new documents and to attract new authors to IR. Individual authors may be interested in the number of downloads of their publications whereas other audiences (faculty, library, university administration) are interested in aggregated data or lists of top downloaded publications. Download counts demonstrate access and visibility and can lead to higher citation rates (Antelman, 2004; Gargouri et al., 2010). The most common IR platforms provide download counts as a basic feature. Item downloads is a meaningful metric if measuring human rather than robot traffic.

Repository managers can supplement the reports generated by their IR platforms with metrics gained from third-party sources, including Web analytics, citation databases, and altmetrics, for example. To connect IR with external databases, it is necessary to link bibliographic metadata with identifiers such as the UT for WoS, PMID for PubMed Central, and DOI for WoS or Scopus (Iriarte et al., 2011). Most repository platforms provide metrics tools for the purpose of assessing growth and access to repositories. Google Analytics as the most popular web analytics system is used by repository managers to track repository visits, user demographics, user behavior, and usage of social media (Bruns and Inefuku, 2015). Whereas Web analytics ascertain visitor demographics and behavior, citations demonstrate usage. Repository platforms can implement citation metrics if the hosting institution has a subscription to SciVerse Scopus API (Konkiel and Scherer, 2013). Some IR provide discovery services to find most cited publications. Early studies have shown that the placement of research papers in institutional repositories can increase citation rates (e.g. Hajjem, Harnad and Gingras, 2006). This may drive institute directors to sign on to these research infrastructures with the promise of improving the reputation of their institution and research staff (Organ, 2006).

Nowadays, most platforms can offer the collection and display of alternative metrics that are based on online activity in social media. These altmetrics supplement existing usage statistics to provide a broader view of research-output impact for the benefit of authors, repository managers, and university administrators alike (Konkiel and Scherer, 2013). In addition to the most popular altmetrics services (Altmetrics, ImpactStory, or Plum Analytics), there are many other possibilities for mining altmetrics for repository content by using web service APIs and open source tools like PLOS's Article Level Metrics package (ibid.). By providing impact measures for grey literature and not only for traditional publications, altmetrics can help authors to document the impact of their complete research output and to understand the readership of their content. Repository managers can use altmetrics to gather numbers beyond common usage statistics to communicate the value in making research output available. The integration of citation metrics and altmetrics enables authors and readers to see the impact of their scholarly work in one place. This convenience can encourage authors and readers to use IR.

All metrics described can be normalized by publication type or author position to create meaningful metrics and are important in communicating with stakeholders. For university administration, IR need to prove they are worth the financial and staff resources allocated to them (Bruns and Inefuku, 2015). For repository managers, repositories need to prove they are worth the time needed to collect and make publications accessible. The report of metrics can lead to an increased use of the repository's services and gathering metrics enables benchmarking of success. The protype web service Repository Analytics & Metrics Portal (RAMP) is supposed to improve the accuracy of IR analytics, providing IR managers with persistent access to accurate counts of file downloads or the potential to aggregate IR metrics across institutions for consistent benchmarking (Baughman, Roebuck, and Arlitsch, 2018).

Conclusion

Repositories are a key service in supporting the mission and goals of their institution and can be seen as a digital embodiment of research activity. IR expand access to research results and thereby reduce the monopoly power of journals. However, IR should be viewed as supplements and not as primary venues for scholarly publishing. To be successful, institutional repositories must be filled with scholarly work that can be searched and cited. Some IR suffer from low participation and only collect a small fraction of an institute's research output (Foster and Gibbons, 2005). Other IR do not contain many primary articles, which raises the question about the purpose of IRs (Arlitsch and O'Brien, 2012). Besides, Internet search engine crawlers face problems when trying to harvest IR because metadata requirements of Google Scholar differ from those for IRs. Thus, some of the content in IR is invisible to scientists using Google Scholar (Arlitsch and O'Brien, 2012). IR can demonstrate the scientific, societal, and economic relevance of research activities and are capable of increasing an institution's visibility and status. Whereas in the past librarians had a service function of supplying scholars with information, they are now in charge of monitoring scholars' performance by producing metrics (Åström, Hansson and Olsson, 2012). One reason for this development is that repository managers have to argue for funding and try to demonstrate the success of IR by using performance indicators. Thus, institutional repositories and bibliometrics as a method of research evaluation have gone through a redefinition of their role and tasks in recent decades. Today, IR serve as tangible indicators of a university's research performance. It requires that repository metrics are comparable across institutions and their application enables benchmarking and the demonstration of contextual value (Cassella, 2010; Thomas, 2007). As there is no established standard of performance indicators, repository managers should be careful with interpretation of metrics. However, the use of data from institutional repositories as a source of bibliometric analyses has its advantages: scientists, librarians, and other administrative staff have to agree and work together to keep IR accurate and up to date. Moreover, the collection and reporting of metrics can encourage the participation in repositories. Another argument in favor of adapting performance indicators is that the value of IR is not in producing upload or download numbers, but in causing changes in scholarly communication (Bruns and Inefuku, 2015).

References

Antelman, K 2004, 'Do Open Access Articles Have a Greater Research Impact?', *College & Research Libraries News*, vol. 65, no. 5, pp. 372–82.

Arlitsch, K & O'Brien, PS 2012, 'Invisible institutional repositories: addressing the low indexing ratios of IRs in Google', *Library Hi tech*, vol. 30, no. 1, pp. 60–81.

Åström, F & Hansson, J 2012, 'How implementation of bibliometric practice affects the role of academic libraries', *Journal of Librarianship and Information Science*, vol. 45, no. 4, pp. 316–22.

Åström, F, Hansson, J & Olsson, M 2011, *Bibliometrics and the Changing Role of the University Libraries*, http://www.diva-portal.org/smash/get/diva2:461857/FULLTEXT01.%20pdf (July 15, 2020).

Ball, R & Tunger, D 2006, 'Bibliometric analysis – A new business area for information professionals in libraries? Support for scientific research by perception and trend analysis', *Scientometrics*, vol. 66, no. 3, pp. 561–77.

Baughman, S, Roebuck, G & Arlitsch, K 2018, 'Reporting Practices of Institutional Repositories: Analysis of Responses from Two Surveys', *Journal of Library Administration*, vol. 58, no. 1, pp. 65–80.

Bruns, T & Inefuku, HW 2015, 'Purposeful Metrics: Matching Institutional Repository Metrics to Purpose and Audience', in *Making Institutional Repositories Work*, pp. 213–34.

Cassella, M 2010, 'Institutional Repositories: an Internal and External Perspective on the Value of IRs for Researchers' Communities', *LIBER Quarterly*, vol. 20, no. 2, pp. 210–25.

Crow, R 2002, 'The Case for Institutional Repositories: A SPARC Position Paper', *ARL Bimonthly Report*, vol. 223, pp. 1–37.

Davis, PM & Connolly, MJL 2007, 'Institutional Repositories: Evaluating the reasons for non-use of Cornell University's installation of DSpace', *D-Lib Magazine*, vol. 13, no. 3/4.

Day, M 2004, Institutional repositories and research assessment, pp. 1–29, University of Bath, UKOLN.

Foster, NF & Gibbons, S 2005, 'Understanding Faculty to Improve Content Recruitment for Institutional Repositories', *D-Lib Magazine*, vol. 11, no. 1.

Gargouri, Y, Hajjem, C, Larivière, V, Gingras, Y, Carr, L, Brody, T & Harnad, S 2010, 'Self-Selected or Mandated, Open Access Increases Citation Impact for Higher Quality Research', *PLOS ONE*, vol. 5, no. 10.

Hajjem, C, Harnad, S & Gingras, Y 2006, 'Ten-Year Cross-Disciplinary Comparison of the Growth of Open Access and How it Increases Research Citation Impact', https://arxiv.org/abs/cs/0606079v2 (July 15, 2020).

Iriarte, P, de Kaenel, I, Krause, JB & Magnenat, N 2011, 'Exploiting and improving institutional repositories for bibliometrics', https://archive-ouverte.unige.ch/unige:23065 (July 15, 2020).

Key Perspectives Ltd. 2009, 'A Comparative Review of Research Assessment Regimes in Five Countries and the Role of Libraries in the Research Assessment Process', *Report commissioned by OCLC Research*.

Konkiel, S & Scherer, D 2013, 'New opportunities for repositories in the age of altmetrics', *Bulletin of the American Society for Information Science and Technology*, vol. 39, no. 4, pp. 22–26.

Organ, MK 2006, 'Download statistics – what do they tell us? The example of research online, the open access institutional repository at the University of Wollongong, Australia', *D-Lib Magazine*, vol. 12, no. 11.

Ramalho Correia, AM & de Castro Neto, M 2002, 'The role of eprint archives in the access to, and dissemination of, scientific grey literature: LIZA – A case study by the National Library of Portugal', *Journal of Information Science*, vol. 28, no. 3, pp. 231–41.

Smith, M, Rodgers, R, Walker, J & Tansley, R 2004, 'DSpace: A Year in the Life of an Open Source Digital Repository System', in *ECDL 2004: Research and Advanced Technology for Digital Libraries*, pp. 38–44.

Thomas, G 2007, 'Evaluating the Impact of the Institutional Repository, or Positioning Innovation Between a Rock and a Hard Place', *New Review of Information Networking*, vol. 13, no. 2, pp. 133–46.

7 Teaching and Training

7.1 Institutions for Bibliometric Qualification
Simone Fühles-Ubach and Miriam Albers

Abstract: The article deals with the significance of bibliometrics in continuing education. Although bibliometry is not a new topic, new demands arise through new developments. With the emergence of social networks and other online media, altmetrics (alternative metrics) have broadened the spectrum of bibliometrics and the need for further education in that area. Furthermore, a competence model for bibliometric tasks that differentiates three levels – entry level, core area, and specialized area – is introduced and assigned to the different levels of librarianship and careers. The *European Summer School for Scientometrics* (ESSS), created because of the small number of continuing education courses on bibliometric topics in German-speaking countries, is presented as well as the main places which offer further education in the field of bibliometrics.

Keywords: further education, continuing education, bibliometric qualification, Altmetrics, ESSS.

Introduction – Research Question

Librarians in scientific and research libraries are experts in handling large amounts of various kinds of data. They understand the publication cultures of the various disciplines and hold independent positions in their institutions. For these reasons, they are qualified to conduct bibliometric analyses as one of the services offered by their institutions. Prerequisites for performing these analyses include access to the corresponding databases, such as Web of Science or Scopus and the availability of trained personnel (Gimpl, 2017, p. 24). Analysis of the curricula of German-speaking universities has shown, however, that neither bachelor nor master degree programmes offer a comprehensive range of corresponding contents/modules. This problem is not limited to German-speaking countries. When Cox et al. (2017) asked participants at a bibliometrics conference in Great Britain whether they had acquired their knowledge of bibliometrics from their studies, only 29% answered in the affirmative. Thus, further education in the field of bibliometrics is necessary, as existing knowledge must not only be kept up to date by instruction in newer developments, such as altmetrics, but gaps in essential knowledge must be addressed in vocational practice. To illustrate this point, as recently as 2016, an overview study of library training courses in Germany found no courses on bibliometrics and only two on informatics (Plewka and

---

Simone Fühles-Ubach, Professor of Statistics and Library Management at the Institute for Information Science at the Technical University of Cologne, simone.fuehles-ubach@th-koeln.de
Miriam Albers, research associate for organisational development at ZB MED – Information Centre for Life Sciences in Cologne, miriam.albers@th-koeln.de

https://doi.org/10.1515/9783110646610-042

Wähler, 2017, p.172, Annex). This article discusses possibilities in continuing education for the extended subject area of bibliometrics in German-speaking countries.

Definition

In contrast to the following chapter, which focuses on the role of bibliometrics in curricula, the study now deals with the significance of bibliometrics in continuing education. According to the definition of the German Education Council from 1970, which is still valid today, continuing education is the "continuation or resumption of organised learning after completion of a first phase of education that has been extended in various ways" (Deutscher Bildungsrat, 1970, p. 197). Continuing education occurs on two levels: academic and professional. The first refers to continuing education, which has been established at many higher education institutions since the Bologna Reform of 1999 as a separate area alongside undergraduate degree programmes (Richter, 2019) and numerous continuing education institutions of the (federal) Länder. The second concerns itself with professional associations, which support continuing education and lifelong learning as part of their mission.

This study is limited to events that focus on bibliometrics as the central topic of a continuing education event. Lectures or discussions on the subject of bibliometrics held at conferences, such as the Librarians' Day or the Library Congress, are not considered, due to the brevity of the lectures and the one-dimensional mediation character of these events. Our focus centers mainly on the transmission of information and less on the "organized learning" aspect of further education.

New Demand through New Developments

Bibliometry is not a new topic; its meaning is only subject to greater fluctuations. Bibliometrics as statistical analysis of publications has been practised since the 1920s, i.e. for almost 100 years (Gingras, 2014). In the 1960s, the topic became known worldwide through the development of the ISI Citation Indices (Thelwall, 2008). Since the turn of the millennium, the topic has been reinforced by the development of the Internet and the dissemination of bibliometric tools and indicators (Journal Impact Factor or h-Index). With the emergence of social networks and other online media, altmetrics (so-called alternative metrics) arose, and, since the introduction of the term in 2010 by Priem and colleagues, has once again significantly broadened the spectrum of bibliometrics (Priem et al., 2010). Altmetrics wants to answer the question as to which scientific papers are most discussed in online media and is, therefore, much more up to date than the citation numbers of scientific publications in journals, which appear with a time lag. The "Altmetric Attention Score" shows how frequently the press, social networks, strategy, and guideline papers, and other online sources cite, discuss, or disseminate scientific publications (Tunger et al., 2017). This is particularly interesting for young scientists who cannot yet look back on a long scientific career with numerous publications. Consequently, these "new" measurements and indicators, which are also offered, for example, by Google Scholar or ResearchGate, enjoy particular popularity. The necessity of dealing with these new developments, which extend the traditional field of bibliometry, is absolutely a given and of special topicality to serve the needs of young scientists.

Competence Model for Further Education in Bibliometrics

Cox et al. (2017) used a questionnaire to ask conference attendees to rate bibliometric tasks as entry level, core, or specialist. Results indicated that the focus of library services to date was in the provision of information literacy to students rather than in the assessment of the quality of academic research services provided by individuals or institutions. They cited a Swedish study (Anström and Hannson, 2013), which sees the main problem areas of librarians in the field of bibliometrics as uncertainty in advanced statistical analyses, indisposition in the assessment of scientists, and danger of being associated with less efficient departments.

This problem could be of central importance, especially for librarians in the upper grade of the civil service who completed a diploma or bachelor's degree at a university of applied sciences (possibly many years ago). Being able to analyze one's own research seems to be an important prerequisite for assessing the research performance of others. This has probably not always been the case for graduates of universities of applied sciences, which were often founded in the 1970s as successor institutions to engineering schools. Research at universities of applied sciences has only become more important in the past 10–20 years. For university graduates, greater proximity to research is more self-evident. This means that the task of assessing the quality of academic research, for example, is obviously closer to the activities of the senior service.

Different Levels of Competence – Entry/Core/Specialized Levels

In this context, however, the question arises as to whether the field of bibliometry in its mediation must not be viewed in a more differentiated way, as numerous other areas can be assigned to the subject in addition to the assessment and evaluation of individual and collective research achievements. This is the starting point for the study by Cox et al. (2017) who, together with librarians, developed a competence model for bibliometric tasks. As a result, three levels emerged: an entry level, a core area, and a specialized area. For the entry level, a rather small scope of tasks was identified (17 out of 99 identified tasks). These concerned explaining basic concepts, calculating key metrics (especially journal metrics), and aspects of professional behavior. With regard to the previously formulated problem of working at the same level with researchers, this area could also be easily covered by librarians without extensive research experience of their own. Forty-eight tasks, i.e. half of identified tasks, form the core area of the competence model. A large part of the tasks revolves around "Awareness raising and responsible use". "Advising on appropriate tools and explaining the differences between results from different tools" is part of the core area, as are publication advice, reading recommendations for journals, support for grant applications, and library collection development. This also includes the area of metrics, which concerns the research performance of individual scientists or entire institutions. About a quarter of all tasks are regarded as specialized fields and include activities that are highly technically-oriented, more in the field of consulting or politics, as well as the evaluation of researchers and institutions for management reasons or personnel development.

European Summer School for Scientometrics (ESSS)

Responding to the lack of pertinent scientometrics education (especially in German-speaking countries) and to the increasing demand (particularly by research quality managers), the University of Vienna (A), the German Centre for Higher Education Research and Science Studies – DZHW (D), and the Katholieke Universiteit Leuven (B) joined cooperatively to found the European Summer School for Scientometrics (ESSS) in 2010. Since 2017, the EC3metrics Group of the University of Granada has been an official partner of ESSS (https://www.scientometrics-school.eu/about.html [July 15, 2020]). The addition of a Spanish partner in 2017 shows that demand is also growing in other countries and that the merger is expanding. The office is located in Vienna, where ESSS 2019 also took place. The summer school takes place over five days, alternating annually among Berlin, Vienna, and Leuven. Topics range from introductory to advanced. The target group consists of decision-makers in science policy and management, scientists and librarians, and is also open to other interested parties from Europe and beyond. In the near future, European Credit Transfer System (ECTS) points will be awarded for continuing education courses. ESSS has secured a total of five renowned partners: Web of Science Group, Elsevier, Digital Science, Science-Metrix, and 1Science (http://www.forschungsinfo.de/Bibliometrie/index.php?id=ESSS [July 15, 2020]).

Information Base and Research Method

Additional providers in the German-speaking area were sought to further our analysis of the training institutions. All providers of library training for academic librarians in Germany, Switzerland, and Austria were systematically researched. In addition, an independent search in well-known search engines was carried out. Furthermore, institutions on whose websites no offerings could be found at present were requested by e-mail for further information on current and/or planned bibliometric information events.

In contrast to universities, continuing education institutions are less standardized. There are no general overviews and no comparable descriptions. In addition, at many continuing education institutions, only the current year's events can be viewed – not those that have already been completed or those planned for the following year. It is, therefore, only possible to get a picture of current offerings at continuing education institutions in mid-2019 and compare these findings, to a limited extent, with the general offerings of the institutions.

Results

In addition to the annual English-language conference (already concluded) and continuing education in the form of EEES (University of Vienna, 2019a), six German-language offerings on bibliometric continuing education were identified in 2019: ZBIW – Zentrum für Bibliotheks- and Informationswissenschaftliche Weiterbildung the Technischen Hochschule (TH) Köln ((TH Köln, 2018, p. 20) (TH Köln, 2019, p. 21)), the Weiterbildungszentrum der Freien Universität (FU) Berlin (FU Berlin, 2019, p. 26), HessFort – bibliothekarische Fortbildung in Hessen (HeBIS-Verbundzentrale, 2019), and the Vereinigung Österreichischer Bibliothekarinnen and Bibliothekare (VÖB) (Universitäts- und Landesbibliothek Tirol, 2019). The Bavarian Library Academy held a workshop in 2017 (Bayerische Staatsbibliothek, 2019). The Suisse librarian training facility "Bibliosuisse" had two workshops (one in German, one in French) in 2016 with fewer participants (seven and eight) in relation to other offers. Both events were for beginners and taught by librarian PhD scientists.

A search of additional education offerings of the professional association Berufsverband Information Bibliothek (BIB), the ekz-Bibliotheksservices, the Bibliothekarische Fortbildung in Niedersachsen, the Fortbildung Sächsische Landesfachstelle für Bibliotheken, the Verein Deutscher Bibliothekarinnen und Bibliothekare (VDB), the Büchereiverband Österreich (BVÖ), and Bibliosuisse (Switzerland) did not produce any results for an offering of bibliometrics in 2019. The EKZ library services reported that the topic is not important for their core target group of public libraries.

Table 1

Provider / Trainer	Title	Duration	Costs	Target Group	Content[1]
TH Köln / Mr. Dr. XX[2]	Bibliometrics I	1 day	165 €	Employees of the information departments of academic and public libraries	– Basics – Databases – Bibliometric indicators – Practical application of knowledge gained from experience
TH Köln / Mr. Dr. XX	Bibliometrics II	1 day	165 €	Employees of the information departments of academic and public libraries – preferably participants in the basics seminar Bibliometrics I	– Analyses at the macro level – Analyses at topic level – Presentation, evaluation, and calculation of complex indicators – Visualization of simple author and institutional cooperation networks – Introduction to patent informetrics
FU Berlin / Mr. Dr. YY	Introduction into the bibliometrics of specific application examples: What can and should bibliometry do?	2 days	220 €	Subject librarians, managers, and employees from scientific libraries who are NOT experts in bibliometrics	– Basics – Databases – Bibliometric indicators – Impact measurement using key figures – Practical application/ bibliometrics in libraries – Open access, altmetrics, and research data management – Future networking
HessFort / Mr. Dr. YY	Workshop: Bibliometrics	1 day	50 €	Scientific staff, librarians, and other interested parties who are already actively involved in bibliometrics	– Basics – Databases – Practical application/ bibliometrics in libraries – Tools for data acquisition and data visualization – Future networking – Open access and research data management

---

1 The contents are summarized here in a shortened keyword form and, as far as possible, are adjusted in the wording.

2 The names are known but have been anonymized for data protection reasons. Identical letters were used for the same person.

Table 1 *(Continued)*

Provider / Trainer	Title	Duration	Costs	Target Group	Content[1]
VÖB (Wien)/ Mr. Dr. ZZ	Bibliometrics and Scientometrics	4 days	550 € (estimated)	Participants of the basic course "Library and Information Studies", staff members in public and scientific libraries	– Quantitative evaluation of scientific research publications – Citation analysis – Impact factors – Data mining[3]
Bibliotheksakademie Bayern / Mrs. AB, Mrs. Dr. CD	Workshop: Bibliometrics	1 day[4]	60 €	Bibliothekare, die einen Einblick in Bibliometrie erhalten und eventuell bibliometrische Beratungen anbieten möchten	– Basics – Academic identity management (Author profiles) – Classic metrics – Alternative metrics – Critical View – Bibliometry in libraries

The overview shows that the trainers are all PhD scientists. Further research shows that, with one exception (Dr. Jovanović), the trainers also work in scientific libraries or have been employed there for a long time, even if they did not have a doctorate in library science. The training of bibliometric services in the library is, therefore, carried out by the senior service, which also corresponds to the findings of the competence model.

However, general conditions of the further training courses offered are very heterogeneous. Duration varies between one and four days, costs are between 50 and 550 euro, and the target group can be employees with or without previous experience, exclusively from academic or public libraries. The contents of courses can only be compared to a limited extent due to differences in descriptions. Topics such as "Fundamentals of Bibliometry", databases (e. g. Web of Science) and basic metrics, such as Impact Factor or Hirsch Index, however, seem to be part of every training course, which correspond to the basic level of the competence model.

In addition, the contents offered differ. On one hand, application of bibliometric methods is taken up as a library service, and attempts are made to create links to other challenges of the publication system, such as Open Access or research data or to establish a more extensive exchange. On the other hand, special topics, such as data visualization, patent informetrics or data mining, are taught. In particular, the background of the trainers and the title of the event, whether as further training or as a workshop, which tends to include exchange, seems to be essential for selection of the contents.

---

[3] A short description of the content in comparison.
[4] The event was the only one to take place in 2017.

In addition to further training for librarians, an independent search on the Internet showed that events for scientists are also offered, some of which are conducted by librarians. For example, the library of the Technical University of Munich offers doctoral students and scientists a four-hour course, "Visibility and Impact of Research – Bibliometry, Scientific Communication and Publication Strategies" (Universitätsbibliothek der Technischen Universität München, 2019). The library of the University of Bielefeld, on the other hand, will present its own services and licensed bibliometric databases in the one-and-a-half-hour course "Bibliometrics" (Universität Bielefeld, 2019).

Summary

Even almost 10 years after the implementation of ESSS, created because of the small number of continuing education courses on bibliometric topics in German-speaking countries, the challenge remains. It is possible to participate in continuing education courses with different foci in Cologne, Berlin, or Frankfurt (HessFort). However, there remains a reluctance to offer further training to librarians, as is evidenced in the limited courses currently available to them. Despite extensive, systematic, and explorative web searches, the limited number of course offerings on bibliometrics is a limiting factor. For the future, a systematic overview, differentiated according to target groups and contents and locations, would be necessary to continuously view, compare, and evaluate such course offerings.

References

Anström, F & Hannsson, J 2013, 'How implementation of bibliometric practice affects the role of academic libraries', *Journal of Librarianship and Information Science*, vol. 45, no. 4, pp. 316–22.

Bayerische Staatsbibliothek 2019, *Workshop: Bibliometrie 28.09.2017*, https://www.bsb-muenchen.de/nc/babcaldetail/?tx_cal_controller%5Bview%5D=event&tx_cal_controller%5Btype%5D=tx_cal_phpicalendar&tx_cal_controller%5Buid%5D=214&tx_cal_controller%5Byear%5D=2017&tx_cal_controller%5Bmonth%5D=09&tx_cal_controller%5Bday%5D=28&cHash=2ea384368fffbc56bd851665353fd518 (July 15, 2020).

Cox, A, Gadd, E, Petersohn, S & Sbaffi, L 2017, 'Competencies for bibliometrics', *Journal of Librarianship and Information Science*, vol. 1, doi: https://doi.org/10.1177/0961000617728111, https://journals.sagepub.com/doi/pdf/10.1177/0961000617728111.

Deutscher Bildungsrat, 1970, *Strukturplan für das Bildungswesen*, Stuttgart.

FU Berlin 2019, *Bibliotheksweiterbildung: Weiterbildungsprogramm in Öffentlichen und Wissenschaftlichen Bibliotheken. Januar bis Dezember 2019 / 89*. Program, https://ssl2.cms.fu-berlin.de/fu-berlin/sites/weiterbildung/PM_weiterbildungsprogramm/pdf/bib/bib.pdf (July 15, 2020).

Gingras, Y 2014, *Bibliometrics and research evaluation: Uses and abuses*, MIT Press, Cambridge MA.

Gimpl, K 2017, *Evaluation von ausgewählten Altmetrics-Diensten für den Einsatz an wissenschaftlichen Bibliotheken*, Master-Thesis, Köln, https://publiscologne.th-koeln.de/frontdoor/deliver/index/docId/1034/file/MAT_Gimpl_Kerstin.pdf (July 15, 2020).

HeBis-Verbundzentrale 2019, *Workshop Bibliometrie*, https://www.hebis.de/de/1gs_fortbildung/kursangebot/2019_09_Bibliometrie.php (July 15, 2020).

Plewka, M & Wähler, L 2017, *Vergleich der Fortbildungsanbieter im Bibliotheksbereich in Deutschland und dem Vereinigten Königreich unter Berücksichtigung der unterschiedlichen Bibliothekssysteme in Hinblick auf Organisation, Angebot und Zugang*, Bachelorarbeit, Technische Hochschule Köln.

Priem, J, Taraborelli, D, Groth, P & Neylon, C 2010, *Altmetrics: A manifesto*, http://altmetrics.org/manifesto (July 15, 2020).

Richter, C 2019, *Wandel der wissenschaftlichen Weiterbildung im Zuge der Digitalisierung*, Bachelorarbeit, Technische Hochschule Köln.

Thelwall, M 2008, 'Bibliometrics to webometrics', *Journal of Information Science*, vol. 34, no. 4, pp. 605–21.

TH Köln 2018, *Weiterbildungsprogramm für Beschäftigte in Bibliotheken und Informationseinrichtungen. 1.Halbjahr 2019*, accessed July 18, 2019, https://www.th-koeln.de/mam/downloads/deutsch/weiterbildung/zbiw/angebote/zbiw_programmheft_1_2019_web.pdf (July 15, 2020).

TH Köln 2019, *Weiterbildungsprogramm für Beschäftigte in Bibliotheken und Informationseinrichtungen. 2.Halbjahr 2019*, accessed July 18, 2019, https://www.th-koeln.de/mam/downloads/deutsch/weiterbildung/zbiw/angebote/zbiw_programmheft_2_2019_web.pdf (July 15, 2020).

Tunger, D, Meier, A & Hartmann, D 2017, *Machbarkeitsstudie Altmetrics*, http://hdl.handle.net/2128/16419 (July 15, 2020).

Universität Bielefeld 2019, *Fortbildungen für Forschende und Lehrende: Bibliometrie*, 2019, https://www.uni-bielefeld.de/pep/fortbildung/ub/bibliometrie.html (July 15, 2020).

Universitätsbibliothek der Technischen Universität München 2019, *Sichtbarkeit und Impact von Forschung – Bibliometrie, wissenschaftliche Kommunikation und Publikationsstrategien*, 2019, https://www.ub.tum.de/kurs/sichtbarkeit-und-impact-von-forschung (July 15, 2020).

Universitäts- und Landesbibliothek Tirol 2019, *Seminarprogramm 4 L: 5. Bibliometrie und Szientometrie*, accessed July 18, 2019, http://www.bibliotheksausbildung.at/weiterbildung/seminarprogramm-4 l.html#bibliometrie (July 15, 2020).

University of Vienna 2019, *History*, 2019, https://www.scientometrics-school.eu/about.html (July 15, 2020).

University of Vienna 2019a, *Programme Leuven 2019*, https://www.scientometrics-school.eu/programme.html (July 15, 2020).

7.2 Bibliometrics in the Curriculum
Simone Fühles-Ubach, Miriam Albers, and Mandy Neumann

Abstract: Do LIS-Schools in German-speaking countries offer (enough) training in the up-and-coming field of bibliometrics, which is or may become central to the work of academic and scientific librarians? This chapter answers the question based on a review of the curricula of German language library studies at the university level. An evaluation of the module books of 34 courses of study revealed that bibliometrics and related topics, such as scientometry or informetry, are not commonly part of the curriculum in library education. At present, bibliometrics is expert knowledge that is taught only occasionally and late in the course of studies. The necessity of increased placement of bibliometric content in the course of studies is discussed.

Keywords: LIS Schools, curricula, scientometry, informetry, courses, modules.

Introduction – Research Question

To describe bibliometrics as a new service for libraries seems inappropriate, given the large number of publications in the early 2000s that discussed its use. Warmbrunn (2015) even describes the library in 2015 as a "natural contact" for bibliometric analysis methods (Warmbrunn, 2015, 19–4). However, this topic has not established itself as a library service either in the perception of librarians or in the expectations of customers. An 2017 analysis of job advertisements in the library field in German-speaking countries by Nowak and Schneckenleithner showed bibliometrics in job advertisements as "practically not in demand" (Nowak and Schneckenleithner, 2017, p. 63). In order to determine whether bibliometrics is a common and widespread part of current Library or Information Studies requirements, the module books of all current courses of study from the wider library and information science environment in German-speaking countries, i.e., Germany, Austria, and Switzerland, were researched and evaluated.

Definition – What are we Talking About?

Bibliometrics is essentially the use of statistical methods for analysis of various media. Bibliometrics is defined as "the measurement of the (formal) written output

---

Simone Fühles-Ubach, Professor of Statistics and Library Management at the Institute for Information Science at the Technical University of Cologne, simone.fuehles-ubach@th-koeln.de
Miriam Albers, research associate for organisational development at ZB MED – Information Centre for Life Sciences in Cologne, miriam.albers@th-koeln.de
Mandy Neumann, software developer with a background in computational linguistics, mandyneumann@gmx.net

of scientists and their perceptions" (Ball, 2014, p. 3). In order to avoid the exclusion of basically similar contents due to different definitions or terminology, the superordinate or related terms of informetry, scientometry, webometry, and altmetrics should also be considered.

As a generic term for bibliometrics, informetry, along with the following terms, refers to the measurement and analysis of information. When limited to scientific information, the term scientometry is used. When referring to analysis of web pages, the term webometry is used (Jovanović, 2012, p. 72).

In addition, there is the area of altmetrics, which Haustein (2016) classifies as part of webometrics, noting that a uniform definition (and thus a consensus on what exactly Altmetrics measures and what conclusions can be drawn from it) are still lacking. Altmetrics records scientific output from online sources, i.e., references from news portals or social media (Haustein, 2016, p. 415 ff). A report by the Expert Group on Altmetrics, commissioned by the European Commission, also argues that classical bibliometrics, together with alternative metrics, should create "complementary approaches to evaluation". The expert group also sees potential in the fact that a broader audience (apart from the closed scientific community) can be included and that information can be collected much more quickly than through conventional metrics (European Commission, 2017).

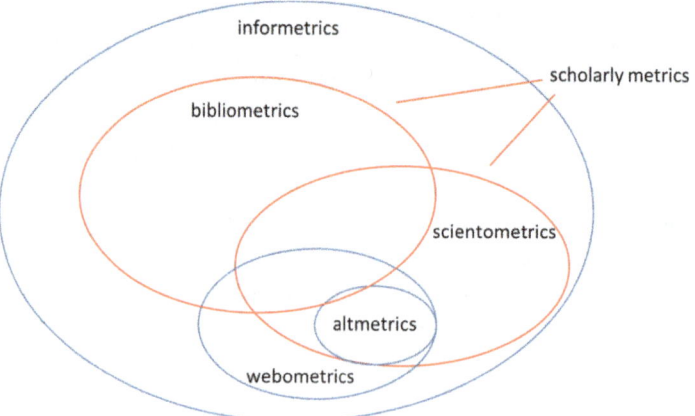

Figure 1: The position of altmetrics in informetrics, according to (Haustein, 2016: S. 416).

Information Base and Research Method

The starting point for our analysis was an in-house database containing current and (as far as publicly accessible) past module books of information science and library studies in German-speaking countries (Germany, Austria, and Switzerland). Relevant study programmes were identified by checking a list[1] from the "Hochschulverband Informationswissenschaft" (Hochschulverband Informationswissenschaft, n.d.), complemented by information from a database[2] of the "Berufsverband Information Bibliothek e.V." (Berufsverband Information Bibliothek e.V., n.d.) and manual research. Study programmes from these lists were included if they contained at least one library-related subject, which was the case for all library study and most of the information science programmes. We set up a MySQL database with relational tables to hold the relevant information on study programmes (e.g. university name and type, programme name, focus and summary) and individual modules (e.g. title, description, workload). The data was collected by copying the information from the available PDF documents and pasting them in the appropriate fields of a self-developed web application for simplified insertion into the database. For easier querying of the data, a Solr index was set up on top of the database. This allowed for searching the textual data by issuing keyword queries via the Solr query interface. To date, the database contains data on more than 2,000 modules from 46 programmes of 20 different universities.

Although module books of previous courses were often accessible in the database, only current, valid module books were evaluated in the analysis. This is because the focus of this study was on the current status of bibliometrics in the curriculum rather than on development.

For this purpose, the module books of a total of 34 courses of study at the following universities in Germany were searched, using six search terms ("bibliometr*", "informetr*OR infometr*", "s*ientometr*", "altmetr*", "webometr*", "metri*"): Humboldt-Universität zu Berlin, Hochschule Darmstadt, Heinrich-Heine-Universität Düsseldorf, Hochschule für Angewandte Wissenschaften Hamburg, Hochschule Hannover, Universität Hildesheim, Technische Hochschule Köln, Universität Konstanz, Hochschule für Technik Wirtschaft und Kultur Leipzig, Archivschule Marburg, Fachhochschule Potsdam, Universität Regensburg, Hochschule der Medien Stuttgart, Technische Hochschule Wildau; in Switzerland: Universität Bern, Hochschule für Technik und Wirtschaft Chur, Fachhochschule Westschweiz (Geneva), Universität Zürich; and Universität Innsbruck in Austria, for a total of nine universities and 10 universities of applied sciences.

---

1 https://web.archive.org/web/20190329123838/http://www.informationswissenschaft.org/institutionen/ (July 15, 2020).
2 https://web.archive.org/web/20190329123634/http://marvin.bibliothek.uni-augsburg.de/cgi-bin/daps2.pl?instliste=hochschule (July 15, 2020).

Results

The search terms "bibliometr*" (nine hits), "informetr*OR infometr*" (seven hits),[3] "s*ientometr*" (seven hits [4]), "altmetr*" (five hits), "webometr*" (one hit), and "metri*" (eight hits) resulted in 20 hits for the module title or module description. Often, different terms referred to the same module. There were no hits for the study programmes of universities in Hamburg, Hanover, Hildesheim, Leipzig, Marburg, Regensburg, Stuttgart, Wildau, Bern, or Geneva. At Hannover University of Applied Sciences and Arts, the term "bibliometr*" was in the module book until 2009.

Other universities, such as HU Berlin, also did not include this content in their degree programmes. Thus, in only 12 (i.e., 35%) of 34 possible courses of study, in the broadest sense, are metric contents provided as part of the curriculum. In Berlin, however, bibliometrics has been part of the curriculum for the longest time, i.e., since 2008.

A more detailed analysis of the module contents showed that the search term "metri*" is used exclusively for web metrics in the field of computer science, except in Potsdam (title of the module "Electronic Publishing") and in the Master's programme in Darmstadt (title of the module "Altmetrics, Social Network Analysis and Bibliometrics" – grey shading in the table). Without these results, the number of hits is reduced to 10 study courses (29% of all study courses) and 15 modules. This rather low occurrence of the topic in the degree programmes alone indicates that bibliometrics is not usually a part of the library and information studies programme qualifications. In seven modules, i.e., slightly less than half the modules, one term (usually bibliometrics and /or informetry) appears in the title of the module. The other titles, such as "Information Services", imply that metric content is only one focus of the course. It is questionable if the complex contents of these areas can actually be conveyed within this framework in such a way that students would be able to use bibliometrics/informetrics in their own research or calculations. As a result, students would be required to learn this information "on the job".

Eight of the modules occur in five different bachelor's degree programmes and seven modules in five master's degree programmes. Surprisingly, therefore, the distribution is almost the same between the two qualification levels. There are clear differences, however, in the weighting and placement of the modules. In the master's programme, the modules are placed and highly weighted, on average, in the second semester with 9.67 ECTS early in the course of study. In the bachelor's programmes, these are placed, on average, in the fourth semester and are weighted less, at 6.75 ECTS. The different weighting could also be due to the overall lower number of modules and semesters in the master's programme, resulting in higher ECTS distributions per module. For five modules in the bachelor's programme, the topics are not includ-

---

[3] The spelling "Infometry" is only used in Chur.
[4] The spelling "Scientometrie" is only used in Berlin.

ed in the title, but only in the module description. This is a sure indicator that bibliometrics in the bachelor's degree is taught rather superficially.

Basically, bibliometrics and related topics do not seem to belong to the basics, but require prerequisite knowledge. This result has also been found in other subject areas. In a worldwide study conducted in 2017, Albers found that the topic of "Open Access" tends to be more of a management topic, i.e., at master's level, and less of an administrative topic, i.e., at the bachelor's level (Albers, 2017, p. 144).

The geographic distribution of the modules (see map) completely excludes the North (Hamburg, Hannover) and the South (Stuttgart, Munich). Bibliometrics is dealt with particularly intensively in the master's programme "Information Science" in Darmstadt and in the bachelor's programme "Library Science" in Potsdam. The reasons for this cannot be determined without knowledge of the study reform process at the universities.

Table 1: International Synopsis of curriculum/ modules in Germany, Austria (A), Switzerland (CH).

Location	Type	Course of study	BA	MA	Title	Sem.	ECTS	Year module book	Hit on
Berlin	Uni	Information Science		X	Bibliometrie, Informetrie, Szientometrie	2	10	2018	Bibliometr*, Informetr*, s*ientometr*, webometr*
Chur (CH)	FH	Information Science		X	Information Topics	2	15	2019	Bibliometr*, Infometr*
Darmstadt	FH	Informationswissenschaft	X		Anwendungsentwicklung	3	5	2018	metri*
		Informationswissenschaft	X		Web Analytics (Web Controlling)	3	5	2018	metri*
		Informationswissenschaft	X		Methoden-Workshop: Business Intelligence 1.0 und 2.0	4	5	2018	metri*
		Informationswissenschaft		X	Informetrie	1	5	2018	Informetr*, s*ientometr*
		Informationswissenschaft		X	Altmetrics, Social Network Analysis und Bibliometrie	2	10	2018	Bibliometr*, Informetr*, s*ientometr*, altmetr*, metri*
		Informationswissenschaft		X	Webanalyse	2	10	2018	metri*

Table 1 *(Continued)*

Loca-tion	Type	Course of study	BA	MA	Title	Sem.	ECTS	Year module book	Hit on
Düsseldorf	Uni	Informationswissenschaft	X		Informetrie[5]	4	14	2013[6]	Informetr*, s*ientometr*
Innsbruck (A)	Uni	Library and Information Studies		X	Bibliometrie und Szientometrie	4	?	2019	Bibliometr*, s*ientometr*
Köln	FH	Bibliothek und digitale Kommunikation	X		Informationsservices	4	6	2019	Bibliometr*
		Bibliothek und digitale Kommunikation	X		Finanzen, Informetrie, Community Development	6	6	2019	Bibliometr*
		Data and Information Science	X		Informetrie, Bibliometrie, Szientometrie und Empirische Forschungsmethoden	6	6	2019	Bibliometr*, Informetr*, s*ientometr*, altmetr*
Konstanz	Uni	Information Engineering	X		Multimedia Database Systems	5	9	2017	metri*
		Computer and Information Science		X	Multimedia Database Systems	1	9	2015	metri*
Potsdam	FH	Bibliothekswissenschaft	X		Forschungsmethoden	3	5	2018	Bibliometr*, Informetr*, altmetr*, metri*
		Bibliothekswissenschaft	X		Informationsressourcen und -dienste 2	3	5	2018	altmetr*
		Bibliothekswissenschaft	X		Elektronisches Publizieren	3	5	2018	metri*
		Bibliothekswissenschaft	X		Informationsverhalten und Wissenschaftssoziologie	6	7	2018	s*ientometr*

---

5 Includes one lecture, one tutorial, and two seminars.
6 The course will be closed in 2022.

Table 1 *(Continued)*

Location	Type	Course of study	BA	MA	Title	Sem.	ECTS	Year module book	Hit on
Zürich (CH)	Uni	Bibliotheks- und Informationswissenschaft		X	Kontext Bibliothekswesen: Schnittstellen und institutionelle Partnerschaften[7]	2	8	2017	Bibliometr*, altmetr*

The overview table shows that the range of offerings in the field of bibliometrics varies greatly among German-speaking universities. Numerous universities with courses in library and information science are not listed in the table, as they don't offer modules in bibliometrics. Although the number of universities of applied science that offer courses in bibliometrics is much larger than the number of universities, five universities are listed in the matrix and four universities of applied sciences.

Although there are far more bachelor's degree programmes than master's degree programmes, the distribution does not correspond. In the broadest sense, bibliometry is a topic in 12 module books of bachelor's programmes, while it is listed in eight master's programmes. This shows that it is apparently an advanced competency that is only addressed in the bachelor's degree programmes in the later semesters or in the master's degree programmes. This situation does not seem to be specific to German universities. A recent study in the UK included a questionnaire that asked respondents if their study requirements had covered bibliometrics. Sixty-five percent of respondents said that their library qualification studies had not included bibliometrics (Cox et.al., 2017).

Of course, these results do not mean that bibliometrics is not included in the teaching at these universities but its role must be considered subordinate, as none of the researched terms appeared in the module books of the courses of studies. This may be because bibliometrics only plays a role in the area of academic and research libraries. As the role of bibliometrics is not relevant to the work of librarians in public libraries, the subject is not addressed (or addressed only tangentially, as an elective or project) in the course of studies. It is, therefore, not possible to speak of a standard for instruction in bibliometrics in the degree programmes or library and information studies or of a comprehensive coverage for universities in German-speaking countries. This is also shown on the map below (fig. 2).

The map shows the locations of the respective universities which offer modules in the different courses of study on the topic "Bibliometrics, Scientometry, or Altmet-

---

[7] Term used in a very large context.

Figure 2: Map of universities offering bibliometric modules in Germany, Austria, and Switzerland.

rics". It is noteworthy that these few sites provided the data base of 34 module books for this study.

Summary

Bibliometrics is taught at universities in German-speaking countries with varying degrees of intensity. Some bachelor's courses do not include this topic in the module books; however, in the master's courses the subject occurs more frequently. Even if the subject area does occur as an elective subject or as a project, however, no comprehensive offering currently exists at the universities studied. If research and meta data management become more important in the future, and if Altmetrics, i.e., indicators from the field of social media, become more defined and widespread, changes in curricular offerings at the university level may be expected and will become an important area for future research.

References

Albers, M 2017, Das Zeitschriftenmanagement Wissenschaftlicher Bibliotheken und die Implikation der Open-Access-Initiative, Dissertation, Berlin, doi: http://dx.doi.org/10.18452/18521.
Ball, R 2014, Bibliometrie. Einfach – verständlich – nachvollziehbar, De Gruyter Saur, Berlin.
Berufsverband Information Bibliothek e.V. n.d., *Liste der Hochschulen* [Online]. DAPS – Datenbank der Ausbildungsstätten, Praktikumsstätten und Studienmöglichkeiten im Bereich Archiv, Bibliothek, Dokumentation, http://marvin.bibliothek.uni-augsburg.de/cgi-bin/daps2.pl?instliste=hochschule, archived at https://web.archive.org/web/20190329123634/http://marvin.bibliothek.uni-augsburg.de/cgi-bin/daps2.pl?instliste=hochschule (July 15, 2020).

Cox, A, Gadd, E, Petersohn, S & Sbaffi, L 2017, 'Competencies for bibliometrics' *Journal of Librarianship and Information Science*, vol. 1, doi: https://doi.org/10.1177/0961000617728111, https://journals.sagepub.com/doi/pdf/10.1177/0961000617728111.

European Commission 2017, Next-generation metrics: Responsible metrics and evaluation for open science, doi: https://doi.org/10.2777/337729.

Haustein, Stefanie 2016, 'Grand challenges in altmetrics: heterogeneity, data quality and dependencies', in *Scientometrics*, no. 108, S. 413–423, https://link.springer.com/content/pdf/10.1007%2Fs11192-016-1910-9.pdf (July 15, 2020).

Hochschulverband Informationswissenschaft n.d., *Institutionen* [online], accessed July 29, 2019, http://www.informationswissenschaft.org/institutionen/, archived at https://web.archive.org/web/20190329123838/http:/www.informationswissenschaft.org/institutionen/ (July 15, 2020).

Jovanović, M 2012, 'Eine kleine Frühgeschichte der Bibliometrie', in *Information. Wissenschaft & Praxis*, Jg. 63, no. 2, S. 71–80.

Nowak, M & Schneckenleithner, C 2017, 'Wohin mit den InformationsexpertInnen? Ergebnisse einer Erhebung zur Berufssituation der Absolventinnen des Grundlehrgangs Library and Information Studies', in *Mitteilungen der VÖB*, Jg. 70, no. 1, S. 42–63.

●Tunger, D, Meier, A & Hartmann, D 2017, Machbarkeitsstudie Altmetrics, http://hdl.handle.net/2128/16419 (July 15, 2020).

Warmbrunn, J 2015, 'Was ist Bibliometrie und was haben Bibliothekare damit zu tun?', in *Bibliometrie –Praxis und Forschung*, no. 4, S. 19-1-19-4.

7.3 The Competent Bibliometrician – A Guided Tour through the Scholarly and Practitioner Literature

Sabrina Petersohn

Abstract: Repeated calls for responsible research metrics and professional codes of conduct in evaluative bibliometrics highlight the need to investigate which qualifications and competencies enable a proficient application of bibliometric methods and indicators. Taking competence research as a point of departure, this chapter delineates salient dimensions of professional competence in bibliometric research evaluation by reviewing a selected subset of the literature. The reviewed literature focuses on handbooks, monographs, and scholarly and practitioner articles that introduce theory and methodology of bibliometrics and showcase applications to scholars and practitioners mainly outside of the scientometric research community. The goal of the chapter is twofold: first, by structuring the presentation of the literature according to major competency dimensions, it offers a frame of reference for studying the growing and increasingly varied literature on bibliometrics in evaluative and policy contexts from the perspective of professional competencies. Second, it provides a brief theoretical reflection on the character of the "competent bibliometrician".

Keywords: evaluative bibliometrics, professional competence, competency dimensions, academic libraries, research management, expertise.

Introduction

The "metric tide" is not ebbing away despite recurrent debates regarding the controversial nature and use of bibliometric indicators in research assessment (Glänzel and Schoepflin, 1994; Ràfols, 2019). Ensuing calls for responsible research metrics and professional codes of conduct highlight the need to investigate which qualifications and competencies enable a proficient application of bibliometric methods and indicators in evaluative contexts (Glänzel and Schoepflin, 1994; Wilsdon et al., 2015; Zhao, 2016).

Taking competence research as a point of departure, this chapter delineates salient dimensions of professional competence in bibliometric research evaluation by reviewing a selected subset of the literature. The review focuses on handbooks, monographs, scholarly and practitioner articles that introduce theory and methodology

---

Dr. **Sabrina Petersohn,** German Centre for Higher Education Research and Science Studies (DZHW), Research Associate Research System and Science Dynamics, Schützenstraße 6a, 10117 Berlin, Germany, petersohn@dzhw.eu

of bibliometrics and showcase applications to scholars and practitioners mainly outside of the scientometric research community. The goal of the chapter is twofold: first, by structuring the literature according to major competency dimensions, it offers a frame of reference for studying the growing and increasingly varied literature on bibliometrics in evaluative and policy contexts. Second, it provides a theoretical reflection on the character of the "competent bibliometrician".

The chapter is structured as follows: first, a working definition of professional competence in bibliometric research evaluation is presented followed by a description of its major competency dimensions. Subsequently, the literature is examined regarding present or required bibliometric competencies, starting with handbooks, monographs, and edited volumes addressing a mixed audience, followed by publications targeted at two major user groups: academic librarians and research managers. Lastly, the idea of the "competent bibliometrician" is discussed from a sociology of professions and a constructivist perspective.

Professional Competence in Bibliometric Research Evaluation – Insights from Competence Research

A discussion of the manifold attempts to capture the meaning of the ambiguous and complex notion of competence is beyond the scope of this chapter (see further Mulder and Winterton, 2017). For the purpose of this review, professional competence (plural: competences) is defined as a generic set of characteristics or capabilities conditional for task performance and problem-solving in a certain profession, occupation, job, role, or situation. A specific competency (plural: competencies) is an element of generic competence and consists of a coherent cluster of knowledge, skills, and attitudes (Mulder, 2014).

Based on Cheetham and Chivers' (1996) holistic model of professional competence, three competency dimensions are distinguished which are relevant for the task of bibliometric research assessment.

1. Cognitive competencies comprise formal or tacit theoretical, abstract, specialist, and technical knowledge as well as knowledge application underpinned by a contextualized understanding of work situations. Domain-specific knowledge includes for example mathematical and statistical foundations of bibliometrics, theories of citation, author level impact measures, and bibliometric techniques such as co-citation analysis.
2. Functional competencies encompass tasks and functions specific to an occupation or profession as well as generic skills such as for example organizing and planning, monitoring, evaluating, implementing as well as literacy, numeracy, or IT skills. Exemplary skills and tasks are downloading references from citation databases, visualizing collaboration patterns, or advising on publication strategies using journal impact factors.

3. Ethical competencies contain personal and professional values and attitudes such as the ability to make sound judgment in work related contexts, sensibility to the needs of others, client-centeredness, duty to keep up to date and to help newcomers to the profession. With regard to the task of assessment metrics users need to be educated about caveats and limitations of bibliometric analyses as well as possible unintended consequences on the individual and system level. Principles for the responsible use of bibliometric data have been laid down in the Leiden Manifesto and the Metric Tide report (Hicks et al., 2015; Wilsdon et al., 2015).

Professional competencies are subject to cumulative learning and training in both formal education and informal qualification processes (Eraut, 1998; Weinert, 2001). In evaluative bibliometrics, qualifications are offered in the form of a major summer school (European Summer School for Scientometrics) or workshops and training courses offered by leading bibliometric research institutes such as the Centre for Science and Technology Studies, Leiden (CWTS), and commercial suppliers of bibliometric tools (see chapter 7.1).

The literature selection was informed by several strategies comprising a search for authoritative books published by seminal scholars in the field of informetrics and scientometrics (Martin et al., 2012), as well as snowballing and cited reference searches of Aström and Hansson (2013), Ball and Tunger (2006), Corrall, Kennan, and Afzaal (2013), Cox et al. (2019), Gumpenberger, Wieland, and Gorraiz (2012), Petersohn (2016), and Schneijderberg and Merkator (2013). The review is selective in nature by focusing on theories, methodologies, and applications pertaining to evaluative bibliometrics.

Codified Knowledge Base of Evaluative Bibliometrics: Monographs and Edited Books

This section highlights the literature that represents core cognitive competencies by reviewing handbooks, monographs, and edited books by leading authors in the field of evaluative bibliometrics.

Ten monographs (Andrés, 2009; Ball, 2018; de Bellis, 2009; Gingras, 2016; Moed, 2005; Moed, 2017; Rousseau et al., 2018; Sugimoto and Larivière, 2018; Todeschini and Baccini, 2016; Vinkler, 2010) and eight edited books (Cronin and Atkins, 2000; Cronin and Sugimoto, 2014; Cronin and Sugimoto, 2015; Ding et al., 2016; Glänzel et al., 2019; Moed et al., 2004; Sugimoto, 2016; van Raan, 1988) have been selected. They vary from classical handbooks representing the state-of-the-art in the discipline, an encyclopedic collection of indices, edited books as Festschriften for esteemed scholars in the field, and technical introductions to methods up to opinionated essays.

Almost all authors apart from de Bellis (2009), Sugimoto (2016), and Cronin and Atkin (2000), who address an interested public in general, aim at a distinct readership comprised of research administrators and managers, policymakers, practitioners, librarians, and information professionals, as well as academics from all disciplines as the ones being affected by bibliometric research evaluation and scholars from Library and Information Sciences (LIS).

Conforming to the nature of handbooks and similar authoritative publications codifying core knowledge in the field, they convey cognitive competencies par excellence. A second competency dimension embraced across this subset of the literature is ethical competencies. With regard to representing state-of-the-art knowledge, the books contribute to well-informed, up to date professional practice. More importantly, they allow for critical and informed judgment of the limitations and caveats of bibliometric data, methods and indicators, thereby fostering professional values such as the responsible use of metrics.

The contributions can be grouped into four distinct "families", each offering a differing emphasis on cognitive and ethical competencies.

1. The "critical-reflexive" family: this group encompasses the books by Cronin and Sugimoto (2014), Cronin and Sugimoto (2015), de Bellis (2009), Gingras (2016), Moed (2005), Moed (2017), Sugimoto (2016), and Sugimoto and Larivière (2018). As different as they are, the main tenet shared by these contributions is to caution against an unquestioned reliance on bibliometrics as science policy tools by emphasizing conceptual problems, validity and accuracy issues, and potentials for misuse and abuse of metrics and rankings, thereby strongly promoting the development of ethical competencies with regard to evaluative bibliometrics.

2. The "classical handbook" family: in this group the contributions by Cronin and Atkins (2000), Glänzel et al. (2019), Moed et al. (2004), van Raan (1988), and Todeschini and Baccini (2016) are assembled. They foster cognitive competencies by representing current advances in theory, methodology, and application of bibliometrics, and scientometrics in a science policy context. All books also permit the acquisition of ethical competencies since they enable readers to stay up to date and understand limitations of bibliometric methods, data and indicators.

3. The "application-oriented" family contains the monographs by Andrés (2009), Ball (2018), and Vinkler (2010). They set out to provide readable introductions to carrying out bibliometric studies including sketching the foundations of and current developments in bibliometrics, providing an overview over central indices and tools as well as types of analyses. The main thrust lies on specialist, yet not overly technical or abstract knowledge geared to knowledge application, keeping in mind basic ethical competencies needed for conducting bibliometric analyses.

4. The "technical-methodological" family is represented by Ding et al. (2016) and Rousseau et al. (2018). They put an emphasis on the mathematical and statistical foundations of scholarly metrics, evaluative techniques, and on providing an

overview over current technologies and methodologies such as statistical and text-based methods, visualization techniques and network tools and analysis. Among the books reviewed, they represent cognitive competencies requiring very technical, formal, and abstract knowledge, yet also conceptual and procedural knowledge lending itself to application for advanced users. A notable exception in displayed competencies is the edited book by Ding et al. (2016) which also illustrates functional competencies by providing step-by-step instructions for using software tools to compute citation or collaboration networks, model topics, or map diversity.

Bibliometric Tasks, Functions, and Roles in Academic Libraries

The literature giving an insight into bibliometric practices and services is dominated by academic librarianship as the most prolific user group. The profession publishes frequently about its bibliometric roles and functions as evidenced by 14 scholarly articles and seven contributions in practitioner journals.

Bibliometric practices and services are planned or established in libraries across the globe: in Europe (Austria, Germany, Ireland, Poland, Sweden, and the United Kingdom), the USA, Canada, New Zealand, Australia, Sub-Saharan Africa, and China. The USA and Australia make up the largest share of the contributions with seven and three papers respectively.

The majority of the contributions consist in descriptions of established or planned services (Ball and Tunger, 2006; Bladek, 2014; Braun, 2017; Byrne, 2019; Drummond and Wartho, 2009; Gumpenberger et al., 2012; Gutzman et al., 2018; Hendrix, 2010; Leiss and Gregory, 2016; Onyancha, 2018; Qiu et al., 2018; Ye, 2019). Six papers report on survey results (Åström and Hansson, 2013; Corrall et al., 2013; Haddow and Mamtora, 2017; Malone and Burke, 2016; Miles et al., 2018; Ryś and Chadaj, 2016). Three articles represent opinion pieces calling for seizing bibliometrics and altmetrics as an opportunity to strengthen the libraries' position against the backdrop of the changing research environment (Herther, 2009; MacColl, 2010; Tattersall, 2017).

In this subset of the literature, all three dimensions of professional competence in bibliometric research evaluation are present. Cognitive competencies are displayed in a different manner compared to the previous section: specialist knowledge about bibliometrics is referenced in smaller scope and detail. However, both cognitive and functional competencies in the field of LIS, comprising for example the handling of databases, information retrieval as well as classification skills and knowledge, are emphasized by half of the contributions as conducive to the development of bibliometric services (Åström and Hansson, 2013; Ball and Tunger, 2006; Bladek, 2014; Braun, 2017; Gumpenberger et al., 2012; Gutzman et al., 2018; Leiss and Gregory, 2016; Miles et al., 2018; Onyancha, 2018).

This subset of the literature lends itself particularly to gain an insight into the array of bibliometric tasks and functions performed. The most common service is training and bibliometrics education, followed by consultations regarding the calculation and use of author-level and journal-level indices. Performance or collaboration analyses as well as benchmarking activities are also undertaken to different degrees of sophistication if the service is formally institutionalized at the library and sufficiently staffed. A higher amount of detail is given in Ball and Tunger (2006) and Gumpenberger et al. (2012) with regard to specific types of analyses such as trend analyses. Braun (2017), Drummond and Wartho (2009), Gutzman et al. (2018), and Leiss and Gregory (2016) are examples of comprehensive descriptions of services including types of reports produced or analyses and visualizations extracted from software tools.

Functional competencies are thus mainly depicted at the level of tasks, less at the level of general skills with the exception of Byrne (2019) and Bladek (2014). They give recommendations on how to set up a program for competency-based bibliometric upskilling and for introducing institutional bibliometric services, emphasizing the need for planning, negotiation, and implementation skills. Collaboration also features as an important skill. Several articles mention the need for collaborating with other organizational units of the university, especially research offices or quality control and planning. Libraries sometimes partner up with research administration and management in providing bibliometric services (Corrall et al., 2013; Leiss and Gregory, 2016)

Whereas the main emphasis lies on depicting functional competencies by presenting bibliometric tasks and functions, a lot can be learned about ethical competencies as well. They are framed predominantly in terms of professional development. This implies that the majority of contributions endorse bibliometric activities as a means to strengthen the position of the library on campus and to enhance the viability of the profession. Some articles also critically discuss challenges associated with the introduction and implementation of bibliometric services (Braun, 2017; Hendrix, 2010) as well as risks to the role of the library as a neutral service provider (Åström and Hansson; 2013). The acknowledgement of lacking bibliometric skills, especially mathematical and statistical skills, illustrates a pronounced professional value of librarianship, namely the emphasis on continuous education and learning (Byrne, 2019; Corrall et al., 2013; Haddow and Mamtora, 2017; Onyancha, 2018). The reflexive trend regarding the responsible use of metrics visible in the section on bibliometric handbooks is perpetuated in parts of the literature by academic librarianship, albeit as a less pronounced facet of ethical competencies than the need and possibility for professional development (Bladek, 2014; Braun, 2017; Haddow and Mamtora, 2017; Gutzman et al., 2018; Leiss and Gregory, 2016; Miles et al., 2018).

Bibliometric Tasks, Functions, and Roles in Research Management and Administration

Although the literature on research management and administration as a developing profession is broad, encompassing characterizations of job roles, tasks, occupational knowledge, and even related competencies (Hockey and Allen-Collinson, 2009; Schneijderberg and Merkator, 2013; Schneijderberg, 2015), no specific reference is made with regard to services provided in evaluative bibliometrics. However, quality control and measurement is regarded as an area where new competencies arise (Krücken et al., 2013).

More specific allusions to the involvement of research managers and administrators in evaluative bibliometrics are garnered from two surveys about the use of bibliometric and altmetric tools by the "end-user community" and an assessment of bibliometric competencies by bibliometric practitioners (Cox et al., 2019; Gadd and Rowlands, 2018; Gadd, 2019). Survey respondents mainly consist of librarians and information professionals, however in both cases about roughly a third of the answers stem from research administrators.

Due to the sparse coverage of bibliometric functions and tasks in the literature on research administration and management, only two relevant publications were retrieved which point to some cues regarding functional and ethical competencies.

A study conducted by the Imperial College London broadly illustrates functional competencies in evaluative bibliometrics. It reports that the management and development of research performance constitutes a main task of British research managers, including the monitoring of research outcomes using research metrics (Green et al., n.d.). The need to support international collaborations also elicits the use of bibliometric indicators. Data are processed and analyzed by means of Current Research Information Systems, leading to the enhancement of the tasks, roles, and remits of the newly formed role of the research information manager.

A qualitative study on academic managers in Sweden investigated the ways in which performance measurements influence the work in research management (Söderlind and Geschwind, 2019). It illustrates the main functions of metrics as focusing devices, enabling priority setting, and decision-making, thereby facilitating institutional governance. Despite being regarded as valuable tools, they are used instrumentally. This study illustrates the professional values and therefore ethical competencies of research managers.

The Competent Bibliometrician – A Concluding Theoretical Reflection

The competency dimensions reviewed across the literature are exemplary of what has been termed the "entity-based" perspective on professional competence that focuses on a distinct applied formal and tacit body of knowledge, skills, and attitudes for accomplishing work tasks (Sandberg and Pinnington, 2009).

The constitution of bibliometric expertise and competence can, however, be studied from differing perspectives. From a constructivist stance, Leydesdorff et al. (2016) and Hammarfelt and Rushforth (2017) contend that bibliometric expertise regarding indicators and data sources does not consist of objective, technical procedures and a priori sets of principles employed by experts such as data producers as well as bibliometricians. Rather, indicators and data are socially constructed boundary objects, constantly modified and (re-) constructed in terms of their use in specific disciplinary and institutional settings. They acquire different meanings and functions according to the differing user groups. According to these authors, a distinction between amateur and professional bibliometrics, or a gradation of competence into levels ranging from novice to expert, does not hold.

A second perspective from the sociology of professions demonstrates how competence in evaluative bibliometrics can be regarded as a particular level or delineated stage of expertise. The attainment of professional status can be the proclaimed ambition of distinct users and producers of research metrics such as academic librarians (Petersohn, 2016) or bibliometric expert organizations (Petersohn and Heinze, 2018). This approach is based on the assumption that abstract knowledge linked to specific work tasks, or cognitive competencies linked to functional competencies, are used in a specific manner to claim professional responsibility for a particular field of expertise (see chapter 2.2). This claim, however, has to be legitimated and defended in different social arenas to become effective and accepted.

It can be concluded that becoming a "competent bibliometrician" is not only about acquiring the three dimensions of professional competence in evaluative bibliometrics. Both theoretical approaches illustrate with their interpretative-relational perspective that competence is an unstable construct based on situated professional judgment, professional demarcations of expertise and the understanding of work, and its contexts (Lindberg and Rantatalo, 2015; Sandberg and Pinnington, 2009).

References

Andrés, A 2009, *Measuring academic research: How to undertake a bibliometric study*, Chandos Publishing.
Åström, F & Hansson, J 2013, 'How implementation of bibliometric practice affects the role of academic libraries', *Journal of Librarianship and information Science*, vol. 45, pp. 316–22.
Ball, R 2018, *An Introduction to Bibliometrics: New Development and Trends*, Chandos Publishing.
Ball, R & Tunger, D 2006, 'Bibliometric analysis-A new business area for information professionals in libraries?' *Scientometrics*, vol. 66, pp. 561–77.
Bladek, M 2014, 'Bibilometrics services and the academic library: meeting the emerging needs of the campus community', *College & undergraduate libraries*, vol. 21, pp. 330–44.
Braun, S 2017, 'Supporting research impact metrics in academic libraries: A case study', *portal: Libraries and the Academy*, vol. 17, pp. 111–27.

Byrne, J 2019, Building a Future-Ready Workforce-Embedding Bibliometric Capabilities at UNSW Library.

Cheetham, G & Chivers, G 1996, 'Towards a holistic model of professional competence', *Journal of European industrial training*, vol. 20, pp. 20–30.

Corrall, S, Kennan, MA & Afzal, W 2013, 'Bibliometrics and research data management services: Emerging trends in library support for research', *Library trends*, vol. 61, pp. 636–74.

Cox, A, Gadd, E, Petersohn, S & Sbaffi, L 2019, 'Competencies for bibliometrics', *Journal of Librarianship and Information Science*, vol. 51, pp. 746–62.

Cronin, B & Atkins, HB 2000, *The web of knowledge: A festschrift in honor of Eugene Garfield*, Information Today.

Cronin, B & Sugimoto, CR 2014, *Beyond bibliometrics: Harnessing multidimensional indicators of scholarly impact*, MIT Press, Cambridge, Massachusetts; London, England.

Cronin, B & Sugimoto, CR 2015, *Scholarly metrics under the microscope*, Information Today Inc/ASIST, Medford, NJ.

de Bellis, N 2009, *Bibliometrics and Citation Analysis: From the Science Citation Index to Cybermetrics*, Scarecrow Press, Plymouth.

Ding, Y, Rousseau, R & Wolfram, D 2016, *Measuring scholarly impact. Methods and practice*, Springer, Cham.

Drummond, R & Wartho, R 2009, 'RIMS: the research impact measurement service at the University of New South Wales', *Australian Academic & Research Libraries*, vol. 40, pp. 76–87.

Eraut, M 1998, 'Concepts of competence', *Journal of interprofessional care*, vol. 12, pp. 127–39.

Gadd, E 2019, 'Influencing the changing world of research evaluation', *Insights*, vol. 32.

Gadd, E & Rowlands, I 2018, 'How can bibliometric and altmetric suppliers improve? Messages from the end-user community', *Insights*, vol. 31.

Gingras, Y 2016, *Bibliometrics and Research Evaluation. Uses and Abuses*, MIT Press, Cambridge, Massachusetts; London, England.

Glänzel, W, Moed, HF, Schmoch, U & Thelwall, M 2019, *Springer Handbook of Science and Technology Indicators*, Springer International Publishing.

Glänzel, W & Schoepflin, U 1994, 'Little Scientometrics, Big Scientometrics ... And Beyond', *Scientometrics*, vol. 30, pp. 375–84.

Green, J, Mcardle, I, Rutherford, S, Turner, T, van Baren, J, Fowler, N, Govaert, P & Weertman, N n.d., Developing tools to inform the management of research and translating existing good practice, JISC Imperial College London.

Gumpenberger, C, Wieland, M & Gorraiz, J 2012, 'Bibliometric practices and activities at the University of Vienna', *Library management*, vol. 33, pp. 174–83.

Gutzman, KE, Bales, ME, Belter, CW, Chambers, T, Chan, L, Holmes, KL, Lu, Y-L, Palmer, LA, Reznik-Zellen, RC, Sarli, CC, Suiter, AM & Wheeler, TR 2018, 'Research evaluation support services in biomedical libraries', *Journal of the Medical Library Association: JMLA*, vol. 106, pp. 1–14.

Haddow, G & Mamtora, J 2017, 'Research support in Australian academic libraries: Services, resources, and relationships', *New Review of Academic Librarianship*, vol. 23, pp. 89–109.

Hammarfelt, B & Rushforth, AD 2017, 'Indicators as judgment devices: An empirical study of citizen bibliometrics in research evaluation', *Research Evaluation*, vol. 26, pp. 169–80.

Hendrix, D 2010, 'Tenure metrics: bibliometric education and services for academic faculty', *Medical Reference Services Quarterly*, vol. 29, pp. 183–89.

Herther, NK 2009, 'Research evaluation and citation analysis: key issues and implications,' *The Electronic Library*, vol. 27, pp. 361–75.

Hicks, D, Wouters, P, Waltman, L, de Rijcke, S & Rafols, I 2015, 'The Leiden Manifesto for research metrics', *Nature*, vol. 520, pp. 429–31.

Hockey, J & Allen-Collinson, J 2009, 'Occupational knowledge and practice amongst UK university research administrators', *Higher Education Quarterly*, vol. 63, pp. 141–59.

Krücken, G, Blümel, A & Kloke, K 2013, 'The managerial turn in higher education? On the interplay of organizational and occupational change in German academia', *Minerva*, vol. 51, pp. 417–42.

Leiss, C & Gregory, K 2016, 'Visibility and impact of research: Bibliometric services for university management and researchers', Proceedings of the IAUTL Conferences.

Leydesdorff, L, Wouters, P & Bornmann, L 2016, 'Professional and citizen bibliometrics: complementarities and ambivalences in the development and use of indicators-a state-of-the-art report', *Scientometrics*, vol. 109, pp. 2129–50.

Lindberg, O & Rantatalo, O 2015, 'Competence in professional practice: A practice theory analysis of police and doctors', *Human relations*, vol. 68, pp. 561–82.

MacColl, J 2010, 'Library roles in university research assessment', *Liber quarterly*.

Malone, T & Burke, S 2016, 'Academic librarians' knowledge of bibliometrics and altmetrics', *Evidence Based Library and Information Practice*, vol. 11, pp. 34–49.

Martin, BR, Nightingale, P & Yegros-Yegros, A 2012, 'Science and technology studies: Exploring the knowledge base', *Research Policy*, vol. 41, pp. 1182–1204.

Miles, R, Konkiel, S & Sutton, S 2018, 'Scholarly Communication Librarians' Relationship with Research Impact Indicators: An Analysis of a National Survey of Academic Librarians in the United States', *Journal of Librarianship and Scholarly Communication*, vol. 6.

Moed, HF 2005, *Citation Analysis in Research Evaluation*, Springer, Dordrecht.

Moed, HF 2017, *Applied evaluative informetrics*, Springer, Cham.

Moed, HF, Glänzel, W & Schmoch, U (eds.) 2004, *Handbook of Quantitative Science and Technology Research. The Use of Publication and Patent Statistics in Studies of S&T Systems*, Kluwer, Dordrecht.

Mulder, M 2014, 'Conceptions of Professional Competence', in S Billett, C Harteis & H Gruber (eds.), *International Handbook of Research in Professional and Practice-based Learning*, Springer, Dordrecht.

Mulder, M & Winterton, J 2017, 'Introduction', in M Mulder (ed.), *Competence-based Vocational and Professional Education: Bridging the Worlds of Work and Education*, Springer International Publishing, Cham.

Onyancha, OB 2018, 'Navigating the rising metrics tide in the 21st century: which way for academic librarians in support of researchers in sub-Saharan Africa?', *South African Journal of Libraries and Information Science*, vol. 84, pp. 1–13.

Petersohn, S 2016, 'Professional competencies and jurisdictional claims in evaluative bibliometrics: The educational mandate of academic librarians', *Education for Information*, vol. 32, pp. 165–93.

Petersohn, S & Heinze, T 2018, 'Professionalization of bibliometric research assessment. Insights from the history of the Leiden Centre for Science and Technology Studies (CWTS)', *Science and Public Policy*, vol. 45(4), pp. 565–578.

Qiu, L, Zhou, E, Yu, T & Smyth, N 2018, Technology Transformations in Research Evaluation Metrics Data: library reference services and research intelligence in China.

Ràfols, I 2019, 'S&T indicators in the wild: Contextualization and participation for responsible metrics', *Research Evaluation*, vol. 28, pp. 7–22.

Rousseau, R, Egghe, L & Guns, R 2018, *Becoming metric-wise: A bibliometric guide for researchers*, Chandos Publishing.

Ryś, D & Chadaj, A 2016, 'Bibliometrics and academic staff assessment in Polish university libraries-current trends', *Liber Quarterly*, vol. 26.

Sandberg, J & Pinnington, AH 2009, 'Professional competence as ways of being: An existential ontological perspective', *Journal of management studies*, vol. 46, pp. 1138–70.

Schneijderberg, C 2015, 'Work Jurisdiction of New Higher Education Professionals', in UC Teichler & K William (eds.), *Forming, Recruiting and Managing the Academic Profession*, Springer, Heidelberg, New York, Dordrecht, London.

Schneijderberg, C & Merkator, N 2013, 'The New Higher Education Professionals', in BM Kehm & U Teichler (eds.), *The Academic Profession in Europe: New Tasks and New Challenges*, Springer, Dordrecht.

Söderlind, J & Geschwind, L 2019, 'Making sense of academic work: the influence of performance measurement in Swedish universities', *Policy Reviews in Higher Education*, vol. 3, pp. 75–93.

Sugimoto, CR 2016, *Theories of informetrics and scholarly communication*, Walter de Gruyter GmbH, Berlin, Boston.

Sugimoto, CR & Larivière, V 2018, 'Measuring research: what everyone needs to know', Oxford University Press, New York.

Tattersall, A 2017, 'Supporting the research feedback loop: Why and how library and information professionals should engage with altmetrics to support research', *Performance Measurement and Metrics*, vol. 18, pp. 28–37.

Todeschini, R & Baccini, A 2016, *Handbook of bibliometric indicators: quantitative tools for studying and evaluating research*, John Wiley & Sons.

van Raan, AFJ (ed.) 1988, *Handbook of Quantitative Studies of Science and Technology*, Elsevier, Amsterdam.

Vinkler, P. 2010. *The evaluation of research by scientometric indicators*, Chandos Publishing.

Weinert, FE 2001, 'Concept of competence: A conceptual clarification', in DS Rychen & LH Salganik (eds.), *Defining and selecting key competencies*, Hogrefe & Huber Publishers, Ashland, OH, US.

Wilsdon, J, Allen, L, Belfiore, E, Campbell, P, Curry, S, Hill, S, Jones, R, Kain, R, Kerridge, S, Thelwall, M, Tinkler, J, Viney, I, Wouters, P, Hill, J & Johnson, B 2015, The Metric Tide: Report of the Independent Review of the Role of Metrics in Research Assessment and Management, HEFCE, London.

Ye, L 2019, 'Chinese Academic Library Research Evaluation Services', *Journal of Library Administration*, vol. 59, pp. 97–128.

Zhao, D 2016, 'Bibliometrics education', *Education for Information*, vol. 32, pp. 121–24.

8 The Future of Bibliometrics

8.1 The Future of Bibliometrics: Where is Bibliometrics Heading?

Rafael Ball

Abstract: Bibliometrics is a system that examines and addresses the most diverse forms and formats of science output. It plays a mediating and supporting role by researching and analysing how and in what form science output can and should look like in the future. In this way, it increasingly acquires a normative moment in the discussion about mass science and its (publication) consequences. The future of bibliometrics is directly dependent on the development of scholarly communication, but it also determines its development and prioritization in a normative way by providing a wide range of metrics. Under the keyword "analytics", it is increasingly possible to collect and analyse the largest and most diverse amounts of data. Profiling will complement bibliometrics and even a single personal "scientist score" could be imagined as the climax of bibliometrics. Whether this is desirable is another question.

Keywords: future of bibliometrics, altmetrics, social scoring, profiling, scientific analytics, judgment, reason.

Bibliometrics is and has always been tied to the development of academic communication; as part of this development, it is inextricably linked to its future and design.

The beginnings of bibliometrics can be traced back to the fundamental issues of summarising and focusing increasing, widely scattered content. Almost immediately after the emancipation of academia, which began at the latest with the foundation of academies and universities and academia as a self-referential system, the number of publications rose on a scale which necessitated summaries and reference literature (Mabe and Mayur, 2001). However, bibliometrics goes one step further than reference literature. Whereas the latter summarises the contents of the publications qualitatively, bibliometric methods compile statistics regarding their perception and re-use in the form of citations. These quantitative methods now directly reflect the significance of the paper in question. With the aid of this (statistical) information, scientists are then able to decide and prioritise what they would like to read and what they can ignore. Originally, bibliometric analyses were intended as an aid for librarians to select and procure relevant literature, which meant they were a holdings management tool (Garfield, 1955).

(Evaluative) information on the significance of papers and their authors was not initially implicit with bibliometrics, even though the majority of the results of bibliometrics are perceived only as such nowadays.

Dr. **Rafael Ball**, Director ETH Libraries and Collections, ETH Zurich, Rämistrasse 101, 8092 Zuerich, Switzerland. Email: rafael.ball@library.ethz.ch

Bibliometrics is developing in parallel with academic communication, albeit with a certain time gap. Therefore, bibliometrics can also be described as a system which examines and highlights a vast range of forms and formats of academic output (de Solla Price, 1976). Especially against the backdrop of the criticism of excessive publication volumes ("publish or perish"), bibliometrics can play a mediating, supportive role by researching and analysing what the academic output of the future might and should look like, and which form it should take. In other words, it is no longer merely an analysis tool in the aftermath of academic output, but rather is increasingly gaining normative momentum in the debate on mass academia and its (publishing) consequences.

The future of bibliometrics thus depends on the development of academic communication and its forms and formats. This means developing adequate methods and metrics to be in a position to make relevant statements regarding the perception and attention of the publications in question. This is the passive (and subordinate) role of bibliometrics.

As mentioned earlier, however, bibliometrics is also becoming part of the (normative) debate on what the academic communication of tomorrow ought to look like. This does not just include the opportunities and limitations of new technologies and their epistemological value, but also the specific question as to whether and how the sheer volume of academic output should be handled.

But let's not get ahead of ourselves.

Academic communication is in a state of radical change and at the end of the third paradigm shift (Ball, 2018).

Digitalisation and the birth of the Internet since the mid-1990s on the one hand and the rise of social media and their huge impact not just on everyday mass communication but also corporate and academic communication on the other have triggered an unprecedented qualitative and quantitative change in academic communication.

Beforehand, there were only minor technical or visual variations in formats and forms in the communication of academic results.

The possibilities of writing papers and book manuscripts in electronic form and the almost instantaneous and free distribution of their content gave the already sharp increase in the volume of academic output in the second half of the twentieth century another major boost. Moreover, the advent of digital distribution units rendered the classic structure categories of distribution formats such as journals, papers and books to some extent redundant. Publishing houses no longer have to wait for all the articles in a journal issue to come in. In the digital age, papers are published in precisely the chronological order in which they are provided by the author or the reviewers.

Social media provided another fresh stimulus when they made their definitive breakthrough with the major media companies such as Facebook, Instagram and Twitter: "Social networks have become strong source collections for statistical mass recording. Their enormous databases aid systematic information acquisition and are used to collect, evaluate and interpret socio-statistical data" (Reichert, 2003, p. 68).

As a result, a new mass medium has emerged, which is also used to disseminate and communicate academic content. Relevant content is supplied, disseminated and at the same time also perceived, passed on and evaluated (cited, liked, retweeted) via these channels. The topic of perceiving academic output is thus taking on a new dimension: bibliometrics, which solely had recourse to citations based on print publications until the 1990s, now also has to increasingly take new media formats and their own specific evaluation and perception systems into account.

Corresponding new methods, tools and metrics were also developed and provided (see Bar-Ilan et al., 2012; Bornmann, 2016; Cronin and Sugimoto, 2014; Fenner, 2014; Haustein et al., 2014). Today, they supplement the classic indicators as "altmetrics" and also refer to these forms of communication in the statements regarding the reception history of academic publications.

Academic communication in the second decade of the twenty-first century is increasingly discovering new dimensions and directions, which is not just connected with the technical possibilities such as multimediality as a standard and the concurrence of Internet technologies, but also and especially with science political activities such as open access and open science.

Open access means free access to academic information for everyone, free of charge. Exclusivity in the form of relevant brands of key journals or publishing houses and their series are becoming increasingly irrelevant, for instance. The open science movement, on the other hand, has another step in its sights: the whole of academia, its processes and procedures should be freely and publicly accessible – ideally as a public platform upon which everyone can see and follow the point where research is and what results can be expected. It goes without saying that the classic publishing formats are also fundamentally scrutinised. Previously, the public had been removed from the internal aspect of academic communication as the "informal part"; what occurred there took place solely within one's own academic community (and with good reason). Only upon publishing the results as a paper, books or conference paper was the inner circle left and the debate crossed from the informal aspect of communication to the formal (Ball, 2014, p. 16).

If open science is realised as consistently as some demand,[1] the distinction between these two areas no longer makes sense. Separation into "unpublished" and "published" becomes futile. At the same time, the status of the "provisional nature" of internal discussions ceases to apply, as does the opportunity to play out and discuss mistakes and doubts, cluelessness and speculation in an internal framework to start with.

---

[1] Open science is, "a way of doing science in which – as best as you can – you make all your research freely available to the public and in real time." (Bradley, cited by Poynder, 2010); "All in all, we are putting openness at the heart of EU research and innovation funding." (Kroes, 2013).

As possible formats for the "publication" of the results of open science processes (where, by definition, the distinction into published and unpublished will no longer be drawn), the dynamic document can be envisaged as an incomplete paper, the "fluid PDF" in the status of a "perpetual beta"; in other words, a platform upon which not only are the results available openly and transparently to everyone, but the entire previous and ongoing process is openly visible to research and can be read and commented upon. Much like a Wikipedia article, research is then permanently updated and refined. In this instance, it is hard to imagine which role "perception metrics" will be able to play in understanding bibliometrics. At most, the measurement of the activities on the platform and their access statistics would be conceivable.

The difference between attention and importance poses another problem. In times of escalating and simultaneously aggressive and subtle marketing, scientists are also acting increasingly strategically. They "market" their results in the best interests of the methods which measure their attention and thus aid a self-perpetuating system. Not only does the selection of "suitable" research topics ("mainstream research") play a part here, but also diverse methods and "tricks" to increase the level of attention (Ball, 2007).

While the ubiquitous use of figures and the translation of quantitative parameters into numerical, easily comparable data is not an invention of the digital age, ever since digitalisation and the opportunities it offers to process enormous quantities of data in an extremely short space of time, quantification has become a core, almost unbridled topic. And so it is not by chance that less attention is paid to the actual results, qualities, processes and judgements than their analysis and perception as the actual result of political, economic or academic action. The aspiration to "be good" has often given way to "looking good" (Ball, 2016). And this is highly problematic for academia, which aspires to gear its own work towards objectivity and getting to the truth, not external conditions.

Bibliometrics is therefore dependent on the development of the forms and formats of academic communication, also helps determine (normatively) their development and prioritisation through the provision of a vast range of metrics services and, moreover, is used to evaluate people, institutions, regions and countries in their rankings.

The latter aspect is increasingly gaining in importance against the backdrop of the digital footprints of individual scientists and their institutions.

Online publications, articles on blogs, forums, Twitter, Facebook and other social media, and on portals with liquid content require new metrics to gauge academic achievements, output and the performance of people and institutions. Moreover, with the increase in free publication and information on the Internet (open access, open science) there are realistic opportunities to have free access to enormous quantities of academic data and take into account big data applications in bibliometrics. In the process, all structured and unstructured data will then be browsed and analysed for evaluation. As a result, the days of the large-scale, once powerful databases that defined bibliometrics like monopolies are numbered if academia is to have all its findings stored in a vast range of forms online in a way that is barrier-free and always accessible along the lines of open data.

The tendency towards comprehensive data acquisition and its evaluation constitutes an additional step in the evaluation of individual performances. Under the banner of "analytics", the aim is to collect and analyse increasingly large, extremely diverse quantities of data. With big data, new contexts are being uncovered that nobody has even thought of or asked about before:

As a consequence, an increasing amount of data on every single one of us is available – including from our private spheres. The image of transparent customers and citizens is no longer a vision of the future; it's a reality (Bachmann et al., 2014, pp. 21–22).

Therefore, transparent scientists are also conceivable (whether open science actually means this consequence or merely tolerates it is open to debate) if all possible data is evaluated, such as unencrypted emails, text messages, articles on social networks, personal profiles, search requests on search engines, Internet searches, publications, presentations, data from ordering, purchasing and payment processes, booking procedures (travel, tickets) shipment tracking, all manner of downloads, data from lab instruments, learning portals, (tracking) data from apps, smartphones, all manner of sensors, communication contact information, navigation devices, vehicle data electronics/sensors, personal sensors, data in the Cloud, data from the household infrastructure, networked PC infrastructure, means of payment/economic data such as bank, discount and credit cards, credit investigation companies, bank and account data, data from registry offices, tax authorities and data from health insurance companies (based on Bachmann et al., 2014, pp. 21–22).

This kind of profiling will be a massive addition to bibliometrics. If vast quantities of (personal and institutional) information is available on scientists above and beyond their publication data and can be compiled and evaluated via search algorithms, before long all this data will yield clues as to the output and performance of individual scientists.

A series of analytical tools such as PLUM Analytics,[2] Figshare,[3] InCites,[4] or SciVal[5] already exist on the market, which adopt an integrated management approach and afford decision makers in academia and research an integrated processing of performance, financial, personal and publishing data.

Data from classic bibliometrics based on the citation and perception of publications will then only be a small part of a comprehensive data evaluation on people and institutions.

---

[2] Plum Analytics: https://plumanalytics.com/ (July 15, 2020).
[3] Figshare: https://figshare.com/ (July 15, 2020).
[4] Web of Science Group: http://researchanalytics.thomsonreuters.com/incites/ (July 15, 2020).
[5] Elsevier: http://www.elsevier.com/online-tools/research-intelligence/products-and-services/scival (July 15, 2020).

In future, scientists and institutions will be given a whole series of scores which not only provide a more comprehensive picture of the academic performance, but also the perception, behaviour, demeanour, appearance and (subjective) credibility. Like it or not, it conforms to the manner and the possibilities of evaluation in the digital Internet age of the twenty-first century. In China, this kind of personal data analysis is already being implemented and used simultaneously as an incentive and penalty system (Marr, 2019). A score similar to that which has long existed in the assessment of economic performance especially in awarding credits can then be transferred to academia.

The h-Index, a simple indicator designed to gauge the importance of publications by a scientist, has become outdated and can be replaced by a digital "scientist score", which takes into account and combines all the available network data by a scientist.

However, the translation of complex, qualitative academic results into a few key figures might prove problematic for academia and its self-image. Unlike economic processes, the success of which can be defined purely in terms of turnover, market share and profit, academia comes down to knowledge, creativity and uncovering truth. Success or failure in science are defined in a fundamentally different way to economics.

Focusing scientists, knowledge management and research sponsors down to a few key figures and bibliometric scores which measure solely perception, but never quality, swiftly leads to adjustment strategies in the interests of the metrics used and their respective value judgements. Thanks to the broad use of the quantification of academic output and the concentration of a few indicators in careers planning, recruitment processes and the allocation of research funding perpetuate and reinforce the system permanently. Not only does the specific focus on perception indicators in academia itself denote a departure from its own inner logic, it also leads – besides the aforementioned "looking good effect" – to a concentration on "mainstream topics" and easily usable contents. Although alternative metrics such as those developed through the measurement of social media impact, links, likes and downloads, for instance, might well undermine the oligopoly of database providers, nothing fundamentally changes in the problematic equation of perception and quality.

The development of figure-based evaluation systems in academia, however, cannot solely be traced back to the (staged or actual) competition in global academia; it is also determined by the growing number of scientists worldwide, the diversification and increase in disciplines and the skyrocketing publication figures.

Decision makers (who are often the scientists themselves) now have little hope of curbing the volume and complexity without quantitative support systems. Anyone who breaks (or has broken) down research results to the "last publishable unit" cannot be surprised by the inundation of publications, rising journal prices, the use of reductionist, quantitative systems in knowledge management and research promotion, or even the loss of critical powers of judgement and the advance of the technocrats. In this respect, academia's justified criticism of the quantification of academic output and the reduction of quality to a handful of key figures in ratings and rankings can be traced back to itself.

References

Bachmann, R., Kemper, G., & Gerzer, T. (2014). *Big Data – Fluch oder Segen?: Unternehmen im Spiegel gesellschaftlichen Wandels.* Heidelberg, München, Landsberg, Frechen, Hamburg: mitp.

Ball, R. (2007). Scholarly communication in transition: The use of question marks in the titles of scientific articles in medicine, life sciences and physics 1966–2005. *Scientometrics,* 79(3), pp. 667–679. doi: https://doi.org/10.1007/s11192-007-1984-5.

Ball, R. (2014). Rafael Ball. *Bibliometrie. Einfach – verständlich – nachvollziehbar.* Berlin/Boston: Walter de Gryter GmbH.

Ball, R. (2016). Scientific profiling instead of bibliometrics: Key performance indicators of the future. *Infozine Special Issue* (S1), pp. 17–19.

Ball, R. (2018, vol. 20 no. 1). The departure from the linear text. *Toruńskie Studia Bibliologiczne,* pp. 11–41.

Bar-Ilan, J., Haustein, S., Peters, I., Priem, J., Shema, H. & Terliesner, J. (2012). 'Beyond citations: Scholars' visibility on the social web', Proceedings of the 17th international conference on science and technology indicators, vol. 52900, pp. 14. Available from: http://arxiv.org/abs/1205.5611. [26 August 2019].

Bornmann, L. (2016). Scientific revolution in scientometrics: The broadening of impact from citation to societal. In C. R. Sugimoto (Ed.), *Theories of Informetrics and Scholarly Communication* (pp. 347–359). Berlin: Walter de Gruyter GmbH.

Cronin, B., & Sugimoto, C. R. (2014). *Beyond Bibliometrics: Harnessing Multidimensional Indicators of Scholarly Impact.* Cambridge: The MIT Press.

de Solla Price, D. (1976, vol. 27 no.5–6). General theory of bibliometric and other cumulative advantage processes. *Journal of the American Society for Information Science,* pp. 292–306.

Elsevier. (2019). *About SciVal.* Retrieved August 30, 2019, from https://www.elsevier.com/solutions/scival.

Fenner, M. (2014). Altmetrics and other novel measures for scientific impact. In S. Bartling, & S. Friesike (Eds.), *Opening Science. The evolving guide on how the internet is changing research, collaboration and scholarly publishing* (pp. 179–189). Cham: Springer International Publishing. Retrieved from https://link.springer.com/book/10.1007/978-3-319-00026-8#editorsandaffiliations.

Figshare. (n.d.). *Figshare home page.* Retrieved August 30, 2019, from https://figshare.com/.

Garfield, E. (1955, vol. 122 no. 3159). Citation indexes for science: A new dimension in documentation through association of ideas. *Science,* pp. 108–111.

Haustein, S., Peters, I., Bar-Ilan, J., Priem, J., Shema, H., & Terliesner, J. (2014). Coverage and adoption of altmetrics sources in the bibliometric community. *Scientometrics,* vol. 101, no. 2, pp. 1145–1163. Retrieved from https://doi.org/10.1007/s11192-013-1221-3.

Kroes, N. (2013). 'Opening up scientific data', Launch of the Research Data Alliance/Stockholm 18 March 2013, speech. Available from: https://europa.eu/rapid/press-release_SPEECH-13-236_en.htm. [26 August 2019].

Mabe, M., & Mayur, A. (2001). Growth dynamics of scholarly and scientific journals. *Scientometrics,* vol. 51 no. 1, pp. 147–162.

Marr, B. (2019, Januar 21). Chinese Social Credit Score: Utopian Big Data Bliss Or Black Mirror On Steroids?, *Forbes*. Retrieved August 30, 2019, from https://www.forbes.com/sites/bernardmarr/2019/01/21/chinese-social-credit-score-utopian-big-data-bliss-or-black-mirror-on-steroids#2959d7365cc6.

Plum Analytics. (2019). *Plum Analytics*. Retrieved August 30, 2019, from https://plumanalytics.com/.

Poynder, R. (2010). 'Interview with Jean-Claude Bradley. The impact of Open Notebook Science', Information today, vol. 27, no. 8. Available from: http://www.infotoday.com/IT/sep10/Poynder.shtml. [26 August 2019].

Reichert, R. (2003). *Die Macht der Vielen. Über den neuen Kult der digitalen Vernetzung.* Bielefeld: Transcript.

Web of Science Group. (2019). *InCites. An objective analysis of people, programs and peers.* Retrieved August 30, 2019, from http://researchanalytics.thomsonreuters.com/incites/.

8.2 Open Science and the Future of Metrics
Tamara Heck

Abstract: With regard to open science developments, scientometrics might play an important role. Scientometrics enable displays of changes in research practices and possibly measurements of the impact of open science initiatives. Conversely, metrics influence researchers' practices and might be applied to achieve a widespread adoption of open science practices. This chapter discusses open science initiatives and goals, the establishment of policies and influences on researchers' practices. With regard to these developments, metrics will be discussed as an evaluation tool for open practices on the one hand, and as an incentive to foster open science on the other. The last part of the chapter refers to the openness of metric analyses.

Keywords: open science, open metrics, incentives, research behavior, open access, open practices, responsible metrics.

Introduction

The term "open science" refers to a discussion of research practices and norms that reaches from spotting a digital transformation in science to proclaiming a scientific revolution that will shift the entire research process. This umbrella term comprises ideas like open access to scientific publications, open data, open peer review, open education and citizen science (open participation). A concrete definition, specifically with regard to open science practices of researchers, has yet to be found. Alongside many relevant bottom-up driven initiatives that focus on single practices of open science to be applied within research communities, larger top-down initiatives like those by the European Commission (European Commission 2016) contribute to the debates of opening up science and increase the visibility of the topic for researchers, infrastructure providers like libraries, political and commercial stakeholders, and society in general.

The transition to a new form of research practice was driven by the development of new digital technologies that offered new ways for researchers to communicate and disseminate their work and to collaborate with colleagues. Parallel to these changes, new forms of measuring and evaluating research became possible. As researchers started to use digital infrastructures of the Web 2.0 and more and more data was available related to scientists and their work, scientometricians and service providers were able to accumulate metrics about the activities of scientists and impact of research (Priem & Hemminger 2010; Priem et al. 2010).

Tamara Heck, Postdoc at the Information Center for Education at DIPF | Leibniz Institute for Research and Information in Education

In most cases, scientometricians followed the principle of measuring "what can be most easily measured" (Wilsdon et al. 2017, p 13). This lead to a variety of new metrics, which are subsumed under the term "altmetrics" (alternative metrics), and represent a counterpart of the more traditional bibliometrics. Measuring research activities on the Web, the question arises whether those metrics are suitable to measure open science practices and the impact open science intends to have.

Bibliometrics have not always been an indicator of demonstrating research practices, but reversely, they influence research practices. Thus, metrics can play an important role in achieving a wide-spread adoption of open science. Both perspectives are part of current discussions.

Open Science Goals

Open science is geared toward enforcing openness in all research processes. Initiators often use visualizations of a researcher circle to show those processes, like the one by Kramer & Bosman (2017). Processes include acts to facilitate the discovery of research results via sharing, disseminating and documenting, writing and publication processes via open access publications and open licenses, and assessment via open peer review and pre-registering studies. The options are as manifold as research practices and approaches. Science 2.0 as the term formerly used for the open science movement resembles the idea of using digital tools to make processes more open. Applying those tools and online services has been demonstrated in a large-scale survey (Kramer & Bosman 2016). To summarize the idea of open science practice, it can be said that open science researchers move from "'publishing as fast as possible' to 'sharing knowledge as early as possible'" (European Union 2016, p. 34).

Open science is said to face current research challenges, which Franzen (2016a) labels the "credibility crisis of research". Relevant for research quality are reproducibility, validity, and comprehensiveness. Making data, methods and results – including none confirmed or negative results – open and accessible contributes to the enhancement of quality and thus credibility within the research community and in society.

Fecher & Friesike (2014) describe five perspectives that each set another focus on open science: open knowledge, open infrastructures, citizen involvement, efficient knowledge creation, and new measurements for science impact. Those perspectives show the multi-dimensionality and complexity of the idea as well as the linkage between the diverse aspects (Bartling & Friesike 2014). The establishment of new measurements is dependent on infrastructures and knowledge creation by researchers.

Open Science Initiatives

It is interesting to note that the so-called second scientific revolution started to rebel against developments that have their origin in the first revolution, i.e. the establishment of the research journal publishing system in the 17th century. Many initiatives started by promoting open access publishing of journal articles. This resulted in diverse open access models, and journal publishers joined this trend[1]. Moreover, the idea of open access expanded to research output like data, source code, methods, and processes like peer-review.

Initiatives of the European Commission (European Commission 2016) include the Open Science Cloud for research data[2], the Open Science Policy Platform to promote and advise the application of open science principles[3] and Open Science Monitor to track open science trends[4]. OpenAIRE[5] is an EU-funded project that started with advice on open access publication, and is meanwhile engaged in several open science activities, like peer-to-peer learning. FOSTER[6] focuses on the teaching and learning of open science and respective awareness among researchers, librarians and other stakeholders. Similarly, the Open Science MOOC[7] launched in 2018 offers ten learning modules, including open learning and the use of open educational resources. The relevant supporting partners are university libraries, infrastructure providers for open research, open access publishers, and communities engaging in those topics.

In accordance with the EU activities, Go FAIR[8] is an initiative funded by the ministries of Germany, the Netherlands and France to support the development of research data services that follow the four principles research data should adhere to: findability, accessibility, interoperability and reusability (Wilkinson et al. 2016).

Besides the larger projects, many smaller research communities have raised awareness for open science. Initiators started to list further world-wide activities and community events[9] – as of summer 2019 there are over 55 entries for communities initiated by research institution offices or researcher groups at department level, with a local focus like a city or country, or with a research discipline focus.

---

1 https://open-access.net (July 15, 2020).
2 https://ec.europa.eu/research/openscience/index.cfm?pg=open-science-cloud (July 15, 2020).
3 https://ec.europa.eu/research/openscience/index.cfm?pg=open-science-policy-platform (July 15, 2020).
4 https://ec.europa.eu/info/research-and-innovation/strategy/goals-research-and-innovation-policy/open-science/open-science-monitor_en (July 15, 2020).
5 https://www.openaire.eu/ (July 15, 2020).
6 https://www.fosteropenscience.eu/ (July 15, 2020).
7 https://opensciencemooc.eu/ (July 15, 2020).
8 https://www.go-fair.org/go-fair-initiative/ (July 15, 2020).
9 https://docs.google.com/spreadsheets/d/1LNF5_bOkRV-RLIF4HYmu-gOemIa4IdfXEer89fM-Vy8/edit#gid=0 (July 15, 2020).

Open Science Policies

Open science research policies are set to define guidelines and strategies to foster open science practices. Those policies are generally established by governments on a national level, research institutions, research funding bodies, or publishers. As it is still unclear what open science practices mean and which aspects should be included (Franzen 2016b), current policies focus on concrete sub-themes of open science, i.e. mostly data and publication. The SPARC analysis reports an increase in research data policies and declarations of intent to establish such (SPARC 2018). Five EU countries added a policy, which adds up to 13 EU countries that have a national policy. However, empirical studies have shown that open access or data policies are not commonly used by commercial publishers (Blahous et al. 2015; Ellison et al. 2019).

Policies either cover instructions on open data only, or as well cover guidelines on open access publication, infrastructure and software. Nosek et al. (2015), for example, suggest a policy model for journal publishers to set incentives for researchers to make their work more transparent. The model includes a range of aspects like sharing of data, methods (e.g. code), pre-registration and fostering replication studies. The types of policies differ from national plans to white papers, and even laws (France, Lithuania), i.e. guidelines are either highly imperative or rather encouraging (SPARC 2018). Those national policies are established on high levels, often involving ministries and national research funders. Policies act as "systematic incentives" (Friesike & Schildhauer 2015) to foster open science practice. Nevertheless, policymakers are aware of the diversity of research institutions and their diverse needs for research data management and quality assurance, which makes it difficult to apply a one-policy solution on a national level.

Open Science practices

Research practices do not seem to keep up with the speed and the enormous effort made by open science initiatives and policies. Data sharing seems to be dependent on individual personality (Linek et al. 2017) and academic reputation within a discipline (Kim 2018). Interviews with researchers give deeper insights into researcher attitudes towards openness. Influencing factors are technical challenges to using open infrastructures, confusing guidelines to handle data sharing, and considerations of research impact and reputation (Levin & Leonelli 2017). Moreover, different research values and ethical considerations are factors that speak against openness on all levels, as researchers fear that open practices compromise their research integrity. Levin & Leonelli (2017) emphasize that current policies establish normative understandings of open science that do not reflect the heterogeneity of research and its contextual factors. Thus, the question is how researchers will practice open research in future, or more specifically how they will be able to practice according to contextual factors and their implied scientific values and ethos that guide their practice (Reichmann 2017)? We need to know more about the effects of open science initiatives and what influences research practice behavior.

Metrics – Evaluating and Incentivizing

For metrics research, the consequences of the open science movement are twofold. Metrics are instruments to evaluate research, and at the same time they are part of the scientific system and as such are applied to act as open science incentives.

Metrics and indicators are part of research evaluation, whereby the goals and uses vary. They can have an epistemological, controlling, or a public oriented function, for example, and may focus on research input or output processes (Hornbostel 2016). Hereby, we have to distinguish between data to be collected and its interpretation, which is applied to judgements on research performance and funding. The Research Core Dataset is a recent German approach to collect data for measuring research output, but it does not suggest concrete indicators (Biesenbender & Hornbostel 2016). In the Australian research assessment (ERA 2018)[10] information on open access research output was collected as an indicator to measure the open access trend. In the recent British research excellence framework[11] open access is even mandatory for journal articles and conference proceedings. Applying metrics as a controlling function with regard to research funding regulation as for example on open access publication means that we introduce new metrical indicators and approaches to assess the fulfillment of open science policies. As such, metrics can be applied as a controlling function for open science goals.

Bibliometrical approaches with an epistemological function are applied to measure the growth of open access publications on a country or discipline level for example. Recent studies have shown that the overall proportion of open access publications is growing (Piwowar et al. 2018). However, there are differences among disciplines. Bosman & Kramer (2018) summarize recent studies and introduce their own method to track open access output. Studies try to apply diverse data sources, i.e. traditional sources like the Web of Science and Scopus, and new services like oaDOI[12] that harvest data from relevant web sources.

Considering the multi-dimensionality of open science, altmetrics can include further indicators to measure research impact. There are diverse options, first of all new researcher activities in addition to authoring scientific publications, i.e. communicating about research (publications, but as well unpublished material) via social media platforms, commenting on colleagues' research. Second, any activities re-

---
10 https://www.arc.gov.au/excellence-research-australia (July 15, 2020).
11 https://www.ref.ac.uk/ (July 15, 2020).
12 https://oadoi.org/ (July 15, 2020).

lating to a researcher's work can be measured, i.e. any persons reads, likes, downloads, or comments. As such, altmetrics may have a potential to measure social impact, i.e. open research participation, by any user online or in other words the society. Though in fact, researchers should be cautious while measuring the social impact of research (Tunger, Clermont & Meier 2018). Open research participation is hard to define. First of all, it is not clear what "open" means. Thus, online research activities can still be limited to the research community that is closed to the public. Second, "research participation" assumes that we claim online activities to be "meaningful" for research. However, "meaningful" and valuable is experienced differently by researchers (Levin & Leonelli 2017). They describe openness and open practices differently and prefer divers forms of openness, like a study on aspects of open peer reviews shows (Ross-Hellauer, Deppe & Schmidt 2017). If metrics are to contribute to monitoring open science, and those measurements are applied to evaluate openness, then we need to agree on what we measure and what value we put on those measured research actions. The EU Open Science Monitor is a trial to aiming at establishing such metrics and indicators (Open Science Monitor Consortium Partners 2019).

Metrics as research evaluation tool are one perspective, another one considers the researchers' view and behaviour. Metrics are an effective way of guiding research practice, or more directly said to change behavioral practice. Similarly to policies and guidelines mentioned above, researchers are guided by metrics to improve their performance and reputation, and to assess peers. A researcher's reputation is highly dependent on the scientific communication system (Heise 2017, p 68), and this communication is represented by (alt)metrics like publications, citations, and social media activities like readership and downloads. As such, applying acknowledged metrics to measure open science practices by researchers can have positive effects. For example, infrastructures that allow the citation of shared research data or open research material increases researchers' reputation through acknowledged citation metrics. Additionally, systems may apply online badges for sharing open data to trigger the awareness of open science practice (Rowhani-Farid, Allen & Barnett 2017).

However, metrics can be misleading incentives. They are subject to "gaming" and studies showed that manipulating one's numbers to increase reputation is easily possible (Tunger, Clermont & Meier 2018; Orduna-Malea, Martín-Martín & Delgado López-Cózar 2016). Moreover, metrics tempting universities and research institutions to establish an "excessively managerial, audit-driven culture", leading actors to focus on things that can be measured only, herewith reduce diversity in research, and tempt researchers to pursue biased incentives (Wilsdon et al. 2017, p 6).

Open Metrics as Imperative

Discussions on the misuse of metrics and their interpretation put metrics themselves in the center of open science practices. Ràfols (2019) stresses that "[...] problems with current use of quantitative evidence [lie...] in the role that STI [science, technology and innovation] indicators play in STI governance" and that is about to change (p. 7). Currently, we see a change in norms and values that research and society embraces. Open science practices become more and more relevant and are required top-down by funders and policy makers and postulated bottom-up by research communities and initiatives. Furthermore, today's research needs to address its societal goals and impact. Future metrics should be framed with regard to this context and use and not be seen as isolated tools (Ràfols, 2019). They need to adapt to the shift in our norms. Moreover, we need to expand data sources to allow more diverse participation in the development of metrics, and to open up metrical processes to raise awareness on the obstacles and options metric come with (Ràfols 2019).

Open metrics need to show transparency with the data and objects they use, as well as with the algorithms applied to analyze these resources (Herb 2016). Infrastructures like for example Impactstory that support research activity analyses open up those processes for anyone, who wants to reproduce metrics (Konkiel, Piwowar & Priem 2014). The Leiden Manifesto, for example, summarizes those claims in ten principles, which guarantee open, transparent, and fair research evaluation (Hicks et al. 2015). Two aspects stressed are the context of evaluation and the need to consider quantitative metrics as well as qualitative evidence by experts.

The EU expert group on altmetrics (Wilsdon et al. 2017) picked up claims on the responsible use of research metrics stated by researchers and their initiatives like DORA[13], whose supporters aim at disposing journal impact factors for funding and promotion assessment in research. With regard to open science, they suggest indicator development for measuring the progress of open science, however, with an awareness on limitations and biases of single indicators.

To summarize, metrics do not come without risks and challenges, either in the sense of applying unfitting data and numbers, or of evoking inappropriate behavior like gaming. Those developments have led to initiatives and claims to introduce rules for applying metrics. One crucial factor is the openness and transparency of metrics themselves.

With regard to open science, metrics have the potential to foster the awareness and acceptance of open science practices. On the one hand, such indicators, properly established, can offer evidence for open science practices and show potentials of improving the support of such. On the other hand, metrics act as incentives to shape research behavior and communication.

It remains an open question to be solved whether we first should concretely define what we mean by open science practices and which practices we would like to foster – which we then can measure properly. Or whether we first should develop more robust and open sets of metrics to a) measure open science, and b) use them as incentives to foster open science practices among researchers. Currently,

---

[13] https://sfdora.org/ (July 15, 2020).

we are investigating both approaches, but we at least should be aware of their interdependencies and influences. Notwithstanding, both the discussion on metrics and open science have one important factor in common: We need to understand the meanings as well as our intended benefits and potential weaknesses of both metrics and open science. Quite possibly, this means that we might need to start more in-depth discussions on scientific values, and how we would like to practice and assess research in future.

References

Bartling, S & Friesike, S 2014, 'Towards Another Scientific Revolution' in *Opening science*, in S Bartling & S Friesike (eds.), pp. 3–15, Springer, New York.

Biesenbender, S & Hornbostel, S 2016, 'The Research Core Dataset for the German science system. Developing standards for an integrated management of research information', *SCIENTOMETRICS*, vol. 108, no. 1, pp. 401–12.

Blahous, B, Gorraiz, J, Gumpenberger, C, Lehne, O, Stein, B & Ulrych, U 2015, 'Forschungsdatenpolicies in wissenschaftlichen Zeitschriften – Eine empirische Untersuchung', *Zeitschrift für Bibliothekswesen und Bibliographie*, vol. 62, no. 1, pp. 12–24.

Bosman, J & Kramer, B 2018, 'Open access levels: a quantitative exploration using Web of Science and oaDOI data'.

Ellison, TS, Koder, T, Schmidt, L, Williams, A & Winchester, CC 2019, 'Open access policies of leading medical journals. A cross-sectional study', *BMJ open*, vol. 9, no. 6, e028655.

European Commission 2016, *Open Innovation, Open Science, Open to the World – a vision for Europe*, http://publications.europa.eu/resource/cellar/3213b335–1cbc-11e6-ba9a-01aa75ed71a1.0001.02/DOC_2 (July 15, 2020).

European Union 2016, *Open Innovation, Open Science, Open to the World. A vision for Europe*, Publications Office of the European Union, Luxembourg, https://publications.europa.eu/de/publication-detail/-/publication/3213b335–1cbc-11e6-ba9a-01aa75ed71a1/language-en (July 15, 2020).

Fecher, B & Friesike, S 2014, 'Open Science: One Term, Five Schools of Thought' in S Bartling & S Friesike (eds.), *Opening science*, pp. 17–47, Springer, New York.

Franzen, M 2016a, 'Open Science als wissenschaftspolitische Problemlösungsformel?' in D Simon, A Knie, S Hornbostel & K Zimmermann (eds.), *Handbuch Wissenschaftspolitik*, Springer Fachmedien, Wiesbaden.

Franzen, M 2016b, 'Open Science als wissenschaftspolitischeProblemlösungsformel?' in D Simon, A Knie, S Hornbostel & K Zimmermann (eds.), *Handbuch Wissenschaftspolitik*, Springer Fachmedien, Wiesbaden.

Friesike, S & Schildhauer, T 2015, 'Open Science: Many Good Resolutions, Very Few Incentives, Yet' in IM Welpe, J Wollersheim, S Ringelhan & M Osterloh (eds.), *Incentives and performance. Governance of research organizations*, pp. 277–89, Springer International Publishing, Cham, s.l.

Heise, C 2017, *Von Open Access zu Open Science: Zum Wandel digitaler Kulturen der wissenschaftlichen Kommunikation*, meson press, Lüneburg, Germany.

Herb, U 2016, 'Impactmessung, Transparenz & Open Science', *Young Information Scientist*, pp. 59–72, http://eprints.rclis.org/29991/1/YIS_1_2016_59_Herb.pdf (July 15, 2020).

Hicks, D, Wouters, P, Waltman, L, Rijcke, S de & Rafols, I 2015, 'Bibliometrics. The Leiden Manifesto for research metrics', *Nature*, vol. 520, no. 7548, pp. 429–31.

Hornbostel, S 2016, '(Forschungs-)Evaluation' in D Simon, A Knie, S Hornbostel & K Zimmermann (eds.), *Handbuch Wissenschaftspolitik*, Springer Fachmedien, Wiesbaden.

Kim, Y 2018, 'Reputation, Trust, and Norms as Mechanisms Leading to Academic Reciprocity in Data Sharing: An Empirical Test of Theory of Collective Action', *Proceedings of ASIS&T AM 2018*, pp. 244–53.

Konkiel, S, Piwowar, H & Priem, J 2014, 'The Imperative for Open Altmetrics', *The Journal of Electronic Publishing*, vol. 17, no. 3.

Kramer, B & Bosman, J 2016, 'Innovations in scholarly communication – global survey on research tool usage', *F1000Research*, vol. 5, p. 692.

Kramer, B & Bosman, J 2017, *Wheel of Open Science practices (editable powerpoint)*, Figshare.

Levin, N & Leonelli, S 2017, 'How Does One "Open" Science? Questions of Value in Biological Research', *Science, Technology & Human Values*, vol. 42, no. 2, pp. 280–305.

Linek, SB, Fecher, B, Friesike, S & Hebing, M 2017, 'Data sharing as social dilemma. Influence of the researcher's personality', *PLoS ONE*, vol. 12, no. 8, e0183216.

Nosek, BA, Alter, G, Banks, GC, Borsboom, D, Bowman, SD, Breckler, SJ, Buck, S, Chambers, CD, Chin, G, Christensen, G, Contestabile, M, Dafoe, A, Eich, E, Freese, J, Glennerster, R, Goroff, D, Green, DP, Hesse, B, Humphreys, M, Ishiyama, J, Karlan, D, Kraut, A, Lupia, A, Mabry, P, Madon, TA, Malhotra, N, Mayo-Wilson, E, McNutt, M, Miguel, E, Paluck, EL, Simonsohn, U, Soderberg, C, Spellman, BA, Turitto, J, VandenBos, G, Vazire, S, Wagenmakers, EJ, Wilson, R & Yarkoni, T 2015, 'Scientific Standards. Promoting an open research culture', *Science (New York, N.Y.)*, vol. 348, no. 6242, pp. 1422–25.

Open Science Monitor Consortium Partners 2019, *Open science monitor methodological note*, https://ec.europa.eu/info/sites/info/files/research_and_innovation/open_science_monitor_methodological_note_april_2019.pdf.

Orduna-Malea, E, Martín-Martín, A & Delgado López-Cózar, E 2016, 'Metrics in academic profiles: a new addictive game for researchers?', *Rev Esp Salud Publica*, vol. 90, pp. 1–5.

Piwowar, H, Priem, J, Lariviere, V, Alperin, JP, Matthias, L, Norlander, B, Farley, A, West, J & Haustein, S 2018, 'The state of OA. A large-scale analysis of the prevalence and impact of Open Access articles', *PEERJ*, vol. 6.

Priem, J & Hemminger, BM 2010, 'Scientometrics 2.0: Toward new metrics of scholarly impact on the social web', *First Monday*, vol. 15, no. 7, https://firstmonday.org/ojs/index.php/fm/article/view/2874/2570 (July 15, 2020).

Priem, J, Taraborelli, D, Groth, P & Neylon, C 2010, *Altmetrics: A manifesto, 26 October 2010*, http://altmetrics.org/manifesto (July 15, 2020).

Ràfols, I 2019, 'S&T indicators in the wild. Contextualization and participation for responsible metrics', *Research Evaluation*, vol. 28, no. 1, pp. 7–22.

Reichmann, W 2017, 'Open Science zwischen sozialen Strukturen und Wissenskulturen', *TATuP Zeitschrift für Technikfolgenabschätzung in Theorie und Praxis*, vol. 26, nos. 1–2, pp. 43–48.

Ross-Hellauer, T, Deppe, A & Schmidt, B 2017, 'Survey on open peer review. Attitudes and experience amongst editors, authors and reviewers', *PLoS ONE*, vol. 12, no. 12, e0189311.

Rowhani-Farid, A, Allen, M & Barnett, AG 2017, 'What incentives increase data sharing in health and medical research? A systematic review', *Research integrity and peer review*, vol. 2, no. 7.

SPARC 2018, *An Analysis of Open Data and Open Science Policies in Europe*, https://sparceurope.org/download/3674 (July 15, 2020).

Tunger, D, Clermont, M & Meier, A 2018, 'Altmetrics. State of the Art and a Look into the Future' in M Jibu (ed.), *Scientometrics*, IntechOpen, London.

Wilkinson, MD, Dumontier, M, Aalbersberg, IJ, Appleton, G, Axton, M, Baak, A, Blomberg, N, Boiten, J-W, da Silva Santos, LB, Bourne, PE, Bouwman, J, Brookes, AJ, Clark, T, Crosas, M, Dillo, I, Dumon, O, Edmunds, S, Evelo, CT, Finkers, R, Gonzalez-Beltran, A, Gray, AJG, Groth, P, Goble, C, Grethe, JS, Heringa, J, 't Hoen, PAC, Hooft, R, Kuhn, T, Kok, R, Kok, J, Lusher, SJ,

Martone, ME, Mons, A, Packer, AL, Persson, B, Rocca-Serra, P, Roos, M, van Schaik, R, Sansone, S-A, Schultes, E, Sengstag, T, Slater, T, Strawn, G, Swertz, MA, Thompson, M, van der Lei, J, van Mulligen, E, Velterop, J, Waagmeester, A, Wittenburg, P, Wolstencroft, K, Zhao, J & Mons, B 2016, 'The FAIR Guiding Principles for scientific data management and stewardship', *Scientific data*, vol. 3, 160018 EP.

Wilsdon, J, Bar-Ilan, J, Frodeman, R, Lex, E, Peters, I & Wouters, P 2017, *Next-generation metrics: Responsible metrics and evaluation for open science*, https://ec.europa.eu/research/open science/pdf/report.pdf#view=fit&pagemode=none (July 15, 2020).

List of Contributors

Heinz Ahn received his PhD in Business Management from RWTH Aachen University (Germany), where he also held a position as Postdoc at the Chair of Environment Economy and Industrial Control. Since 2008, he is Full Professor and CEO of the Institute of Management Control & Business Accounting at the Technische Universität Braunschweig (Germany). His research focuses on instruments for planning, measuring and managing the performance of companies, their subunits and their actions. The respective research outcome is published regularly in leading international journals, mainly comprising the following three topics: cost management, KPI-based planning concepts, performance control.

Miriam Albers (born 1980) is a research associate for organisational development at ZB MED – Information Centre for Life Sciences in Cologne since March 2020.
She studied library science as well as psychology. She worked for the head office of Fraunhofer-Gesellschaft for the central information unit. She also worked as a lecture for Institute for Information Science at the Technical University of Cologne in sectors such as human resource management, project management, electronic publishing or empirical methods. She graduated her PhD cooperative at Technical University of Cologne and Humboldt University on the subject of "Journal management at academic libraries and the implication of the open access initiative".
At the moment, she works on an innovative project dealing with the opportunity of using bibliometric methods for user studies and the design of new library services.

Valeria Aman studied Library and Information Science at the Humboldt University of Berlin and the Royal School of Library and Information Science in Copenhagen. She was employed at the iFQ from May 2013 to December 2015 and conducted several bibliometric analyses and evaluations. With the move to DZHW in 2016, she started her PhD on the knowledge transfer of internationally mobile scientists. Within the Competence Centre for Bibliometrics she participates in the development of a robust data infrastructure for bibliometric applications.

Fredrik Åström is a Reader in information studies and works as a bibliometrics expert at Lund University. His field of expertise is on issues related to scholarly communication and research evaluation, drawing on methods and theories from information studies as well as sociology of science. Recently, Åström's main line of research has been on research evaluation practices, with a particular focus on the use of bibliometrics in research assessments and evaluations.

Rafael Ball has been Director of ETH Library Zurich, Switzerland, since 2015. He holds doctorates in biology and science history and studied biology, Slavonic studies and philosophy at the Universities of Mainz, Warsaw and Moscow. He complete a two-year postgraduate qualification as a scientific librarian in 1996 and was head of Central Library in the Research Center Juelich, Germany from 1996 to 2008. Ball was Director of the University Library of Regensburg from 2008 to 2015. He has written and edited numerous publications, and is a dedicated speaker and a lecturer at various universities. His main work and research interests are the library of the future, science communication and the role of the printed book in the digital age.

Ingrid Bauer holds a PhD in chemistry as well as a degree in Library Science (Final theses in German: "Google Scholar: data source of the future?" / "Google Scholar – Datenquelle der Zukunft?"). After several years working in the area of international research funding she started working at the library of TU Wien in the year 2014, where she was Head of the subject library for Chemistry and Engineering and established bibliometric services at TU Wien. Since 2019 she works in the area of quality management and university development at the rector's office of TU Wien.

Clemens Blümel is a researcher at DZHW Berlin. He studied sociology, communication studies and psychology and has worked at the Fraunhofer Institute for Systems and Innovation Research as well as at Humboldt-University. His current research focuses on innovation in scholarly communication and digital scholarly practices as well as on novel digital metrics for research and scholarship.

Pei-Shan Chi is a researcher of ECOOM bibliometric team at KU Leuven. She holds a BA and MA in library and information science from National Taiwan University. After working in industry and academia, she completed a PhD at the Institute of Library and Information Science, Humboldt-Universität zu Berlin. Her research interests include bibliometric analysis, indicator development and research evaluation in the social sciences and humanities.

Tindaro Cicero graduated magna cum laude in Statistics from the University of Messina in 2008, earned a Master of Science degree in 2011 and a PhD degree in 2012 in Business Engineering at University of Rome "Tor Vergata". He is now working at ANVUR, the Italian Agency for the Evaluation of Universities and Research, where since 2017 he is leader of the "National Scientific Qualification and post-graduate degrees accreditation" unit. His main research interests are statistics applied to research evaluation and bibliometrics.

Marcel Clermont, since 2018, is professor for business science with emphasis on management and financial accounting at Duale Hochschule Gera-Eisenach, Germany. His research focusses on performance measurement and management in general and on the non-profit sector in particular (in particular the performance evaluation of universities and theaters). He has published several papers in this context and managed different third-party-funded projects.

Jennifer D'Souza is a Postdoctoral Researcher at the TIB Leibniz Information Centre for Science and Technology University Library in the Data Sciences and Digital Libraries group. Her research interests mainly include developing supervised machine learning techniques for natural language processing to facilitate text mining and automated information extraction. Aside from this, she is also interested in scientometrics.

Farshid Danesh has a BA, MA, and Ph.D. in Knowledge and Information Management. He obtained his Ph.D. degree from the Ferdowsi University of Mashhad in 2013. He is now an Assistant Professor at Regional Information Center for Science & Technology (RICeST), researching and teaching in the Information Management Research Department. His research interests are Scientometrics, Bibliometrics, Scholarly communications, Quantitative research methods, Information visualization, Data analytics, and Social Network analysis.

Koenraad Debackere is a Professor of Innovation Management and Policy at KU Leuven. He is Promotor-Coordinator of ECOOM. His research has focused on the development and use of indicators measuring the effects of science and innovation policy, the role of entrepreneurial universities in economic development and the management and growth of knowledge-intensive companies.

Tahereh Dehdarirad is a researcher and bibliometric analyst at Chalmers University of Technology, Sweden. She obtained her PhD degree in 2016 from the University of Barcelona, Spain. In her thesis, she studied gender differences in science and higher education using bibliometric indicators. In 2019, she began a project funded by GENIE (Gender Initiative for Excellence) at Chalmers to study the scientific performance of female and male scholars at Chalmers from a bibliometric perspective. Her research interests include scientometrics, gender differences in science, social media data analysis and metrics, open access (science) and public engagement in science. A complete list of her publications can be found at https://orcid.org/0000–0003–2529–962X (July 15, 2020).

Hélène Draux works as a Research Data Scientist at Digital Science. After completing a master's degree in Geographic Information Systems, she researched the use of maps during public involvement in decision-making, discussing differences between paper and online maps. She developed a keen interest in visualisation, not only through maps but also (info)graphics. She has worked in the field of bibliometrics since 2017, and in this capacity has published blog articles and analyses in the Digital Research Report series.

Dorte Drongstrup is a Research Librarian at the University Library of Southern Denmark, where she does research within the domain of Scientometrics and Scholarly Communication and performs research evaluations. Drongstrup has an MS in Library Science from the Royal School of Library and Information Science and a PhD in Business and Social Sciences from Aarhus University.

Leo Egghe was born in 1952 and has three children. He has a Doctorate in Mathematics (University of Antwerp, 1978) and a Ph.D. in Information Science (City University London, 1989). He was the Chief Librarian of the University of Hasselt from 1979 to 2017 and Professor of Library and Information Science in the University of Antwerp from 1983 to 2016 where he taught courses on informetrics and information retrieval. He has also been visiting professor in several scientific institutes across the world, and has conducted several development projects in Africa. He (together with R. Rousseau) organized the first ISSI conference in 1987 (the name ISSI was given later). In 2001 he (together with R. Rousseau) received the Derek De Solla Price Award. He is the Founding Editor-in-Chief of the Elsevier journal *Journal of Informetrics* which started in 2007. He has (co-) authored more than 300 scientific publications (most of them in JCR source journals) as well as five books. His main interests are the mathematical development of the theory of power laws (Zipf, Lotka, which resulted in a book, published by Elsevier in 2005) and impact measures. In 2006 he invented the well-known g-index.

Grischa Fraumann is a Research Assistant at the TIB Leibniz Information Centre for Science and Technology in the R&D Department, and a PhD Fellow at the University of Copenhagen in the Department of Communication. He is also a Research Affiliate at the "CiMetrias: Research Group on Science and Technology Metrics" at the University of São Paulo (USP). His research interests include altmetrics, higher education research, and research policy.

Simone Fühles-Ubach (born 1966) is Professor of Statistics and Library Management at the Institute for Information Science at the Technical University of Cologne.

She studied library and information science as well as administrative sciences. She worked for almost eight years in various positions in the administration of the German Bundestag, most recently as Coordinator for New Media. At the same time, she completed her doctorate at Humboldt University on the subject of "Uncertainty in databases and retrieval systems". Her work was awarded the Erich Pietsch Prize of the German Society for Information in 1998. Since 1998 she has been a professor at the TH Köln, and from 2010–2018 was Dean of the Faculty of

Information and Communication Sciences. Since 2018 she has also been an internal member of the University Council of the TH Köln.

Stephan Gauch holds a degree in social science and methods of empirical social research and a PhD in economics, about the interlinkage between research and standardization in ICT. He has been pioneering new sources of data for indicator construction, e.g. the use of trademarks as innovation indicators in services or standards as indicators for diffusion and coordination of innovation. Over time, his interests have shifted towards performativity of quantification, specifically in the field of bibliometrics. Currently, he is head of a group at Humboldt-Universität zu Berlin that aims to develop the notion of "reflexive bibliometrics" integrating semiotics, sociology of science and practices of bibliometric research.

Aldis Gedutis is a senior researcher at Centre for Studies of Social Change (Klaipeda University, Lithuania). He is a philosopher of science specialising in social studies of science, philosophy and sociology of the humanities, and evaluation practices of social sciences and humanities.

Mohammad Reza Ghane is an Associate Professor in LIS at Regional Information Center for Science and Technology (RICeSt), Iran. He has a bachelor degree in English language and Literature and both master and Ph.D. degrees in Library and Information Science (LIS).

He has been managing director of the Iranian LIS Association (South Region Branch) since 2015. As part of his educational duties, he teaches research methods, inferential statistics, research evaluation, webometrics, and Science policy. His peer review capacity comes back to his responsibility as managing editor of *International Journal of Information Science and Management* (IJISM) since 2003 (https://ijism.ricest.ac.ir/index.php/ijism/about/editorialTeam [July 15, 2020]), and his participation in peer reviewing and publishing for many Iranian and international journals of LIS such as *Scientometrics, Journal of Information Science, The Electronic library, Learned Publishing, SAGE Open*, and *Serials Review* among others. He has frequently been a reviewer for major LIS journals in Iran such as *Human Information Interaction* (https://hii.khu.ac.ir/en [July 15, 2020]), *International Journal of Information Science and Management (IJISM), Interdisciplinary Studies in the Humanities* (http://www.isih.ir/ [July 15, 2020]), *National Studies on Librarianship and Information Organization* (NASTINFO) (http://nastinfo.nlai.ir/journal/about?lang=en [July 15, 2020]) and *Iranian Journal of Information Processing & Management* (https://jipm.irandoc.ac.ir/index.php?slc_lang=en&sid=1 [July 15, 2020]). In addition, his knowledge on the administrative process of publishing dates back to his position as the head of the publication office at RICeST, which he held for several years. Mohammad has held many workshops for researchers and students on academic writing and publishing, research evaluation, and open access. From the methodological perspective, he has studied and researched through several research methods, and has translated a book into Persian entitled *Statistical Methods for the Information Professional: A Practical, Painless Approach to Understanding, Using, and Interpreting Statistics*, a handbook for graduate students and researchers in Iran. His most recent research work is an authored book, *Open access and Rethinking Scholarly Communication* (in press).

Wolfgang Glänzel is Director of the Centre for R&D Monitoring (ECOOM) and Full Professor at KU Leuven. He is also affiliated with the Department of Science Policy and Scientometrics at the Library of the Hungarian Academy of Sciences in Budapest (Hungary). Glänzel studied mathematics at Eötvös Lorand University (ELTE) in Budapest. He holds a Doctorate in Mathematics from ELTE, obtained in 1984, as well as a PhD in the Social Sciences obtained from Leiden University (The Netherlands) in 1997. His research activities comprise probability theory and mathematical statistics, quantitative science studies and research policy. Wolfgang Glänzel has published numerous journal articles, proceedings and book chapters, and has co-authored/coedited several books. He is Secretary-Treasurer of the International Society for Scientometrics and Informetrics (ISSI), Editor-in-Chief of the international journal *Scientometrics*, and Academic Editor of the multidisciplinary OA journal *PLoS ONE*.

Juan Gorraiz studied physics at the University of Madrid and at the University of Vienna, where he obtained his Doctor's degree. He is Head of the Bibliometrics and Publication Strategies Department of the Library and Archive Services, University of Vienna, which is specialized in supporting both researchers and decision-makers in research administration. He has been engaged in bibliometric analyses and studies since 2001. Moreover, he has been teaching information retrieval and bibliometrics at the university course "Library and Information Studies" since 1992. Apart from his ongoing commitment to the esss, he has contributed outstanding services to the scientometric community as an organizer and programme chair of the "10th International Conference on Science & Technical Indicators" in 2008 in Vienna as well as an organizer of the "14th International Society of Scientometrics and Informetrics Conference" in 2013 in Vienna. Last but not least, he is one of the initiators of the "European Summer School for Scientometrics" (esss), where he is engaged as steering committee member and lecturer.

Christian Gumpenberger has a Doctor's degree in Veterinary Medicine from the University of Veterinary Medicine Vienna and a Master's degree in Library and Information Studies from Danube University Krems. He was Head of the Department of Public Services and Reference Librarians at the University Library of the University of Veterinary Medicine Vienna, Head of the Novartis Knowledge Center Vienna, as well as Global Project Manager for the Novartis Institutional Repository Project & Open Access Champion at Novartis. He has also ran his own information consultancy business focusing on project management in the field of new trends in scholarly communication, especially Open Access. Christian was also Coordinator of the Council of Austrian University Libraries from 2010 to 2020. Since 2020, he has also been Head of Department for Bibliometrics and Publication Strategies at the University of Vienna.

Björn Hammarfelt is an associate professor at the Swedish School of Library and Information Science (SSLIS), University of Borås. His research is situated at the intersection of information studies and sociology of science, with a focus on the organization, communication, and evaluation of research. His recent work has mainly been focused on how scholars use and respond to bibliometric measurement.

Robin Haunschild studied chemistry in Hannover and Marburg. After two postdoctoral positions (Rice University in Houston, TX and Karlsruhe Institute of Technology including a Carl-Zeiss fellowship for two years he joined the Central Information Service for the institutes of the chemical, physical, and technical section of the Max Planck Society in 2014. See also his publications and their citations available under Google Scholar https://scholar.google.de/citations?user=kDfateQAAAAJ&hl=de. His current research interests include the study of bibliometrics and altmetrics as well as their application to specific fields of natural sciences, e.g., chemistry and climate change. He has served as a reviewer for more than 40 journals in recent years, and he is a member of the Editorial Board of the journal Information since 2019. In 2020, he joined the Editorial Boards of the journals *Scientometrics* and *Journal of Informetrics*.

Tamara Heck is Postdoc at the Information Center for Education at DIPF | Leibniz Institute for Research and Information in Education. She is responsible for research concerned with information management and infrastructures within the educational field. Her current research focuses on research behavior and the adaptation of open science practices, with the goal to disclose the development of scientific work and norms. These aspects include questions on the influence of open science on higher education and the development of open processes in learning and teaching, like applying open educational resources, open pedagogy and open infrastructures. Further research is concerned with information literacy and its implications on the adaptation of new information behavior and practices in work-related contexts.

Thomas Heinze is professor of organizational sociology and deputy director at the Interdisciplinary Center for Science and Technology Studies (IZWT) at the University of Wuppertal. He studied Sociology and Economics at the Universities of Trier and Stirling (Diploma 2000), obtained a PhD in Administrative Science at the University of Speyer (2005) and a habilitation in Sociology at the University of Bamberg (2010). He served as guest professor at Gothenburg University (2013), Arizona State University (2017), and California Institute of Technology (2018). His research interests include the emergence and diffusion of scientific breakthroughs, public research organizations, research evaluation, theories of institutional change, organizational theory, and comparative historical sociology

Kim Holmberg is a Senior Researcher at the Research Unit for the Sociology of Education (RUSE) at the University of Turku. His research interests include altmetrics, webometrics, bibliometrics, scholarly communication in digital environments, social network analysis, and studying various other phenomena on the Web in general and in social media in particular, mainly using quantitative methods.

Arlette Jappe is senior researcher at the Interdisciplinary Center for Science and Technology Studies (IZWT) at the University of Wuppertal. She studied Psychology at Free University Berlin (Diploma 2001) and obtained a PhD in Sociology at Bielefeld University (2007). She was researcher at the Fraunhofer Institute for System and Innovation Research in Karlsruhe (2001–2012) and has broad experience in science and innovation policy research. Her research interests include research organizations and institutional renewal, bibliometric research methods, research evaluation, and research capacity development in sustainability science.

Miloš Jovanović is currently the head of unit of the group "Tools and Methods" at the Fraunhofer Institute for Technological Trend Analysis INT in Euskirchen, Germany. His group works on developing and scanning for new IT-tools and methods that can be employed for scientific work at their institute. His research focuses on bibliometrics, patentometrics, and recently altmetrics and the visualization of data. He also worked in FP7 and H2020 projects for the EU Commission as project coordinator and work package leader. He studied modern history, politics, media science and information science at the Heinrich-Heine-University in Düsseldorf and finished his PhD working on a scientometric method to classify technologies into basic or applied science.

Johanna Krolak is a doctoral student at the Central Library of Forschungszentrum Jülich and is currently working on the topic of quantifying research efficiency in the German university system. In addition to her research activities, she is the Chief Financial Officer of the kombabb Competence Centre for Disability, Studies and Profession NRW, Germany. She obtained a diploma in economics at the Rheinische Friedrich-Wilhelms-University in Bonn and a diploma in business administration at the FernUniversität in Hagen.

Emanuel Kulczycki is the head of Scholarly Communication Research Group (the Adam Mickiewicz University in Poznań) and a policy advisor to the Ministry of Science and Higher Education in Poland. From 2018 to 2020 he has been the chair of the European Network for Research Evaluation in the Social Sciences and the Humanities (ENERSSH). His recent papers were published in Nature, Research Evaluation, Journal of Informetrics and Scientometrics (more information: emanuelkulczycki.com).

Steffen Lemke is a member of the Web Science team at ZBW Leibniz Information Centre for Economics, where he is completing a PhD in Computer Science. He holds a master's degree in business information systems from Kiel University. Steffen does research in topics related to scientometrics and science communication and has a particular interest in evaluation systems of science and how they affect the ways researchers work.

Emilio Delgado López-Cózar is a Professor at the Facultad de Comunicación y Documentación of the Universidad de Granada. He holds a PhD in Library & Information Science. His research interests are focused on the analysis of the new sources of information and scientific evaluation (e. g., search engines like Google Scholar) and the new metrics used to measure the visibility and the impact of scientific activity (Altmetrics).

Marion Maisonobe is a CNRS Researcher specialized in the geography of science. Her work covers research on the global geography of the world contemporary production, on the world network of collaborations between cities at several geographical scales, and on the spatial dynamics of specific fields of knowledge production which include DNA Repair, Green Chemistry, Urban Modelling, and Marine Science. From a methodological point of view, Marion Maisonobe has special interests in network analysis, the monitoring of the diffusion of ideas and innovation, as well as the data-visualization of global exchanges. She is very keen in initiating the development of reproducible research methods and to this aim she contributes to the development of the NETSCITY application, which allows geocoding, mapping, and analyzing the geography of bibliographic corpuses, extracted from the WoS and Scopus, at the world level.

Marco Malgarini was appointed in 2012 as Senior Manager for Research Evaluation at ANVUR, the Italian national agency for the evaluation of universities and research institutes. Marco is an economist specialized in econometrics and statistical analysis, and has published widely in national and international journals on economic and statistical issues. He is a member of the European RTD Evaluation Network and of the G7 Working Group on Research Assessment. His current research interests include research evaluation, research policies, scientometrics and the use of indicators in evaluation procedures.

Ali Mardani-Nejad is a graduate in Knowledge and Information Science (KIS). He attained a Master's degree from Allameh Tabatabai University in Tehran, Iran. Currently he is a lecturer, researcher and member of Young Researchers and Elite Club of Islamic Azad University Najafabad Branch. His research interests are webometrics, scientometrics, E-learning, website quality, websites improvement, and university ranking systems.

Ben McLeish has worked within scholarly communication services and discovery and data platforms for 16 years, beginning with Wiley in 2004. He has worked at Digital Science for six years focusing on the adoption of altmetrics within Europe. He was born and raised in what was West Germany, leaving a few months after the fall of the Berlin Wall. He lives and works in North Yorkshire.

Jafar Mehrad is founder of the Islamic World Science Citation Center (ISC) & Regional Information Center for Science and Technology (RICeST). He is also academician and Professor of Knowledge and Information Sciences at the Department of Knowledge & Information Sciences, Faculty of Education & Psychology, Shiraz University, Shiraz, Iran.

Andreas Meier is currently working at the Central Library of Juelich Research Center. As a member of the group Data and Metrics, he is working on the topics of bibliometrics and altmetrics. Meier studied Information Science at the Heinrich Heine University in Duesseldorf and graduated with a Master's degree.

Bernhard Mittermaier has been working since 2004 at the library of Forschungszentrum Jülich (Germany), since 2008 in the role of head of the library. His education includes a diploma in chemistry, a PhD in analytical chemistry at the University of Ulm and a M.A. (LIS) in library and information science at the Humboldt University Berlin. Mittermaier is also a member of the DEAL project group and negotiation team and the project group of the National Open Access Contact Point OA2020-DE. His main interests are Open Access including the development of the German Open Access Monitor, licence negotiations, and bibliometrics (publications: http://juser.fz-juelich.de/search?ln=de&p=aid:P%3 A(DE-Juel1)133810; ORCID: http://orcid.org/0000 – 0002 – 3412 – 6168 [July 15, 2020]).

Rogério Mugnaini is Professor of Library and Information Science at the University of São Paulo (USP), where he leads the research group "CiMetrias: Research Group on Science and Technology Metrics". His research interests include bibliometrics, scientometrics, national scientific production, indicators, information sources, and research policy.

Rüdiger Mutz is a Senior Researcher at the Center for Higher Education and Science Studies (CHESS), University of Zurich. His research focuses on research evaluation on the base of peer review procedures and bibliometrics, methodological-statistical questions of research on higher education (e.g. bias-corrected ranking procedures, interrater reliability), and meta-analyses.

Mandy Neumann is a software developer with a background in computational linguistics. She used to work in several research projects with foci on text mining, information extraction and web scraping. As a researcher and developer at TH Köln – University of Applied Sciences, she addressed problems regarding data collection and analysis in the bibliographic domain.

Kaltrina Nuredini is a researcher at ZBW Leibniz Information Centre for Economics and currently in the last year of her PhD. Her background is in computer science with research focus in Web Science. Her current research interests are in investigating altmetric attention for journals and their articles.

Michael Ochsner is a senior researcher at the Centre of Excellence in Social Sciences, FORS, Lausanne, Switzerland and a scientific collaborator at the Professorship for Social Psychology and Research on Higher Education, D-GESS, at ETH Zurich, Switzerland. He is a survey methodologist and sociologist specialising in research evaluation in the social sciences and humanities, international surveys, welfare policy and work-life conflict. He is vice-president of EvalHum, an international association for research evaluation in the social sciences and humanities and an associate editor of the journal Palgrave Communications.

Enrique Orduña-Malea is Assistant Professor in the Department of Audiovisual Communication, Documentation and History of Art (DCADHA) at the Polytechnic University of Valencia (Spain). He holds a PhD in Library and Information Sciences, a Master Degree in Multichannel Contents Management, a MA in Library & Information Science, and a Technical Telecommunications Engineer Degree. His research interests are focused on the study of contents, users and organisations on the Web through informetric methods.

David A. Pendlebury is Head of Research Analysis at the Institute for Scientific Information (ISI), a part of Clarivate Analytics. Since 1983 he has used *Web of Science* data to study the structure and dynamics of scientific and scholarly research. He worked for many years with ISI founder Eugene Garfield. With Henry Small, Pendlebury developed *Essential Science Indicators*, which provides publication and citation data on influential individuals, institutions, journals, and countries, identifies highly cited papers, and defines research fronts representing contemporary activity at the specialty level.

Ginevra Peruginelli, researcher at IGSG-CNR, has a degree in Law (1999), a Master's degree in Computer Science at the University of Northumbria (2005) and a PhD in Telematics and Information Society (2008). Since 2018, she is the Secretary of Free Access to Law Movement. She is a member of the Scientific Council of the Department of Social Sciences and Humanities, Cultural Heritage, CNR. She collaborates in several European projects on legal informatics and is the author of many scientific works and editor of books on ICT and legal information. Orcid: 0000–0002–9331–4476.

Isabella Peters has been Professor of Web Science at ZBW Leibniz Information Centre for Economics and Chair of the Web Science research group at Kiel University since 2013. She received her PhD in Information Science at the Heinrich Heine University in Düsseldorf. Her research focuses on user-generated content, social media, and their potential for assessing scholarly communication, i.e. altmetrics, and open science. She was a member of the European Expert Group on Altmetrics and co-chaired the LIBER working group on alternative metrics.

Sabrina Petersohn has been a researcher at the German Centre for Higher Education Research and Science Studies – DZHW since 2017. Currently, she is principal investigator of a research project investigating task profiles and competencies in IT-supported research reporting. She holds a PhD in sociology from the University of Wuppertal and a Master's degree in sociology, political sciences and public law from the University of Potsdam, Germany. Her dissertation project dealt with the professionalization of bibliometric research evaluation. Previously she worked as a doctoral researcher at the University of Wuppertal (2016–2017) and at the GESIS Leibniz Institute of Social Sciences in Cologne (2012–2016). Her current research interests revolve around the governance of science, science policy, research evaluation, the professionalization of bibliometrics, research information, research administration and management as well as the role of academic libraries and qualitative methods.

Ronald Rousseau is a researcher at KU Leuven (Belgium) and at the University of Antwerp (Belgium). His main interest is in mathematical aspects of citation analysis. He obtained a Ph.D. in mathematics from KU Leuven (in 1977) and a Ph.D. in Library and Information Science from Antwerp University (in 1992). In 1983 he obtained a Habilitations degree from KU Leuven. He was the recipient of the Price of the Belgian Academy of Science (1979) and of the Derek J. de Solla Price award for scientometrics (2001). From 2007 to 2015 he was the elected president of the International Society for Scientometrics and Informetrics (ISSI).

Elías Sanz-Casado is Full Professor in the Department of Library and Information Science at the Carlos III University of Madrid, Director of the research group "Laboratory for Metric Information Studies" (LEMI), and leads the "Research Institute for Higher Education and Science" (INAECU) which is made up of members of Carlos III University of Madrid and Autonomous University of Madrid. His main research lines are research evaluation of scientific areas and institutions, designing and developing of bibliometric indicators for research evaluation on sciences, social sciences and humanities disciplines, and creating and developing university rankings.

Niels Taubert is the head of the working group Bibliometrics and a sociologist of science, technology, and digital media by training. His main areas of research are the conception and the operation of openness in different social fields (open source software development, open access, open science, and open science governance), and the digitisation of science.

Dirk Tunger studied Information Science in Hamburg at the University of Applied Sciences and received his doctorate in Information Science from the University of Regensburg in 2007. From 2003 to 2017, he worked as an information scientist at the Central Library of Forschungszentrum Jülich. During this time, he worked as a research associate on the establishment and further development of the "Bibliometrics" working group, which has been headed by him. Since 2018, Dirk Tunger has been a research associate in the Center of Excellence "Analyses, Studies, Strategy" of the Project Management at Forschungszentrum Jülich in the field of evaluation and impact analysis. Currently, he is also working as a project lead at the Institute of Information Management of TH Köln in the project UseAltMe, whose goal is the development of indicators for Altmetrics.

Anthony (Ton) F.J. van Raan, Professor of Quantitative Studies of Science, founder and director until 2010 of the Centre for Science and Technology Studies, Leiden University. PhD in physics (Utrecht, 1973), physics research in Utrecht, Bielefeld and Leiden, visiting scientist in the US, UK, and France; 1985 field switch to science studies. Winner of the Derek de Solla Price Award 1995. Main interests involve the application of bibliometric indicators in research evaluation, mapping of science, statistical properties of indicators, scaling behaviour of universities and cities. He has published (as author and co-author) around 30 articles in physics and 200 in science and technology studies. He is editor of the Handbook of Quantitative Studies of Science and Technology and member of the editorial board of the international journals Scientometrics, Research Evaluation, and Quantitative Science Studies. Professor Van Raan's advisory work has been frequently used by the government of the Netherlands, other European Union member states, the European Commission, the OECD, European scientific organizations such as the Netherlands Organization for Scientific Research (NWO), Royal Netherlands Academy of Sciences (KNAW), Deutsche Forschungsgemeinschaft (DFG), Fraunhofer Gesellschaft and by the business sector (Elsevier). He recently has been member of the Expert Group on Monitoring and Evaluation of the European Research Council (ERC). On the occasion of his retirement as CWTS director he was awarded with the royal distinction of Knight in the Order of the Dutch Lion. More information can be found at http://www.cwts.nl/tvr/ (July 15, 2020).

Juergen Wastl leads the Digital Science consultancy portfolio, supporting research institutions, funding bodies, governments and other institutions with research capabilities to make better use of data to inform their strategies and decisions. A molecular biologist and biochemist by training, Juergen has held roles in project management and research strategy in Industry and Higher Education. Before joining Digital Science he headed the research information team in the Research Strategy Office at the University of Cambridge. In this role he was responsible for the development and advancement of tools and applications to meet a diverse set of research information needs. He supported a variety of internal and external research evaluation exercises and contributed to the University's extensive Strategic Research Review process with analyses and reports. Since October 2019 he has also been Associate Director at the Research on Research Institute.

Index

A-index 173
Academia.edu 196, 206f., 217, 256, 258, 260, 267, 341
Academic collaborations 319, 325
Academic communication 499–502
Academic output 195, 500f., 504f.
Academic Ranking of World Universities (ARWU) 35, 301–304, 306
Academic Social Networks (ASN) 22, 256–258, 265–269, 275
Accountability in academia 291
Alan Prichard 20
Alfred Lotka 9, 20, 107f., 112, 115, 307
Allocating resources 291, 294
Allocation 23, 54f., 94, 125, 291–293, 388, 457, 504
Alternative publishing 266
Altmetric Attention Score 209, 219, 222, 428, 466
Altmetric.com 192, 196, 204, 209, 222, 235, 241f., 256
Altmetric donut 216
Altmetric Explorer 216
Altmetrics 59f., 65, 69, 84, 117, 120, 125, 135, 140f., 145, 181–189, 191–193, 195–197, 201–212, 215–224, 231, 233, 235, 237, 242, 256, 258, 265, 277, 281f., 428, 455, 458f., 465f., 470, 476, 478f., 482, 489, 491, 499, 501, 508, 511f.
Altmetrics classifications 201
Altmetrics Concept 192
American Physical Society 78
Article-level metrics 203, 209, 235f., 238, 241f., 428
Arts & Humanities Citation Index (A&HCI) 29, 399
ArXiv 240, 340, 344f., 456
Attention 15, 209f., 215–220, 222f., 231, 235–237, 242, 255, 258, 261, 267, 291, 302, 304, 307, 349f., 428, 431, 433, 500, 502
Author By-line Order 344
Author order 303, 397, 399–402

Benchmarking 59, 299–301, 451f., 459f., 490
Bibliometric Performance 117, 319
Bibliometric practices 489

Bibliometric report 221, 223f., 230
BibSonomy 206
Blind peer review 78
Blogger 206
Bradford's law 307

Centre for R&D Monitoring at KU Leuven 21
Chord diagram 365, 370
Citation count 35, 85, 107, 292, 294, 339
CiteULike 206, 257
Clarivate Analytics 27, 29, 36, 81, 236, 431f., 434
Co-authorship 118, 260, 313, 324, 372, 397f., 400, 402, 426
Cole and Eales 9
Collaborative publications 320
Competence Centre for Bibliometrics 21
Competence in bibliometric 485f., 489
Complex indicators 470
Conference Proceedings Citation Index (CPCI) 22, 29, 191
Continuing education 465f., 468f., 472
Continuous Convex Bibliometric Theory 111
COUNTER 217
Credibility crisis 508
Cross-gender Collaboration 343
Crown indicator 56, 60
Current Contents 27, 30f., 438, 440, 445f.
Curriculum 79, 475, 477f.
Cybermetrics 191, 193–195, 197

Derek de Solla Price 12, 14, 20, 32, 36, 54
Dimensions 22, 375, 421–428
Double-blind peer review 78
Double boom cycle 313

Education in Bibliometrics 467
Elsevier 22, 53, 55, 216, 223, 267, 276, 344, 423, 468
Eugene Garfield 11, 13–15, 23, 27–36, 54, 400, 441
European Network of Indicators Designers (ENID) 67
European Summer School for Scientometrics (ESSS) 21, 465, 468, 472, 487
Evaluative bibliometrics 23, 33, 54, 91, 93, 95f., 117f., 485, 487, 491f.

Evaluative citation analysis (ECA)   94–96
Ex post evaluation   292
Expert Group on Altmetrics   476, 513

F1000   82, 207 f.
Facebook   195 f., 204, 206–209, 216, 218, 220, 242 f., 256 f., 266, 341, 500, 502
Field-normalized indicators   85
Field-Weighted Citation Impact (FWCI)   320, 323 f.
Field Weighted Citation Impact indicator   319
FigShare   206, 503
Flow Charts   370
Funding   23, 32, 34, 54, 59, 62, 82, 126, 129, 291–294, 300, 351–353, 388, 399, 402, 421–423, 426, 460, 511, 513
Future of bibliometrics   500
Future research   80, 311 f., 319, 377, 482

G-index   171, 173
Gaming   35, 129, 295, 512 f.
Gender differences   335, 339–342, 344 f., 347 f., 351–354
Gender imbalance   335, 354
German Centre for Higher Education Research and Science Studies (DZHW)   468
GitHub   206, 236
Google Scholar   22, 35, 62, 231, 260, 313, 336, 456, 459, 467
Grant peer reviews   82, 85
Grants   77, 125, 292, 296, 353, 365, 369, 421–424, 426–428

H-index   35, 60, 83, 94, 107, 114 f., 294, 301, 335, 338, 340 f., 347 f., 353 f., 466, 471, 504
High-ranking journals   81
Hirsch, Jorge   169

Impact of Gender on Collaboration   342
ImpactStory   209, 237, 242, 459, 513
Importance   15, 29, 32, 54, 56, 60, 113, 121, 193, 291 f., 294, 306, 315, 319, 426, 467, 502, 504
Indexing services   193 f.
Informetrics   21, 193 f., 196 f., 203, 470 f., 478, 487
Institute for Scientific Information (ISI)   11–14, 27, 29–36, 54 f., 58, 235, 379, 381, 431 f., 434, 437, 441, 452, 466

Institutional Repository (IR)   216, 457
Institutionalization of bibliometric   20
Instiute for Scientific Information (ISI)   32
International collaboration   57 f., 319–321, 324, 326, 342, 344, 491
International Society for Scientometrics and Informetrics (ISSI)   21, 66, 422, 447
Islamic World Science Citation Center (ISC)   431–441, 445–449, 452
ISSI conference   56, 336
ISSI Quarterly Newsletter   67–69

Jorge Hirsch   83, 108, 114
Journal Citation Report (JCR)   15, 23, 27, 29 f., 81, 300, 437 f., 440, 452
Journal Impact Factor (JIF)   23, 29 f., 81, 85, 94, 194, 262, 294, 335, 338, 340, 353, 428, 433, 439, 466, 486, 513
Journal of Scientometric   21

Karolinska Institute   21

Leiden Centre for Science and Technology Studies (CWTS)   21, 33 f., 53, 55–60, 95 f., 303, 422, 487
Leiden manifesto on research metrics   294
Leiden Ranking   59 f., 303, 305
Loop   267

Marriage and Marital Status   350
Mendeley   196, 206–209, 211, 224–226, 229, 239, 242 f., 257 f., 261, 266 f., 341 f.
Mendeley Reader Counts   283
Metrics aggregators   235
Misleading incentives   512

National citation indexing system   431
National Research Assessment   58, 84 f., 99–103
Netometrics   193
Network analysis   313, 365, 375, 384, 398, 478 f.
Networks   20, 60, 94, 107, 255, 313, 343, 365, 369, 372 f., 375, 384, 470, 489
New metrics   135 f., 143, 192, 221–223, 230, 256, 261, 428, 502, 508
Normalization   60, 222
Normalized Citation Score   371

Oone-dimensional bibliometrics   107

Open Access 60, 96, 128, 216, 235, 257 f., 268, 303, 427, 455–457, 470 f., 479, 501 f., 507–511
Open metrics 507, 512 f.
Open peer review 78, 80, 128 f., 507 f., 512
Open science 60, 125, 128, 261, 296, 501–503, 507–514

Past performance assessment 79
Patent 53, 57 f., 118, 209, 215, 218 f., 312–314, 365, 369 f., 381, 384–387, 389, 421, 423, 426–428, 470 f.
Patent analysis 54, 57, 311
Patentometric analysis 314
Patentometrics 311, 313–315
Patentometry 314
Paul Otlet 10
Peer review 34, 55, 57 f., 77–86, 94, 96, 117, 121, 125–129, 208 f., 218, 230, 292, 294, 302, 434 f., 437 f., 452, 456
Peer review system 136, 138
Perception metrics 502
PLOS 208 f., 230, 235–238, 240–243, 459
Plum print 223
PlumX Metrics (Plum Analytics) 235, 241 f., 459, 503
Productivity 9, 20, 23, 81, 108, 230, 294, 320, 335–339, 345–354, 381, 397–402, 435, 441, 458
Profiling 503
Project funding 292 f., 295

QS World University Ranking 301

Ranking 8, 13, 15, 59, 83–86, 121, 204, 219, 261, 276, 292, 294, 296, 299–307, 434, 438–440, 449, 452, 488, 502, 505
Readership counts 206, 243
Recruitment process 82 f., 504
Regional Information Center for Science and Technology (RICeST) 433 f.
Replicability 138, 144
Repository Analytics & Metrics Portal (RAMP) 459
Reputational control 91, 94 f., 292
Research assessment 35, 77, 84, 91, 93–96, 212, 221, 291 f., 295, 365, 431, 437, 455, 457 f., 485 f., 511
Research collaboration 303, 319 f., 323 f., 342, 398

Research evaluation 20, 23 f., 33 f., 53 f., 58, 84, 107 f., 207, 211, 259, 261, 265, 267 f., 275, 277, 293, 421, 426, 433, 455, 457, 460, 485 f., 488 f., 511–513
Research evaluation system 291 f., 295, 434, 437
Research funder 93, 421, 427, 510
Research funding 23, 34, 94 f., 117, 125, 128, 292, 302, 397, 504, 510 f.
ResearchGate 22, 206 f., 217, 255 f., 258, 260 f., 265–269, 271 f., 275–278, 467
Reviewer 78–80, 126–129, 222, 427, 500
Robert Merton 12, 32–34, 77
Royal Society of Chemistry 78

San Francisco Declaration on Research Assessment (DORA) 23, 202, 513
Scholarly communication 30, 80, 192, 194, 203, 206 f., 255–257, 259, 262, 265, 455 f., 460
Scholarly publishing 77, 80, 195, 202, 455–457, 459
Scholarlyhub 267
Science 2.0 508
Science Citation Index (SCI) 11–13, 20, 22 f., 27–34, 54 f., 58, 191, 193, 381 f., 399 f., 432, 441 f., 445
Scientific impact 209, 294, 303, 319 f., 324, 326 f., 350, 452
Scientific legitimacy 92
Scientist score 504
Scientometrics 2.0 135 f., 139–141, 144–146, 203
Scimago Lab 21
Scopus 22, 59, 118, 128, 202, 207, 223–226, 239–241, 268, 302, 313, 320, 324, 336, 341, 390, 431, 437, 441, 458, 465, 511
Scoring system 219
Second scientific revolution 509
Self-marketization of scientists 257
Shanghai Ranking 59, 302
SIR SCImago Institutions Ranking 302, 304 f.
SlideShare 206
Social impact 60, 208, 512
Social media 59 f., 195–197, 201–203, 205–212, 215, 219, 221–224, 226, 229, 231, 233, 235 f., 242, 266, 269, 369, 458 f., 476, 482, 500, 502, 504, 512
Social media metrics 62, 203, 265, 335, 338, 341, 353

Social media platform 195, 201–205, 207, 210–212, 511
Social network platforms 266
Social Sciences Citation Index (SSCI) 13, 22, 29, 191, 399
Sociology of science 19, 27, 34, 56, 378
Standardization 222, 380

Technological Trend Analysis (TTA) 311–315
Tenure decision 23, 82, 85f.
Thomson Reuters 27, 34, 36, 58, 302
Times Higher Education World University Ranking (THE-WUR) 301–303
Training course 465, 471, 487
Twitter 120, 195, 203–211, 215, 217f., 220, 224–226, 233, 238, 241–243, 341, 500, 502
Two-dimensional bibliometrics 107f.

University Ranking 35, 59, 295, 299, 302–305, 307, 439, 449, 451f., 455

Visibility of female and male scholars 338

Web Impact Factor (WIF) 194f.
Web of Science 27, 29, 54, 58, 82, 94f., 118, 128f., 202, 207, 223, 240, 303, 313, 336, 378, 385, 390f., 399, 432, 465, 468, 471, 511
Webometrics 59, 191, 193–195, 203, 313, 476
Webometry 193, 476
WordPress 206

Zipf's law 8, 10, 108, 307
Zotero 206

www.ingramcontent.com/pod-product-compliance
Lightning Source LLC
Chambersburg PA
CBHW081022240426
43668CB00031B/2347